APPLYING CAREER DEVELOPMENT THEORY TO COUNSELING

FIFTH EDITION

Richard S. Sharf
University of Delaware

BROOKS/COLE
CENGAGE Learning™

Australia • Brazil • Japan • Korea • Mexico • Singapore • Spain • United Kingdom • United States

BROOKS/COLE
CENGAGE Learning

Applying Career Development Theory to Counseling, Fifth Edition
Richard S. Sharf

Publisher/Executive Editor:
Marcus Boggs

Acquisitions Editor: Seth Dobrin

Assistant Editor: Allison Bowie

Editorial Assistant: Diane Mars

Technology Project Manager:
Andrew Keay

Marketing Manager: Trent Whatcott

Marketing Assistant: Ting Jian Yap

Marketing Communications Manager:
Tami Strang

Project Manager, Editorial Production:
Abigail Greshik

Creative Director: Rob Hugel

Art Director: Caryl Gorska

Print Buyer: Paula Vang

Permissions Editor: Bob Kauser

Production Service: Pre-Press PMG

Copy Editor: Pre-Press PMG

Cover Designer: Laurie Anderson

Cover Image: Réunion des Musées
Nationaux/Art resource, NY

Compositor: Pre-Press PMG

For product information and technology assistance, contact us at: **Cengage Learning Academic Resource Center, 1-800-423-0563**

For permission to use material from this text or product, submit all request online at **www.cengage.com/permissions.**
Further permissions questions can be e-mailed to **permissionrequest@cengage.com.**

Library of Congress Control Number: 2008941255

Student Edition:

ISBN-13: 978-0-495-80470-3

ISBN-10: 0-495-80470-3

Brooks/Cole, Cengage Learning
10 Davis Drive
Belmont, CA 94002-3098
USA

Cengage Learning products are represented in Canada by Nelson Education, Ltd.

For your course and learning solutions, visit **academic.cengage.com.**

Purchase any of our products at your local college store or at our preferred online store **www.ichapters.com.**

Printed in the United States of America
1 2 3 4 5 6 7 8 9 12 11 10 9

Brief Contents

iii

CONTENTS

v

APPENDICES

PREFACE FOR STUDENTS

NOW

The purpose of this textbook is to provide background information that you may use in working with clients who have concerns about problems at work or making a career choice. Part One of this book describes several views of how people make career choices and deal with adjusting to working, along with suggestions for counseling them. Part Two examines how individuals deal with career choice and work issues in childhood, adolescence, adulthood, and retirement. Job loss and sexual harassment also are discussed. Part Three explains specific issues such as the role of parents and others on career choice. Cognitive and behavioral approaches to career development also provide useful views on career counseling. Part Four integrates different theories or approaches to career counseling.

To make the book practical for your use with clients, I have included case examples and client—counselor dialogues. Theories of career development are based on research that often uses tests and inventories. A number of tests and inventories are integrated with theories in this textbook. I've explained how you might use them in career counseling.

LATER

This textbook can help you when you are doing career counseling with clients both when in graduate school and when working as a counselor or mental health professional. Not all career counseling is done by counselors who call themselves career counselors. A number of former students have told me that they have done career counseling with clients, when they did not expect that they would be doing so. I have tried to make this a book that will be a useful source for you when you are active in the counseling or mental health profession. Consulting the text at a later time can help you in understanding work related concerns and career choice issues when counseling individuals with such problems.

Some of you may be preparing for a licensing or certification examination based on CACREP guidelines. Appendix A describes CACREP standards for career issues and lists the page numbers that cover each of the standards.

I have also developed a student manual that contains exercises which can be used in individual or group career counseling. These exercises provide a practical means of helping clients with career choice and work issues. The Student Manual also has many practice multiple choice questions that can be useful in preparing for classroom or other examinations.

Richard S. Sharf

Preface for Instructors

Students taking a beginning graduate course in career guidance, career theory, or career counseling want to know how to assist clients with career concerns. This book will help them relate career theory and research to the practice of counseling, aiding them in their practicum, their internship, and their jobs as counselors. In this fifth edition of *Applying Career Development Theory to Counseling*, I show how each career development theory can be used in counseling. Each theory gives special insight into various perspectives on career development as it affects career counseling. Furthermore, the theories organize facts into a comprehensive system for students to understand and to use, rather than overwhelm them with unrelated lists of information.

Case examples are a special feature of this book. For each theory and its significant constructs, one or more cases are used to illustrate the conceptual approach of the theory. The examples are given in a dialogue between the counselor and the client. In the dialogue, the counselor's conceptualization follows most counselor statements and appears within brackets. This approach provides a direct application of the theory to counseling practice, making the book useful to both students and practicing counselors. In a few places, narrative descriptions of cases are used to illustrate theories.

THE FIFTH EDITION

New to the fifth edition are several significant additions. These additions are listed below by chapter:

Chapter 3: "Occupations: Information and Theory." In the previous editions, this was Chapter 15 and was titled "The Labor Market: Sociological and Economic Perspectives." This chapter has been moved to follow "Trait and Factor Theory"

(Chapter 2). It is presented as a further development of Step 2 in trait and factor theory, giving more detail about occupational information. With previous editions, many instructors used this chapter after the chapter on trait and factor theory; therefore, it seemed appropriate to move it there. Occupational information for the United States labor market has also been updated in this edition.

Chapter 7: "Career Development in Childhood." Gottfredson's theory of Self-Creation, Circumscription, and Compromise has been significantly revised. There is a greater emphasis on childhood cognitive development than in the previous editions. Also, Chapter 7 describes how Gottfredson has developed the compromise aspect of her theory by examining three difficulties that young people have in making career decisions.

Chapter 8: "Adolescent Career Development." The theory and stages of Ginzberg and his colleagues have been removed from this edition because there has been little or no research on this theory in the last ten years. The emphasis of this chapter is on Super's work on adolescent career development, along with the work of Vondracek and his colleagues. Vondracek's work on vocational identity is described more thoroughly in this edition than in past editions.

Chapter 10: "Adult Career Crises and Transitions." In the section on career transitions, the discussion of the boundaryless careers has been expanded to include protean careers.

Chapter 11: "Constructivist and Narrative Approaches to Career Development." The section on personal construct psychology, including discussion of the vocational rep test and laddering techniques, has been removed from the chapter. It has been replaced by Savickas's career construction theory, which integrates narrative counseling with other career development theories. Savickas's approach is receiving considerable current interest.

Chapter 12: "Relational Approaches to Career Development." Roe's work on the effects of parental attitudes on the career development of children has been decreased in size because it is no longer a topic of research. The sections on parent–child career interactions and family systems therapy have been expanded.

Chapter 14: "Social Cognitive Career Theory." In previous editions, this chapter only discussed the social cognitive career model of career choice. This chapter now focuses mainly on this model, but also describes the models of the development of interests, predicting educational and occupational performance, and predicting work and life satisfaction. A considerable amount of new research studies has also been added to this chapter.

Chapter 16: "Theories in Combination." A large table, Table 16.1, has been added to summarize the major concepts covered in each theory. I have separated the concepts by theory and by chapter. The table can be used for studying the materials in this book and it can also be used when doing career counseling to remind students about the various theories and their approaches to career development. A new integrative approach to career development is also explained. Lapan and Turner have developed a contextually responsive career counseling system for young people that was developed by using several theories described in this text. It serves as an example of ways to integrate career development theories.

The previous Appendix A contained the ethical guidelines of the National Career Development Association. The guidelines have been revised and greatly expanded and are now too lengthy for this book. Students are referred to the NCDA Web site for the guidelines. Because of the current interest in CACREP standards, Appendix A now lists those standards, along with information as to how the various sections and chapters of this book meet each of them. Standards for 2001 and a draft of 2009 standards are listed.

Each chapter in this fifth edition has been revised to reflect the results of new research and changes in the theory, where there have been changes. Although research that has been done outside of the United States has less impact, it continues to make a major contribution to career development research and is included in this edition.

SPECIAL CONSIDERATIONS IN EACH CHAPTER

Each career development theory is discussed in terms of its implication for using occupational information, for using tests and inventories, and for special issues that may affect the application of the theory. Some theories use an occupational classification system; others specify how occupational information can be used in counseling. Yet other theories have relatively little to say about the use of occupational information. Because occupational information (and educational information) is such an important part of career counseling, special efforts are made to link theory and career information. Many theories use test and inventories both as a means of researching career development theory and as tools for the counselor to use in helping clients assess themselves. This book focuses on assessment instruments as they relate to theories and does not assume knowledge of assessment issues, although some information about reliability and validity is presented. Also, career development theories provide insight into possible conflicts between counselor values and client values, which may present problems to the counselor. When choosing among theories, occupational information and information about assessment can help students to select the career-development theories that will assist them most in their work as counselors.

In each chapter, a section addresses the application of theories of career development to women and culturally diverse populations. Theories vary greatly in how they address the issues of women. For example, Gottfredson's career development theory deals specifically with career issues of women. Other theories deal only tangentially with women's career choice issues. Many career development theories were originally created for white men and were later expanded to include women and diverse cultural groups. This fifth edition reflects an increase in research on the career development issues of culturally diverse populations. This is a particularly challenging issue to address because there is a wide variety of cultural groups and differences within cultural groups. For example, there are many significant cultural differences among Native American tribal groups. Also, some career development issues may be different for African Americans compared with those of African descent in other countries. Included in the emphasis on cultural diversity is a reference to research done in other countries, especially Europe and Asia.

CONTENTS OF THIS BOOK

This book is divided into an introduction and four parts: "Trait and Type Theories" (Part One), "Life-Span Theory" (Part Two), "Special Focus Theories" (Part Three), and "Theoretical Integration" (Part Four). Trait and type theories emphasize the assessment of interest, abilities, achievements, personality, and values, together with the acquisition of occupational information. Life–span theory follows a chronological approach, studying people across broad stages in the life span. Special focus theories include the application to career development issues of research in psychology, such as constructivist theory and learning theory. Theoretical integration deals with how these theories can be combined for effective career counseling. The last chapter (Chapter 16) also discusses the relevance of career development areas to special issues such as noncounseling interventions, group counseling, and job placement, among other concerns. Chapter 1 briefly describes each chapter.

COURSE APPLICATION

This book is intended for a beginning graduate course of which career issues are a major component. The book can be used in different ways, depending on whether the emphasis of the course is on career counseling, career assessment, career guidance, or career theory.

Whereas most books that describe career counseling prescribe the method or many components of methods, this book presents a number of different theoretical and conceptual approaches to career counseling. After studying these various approaches, the student can decide which theories will be most helpful to him or her in counseling work. In general, the chapters are independent of each other, and not all chapters need to be assigned. Because trait and factor theory represents a straightforward approach to career choice and adjustment, it is often an appropriate starting place. Also, since Chapter 3 expands on occupational information described in Chapter 2, it may be appropriate to use the two chapters in sequence.

The assignment of career tests and inventories, together with their manuals, can be combined with the use of this book. Table 16.2 on pages 470-471, lists the tests and inventories referred to in this book and the theory with which they are associated. Trait and factor theories make the most use of the tests and inventories; life-span theory, decision-making theory, social learning theory, and constructivist approaches make less direct use of them.

Appendix A describes the CACREP criteria and how each of the CACREP criteria relates to topics covered in this book. Some criteria are covered thoroughly, such as career theory, the most obvious example. Others, such as instructional career guidance in the classroom, receive less coverage. However, this book does provide a background for designing guidance activities and programs.

SUPPLEMENTS

A student manual, which was available for the fourth edition, has been revised and is now available for this edition. Several features, in addition to sample questions, are provided. Career development exercises are provided with two purposes. The first purpose is to have students understand their own career development by using the theory or theories described in the chapter. The second purpose is to provide students with exercises that they may use in their counseling work as students or professionals. Another section of the student manual uses a case study approach to learning the theory. At various points in the case, multiple-choice questions are asked about the case. Open-ended questions are asked about how theory addresses general and cultural issues. The final section has multiple-choice and true or false review questions. Attention has been given to making the student manual interesting and relevant.

To provide instructors with materials that they may use in the classroom and to assist in preparation of lectures and examinations, I have expanded the instructor's manual. I have included numerous discussion questions for each chapter, as well as suggestions for role-playing of counseling in class. For examinations, I have prepared more than 500 multiple-choice questions (some questions that appeared in the previous edition of the manual have been revised for clarity). Also, I have expanded the Power Point slides that instructors may use in their classroom presentations. I believe that all the materials I have provided will suggest other classroom exercises, slides, or examination questions that instructors may wish to develop for their own purposes.

ACKNOWLEDGMENTS

Many people have been extremely helpful in reading one or more chapters of the book. I would like to thank the following people who have read and commented on the fifth edition of this book: Michael B. Johnson, University of Texas—Pan American; Deborah G. Haskins, Loyola College in Maryland; Andrew J. Finch, Vanderbilt University, Peabody; Justin C. Perry, Cleveland State University; LeeAnn M. Eschbach, University of Scranton; Amanda C. Healey, Old Dominion University; Shannon Ray, Nova Southeastern University; and J. Barry Mascari, Kean University.

I would also like to thank Karen J. Forbes of Lafayette College and Matthew R. Elliott of Holy Cross College, who read several early chapters, making suggestions for the ultimate form that this book would take. The following people read, commented on, of supplied materials for chapters in this book: Linda Gottfreson, James E. Hoffman, Lawrence Hotchkiss, Janice Jordan, Charles Link, Mary C. Miller, and Steven M. Sciscione of the University of Delaware; Janet Lenz, Gary Peterson, Robert Reardon, and James Sampson of Florida State University; Debra Bloch of the University of Maryland at Baltimore; David Blustein of Boston College; Rene V. Dawis of the University of Minnesota; Kimberly Ewing of Loyala University of Baltimore; Gail Hackett of the University of Arizona; John L. Holland; Richard T. Lapan of the University of Massachusetts; David Lubinski of Vanderbilt University; John D. Krumboltz of Stanford University; Robert Lent of the University of

Maryland; James Rounds of the University of Chicago; Mark L. Savickas of Northeastern Ohio Universities College of Medicine; Michael Smith of McGill University; Susan Phillips of the State University of New York at Albany; Terence J. G. Tracey of Arizona State University; Fred Vondracek of Pennsylvania State University; Colleen Teixeira and Stephanie White of the United States Bureau of Labor Statistics; and Richard Young of the University of British Columbia.

The staff of the Library of the University of Delaware were very helpful in providing resources and assistance for writing this new edition. I would especially like to thank Susan Brynteson, Director of Libraries and Jonathan Jeffrey, Associate Librarian for their assistance. Finally, I would like to thank my wife, Jane, for her patience and understanding when this book was being prepared.

Richard S. Sharf

INTRODUCTION

CHAPTER I

CHAPTER HIGHLIGHTS

The Role of Theory in Psychology

Counselors' Use of Career Development Theory

Counselor Skills

Goals of Career Counseling

Goals, Career Development Theory, and Ethics

Career Development of Women

Career Development of Culturally Diverse Populations

What's Ahead

Being satisfied with one's career is one of the most important aspects of an individual's personal happiness. Career concerns occur throughout one's lifetime. As young children are exposed to their parents' occupations, television programs, and the people around them, they become aware of career opportunities and choices. This exposure becomes broader and deeper throughout elementary school, middle school, and high school. It is difficult for students not to be overwhelmed by the many choices of occupations facing them. After high school, temporary and transitional occupations are often chosen, with continued adjustment throughout one's life span to increase career satisfaction. During retirement, questions of career satisfaction may be important. Because approximately half of a person's waking hours is spent working, dissatisfaction with career demands can spread into other parts of one's life. It is not uncommon for job dissatisfaction to affect relationships with family and friends. People who are dissatisfied with their work or find it boring or monotonous must look for satisfaction in other areas of their lives, such as leisure and family. For many people, however, these other satisfactions do not compensate for the frustration they experience at work. The opportunity to help someone adjust to a selected career is an opportunity to affect a person's life positively, in meaningful and significant ways.

The knowledge that several hours spent in counseling can greatly influence the outcome of an individual's life is an exciting challenge to the counselor. Individuals unfamiliar with career counseling have sometimes compartmentalized counseling by saying there is personal counseling, and then there is career counseling. In editing a special section of *The Career Development Quarterly*, Linda Subich (1993) asked the question: "How personal is career counseling?" She received 32 submissions, of which 10 were published. The clear, virtually unanimous answer was "Very personal." These respondents recognized that personal issues pervade career counseling, and that career issues are often prominent in personal counseling, thus making the distinction between the two moot. A survey of experts in vocational psychology shows that they use the same counseling skills in dealing with career issues as they do in dealing with other personal counseling issues (Whiston, Lindeman, Rahardja, & Reed, 2005). Career counseling can include discussion of many different personal, familial, and cultural issues (Maxwell, 2007). In dealing with college students, Hinkelman and Luzzo (2007) show how personal issues affect career development and vice versa. These articles point out the personal nature of career counseling from many different vantage points. Because career issues do not always have the immediate impact on counselors that negative or stressful events or feelings may have, career issues may be neglected or dismissed if they are not examined thoroughly.

A wide variety of approaches have been used in career counseling, some of which adapt techniques from personal counseling. For example, Nevo and Wiseman (2002) use Mann's short-term dynamic psychotherapy as a model for career counseling. This model stresses the importance of the therapeutic relationship, client activities over their life span, and active counselor participation. Other writers address career counseling for individuals with marital concerns such as those of battered women (Brown et al., 2005). Recently, attention has been given to gay and lesbian clients. For lesbian, gay, and bisexual youth, sexual identity conflicts and lack of social support can interfere with or slow the process of career decision making (Schmidt & Nilsson, 2006). Focusing on lesbian clients, Bieschke and Toepfer-Hendey (2006) suggest a model of career counseling to help them deal with personal and social issues affecting career concerns. Increasingly, counselors are applying techniques from personal counseling to a variety of culturally diverse groups and to a variety of issues, such as those described in this paragraph.

In this textbook, numerous case examples are used to illustrate the application of career development theory to counseling. Most of the examples have personal and career components. For instance, Winifred (Chapter 4) is a 45-year-old farmer who is faced with the difficulty of changing jobs after experiencing chronic back pain. Chester (Chapter 5) is a high school dropout whose boredom and frustration with his life and work are affecting his personal life. George (Chapter 6) is tense and anxious at work and has difficulty dealing with the employees who he supervises. Arthur (Chapter 7), a fourth-grade student, is starting to fall behind in school, is withdrawing from his peers, and is frustrated by reading. Personal issues confront Chad (Chapter 8) as he decides between selling drugs and staying in school to prepare for a career. Matthew (Chapter 9) is 64 years old and is confused and afraid as he faces imminent retirement. Having been laid off from a job that he has had for 23 years, John, who is 55, is angry and depressed (Chapter 10). The trauma of sexual harassment and racial discrimination forces Roberta (Chapter 10) to deal with her anger and the perpetrators of the harassment. Dennis, a 25-year-old grocery store manager, lives at home and struggles to cope with his father's negative views of him (Chapter 11). Lacking self-confidence and tending to procrastinate, Tiffany is having difficulty leaving a job she dislikes in order to train for a new career (Chapter 11). Maria (Chapter 12), a high school junior, is unsure of her ability to make decisions. Planning to be a professional football player, Xavier has broken his leg and is upset that his dreams for the future now seem uncertain (Chapter 13). Sharon (Chapter 14) is unsure of herself, especially her academic ability; this lack of self-efficacy plays a role in her dilemma about her career choice. Her reactions are affected by her relationships with her friends and family. Parnell's (Chapter 15) disciplinary problems in college have put stress on his relationships with his family members and have caused him to think about his decisions regarding his future career and his decision making in general. A spiritual approach to career decision making is illustrated through Bonnie's experiences (Chapter 15). Bonnie is not sure whether to attend college and must contend with her mother's hurt feelings. These are a sampling of some of the cases that appear in this textbook, many of which are concerned with both personal and career issues.

Life issues and problems occur at many different times. The developmental nature of career concerns can be seen in the case of Lucy, who is discussed in Chapters 7, 8, and 9. As a fifth-grade student, she is upset about her mother's forcing her father out of the house, and her reaction affects her interactions at school and within her family. At 15 years old, the pressures on Lucy from her father and her boyfriend to go to nursing school rather than to medical school are affecting her self-confidence and her ability to make decisions. At 28 years old, Lucy is hurting from the breakup of a 3-year relationship and is deciding whether to return to school to become a physician. These personal and career issues are intertwined, as they are for many clients.

One definition of *career* refers to roles individuals play over their lifetime (Niles & Harris-Bowlsbey, 2002). The roles may include leisure and community service, as well as other activities. The case studies presented in this book offer snapshots of a person's career or an aspect of a person's working and leisure behavior. In this textbook, *career choice* applies to decisions that individuals make at any point in their career about particular work, leisure, or other activities that they choose to pursue at that time. The focus is on the individual, in contrast to the terms *job*, *occupation*, and *work*. In this textbook, jobs refer to positions requiring similar skills within one organization. Occupations refer to similar jobs found in many organizations. Occupations exist regardless of whether individuals are employed in them. Career refers to the lifetime pursuits of the individual. *Work*, a term used occasionally in this text, refers to purposeful activity to earn money or other reward and possibly to produce a product or service for others. Although *work* often is used to describe an unpleasant activity, work can be pleasant and rewarding economically, spiritually, socially, or personally. Other authors may define work as effort spent in an activity, or they may have other definitions of work.

Career development theory can serve as a guide for career counseling and for problems similar to those described earlier. By tying together research about career choice and adjustment with ideas about these issues, career development theorists have provided a conceptual framework within which to view the types of career problems that emerge during a person's lifetime. To understand these theories, I wish to first discuss the role of theory in psychology.

THE ROLE OF THEORY IN PSYCHOLOGY

In reviewing the role of theory in psychology, Heinen (1985) describes theory as "a group of logically organized laws or relationships that constitute explanation in a discipline" (p. 414). Theory has been particularly important in the development of physical and biological science. Within psychology, theory has made a distinct impact in the area of learning. When applied to career development, theory becomes cruder and less precise. Career development theory attempts to explain behavior that occurs over many years and is made up of reactions to thousands of situations, experiences, and people, such as school, hobbies, and parents.

Regardless of the type of theory, there are certain general principles for judging the appropriateness of a theory. The following are criteria by which career development theories can be evaluated (Fawcett & Downs, 1986; Franck, 2002; Hanzel, 1999; Snow, 1973).

1. *Theories should be explicit about their rules and theorems. Terms that are used in describing these rules should be clear.* Theories that attempt to explain how people make career choices often have difficulty in defining terms such as *growth, development,* and *self-concept.* Theorems about career selection are also difficult to make. In general, the broader the theory, the more difficult it is to be specific about the terms that are used.

2. *Theories should be precise about the limitations of their predictions. Theories differ in the breadth of behavior that they attempt to predict.* For example, some theories attempt to explain career development for women, some for both men and women, and some for people of different age groups. Some theories attempt to explain vocational choice, whereas others try to explain how people adjust to this choice; still others explain both. It is important to understand what the subject of the theory is. It is unfair to criticize a theory for not doing something that it does not set out to do.

3. *When theories are developed, they need to be tested.* Testing a theory is accomplished by doing research that can be expressed in terms of quantitative relationships. By doing research studies that use clear and measurable terms, investigators can best determine if data are in agreement with the theory. Within the field of career development, it is sometimes difficult to determine whether research supports a theory. The reason may be that an investigator has defined terms in a different way from the theorist or has used an unrepresentative sample to make predictions or generalizations. For example, if a theorist attempts to explain how

all people make choices, the research samples should include both men and women across a broad range of cultural, social, and financial backgrounds. Sometimes evidence from a research study is unclear, supporting some propositions of a theory but not others, or supporting the theory for some populations but not others. A helpful method for confirming theoretical constructs is to develop inventories that define constructs and relate them to other constructs within the theory, as well as to other theories and instruments. By the accumulation of such information, construct validity is established for the theory and the instrument.

   4. *A theory needs to be consistent and clear.* A theory should provide constructs that have a logical relationship to each other. To be clear, the theory should not be too complex. It should provide the simplest way to explain propositions. However, there is the danger of oversimplification. Essential components should not be left out of a theory. Because vocational theorists attempt to explain exceedingly complex behavior, it is only natural that they may oversimplify their theories. In doing so, they may provide a useful and understandable guide for the counselor.

   In summary, a theory needs to be explicit about its theorems and terms. Furthermore, it needs to be clear about what it is theorizing and the breadth of its propositions. In addition, research should be able to provide positive or negative support for the theory. Sometimes research findings add to and further develop a theory, showing that it is open to change. Also, a career development theory, while being neither too simple nor too complex, must provide a useful way of explaining and understanding career development.

   Judgments about the soundness and relative utility of theories are difficult for the counselor to make. Osipow and Fitzgerald (1995) and Brown (2002), among others, have attempted to evaluate how well career development theories meet criteria similar to those described earlier. Although research will receive comment, the primary focus of this textbook is the application of the theory by the counselor. I have determined that most of the theories included in this textbook meet, at least minimally, the four criteria listed earlier. Some theories are quite new and have not yet met these criteria, but they provide new ideas for counselors to consider.

   A broad approach to the application of theory to career development and to psychology in general has been taken by Dawis (2000, 2002). He argues that the Person–Environment Fit model can be used as a way of understanding the important aspects of psychological science. He believes that by studying the interaction between individuals and their environment, researchers will have an excellent model for studying many psychological issues, including career choice and development. Other writers have examined different approaches to the study of the Person–Environment Fit model that can be used depending on the variables being studied (Edwards, Cable, Williamson, Lambert, & Shipp, 2006; Jansen & Kristof-Brown, 2006). Almost all of the theories in this book, especially Chapters 2 through 6, can be viewed from this broad perspective as they focus on how individuals interact with their environment (for example, school, work, and families). However, the Person–Environment Fit model is too broad to be applied by counselors without more specifications; therefore, I discuss theories that are more detailed and specific about career development.

COUNSELORS' USE OF CAREER DEVELOPMENT THEORY

When selecting theories of career development to apply, counselors must not only have confidence in the theory, as described in the previous section, but they also must make judgments about the advisability of using that theory with their clients. Furthermore, counselors need to consider their own view and style of counseling or psychotherapy. Their theory of counseling is likely to influence their selection of a theory of career development. The counselor also needs to select a theory of career development that is manageable and relatively easy to draw on in a counseling session. These three concepts are discussed in more detail in the following sections.

CLIENT POPULATION

Counselors work in a wide variety of settings and are likely to encounter a preponderance of one or another type of career problem. For example, elementary school and middle school counselors work with students who are at the beginning of the career information and selection process. High school and college counselors tend to help their clients with vocational choice, development of alternatives, and job placement. Although employment counselors deal with some of the same issues as high school and college counselors, they may encounter more issues related to satisfaction with and adjustment to a job. Some counselors work in business and industry with a limited number of professions, such as accounting and engineering. These counselors are likely to be involved in issues of work satisfaction, adjustment, and promotion. Vocational rehabilitation counselors and other counselors who work with clients who are physically and mentally challenged deal not only with the issues mentioned earlier but they also must judge the applicability of the theory to the challenges of their clientele. Moreover, retirement issues have become a greater concern of counselors in recent years. Choosing new, part-time, or volunteer work and scaling down the demands of current work are issues that retirement counselors often consider.

Pastoral counselors, physicians, clinical psychologists, and psychiatrists work in settings where their clients may have career choice or adjustment issues that are related to other problems. Although career concerns may not be the presenting problem for the clients of these and other mental health workers, they may still be significant issues. Furthermore, the gender of the client can be an important variable in theory selection. Counselors can ask themselves if a theory is as appropriate for younger as older individuals. Because career development theories differ in the age range that they choose to explain, it is for the counselor to decide whether a particular career development theory is appropriate for the population with which he or she works.

THEORIES OF COUNSELING AND THEORIES OF CAREER DEVELOPMENT

Like counseling theories, many theories of career development are derived from theories of personality. Often, it is difficult to clearly distinguish theories of counseling and of career development from theories of personality.

In general, counseling and psychotherapy theories tend to be a subset of personality theories used to bring about a desired change in feeling, thinking, or behavior. Similarly, some theories of career development tend to be a subset of personality theories, which include how people relate to work and career issues. Therefore, because personality, counseling, and career development theory are highly interrelated, it is natural for counselors who prefer a certain personality theory or theory of counseling to be drawn to a compatible career development theory.

Because theories of personality and counseling form the core of a counselor's training, they tend to influence the counselor's selection of a theory of career development. Rarely would the selection of a theory of career development determine a counselor's theory of personality or career counseling. For example, counselors attracted to Jungian theory may wish to use the Myers–Briggs theory of types. Those counselors who use rational emotive behavior therapy, behavioral therapy, or cognitive therapy may find trait and factor theory, Holland's theory of types, social learning, and cognitive information processing approaches to be particularly helpful. Many counselors are eclectic in their practical orientation; that is, they may draw from many theories. Although it is helpful to be open to the value of all theories of career development, it is important to remember the connection between career development theory and counseling theory. The theories presented in this book differ in terms of how similar they are to theories of personality, with a few being quite different.

Chunking

The concept of chunking is important for counselors to consider when selecting a theory of career development. Unlike computers, counselors have a limited ability to remember information. Psychologists have studied the limited capacity of both short- and long-term memory. In studying short-term memory, Miller (1956) suggested that people can process five to nine concepts, ideas, numbers, words, or sentences at a time. This processing is done by grouping concepts or ideas and is called *chunking*. Chunking is a concept that is used in teaching to help individuals improve their learning (Bodie, Powers, & Fitch-Hauser, 2006). It has also been studied in order to help researchers understand how individuals develop expertise in different areas of learning (Gobet, 2005). Research has extended knowledge about chunking by examining physiological aspects of learning. Studies of brain-wave frequency and the cerebral cortex suggest that working memory handles about seven items at a time (Glassman, 1999; Wickelgren, 1999). The concept of chunking has been extended to understand the thinking of novice and experienced psychotherapists, with experienced psychotherapists chunking more information than inexperienced psychotherapists (Ettelson, 2002).

There is value in applying the concept of chunking to the use of career development theory in career counseling. Theories that have three or four basic constructs are likely to be learned relatively easily. Theories with up to eight or nine concepts may be remembered and used with some difficulty, depending on how often the concepts are reused in counseling. For example, John Holland has a theory that describes six basic types of people and work environments, which is explained in Chapter 5. Having relatively few types makes the process of remembering them easier for counselors than if there were more types. Theories with more than eight or nine concepts are likely to present a retention problem for the counselor when he or she is starting to put a theory into practice. One solution is to divide the theory into several chunks. It is important to do this, because counselors need to learn information about a number of subjects, such as helping skills, career assessment, and occupational information, when assisting clients in career decision making.

COUNSELOR SKILLS

The primary purpose of this book is to describe the usefulness of career development theory in counseling people with problems of career choice and adjustment. Information about theories can be combined with helping skills, which are often based on the early work of Carl Rogers (1951). Since the 1940s, career assessment has also been an integral part of career counseling. Furthermore, the use of occupational information as found in pamphlets, books, and computers is a necessary component of career counseling. These three areas of knowledge—helping skills, testing, and providing occupational information—are described in the following sections in terms of their relation to career development theory.

HELPING SKILLS

Since the early 1980s, a number of books have described helping skills. The authors of these books appear to agree generally on the helping skills necessary for change in most counseling situations, including career counseling. Their work is based on the views of Carl Rogers (1958), who specifies four basic conditions necessary for counseling change: unconditional positive regard, genuineness, congruence, and empathy.

Unconditional positive regard can be described as the acceptance of a person as being worthwhile and valuable, regardless of age, gender, race, or what he or she has done. Genuineness refers to sincerity—the need for the counselor to be honest with the client. Congruence requires that the counselor's voice tone, body language, and verbal statements be consistent with one another. Finally, empathy refers to the ability to communicate to the client that the counselor understands the client's concerns and feelings from the point of view of the client. These four basic conditions have become the cornerstone of research involving more than 260 studies.

Truax and Carkhuff (1967) and Carkhuff and Berenson (1967) have done considerable research to further define and develop Rogers's work. Recently, Chang, Scott, and Decker (2008), Egan (2007), Ivey and Ivey (2008), and Okun and Kantrowitz (2008) have provided methods for learning the basic or core helping skills. In addition, these authors have emphasized (to varying degrees) other important skills such as asking open-ended and nonbiased questions. In addition to discussing, paraphrasing, and reflecting feelings (basic empathic listening skills), these authors have explained important issues of confrontation and the need for concreteness and specificity. They also have provided texts for courses in basic counseling skills or helping relationships. A detailed explanation of these skills goes beyond the scope of this book. However, I describe the most common interventions and counseling techniques that are likely to be used in career counseling. These interventions are used in many of the case examples that are found throughout this book.

ATTENDING SKILLS A basic counseling skill is the counselor's nonverbal presence in the counseling situation. In an attending position, counselors face their clients squarely, adopting an open posture (legs and arms not crossed) and leaning slightly toward the other person. Maintaining good eye contact, but not staring, is natural for people who are having a deep conversation. Counselors also maintain a relaxed, rather than tense or fidgety, presence. These skills are used primarily in North America when addressing clients. In other cultures, people may show attentiveness in other ways (Egan, 2007).

QUESTIONS Questions are used to get specific information or to help clients describe or elaborate on certain subjects, feelings, or events. Closed-ended questions request specific information, and the answers are often of the "yes" or "no" variety. Open-ended questions encourage a broader response, asking the client to explain more fully the what, how, when, or where of a situation, feeling, or event. Both types of questions are illustrated in the following dialogue:

CO: What grade did you get in English last year? [Closed-ended question]
CL: I got an A.
CO: Did you like the class? [Closed-ended question]
CL: Yes, it was OK.
CO: What did you learn about in class? [Open-ended question]
CL: We studied modern writers, and I learned how to critique short stories. I was surprised that my ability to develop a good paragraph really changed during the course. My teacher was very helpful and complimented me about my progress.
CO: How does that affect your thoughts about college? [Open-ended question]
CL: It really gets me thinking. I hadn't known that I could write that well. The short reviews we did in class really made me more comfortable with writing and made me think, 'Hey, I can do more of this.' I could even do it in college.

As shown here, open-ended questions usually elicit a much broader explanation from the client than do closed-ended questions. Questions, in general, and especially closed-ended questions tend to place the burden of the interview on the counselor. In a sense, if questions are used frequently, clients develop an expectation that if they answer the questions the counselor will provide a solution to the problem. In this book, questions are used sparingly in the case examples. Rather, the counselors in the examples are more apt to use reflections of client statements.

STATEMENTS AND REFLECTIONS By rephrasing what the client has said, counselors focus on the cognitive or emotional content of a client's statement. When a client makes a statement, restating it directs attention to the situation, the person, or the general idea. The client thus is encouraged to add to or to develop his or her statement. Restatements may reflect not only the words of the client, but also the voice tone, gestures, and facial expressions. Because information and affect are attached to career issues, it is often helpful to make content and feeling reflections. Feeling reflections contain (or imply) an emotional word or phrase. Content reflections focus on the information that the client provides.

CL: My work is so boring. All I do is wait on one customer after another. I ring up the sale. Give the customer the receipt. Ring up the sale. Give the customer the receipt. And on and on.

CONTENT REFLECTION: Each day you perform the same actions over and over again.
FEELING REFLECTION: Waiting on customers is really boring you and annoying you. You can't wait till the day is over.

In this situation, the content reflection tells only a small part of the story. The feeling reflection provides a fuller expression of the client's experience. In the cases in this book, when feeling or emotional content is provided in the client's statement, the counselor's response usually reflects the affective component. Content reflections tend to be used mainly when the counselor perceives little affect.

CONTINUATION RESPONSES   Often, in career counseling (and other counseling), it can be helpful to request more information. A nonverbal gesture such as nodding or using a hand movement invites a client to continue. Verbal comments include: "Tell me more," "Can you say more about that?" "Go on," "Hmm," "And then?" and "And what happened then?" The following brief example attempts to clarify the usefulness of continuation responses.

CO: What are your plans for next year? [Open-ended question]
CL: I think that I'm going to work in the department store's hardware department. I've done it for three years, and it's easy to continue to do so. Besides, I really think I need to get more money before I can continue college.
CO: Say more about that, if you would. [Continuation response]
CL: It's easy to stay in the hardware department. I know it really well, but I'm not getting very far with it. Sometimes I think I should go back to school anyway, even though I don't have the money, and just hope things will work out.
CO: Hmm. Tell me more. [Continuation response]
CL: I don't think that I have the money, but maybe I can get my father to take out a loan. He really doesn't want to, but if I'm really persuasive, maybe he can help me. It sure would be better than having to be back in that old job.

When discussing career issues, continuation techniques bring out more information than the client may volunteer at first. The career development theories in this book focus on the client as an important informational resource about himself or herself. Thus, continuation responses are frequently seen in the examples.

GIVING INFORMATION, NOT OPINION   Often, counselors give clients information about educational or occupational opportunities. It is important that this information be accurate, up to date, and clear. Biased information can be destructive and confusing to the client. Opinions that are given by the counselor represent only one person's view. However, because clients are likely to view counselors as experts, the counselors' opinions may be perceived as being information or *the truth*. Counselors who give opinions risk discouraging or encouraging a client inappropriately.

CL: Now, after I've completed my first year of college, I have a C average. I'm not sure whether I should revise my plans to go to medical school.
OPINION 1: I think that you should revise your plans. Students with a C average have little chance of getting into medical school.
OPINION 2: Things are likely to get better. You still have a chance to pull your grades up and probably get into medical school.

QUESTION ABOUT
INFORMATION: What do you think about your chances of getting into medical school? [The counselor wants to know what the basis of the client's information is.]

CL: I realize that most students have to have an A-minus average to go to medical school, but I think I can raise my grades.

INFORMATION: You may find it helpful to go to the premed adviser to get more information about how students have done here in getting into medical school. [The counselor does not have the specific information that the client needs on hand but directs the client to an appropriate source.]

Although individuals with a C average in their freshman year in college may find it difficult to be admitted to medical school, there are some exceptions. The counselor assumes a powerful role if she or he gives Opinions 1 or 2. The theories that are discussed in this book assume that the client, rather than the counselor, is the decision maker; thus, the counselor should provide guidance for career decision-making and accurate information, rather than opinions.

REINFORCEMENT   A behavioral technique, verbal reinforcement of the client's behavior is often used in career counseling. This technique is particularly featured in Chapter 13, which describes social learning theory. In verbal reinforcement, it is the client's behavior that is reinforced, rather than the client.

CL: I've been wanting to tell my boss that he's been giving me too many assignments lately. I've been afraid to do so, and I've been really anxious. I'm afraid that he will be really mad at me and tell me I'll have to leave my job. This is something I don't want to do. It's a great job otherwise. This has bugged me so much that I've been losing sleep over it, and I'm really starting to feel depressed. Finally, I got up the courage and talked to my boss and told him exactly what it was that was bothering me. He was understanding and I was really relieved.

CO: That's terrific. You did something that you have wanted to do for quite a while. You explained the problem and the difficulties, and you got satisfaction. That's wonderful.

If the client had said, "I told my boss all these things, and he got really angry," the counselor might have replied, "You did what you wanted to do. You explained the problem to him specifically and told him how it was bothering you. It's great that you were able to do so. It's too bad that he didn't respond the way you wanted him to." In both cases, the counselor is reinforcing the client's behavior. A common behavior that counselors reinforce is information seeking. For example, when a client has read about or talked to people in a particular profession, counselors may say, "That's terrific that you spent so much time in finding out about that. Great!"

FAMILY BACKGROUND EXPLORATION   Chapter 12, which focuses on relational approaches to career development, discusses ways of exploring the role of the family (and others) in career decision making. For example, the genogram is a method of diagramming family relationships and is a tool for discussing the relationship of clients' career plans to those of their families.

ASSESSMENT INTERPRETATION   An important career-counseling intervention is interpretation of tests and inventories. Discussed particularly in the theories that are explained in Part One, test and inventory interpretation provides information about the client to the client. In interpreting tests or inventories for clients, counselors use many of the skills that have been described in this chapter. Throughout the book, examples of assessment interpretation are given for interest, ability, value, and personality tests and inventories. Some of the specific knowledge that is needed to make accurate assessment interpretations is discussed briefly in the following section. Assessment interpretation, like many of the techniques described in this textbook, is helpful in career counseling. Other techniques, such as confrontation, self-disclosure, and counselor interpretations, can also be helpful and are described in some of the books cited earlier.

Most career development theories do not specify counseling techniques. Rather, they provide a way of comprehending and organizing the information that is contained in counseling sessions. The tools that produce this information are the content and feeling reflections, open-ended questions, and other techniques mentioned previously. Career development theory, which may indirectly (and sometimes directly) affect the technique used, aids the counselor in understanding the client. It is likely that the counselors using trait and factor theory will ask more questions and will use fewer feeling reflections than those who apply Super's lifespan theory. However, this does not have to be the case. This book focuses on making use of career development theory in conceptualizing career counseling when assisting a client.

ASSESSMENT INSTRUMENTS

Two types of assessment instruments are discussed in this textbook: tests and inventories. The term *test* refers generally to ability and achievement tests on which there are correct answers and on which individuals attempt to perform as well as possible ("maximum performance"). The term *inventory* refers to instruments that solicit a preference or viewpoint from the client and have no "right" or "wrong" answers. Common inventories used in counseling measure interests, values, and personality. Career development theories differ in the weight they give to the importance of tests and inventories in the career development process. Tests and inventories have been in wide use for career counseling since the 1930s and 1940s. Extensive test development took place during World War II because of the need to assign men and women to the military tasks for which they were best suited. Although originally designed for the selection of employees, tests and inventories have been particularly useful in counseling. To be competent in test or inventory selection, counselors need to understand measurement concepts such as normative information, reliability, and validity. Because these concepts are so important in understanding assessment, they are described briefly in the following sections. However, these descriptions do not take the place of a course or text on psychological measurement.

NORMS   It is useful to compare a client's score on a test or inventory with a normative sample (norms) that is used in developing a standard for scoring (Neukrug & Fawcett, 2006). Such a sample should be normal scores—that is, those that are typical of a population. Sometimes, norms are based on a general population; at other times, they are based on specific groups, such as high school students, accountants, or former drug abusers. In some cases, norms are listed separately for male and female individuals; in other cases, they are combined. Norms are also sometimes separated for people of different genders or ages. Good norms are helpful in providing counselors with a full understanding of the basis of the comparisons that they will make. For example, a counselor usually would not want to compare a 12th-grade client's biology achievement score with the scores of 9th-grade students. Although national norms are used frequently, it is sometimes helpful to have local norms, to compare students within a school system or a state.

Norms typically are presented in percentile scores, which are easy to understand because counselors can see the percentage of individuals with results above or below a particular score. Often, standard scores are used because, unlike percentile scores, they provide for a uniform difference between each score. Thus, the difference between 50 and 55 is the same as the difference between 70 and 75, which is not true of percentages. It is important for counselors who wish to use the tests or inventories that are described in this book to read a test manual to learn about norms and to decide, where appropriate, which norms to use.

RELIABILITY   To be used, a test or inventory must be dependable and consistent. If a student takes a test or inventory one time, the score that he or she receives a second time should be similar. A test or inventory that has perfect reliability would be one on which everyone's scores were in the same relative position on every additional administration of the instrument. There are two major sources of unreliability: variation in human performance and variation in the technical aspects of measurement. For example, a measurement of math ability should be more stable than a measure of depression, which varies according to mood. Error may be caused by the testing conditions, such as lighting, heat or cold, and poor instructions. On many instruments, the reliability coefficients usually exceed .80, but there are some situations in which an acceptable reliability may be less. Reliability may be measured by administering the same instrument on two different occasions or two different forms of the same test on different occasions. Split-half reliability is obtained by dividing a single test or inventory into two comparable halves, and then comparing the results from the two halves. Yet another measure is interitem consistency, which is arrived at by examining the average intercorrelations among the items on an assessment instrument. Knowledge of the reliability of an instrument is important in deciding whether to use it with clients.

VALIDITY   Does a test or inventory measure what it is supposed to measure? Does a measure of English skills really measure skills in English? How well a test or inventory measures what is requested of it is referred to as *validity* (Neukrug & Fawcett, 2006). For a test or inventory to be valid, it must first be reliable; that is, it must be a consistent measure of a trait or other variable. Different types of scales require different types of validity. *Content validity* refers to the actual content of the items. The items should reflect the area (for example, knowledge of algebra) that the instrument is attempting to measure. *Concurrent validity* is a measure against a specific criterion. For example, scores on a test of clerical ability can be compared with the performance of secretaries who have established clerical abilities. *Predictive validity* also refers to a criterion, but one that applies to the future. For example, a test of clerical aptitude should predict how well applicants for secretarial positions will perform on clerical aspects of their positions in a year from that date. *Construct validity* is more complex, referring to whether the scales make psychological sense and are related to the variables to which they should be related. A depression inventory should be related to other inventories of depression or psychiatric ratings of depressed people on specific symptoms of depression. Test and inventory manuals provide the counselor with information on these types of validity. An assessment instrument that is not valid has little value for the counselor. This book mentions many tests and inventories, and all have at least moderate validity in some, but not all, of the four types of validity described here.

Assessment instruments play two major roles in career development theory. First, tests and inventories can be used to develop and verify a theory. Second, tests and inventories can provide the counselor with information that can then be used as a means of understanding the client from the point of view of career development theory. For example, John Holland developed and used the Self-Directed Search and the Vocational Preference Inventory as a way to test the constructs of his theory. Another example is Super's career development theory. Donald Super developed the Values Scale and the Career Development Inventory, among many other inventories. Other investigators have developed career maturity scales, all of which can be used to research various aspects of Super's theory. Counselors can use these instruments to develop knowledge about the client that they can then relate directly to a theoretical context.

For the counselor, tests and inventories have three major features: selection, administration, and interpretation. Norms, reliability, and validity are important considerations in deciding which tests or inventories to select. Test and inventory selection may also be based on theoretical concepts that are relevant to the clients, which are discussed further in this textbook. Administration is described in detail in each test manual, and different considerations apply to individual and group test-taking procedures. Interpreting a test or inventory requires knowledge of both the client and the assessment instrument. This textbook provides examples of test and inventory interpretation to show how a counselor may discuss portions of results with a client.

PROVIDING OCCUPATIONAL INFORMATION   Career counseling differs from other types of counseling in its reliance on occupational and educational information. Over 30 years ago, Hoppock (1976) described in detail the information that counselors should know about occupations and the importance of occupational information in counseling. His advice about what counselors should know about occupational information is still valuable now:

- Know where their clients get their first jobs or where their clients go to work after they have completed counseling.
- Determine the principal employment opportunities in their local area. The geographic area within which college students search for jobs is likely to be much larger than for high school students, who are more likely to look for work close to home.

- Learn about occupations that are being considered by their clients, so they can provide information appropriate for their clients.
- Learn about at least one occupation that is central to each of three of the most important and largest local employers. This will entail visiting and developing contacts with these employers.
- Know how to obtain information and to evaluate it for accuracy and usefulness.

Essentially, counselors need to know certain types of information and specific sources of career information. The types of information that are perhaps most important include descriptions of the occupation, working conditions, qualifications required by the job duties, beginning and average salaries, employment outlook, education (courses, majors, or degrees) required by the job, and where one can get more information about the occupation. Information related to these topics is provided in publications such as the *Occupational Outlook Handbook* (2008) and the *Encyclopedia of Careers and Vocational Guidance* (Ferguson, 2007), which also have online versions. These publications offer occupational information about a broad and representative sample of occupations. In addition, pamphlets produced by publishers specializing in occupational information and by trade organizations describe hundreds of occupations that are available. Textbooks and courses on occupational information deal fully with these topics and are helpful for effective career counseling. Furthermore, a number of computerized guidance products such as DISCOVER (ACT, 2007) and SIGI³ (VALPAR, 2007) provide occupational information together with career assessment.

Career development theories vary widely in the attention that they direct to occupational information. For example, Holland's theory provides a system for classifying all occupational information through the use of six categories. Holland provides an identifiable code for each occupation that has clear meaning according to his theory. In contrast, the Myers–Briggs theoretical formulation focuses almost entirely on the person's type and not on occupational information. Super and colleagues (Starishevsky & Matlin, 1963) used the term *occtalk* to describe occupational information that clients learn; they used the term *psychtalk* to delineate the views that clients have of themselves. For instance, the statement "It is helpful for musicians to know a number of instruments" is an example of occtalk, whereas "I enjoy learning music theory" is an example of psychtalk. This example illustrates how theorists have built a bridge between occupational information and information about the client from a counseling interview. Although occupational information is described in this chapter, it is explained in detail in Chapter 2 as a means of classifying careers and in Chapter 3 as a way of learning information about the labor market. Classifying occupations and learning about the labor market are two important aspects of occupational information.

How Career Development Theory Relates to Career Counseling

Just as counseling theories provide a framework for the conceptualization of client problems, career development theory provides a framework for helping with a client's career problems. Career development theory can be considered the part of the process of career counseling that offers a means of conceptualizing career concerns. Basic helping skills are the essential ingredient in bringing about change and progress in career issues. Assessment instruments, as well as occupational information, can be seen as additional information that aids in the conceptualization process. Counseling skills are used to provide feedback about tests and inventories or to give information about occupations. Overall, it is career development theory that can give counselors an idea of how they are going to help their clients and what the eventual outcome of counseling may be. The goal directedness that career development theory can provide gives counselors, particularly beginning counselors, a sense of confidence.

GOALS OF CAREER COUNSELING

The two most common goals of career counseling are the selection of an occupation and the adjustment to an occupation. As shown in Chapters 7 and 8, career selection usually takes place any time after the age of 14 years, but most commonly during high school, college, or both. When helping a client in the process of choosing occupations, counselors often use information about the client's satisfaction with any previous work. When adults are trying to find more satisfaction in an occupation, they often question their current career choice and review their reasons for seeking that occupation. This may happen at any time during a person's working life. Some theorists, such as Dawis and Lofquist (1984), focus on vocational adjustment, as well as vocational selection. Implicit in all career development theories is the notion that the client, rather than the counselor, makes the final choice.

Goals, whether explicit or implicit, are essential to counseling. Goals serve as a guide for the work that is done in the counseling session. An example of making goals explicit is when the counselor and the client agree that the purpose of counseling is to select from appropriate career alternatives. An example of making goals implicit is when the counselor assumes that the client wishes to select appropriate career alternatives. Whether the goals are explicit or implicit, the use of career development theories can make goals clear and specific for the counselor.

For each theory in this book, methods of conceptualizing theoretical constructs in terms of counseling goals are described to the extent that the theory permits. A counselor using theoretical constructs in conceptualizing client goals should have a sense of how well the counseling is progressing, what (in general) should happen next in the counseling, and what needs to take place for the counseling to be completed. These goals and their implementation may not be identical for all people. Ethical standards help counselors meet their clients' goals in constructive and appropriate ways.

GOALS, CAREER DEVELOPMENT THEORY, AND ETHICS

To assist clients in issues related to career development, counselors must behave ethically. Ethics, at the most basic level, are standards of behavior developed by a group of people to which members of that group should behave. They often overlap with laws, which are standards developed and enforced by governmental bodies. For counselors and other mental health practitioners, there are professional and governmental organizations that have developed codes of ethics that counselors and mental health practitioners must follow, regardless of whether they are members of the organization, to guide them in ethically meeting their clients' goals.

There are ethical codes for psychiatrists, other physicians, nurses, clergy, social workers, psychologists, mental health counselors, marriage counselors, career counselors, and others. All of these codes of ethics are similar in intent and content. Differences tend to be quite minor and reflect the goals of the particular profession. Three of the most relevant sets of ethical standards for this textbook are those developed by the American Psychological Association (APA), the American Counseling Association (ACA), and the National Career Development Association (NCDA). Ethical standards of the NCDA (2007) are especially relevant to the focus of this textbook. They are discussed later in this section.

Ethical principles provide an overview of ethical standards and a framework for understanding ethical standards. Five moral standards are the foundation for the ethical principles of most codes of ethics in the helping professions (Corey, Corey, & Callanan, 2007; Van Hoose, 1986; Welfel, 2008), These standards reflect the values of those working in the helping professions, including career counselors, as they view their interactions with and responsibilities to clients. The five moral principles are autonomy, nonmaleficence, beneficence, justice, and fidelity.

Autonomy

Counselors respect that clients make their own decisions. Clients control their own lives and make their own choices. Counselors help clients to develop independent decision-making skills. Counselors refrain from judging clients' values.

Nonmaleficence

Basically, counselors do no harm. They do not hurt or manipulate clients for their own gain. Taking care not to inadvertently hurt clients is one aspect of the principle.

Beneficence

More than just avoiding causing harm to the client, counselors should seek to help clients by promoting health and well-being. Promoting the welfare of their clients is essential to this counseling principle.

Justice

Justice refers to fairness in dealing with clients and other professionals. Included in the principle of justice are appropriate setting of fees, access to counseling services, provision of high-quality services, and the fair treatment of others. Treating one person fairly while not violating the rights of another can be challenging.

Fidelity

Honoring commitments to clients, colleagues, and students is the essence of the principle of fidelity. Adherence to standards of confidentiality aids in the promotion of a trusting relationship with clients. An honest relationship with a client prohibits a counselor from exploiting a client for the counselor's needs.

This set of principles underlies the ethical codes of both ACA and NCDA. NCDA is a division of ACA. These principles provide only an overview of the purpose of ethical codes. University courses and textbooks give a much fuller description of ethical codes than can be provided in this book. However, I believe it is helpful to give more information about ethics as it relates to career counseling concerns.

The ethical standards of the NCDA Code of Ethics (2007) are grouped into nine sections:

A: The Professional Relationship

B: Confidentiality, Privileged Communication, and Privacy

C: Professional Responsibility

D: Relationships with Other Professionals

E: Evaluation, Assessment, and Interpretation

F: Use of the Internet in Career Services

G: Supervision, Training, and Teaching

H: Research and Publication

I: Resolving Ethical Issues

These standards are outlined in a 50-page description. Although they may seem overwhelming at first, there are some general guidelines. In cases of uncertainty, it is best to do nothing and seek consultation with colleagues or supervisors. It is often helpful to make notes about consultations that you have participated in. Professional organizations may offer expert advice on ethical matters.

Career development theories explain how people adjust to work issues, make career choices, and change their career goals as they develop. Career theorists assume that their theories will be applied ethically. All aspects of theories described in this book fit within ethical standards of APA, ACA, and NCDA. The theories in this text provide counselors with a knowledge base that they can use to ethically help their clients. Helping clients, regardless of gender or cultural background, is important both to the client's career development and to the ethical practices of career counseling.

CAREER DEVELOPMENT OF WOMEN

Some career development theories were created before 1960 and were based solely on research on white male individuals from middle-class or upper-middle-class families. Although most of these theories have since incorporated women into their sampling and theoretical statements, career development theorists have been criticized for their neglect of women's career development issues. The role of women in the workplace has changed greatly since the early 1960s. Because women represent more than half the population of the United States and of the world, it is particularly important to illustrate the application of career development theories to women.

Each chapter in this book devotes a section to dealing with applications of theory to career counseling issues for women. In some chapters, the section is quite brief, because the theory may not be sufficiently detailed and researched to include information about women. In other chapters, especially those reviewing life-span and social cognitive career theory, much space is devoted to career development issues for women, as well as to examples of counselor conceptualizations of client concerns. Theories of women's life-span career development are included in Part Two. There is approximately equal representation of men and women in the case examples illustrating career development theory.

CAREER DEVELOPMENT OF CULTURALLY DIVERSE POPULATIONS

Culture may refer to a variety of different groupings including social class, religion, disabilities, age, sexual identification, and ethnicity. All of these are discussed at some point in this book. However, the section "Culturally Diverse Populations" will refer to geographical or ethnic groups, as that has been a major focus of career development interest and research. Because there are so many ethnic and geographical cultures throughout the world, discussion of the career development of culturally diverse populations is more complex than the discussion of differing career concerns between men and women. No theories of career development have been formulated to apply specifically to one culture or another. However, research has been done on the applicability of particular career development theories to specific cultural groups. This book presents this research where I believe it will help in understanding the context of the theory for a particular group.

Within the field of career development, more research has been done on African Americans than on other cultural groups. Some research has also studied the career development of Latinos, Asians, and Native Americans, but even these groups do not represent uniform cultural backgrounds. For example, an Asian group can include people from Japan, China, Vietnam, Cambodia, and India, as well as many other nations. Within each of these nationalities are groups that may have little in common with each other. For example, there are many regions in India that do not share a common language, religion, or social customs. Immigrants to the United States may come as refugees from wars. During and after the Vietnam War, many Vietnamese people came to the United States seeking employment after being forced to flee their country. Discussion of these different cultures is beyond the scope of this book and can be found in other sources (for example, Atkinson, Morten, & Sue, 1998; Diller, 2007; and Lum, 2007), although their emphasis is not on career or employment issues. This book gives some examples of the conceptualization of career development issues when counseling people from some of these cultures, but it is not possible to include examples from all cultures.

In this book, the term *culturally diverse populations* is used to designate African Americans, Africans, Latinos, Native Americans, and Asian/Pacific Islanders. The term *minority* is reserved for people who represent a minority of a given population. Worldwide, people of color are a majority and white people are a minority.

WHAT'S AHEAD

The theories described in this book are grouped into four parts: Trait and Type Theories (Part One), Life-Span Theories (Part Two), Special Focus Theories (Part Three), and Theoretical Integration (Part Four).

Part One deals with characteristics or types of people, focusing on the behavior and concerns of a person at the present moment. Chapter 2 discusses the earliest formal theory of career development: trait and factor theory. This theory deals with the study of interests, values, aptitudes, and other traits that are used in assisting clients with career decisions. Chapter 2 serves as a general approach to trait and factor theory. Chapter 3 describes occupational information (a part of trait and factor theory) in detail. It also describes the views of sociologists and economists about the labor market, examining such issues as social status and discrimination toward women and culturally diverse populations in areas of job entry, advancement on the job, and salaries. Chapters 4, 5, and 6 are specific examples of trait and factor theory. Chapter 4 explains Lofquist and Dawis's theory that focuses on adult adjustment to work. Chapter 5 describes John Holland's typology of people and environments, including an explanation of the six Holland types and their application to career counseling. Another typology, based on Carl Jung's approach to personality theory and featuring the Myers–Briggs view of personality types as it affects career development, is the focus of Chapter 6.

Part Two includes life-span theories, focusing on four aspects of life-span development: childhood (Chapter 7), early adolescence (Chapter 8), late adolescence and adulthood (Chapter 9), and adult career crises and career transitions (Chapter 10). This format is followed for several reasons. Super's life-span theory is more developed than other life-span theories, having produced more research and instrumentation. Most other life-span theories do not cover the entire life span. Furthermore, the conceptualization of career counseling is similar among all life-span theories. Chapters 7, 8, and 9 use Super's theory as the basis for explaining career development concepts. Gottfredson's theory, which focuses on gender role and career choice, provides an explanation for the career development of children (Chapter 7). The work of Fred Vondracek and his colleagues on vocational identity provides a view of adolescent career development that supplements Super's theory (Chapter 8). Chapter 10 uses Hopson and Adams's theory of adult transitions to discuss career crises. It is placed within the context of Super's life-span theory.

In Part Three, additional theories emphasize various aspects of career development. Chapter 11 explains two different constructivist approaches—ways of viewing individuals as creating their own views of events and relationships in their lives. Chapter 12 describes the influence of relationships on career choices. This includes relationships of the client with parents, other family members, teachers, friends, and others. Chapter 13 reviews Krumboltz's behavioral approach to career decision making, together with career counseling techniques, based on social learning theory. Social cognitive career theory examines the relationship of self-efficacy and expected outcome to career choice (Chapter 14). A particular focus of this theory are the barriers to career choice that face women and culturally diverse populations. Chapter 15 examines how one makes career decisions, by comparing a spiritual approach versus a cognitive information-processing perspective on career decision making.

Part Four shows counselors how to integrate several theories in their counseling conceptualization. This part gives examples of how this integration can take place (Chapter 16), depending on the work setting and the counselor's theoretical preferences. Also discussed are special issues such as the use of computer guidance programs, career group counseling, and job placement counseling.

Each chapter follows the same format. The first part of the chapter describes a specific theory and its important constructs. Integrated into the description of the theories is information about counseling strategies, with examples of how to conceptualize client concerns by using theoretical constructs. Brief dialogues between counselor and client, which include counselor conceptualizations, illustrate the application of each career development theory. The use of dialogue enables readers to learn about the thought process a counselor goes through to conceptualize a client problem.

Occasionally, narrative case studies are also used. Included in each chapter is a discussion of how the theory incorporates testing and occupational information. Applicability to women and culturally diverse populations is also described, with reference to reviews of the literature and general research findings. Another section of each chapter deals with counselor problems in applying the theory, including feelings and thoughts counselors may have that interfere with applying a particular theoretical approach. After reading each chapter, readers should have a clear idea of how to think about client problems by using a particular theory.

There are several ways readers can apply the information in this book to make it more meaningful for them. Readers who counsel clients can try to picture a client and think about his or her presenting concerns in terms of a particular theory. Another approach is to think of one's own life or that of friends or family in terms of the theory. For students, an effective way of integrating career development theory into counseling is to role-play counseling situations with other students, using a particular theoretical orientation. All of these approaches are likely to make the material seem more helpful and applicable.

REFERENCES

ACT, Inc. (2007) DISCOVER (Windows) [Computer Software]. Iowa City, IA. Author.

Atkinson, D. R. (2004). *Counseling American minorities: A cross-cultural perspective* (6th ed.). Boston: McGraw-Hill.

Atkinson, D. R., Morten, G., & Sue, D. W. (1998). *Counseling American minorities: A cross-cultural perspective* (5th ed.). Boston: McGraw-Hill.

Bieschke, K. J., & Toepfer-Hendey, E. (2006). Career counseling with lesbian clients. In W. B. Walsh & M.J. Heppner (Eds.). *Contemporary topics in vocational psychology* (2nd ed., pp. 361–385). Mahwah, NJ: Erlbaum Associates.

Bodie, G. D., Powers, W. G., & Fitch-Hauser, M. (2006). Chunking, priming and active learning: Toward an innovative and blended approach to teaching communication-related skills. *Interactive Learning Environments, 14*(2), 119–135.

Brown, C., Linnemeyer, R. M., Dougherty, W. L., Coulson, J. C., Trangsrud, H. B., & Farnsworth, I. S. (2005). Battered women's process of leaving: Implications for career counseling. *Journal of Career Assessment, 13*(4), 452–475.

Brown, D., & Associates (Eds.). (2002). *Career choice and development* (4th ed.). San Francisco: Jossey-Bass.

Carkhuff, R., & Berenson, B. (1967). *Beyond counseling and therapy*. New York: Holt, Rinehart & Winston.

Chang, V. N., Scott, S. T., & Decker, C. L. (2008). *Developing helping skills: A step-by step-approach*. Belmont, CA: Brooks/Cole.

Corey, G., Corey, M. S., & Callanan, P. (2007). *Issues and ethics in the helping professions* (7th ed.). Belmont, CA: Thomson Brooks/Cole.

Dawis, R. V. (2000). The person-environment tradition in counseling psychology. In W. E. Martin Jr., & J. L. Swartz (Eds.), *Person-environment psychology: Clinical and counseling applications for adolescents and adults* (pp. 91–111). Mahwah, NJ: Erlbaum.

Dawis, R. V. (2002). Person-environment-correspondence theory. In D. Brown & Associates (Eds.), *Career choice and development* (4th ed., pp. 427–464). San Francisco: Jossey-Bass.

Dawis, R. V., & Lofquist, L. H. (1984). *A psychological theory of work adjustment.* Minneapolis, MN: University of Minnesota Press.

Diller, J. V. (2007). *Cultural diversity: A primer for the human services* (3rd ed.). Belmont, CA: Brooks/Cole.

Edwards, J. R., Cable, D. M., Williamson, I. O., Lambert, L. S., & Shipp, A. J. (2006). The phenomenology of fit: Linking the person and environment to the subjective experience of person-environment fit. *Journal of Applied Psychology, 91*(4), 802–827.

Egan, G. (2007). *The skilled helper: A problem management and opportunity-development approach to helping* (8th ed.). Belmont, CA: Brooks/Cole.

Ettelson, D. M. (2002). The effect of experience level and cognitive style on therapist thoughts and intentions. *Dissertation Abstracts International: Section B, 63* (5-B), 2579.

Fawcett, J., & Downs, F. S. (1986). *The relationship of theory and research.* Norwalk, CT: Appleton-Century-Crofts.

Ferguson, L. G. (Ed.). (2007). *Encyclopedia of careers and vocational guidance* (14th ed.). New York: L.G. Ferguson.

Franck, R. (Ed.). (2002). *The explanatory power of models: Bridging the gap between empirical and theoretical research on the social sciences.* Boston: Kluwer.

Glassman, R. B. (1999). Hypothesized neural dynamics of working memory: Several chunks might be marked simultaneously by harmonic frequencies within an octave of brain waves. *Brain Research Bulletin, 50,* 77–93.

Gobet, F. (2005). Chunking models of expertise: Implications for education. *Applied Cognitive Psychology, 19*(2), 183–204.

Hanzel, J. (1999). *The concept of scientific law in the philosophy of science and epistemology: A study of theoretical reason.* Boston: Kluwer.

Heinen, J. R. (1985). A primer on psychological theory. *Journal of Psychology, 119,* 413–421.

Hinkelman, J. M., & Luzzo, D. A. (2007). Mental health and career development of college students. *Journal of Counseling & Development, 85*(2), 143–147.

Hoppock, R. (1976). *Occupational information.* New York: McGraw-Hill.

Ivey, A. E., & Ivey, M. B. (2008). *Essentials of intentional interviewing: Counseling in a multicultural world.* Belmont, CA: Brooks/Cole.

Jansen, K. J., & Kristof-Brown, A. (2006). Toward a multidimensional theory of person-environment fit. *Journal of Managerial Issues, 18*(2), 193–212.

Lum, D. (2007). *Culturally competent practice: A framework for understanding diverse groups and justice issues* (3rd ed.). Belmont, CA: Brooks/Cole.

Maxwell, M. (2007). Career counseling is personal counseling: A constructivist approach to nurturing the development of gifted female adolescents. *The Career Development Quarterly, 55*(3), 206–224.

Miller, G. A. (1956). The magical number seven, plus or minus two: Some limits on our capacity to process information. *Psychological Review, 63,* 81–97.

National Career Development Association. (2007). *2007 NCDA code of ethics.* http://www.ncda/pdf/code_of_ethicsmay-2007.pdf.

Neukrug, E. S., & Fawcett, R. C. (2006). *Essentials of testing and assessment: A practical guide for counselors, social workers, and psychologists.* Belmont, CA: Brooks/Cole.

Nevo, O., & Wiseman, H. (2002). Incorporating short term dynamic psychotherapy principles into career counseling: A theoretical and practical approach. *Journal of Career Development, 28,* 227–245.

Niles, S. G., & Harris-Bowlsbey, J. A. (2002). *Career development interventions in the 21st century.* Upper Saddle River, NJ: Merrill Prentice Hall.

Occupational outlook handbook. (2008). Washington, DC: U.S. Department of Labor.

Okun, B. F., & Kantrowitz, R. E. (2008). *Effective helping: Interviewing and counseling techniques* (7th ed.). Belmont, CA: Brooks/Cole.

Osipow, S. H., & Fitzgerald, L. F. (1995). *Theories of career development* (4th ed.). Boston: Allyn & Bacon.

Rogers, C. (1951). *Client-centered therapy.* Boston: Houghton Mifflin.

Rogers, C. (1958). The characteristics of a helping relationship. *Personnel and Guidance Journal, 37,* 6–16.

Schmidt, C. K., & Nilsson, J. E. (2006). The effects of simultaneous developmental processes: Factors relating to the career development of lesbian, gay, and bisexual youth. *The Career Development Quarterly, 55*(1), 22–37.

Snow, R. E. (1973). Theory construction for research and testing. In R. W. Travers (Ed.), *Second handbook of research on teaching* (pp. 77–112). Chicago: Rand McNally.

Starishevsky, R., & Matlin, N. A. (1963). A model for the translation of self-concept into vocational terms. In D. E. Super, R. Starishevsky, N. A. Matlin, & J. P. Jordaan (Eds.), *Career development: Self-concept theory* (Research Monograph No. 4, pp. 33–41). New York: College Entrance Examination Board.

Subich, L. M. (1993). How personal is career counseling? *The Career Development Quarterly, 42,* 129–131.

Truax, C. B., & Carkhuff, R. R. (1967). *Toward effective counseling and psychotherapy. Training and practice.* Chicago: Aldine.

VALPAR, International. SIGI [3]. [Computer Program]. Tucson, AZ: Author (2007).

Van Hoose, W. H. (1986). Ethical principles in counseling. *Journal of Counseling and Development, 65,* 168–169.

Welfel, E. R. (2006). *Ethics in counseling & psychotherapy* (3rd ed.). Belmont, CA: Thomson Brooks/Cole.

Whiston, S. C., Lindeman, D., Rahardja, D., & Reed, J. H. (2005). Career counseling process: A qualitative analysis of experts' cases. *Journal of Career Assessment, 13*(2), 169–187.

Wickelgren, W. A. (1999). Webs, cell assemblies, and chunking in neural nets: Introduction. *Canadian Journal of Experimental Psychology, 53,* 118–131.

TRAIT AND TYPE THEORIES

Trait and type theories were the first career development theories to be described. In general, they were developed to analyze traits or characteristics of individuals with the intention of matching these traits with qualifications required by jobs. Groups of traits or characteristics could be combined so that specific types of individuals could be identified. Likewise, job qualifications and work requirements could be combined to describe types of work.

In this part, four trait or type theories are presented. Trait and factor theory, which is described in Chapter 2, assesses characteristics of people and characteristics of jobs; these characteristics are then matched to help an individual select an occupation. Chapter 3 continues the description of trait and factor theory by elaborating on occupational information. First, information about the United States labor market is discussed, then sociological and economic theories about work and occupations are explained, giving different perspectives about occupations and work. As described in Chapter 4, work adjustment theory provides a framework for assessing an individual's needs and skills so that they can be matched with similar needs and skills required by a small group of different occupations. Holland's typological theory, which is the focus of Chapter 5, describes six types of people and six types of environments. The counselor assists in career selection by matching the person with the environment. Myers-Briggs type theory, which is introduced in Chapter 6, describes ways of perceiving and judging the world. Matching an individual's style of judging and perceiving with the styles of judging and perceiving used by people employed in certain careers can assist an individual in finding a compatible work environment. Each of these theories shares the goal of accurately measuring characteristics or types of individuals so that they can be matched with characteristics or types of work to provide assistance in career selection.

TRAIT AND FACTOR THEORY

CHAPTER 2

CHAPTER HIGHLIGHTS

Step 1: Gaining Self-Understanding

Example of Step 1

Step 2: Obtaining Knowledge about the World of Work

Step 3: Integrating Information about One's Self and the World of Work

Applying the Theory to Women

Applying the Theory to Culturally Diverse Populations

Counselor Issues

In 1909, Frank Parsons described his concept of vocational guidance in his book *Choosing a Vocation*. In a special section of the *Journal of Career Development*, Hartung and Blustein (2001) described these views and Parsons's contribution to career development. Parsons's views became the foundation for what later evolved into trait and factor theory. The term *trait* refers to a characteristic of an individual that can be measured through testing. *Factor* refers to a characteristic that is required for successful job performance; it also refers to a statistical approach used to differentiate important characteristics of a group of people. Thus, the terms *trait* and *factor* refer to the assessment of characteristics of the person and the job.

Assessment of traits is referred to in the first and most crucial of the steps Parsons identified that describes his approach to occupational selection. Parsons

(1909) proposed that, to select an occupation, an individual ideally should have the following information:

1. A clear understanding of yourself; your attitudes, abilities, interests, ambitions, and resource limitations; and their causes
2. A knowledge of the requirements and conditions of success, advantages and disadvantages, compensation, opportunities, and prospects in different lines of work.
3. True reasoning on the relations of these two groups of facts

Frank Parsons's book, derived from his work in career counseling with adolescents in the Boston area, was not the only contribution to the development of trait and factor theory. At about the same time, Elton Mayo at Harvard and Frederick Taylor, who was working in business, were doing early industrial psychological work that involved the study of working conditions such as fatigue and boredom. They developed various ways to study how an individual reacts to his or her work environment. It was natural that their objective measurements would fit into the discipline of trait and factor psychology. In the 1930s and 1940s, particularly during World War II, much work was done on assessing abilities of personnel. It was necessary for the U.S. Employment Service and the War Manpower Commission to develop a research testing and placement program so that Americans would be better able to serve the war effort. One of the most important tests that grew out of that program was the Army General Classification Test. This test set new standards for test development and was used to select recruits for a wide variety of tasks. Many other tests also were developed through federal funding. This gave a boost to the assessment techniques that were needed for the development of trait and factor theory. After World War II, research continued in the area of assessment; much of this research was done at the University of Minnesota. In fact, trait and factor theory has also been called the *Minnesota point of view*, as well as *actuarial counseling.*

The most well-known contributor to "the Minnesota point of view" was Edmund G. Williamson, Dean of Students at the University of Minnesota between 1941 and 1969. His writings epitomize the trait and factor approach (Williamson, 1939, 1965). Although Williamson, like Carl Rogers, was concerned with the whole person, his approach was entirely different from Rogers's and was labeled *directive*, in contrast to the nondirective approach of Carl Rogers. Among Williamson's methods were information giving and direct suggestion. It was his view that the counselor should share his or her wisdom with the client in guiding the client to a correct decision. In contrast, Rogers emphasized reflection of the client's feelings rather than imparting information. Williamson's approach has been criticized by a number of writers (Aubrey, 1977).

There is little research supporting or refuting trait and factor theory itself as a viable theory of career development. Rather, the extensive and vast research that has been done has related traits and factors to one another or has established the validity and reliability of measurements of traits and factors. Developers of tests and inventories have correlated aptitudes, achievements, interests, values, and personality with each other. When validating and developing tests, it is necessary to relate the scales of one test to the scales of very similar tests.

This chapter takes a broad view of trait and factor theory to show how it can be used to conceptualize career development. Parsons's (1909) century-old concepts have been embellished by integrating tests and occupational information with his precepts. Parsons characterized the first step of career choice as gaining "a clear understanding of yourself, your attitudes, abilities, interests, ambitions, resource limitations, and causes" (p. 5). This chapter approaches this step in terms of aptitudes, achievements, interests, values, and personality to reflect five types of assessment that have emerged as important to career counseling. Parsons's second step is obtaining "a knowledge of the requirements and conditions of success, advantages and disadvantages, compensation, opportunities, and prospects in different lines of work" (p. 5). This chapter discusses how the counselor can assist the client in gaining knowledge of occupations. For the third step, Parsons said that a wise choice is made by "true reasoning on the relations on these two groups of facts" (p. 5). This chapter considers integration of information about one's self and the world of work, giving a focus that is not limited to the use of counselors' cognitive skills, but that also includes reflecting and questioning skills. Information regarding various traits and factors in women and culturally diverse populations also are given, followed by a discussion of potential counseling difficulties in using trait and factor theory.

STEP 1: GAINING SELF-UNDERSTANDING

When Parsons and early career counselors started to help young people choose a career, they had few tests, inventories, or occupational information available to them. They relied primarily on interviews and discussions with clients. Asking clients what they enjoyed doing (interests) and how well they did it (aptitude and achievement) was an important method of helping the client gain self-understanding. As clients talked about aspects of their life that were important to them (their values), the counselor was able to make a further assessment. As the counselor observed the clients and listened to their comments about themselves and others, the counselor could make observations about the clients' personality. The counseling interview continues to be an important part of the trait and factor assessment process. However, the development of tests and inventories has given counselors additional useful tools.

Since the beginning of the 20th century, psychologists have been productive in the development of assessment instruments. These are reviewed in the *Fifteenth Mental Measurements Yearbook* (Plake, Impara, & Spies, 2003) and in *Tests in Print VI* (Murphy, Plake, Impara, & Spies, 2002), which lists 2,780 instruments, of which 82 are achievement batteries, 210 are intelligence and academic aptitude tests, 540 are vocational inventories, and 629 are personality inventories. It is, of course, practically impossible for the counselor to become familiar with each of these tests and inventories. This chapter describes only a few well-accepted assessment instruments that counselors are likely to use in the trait and factor approach and that are frequently used by counseling psychologists (Herr, Cramer, & Niles, 2004). This does not necessarily mean that these are the best instruments, but they are used widely and are different enough from each other that their main features can be contrasted. *A Counselor's Guide to*

Career Assessment Instruments (Kapes & Whitfield, 2001) presents reviews of most of the instruments described in this textbook. In addition, many of these tests and inventories are available online. When a counselor chooses an instrument to use with clients, the counselor may incorporate the concepts of the tests or inventories into his or her thinking about the client. For example, a counselor attempting to conceptualize a client's sociability may use the definition of *sociability* on the Sociability scale of the California Psychological Inventory rather than invent a new definition of sociability. It is the purpose of this chapter not to evaluate these tests and inventories, but rather to show how they can be used in conceptualizing clients' career concerns.

The five basic traits and factors that can be assessed by testing and interviewing are aptitudes, achievements, interests, values, and personality. The following sections consider each of these areas in turn.

APTITUDES

The terms *aptitude, ability,* and *achievement* are easily confused, as are the tests that measure these traits. It is helpful to make the following distinctions: An achievement test is designed to reveal how much an individual has learned; an ability test measures maximum performance and reveals the level of a person's present ability to perform a task; and an aptitude test reveals a person's probable future level of ability to perform a task (Aiken & Groth-Marnat, 2007). That is, these tests measure past achievement, present ability, and future aptitude. Often, determining whether a test measures ability, aptitude, or achievement can be difficult. For example, the assessment of past achievement may provide a measure of possible aptitude. Aptitude tests have been particularly attractive to clients who believe that, if they can find the occupations in which they have aptitude, they can predict their future success in a specific occupation. Unfortunately, aptitude tests measure a number of general aptitudes, and no aptitude tests exist that are precise enough to predict with certainty the eventual success of an individual.

Aptitude tests have been used to predict future success in either further educational endeavors or in occupational training. Table 2.1 lists a sample of well-known aptitude tests, together with their subtests. The first two tests listed—the College Board Scholastic Assessment Test (SAT) and the American College Testing Assessment Program: Academic Test (ACT)—are used for predicting college success. The Differential Aptitude Tests (DAT) are used to assist people in selecting a career. The U.S. Department of Labor O*NET Ability Profiler (AP), now used in place of the General Aptitude Test Battery (GATB), is used only for counseling, whereas the GATB was used for both counseling and selection. The Armed Services Vocational Aptitude Battery (ASVAB) is used by the United States Armed Services for counseling and selection. Note that all five of the tests measure verbal and quantitative (mathematical or numerical) aptitudes.

Measurement of verbal and mathematical aptitudes is common to almost all academic aptitude tests. Note also that fewer subtests are used for measuring college aptitude than are used for predicting aptitude for occupations not requiring college skills, such as secretary, mechanic, and electronics technician. Furthermore, the

TABLE 2.1 | FIVE APTITUDE TESTS AND THEIR SUBTESTS

College Board Scholastic Assessment Test (SAT)	ACT Assessment Program: Academic Tests (ACT)	Differential Aptitude Tests (DAT)	U.S. Department of Labor O*NET Ability Profiler (AP)	Armed Services Vocational Aptitude Battery (ASVAB)
Verbal	English usage	General learning	Verbal Ability	Coding speed
Mathematical	Mathematics usage	Verbal reasoning	Arithmetic Reasoning	Word knowledge
Standard written English	Social studies reading	Numerical ability	Computation	Arithmetic reasoning
	Natural sciences reading	Abstract reasoning	Spatial Ability	Tool knowledge
		Clerical speed and accuracy	Form perception	Space perception
		Mechanical reasoning	Clerical perception	Mechanical comprehension
		Space relations	Motor coordination	Shop information
		Spelling	Finger dexterity	Automotive information
		Language usage	Manual dexterity	Electronics information

DAT, GATB, and ASVAB give occupational profiles that match high scores on various aptitudes. Thus, one can look up an occupation in one of the test manuals and find the scores that are needed on various subtests for suggested entry into that specific occupation. These scores should be considered guidelines rather than requirements. Research on the validity of these instruments continues to be important. The ASVAB has been shown to improve aspects of career decision making and to enhance self-knowledge in high school students (Baker, 2002).

More than most other types of tests, the aptitude test that a counselor uses depends on his or her setting. For example, high school and college counselors in the eastern and western parts of the United States tend to use the SAT, whereas their colleagues in the Midwestern states tend to use the ACT. Counselors working at a federal employment service are likely to use the AP, whereas those working with the military or prospective applicants to the military will use the ASVAB. The selection of appropriate norms is necessary, so that clients' aptitudes are compared with an appropriate comparison group. Clients' self-estimates of their aptitudes can be useful, so that comparisons can be made with measured aptitudes, allowing the client to develop a fuller understanding of his or her aptitudes. Prediger (2004) points out that self-estimates of ability often are as predictive of academic or other performance as ability tests. However, college students are more likely to overestimate their abilities than to underestimate them (Gati, Fishman-Nadav, & Shiloh, 2006). In addition, self-estimates of ability can provide assessment in areas for which ability tests are seldom available. Examples of these areas are artistic and literary ability, helping others, meeting people, sales, and leadership.

Although discussion with a client may produce information to make an objective judgment about aptitude and abilities, counselors should be wary of making *predictions* about a client's success on the basis of aptitude test scores. It is one thing for employers to make selections based on aptitude; it is another for a counselor to say to a client, "You could not become a physician because your scores are not high enough." There are examples in our society of how the client proved the counselor wrong by doing much better than was predicted. Clients are in a better position than the counselor to determine the risk they are willing to take in trying to enter an occupation in which they would appear to have little chance for success. Clients must live with the effects of their decisions. For example, a client with mediocre grades who has always wanted to be a doctor but who does not apply to medical school may regret that decision for many years.

ACHIEVEMENT

Achievement refers to a broad range of events that individuals participate in and accomplish during their lifetime. These can be separated into three types of achievements. The first type is academic accomplishment, measured most often by grades, but also by honors and specific test scores. The second type is accomplishments in work, such as tasks completed and supervisor ratings. The third type, and the one that most easily fits with the trait and factor approach, pertains to tests of achievement for certification or entry into an occupation.

Over the years, research studies have shown that the best single predictor of academic performance is previous academic performance. That is, one can predict performance in college better from high school grades than from aptitude test scores, with aptitude tests accounting for about 15% of the variance in predicting college grades (Leman, 1999). In fact, high school grades can be given twice the weight of scholastic aptitude tests when predicting college grades (Astin, 1993). Also, accomplishments that were attained at work, through hobbies, or through extracurricular activities can be useful in determining the nature of an individual's abilities and achievements. These accomplishments can be diverse and include such activities as athletic honors, ability to help a sick person, ability to type a paper quickly, ability to tally numbers with speed and accuracy, and ability to give a speech in front of an audience. Recently, other variables, such as conscientiousness and attendance at class (Conard, 2006) and being able to discipline oneself academically (Robbins, Allen, Casillas, Peterson, & Le, 2006; Duckworth & Seligman, 2005) have been identified as important factors in predicting academic achievement in college.

Achievement can be measured quantitatively through tests that are used for licensure, certification, or entry into a particular field or profession. For example, psychologists, doctors, nurses, and lawyers must pass board examinations of a particular state before becoming licensed to do their specific work. Similarly, plumbers, police officers, and many other professionals must take tests before advancing from one level to another. The wide range of achievement tests currently available includes tests pertaining to the following careers:

Accountant	Life insurance agent	Professional counselor
Actuary	Mechanic	Psychologist
Artist	Musician	Real estate agent
Cosmetologist	Nurse	Teacher
Dietician	Physician	Typist
Electrician	Plumber	X-ray technician
Funeral director	Police officer	

What characterizes all of these tests is that they are specific to a given task or profession. For example, the best test of typing ability is to obtain a typing sample from an individual. A written or multiple-choice test about typing would not be adequate. Likewise, the best test of artistic or musical ability is to look at a portfolio of artwork or listen to a musical audition.

One of the problems in using client self-report of accomplishments, such as helping someone in distress, is that people in the United States and Japan (and other countries) are often taught to be modest about their achievements. Encouragement is often needed for people to accurately present their successes. Emphasizing these accomplishments can be useful because they may serve as building blocks for further accomplishments. For example, if a student has successfully presented a project at a science fair, that becomes a starting place to discuss other types of projects and science interests that the person may have.

Interests

Over the years, interests have become the most important trait used in occupational selection. The reason is that occupational entry can be predicted more accurately from interests than from aptitude for individuals with many abilities who are able to choose from a wide range of occupations. Reviews of the relationship between interests and abilities have shown a small but significant correlation between the two ($r=.20$) (Ackerman & Heggestad, 1997; Lent, Brown, & Hackett, 1994). Tracey and Hopkins (2001) find that both interests and self-estimates of ability predict occupational choice, but interests are more predictive of ability than are self-estimates. Using a variety of measures of interest and intelligence, Proyer (2006) found that scientific and technical interests were related to spatial ability more strongly than other interests were to a variety of abilities. Often, interests and ability are discussed together in career counseling.

Some individuals may like some things that they do not do well, and others may be good at activities they do not like. Unlike aptitude tests, interest inventories have scales for specific occupations. Two particularly well-known interest inventories that use occupational scales are the Kuder DD and the Strong Interest Inventory (SII). By measuring the interests of successful and satisfied people in an occupation, the authors of these instruments were able to develop a scale that compares the interests of these individuals with the interests of those who are unsure of their career choice. Such scales tend to predict occupational success and satisfaction many years after the inventory was taken (Hansen & Dik, 2005).

In addition to occupational interests, general areas of interest have been measured. Whereas occupational interest scales describe interests of people in a specific occupation, such as secretary, basic interest scales measure interests in activities, such as office practices. An office service interest scale may include tasks such as typing, taking dictation, and answering the phone. To use another example, a mathematics scale may measure interests in abstract math and computation, whereas a mathematician scale measures the similarity of the interests of the test-taker to the interests of those who are employed as mathematicians. Several inventories measure a broad spectrum of general interests. Three of these inventories are listed in Table 2.2: the Kuder Career Search (KCS), the Basic Interest Scales of the SII, and the California Occupational Preference Survey (COPS). Note that the COPS has separate professional and skilled interest scales for five different interest areas. In general, the basic interest scales are quite similar for all three of the inventories. Any one of these inventories can provide a framework for categorizing interests in counseling.

The counselor can more easily understand the client's experience by using a particular structure to evaluate a client's interests. For example, if a counselor uses the 10 interest scales of the KCS as a framework, he or she can categorize the client's discussion of preferences during an interview. If a client talks of enjoying painting and drawing throughout his school experience, as well as writing for high school and college publications, the counselor can conceptualize and categorize these interests as art and communications. Later, when the client talks about enjoying going to art museums and discussing art with friends, this same conceptualization of artistic interests can be made. Having this frame of reference allows the counselor to group concepts and ideas that come from the counseling interview. If the counselor then administers the KCS to the student, the counselor can get further validation of the client's interest in art if the score is high. If the score is low, the counselor can discuss the discrepancy between the client's expressed interest in art and low inventoried interest in art. When selecting inventories to use with clients, it is helpful to use those that make conceptual sense to the counselor. For example, it is possible but more difficult to use the SII Basic Interest Scales as a conceptual base when using the KCS. Trying to conceptualize or chunk 10 scales (KCS), 14 scales (COPS), or 23 scales (SII) can be difficult. Holland's theory (see description in Chapter 5) uses only six scales or constructs. When discussing a client's interests in one trait, it is often helpful to discuss abilities and achievements in that trait at the same time. This helps the counselor to better organize the client's previous experiences and to use fewer chunks of material.

VALUES

Neglected by many trait and factor counselors, values represent an important but difficult concept to measure. Of a sample of 3,570 college freshmen, 29% said they were seeking careers that reflected their interests, but 47% said they were seeking careers consistent with their values (Duffy & Sedlacek, 2007). For career counseling, two types of values are considered important: general values and work-related values. Table 2.3 lists the 6 general values that are found in the Study of Values (SV) and the 21 work values listed in the Values Scale (VS). Table 2.3 shows the contrast between the general values of the SV, recently revised

TABLE 2.2 | THREE INTEREST INVENTORIES AND THEIR SCALES

Kuder Career Search (KCS)	Strong Interest Inventory (SII) Basic Interest Scales	California Occupational Preference Survey (COPS)
Nature	Athletics	Consumer economics
Mechanical	Computer Hardware & Electronics	Outdoor
Computations		Clerical
Science/Technical	Counseling & Helping	Communication
Sales/Management	Culinary Arts	Science—professional
Art	Entrepreneurship	Science—skilled
Communications	Finance & Investing	Technology—professional
Music	Healthcare Services	
Human services	Human Resources & Training	Technology—skilled
Office detail	Law	Business—professional
	Management	Business—skilled
	Marketing & Advertising	Arts—professional
	Mathematics	Arts—skilled
	Mechanics & Construction	Service—professional
	Medical Science	
	Military	
	Nature & Agriculture	
	Office Management	
	Performing Arts	
	Politics & Public Speaking	
	Programming & Information Systems	
	Protective Services	
	Religion & Spirituality	
	Research	
	Sales	
	Science	
	Social Sciences	
	Taxes & Accounting	
	Teaching & Education	
	Visual Arts & Design	
	Writing & Mass Communication	

TABLE 2.3 | TWO VALUES INVENTORIES AND THEIR SCALES

Study of Values (SV)	Values Scale (VS)
Theoretical	Ability utilization
Economic	Achievement
Aesthetic	Advancement
Social	Aesthetics
Political	Altruism
Religious	Authority
	Autonomy
	Creativity
	Economic rewards
	Lifestyle
	Personal development
	Physical activity
	Prestige
	Risk
	Social interaction
	Social relations
	Variety
	Working conditions
	Cultural identity
	Physical prowess
	Economic security

by Kopelman, Rovenpor, & Guan (2003), and the more specific work-related values of the VS. However, counselors might not make use of any value inventories, preferring to conceptualize work values or general values rather than to measure them. One reason is that it is difficult to develop a reliable and valid values inventory, because these concepts are often elusive and cannot be predicted easily.

Values, as difficult to assess as they may be, are often helpful to clients who are deciding on a career direction (Rounds & Armstrong, 2005). For example, the client who wishes to help others may feel that this desire is more important than any of his or her other traits or factors, such as interests or abilities. In such a case, the counselor helps the client find an interesting way to satisfy his or her values. For example, a client who wishes to help the homeless may pursue social work or business management, depending on the direction of the client's interests. The value of helping others is called altruism on the VS.

Although most literature on values examines those in the United States, newer research has focused on value scales for individuals outside of North America, as well as individuals who have recently moved to the United States. Values of Korean and Korean-American high school students have been compared on the Asian Values Scale (Lee, 2006). The Asian American Values Scale was developed by determining five important components of Asian American values (Kim, Li, & Ng, 2005). Another instrument, the European American Values Scale for Asian Americans, provides yet another view of assessing values (Hong, Kim, & Wolfe, 2005). These scales illustrate the importance of examining values across different cultures.

Being able to label a value and compare it with other values can be useful for the counselor. Although the list of 21 work values in the VS is long, it does give the counselor a framework to assess the values important to a client. Some counselors may prefer to use a shortened version of such a list of values, whereas others may be satisfied using the six values of the SV.

PERSONALITY

The measurement of personality has been an important area of study for the last 80 years. Although much of the work has centered on abnormal personality, with the development of the Minnesota Multiphasic Personality Inventory-2 (MMPI), the Rorschach, and the Thematic Apperception Test (TAT), work has also been done in the area of normal personality. For comparison, two different measures of personality that give insight into the conceptualization of personality for vocational selection are listed in Table 2.4. These two instruments are the California Psychological Inventory (CPI) and the Sixteen Personality Factor Questionnaire (16 PF). The CPI represents a commonsense or folk approach to personality, and the 16 PF represents a statistical approach.

The CPI, developed by Harrison Gough (Gough & Bradley, 1996), uses 20 scales to measure different aspects of personality. The terms used are inoffensive ones to which clients might not object and are called "folk scales" (Table 2.4). Gough used many items from the MMPI to develop this inventory; however, the two inventories are different in that the MMPI uses pathological terminology and the CPI does not. For example, the MMPI uses scale names such as "schizophrenia" and "hypochondriasis," whereas the CPI uses names such as "self-control" and "flexibility." People who score high on flexibility are likely to be rated by others as flexible. Such comparisons between scores on a scale and ratings by experts or peers were widely used in developing the CPI. The scale names represent terms that counselors can use when trying to assess the characteristics of individual clients.

The 16 PF lists 16 primary personality factors. These are presented using a bi-polar method, indicating the two extremes of each trait. Examples are cool versus warm, submissive versus dominant, and shy versus bold. These factors are similar in many ways to the 20 scales of the CPI; the difference is in their development. A statistical technique, factor analysis, was used to try to make the scales as different from each other as possible. These factors can be useful in conceptualizing a client who is trying to make occupational selection decisions.

Personality profiles have been developed using the CPI and the 16 PF for individuals in a variety of occupations. Therefore, a counselor is able to match the profile of a client with an appropriate occupational pattern. Personality inventories are more difficult to learn to use than are ability, achievement, interest, or values tests or inventories because of the complexity of the variables involved and their abstraction. In addition, personality inventories may present a cultural

TABLE 2.4	Two Personality Inventories and Their Scales
California Psychological Inventory (CPI)	**Sixteen Personality Factor Questionnaire (16 PF)**
Dominance	Cool vs. warm
Capacity for status	Concrete thinking vs. abstract thinking
Sociability	Affected by feelings vs. emotionally stable
Social presence	Submissive vs. dominant
Self-acceptance	Sober vs. enthusiastic
Independence	Expedient vs. conscientious
Empathy	Shy vs. bold
Sense of well-being	Tough-minded vs. tender-minded
Responsibility	Trusting vs. suspicious
Socialization	Practical vs. imaginative
Self-control	Forthright vs. shrewd
Tolerance	Self-assured vs. apprehensive
Good impression	Conservative vs. experimenting
Communality	Group-oriented vs. self-sufficient
Achievement via independence	Undisciplined self-conflict vs. following self-image
Achievement via conformance	
Intellectual efficiency	Relaxed vs. tense
Psychological-mindedness	
Flexibility	
Femininity/Masculinity	

bias reflecting the culture of the developers or the sample used for measuring participants' personality. In fact, many counselors who use the trait and factor approach may not use personality tests at all. However, both personality and interest inventories can assist counselors as they develop a broader understanding of their clients (Swanson & D'Achiardi, 2005). For example, an accountant may have needs for order and deference that may influence occupational selection, as does an interest in business, accounting principles, and math. Furthermore, intelligence and mathematical ability are likely to be important factors in the choice of accounting. Being able to integrate the concepts of order and deference with interests, abilities, achievements, and values is helpful.

Example of Step 1

Jack, a white freshman at a large university, is undecided about his career choice. He has already met with the counselor for one session and has gone over his results on the KCS, the VS, and the CPI (Table 2.5). The counselor now has his

TABLE 2.5 | JACK'S HIGH AND LOW SCORES ON SELECTED TESTS AND INVENTORIES

	SAT	KCS	VS	CPI
High	Verbal	Art	Creativity	Social presence
		Sales/Management	Ability utilization	Socialization
Low	Math	Nature	Economic security	Independence
		Computations	Altruism	
		Office detail		

Abbreviations: SAT, College Board Scholastic Assessment Test; KCS, Kuder Career Search; VS, Values Scale; CPI, California Psychological Inventory.

SAT results. The following dialogue might occur in the second session as the counselor attempts to integrate the test results. Assessment results are usually discussed interactively rather than just reported or delivered to the client, because the results usually have a deeper impact with an interactive approach, and the counselor may be seen as more expert and trustworthy than when results are just reported (Hanson, Claiborn, & Kerr, 1997). Osborn, and Zunker (2006) go into detail about assessment interpretation, whereas the following dialogue focuses on conceptualizing the client's use of information about his traits taken from assessment instruments.

CL: Some of my courses this semester are really boring. I wish I didn't have so many course requirements.

CO: I'd like to hear more about them. [Detail is needed to evaluate the client's experience in terms of his various traits and factors.]

CL: Calculus is a nuisance. It takes a lot of time, there doesn't seem to be any use for it, and I just feel so bored after the class. My history course isn't much better—medieval civilization is not exactly earthshaking to me. I knew I had to take a history course, but maybe I should have taken something else.

CO: Having to fulfill requirements is really quite difficult for you. [With low SAT and KCS scores, it is not surprising that Jack is having difficulty with math and does not like it. The counselor lets Jack determine what he wants to talk about next by using a feeling reflection.]

CL: Fortunately, not all my courses are so bad. My speech course is easy and kind of fun. I've enjoyed standing up in front of the class and trying to capture the attention of the other students, which really is a challenge, as many of them like the class as much as I like math. That class reminds me a bit of when I worked at carnival concessions two summers ago and I had to give a spiel to people about why they should play a game.

CO: It sounds like fun, trying to present yourself in an impressive way to others. It reminds me of what we were talking about last time when we were going over the California Psychological Inventory. [The counselor makes a direct connection between the client's high score on the Social Presence scale of the CPI and his desire to present his work in the speech class and to be involved in the carnival situation.]

CL: Yes, I sure enjoy the attention I get. It's kind of fun. I remember when I first came to visit this campus; I was impressed with the guy who showed us around. In fact, even though I'm just a freshman, I think I want to try to see if I can give campus tours, too.

CO: You really are enjoying doing a lot of things that get you out in front of others. [Jack seems quite aware and accepting of his own enjoyment of getting the attention of others.]

CL: I guess so. I'm all over the place. I've got our whole dorm working on this massive homecoming float. It really looks good. I think we're going to win first prize.

CO: You really seem to enjoy designing and developing new things. [The counselor is aware of the client's high score on Creativity on the Values Scale and chooses to comment on this trait of the client without mentioning the score itself.]

CL: Yes, I don't know how to find time to study sometimes, but I also seem to manage. There's so much to learn here and so much to do. I need some 48-hour days.

CO: It really is hard to decide what to do sometimes. [The CPI results alerted the counselor to Jack's interest in socializing and communicating with others, and Jack's ability utilization score on the VS indicated his desire to use his skills. The counselor is also aware that this may create some problems for Jack in deciding what to do. Note that the counselor combines reflective responses with trait and factor conceptualization.]

STEP 2: OBTAINING KNOWLEDGE ABOUT THE WORLD OF WORK

Occupational information is the second ingredient of trait and factor theory. It is the counselor's role to help the client gather occupational information. To do this, it is not necessary to rely solely on the counselor's knowledge of occupations, but also to use many resources to supplement this knowledge. There are three aspects of occupational information to consider. The first aspect is the type of information; for example, a description of the occupation, the working conditions, or the salary. The second important aspect is classification. There are several classification systems that enable the client and the counselor to see thousands of occupations organized in meaningful ways. Third, it is helpful to know the trait and factor requirements for each occupation that a person is seriously considering. For example, if a client is thinking about becoming a veterinarian, it is helpful to know which aptitudes, achievements, interests, values, and personality traits are related to satisfaction with veterinary medicine.

TYPES OF OCCUPATIONAL INFORMATION

Occupational information is available from a variety of different sources. These sources include booklets made available by professional trade associations, pamphlets available through publishers that specialize in producing occupational information, and lengthier books or encyclopedias. Furthermore, occupational information is available on CDs and DVDs, as well as through computer-based information systems and many Web sites. At its most basic level, almost all occupational information includes a description of the occupation, the qualifications required for entry, the necessary education, the working conditions, the salary, and the employment outlook. Many publications go beyond this by giving information about career ladders, similar occupations, examples of people working in the profession, and special information for women and culturally diverse populations. The next section provides a more detailed explanation of the types of occupational information.

It is impossible for counselors to remember all the information about many occupations. Perhaps the most important type of information for counselors to know is the description of an occupation. Beyond that, it is helpful to have books such as the *Occupational Outlook Handbook* (OOH) (2008), which is issued every 2 years and provides detailed information about more than 250 occupations. The OOH is also available online and is linked to several inventories, such as the KCS. Occupational information changes from year to year, which makes matters even more complex. Specifically, the salary and employment outlook is likely to vary. Furthermore, these two variables are apt to differ depending on what section of the United States one lives in. For example, plumbers make a higher salary in New York City than they do in Des Moines, Iowa, or Augusta, Maine. When evaluating occupational information, it is useful to examine language, content, and pictures for race or gender bias. Herr, Cramer, and Niles (2004) provide many resources for obtaining career information, including publishers and organizations.

The National Career Development Association (1991) has published guidelines that address the quality and content of occupational information. Regarding quality, questions such as the following are asked: Are the written information and pictures accurate and nonbiased with regard to gender and race? Is the information clear and interesting, and is it appropriate for the intended audience? Is the material updated frequently? Regarding content, the following areas are covered: the duties and nature of the work, the physical activities required, social and psychological satisfactions and dissatisfactions, the type of preparation required, earnings and benefits, advancement possibilities, the employment outlook, part-time and volunteer opportunities for exploring the occupation, related occupations, sources of training, and sources of additional information. Readers can see how these topics are covered by examining a description of one occupation in the *Occupational Outlook Handbook* (2008). The National Career Development Association (2008) has also published guidelines for the Use of the Internet for Provision of Career Information and Planning Services to assist counselors in making appropriate use of the Internet with their clients.

CLASSIFICATION SYSTEMS

Because it is easy to become overwhelmed by the volume of information available to counselors and clients, it is essential to have a way to organize occupational information. Classification systems have been developed to fill this need. Three different government classification systems are based on analyzing definitions of occupations and work functions. In addition, Holland's classification of occupations (Chapter 5) has been based on research into the six categories of his theory. Some classification systems are developed through statistical procedures such as factor analysis to determine groupings of occupations based on data from interest inventories (Armstrong, Smith, Donnay, & Rounds, 2004).

The most comprehensive listing of occupations is the *Dictionary of Occupational Titles* (DOT); the most recent edition was published in 1991 by the U.S. Department of Labor. It classifies about 12,000 occupations that existed in the United States as of 1991. To organize these occupations, it uses a nine-digit code. The first three numbers designate an occupational group. The first digit identifies 1 of 9 broad categories, the second digit breaks up the occupations into 82 divisions (Table 2.6), and the third digit divides the occupations into 559 groups. For example, the occupation of counselor has 045 as the first three digits. The 0 refers to professional, technical, and managerial occupations. The 04 applies to occupations in the life sciences. Within that division, 045 designates occupations in

TABLE 2.6	DICTIONARY OF OCCUPATIONAL TITLES: TWO-DIGIT OCCUPATIONAL DIVISIONS

0/1	*Professional, Technical, and Managerial Occupations*
00/01	Occupations in architecture, engineering, and surveying
02	Occupations in mathematics and physical sciences
03	Computer-related occupations
04	Occupations in life sciences
05	Occupations in social sciences
07	Occupations in medicine and health
09	Occupations in education
10	Occupations in museum, library, and archival sciences
11	Occupations in law and jurisprudence
12	Occupations in religion and theology
13	Occupations in writing
14	Occupations in art
15	Occupations in entertainment and recreation
16	Occupations in administrative specializations
18	Managers and officials, n.e.c.*
19	Miscellaneous professional, technical, and managerial occupations
2	*Clerical and Sales Occupations*
20	Stenography, typing, filing, and related occupations
21	Computing and account-recording occupations
22	Production and stock clerks and related occupations
23	Information and message distribution occupations
24	Miscellaneous clerical occupations
25	Sales occupations, services
26	Sales occupations, consumable commodities
3	*Service Occupations*
30	Domestic service occupations
31	Food and beverage preparation and service occupations
32	Lodging and related service occupations
33	Barbering, cosmetology, and related service occupations
34	Amusement and recreation service occupations
35	Miscellaneous personal service occupations
36	Apparel and furnishing service occupations
37	Protective service occupations
38	Building and related service occupations
4	*Agricultural, Fishery, Forestry, and Related Occupations*
40	Plant farming occupations
41	Animal farming occupations
42	Miscellaneous agricultural and related occupations
44	Fishery and related occupations
45	Forestry occupations
46	Hunting, trapping, and related occupations
5	*Processing Occupations*
50	Occupations in processing of metal
51	Ore refining and foundry occupations
52	Occupations in processing of food, tobacco, and related products
53	Occupations in processing of paper and related materials

TABLE 2.6 | CONTINUED

54	Occupations in processing of petroleum, coal, natural and manufactured gas, and related products
55	Occupations in processing of chemicals, plastics, synthetics, rubber, paint, and related products
56	Occupations in processing of wood and wood products
57	Occupations in processing of stone, clay, glass, and related products
58	Occupations in processing of leather, textiles, and related products
59	Processing occupations, n.e.c.*
6	*Machine Trades Occupations*
60	Metal machining occupations
61	Metalworking occupations, n.e.c.*
62/63	Mechanics and machinery repairers
64	Paperworking occupations
65	Printing occupations
66	Wood machining occupations
67	Occupations in machining stone, clay, glass, and related materials
68	Textile occupations
69	Machine trades occupations, n.e.c.*
7	*Benchwork Occupations*
70	Occupations in fabrication, assembly, and repair of metal products, n.e.c.*
71	Occupations in fabrication and repair of scientific, medical, photographic, optical, horological, and related products
72	Occupations in assembly and repair of electrical equipment
73	Occupations in fabrication and repair of products made from assorted materials
74	Painting, decorating, and related occupations
27	Sales occupations, commodities, n.e.c.*
29	Miscellaneous sales occupations
75	Occupations in fabrication and repair of plastics, synthetics, rubber, and related products
76	Occupations in fabrication and repair of wood products
77	Occupations in fabrication and repair of sand, stone, clay, and glass
78	Occupations in fabrication and repair of textile, leather, and related products
79	Benchwork occupations, n.e.c.*
8	*Structural Work Occupations*
80	Occupations in metal fabricating, n.e.c.*
81	Welders, cutters, and related occupations
82	Electrical assembling, installing, and repairing occupations
84	Painting, plastering, waterproofing, cementing, and related occupations
85	Excavating, grading, paving, and related occupations
86	Construction occupations, n.e.c.*
89	Structural work occupations, n.e.c.*
9	*Miscellaneous Occupations*
90	Motor freight occupations
91	Transportation occupations, n.e.c.*
92	Packaging and materials handling occupations
93	Occupations in extraction of minerals
95	Occupations in production and distribution of utilities
96	Amusement, recreation, motion picture, radio, and television occupations, n.e.c.*
97	Occupations in graphic art work

*n.e.c. is an abbreviation for "not elsewhere classified."

Source: Based on *Dictionary of occupational titles* (4th ed.). (1991). Washington, DC: U.S. Department of Labor, Employment and Training Administration. 1991.

psychology. The next three digits relate to three ways of doing tasks. The fourth digit describes how the individual deals with data, the fifth digit indicates how a person deals with people, and the sixth digit describes how a person uses things. The assignment to categories of data, people, and things is based on an analysis of the tasks done by people in the occupation. The last three digits indicate the alphabetical order of the occupational titles that have the same six-digit code. Many other sources give further details of this system, for example, *Improved Career Decision Making Through the Use of Labor Market Information* (1991), which is also a U.S. Department of Labor publication. The DOT classification system continues to be used by counselors and by test publishers to classify occupations. However, in 1998, the U.S. government replaced it with the O*NET classification system. Working from the *Dictionary of Occupational Titles*, hundreds of people worked together to develop the O*NET, the *Occupational Information Network*, which replaced the DOT. Unlike other classification systems, the O*NET was designed to be presented on the computer so that it could be updated frequently. Table 2.7 lists the 9 sections and the 103 major groupings of the O*NET.

Whereas the DOT contains 12,741 occupational titles, the O*NET has information on about 1,170 occupations. Over the years, new occupations will be added to this database. What makes this classification system so different from others is that each occupation has about 445 data descriptors. Contrast this with the eight descriptors that are used in the *Occupational Outlook Handbook*—nature of the work, working conditions, employment, training, job outlook, earnings, related occupations, and sources of additional information.

Although 445 descriptors are available, this does not mean that all are used for each occupation. Most individuals will not use the O*NET itself, but will look at a version that has been abstracted from the O*NET onto the computer or into a book such as *The O*NET Dictionary of Occupational Titles* (Farr & Shatkin, 2007). The information that is provided in this book includes 14 relevant descriptions, not 445. The six categories of O*NET descriptors are described below. Because the 6 categories of 445 descriptors include so many characteristics, only the more common ones are listed.

1. *Worker characteristics* include abilities, interests, and work styles. Among the *abilities* are cognitive (verbal, numerical, perceptual, and spatial), psychomotor (manual and finger dexterity), physical (strength, endurance, balance, and coordination), and sensory abilities (visual, auditory, and speech). *Interests* are represented by the six Holland types (see Chapter 5). Included under interests are occupational values such as ability utilization, achievement, variety, compensation, and advancement. *Work styles* include achievement in interpersonal orientations, social influence, adjustment, independence, and practical intelligence.

2. *Worker requirements* include skills that are basic, as well as specific knowledge requirements. Educational requirements are also a part of this category. *Basic skills* refer to reading comprehension, active listening, writing, speaking, math, and science, whereas *process skills* include critical thinking, active learning, learning strategies, and monitoring. *Cross-functional skills* are social (persuading, negotiating, and instructing), problem solving, and technical abilities (testing, maintaining, repairing); judging and decision making; and managing time and finances. *Knowledge requirements* refer to principles and facts about a variety of subjects such as business,

TABLE 2.7 | O*NET OCCUPATIONS WITHIN GROUPINGS OF RELATED JOBS

Section 1 Executives, managers, and administrators
13– – – General managers
15– – – Specialty managers
190– – Executives
199– – Services managers

Section 2 Professional and support specialists, financial specialists, engineers, scientists, mathematicians, social scientists, social services workers, religious workers, and legal workers
211– – Financial specialists
213– – Purchasers and buyers
215– – Human resource workers
219– – Inspectors and compliance officers
219– – Management support workers
221– – Engineers
223– – Architects and surveyors
225– – Engineering technologists and technicians
241– – Physical scientists
243– – Life scientists
245– – Life and physical sciences technologists and technicians
251– – Computer scientists
253– – Mathematical scientists and technicians
271– – Social scientists
273– – Social service workers
275– – Religious workers
281– – Lawyers and judges
283– – Legal assistants

Section 3 Professional and support specialists, educators, librarians, counselors, health care workers, artists, writers, performers, and other professional workers
311– – College and university faculty
313– – Preschool, kindergarten, elementary, secondary, and special education teachers and instructors
315– – Librarians, curators, and counselors
321– – Diagnosing and treating practitioners (health)
323– – Medical therapists
325– – Health care providers
329– – Medical technologists and technicians
340– – Artistic, creative, and entertainment providers
39– – – Other professional, paraprofessional, and technical workers

Section 4 Sales workers
410– – Sales supervisors and managers
430– – Sales agents
490– – Technical, wholesale, and retail sales workers
499– – Sales consultants and estimators

Section 5 Administrative support workers
510– – Administrative supervisors
531– – Financial transaction workers
533– – Insurance specialists
535– – Investigators and collectors

(continued)

TABLE 2.7 | CONTINUED

537– –   Government clerks
538– –   Travel and hotel clerks
539– –   Other clerical workers
551– –   Secretaries
553– –   General office support workers
560– –   Office machine operators
571– –   Communications equipment operators
573– –   Mail clerks, carriers, and messengers
580– –   Material recording, scheduling, and distributing workers

Section 6   Service workers
610– –   Service supervisors and managers
620– –   Private household workers
630– –   Protective services workers
650– –   Food service workers
660– –   Medical assistants and aides
670– –   Cleaning and building service workers
680– –   Personal service workers

Section 7   Agricultural, forestry, and fishing workers
720– –   Agriculture, forestry, and fishing supervisors
730– –   Timber cutting and related logging workers
790– –   Plant and animal workers
798– –   Farm workers
799– –   Other agricultural workers

Section 8   Mechanics, installers, repairers, construction trades, extractive trades, metal and plastic working, woodworking, apparel, precision printing, and food processing workers
810– –   Blue-collar worker supervisors
830– –   Inspectors, testers, and graders
851– –   Industrial equipment mechanics
853– –   Motor vehicle mechanics
855– –   Communications equipment mechanics
857– –   Line installation and electronic equipment repairers
859– –   Other mechanics, installers, and repairers
871– –   Carpenters, drywall workers, and lathers
872– –   Electricians
873– –   Masons, concrete workers, tile setters, and reinforcing metal workers
874– –   Painters and paper hangers
875– –   Plumbing workers
876– –   Flooring installers
877– –   Highway and rail workers
878– –   Other construction workers
879– –   Extractive trade workers
891– –   Metal working and plastics working occupations
893– –   Woodworking occupations
895– –   Apparel occupations

Section 9   Machine setters, operations, and tenders, production workers, hand workers, plant and systems workers, transportation workers, and helpers
911– –   Machine cutting, trimming, drilling, grinding, and polishing setters, operators, and tenders

TABLE 2.7	CONTINUED

913– –	Punching, pressing, extracting, rolling, and forming machine setters and operators
917– –	Metal fabricating machine setters, operators, and related workers
919– –	Molding, casting, plating, and heating machine setters, and operators
921– –	Other metal and plastic machine setters and operators
923– –	Woodworking machine setters and operators
925– –	Printing, binding, and related machine setters and operators
927– –	Textile and related machine setters, operators, and related workers
929– –	Other machine setters, operators, and tenders
931– –	Precision production occupations
939– –	Hand workers, including assemblers and fabricators
950– –	Plant and systems occupations
971– –	Motor vehicle operators
973– –	Rail transportation workers
975– –	Water transportation and related workers
977– –	Air transportation workers
978– –	Other transportation-related workers
979– –	Material moving equipment operators
981– –	Helpers—mechanics and repairers
983– –	Helpers—construction
985– –	Helpers—feeders and offbearers
987– –	Helpers—material movers
989– –	Helpers—production, washing, and packing
990– –	Military

Source: O*NET Database. (1998). U.S. Department of Labor, Washington, DC.

engineering, math, and communication. *Education requirements* refer to the level of education required for a specific subject.

3. *Experience requirements* describe specific preparation or work experience. Licenses or certificates are also used to identify levels of skill or performance needed to enter an occupation.

4. *Occupation requirements* are presented as general types of work activities, the context of the organization, and the context of the work. *General types of work activities* are those that occur in many types of jobs. They include getting information needed to do the job, processing and evaluating information, making decisions, solving problems, performing physical and technical work, and communicating with others. *Organizational contexts* refer to the way that people do their work. Some of the organizational context factors include the amount of control the workers have in making decisions, the variety of skills used in the work, autonomy, feedback, recruitment and selection of employees, training and development, and pay and benefits. *Work contexts* are the social and physical factors that affect how individuals do their work. These include methods of communication, job interactions, the work setting, job hazards, physical demands, challenging nature of the work, and the pace and schedule of the work.

5. *Occupation-specific requirements* describe characteristics of each occupation in terms of skills, knowledge, tasks, duties, machines, tools, and equipment.

6. *Occupational characteristics* include information about the occupation, such as job opportunities and pay.

The vast amount of information available in the O*NET can be overwhelming. The information abstracted above has been taken from Lock (2005). Because this information is so comprehensive, *The O*NET Dictionary of Occupational Titles* (Farr & Shatkin, 2007) provides one of the best resources for understanding and using the O*NET. Included in this book are crosswalks (a bridge or cross-reference) to the Dictionary of Occupational Titles, the *Guide for Occupational Exploration* (GOE), and descriptions of 218 of the O*NET data elements. There is also information on the O*NET database's structure and development, as well as an alphabetical index of O*NET job titles.

The 14 descriptors that are provided in *The O*NET Dictionary of Occupational Titles* are listed briefly below. This information is similar to that provided by the *Dictionary of Occupational Titles*.

- *O*NET Number*—Each O*NET occupation has its own number that relates to occupational groups and subgroups within the O*NET.
- *O*NET Occupational Title*
- *Occupational Handbook Titles*
- *O*NET Occupational Description*—This contains a brief description of the job followed by a list of occupational tasks performed by individuals working in that occupation.
- *Yearly Earnings*—This is the average pay received by those working in specific occupational fields.
- *Education*—This includes education, training, and work experience required for entry into the occupation.
- *Knowledge*—This includes knowledge that is required for the job that may come from sources such as high school, college, training programs, self-employment, or other life experiences.
- *Abilities*—These are enduring attributes that are required for the job and do not change over time.
- *Skills*—These are the many small skills that may be needed for each job.
- *General Work Activities*—These include both basic and complex work activities.
- *Job Characteristics*—These include such information as interacting with others, mental processes, role relationships, communication methods, and other characteristics.
- *The Guide for Occupational Exploration Groupings (GOE)*
- *Classification of Instructional Programs*—This is a system of categorizing training and educational programs and courses.
- *Related Dictionary of Occupational Titles Jobs*—This includes the nine-digit DOT code and the title for related DOT jobs.

Another government classification system, the *Guide for Occupational Exploration* (Farr, Ludden, & Shatkin, 2007), uses a three-digit code somewhat similar to the first three digits of the DOT code. The difference is that the codes are more related to the interest requirements of occupations than are the DOT codes. The 12 basic interest areas are listed in Table 2.8. The GOE lists occupations in 348 subgroups, with the DOT code given for each code or occupation in the

TABLE 2.8	GUIDE FOR OCCUPATIONAL EXPLORATION SYSTEM: INTEREST AREAS, WORK GROUPS, AND SUBGROUPS

01	*Artistic*	06.03	Quality control
01.01	Literary arts	06.04	Elemental work: Industrial
01.02	Visual arts	07	*Business Detail*
01.03	Performing arts: Drama	07.01	Administrative detail
01.04	Performing arts: Music	07.02	Mathematical detail
01.05	Performing arts: Dance	07.03	Financial detail
01.06	Craft arts	07.04	Oral communications
01.07	Elemental arts	07.05	Records processing
01.08	Modeling	07.06	Clerical machine operation
02	*Scientific*	07.07	Clerical handling
02.01	Physical sciences	08	*Selling*
02.02	Life sciences	08.01	Sales technology
02.03	Medical sciences	08.02	General sales
02.04	Laboratory technology	08.03	Vending
03	*Plants and Animals*	09	*Accommodating*
03.01	Managerial work: Plants and animals	09.01	Hospitality services
		09.02	Barber and beauty services
03.02	General supervision: Plants and animals	09.03	Passenger services
		09.04	Customer services
03.03	Animal training and service	09.05	Attendant services
03.04	Elemental work: Plants and animals	10	*Humanitarian*
		10.01	Social services
04	*Protective*	10.02	Nursing, therapy, and specialized teaching services
04.01	Safety and law enforcement		
04.02	Security services	10.03	Child and adult care
05	*Mechanical*	11	*Leading-Influencing*
05.01	Engineering	11.01	Mathematics and statistics
05.02	Managerial work: Mechanical	11.02	Educational and library services
05.03	Engineering technology	11.03	Social research
05.04	Air and water vehicle operation	11.04	Law
05.05	Craft technology	11.05	Business administration
05.06	Systems operation	11.06	Finance
05.07	Quality control	11.07	Services administration
05.08	Land and water vehicle operation	11.08	Communications
05.09	Materials control	11.09	Promotion
05.10	Crafts	11.10	Regulations enforcement
05.11	Equipment operation	11.11	Business management
05.12	Elemental work: Mechanical	11.12	Contracts and claims
06	*Industrial*	12	*Physical Performing*
06.01	Production technology	12.01	Sports
06.02	Production work	12.02	Physical feats

Source: Based on *Guide for Occupational Exploration*. (1979). U.S. Department of Labor, Washington, DC.

subgroup. Because the GOE makes more intuitive sense to the client, using the GOE requires less assistance from the counselor than using the DOT.

A more complex system is the *Standard Occupational Classification Manual* (SOC, 2000). It has three levels: major groups, minor groups, and broad occupations. The SOC code clusters jobs by similar work function, rather than by interests, as in the GOE. The 23 major groups that make up this classification system are listed in Table 2.9, together with the 98 minor groups. The SOC was developed to bridge the DOT and a classification system used by the U.S. Census Bureau. Also, it was designed to be comprehensive and to be used by many federal agencies. Because these four classification systems—DOT, O*NET, GOE, and SOC—all attempt to classify several thousand occupations, they are helpful tools for the counselor in organizing a large amount of material.

TRAIT AND FACTOR REQUIREMENTS

Occupational information can be related directly to the client's traits. Information about required aptitudes, achievements, interests, values, and personality is contained in occupational pamphlets and books. For example, when reading that a lawyer must learn the law, must write arguments, and so forth, a client can ask himself or herself if he or she is interested in doing those activities. When the qualifications and the educational requirements of an occupation are explained in occupational resources, clients can determine whether they have the necessary ability to proceed into that occupation. With regard to working conditions, a client can decide whether he or she has the appropriate personality and abilities to find the working conditions satisfying. For example, a person with a need for organization and cleanliness may find work in factories with dirt and scrap parts objectionable. A client's values are tested when the client must consider if the salary is sufficient or if the employment outlook is too risky. Occupational literature contains information that allows a client to assess the fit between his or her aptitudes, achievements, interests, values, and personality and the occupation being described.

WHAT THE COUNSELOR NEEDS TO KNOW

Because thousands of occupations are open to clients, it is helpful for the counselor to be able to decide what he or she must know about occupations. For example, if a counselor uses the Strong Interest Inventory (SII), it is helpful to know the descriptions of all occupations listed, because clients are likely to ask about them. If a counselor uses a personality inventory or an aptitude test such as the ASVAB, it is beneficial to have at hand a list of occupations that match scores on those inventories or tests. Often, the classification system that the counselor uses is determined by the classification system used by the occupational library in his or her setting. The counselor can direct the client to appropriate occupational information by making use of an organized library. Then the client can read information not only about a specific occupation, but also about occupations with similar codes. For example, by looking under the DOT code with the first three digits of 045, the client will find information about several different kinds of counseling and psychology occupations.

TABLE 2.9	STANDARD OCCUPATIONAL CLASSIFICATION SYSTEM: 23 MAJOR GROUPS AND 98 MINOR GROUPS

11–0000	*Management Occupations*
11–1000	Top executives
11–2000	Advertising, marketing, promotions, public relations, and sales managers
11–3000	Operations specialties managers
11–9000	Other management occupations
13–0000	*Business and Financial Operations Occupations*
13–1000	Business operations specialists
13–2000	Financial specialists
15–0000	*Computer and Mathematical Occupations*
15–1000	Computer specialists
15–2000	Mathematical science occupations
15–3000	Mathematical technicians
17–0000	*Architecture and Engineering Occupations*
17–1000	Architects, surveyors, and cartographers
17–2000	Engineers
17–3000	Drafters, engineering, and mapping technicians
19–0000	*Life, Physical, and Social Science Occupations*
19–1000	Life scientists
19–2000	Physical scientists
19–3000	Social scientists and related workers
19–4000	Life, physical, and social science technicians
21–0000	*Community and Social Services Occupations*
21–1000	Counselors, social workers, and other community and social service specialists
21–2000	Religious workers
23–0000	*Legal Occupations*
23–1000	Lawyers, judges, and related workers
23–2000	Legal support workers
25–0000	*Education, Training, and Library Occupations*
25–1000	Postsecondary teachers
25–2000	Primary, secondary, and special education school teachers
25–3000	Other teachers and instructors
25–4000	Librarians, curators, and archivists
25–9000	Other education, training, and library occupations
27–0000	*Arts, Design, Entertainment, Sports, and Media Occupations*
27–1000	Art and design workers
27–2000	Entertainers and performers, sports and related workers
27–3000	Media and communications workers
27–4000	Media and communications equipment workers
29–0000	*Health Care Practitioners and Technical Occupations*
29–1000	Health diagnosing and treating practitioners
29–2000	Health technologists and technicians
29–9000	Other health care practitioners and technical occupations
31–0000	*Health Care Support Occupations*
31–1000	Nursing, psychiatric, and home health aides
31–2000	Occupational and physical therapist assistants and aides
31–9000	Other health care support occupations
33–0000	*Protective Service Occupations*
33–1000	First–line supervisors/managers, protective service workers

(continued)

TABLE 2.9 | CONTINUED

33–2000	Fire fighting and prevention workers
33–3000	Law enforcement workers
33–9000	Other protective service workers
35–0000	*Food Preparation and Serving–Related Occupations*
35–1000	Supervisors, food preparation and serving workers
35–2000	Cooks and food preparation workers
35–3000	Food and beverage serving workers
35–9000	Other food preparation and serving-related workers
37–0000	*Building and Grounds Cleaning and Maintenance Occupations*
37–1000	Supervisors, building and grounds cleaning and maintenance workers
37–2000	Building cleaning and pest control workers
37–3000	Grounds maintenance workers
39–0000	*Personal Care and Service Occupations*
39–1000	Supervisors, personal care and service workers
39–2000	Animal care and service workers
39–3000	Entertainment attendants and related workers
39–4000	Funeral service workers
39–5000	Personal appearance workers
39–6000	Transportation, tourism, and lodging attendants
39–9000	Other personal care and service workers
41–0000	*Sales and Related Occupations*
41–1000	Supervisors, sales workers
41–2000	Retail sales workers
41–3000	Sales representatives, services
41–4000	Sales representatives, wholesale and manufacturing
41–9000	Other sales and related workers
43–0000	*Office and Administrative Support Occupations*
43–1000	Supervisors, office and administrative support workers
43–2000	Communications equipment operators
43–3000	Financial clerks
43–4000	Information and record clerks
43–5000	Material recording, scheduling, dispatching, and distributing workers
43–6000	Secretaries and administrative assistants
43–9000	Other office and administrative support workers
45–0000	*Farming, Fishing, and Forestry Occupations*
45–1000	Supervisors, farming, fishing, and forestry workers
45–2000	Agricultural workers
45–3000	Fishing and hunting workers
45–4000	Forest, conservation, and logging workers
47–0000	*Construction and Extraction Occupations*
47–1000	Supervisors, construction and extraction workers
47–2000	Construction trades workers
47–3000	Helpers, construction trades
47–4000	Other construction and related workers
47–5000	Extraction workers
49–0000	*Installation, Maintenance, and Repair Occupations*
49–1000	Supervisors of installation, maintenance, and repair workers
49–2000	Electrical and electronic equipment mechanics, installers, and repairers
49–3000	Vehicle and mobile equipment mechanics, installers, and repairers
49–9000	Other installation, maintenance, and repair occupations

TABLE 2.9 | CONTINUED

51–0000	*Production Occupations*
51–1000	Supervisors, production workers
51–2000	Assemblers and fabricators
51–3000	Food processing workers
51–4000	Metal workers and plastics workers
51–5000	Printing workers
51–6000	Textile, apparel, and furnishings workers
51–7000	Woodworkers
51–8000	Plant and systems operators
51–9000	Other production occupations
53–0000	*Transportation and Material Moving Occupations*
53–1000	Supervisors, transportation and material moving workers
53–2000	Air transportation workers
53–3000	Motor vehicle operators
53–4000	Rail transportation workers
53–5000	Water transportation workers
53–6000	Other transportation workers
53–7000	Material moving workers

Source: Based on *Standard Occupational Classification Manual.* (1998). U.S. Department of Commerce, Washington, DC.

Counselors should also be aware that new occupations are continually being developed. "Web designer" and "information architect" did not exist as occupations in the 1960s. Because occupations are being added to the job market at a relatively fast rate, the O*NET was designed to be continually updated in an online format. Book versions of the O*NET are printed from computer versions occasionally, but they are not as up to date as the online version. The O*NET reflects the rapid growth in new technological occupations in the labor market.

EXAMPLE OF STEP 2

As Jack and the counselor discuss Jack's experience and assessment results (see Table 2.5), they arrive at several occupations that Jack may want to examine. They have chosen these occupational titles because these are occupations that seem to fit some of Jack's interests, aptitudes, and values and his personality.

CL: Although I had thought of sales before, I had never given it much thought because my knowledge of sales was limited to door-to-door or telephone sales, and I never really liked that.

CO: There is a wide variety of sales occupations, and I can help you learn about them by showing you information about some of the job descriptions that we have in our career library. [The counselor is aware that books such as the *Occupational Outlook Handbook* and booklets on occupations may be a good start in broadening Jack's knowledge about sales. The counselor does not need to know all of the sales occupations that exist. If he or she wishes to find as large a number of sales occupations as possible, then the O*NET titles will provide that information.]

CL: Although sales seems OK, I'm still interested in doing artwork. But, on the other hand, I don't want to be a starving artist. There must be some ways to use art and still make a living.

CO: There are. Although some artistic occupations are extremely competitive, there are some that are not as competitive. It is really worth looking into some of these, such as graphic arts. [Even though painting for a living is competitive, it is not appropriate to discourage the client from learning more about this occupation or others like it. The counselor wishes to encourage the client to read about a wide variety of artistic occupations that may include the use of drawing, painting, or sculpting.]

CL: I haven't taken any art courses in college, but in high school last year, I worked closely with my art teacher. Perhaps that's something that I should look into.

CO: Maybe you will be able to talk to your teacher during your vacation. [Jack is being encouraged to get occupational information. Even though the test and inventory scores may not fit with art teaching as much as they may with other occupations, it is helpful to encourage Jack to make this decision himself. This decision is best made after getting more information about being an art teacher.]

CL: When I think of it, there are a lot of people I know in careers that I'm considering. And some in careers I'm really not considering. My uncle sells Cadillac cars in Philadelphia.

CO: Even though you're not considering selling cars, you're interested in sales. Perhaps you could talk to him about sales. [Getting information from all sources, both direct and indirect, is helpful.]

CL: Yes, but my uncle's like me. He'll probably try to sell me on selling.

CO: But you're able to separate the good information from opinion. Furthermore, you can compare what he says with information that you learn when you read about sales occupations. [Being aware of the subjectivity of one person's impressions of an occupation, the counselor encourages Jack to consult other sources of more objective information, such as books or pamphlets.]

STEP 3: INTEGRATING INFORMATION ABOUT ONE'S SELF AND THE WORLD OF WORK

According to trait and factor theory, this third step, integrating information about one's self and about occupations, is the major goal of career counseling. As mentioned earlier, the manuals that accompany some tests and inventories indicate which occupations match specific patterns of scores.

Furthermore, occupational information has within it material indicating the aptitudes, achievements, interests, values, and personality characteristics required for each occupation. In a sense, the matching is built into the first two steps of trait and factor theory. However, this is simpler in theory than it is in practice. It is possible for a person's abilities, as measured on the ASVAB, to suggest one set of occupations, whereas their interests, as measured on the SII, suggest another group of occupations, and then their personality, as measured on the 16 PF, suggests a third group of occupations. There may also be disagreement among instruments that measure the same trait, emphasizing the fallibility of assessment and the need for care in assessment interpretation. In addition to the fallibility of assessment instruments is the notion that much information that is useful in making career decisions may not come necessarily from tests and inventories but from the counseling interview.

Tests and inventories are not the only methods for measuring and assessing traits. Computer guidance systems tend to fit neatly into trait and factor theory.

They often combine tests and occupational information in such a way that clients can meet their own individual needs for self-assessment and occupational information. Two of the more comprehensive systems are SIGI^3, formerly called SIGI PLUS (VALPAR, 2007) and DISCOVER (ACT, Inc., 2007). Both systems allow an opportunity to measure interests, values, and self-reported competencies. These systems do not measure personality, but they do provide assessment of work values. Occupational information is then matched with the student's competencies, values, and interests, so that the student can examine information about occupations that match his or her self-assessment. Both instruments provide an opportunity to help with the decision-making process by reducing a list of occupational alternatives. In fact, DISCOVER allows the opportunity to put into the system scores from a number of instruments, such as those that have been discussed earlier.

One advantage that both SIGI^3 and DISCOVER have over the tests and inventories previously described is that the computer programs are interactive. That is, as a student answers some questions and receives information, he or she can choose to move to any one of several sections. There is interplay of information between the client and the computer, resulting in immediate feedback to the client. Computers can be used instead of or with other tests or inventories. However, tests, inventories, and computers cannot help clients in working out difficult and unusual concerns, such as parental pressure to enter an unwanted occupation.

How the Counselor Can Help

The process of counseling by using trait and factor theory requires moving between the assessment of one's self and occupational information. Because much occupational information can be obtained outside the counseling session, most of the focus within the session is on self-assessment.

Counselors have available to them a full range of helping skills (see Chapter 1). In using trait and factor theory, a counselor need not be limited to making suggestions and giving information. Both reasoning and feelings are important in making a career decision. When a client expresses a feeling, it is often helpful to find the reason behind it. For example, if a client says, "I wouldn't like to be a nurse," the counselor can respond in a number of ways, for example, "What is it about nursing that you don't like?" or "Nursing doesn't feel right to you?" By doing this, the counselor is likely to find out the cause of these feelings. If the client replies, "I don't have what it takes to get into a nursing school," the counselor can reply, "You believe a nursing school wouldn't accept you" (content reflection), "You feel anxious about entering a nursing school" (feeling reflection), or "What makes you think you couldn't enter a nursing school?" (open question). These are examples of helping skills that would assist the student in exploring his or her interest or abilities in nursing. Counseling can proceed by repeatedly going over a client's aptitudes, achievements, interests, abilities, and values until an understanding is reached.

As counseling progresses, it may be important to get more specific occupational information, as well as more specific information about interests, aptitudes, achievements, values, and personality. An excellent way to do this is for the client to talk with people in a specific job. The client can obtain even more detailed information by trying out an activity as a volunteer or part-time worker. For example, if a student is trying to choose between becoming an occupational therapist and a salesperson, it may be helpful to get a summer job as a salesperson in a retail store and volunteer in a hospital to work in the occupational therapy field. A potential problem is that occasionally one may work in a setting that is unrepresentative because of low morale, inadequate administrative structure, or unhelpful colleagues. Counselors can help the client separate the setting from the idiosyncrasies of the work setting. As occupational experience and exploration in the counseling session help the client define his or her interests and ability more clearly, the client moves toward a career decision.

Although a career decision has been reached, it may be only temporary. Career counseling can be repeated at various times in the client's lifetime. Traits and factors can be reassessed as clients have new experiences that affect their assessment of their aptitudes, achievements, interests, values, and personality.

EXAMPLE OF STEP 3

The following dialogue is from a session that occurred after Jack had talked to others and read about occupations that interest him.

CL: Some of the information that I read was really helpful. I hadn't realized that there were so many different types of sales occupations and so many different places where you could work.

CO: That's great. It sounds as if you've done a lot of work. [The counselor chooses to reinforce the client's information seeking. Without occupational information, career counseling will be unsuccessful.]

CL: I think I would really like to take more art courses, perhaps in graphic arts. I know that graphic arts is a competitive field; at least that's what the material said. But I still think it would be good for me.

CO: Tell me a little more about what you like about it. [The counselor is aware of Jack's low score on economic security on the VS. His lack of concern about the competitiveness of graphic arts seems consistent with this.]

CL: Well, there is really an opportunity to draw, to be precise, to create new things. I could see myself doing advertising work.

CO: The artistic work really seems to fit you. [Jack's high scores on art on the KCS and creativity on the VS are consistent with this statement.]

CL: When I was looking in the career library, I found information about public relations. That got me thinking, too, because you can use all kinds of methods to try to persuade people to a certain point of view. I guess I hadn't realized that there are a lot of ways of doing this. I suppose you can do this artistically, as well as by talking to people.

CO: That's a clever way of looking at that. Perhaps you can combine several interests of yours. [Reinforcing the client's insight into how to combine art and sales/management interests, as indicated on the KCS, helps to move the client further along in his decision-making process.]

CL: I wonder if you can really do this in public relations or maybe advertising.

CO: Perhaps we can find some people for you to talk to about this idea. [The counselor realizes that written occupational information may not be enough to satisfy Jack's curiosity. The counselor is prepared to provide other resources to help Jack clarify his career decision making. Note how the counselor moves back and forth between self-assessment and occupational information, gradually moving the client closer to a career decision.]

APPLYING THE THEORY TO WOMEN

Differences in the abilities, achievements, values, personality, and interests of men and women have been a frequent source of study. Much research has focused on the differences between men and women in their real and perceived mathematical and verbal ability, resulting in differential educational and occupational achievements by men and women. Although the values and interests of men and women are becoming more similar, there are some significant variations. This section focuses on these issues.

Contrasting the abilities of men and women yields complex results (Suzuki & Ahluwalia, 2003). When studied in detail, some differences show that some verbal skills and some math skills are areas in which women perform better than men, whereas in other verbal and math skills, men perform better than women. It has been suggested that these differences are because of both socialization and physiological differences in the way that the brain operates and functions. On general measures of intelligence, such as the Wechsler Adult Intelligence Scale, Third Edition, there are no useful differences between genders. Individual differences are far greater than gender differences.

Attention has been given to women in math and science, because women are underrepresented in these areas. Betz and Fitzgerald (1987) point out that those women who continue to study math have a much broader range of career options than those who do not. Studying eighth graders, Mau (2003) reports that girls tend to be less persistent than boys in pursuing math and science occupations. Girls in the sample had lower scores on math self-efficacy than did boys; scores on reading self-efficacy were similar for boys and girls. In research on ninth-grade girls' views about math, the girls who believed they were competent in math were also likely to do well in math and to express intentions to take more math courses (Crombie et al., 2005). Related to the differing achievements of women in school and in careers is their attitude toward their ability to be successful.

Personality factors such as confidence and self-esteem have been a focus of research that attempts to explain the different levels of accomplishment and ability of women compared with men. Chipman, Krantz, and Silver (1992) report that math anxiety negatively affects interest in science careers. Well-adapted or vocationally secure women have been documented as sharing strong interest and ability in the sciences (Meldahl & Muchinsky, 1997). Related to this is the concept of self-efficacy (Chapter 14, "Social Cognitive Career Theory," contains a more detailed discussion). The research on math self-efficacy, as reviewed by Fouad, Helledy, and Metz (2003), shows that women are often less confident and more anxious about their math ability than are men.

Lack of self-confidence about career-related activities is not confined to math. For example, Swanson and Lease (1990) report that women rate the general abilities of peers greater than their own abilities, whereas men rate the abilities of peers lower than their own abilities. Read (1994) claims that women in nontraditional training programs have greater confidence in being able to succeed in school and on the job than do women in traditional and gender-balanced programs. In a study of 198 working women aged 18 to 55 years, Betsworth (1999) reports that the women significantly underestimate their abilities on general learning ability, verbal ability, spatial ability, form perception, clerical perception, and motor coordination. In a study of 201 adults, Furnham (2002) reports that women rate their numerical ability lower than do men. These studies show that the lack of self-esteem and confidence of many women has kept them from greater educational and occupational accomplishments.

In a broad sense, the interests of men and women have been shown to be different (Fouad, 2002; Suzuki & Ahluwalia, 2003; Tracey, Robbins, & Hofsess, 2005). Interest inventories have revealed that, in general, women have more interest in artistic, clerical, and social occupations than men. Conversely, they have less interest in scientific and technical occupations (Fouad, Helledy, & Metz, 2003). One of the problems in measuring interests has been that early forms of interest inventories were often gender biased. For example, separate forms were used for men and women, and occupational titles were often male-oriented, such as mailman rather than mail carrier (Fouad, Helledy, & Metz, 2003). Although interest inventories have been improved to measure interests more accurately, without gender bias contaminating the assessment, interest inventories still reflect social values about occupations; for example, social values that women should enter occupations such as teaching, nursing, and social work continue to exist. For counselors, the challenge is to help women develop occupational interests in areas such as science and math.

Some research has focused on the different values that men and women have regarding work. Gender-role stereotyping and the effects of limiting the range of occupations that women consider, as well as their attitude toward work, is a significant aspect of Brown's (2002a, 2002b) theory of the role of work values in each individual's life. In terms of commitment to work, Luzzo (1994) reports that college women have a stronger commitment to work than do college men. Lips (1992) writes that college women rate people-related values and intrinsic values higher than do college men. This finding was supported by Duffy and Sedlacek's (2007) research on the values of college first-year students. Although there are differences in the values of men and women within various professions and occupations, the differences in the career values of men and women appear to be decreasing, with both male and female individuals valuing accomplishment, salary, security, and so on.

Although differences in abilities, achievements, personality, interests, and values between men and women do exist, they are often rather small. The differences between workers within occupational groups are often much greater than those between men and women in general. Being aware of how men and women differ on various traits and factors may help counselors attend to societal pressures on their female clients, while attempting to maximize their educational and occupational opportunities.

APPLYING THE THEORY TO CULTURALLY DIVERSE POPULATIONS

Regarding the traits of culturally diverse individuals, perhaps the most research has focused on the interests and work values of different cultural groups. For the purposes of this section, the interests and work values of Asian Americans, African

Americans, Hispanics, and Native Americans are discussed. Related to the formation of work values is the availability of occupational information. It is not valid to assume that occupational information is equally available to all people in the United States.

Research on the interests of culturally diverse people has focused mainly on measures of interests. Fouad (2002) examined the interest structure of African Americans, Asian Americans, European Americans, Hispanics/Latinos, and Native Americans on the SII. Assessing interests of about 70,000 eighth-, tenth-, and twelfth-grade students, Tracey et al. (2005) found only small differences among the interests of different cultural groups, as did Fouad (2002). Using a sample of more than 55,000 employed adults, Lattimore and Borgen (1999) report that the SII generally predicted the interests of African Americans, Hispanic Americans, Asian Americans, and Native Americans as well as it did the interests of white individuals. Examining the interests of Chinese college students, Tang (2001) reports that, in general, the interests of the students fit with the structure of the General Occupational Themes and the Basic Interest Scales of the Strong Interest Inventory. Tracey, Watanabe, and Schneider (1997) caution that some models of career interests that fit U.S. students do not apply to Japanese students. Leung, Ivey, and Suzuki (1994) write that Asian American college students have interests in social occupations, as well as scientific and technical occupations, in contrast to the traditional view that Asian American interests are primarily in the scientific fields. Much of the research has used Holland's inventories (Chapter 5). Currently, there is not sufficient information to reveal how accurately interest inventories measure the likes and dislikes of culturally diverse people.

In his discussion of the work values of different cultural groups, Axelson (1999) describes studies that emphasize the various characteristics of cultural groups but cautions against generalizing about the behavior of individuals within a particular cultural group. Observing that Asian Americans are often willing to adopt the work values of a new culture and assimilate into it, Sue (1975) states that this is due, in part, to the development of independent work behavior in their native country. Studying the values of adolescents in Hong Kong, Lau and Wong (1992) claim that the adolescents value personal and competency factors, enjoyment, and security, in contrast to independence and obedience. This finding contradicts traditional views of the values of Chinese adolescents. In addition, a study of South Asian Americans has shown that those who are less comfortable with American culture are more likely to be interested in stereotypical Asian occupations than those South Asian Americans who are more comfortable with American culture (Castelino, 2005).

Career Counseling for African Americans (Walsh, Bingham, Brown, & Ward, 2001) raises a number of issues that affect the career counseling of African Americans. These issues include the importance for counselors to be aware of the effect of slavery and discrimination on African Americans. The book also makes suggestions for assessing career needs of African Americans and for attending to career counseling issues. Bingham and Ward (2001) raise the issue of African Americans being overrepresented in social service occupations. They also criticize trait and factor theory for not having used enough African American subjects in research studies. In an article describing characteristics of professional African

American women, Pearson and Bieschke (2001) emphasize the importance of the family, as well as relationships in the family, in providing support for education, encouragement, and finances.

Studying Mexican Americans, Gowan and Trevino (1998) report that men are more likely to hold traditional views of the roles of women in the workplace than are women. Developing a model to explain the educational plans and career expectations of Mexican American high school girls, McWhirter, Hackett, and Bandalos (1998) offer evidence to show that cultural influences are more important than gender in predicting career expectations of Mexican American girls. In general, Mexican American high school students report encountering more barriers associated with ability, preparation, motivation, and support than do white high school students (McWhirter, Torres, Salgado, & Valdez, 2007). Zuniga (2005) found that parental involvement was particularly important in predicting academic performance of adolescent Latino males.

Regarding Native Americans, Juntenen, Barraclough, Broneck, Seibel, Winrow, and Morin (2001) point out that the values of Native Americans are different from those of white individuals in the United States. Native Americans tend to be concerned about work as it relates to their entire community. Awareness of living in two worlds ("white" and "Indian") is also important. In addition, Clark (2002) emphasizes the need in the Native American population to feel a sense of community and a sense of control at work. In a study of Native American urban middle school students, a variety of career exploration skills was shown to help the students develop their interests, beliefs about vocational self-efficacy, and other positive attributes (Turner et al., 2006).

These articles are examples of the findings on different cultural values among culturally diverse people. Such generalizations help us to recognize the variety of work values that exist in society. Differences in work values and interests combined with limited access to occupational information make the career choice process difficult for nonwhite people in the United States. Being aware of such information can help counselors avoid making assumptions about the occupational knowledge and values of their clients.

COUNSELOR ISSUES

One concern about trait and factor theory is its emphasis on assessment. Preferably, a client will not leave the final counseling session saying, "The test told me I should be a ..." Although tests and inventories are used in trait and factor counseling, they are not necessarily the determinant of a final career choice. Because some clients may be looking for a quick solution, it is easy to allow the client to avoid the responsibility of making a career decision. Beginning counselors may find themselves giving assessment information rather than using more difficult counseling skills such as content and feeling reflections.

Trait and factor theory is deceptively simple. It is easy for the beginning counselor to develop a style in which he or she asks questions and the client gives answers. Because tests and inventories seem so authoritative to the client, they can prevent an easy interaction and rapport between the client and the counselor. However, by taking ample time to leave the assessment information and discuss relevant client personal experience, the counselor can help the client accept responsibility for career decision making.

Another reason that trait and factor theory is so deceptively simple is that the three basic tenets of the theory provide an overview but do not provide many details. Trait and factor theory does not provide a guide to which tests or inventories the counselor should include in his or her repertoire. It is up to the counselor to choose from hundreds of tests and inventories and to choose which traits and factors are most important. Conceptually, the theory provides less guidance for the counselor than do most of the other theories discussed in this book.

Trait and factor theory is a static, rather than a developmental, theory. It does not focus on how achievements, aptitudes, interests, values, and personalities grow and change; rather, it focuses on identifying traits and factors. However, this does not mean that this information cannot be useful in counseling. The counselor needs to help the client assess his or her interests and abilities. One way to do this is to discuss how these interests or aptitudes have changed over a period of years. This is certainly permissible within the guidelines of trait and factor theory; however, it is not emphasized. Often, the discussion of previous choices is helpful in making a current choice. Thus, past traits and factors and their evolution may be useful in assessing current traits and factors.

Another problem that counselors may encounter is the difference between their own aptitudes, achievements, interests, values, and personality and those of the client. In particular, if the counselor has work values that are very different from those of the client, the counselor should recognize this and be tolerant. Counselors often value altruism and good working relationships with their associates. They need to be careful to understand those who do not value these factors but prefer prestige or management, which counselors might not value. This and the other issues mentioned above may make trait and factor theory one of the more difficult theories for a counselor to implement.

SUMMARY

Being the oldest and arguably the most widely used of all career development theories, trait and factor theory focuses on the match between an individual's aptitudes, achievements, interests, values, and personality and the requirements and conditions of occupations. Having obtained relevant information, the counselor and client work to bring about a match between the individual and the world of work. This approach relies heavily on the use of tests and inventories to measure aptitudes, achievements, interests, values, and personality. In selection of assessment instruments, the theory is vague, allowing the counselor to select those instruments that seem most appropriate to the counselor and the client. Selection of tests and inventories may determine the occupational classification system that the counselor will use. Such a system is helpful to the client in organizing information about occupations. The research focus in trait and factor theory has been on the traits and factors themselves, rather than on the applicability of the theory as a career counseling approach. Additional research has been done delineating the aptitudes, achievements, interests, values, and personalities of women and culturally diverse people. However, there is a vast need for more research, particularly on the latter group. The general trait and factor theory described in this chapter can be seen as an outline for the more highly defined trait and factor theories of Holland (Chapter 5) and Lofquist and Dawis (Chapter 4).

REFERENCES

Ackerman, P. L., & Heggestad, E. D. (1997). Intelligence, personality, and interests: Evidence for overlapping traits. *Psychological Bulletin, 121,* 219–245.

ACT, Inc. (2007) DISCOVER (Windows). Iowa City, IA. Author.

Aiken, L. R., & Groth-Marnat, G. (2007). *Psychological testing and assessment* (12th ed.). Boston: Allyn & Bacon.

Armstrong, P. I., Smith, T. J., Donnay, D. A. C., & Rounds, J. B. (2004). The Strong ring: A basic interest model of occupational structure. *Journal of Counseling Psychology, 51,* 299–313.

Astin, A. W. (1993). *What matters in college? Four critical years revisited.* San Francisco: Jossey-Bass.

Aubrey, R. F. (1977). Historical development of guidance and counseling and implications for the future. *Personnel and Guidance Journal, 55,* 288–295.

Axelson, J. A. (1999). *Counseling and development in a multicultural society* (3rd ed.). Pacific Grove, CA: Brooks/Cole.

Baker, H. E. (2002). Reducing adolescent career indecision: The ASVAB career exploration program. *Career Development Quarterly, 50,* 359–370.

Betsworth, D. G. (1999). Accuracy of self-estimated abilities and the relationship between self-estimated abilities and realism for women. *Journal of Career Assessment, 7,* 35–43.

Betz, N. E., & Fitzgerald, L. F. (1987). *The career psychology of women.* Orlando, FL: Academic Press.

Bingham, R. P., & Ward, C. M. (2001). Career counseling with African American males and females. In W. B. Walsh, R. P. Bingham, M. T. Brown, & C. M. Ward (Eds.), *Career counseling for African Americans* (pp. 49–76). Mahwah, NJ: Erlbaum.

Brown, D. (2002a). The role of work values and cultural values in occupational choice, satisfaction, and success: A theoretical statement. In D. Brown and Associates (Eds.), *Career choice and development* (4th ed., pp. 427–464). San Francisco: Jossey-Bass.

Brown, D. (2002b). The role of work and cultural values in occupational choice, satisfaction, and success: A theoretical statement. *Journal of Counseling and Development, 80,* 48–56.

Castelino, P. (2005). Factors influencing career choices of South Asian Americans: A path analysis. *Dissertation Abstracts International Section A: Humanities and Social Sciences, 65* (8–A), 2906.

Chipman, S. F., Krantz, D. H., & Silver, A. (1992). Mathematics anxiety and science careers among able college women. *Psychological Science, 3,* 292–295.

Clark, S. C. (2002). Employee's sense of community, sense of control, and world family conflict in Native American organizations. *Journal of Vocational Behavior, 61,* 92–108.

Conard, M. A. (2006). Aptitude is not enough: How personality and behavior predict academic performance. *Journal of Research in Personality, 40*(3), 339–346.

Crombie, G., Sinclair, N., Silverthorn, N., Byrne, B. M., DuBois, D. L., & Trinneer, A. (2005). Predictors of young adolescents' math grades and course enrollment intentions: Gender similarities and differences. *Sex Roles, 52*(5–6), 351–367.

Dictionary of occupational titles (4th ed.). (1991). Washington, DC: U.S. Department of Labor, Employment and Training Administration.

Duckworth, A. L., & Seligman, M. E. P. (2005). Self-discipline outdoes IQ in predicting academic performance of adolescents. *Psychological Science, 16* (12), 939–944.

Duffy, R. D., & Sedlacek, W. E. (2007). The work values of first-year college students: Exploring group differences. *Career Development Quarterly, 55,* 359–364.

Farr, J. M., Ludden, L. L., & Shatkin, L. (2007). *Guide for occupational exploration* (4th ed.). Indianapolis, IN: JIST Works.

Farr, J. M., & Shatkin, L. (2007). *The O*NET dictionary of occupational titles* (4th ed.). Indianapolis, IN: JIST Works.

Fouad, N. A. (2002). Cross-cultural differences in vocational interests: Between groups differences on the Strong Interest Inventory. *Journal of Counseling Psychology, 49,* 283–291.

Fouad, N. A., Helledy, I. I., & Metz, A. J. (2003). Effective strategies for career counseling with women. In M. Kopala & M. A. Keitel (Eds.), *Handbook of counseling women* (pp. 131–151). Thousand Oaks, CA: Sage.

Furnham, A. (2002). Sex differences in self-rated ability. *Social Behavior & Personality, 30,* 185–194.

Gati, I., Fishman-Nadav, Y., & Shiloh, S. (2006). The relations between preferences for using abilities, self-estimated abilities, and measured abilities among career counseling clients. *Journal of Vocational Behavior, 68*(1), 24–38.

Gough, H. G., & Bradley, P. (1996). *California Psychological Inventory: Administrator's guide* (3rd ed.). Palo Alto, CA: Consulting Psychologists Press.

Gowan, M., & Trevino, M. (1998). An examination of gender differences in Mexican-American attitudes toward family and career roles. *Sex Roles, 38,* 1079–1093.

Hansen, J. C., & Dik, B. J. (2005). Evidence of 12-year predictive and concurrent validity for SII occupational scale scores. *Journal of Vocational Behavior, 67* (3), 365–378.

Hanson, W. E., Claiborn, C. D., & Kerr, B. (1997). Differential effects of two test interpretation styles in counseling: A field study. *Journal of Counseling Psychology, 44,* 400–405.

Hartung, P. J., & Blustein, D. L. (2002). Reason, intuition, and social justice: Elaborating on Parsons career decision-making model. *Journal of Counseling and Development, 80,* 41–47.

Herr, E. L., Cramer, S. H., & Niles, S. G. (2004). *Career guidance and counseling through the life span: Systematic approaches* (6th ed.) Boston: Allyn & Bacon.

Hong, S., Kim, B. S. K., & Wolfe, M. M. (2005). A psychometric revision of the European American values scale for Asian Americans using the Rasch model. *Measurement and Evaluation in Counseling and Development, 37*(4), 194–207.

Improved career decision making through the use of labor market information. (1991). Garrett Park, MD: Garrett Park Press.

Juntunen, C. L., Barraclough, D. J., Broneck, C. L., Seibel, G. A., Winrow, S. A., & Morin, P. M. (2001). American Indian perspectives on the career journey. *Journal of Counseling Psychology, 48,* 274–286.

Kapes, J. T., & Whitfield, E. A. (Eds.). (2001). *A counselor's guide to career assessment instruments* (4th ed.). Tulsa, OK: National Career Development Association.

Kim, B. K., Li, L. C., & Ng, G. F. (2005). The Asian American Values Scale—multidimensional: Development, reliability, and validity. *Cultural Diversity & Ethnic Minority Psychology, 11*(3), 187–201.

Kopelman, R. E., Rovenpor, J. L., & Guan, M. (2003). The study of values: Construction of the fourth edition. *Journal of Vocational Behavior, 62,* 203–220.

Lattimore, R. R., & Borgen, F. H. (1999). Validity of the 1994 Strong Interest Inventory with social and ethnic groups in the United States. *Journal of Counseling Psychology, 46,* 185–195.

Lau, S., & Wong, A. K. (1992). Value and sex-role orientation of Chinese adolescents. *International Journal of Psychology, 27,* 3–17.

Lee, S. B. (2006). Asian Values scale: Comparisons of Korean and Korean-American high school students. *Psychological Reports, 98*(1), 191–192.

Leman, N. (1999). *The big test: The secret history of the American meritocracy.* New York: Farrar, Straus & Giroux.

Lent, R. W., Brown, S. D., & Hackett, G. (1994). Toward a unifying social cognitive theory of career and academic interest, choice and performance. *Journal of Vocational Behavior, 45,* 79–122.

Leung, S. A., Ivey, D., & Suzuki, L. (1994). Factors affecting the career aspirations of Asian Americans. *Journal of Counseling & Development, 72,* 404–410.

Lips, H. M. (1992). Gender and science-related attitudes as predictors of college students' academic choices. *Journal of Vocational Behavior, 40,* 62–81.

Lock, R. D. (2005). *Taking charge of your career direction* (5th ed.). Pacific Grove, CA: Brooks/Cole.

Luzzo, D. A. (1994). An analysis of gender and ethnic differences in college students' commitment to work. *Journal of Employment Counseling, 31,* 38–45.

Mau, W. C. (2003). Factors that influence persistence in science and engineering career aspirations. *Career Development Quarterly, 51,* 234–293.

McWhirter, E. H., Hackett, G., & Bandalos, D. L. (1998). A causal model of the educational plans and career expectations of Mexican American high school girls. *Journal of Counseling Psychology, 45,* 166–181.

McWhirter, E. H., Torres, D. M., Salgado, S., & Valdez, M. (2007). Perceived barriers and postsecondary plans in Mexican American and white adolescents. *Journal of Career Assessment, 15*(1), 119–138.

Meldahl, J. M., & Muchinsky, P. M. (1997). The neurotic dimension of vocational indecision: Gender comparability? *Journal of Career Assessment, 5,* 317–331.

Murphy, L. L., Plake, B. S., Impara, J. C., & Spies, R. A. (2002). *Tests in print VI.* Lincoln, NE: University of Nebraska Press.

National Career Development Association. (1991). *Guidelines for the preparation and evaluation of career on occupational information literature.* Retrieved, from National Career Development Association website: www.ncda.org/about/polcoil.html (accessed September, 22, 2007).

National Career Development Association. (2008). *NCDA Guidelines for the Use of the Internet for Provision of Career Information and Planning Services.* Retrieved from National Career Development Association website: www.ncda.org/.

Occupational outlook handbook. (2008). Washington, DC: U.S. Department of Labor.

Osborn, D. S., & Zunker, V. G. (2006). *Using assessment results for career development* (6th ed.). Pacific Grove, CA: Brooks/Cole.

Parsons, F. (1909). *Choosing a vocation.* Boston: Houghton Mifflin.

Pearson, S. M., & Bieschke, K. J. (2001). Succeeding against the odds: An examination of familial influences on the career development of professional African American women. *Journal of Counseling Psychology, 48,* 301–309.

Plake, B. S., Impara, J. C., & Spies, R. A. (Eds.). (2003). *The fifteenth mental measurements yearbook.* Lincoln NE: University of Nebraska Press.

Prediger, D. J. (2004). Career planning validity of self-estimates and test estimates of work-relevant abilities. *Career Development Quarterly, 52,* 202–211.

Proyer, R. T. (2006). The relationship between vocational interests and intelligence: Do findings generalize across different assessment methods? *Psychology Science, 48*(4), 463–476.

Read, B. K. (1994). Motivational factors in technical college women's selection of nontraditional careers. *Journal of Career Development, 20,* 239–258.

Robbins, S. B., Allen, J., Casillas, A., Peterson, C. H., & Le, H. (2006). Unraveling the differential effects of motivational and skills, social, and self-management measures from traditional predictors of college outcomes. *Journal of Educational Psychology, 98*(3), 598–616.

Rounds, J. B., & Armstrong, P. I. (2005). Assessment of needs and values. In Brown, S. D. & Lent R.W. (Eds.) *Career development and counseling: Putting theory and research to work* (pp. 305–329). Hoboken, NJ: Wiley.

Standard occupational classification manual. (2000). Washington, DC: U.S. Department of Commerce.

Sue, D. W. (1975). Asian-Americans: Social-psychological forces affecting their life styles. In J. S. Picou & R. E. Campbell (Eds.), *Career behavior of special groups: Theory, research, and practice* (pp. 97–121). Columbus, OH: Merrill.

Suzuki, L. A., & Ahluwalia, M. K. (2003). Gender issues in personality, cognitive, and vocational assessment of women. In M. Kopala & M. A. Keitel (Eds.) *Handbook of counseling women* (pp. 119–130). Thousand Oaks, CA: Sage.

Swanson, J. L., & D'Achiardi, C. (2005). Beyond interests, needs/values, and abilities: Assessing other important career constructs over the life span. In Brown, S. D. & Lent R.W. (Eds.) *Career development and counseling: Putting theory and research to work* (pp. 353–381). Hoboken, NJ: Wiley.

Swanson, J. L., & Lease, S. H. (1990). Gender differences in self-ratings of abilities and skills. *Career Development Quarterly, 38,* 347–359.

Tang, M. (2001). Investigation of the structure of vocational interests of Chinese college students. *Journal of Career Assessment, 9,* 365–380.

Tracey, T. J. G., & Hopkins, N. (2001). Correspondence of interests and abilities with occupational choice. *Journal of Counseling Psychology, 48,* 178–189.

Tracey, T. J. G., Robbins, S. B., & Hofsess, C. D. (2005). Stability and change in interests: A longitudinal study of adolescents from grades 8 through 12. *Journal of Vocational Behavior, 66*(1), 1–25.

Tracey, T. J. G., Watanabe, N., & Schneider, P. L. (1997). Structural invariance of vocational interests across Japanese and American cultures. *Journal of Counseling Psychology, 44,* 346–354.

Turner, S. L., Trotter, M. J., Lapan, R. T., Czajka, K. A., Yang, P., & Brissett, A. E. A. (2006). Vocational skills and outcomes among Native American adolescents: A test of the integrative contextual model of career development. *The Career Development Quarterly, 54*(3), 216–226.

VALPAR, International. SIGI[3] [Computer Program]. Tuscon, AZ: Author.

Walsh, W. B., Bingham, R. P., Brown, M. T., & Ward, C. M. (Eds.). (2001). *Career counseling for African Americans.* Mahwah, NJ: Erlbaum.

Williamson, E. G. (1939). *How to counsel students.* New York: McGraw-Hill.

Williamson, E. G. (1965). *Vocational counseling.* New York: McGraw-Hill.

Zuniga, K. M. (2005). The influence of individual characteristics and parenting behaviors on adolescent academic performance. *Dissertation Abstracts International Section A: Humanities and Social Sciences, 65* (9–A), 3591.

3 | OCCUPATIONS: INFORMATION AND THEORY

CHAPTER HIGHLIGHTS

The United States Labor Market

Sociological and Economic Approaches

Youth Employment

The Effect of the Work Environment on the Individual

Status Attainment Theory

Human Capital Theory

The Structure of the Labor Market

Women and Discrimination in the Workplace

Culturally Diverse Individuals and Discrimination in the Workplace

This chapter is a continuation of trait and factor theory (Chapter 2), as it elaborates on Stage 2—Obtaining Knowledge about the World of Work. Counselors should not only help clients assess interests, personality, values, and abilities, but also provide information about occupations and the labor market. First, I give an overview of the labor market that includes the trends of growth in industries and occupations as they affect adults and youths. The fields of sociology and economics provide information about various aspects of the labor market, as well as occupations. Sociologists and economists study group behavior; psychologists study how the individual affects his or her environment. Almost all other chapters in this book focus on a psychological rather than economic or sociological view. As a result of research, some models or theories have been developed that point out inequities or obstacles in the labor market that may affect the earnings or success of different individuals. When thinking about the U.S. labor market (and the labor markets of some other countries), individuals often have held the view that "Each person has an equal opportunity to succeed or fail on his or her own." Often, this assumption is oversimplified and false. A number of factors beyond the control of individuals may affect their eventual career choice and success. An individual's life may be significantly impacted by losing out to another person when applying for a job or a promotion. Furthermore, some individuals are taught to value an education and have consistent, helpful parenting and financial support to pay for schooling, whereas others do not. Discrimination because of gender or race is another variable that greatly affects people's career choices and financial and personal success. After describing some basic facts about the U.S. labor market, this chapter examines each of these factors as they influence how individuals deal with the labor market.

THE UNITED STATES LABOR MARKET

A labor market serves to fulfill the needs of citizens of a state, a nation, or the world. Job availability is related to the demand of individuals for food, shelter, clothing, health services, transportation, entertainment, fire and police protection, and so forth. The information about the U.S. labor market in Table 3.1 describes the broad occupational groups in which individuals were employed in 2006 and their predicted increases (and decreases). Employment change also is predicted in Table 3.1 for the year 2016, with computer and mathematical occupations as well as community and social services occupations being the groups that are likely to experience the greatest increases. Farming, fishing, and forestry, as well as production (manufacturing) occupations, are predicted to have a decrease in growth between 2006 and 2016.

Further information about general occupational trends can be obtained by examining growth and replacement needs. Growth refers to the need for new workers to meet demands of an occupation beyond the needs that are met by replacing existing workers. Workers leave occupations for a variety of reasons: transferring to other occupations, retiring, returning to school, assuming household duties, or choosing not to work. Of about 50 million estimated job openings between 2006 and 2016, about 68% will be because of replacement needs (*Occupational Outlook Handbook*, 2008). As shown in Figure 3.1, growth will be greatest in service areas that include healthcare support (such as dental and nursing assistants), protective service (policing, guarding, and firefighting), food preparation, cleaning and maintenance work, and personal care services (such as barbers, childcare workers, and flight attendants). Professional specialty areas that include teachers, counselors, librarians, computer programmers, mathematicians, nurses, and physicians are another area of growth. Because of turnover, as well as other replacement factors, service occupations are projected to have the largest number of job openings (approximately 12 million). In general, replacement needs are greatest in occupations with relatively low pay and limited training requirements. Some occupations, such as clerical ones, may have limited growth because of office automation.

TABLE 3.1 | EMPLOYMENT (IN THOUSANDS) BY BROAD OCCUPATIONAL GROUPS (2006) AND PROJECTED CHANGE (2006–2016)

Occupational Group	Employment						Change	
	Number		Percent Distribution					
	2006	2016	2006	2016			Number	Percent
Total, all occupations	150,620	166,220	100.0	100.0			15,600	10.4
Management occupations	15,397	16,922	5.8	5.6			533	6.1
Business and financial operations occupations	6,608	7,671	4.4	4.6			1,063	16.1
Professional and related occupations	29,819	34,790	19.8	20.9			4,970	16.7
Computer and mathematical occupations	3,313	4,135	2.2	2.5			822	24.8
Architecture and engineering occupations	2,583	2,851	1.7	1.7			268	10.4
Life, physical, and social science occupations	1,407	1,610	0.9	1.0			203	14.4
Community and social services occupations	2,386	2,927	1.6	1.8			541	22.7
Legal occupations	1,222	1,367	0.8	0.8			145	11.8
Education, training, and library occupations	9,034	10,298	6.0	6.2			1,265	14.0
Arts, design, entertainment, sports and media occupations	2,677	2,982	1.8	1.8			305	11.4

Healthcare, practitioners and technical occupations	7,198	8,620	5.2	4.8	1,423	19.8
Service occupations	28,950	33,780	20.3	19.2	4,830	16.7
Healthcare support occupations	3,723	4,720	2.8	2.5	997	26.8
Protective service occupations	3,163	3,616	2.2	2.1	453	14.3
Food preparation and serving-related occupations	11,352	12,789	7.7	7.5	1,436	12.7
Building and grounds cleaning and maintenance occupations	5,745	6,595	4.0	3.8	850	14.8
Personal care and service occupations	4,966	6,060	3.7	3.3	1,094	22.0
Sales and related occupations	15,985	17,203	10.4	10.6	1,218	7.6
Office and administrative support occupations	24,344	26,089	15.7	16.6	1,745	7.2
Farming, fishing, and forestry occupations	1,039	1,110	0.6	0.7	−28	−2.7
Construction and extraction occupations	8,295	9,079	5.5	5.5	785	9.5
Installation, maintenance, and repair occupations	5,883	6,433	3.9	3.9	550	9.3
Production occupations	10,675	10,145	6.1	7.1	−528	−4.9
Transportation and material moving occupations	10,233	10,695	6.4	6.8	462	4.5

Note: Numbers may not equal the total or 100% because of rounding.

Source: U.S. Department of Labor. (2008). *National Employment Matrix, Table 4*, Washington, DC: U.S. Bureau of Labor Statistics.

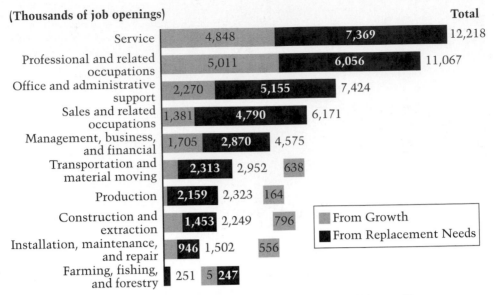

(Thousands of job openings)   Total

Service	4,848	7,369	12,218
Professional and related occupations	5,011	6,056	11,067
Office and administrative support	2,270	5,155	7,424
Sales and related occupations	1,381	4,790	6,171
Management, business, and financial	1,705	2,870	4,575
Transportation and material moving	2,313	2,952	638
Production	2,159	2,323	164
Construction and extraction	1,453	2,249	796
Installation, maintenance, and repair	946	1,502	556
Farming, fishing, and forestry	251	5	247

■ From Growth
■ From Replacement Needs

FIGURE 3.1 | PROJECTED GROWTH IN JOB OPENINGS BY MAJOR OCCUPATIONAL GROUPS, 2006–2016.

Source: Reproduced from *Occupational Outlook Quarterly* (p. 11). (Fall 2007). Washington, DC: Department of Labor, Bureau of Labor Statistics.

The occupations predicted to grow fastest in the United States from 2006 to 2016 cover a wide range of careers. As shown in Figure 3.2, the 20 fastest-growing occupations include health care and computing. The fastest-growing occupations in health care include veterinary technologists and assistants, veterinarians, medical assistants, physical therapy assistants, pharmacy assistants, and dental hygienists. Also, there will be growth in the mental health field for substance abuse and behavioral disorder counselors, social and human service assistants, mental health counselors, and mental health and substance abuse social workers. Occupations such as home health and home care aides often have high turnover. Also, computer-related occupations are among the fastest growing occupations. Examples of some of these are network systems and data communication analysts, computer software engineers, database administrators, and computer systems analysts.

Clearly, the amount of education is closely related to income and the rate of participation in the labor force. Figure 3.3 shows the vast differences in annual salary in 2007 between those with only a high school education ($31,408) and those with a master's degree ($60,580). Individuals with a bachelor's degree ($51,324) earn, on average, twice as much as individuals who do not graduate from high school ($22,256). The more education that individuals have, the lower the rate of participation in the labor force for their category of education. Those with some high school education (46.6%) have a rate of participation in the labor force that is considerably lower than those with a bachelor's degree (77.5%). These data emphatically point out the economic value of an education.

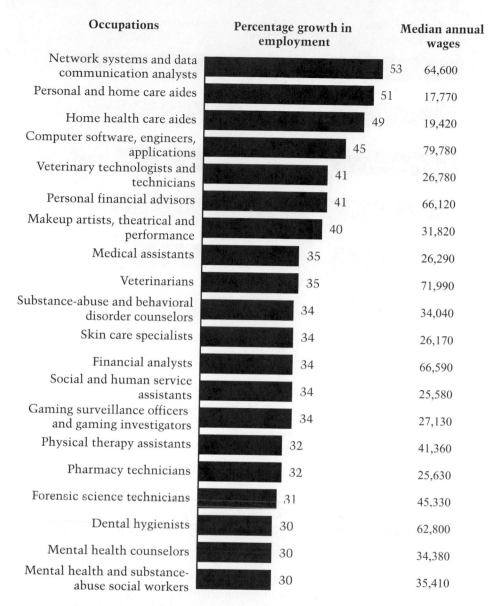

Occupations	Percentage growth in employment	Median annual wages
Network systems and data communication analysts	53	64,600
Personal and home care aides	51	17,770
Home health care aides	49	19,420
Computer software, engineers, applications	45	79,780
Veterinary technologists and technicians	41	26,780
Personal financial advisors	41	66,120
Makeup artists, theatrical and performance	40	31,820
Medical assistants	35	26,290
Veterinarians	35	71,990
Substance-abuse and behavioral disorder counselors	34	34,040
Skin care specialists	34	26,170
Financial analysts	34	66,590
Social and human service assistants	34	25,580
Gaming surveillance officers and gaming investigators	34	27,130
Physical therapy assistants	32	41,360
Pharmacy technicians	32	25,630
Forensic science technicians	31	45,330
Dental hygienists	30	62,800
Mental health counselors	30	34,380
Mental health and substance-abuse social workers	30	35,410

Average growth of all occupations is 10%

FIGURE 3.2 | PERCENTAGE GROWTH IN EMPLOYMENT (PROJECTED 2006–2016, IN THOUSANDS) FOR OCCUPATIONS HAVING THE MOST NEW JOBS. MEDIAN EARNINGS ARE LISTED FOR EACH OCCUPATION AND REPRESENT DATA AS OF MAY, 2006.

Source: Reproduced from Occupational Outlook Quarterly (p. 13). (Fall, 2007). Washington, DC: Department of Labor, Bureau of Labor Statistics, by permission.

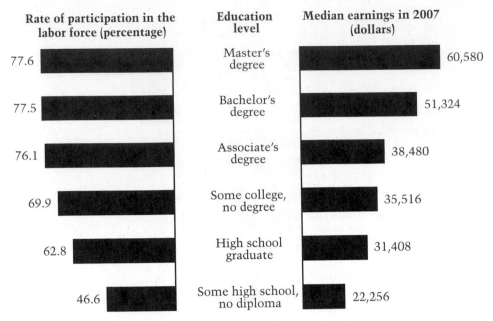

Rate of participation in the labor force (percentage)	Education level	Median earnings in 2007 (dollars)
77.6	Master's degree	60,580
77.5	Bachelor's degree	51,324
76.1	Associate's degree	38,480
69.9	Some college, no degree	35,516
62.8	High school graduate	31,408
46.6	Some high school, no diploma	22,256

FIGURE 3.3 | MEAN ANNUAL EARNINGS AND RATE OF PARTICIPATION IN THE LABOR FORCE FOR PEOPLE 25 YEARS AND OLDER BY HIGHEST LEVEL OF EDUCATION FOR 2007.

Salary data from Table A-17, p. 4. Usual weekly earnings of employed full-time wage and salary workers by educational attainment, age, sex, and race. Annual average, unpublished Occupation and Industry Table from the Current Population Survey. Participation rate from Table 10, Current Population Survey. Employment status of the civilian noninstitutional population by educational attainment, age, sex, race (2007).

Source: From Bureau of Labor Statistics, Washington, DC, 2007.

This brief overview of the U.S. labor market mentions only the most important features. In general, there is considerable predicted increase for occupations that require technical skills, such as network systems analysts and veterinarians and veterinary technologists and assistants. However, there will also be a great need for service workers such as retail salespersons and cashiers. Salary continues to be greatly affected by the type and amount of education that individuals have. More information on the employment of women, African Americans, Latino/as, and Asians is presented later in this chapter. Additional information about local labor markets can be obtained from the *Occupational Outlook Handbook* (2008). With so much information available to counselors from so many sources, it is important to present only highly relevant information to clients, so that they will not be overwhelmed by the data.

SOCIOLOGICAL AND ECONOMIC APPROACHES

In addition to information and predictions about the labor market, there is also research about the labor market as a social organization. Whereas psychology is primarily concerned with the study of individual behavior, sociology and economics emphasize the study of social organizations. The other chapters in this book are concerned with how to make career choices and decisions or adjust to career circumstances. Sociologists and economists approach the question of career choice from an entirely different perspective. Sociologists study the development, organization, and operation of human society. Economists study the production, distribution, and consumption of goods and services. More specifically, sociologists have examined family, cultural, and other social factors that predict career choice, as well as variables such as unemployment and pay distributions by industry. In addition, they have studied the patterns of customs, interactions, and professional development of hundreds of different legal and illegal occupations. Economists have investigated factors such as unemployment, pay distribution by industry, job title, gender, and race, which are all factors directly related to a person's career development. For both economists and sociologists, ability, interests, values, and career decision making, among other variables, are studied when trying to predict labor market or work behavior. Because sociologists and economists focus on social organizations and counselors focus on counseling individuals, not organizations, the application of sociological and economic theories is indirect.

Both psychologists and sociologists have studied how societal factors and pressures affect adolescent workers, whether working part time or full time. In general, psychologists examine how the individual shapes and alters the environment through job choice or work adjustment. A sociological perspective on unemployment, part-time employment, and underemployment of youths provides an interesting view on entry into the workforce. Several sociologists and economists have suggested ways in which the workplace changes the individual. This different frame of reference provides new insights into the worker and the workplace.

Several theories have been the subject of a large number of research investigations. A theory that has prompted study by many sociologists is the status attainment model, which predicts the prestige level of a person's job from an individual's social (particularly family) background. The primary economic theory related to career development is human capital theory. Human capital theory suggests that individuals invest in their own education and training to achieve a higher-paying job with more prestige. Criticism of this model has led to the study of the structure of labor markets. Investigators have divided the labor market into segments. In the lowest segment, the labor market is made up of low-paying jobs that offer little chance of advancement. The opposite is found in the highest segment.

Related to status attainment and human capital theory is the study of the organizational and societal treatment of women and minorities, which critiques and elaborates on these theories. Much research has documented that women and minorities hold different types of jobs from white males, are paid less, and have less chance of advancement. Although these theories and the resulting research do not provide a method of conceptualizing career counseling, they do yield insights into the world of work that a counselor can apply in both career choice and work-adjustment counseling.

YOUTH EMPLOYMENT

Providing an overview of youth employment is difficult, because youths are not a homogeneous group (Blau & Kahn, 2002; Kerckhoff, 2002; Mortimer, 2003, 2007). When discussing youths, researchers often use the ages of 15 to 24 years, but this range is not used uniformly. Not surprisingly, different issues impact younger and older "youths." Although about 10.4% of U.S. students drop out of high school, only about 6.0% of Caucasian and 2.7% of Asian students did, compared with 10.4% of African American and 22.4% of Hispanic students in 2005 (Student Effort and Educational Progress, 2007). With regard to high school graduates, some leave to get full-time employment and start a career, whereas others may leave school with no specific employment in mind. Not only are there differences in age, but there are differences in gender. Even in part-time jobs, young women may make 70% to 75% of the male wage, even though they may work about the same hours after school and when employed full time (Desmarais & Curtis, 1999). However, this disparity is likely to become smaller by the 12th grade (Mortimer, 2003). Motivation of youths toward work may also depend on socioeconomic status. Some youths may work to supplement the income of their parents or to pay for their future education, whereas others may seek employment for spending money for cars or entertainment. These differences in motivation produce different attitudes toward work.

A recent concern has been not only the quantity (number of hours) of work, but also the quality of employment (Cherry, 2001; Mortimer, 2003, 2007). Many jobs for young workers are in the lower-level service industries such as food service and retail work. Fewer jobs are available to youth in public administration, health, social service, and education. One reason is the entry-level or job requirements in the health, social service, and education. Studies on part-time work (Mortimer, 2003) indicate that it can have positive and negative effects on future employment. For youth who have had economic barriers, moderate part-time work along with academic progress predicts educational attainment (Mortimer, 2007). Stinebrickner (2003) reports that work for first-semester college students can negatively affect grades, but cautions that various personal factors may make part-time work appropriate for many adolescents. Working too many hours per week for high school students can lead to problem behavior in school, minor delinquent acts, and alcohol use (Mortimer, 2003). This is particularly true when individuals work more than 20 hours per week. However, there are examples of individuals working more than 20 hours per week who develop a sense of mastery and improved school behavior. The type of part-time employment may make a difference as well; 8th-, 10th-, and 12th-grade students employed in farm work showed decreasing test scores in most grades (Sakurai, 2006). Some jobs lead to more personal satisfaction and better attitudes toward work, whereas others may be routine or even expose individuals to dangerous work conditions. The work-related attitudes that youth learn can have an impact on their later attitudes toward full-time work.

Part-time work can help by giving students a sense of autonomy. Because part-time jobs often pay at a lower hourly rate than full-time jobs, employers may prefer part-time workers. With part-time work, individuals also have more control over their jobs, often having input into when they work, thus reducing employee turnover. Jobs also can offer individuals an opportunity to use and develop job skills and to become more responsible in their work and their relationships with coworkers (Mortimer, 2003).

Youths are more likely than adults to be underemployed. Older individuals who have more experience or on-the-job training are able to get better jobs. Sometimes employers may perceive youths as being more likely to quit, less responsible, and less productive than older workers. Rosenbaum (1999) notes that employers may not trust youths, particularly low-income and minority youths, to work effectively. Rosenbaum (2001) states that, although employers may have information about young workers from teachers and counselors, employers may distrust the information and rely on impressions during job interviews. Thus, young people may experience a type of "age discrimination" based on stereotypes of their work attitudes and abilities, and therefore face underemployment.

In high school, girls show a greater commitment to family life than do boys (Mortimer, 2003). Studying 2,954 white youths, Koenigsberg, Garet, and Rosenbaum (1994) report that young women with children who enter the labor force considered parenting, rather than providing financially for their family, as their major responsibility, whereas young men with children reported the opposite. In rural China, the educational aspirations that mothers have for their daughters may be limited in mothers who hold traditional gender values (Zhang, Kao, & Hannum, 2007). In another study of 3,828 young men and women, Pirog and Magee (1997) note that both men and women can suffer in terms of reduced educational attainment, earning capabilities, and ability to support their children when they take on parental responsibilities. In a general overview of the different experiences of young men and women in the job market, Mortimer (2003) states that young women view their jobs more favorably than young men do. Young women are more likely than young men to appreciate the opportunity to help others in their work and to have good relationships with supervisors. This finding emphasizes the importance of gender differences in youths' attitudes toward work.

Recent studies show the importance of both ethnicity and gender as they relate to the experience of young people who enter the work force. In China, ethnic background has been found to have an impact on the prestige level of occupations that youths will eventually enter (Hannum, 2002). In Germany, where the connection between school and work is closer than in the United States, women are more likely to complete school before having their first child (Mortimer, Oesterle, & Kruger, 2005). In the United States, African American high school graduates often value education more than white youths and are more optimistic about opportunities for future success relative to white youths (Sakura-Lemessy, 2002). However, young African American women have higher unemployment rates than young white women (Reid, 2002). This is partly because of discrimination experienced by young African American women, more employment in seasonal or temporary jobs, and family issues. Thus, young people's experiences in the labor market vary because of cultural and gender issues. For counselors working in schools, it is important to attend to cultural factors that affect the experiences of their young clients.

For counselors, this information suggests the importance of discussing attitudes toward work and actual work demands with their young clients. It is helpful to discuss what individuals expect to get from their work. Is it just income, or is there an opportunity to explore new areas of interest? When discussing students' work experiences, it can be helpful to ask about employer attitudes, relationships with coworkers, new skills learned, and advancement opportunities for both part-time and full-time workers.

THE EFFECT OF THE WORK ENVIRONMENT ON THE INDIVIDUAL

Just as an individual has an effect on his or her work—for example, producing a good performance or performing effectively—so does the work have an effect on the individual. The impact of the work on the individual has been a focus of Melvin Kohn's (2006) research. Kohn and Schooler (1983) and Schooler (1998) have studied the effect that work and the individual have on each other. They have studied how complex work can help individuals increase their ability to deal effectively with complex intellectual tasks. Conversely, individuals can lose their ability to solve complex problems if they no longer deal with challenging tasks.

The work of Kohn and his colleagues shows that having an unchallenging job may lead to a loss of intellectual skills (Kohn, 2006; Mainquist & Eichorn, 1989; Schooler, Mulatu, & Oates, 1999). Kohn and Schooler (1978) have studied "substantive complexity," which they define as "the degree to which the work requires thought and independent judgment" (p. 30). They report that the intellectual demands of a job influenced workers' intellectual ability more than workers' ability affected how they approached their work. In a follow-up study, Kohn and Schooler (1982) reported that job conditions affected an individual's psychological functioning more than an individual's psychological functioning affected his or her job. Applying this theory to workers, unemployed individuals, and those doing housework in the Ukraine and Poland, Kohn et al. (2002) stated that complexity in any of the tasks done by these individuals was related to intellectual flexibility, self-directedness of orientation, and a sense of well-being. In the United States, complex household work increased intellectual flexibility for both men and women, but decreased self-confidence was associated with complex household work for men and increased self-confidence for women (Caplan & Schooler, 2006). In a national longitudinal study of employed men and women in the United States, Schooler, Mulatu, and Oates (1999) confirmed that substantive complexity of work significantly increased levels of intellectual functioning in the sample. This was especially true in the older half of the sample. The following example illustrates the effects of work on an individual.

For four years, Pedro has worked in a factory, where he assembled computer hardware. He has been promoted to a supervisor's job, and this assignment requires that he use writing and mathematical skills that he has not used since high school graduation. His job requires independent decision making based on reading manuals and talking to workers. As a result, his reading ability has improved, although he had to struggle at first to improve his math and writing skills. In a sense, the demands of Pedro's job have required that he become more intelligent. Not all organizations provide individuals such opportunities to develop their skills.

STATUS ATTAINMENT THEORY

Status attainment theory concerns issues regarding the relative role of achievement and social status in influencing occupational selection. Most research on status attainment theory has been on intergenerational change, sometimes called vertical mobility, and has focused on predicting an individual's occupational role from the father's occupations. Of particular note is the early work by Blau (1956) and Blau and Duncan (1967). They, together with other researchers, found that they could predict the socioeconomic status of an individual's first job, which would then predict a current job, from the father's occupation and education.

As research continues on the status attainment model and issues related to it, it becomes more and more complex. Originating about 60 years ago, this theory provides a guideline for researchers to study how variables such as intelligence, teacher influences, and mother's and father's occupational choices can predict an individual's career choice (Hauser, 2005). Figure 3.4 outlines the path of prediction leading from variables concerning family status and cognitive functioning to the eventual prediction of occupational attainment. Family status includes the father's occupational and socioeconomic status, income, and education. A second group of variables measures educational performance (for example, aptitude tests and school grades). Both sets of variables affect social–psychological processes, which include the educational and occupational aspirations of adolescents, the amount of parental and teacher encouragement to attend college, and peers' plans to attend college. These social–psychological processes then act to predict educational attainment, which is measured by the number of years of schooling. The number of years of schooling then leads to the prediction of occupational attainment measured by the status or prestige levels of the career. Sheridan's (2002) study of family background, mental ability, and others' influence confirms that many of these variables have stable effects on individuals' later occupational choice. In a study in Scotland, both father's social class and childhood cognitive ability were found to be important predictors of occupational status both in their children's first occupation and at mid-life (Deary et al., 2005). Wilson (1989) emphasizes the influence that an adolescent's view of his or her future has on persistence in school. Wilson states, "Staying [in school] is the strongest known determinant of subsequent career" (p. 71). However, reevaluating their work on status attainment, Duncan (2005) stated that father's occupation was not as predictive of sons' or daughters' occupational status as was originally thought.

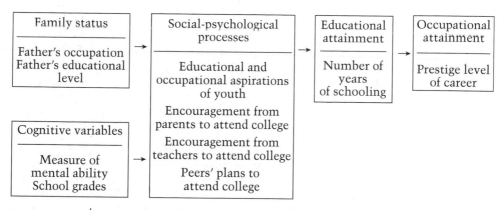

FIGURE 3.4 | ABRIDGED OUTLINE OF AN EARLY VERSION OF THE WISCONSIN MODEL OF STATUS ATTAINMENT.

Source: From "Sociological perspectives on work and career development," by L. Hotchkiss and H. Borow, in *Career choice and development* (2nd ed.), by D. Brown and L. Brooks, and Associates. Copyright © 1990 by Jossey-Bass, Inc. Reprinted by permission.

An area that has received a considerable amount of recent attention is family influences on career choice and occupational status. Knowing the mother's occupation is an important factor in predicting the child's later occupational attainment. In a survey of 4,756 individuals, Khazzoom (1997) reported that mothers' occupations were especially helpful in predicting daughters', as well as sons', occupational attainment. Examining ways in which mothers influence the career choice of their children, Simpson (2003) found mothers often supported the choice of nontechnical college majors, whereas fathers supported technical college majors. Mothers often do this by being emotionally supportive of their children. Agreeing that a mother's emotional and occupational status has an important influence on the child's occupational choice, Korupp, Ganzeboom, and Van Der Lippe (2002) noted that parental influence decreases over time. Using a sample of 5,027 students from the Netherlands, Korupp, Sanders, and Ganzeboom (2002) reported that the father's occupational status had a larger influence on the occupational choice of a son or daughter than the mother's occupational status. Examining family functioning, Biblarz and Raftery (1993) reported that divorce and separation increased the probability that individuals will be in the lowest status jobs rather than the highest. Also, domestic violence against women can contribute to their lower status attainment and lower earnings (Lloyd, 1997). These studies point out the influence of family expectations and functioning on the career plans and concerns of young people and adults.

Culture also has been studied as a factor in status attainment theory. Studying 6,885 new entries to the job market, Waight (1998) reported that African Americans and women do not attain the same levels of occupational status as white men, because of race and gender issues. Among Latino/as in the United States, being bilingual was predictive of higher status attainment of males and females in ways that are related to types of family interactions (Blair & Cobas, 2006). In Vietnam (Korinek, 2006), an individual's occupational status is predicted by parental status as determined by membership in the Communist Party. In China (Chen, 2006), Communist Party membership was also a predictor of occupational success. Comparing the role of mental ability as a determinant of career success in Estonia to that of the United States, Strenze (2006) reported that social status was a stronger predictor of success in Estonia than mental ability. In the United States, mental ability was found to be a stronger predictor of success than social status. Davies, Heinesen, and Holm (2002) reported that Danish adolescents tended to make career choices so that their career achievements will not be less prestigious than those of their parents. In Kenya, cultural factors affected how long children are enrolled in school and their later occupational attainment (Buchmann, 1998). Cultural factors include expectations of children contributing to family income and views of discrimination toward women in the workplace. Such studies provide information about how cultural factors affect educational and occupational planning.

Although status attainment theory has been useful in predicting occupational attainment, it also has been the subject of criticism. Sonnenfeld (1989) stated that status attainment theory has been unable to adequately explain later status changes once an individual has begun employment. He criticizes status attainment theory for failing to use recent data and for not looking at changes in occupational status within a career. Furthermore, status attainment theory has not paid attention to changing social values that have led to less agreement on the definition of a successful career. Most important, he believes that status within a company, rather than occupational attainment, should be measured. These comments notwithstanding, status attainment theory is relevant to career decision making and work-adjustment counseling.

Status attainment theory calls attention to important variables that psychological theories tend to omit. Of the theorists discussed elsewhere in this book, only Gottfredson (2005) deals with sociological variables in career development theory. The variables that status attainment theory emphasizes are the importance of prestige, the status of the family, and encouragement to seek higher education. Although the United States is considered a land of equal opportunity, status attainment theory states that, in reality, one's occupational position is determined to a great extent by one's family's status (and until recently, one's father's status). Related to research on status attainment, studies of health in poor families have found that poor health is a limiting factor in attaining social status (Haas, 2006; Pearlin, Schieman, Fazio, & Meersman, 2005). Knowledge of status attainment theory may help a counselor who is working with a client from a low socioeconomic background think about some of the factors that are necessary for the client to attain an occupation that is much higher in status than that of his or her family. As discussed earlier, one of the factors related to status is lack of parental encouragement to succeed. Adolescents from a low socioeconomic background may lack parental, peer, and teacher encouragement to seek higher education. Furthermore, this background may inhibit accurate occupational aspirations.

The challenge for the counselor is to provide support and information that will help a client counter sociological processes that may interfere with making full use of her or his intellectual abilities. Status attainment theory does not explain how to do this. Rather, status attainment theory underscores the importance of making special efforts to open areas of the labor market to clients that may otherwise have considered these areas closed. An example of a counselor dealing with an individual from a low socioeconomic background is given next.

Betty, a 15-year-old African American high school sophomore, lives in Chicago. Her mother is unmarried and works for a large industrial cleaning firm in the downtown section of Chicago. Betty has two younger sisters who are still in school. Her older sister is enrolled in a nursing program. Betty has been working after school for a fast-food chain. Now, as she approaches 16 years of age, she is considering dropping out of school and working full time for the restaurant. In the following brief excerpt, she is discussing these plans with her guidance counselor:

CL: Since I've been working at this job, I've finally been able to buy some of the clothes that I always wanted. My mother needs some of the money, too, so she takes some.

CO: Sounds as if that's made you feel useful. [The counselor comments on Betty's sense of productivity.]

CL: Yeah, feels like I'm doing something that makes sense with my life, not just sitting around in school reading stuff that seems boring.

CO: School doesn't make sense to you? [The counselor wants to challenge Betty's sweeping view of school.]

CL: Well, I guess it does. I have learned to read pretty much. I've gotten A's and B's. I thought everybody learned to read. Some of the kids I work with can barely write their names. They can hardly read the menus.

CO: Does that limit what they can do? [The counselor wants Betty to assess her own view of the relationship between schooling and advancement.]

CL: It sure does. It looks as if they'll never make more than seven or eight dollars an hour.

CO: How much do you think you can make at this job? [The counselor starts to examine the limitations of fast-food counter work as a full-time job.]

CL: Maybe $300 a week.

CO: That's about $15,000 a year. Does that seem like much to you?

CL: No, not really.

CO: How much would you like to earn? [The counselor is helping Betty start to think about the type of future she would like to have.]

CL: A lot more than that. My mother earns about $18,000 a year, and that's terrible.

CO: What do you think you would have to do to earn more?

CL: Everybody tells me that to earn money, you need to go to college. I could never do that.

CO: Why not? [The counselor wants to question Betty's negative assumptions about her abilities and her potential future.]

CL: We don't have any money to go to college, that's for sure.

CO: There are scholarships available. Students from this school with no support from their parents have gone on to do well in college. Something I can do to help you is to show you how you can get financial aid and to make suggestions about school. Your work is good in school—your grades show it, and your teachers say it. I can help you figure out what you want to do and where you can go to school. [The counselor offers direct support and encouragement to help Betty make positive steps toward her future choices. Betty is unaware of the alternatives available to her. The counselor will help.]

CL: You think I can do this?

CO: Yes, I do. I want to show you how and help you with it.

Having a plan to follow will help the counselor counter Betty's discouragement. The counselor will empower Betty to look at her options. Having established contacts with local colleges and having obtained information about financial aid, the counselor is in a position to suggest to Betty how to find an alternative to a job that does not sufficiently use her abilities.

HUMAN CAPITAL THEORY

The basic idea behind human capital theory is that individuals invest in their own education and training so that they will receive increased lifetime earnings (Becker, 1964; Wachter, 1974). In economics, human capital theory tends to look at earnings in the labor force as they affect a company or government. Here, we will focus on human capital theory as it applies to individuals. Career earnings are seen as a function of ability, education, and training, combined with the effort to produce effectively (Beattie, 2002). Education is viewed as an investment that, when combined with appropriate job experience, will produce a desired income. Individuals (and their families) invest money in college or other training at an early point in an individual's career. This investment is realized some years later, when an individual starts to receive pay for his or her work. For example, in a study of

2,087 Colombian workers, Psacharopoulos and Velez (1992) reported that education had a positive impact on individuals' earnings, even when controlling for ability. Parent (2002) has studied the predictive ability of human capital theory and supports its use, particularly for men with a high school degree. In human capital theory, the individual is viewed somewhat as a firm or a company: If health care and moving expenses will help improve earning power, then these, similar to educational expenses, can be seen as investments in one's eventual lifetime earnings.

Human capital theory has been applied to high school and college students. For example, Worth (2002) reported that youths tend to be committed to the idea of investing in education to get a better job, although this is less true for students who do not complete their education. However, in a sample of more than 5,000 youths, Bedard (2001) found that those living in a labor market that does include universities have higher drop-out rates than those living in a nonuniversity environment. For college students who have transferred to a different university, Hilmer (2002) reported that human capital theory was supported regardless of the quality of either the first institution attended or the institution from which the student graduated. Testing the validity of human capital theory continues to be done under a variety of conditions.

In some ways, human capital theory can be seen as an endorsement of trait and factor theory. Like trait and factor theory, human capital theory emphasizes the role of the assessment of interests and abilities in selecting an occupation. Human capital theory differs from trait and factor theory in that it emphasizes career choice as a long-term process and investment and focuses on income.

Counselors may use information culled from human capital theory to comment on an individual's choice of part-time or summer work in terms of how it will help that individual develop income over his or her lifetime. Furthermore, individuals who do not have sufficient income to pay for investment in the type of education they want may view immediate work as an investment. For example, an individual who wishes to become a physician but cannot pay for the necessary education may choose to go to college for 2 years, work as an emergency medical technician for 2 years, return to college for 1 year, work as a technician for 2 years, finish college in 1 year, work as a registered nurse for 3 years, and then go to medical school. In terms of human capital theory, this process could be viewed as a carefully planned, long-term investment. However, the older an individual is when his or her education is completed, the less time there is to collect on the investment.

Human capital theory has been criticized because its goal is a monetary reward. Often, individuals have other goals, such as being elected to political office, helping others, or having leisure time. More recently, investigators of human capital theory have considered work as an investment that has nonmonetary payoffs. When an individual has multiple goals, such as a high income and helping others, investing in his or her abilities, preferences, and values toward these goals becomes much more complex. Thus, one of the advantages of occasionally thinking about the client in terms of human capital theory is that long-term investment is emphasized, and the individual's future development is considered. In this aspect of planning, human capital theory resembles the developmental work of Donald Super (Chapter 7).

Human capital theory assumes that the labor market is open equally to all workers. This assumption has generated much criticism and has been partially responsible for a vast amount of research demonstrating the oversimplification of human capital theory. For example, Tomaskovic-Devey, Thomas, and Johnson (2002) observed that minorities typically take longer to find jobs than white individuals and have less access to jobs that provide significant on-the-job training. These factors influence the type of job and the amount of money individuals earn. Low-income urban women tended to find jobs through informal contacts such as friends and family (Rankin, 2003). This tends to limit access to good jobs, thus limiting earnings, which challenges the accuracy of human capital theory. Studying low-income urban families, Coley, Bachman, Votruba-Drzal, Lohman, and Li-Grining (2007) found that those women who invested in more education were more likely to have stable, higher-paying jobs than those with less education. Similarly, Zhan (2006) found that single mothers who had previous education or job training had higher wages than those who did not. Gheorghiu-Stephens (2005) suggested that women in both formerly socialist and Western capitalist countries derive fewer benefits from investments in education and training than do men. Bayley (1997) reported that African American college-educated women tended to defer having families more than white college-educated women. In doing so, African American women were earning capital from their investment in their education as predicted by human capital theory. These observations about the complexities of the labor market form the rationale for the rest of this chapter. Human capital theory does not consider job discrimination against women and people from different cultural backgrounds in predicting individual earnings. Also, some research has focused on inequalities in different types of organizations. This work is related to research that explores characteristics of the structure of the labor market.

THE STRUCTURE OF THE LABOR MARKET

Human capital theory assumes that all individuals have an equal opportunity to compete in the labor market. Sociologists and economists have long recognized that this is not true. Disadvantaged and underprivileged groups, in particular, tend to enter different types of jobs from those who are more privileged. Certain types of jobs share similar characteristics. The first approach to characterizing types of jobs was dual-economy (or dualistic) theory (Berger & Piore, 1980). Although originally used to describe two different types of labor markets, dualistic theory gradually evolved into a way of seeing a variety of discontinuous segments in the labor market. Originally, primary employers were seen as holding a monopolistic or oligopolistic market share, as using advanced technology, and as being nationally or internationally involved in commerce (Brand, 1997). These large firms offered higher wages, job stability, and more chances for advancement than did those in the secondary labor market. Retail sales and fast-food businesses are examples of the secondary labor market. These jobs usually pay minimum wage or a little more, offer little chance of advancement, and have a relatively high turnover. It was hypothesized that workers who were a part of the primary labor market were not likely to move to the secondary labor market, and vice versa. Since this early work, others have taken different approaches to studying the structure of the labor market (Kalleberg & Leicht, 2002). One approach is to examine how workers themselves perceive the structure of the labor market (Berntson, Sverke, & Marklund, 2006).

Some studies have revealed a more complex structure in the labor market than that suggested by dualistic theory. Piore and others (Berger & Piore, 1980; Piore, 1975, 1979; Piore & Sable, 1984) suggested three levels of the labor market. They categorized secondary work as situations that have low pay, poor working conditions, and low social status. Little security or advancement is available in these jobs, and little skill is required of the worker. Relationships with supervisors tend to be personal and informal. Members of this labor force tend to be women, adolescents, and migrants, and the turnover is frequent.

Piore and others divide the primary sector into two tiers. The lower tier of the primary sector is more substantial than the secondary market. There is more status, better working conditions, more chance for advancement, and better pay. More skill is required of the workers, and more formal training is necessary. Relationships between workers and supervisors may be informal, or may be controlled by more formal union relationships. Wages are likely to be set through collective bargaining, rather than by the employer. In contrast, the upper tier of the primary market consists of managerial and professional occupations. These jobs offer higher pay, status, prestige, security, and opportunities for advancement. They require more education before employment than do jobs in the lower tier. In general, the worker has more autonomy than in the lower tier, and relationships between supervisors and workers are less important and less formal than in the lower tier.

Not all jobs fit into the primary or secondary labor markets. Piore and colleagues have stated that craft jobs are difficult to classify (Berger & Piore, 1980). They tend to fall between the upper and lower tiers of the primary sector. Craft work is similar to the work done by those in the lower tier, because it is often learned on the job and formal relationships between workers and supervisors exist. However, craftspeople tend to work independently, a characteristic of workers in the upper tier. Craft work includes occupations such as master plumber, electrician, and pipe fitter. One focus of research has been to discover how work is learned and how that learning is applied in each of the four strata of the job market.

Another classification of labor market segments involves a method of describing economies in developing countries (Hodson & Sullivan, 2008). Tertiarization refers to countries that develop a service economy without having an economy that is based on manufacturing products. In this type of labor market, the first sector is agriculture and mining, the second sector is manufacturing, and the third (tertiary) is service. The service sector includes many unskilled jobs such as servant, waitperson, sales clerk, and selling flowers or newspapers. In the United States, agriculture and mining are small compared with manufacturing. In developing countries, the reverse is often true, with manufacturing being limited to the processing of agricultural and mining materials. This may force many workers into low-paying service work, leaving relatively few workers in skilled manufacturing jobs. In Latin America and the Caribbean in 2005, for example, 62.5% of the labor force worked in the service sector and only 17.1% in the manufacturing sector (Hodson & Sullivan, 2008). Tertiarization provides a way of viewing labor markets of countries that are quite different from those in the United States and the European Union.

Hodson and Sullivan (2008) present a way of viewing future changes in the labor market by looking at two major sectors: innovative and marginal. The innovative sector is based on technology. This sector is somewhat similar to Piore's primary sector. Workers would be highly educated and well paid. They are likely to be involved in teams or organizational management. They might even own shares in the firm. Training for new skills and job security would characterize the innovative sector. In contrast, the marginal sector, similar to the secondary sector in dual-economy theory, would pay poorly and offer few benefits. Restaurant work and retail trade are examples of work in the marginal sector. There is likely to be little help or support from employers in terms of advancement or education.

Recent research provides some examples of current issues that may affect different sectors of the labor market. Giesecke and Gross (2003) discussed the growth of the temporary job market and how it has limitations similar to those found in the secondary or marginal labor market. Another issue is that of working at home (Felstead, Jewson, Phizacklea, & Walters, 2002). Working at home not only includes telecommuting by doing primary or innovative sector work from home, but also assembling or doing piecework from home that fits with the secondary or marginal sector. The growth in assembling or doing piecework at home, similar to temporary work, is apt to give workers few opportunities for advancement, benefits, increased pay, or opportunities for education.

For counselors, the value of understanding the structure of labor markets is the emphasis on factors external to the client. The primary emphasis of the psychological theories that are discussed in all the other chapters in this book is the individual and individual choice. This chapter calls attention to basic differences in broad segments of the working world. Whether the counselor thinks of the labor market in terms of two, three, four, or more sectors is not as important as that counselors should be aware that there are broad differences in hiring practices, work relationships, advancement possibilities, and earnings in various categories of jobs. This information is particularly helpful to those who counsel adolescents who are beginning their encounter with the labor market and are likely to start in low-level jobs. This information is helpful in counseling, so that the client and the counselor can examine how to move to better sectors of the labor market. Counselors can help teenagers become aware that many jobs (primary) will not be available to them without more education and experience. However, experience gained on jobs will help to develop personal skills such as reliability and cooperation.

An awareness of occupational information about local employers is helpful to the counselor. Such information includes detailed knowledge of major local employers regarding specific jobs, hiring practices, pay scales, and so on. Knowledge of labor market structure provides a rationale for assessing such information. Counselors can get information that they can give to clients about wages, job stability, chances for advancement, and turnover. This information will help clients understand the long-range implications of taking relatively dead-end jobs, which pay low salaries, have a rapid turnover, and offer little chance for advancement.

WOMEN AND DISCRIMINATION IN THE WORKPLACE

Sociologists and psychologists have studied the effect of gender on career outcomes (Dipboy & Collela, 2005; Rosigno, 2007; Fassinger, 2008). Some of this research has been in the context of status attainment theory, human capital theory, or research on the structure of labor markets. Other studies have examined the effect of gender as it may lead to lower pay, fewer chances for advancement, as well as occupational segregation, which results in women working in occupations with lower prestige than those of men.

In describing discrimination in hiring and promotion, Browne (1999) and England and Farkas (1986) list four determinants of discrimination: taste discrimination, monopoly, error, and statistical generalization. Becker (1957) discusses *taste discrimination* as a preference not to employ members of a particular group. If employers do not hire women, fewer jobs will be available to them, and therefore wages will be lower. The *monopoly model of discrimination* occurs when an organized group agrees to exclude another group from positions. For example, an all-male trade union's decision not to allow women into the union is an example of the "monopoly" model of discrimination. *Error discrimination* refers to employers who do not have discriminatory taste but may underestimate the ability of women to perform the same work as men. *Statistical discrimination* happens when an employer applies generalizations about a group of people to an individual (Padavic & Reskin, 2002). England and Farkas (1986) give this example: "If employers correctly observe that, on average, women have less mechanical knowledge than men, they may decide not to hire any women in positions requiring mechanical knowledge, screening out even those atypical ones with extensive mechanical skills" (p. 160). Whatever the form of discrimination, it acts to limit women's attainment in many ways.

To understand the employment issues of women in the workplace, it is helpful to examine unemployment data, the distribution of women in various occupations, and the salaries of women. As shown in Table 3.2, in the United States, women tend to have similar unemployment rates compared with men. Note that U.S. Bureau of Labor Statistics employment rates include only those individuals who are actively looking for work and receiving unemployment benefits. These rates exclude individuals who are able to work but are not interested in doing so and individuals who would like to work but are discouraged because they believe they will

TABLE 3.2 | UNEMPLOYMENT RATES IN PERCENTAGES BY DEMOGRAPHIC GROUP (2007)

Age (Years)	White Male	White Female	African American Male	African American Female	Asian Male	Asian Female	All
16–17	17.0	14.1	40.1	26.4	12.4	19.2	17.5
18–19	14.8	10.6	30.2	24.7	10.1	12.9	14.5
20–24	7.6	6.2	16.9	13.6	6.9	4.2	8.2
25–54	3.3	3.4	6.9	6.2	2.7	3.0	3.7
55–64	3.0	2.8	5.2	3.7	3.7	3.6	3.1
Total	4.2	4.0	9.1	7.5	3.1	3.4	4.6

Source: Data from the Current Population Survey, U.S. Department of Labor. (2007). *Employment status of the civilian noninstitutional population by detailed occupation, sex and race. 2007, Table 2.* Washington, DC: U.S. Bureau of Labor Statistics.

not be able to find work. Unemployment rates appear to differ markedly more by race than by gender, especially for individuals under the age of 20. However, although men's and women's unemployment rates are similar, women tend to move in and out of the labor force more frequently than men, and women may be involved in family responsibilities that require them to temporarily drop out of the labor force. When they do look for work, they may accept work that men would not consider. For these reasons, the types of occupations that women enter tend to pay less and to have less prestige than typically male-dominated occupations.

In general, the wages of women in the United States are less than those of white men (see Table 3.4). This difference is more dramatic for African American and Hispanic or Latina women than for Asian and Caucasian women. In New York City, female high school graduates tended to have less access to higher paying jobs than men because they did not have the needed specific vocational training (Skinner, 2002).

Studying differences in the pay of women compared with men in 22 countries (including Europe and Japan), Blau and Kahn (2003) reported that the gap between genders is decreasing. This is partly because of a narrower range of salaries in most occupations and collective bargaining that tends to treat men's and women's wages similarly. Cheung (2002) notes that the problem for women in Hong Kong is lack of access to paid work rather than lack of equality of earnings. In Brazil, women are paid less than similarly qualified white men (Lovell, 2006). In Holland, being extraverted was related to increased wages for men, but not for women (Gelissen & de Graaf, 2006). Thus, pay inequalities for women can vary, depending on cultural factors.

A detailed analysis of women's role in the labor force revealed several interesting findings. Studying the values of 7,436 full-time workers from 12 different nations, Rowe and Snizek (1995) reported no differences between men and women in how much they valued high income, security from being fired, free time, advancement, and a feeling of accomplishment. Rather, differences in valuing these variables depended on age, education, and occupational prestige. Stratton (2003) has analyzed unpaid housework that married men and women do. She finds that married women spent more time on housework than their husbands, and that this is true even in households where women earn more than husbands. In *Women, Family, and Work* (Moe, 2003), 12 chapters describe particular factors, such as marriage, housework, and child care, that affect women's earnings and stress while working.

Although discrimination against women in the labor force continues, a gradual gender desegregation of occupations has taken place since the mid-1960s. The term *gender segregation* refers to the difference in distribution of men and women in various occupations or jobs. As Table 3.3 illustrates, women have less than 35% of the high-paying, high-prestige professional jobs, such as engineer, physician, and lawyer, and they have more than 80% of lower-paying, less prestigious professional jobs, such as registered nurse and elementary teacher. In nonprofessional occupations, women represent 96% of secretaries and 89% of maids and housekeeping cleaners. Men dominate the higher-paying nonprofessional occupations such as truck driver and installation, maintenance, and repair occupations. For women to enter the trades or become mechanics often means entering occupations in which they might encounter discrimination. Characteristics of such women include a sense of innate

TABLE 3.3 | EMPLOYED PERSONS BY SELECTED OCCUPATIONS, SEX, AND RACE (2007)

Occupation	Total Employed (in thousands)	Percent of Total			
		Women	African American	Asians	Hispanics
Engineers and architects	2,932	14.4	5.3	9.7	6.4
Physicians	888	30.0	5.6	16.9	5.2
Registered Nurses	2,629	91.7	9.9	7.9	4.6
Management	15,486	37.5	6.3	4.5	7.4
Teachers, postsecondary	1,261	46.2	5.6	11.7	4.2
Teachers, elementary and middle school	2,943	80.9	10.3	1.6	6.9
Lawyers	1,001	32.6	4.9	2.6	4.3
Counselors	686	65.9	18.6	2.9	8.3
Sales occupations	16,698	49.6	9.9	4.7	11.3
Secretaries and administrative assistants	3,401	96.7	9.0	2.2	9.3
Food preparation workers	681	61.2	12.2	5.3	23.4
Nursing, psychiatric, and home health aides	1,871	88.3	33.6	4.2	13.8
Janitors and building cleaners	2,080	34.2	19.2	3.2	28.0
Maids and housekeeping cleaners	1,427	89.2	17.6	3.3	40.4
Installation, maintenance and repair occupations	5,245	3.9	8.3	3.1	13.8
Truck drivers and delivery/sales workers	3,460	5.3	13.8	1.4	17.5
Bus drivers	578	51.6	26.8	1.1	11.3

Source: Data from the Current Population Survey U.S. Department of Labor. (2007). *Employed and experienced and unemployed persons by occupation, sex, and race. Table 1.* Washington, DC: U.S. Bureau of Labor Statistics.

ability, high self-esteem, a wish to be independent, and exposure to good role models (Greene & Stitt-Gohdes, 1997).

One reason for gender desegregation is growth in the service sector, which has caused men to enter occupations that traditionally have been female occupations, such as nursing and teaching (Padavic & Reskin, 2002). Cotter, DeFiore, Hermsen, Kowalewski, and Vanneman (1995) suggest that the influx of women into traditionally male occupations will be a stronger force in occupational desegregation than an increase in men entering traditionally female occupations. Cotter et al. also suggest

TABLE 3.4 | EARNINGS AS A PERCENTAGE OF WHITE MALE EARNINGS FOR
FULL-TIME WORKERS OLDER THAN 16 YEARS (2007)

	Median Weekly Earnings (dollars)	Percent of White Male Earnings
Women		
African American	533	62%
Hispanic or Latina	473	55%
Asian	731	84%
Caucasian	660	76%
Men		
African American	600	69%
Hispanic or Latino	520	60%
Asian	936	108%
Caucasian	866	100%

Source: Data from U.S. Department of Labor. (2008). Data taken from Table A-1. Usual weekly earnings of employed full-time wage and salary workers, by age, sex, race, and Hispanic or Latino ethnicity and non-Hispanic ethnicity, Annual average 2007, not seasonally adjusted. (Unpublished Occupation and Industry Table from the Current Population Survey.) Washington, DC: U.S. Bureau of Labor Statistics.

several other reasons for continuing occupational desegregation: As occupations grow in the numbers needed, both men and women are likely to seek entry, thus desegregating a particular field. Equal employment legislation continues to have an impact on reducing gender discrimination, particularly in public service jobs. Also, because women generally are paid less than men, employers have an economic incentive to hire more women. In England, in the teaching profession—a traditionally female occupation—women were less likely than men to enter school management positions (Moreau, Osgood, & Halsall, 2007). Cohen and Huffman (2003) show that wages are lower in occupations with a high percentage of women. In large cities in China, as more women entered certain jobs, wages tended to decline relative to other jobs (Shu, 2005). Although gender segregation exists, many societal forces contribute to a gradual desegregation.

The above description discusses discrimination from an economic and socio-logical, rather than from a psychological, point of view. Chapter 7 explains Gottfredson's contribution to the role of gender discrimination in the career development of young children. She believes that children develop an orientation to gender roles between the ages of 6 and 8 years that has an important influence on their career choices for the rest of their lives. Chapter 7 discusses studies of gender-role stereotyping among children and within the educational system. In Chapter 8, there are examples of the effects of gender-role stereotyping of adolescents in the social and educational systems. Some of the difficulties that women have in dealing with labor force expectations at various times in their adult lives are examined in Chapter 9 from the point of view of Donald Super and others. In explaining some of the career crises that women are likely to experience in their adult lives, Chapter 10 illustrates the potential problems of leaving and reentering the workforce, sexual harassment, and discrimination. These chapters describe the effects of gender-role stereotyping and discrimination at various stages in women's lives. In contrast, sociological and economic research described in this chapter demonstrates the effects of discrimination on occupational attainment and earnings.

Counselors may find it difficult to use the information about gender-role stereotyping and gender discrimination in terms of earnings and occupational attainment. Social cognitive career theorists (as described in Chapter 14) emphasize the importance of being attuned to women's lack of confidence in academic areas, such as math and science, and in pursuing nontraditional careers. Challenging self-limiting assumptions and reinforcing women's strengths help to increase career self-efficacy beliefs. Career counselors can help female clients by examining traditional gender roles and the effects of society on these roles. Learning about the actual differences between men and women in earnings and occupational attainment may also be of value. Sometimes, counselors are in a position to influence the educational or social system in their setting. For example, high school guidance counselors may be able to identify teachers or counselors in a high school who are suggesting educational or career paths to students based on their gender. The counselors may then take action to correct this problem. Successful women can be excellent role models for other women, as Krumboltz (Chapter 13) suggests in describing the importance of modeling in social learning theory.

Although the above ideas may be helpful, even more basic in counseling women on career issues is the identification of one's own bias. Because counselors also have been raised in a society that treats men and women quite differently, they may unconsciously have developed societal values that affect their counseling. Recognizing one's gender bias without becoming upset with oneself is valuable for counselors. In the example below, a counselor uses an internal dialogue to recognize stereotyping.

Judy has been working as a secretary at the same company since she graduated from high school 7 years ago. Now 25 years old, she is married, has no children, and has sought counseling because she feels limited in her job. Judy is fashionably dressed, and her appearance shows that she has spent time and effort to make herself look attractive. Following is an excerpt from Judy's counseling session:

CL: The people I work with are so nice to me, and it's so much fun talking with them, but I'm not sure that I like my work anymore. I'm doing the same thing each day. In fact, I'm doing more typing than I ever have before. My boss keeps giving me more and more tapes to transcribe.

CO: Can you tell me a little bit more about what is happening at work?

CL: Well, my boss is a sales manager with lots of salespeople under him. I am always busy taking calls from the salesmen and relaying messages to my boss. Then I have plenty of typing to do. I do pretty well. My boss is always telling me how well I do. He's given me pretty good pay raises. I don't get anything like the salesmen, but I guess, compared with other secretaries, I do pretty well. When the work eases up some, I certainly like it better, but maybe there is something else I'd like.

CO: What other options have you considered? [Counselor to self: "I wonder what she's complaining about? She's got a good job. She's making pretty good money. Why would she want to leave? Wait, what am I thinking? Why am I making assumptions for her? It is not my role to determine what's best for her. I am making assumptions about her role as a secretary, that it's a good one for her. Watch it!"]

CL: I'm not sure, but I've thought of being a salesperson like the men who work in our company. I think I could do that, but the company seems to hire just men.

CO: [To self: "Let me get back on track now."] We can consider a number of fields, including becoming a salesperson in your company. If there are barriers, we can look at ways to cross them. For now, let's not close any options. [The counselor is aware that before her last statement Judy had used the term *salesmen* and perhaps she sees their type of work as not being open to her.]

Because gender-role stereotyping is so pervasive in so many cultures, it is important to be alert to how such values affect the counselor. In the example above, the counselor became aware of the biases before they affected the client. Unless counselors can eliminate their own bias, their other efforts to help female clients will be limited.

CULTURALLY DIVERSE INDIVIDUALS AND DISCRIMINATION IN THE WORKPLACE

Just as discrimination is a barrier to occupational attainment and earnings for women, so it is also for culturally diverse populations. Racism not only impacts earnings, access to jobs and promotions, and access to job training and education, but can also affect psychological health (Blustein, 2008). Because many studies in sociology and economics rely on large samples for their research, most work in the United States has focused on the largest minority group, African Americans. Most of the discussion in this section examines the amount and nature of discrimination against African Americans. In general, the arguments against the effectiveness of human capital theory and status attainment for women given in the previous section also apply to African Americans.

The racial discrimination that African Americans and Latino/as (Hispanics) experience in the United States is reflected in employment and wage statistics. As shown in Table 3.2, the unemployment rate for African Americans and Latino/as in 2007 was much greater than the rate for whites and Asians. For African American youths 16 to 17 years old, the rate was extremely high—about one-third were unemployed. Not only is unemployment higher for African Americans and Latino/as, but the types of occupations they work in differ greatly. As shown in Table 3.3, Hispanics and African Americans tend to make up a relatively small proportion of the workers in high-skill jobs (see the top of Table 3.3) and a much larger proportion of the workers in semiskilled and unskilled jobs (see the bottom of Table 3.3). Furthermore, the salaries of African Americans and Hispanic and Latino/a individuals from different Latin American countries tend to be from about one-half to one-quarter less than those of white or Asian male individuals (Table 3.4). Explaining differences in unemployment and wages has been the task of many sociologists and economists.

Many investigators have examined a variety of factors preventing people from culturally diverse populations from attaining high-status jobs, high wages, and lower unemployment rates. Quillian (2006) has reviewed studies of racial attitudes towards African Americans and (to a lesser extent) Hispanics. His review shows that white Americans support the idea that all individuals should be treated equally

regardless of race. However, white Americans, in general, endorse stereotypical beliefs and doubt that individuals experience racial discrimination. A common belief
of white Americans is that African Americans and Hispanics do not work hard
enough. Although the United States passed the Civil Rights Act in 1964, businesses and other organizations have brought about only some desegregation in the
work place (Tomaskovic-Devey & Stainback, 2007). Regarding management positions, desegregation has been primarily in jobs in low wage industries and organizations in which individuals are likely to manage others from their own status
group. In professional jobs, there has been less discrimination than in other
areas of the workforce due to desegregation in colleges and universities, which
are part of the path to job entry (Tomaskovic-Devey et al., 2006; Tomaskovic-
Devey & Stainback, 2007). Recent studies of wages show that white Americans
continue to have significantly higher earnings than African Americans or Hispanic
men (Tomaskovic-Devey, Thomas & Johnson, 2005). Reviewing several studies of
labor market success, Quillian (2006) found that white applicants had higher rates
of success in getting callbacks for job interviews and in getting job offers than did
African Americans or Hispanics. Browne (1999) showed that one reason for the
high unemployment of less-educated young African American men is the shift in
the labor market away from manufacturing, a segment of the labor market that traditionally has employed less-educated young African Americans, to the service sector. Browne (1999) summarized several studies that show that when African
Americans and white adolescents or adults with similar résumés look for jobs,
African Americans experience more discrimination. Racial discrimination in housing is another factor, because some Americans find it difficult to find housing
outside of inner-city areas, where unemployment is higher than in the suburbs
(Brueckner & Zenou, 2003). Moving to better neighborhoods helped improve economic opportunities, as well as feelings of self-efficacy (Rosenbaum, Reynolds, &
Deluca, 2002). Quillian (2006) provides an overview of discrimination and problems that affect African Americans in both housing and the workplace.

Discrimination is found in many types of work in which African Americans are
engaged. African American executives often develop different styles to relate to
white executives than to other African American executives that help them deal
with issues of discrimination (Anderson, 2001). African American executives sometimes encounter firms that have been inconsistent in complying with affirmative action rules, as well as recruitment, retention, and promotion procedures (Phelps &
Constantine, 2001). In a comparison of African American and white assistant college football coaches, African American coaches reported less career satisfaction
and fewer promotions than did white coaches (Sagas & Cunningham, 2005).
Comparing wages for marginal (not highly sought after) professional basketball
players in the National Basketball Association, the salaries of nonwhite players
were significantly less than those of white players (Kahn & Shah, 2005). These
studies are examples of discrimination experienced by African Americans that may
occur in some occupations.

Some writers have examined a variety of political, economic, and psychological
variables affecting the progress of African Americans in the United States and
elsewhere (Cherry, 2001; Herr, Cramer, & Niles, 2004). Reviewing writings on the
experience of young African American men in the labor market, Skinner (1995)

criticizes human capital theory, concluding that the payoff of investments in high school and college education is declining for young African American men. He urges that attention be given to discrimination in housing, hiring, and job promotion, together with an effort to promote full employment and improved urban housing. Skinner also finds support for a dual labor market, with a large proportion of young African American men working for service employers (in the secondary labor market) in large urban cities. Reid (2002) notes that young African American women leave full-time employment at higher rates than young white women because they may work in temporary or seasonal jobs, may be afraid of being laid off, or for other reasons. In a study of 181 African American working women, Yamini-Benjamin (2007) reported significant stress and lack of job satisfaction associated with racial discrimination at work. Effects of racial discrimination towards blacks are not limited to the United States. In England, African-Caribbean women reported more work stress due to racial discrimination than did African-Caribbean men, or Bangladeshi or white individuals (Wadsworth et al., 2007). Thus, there are many barriers that African Americans and others of African descent face as they enter the labor force. Some of the reasons for these barriers have a long history.

Ogbu (1989, 1993, 1997, 2004) finds that African American children's orientation to society is unlike that of white children. Furthermore, he differentiates between the cultural orientation of minority children who are of immigrant origins and those, such as African Americans, who are an involuntary minority group, having been brought to the United States as slaves. He believes that African American children's view is a product of the current and past collective experience of African American people in the workforce. Furthermore, he believes that this heritage applies to middle-class, as well as lower-class, African Americans.

Another view expressed by Ogbu (1989, 1993, 1997, 2004) is that the experience of African Americans, as an involuntary minority group, in looking for work has led them to believe that getting ahead is important. However, this belief has not led to concentration on academic work or academic effort. He believes that African Americans perceive a job ceiling (being denied entrance to high-paying jobs). This perception, in turn, has led to a negative perception of the value of education. He believes that African American youths perceive school learning as a threat to their sense of identity and security, rather than as an opportunity for advancement. His research suggests a sense of disenfranchisement and a distrust of white Americans. Despite their distrust, young African Americans often have high occupational hopes. Ogbu's views are controversial and have been challenged by Hubbard (2005) and Lundy and Firebaugh (2005).

An important counseling issue is how to help African Americans (and other minority groups) to realize their goals. Strengthening work-related attitudes and information can be helpful. Using community, school, and parental resources to help minority adolescents develop attitudes that will be effective in the labor market is an appropriate counseling goal. The challenge to counselors is great because nonwhite people are, in general, less likely than white people to have access to counseling resources.

Just as there are stereotyped attitudes in the United States toward women, there is prejudice toward different cultural groups. It is difficult for people, counselors included, not to be exposed to and incorporate prejudices and discrimination. It is important for counselors to recognize and cope with any of their own attitudes that will prevent effective counseling of culturally diverse people. Sometimes, reactions are visceral rather than conscious, as the following example shows.

Brian is an African American freshman at a large Midwestern university. He has been recruited on an athletic scholarship to play football. He is a large man— 6 feet 3 inches tall and 260 pounds in weight. Like many other freshmen, he has found the transition from high school to college difficult. His football coach, sensing that Brian is unsure about his major and his course performance, recommends counseling. The following dialogue is from the beginning of Brian's counseling interview:

CO: How can I help you, Brian?

CL: Coach sent me here because he knows that I might be headed for some trouble.

CO: Can you tell me more about this? [Since walking with Brian from the waiting room, the counselor has been aware of a feeling right in the middle of the stomach. There is a sense of fear, but there seems to be no reason for it. Brian is pleasant and friendly. The counselor becomes aware that the fear is not due to Brian; rather, it comes from old feelings of prejudice based on skin color and body size. Being aware of these feelings reduces the counselor's physical sense of anxiety. The counselor starts to relax and focus away from old feelings and toward Brian.]

CL: I received a D in math and a D in science, and I'm worried.

CO: It feels really bad for you to get those grades now. I want to see what I can do to help you. [As the counselor's upper body moves slightly toward Brian, so does the counselor's attention. The counselor now is genuinely interested in Brian, and personal distractions have diminished.]

Not all counselors become aware of their feelings so quickly; some never become aware of them. If the counselor continues to feel tension or negative feelings toward the client because of prejudice, the effectiveness of counseling will be greatly diminished. If the counselor believes that African Americans are better in some professions than in others, the counselor will be doing a disservice to clients. Feelings and beliefs of prejudice are likely to undermine counseling, no matter what else the counselor does.

In addition to identifying their own prejudices, counselors often need to help their clients deal with the discrimination that they encounter in the job application process or in the workplace. Familiarity with affirmative action guidelines and legal procedures that address grievances is helpful. However, counselors may find assertiveness techniques useful in dealing with job discrimination. Examples of dealing with discrimination are given in Chapter 10.

SUMMARY

Unlike the other chapters in this book, this chapter focuses on occupational information and the influence of social and economic factors on the labor market as it affects an individual's career development. Data is presented showing the numbers of individuals working in different occupations in the United States and projections as to the growth of occupations over a 10-year period. Different sociological and economic theoretical positions provide different views of the labor market. Of particular interest to counselors is the effect of unemployment and underemployment on youths. Some sociologists have studied how the environment affects the individual, an approach quite dissimilar to that of psychologists, who are concerned with individuals making choices and influencing their environment. An area much studied by sociologists is status attainment theory, which emphasizes the importance of parental and aspirational variables in occupational attainment. Developed by economists, human capital theory views individuals as investing in themselves, their education, and training to increase their lifetime earnings. Study of the structure of labor markets questions human capital theory, suggesting that there are different types of labor markets that provide different pay rates, opportunities for advancement, and working conditions. The study of discrimination, which has been well-documented for both women and people from nonwhite cultures, also addresses the oversimplification of human capital theory. Each theory, as well as research on the discrimination against women and minorities in the United States, provides insights that counselors may use in their work.

References

Anderson, E. (2002). The social situation of the black executive: Black and white identities in the corporate world. In B. R. Hare (Ed.), *2001 Race odyssey: African Americans and sociology* (pp. 316–343). New York: Syracuse University Press.

Bayley, L. J. (1997). Using higher education for aspirational attainment: An American perspective. *International Studies in Sociology of Education, 7*, 213–227.

Beattie, I. R. (2002). Are all adolescent econometricians created equal? Racial, class, and gender differences in college enrollment. *Sociology of Education, 75*, 19–43.

Becker, G. S. (1957). *The economics of discrimination.* Chicago: University of Chicago Press.

Becker, G. S. (1964). *Human capital.* New York: Columbia University Press.

Bedard, K. (2001). Human capital versus signaling models: University access and high school dropouts. *Journal of Political Economy, 109*, 749–775.

Berger, G. S., & Piore, M. J. (1980). *Dualism and discontinuity in industrial societies.* New York: Cambridge University Press.

Berntson, E., Sverke, M., & Marklund, S. (2006). Predicting perceived employability: Human capital or labour market opportunities? *Economic and Industrial Democracy, 27*(2), 223–244.

Biblarz, T. J., & Raftery, A. E. (1993). The effects of family disruption on social mobility. *American Sociological Review, 58*, 97–109.

Blair, S. L., & Cobas, J. A. (2006). Gender differences in young Latino adults' status attainment: Understanding bilingualism in the familial context. *Family Relations, 55*(3), 292–305.

Blau, F. D., & Kahn, L. M. (2002). *At home and abroad: U.S. labor-market performances in international perspective.* New York: Russell Sage.

Blau, F. D., & Kahn, L. M. (2003). Understanding international differences in the gender pay gap. *Journal of Labor Economics, 21*, 106–143.

Blau, P. M. (1956). Social mobility and interpersonal relations. *American Sociological Review, 21*, 290–295.

Blau, P. M., & Duncan, O. D. (1967). *The American occupational structure.* New York: Wiley.

Blustein, D. L. (2008). The role of work in psychological health and well-being: A conceptual, historical, and public policy perspective. *American Psychologist, 63*(4), 228–240.

Brand, H. (1997). Global capitalism and the decay of employment policy. *Dissent, 44*, 56–62.

Browne, I. (1999). Employment and earnings among Latinas and African American women. In I. Browne (Ed.), *Latinas and African American women at work* (pp. 1–31). New York: Russell Sage Foundation.

Brueckner, J. K., & Zenou, Y. (2003). Space and unemployment: The labor-market effects of special mismatch. *Journal of Labor Economics, 21,* 242–266.

Buchmann, C. (1998). Family background, parental perceptions and labor demand: The determinants of educational inequality in contemporary Kenya. Paper presented at the International Sociological Association.

Caplan, L. J., & Schooler, C. (2006). Household work complexity, intellectual functioning, and self-esteem in men and women. *Journal of Marriage and Family, 68*(4), 883–900.

Chen, C. J. (2006). Elite mobility in post-reform rural China. *Issues & Studies, 42*(2), 53–83.

Cherry, R. (2001). *Who gets the good jobs? Combating race and gender disparities.* New Brunswick, NJ: Rutgers University Press.

Cheung, C. (2002). Gender differences in participation and earnings in Hong Kong. *Journal of Contemporary Asia, 32,* 69–90.

Cohen, P. N., & Huffman, M. L. (2003). Individuals, jobs, and labor markets: The devaluation of women's work. *American Sociological Review, 68,* 442–463.

Coley, R. L., Bachman, H. J., Votruba-Drzal, E., Lohman, B. J., & Li-Grining, C. P. (2007). Maternal welfare and employment experiences and adolescent well-being: Do mothers' human capital characteristics matter? *Children and Youth Services Review, 29*(2), 193–215.

Cotter, D. A., DeFiore, J., Hermsen, J. M., Kowalewski, B. M., & Vanneman, R. (1995). Occupational gender desegregation in the 1980s. *Work and Occupations, 22,* 3–21.

Davies, R., Heinesen, E., & Holm, A. (2002). The relative risk aversion hypothesis of educational choice. *Journal of Population Economics, 15,* 683–713.

Deary, I. J., Taylor, M. D., Hart, C. L., Wilson, V., Smith, G. D., Blane, D., et al. (2005). Intergenerational social mobility and mid-life status attainment: Influences of childhood intelligence, childhood social factors, and education. *Intelligence, 33*(5), 455–472.

Desmarais, S., & Curtis, J. (1999). Gender differences in employment and income experiences among young people. In J. Barling & E. K. Kelloway (Eds.), *Young workers: Varieties of experience* (pp. 59–88). Washington, DC: American Psychological Association.

Dipboye, R. L., & Colella, A. (2005). *Discrimination at work: The psychological and organizational bases.* Mahwah, NJ: Erlbaum.

Duncan, O. D. (2005). Methodological issues in the analysis of social mobility. In N. J. Smelser & S. M. Lipset (Eds.), *Social structure & mobility in economic development* (pp. 51–97). New Brunswick, NJ: Transaction.

England, P., & Farkas, G. (1986). *Household, employment, and gender: A social, economic, and demographic view.* New York: Aldine.

Fassinger, R. E. (2008) Workplace diversity and public policy: Challenges and opportunities for psychology. *American Psychologist, 63*(4), 252–268.

Felstead, A., Jewson, N., Phizacklea, A., & Walters, S. (2002). The option to work at home: Another privilege for the favored few? *New Technology, Work, and Employment, 17,* 204–223.

Gelissen, J., & de Graaf, P. M. (2006). Personality, social background, and occupational career success. *Social Science Research, 35*(3), 702–726.

Gheorghiu-Stephens, C. (2005). Does commitment matter? A comparative gender analysis of work commitment and labor market outcomes in western-capitalist and former-socialist countries. *Dissertation Abstracts International, A: The Humanities and Social Sciences, 66*(6), 2404-A.

Giesecke, J., & Gross, M. (2003). Temporary employment: Chance or risk? *European Sociological Review, 19,* 161–177.

Gottfredson, L. S. (2005). Applying Gottfredson's theory of circumscription, compromise in career guidance and counseling. In S. D. Brown & Lent, R. W. (Eds.), *Career development and counseling* (pp. 71–100). Hoboken, NJ: Wiley.

Greene, C. K., & Stitt-Gohdes, W. L. (1997). Factors that influence women's choices to work in the trades. *Journal of Career Development, 23,* 265–278.

Haas, S. A. (2006). Health selection and the process of social stratification: The effect of childhood health on socioeconomic attainment. *Journal of Health and Social Behavior, 47*(4), 339–354.

Hannum, E. (2002). Educational stratification by ethnicity in China: Enrollment and attainment in the early reform years. *Demography, 39,* 95–117.

Hauser, R. M. (2005). Survey response in the long run: The Wisconsin longitudinal study. *Field Methods, 17*(1), 3–29.

Herr, E. L., Cramer, S. H., & Niles, S. G. (2004). *Career guidance and counseling through the lifespan: Systematic approaches* (6th ed.). Boston: Allyn & Bacon.

Hilmer, M. J. (2002). Human capital attainment, university quality, and entry-level wages for college transfer students. *Southern Economic Journal, 69,* 457–469.

Hodson, R., & Sullivan, T. A. (2008). *The social organization of work* (4th ed.). Belmont, CA: Wadsworth.

Hubbard, L. (2005). The role of gender in academic achievement. *International Journal of Qualitative Studies in Education, 18*(5), 605–623.

Kahn, L. M., & Shah, M. (2005). Race, compensation and contract length in the NBA: 2001–2002. *Industrial Relations, 44*(3), 444–462.

Kalleberg, A. L., & Leicht, K. T. (2002). United States. In D. B. Cornfield & R. Hodson (Eds.), *Worlds of work: Building an international sociology of work* (pp. 87–110). New York: Kluwer.

Kerckhoff, A. C. (2002). The transition from school to work. In J. F. Mortimer & R. W. Larson (Eds.), *Changing adolescent experience: Societal trends and the transition to adulthood* (pp. 52–87).

Khazzoom, A. (1997). The impact of mothers' occupations on children's occupational destinations. *Research in Social Stratification and Mobility, 15,* 57–89.

Koenigsberg, J., Garet, M. S., & Rosenbaum, J. E. (1994). The effect of family on the job exits of young adults: A competing risk model. *Work and Occupations, 21,* 33–63.

Kohn, M. L. (2006). *Change and stability: A cross-national analysis of social structure and personality.* Greenbrae, CA: Paradigm Press.

Kohn, M. L., & Schooler, C. (1978). The reciprocal effects of the substantive complexity of work and intellectual flexibility: A longitudinal assessment. *American Journal of Sociology, 84,* 24–52.

Kohn, M. L., & Schooler, C. (1982). Reciprocal effects of job conditions and personality. *American Journal of Sociology, 87,* 1257–1286.

Kohn, M. L., & Schooler, C. (1983). *Work and personality.* Norwood, NJ: Ablex.

Kohn, M. L., Zaborowski, W., Janicka, K., Khmelko, V., Mach, B. W., Heyman, C., & Podobnik, B. (2002). Structural location and personality during the transformation of Poland and Ukraine. *Social Psychology Quarterly, 65,* 364–385.

Korinek, K. M. (2006). The status attainment of young adults during market transition: The case of Vietnam. *Research in Social Stratification and Mobility, 24*(1), 55–72.

Korupp, S. E., Ganzeboom, H. B., & Van Der Lippe, T. (2002). Do mothers matter? A comparison of models of influence of children's educational attainment. *Quality and Quantity, 36,* 17–42.

Korupp, S. E., Sanders, K., & Ganzeboom, H. B. (2002). The intergenerational transmission of occupational status and sex-typing at children's labor market entry. *European Journal of Women's Studies, 9,* 7–29.

Lloyd, S. (1997). The effects of domestic violence on women's employment. *Law and Policy, 19*, 139–167.

Lovell, P. A. (2006). Race, gender, and work in Sao Paulo, Brazil, 1960–2000. *Latin American Research Review, 41*(3), 63–87.

Lundy, G. F., & Firebaugh, G. (2005). Peer relations and school resistance: Does oppositional culture apply to race or to gender? *Journal of Negro Education, 74*(3), 233–245.

Mainquist, S., & Eichorn, D. (1989). Competence in work settings. In D. Stern, & D. Eichorn (Eds.), *Adolescence and work* (pp. 327–367). Hillsdale, NJ: Erlbaum.

Moe, K. S. (2003). (Ed.). *Women, Family, and Work: Writings on the economics of gender.* Malden, MA: Blackwell.

Moreau, M., Osgood, J., & Halsall, A. (2007). Making sense of the glass ceiling in schools: An exploration of women teachers' discourses. *Gender and Education, 19*(2), 237–253.

Mortimer, J. T. (2003). *Working and growing up an American.* Cambridge, MA: Harvard University Press.

Mortimer, J. T. (2007). Educational and work strategies from adolescence to early adulthood: Consequences for educational attainment. *Social Forces, 85*(3), 1169–1194.

Mortimer, J. T., Oesterle, S., & Kruger, H. (2005). Age norms, institutional structures, and the timing of markers of transition to adulthood. *Advances in Life Course Research, 9*, 175–203.

Occupational Outlook Handbook (2008). Washington, DC: U.S. Department of Labor.

Ogbu, J. (1989). Cultural boundaries and minority youth orientation toward work preparation. In D. Stern & D. Eichorn (Eds.), *Adolescence and work* (pp. 101–140). Hillsdale, NJ: Erlbaum.

Ogbu, J. (1993). Differences in cultural frame of reference. *International Journal of Behavioral Development, 16*, 483–506.

Ogbu, J. (1997). African American education: A cultural ecological perspective. In H. P. McAdoo & H. Pipes (Eds.), *Black families* (3rd ed., pp. 234–250). Thousand Oaks, CA: Sage Publications.

Ogbu, J. U. (2004). Collective identity and the burden of "acting white" in black history, community, and education. *Urban Review, 36*(1), 1–35.

Padavic, I., & Reskin, B. (2002). *Women and men at work* (2nd ed.). Thousand Oaks, CA: Sage.

Parent, D. (2002). Matching, human capital and the covariance structure of earnings. *Labour Economics, 9*, 375–404.

Pearlin, L. I., Schieman, S., Fazio, E. M., & Meersman, S. C. (2005). Stress, health, and the life course: Some conceptual perspectives. *Journal of Health and Social Behavior, 46*(2), 205–219.

Phelps, R. E., & Constantine, M. G. (2001). Hitting the roof: The impact of the glass ceiling effect on the career development of African Americans. In W. B. Walsh, R. P. Bingham, M. T. Brown, & C. M. Ward (Eds.), *Career counseling for African Americans* (pp. 161–176). Mahwah, NJ: Erlbaum.

Piore, M. J. (1975). Notes for a theory of labor market stratification. In R. L. Edwards, M. Riech, & D. M. Gordon (Eds.), *Labor market segmentation* (pp. 125–150). Lexington, MA: Heath.

Piore, M. J. (1979). *Birds of passage: Migrant labor and industrial societies.* New York: Cambridge University Press.

Piore, M. J., & Sable, C. F. (1984). *The second industrial divide: Possibilities for prosperity.* New York: Basic Books.

Pirog, M. A., & Magee, C. (1997). High school completion: The influence of schools, families, and adolescent parenting. *Social Science Quarterly, 78*, 710–724.

Psacharopoulos, G., & Velez, E. (1992). Schooling, ability, and earnings in Colombia, 1988. *Economic Development and Cultural Change, 40,* 629–643.

Quillian, L. (2006). New approaches to understanding racial prejudice and discrimination. *Annual Review of Sociology, 32,* 299–328.

Rankin, B. (2003). How low-income women find jobs and its effects on earnings. *Work and Occupations, 30,* 281–301.

Reid, L. L. (2002). Occupational segregation, human capital, and motherhood: Black women's higher exit rates from full-time employment. *Gender & Society, 16,* 728–747.

Rosenbaum, J. E. (1999). Institutional networks and informal strategies for improving work entry for youths. In W. R. Heinz (Ed.), *From education to work: Cross-national perspectives* (pp. 235–259). New York: Cambridge University Press.

Rosenbaum, J. E. (2001). *Beyond college for all: Career paths for the forgotten half.* New York: Russell Sage.

Rosenbaum, J. E., Reynolds, L., & Deluca, S. (2002). How do places matter? The geography of opportunity, self-efficacy and a look inside the black box of residential mobility. *Housing Studies, 17,* 71–82.

Rosigno, V. J. (2007). *The face of discrimination: How race and gender impact work and home lives.* Lanham, MD: Rowman & Littlefield.

Rowe, R., & Snizek, W. E. (1995). Gender differences in work values: Perpetuating the myth. *Work and Occupations, 22,* 215–229.

Sagas, M., & Cunningham, G. B. (2005). Racial differences in the career success of assistant football coaches: The role of discrimination, human capital, and social capital. *Journal of Applied Social Psychology, 35*(4), 773–797.

Sakurai, R. (2006). Youth employment in agriculture in the U.S.: Does it encourage student academic achievement? *Dissertation Abstracts International, A: The Humanities and Social Sciences, 66*(8), 2888-A.

Savickas, M. L. (2002). Career construction: A developmental theory of vocational behavior. In D. Brown & Associates (Eds.), *Career choice and development* (4th ed., pp. 149–205). San Francisco: Jossey-Bass.

Schooler, C. (1998). Environmental complexity and the Flynn effect. In U. Neisser (Ed.), *The rising curve: Long-term gains in IQ and related measures* (pp. 67–79). Washington, DC: American Psychological Association.

Schooler, C., Mulatu, M. S., & Oates, G. (1999). The continuing effects of substantively complex work on the intellectual functioning of older workers. *Psychology and Aging, 14,* 483–506.

Sheridan, J. T. (2002). Occupational attainment across the life course: Sources of stability and change in three occupational characteristics (Doctoral dissertation, University of Wisconsin–Madison, 2002). *Dissertation Abstracts International, 62/7,* 2577-A.

Shu, X. (2005). Market transition and gender segregation in urban China. *Social Science Quarterly, 86* (supplement, 1299–1323.).

Simpson, J. C. (2003). Mom matters: Maternal influence on the choice of academic major. *Sex Roles, 48,* 447–460.

Simpson, P. A., & Stroh, L. K. (2002). Revisiting gender variation in training. *Feminist Economics, 8,* 21–53.

Skinner, C. (1995). Urban labor markets and young black men: A literature review. *Journal of Economic Issues, 29,* 47–65.

Skinner, C. (2002). High school graduate earnings in New York City: The effects of skill, gender, race, and ethnicity. *Journal of Urban Affairs, 24,* 219–238.

Sonnenfeld, J. A. (1989). Career system profiles and strategic staffing. In M. B. Arthur, D. T. Hall, & B. S. Lawrence (Eds.), *Handbook of career theory* (pp. 202–224). New York: Cambridge University Press.

Stinebrickner, R. (2003). Working during school and economic performance. *Journal of Labor Economics, 21,* 473–490.

Stratton, L. S. (2003). Gains from trade and specialization: The division of work in married couple households. In K. S. Moe (Ed.), *Women, family, and work: Writings on the economics of gender* (pp. 65–84). Malden, MA: Blackwell.

Strenze, T. (2006). Who gets ahead in Estonia and America? A comparative analysis of mental ability and social origin as determinants of success. *Trames, 10*(3), 232–254.

Student Effort and Educational Progress. (2007). Dropout ratios of 16- to 24-year-olds by race/ethnicity, 2005. Washington, DC: National Center for Educational Statistics, U.S. Department of Education.

Tomaskovic-Devey, D., & Stainback, K. (2007). Discrimination and desegregation: Equal opportunity progress in U.S. private sector workplaces since the civil rights act. *The Annals of the American Academy of Political and Social Science, 609*(1), 49–84.

Tomaskovic-Devey, D., Stainback, K., Taylor, T., Zimmer, C., Robinson, C., & McTague, T. (2006). Documenting desegregation: Segregation in American workplaces by race, ethnicity, and sex, 1966–2003. *American Sociological Review, 71*(4), 565–588.

Tomaskovic-Devey, D., Thomas, M., & Johnson, K. R. (2002). The emergence of racial earnings inequality across the career: A fixed effects model for estimating the contributions of exogenous and endogenous human capital. Paper presented at the Southern Sociological Society.

Tomaskovic-Devey, D., Thomas, M., & Johnson, K. (2005). Race and the accumulation of human capital across the career: A theoretical model and fixed-effects application. *American Journal of Sociology, 111*(1), 58–89.

Wachter, M. L. (1974). Primary and secondary labor markets: A critique of the dual approach. *Brookings Papers on Economic Activity, 3,* 637–693.

Wadsworth, E., Dhillon, K., Shaw, C., Bhui, K., Stansfeld, S., & Smith, A. (2007). Racial discrimination, ethnicity and work stress. *Occupational Medicine, 57*(1), 18–24.

Waight, J. (1998). Income stratification at retirement: Continuity or change? *Research in Social Stratification and Mobility, 16,* 271–287.

Wilson, A. B. (1989). Dreams and aspirations in the status attainment model. In D. Stern & D. Eichorn (Eds.), *Adolescence and work* (pp. 49–73). Hillsdale, NJ: Erlbaum.

Worth, S. (2002). Education and employability: School leavers' attitudes to the prospect of non-standard work. *Journal of Education and Work, 15,* 163–180.

Yamini Benjamin, Y. I. (2007). Moving toward a better understanding of black women's work adjustment: The role of perceived discrimination and self-efficacy in predicting job satisfaction and psychological distress in black women. *Dissertation Abstracts International: Section B: The Sciences and Engineering, 67*(10-B), 6085.

Zhan, M. (2006). Economic mobility of single mothers: The role of assets and human capital development. *Journal of Sociology & Social Welfare, 33*(4), 127–150.

Zhang, Y., Kao, G., & Hannum, E. (2007). Do mothers in rural china practice gender equality in educational aspirations for their children? *Comparative Education Review, 51*(2), 131–157.

WORK ADJUSTMENT THEORY

Work adjustment theory is the outgrowth of more than 35 years of research by René Dawis and Lloyd Lofquist and their colleagues. Their work, which reflects the trait and factor approach of the University of Minnesota, evolved into a growing body of research that led to several revisions and refinements of their theory. In the process of this development, the Work Adjustment Project was designed to provide improved rehabilitation services for vocationally challenged clients. At the University of Minnesota, an adult Vocational Assessment Clinic treated clients, and a Vocational Psychology Research unit was designed to develop and score the tests and inventories that are part of work adjustment theory. Originally designed to meet the needs of vocational rehabilitation clients, the theory is now applicable to adults who wish to make career choices or those who are experiencing work adjustment problems.

Work adjustment theory (Dawis & Lofquist, 1984) consists of 18 propositions and corollaries. The current theory (Dawis, 2005; Griffin & Hesketh, 2005; Hesketh & Griffin, 2005) is based on research that has modified earlier work (Dawis, England, & Lofquist, 1964; Dawis, Lofquist, & Weiss, 1968; Lofquist & Dawis, 1969). Each of these statements of theory had as a goal the prediction of work adjustment. Dawis and Lofquist (1984) define work adjustment as a "continuous and dynamic process by which a worker seeks to achieve and maintain correspondence with a work environment" (p. 237). That is, work adjustment is indicated by the length of time, or tenure, on the job. This concern with job tenure and a similar concept, job performance, distinguishes work adjustment theory from most other theories described in this book, which are concerned with career selection or work adjustment but not actual performance on the job.

There are two major components to the prediction of work adjustment (and therefore tenure): satisfaction and satisfactoriness. *Satisfaction* refers to being satisfied with the work that one does. In contrast, *satisfactoriness* refers to the employer's satisfaction with the individual's performance. That is, satisfaction refers to the extent to which an individual's needs and requirements are fulfilled by the work that he or she does. Satisfactoriness concerns the appraisal of others, usually supervisors, of the extent to which an individual adequately completes the work that is assigned to him or her; it also is of interest to industrial and organizational psychologists.

"Satisfaction is a key indicator of work adjustment," state Lofquist and Dawis (1984, p. 217). Satisfaction is important because the individual must be satisfied with many aspects of the work, such as salary and type of work task. This chapter focuses primarily on the individual's satisfaction with work. However, work adjustment theory is also concerned with other indicators of satisfaction and satisfactoriness, including the amount of turnover, absenteeism, and tardiness on the job; devotion to a job; job morale; and productivity on a job. These aspects of job performance are all indicators of work adjustment. The work environment must satisfy the individual's needs, and the employee must have the requisite skills to meet the job's needs.

Skills and needs are observable entities that are the essence of work personality. However, hundreds of skills may be required in different types of jobs, as well as many needs; therefore, measurement of skills and needs is awkward and difficult. Dawis and Lofquist (1984) propose the concept of abilities, which combines the common elements of skills required in many jobs. In a similar vein, values serve to group needs together in a meaningful way. Much of these researchers' theoretical work concerns the discussion and measurement of abilities and values. They also discuss personality style and interests. Their experimental work on personality styles and adjustment styles is not as highly developed as is their work on needs and values. They view interests as a derived construct, being a reflection of ability–value relationships.

In describing work adjustment theory, a specific application of trait and factor theory, an approach similar to that used in Chapter 2, "Trait and Factor Theory," is used in this chapter. Work adjustment theory is a specific example of general trait and factor theory in that it makes use of clearly defined concepts and follows an articulated theoretical model. The first section of this chapter is concerned with assessing abilities, values, personality, and interests (similar to Parsons's first step). Because abilities and values are the major emphasis of Lofquist and Dawis's (1984) work, they receive the most attention. The second section (also similar to Parsons's second step as discussed in Chapters 2 and 3 of this text) is concerned with knowledge of the requirements and conditions of occupations. In this section, abilities required by work and reinforcement of individual needs are discussed. The third section (similar to Parsons's third step) outlines the matching of the abilities and values of an individual with the abilities required by the job and the reinforcers provided by the job.

Work adjustment theory also has implications for helping clients with adjustment problems (Griffin & Hesketh, 2005; Hesketh & Griffin, 2005), such as problems with coworkers and superiors, boredom, inability to meet job demands, and retirement, as well as many other issues. In addition, work adjustment theory provides some psychometric data on the ability and values differences of women and culturally diverse populations. This is not a major focus of the theory, however, because it is concerned with differences among individuals not group differences. In the following sections, I follow the three steps of trait and factor theory described in Chapter 2.

STEP 1: ASSESSING ABILITIES, VALUES, PERSONALITY, AND INTERESTS

Consistent with trait and factor theory, measurement of values and abilities is crucial to the understanding of work adjustment theory. To assess abilities, Dawis and Lofquist (1984) make use of the General Aptitude Test Battery (GATB) that was developed by the U.S. Department of Labor (1982). As a measure of values and needs, they have developed the Minnesota Importance Questionnaire (MIQ; Rounds, Henly, Dawis, Lofquist, & Weiss, 1981), which is critical to the use and understanding of work adjustment theory. They have also developed measures of personality style and adjustment style as they relate to work adjustment (Lawson, 1993). Because Dawis and Lofquist (1984) see interests as an expression of abilities and values, their focus is on ability and value assessment. The following sections discuss and illustrate each of the components of work adjustment theory.

ABILITIES

Dawis and Lofquist (1984) define abilities as "reference dimensions for skills" (p. 233). Abilities are viewed as encompassing aptitudes, which are predicted skills, in contrast to acquired skills. For Dawis and Lofquist, the notion of abilities is needed to conceptualize a vast array of work skills. The latter can include typing, waiting on tables, fixing teeth or engines, planing wood, plastering walls, selling insurance policies, and so forth. There are hundreds, perhaps thousands, of such skills. Ability tests measure factors common to many skills. Many ability tests measure between 8 and 15 ability dimensions. Dawis and Lofquist (1984) describe the General Aptitude Test Battery (GATB) (U.S. Department of Labor, 1982) as an example of a measure of ability. The GATB is used widely by employment counseling agencies. Its predictive validity (Farrell & McDaniel, 2001) and its use with the O*NET (*Occupational Information Network* online) (Jeanneret & Strong, 2003; Gore & Hitch, 2005; Rounds &

Armstrong, 2005) are examples of current research and development. The GATB manual (U.S. Department of Labor, 1982) provides a list of abilities that are needed in a vast variety of jobs. A new version of the GATB, the *Ability Profiler*, currently is available, but occupations have not been linked to work adjustment theory. The scales are very similar to the GATB scales and are shown in brackets in the following description of the GATB scales, which measure nine specific abilities:

G—General learning ability [Not in Ability Profiler]: Overall ability to learn, as well as general knowledge

V—Verbal ability [Both GATB and Ability Profiler]: Understanding of words and paragraphs

N—Numerical ability [Computation]: Ability to perform basic arithmetic skills

[Arithmetic Reasoning]: Ability to use basic mathematical and logical skills to solve problems that may occur at work, including skills of gathering and sorting information to solve problems

S—Spatial ability [Both GATB and Ability Profiler]: Ability to see objects in space and understand relationships between two- and three-dimensional objects

P—Form perception [Both GATB and Ability Profiler]: Ability to see details in two- or three-dimensional drawings and to make discriminations in shapes and shadings

Q—Clerical ability [Clerical perception]: Ability to see differences in tables and lists that include both words and numbers

K—Eye/hand coordination [Motor coordination]: Ability to coordinate hand movements with visual perception

F—Finger dexterity [Both GATB and Ability Profiler]: Ability to move small objects quickly and with precision

M—Manual dexterity [Both GATB and Ability Profiler]: Ability to use hands and arms in manipulating objects quickly and skillfully.

Although other abilities could be used in addition to those listed above, Dawis and Lofquist used the nine abilities of the GATB in their application of work adjustment theory. Other ability tests could be used that would be consistent with work adjustment theory, but the GATB is the most practical because of the information it provides for counselors to use in matching jobs with an individual's abilities and values. In general, the GATB incorporates abilities required for many jobs and measures a broader base of abilities than many academic aptitude tests. For example, one would expect an electrician to have, among other abilities, numerical ability, form perception, and eye/hand coordination, which are all measured by the GATB (and the Ability Profiler).

VALUES

Just as abilities represent a distillation of many work skills, values represent a grouping of needs. Unlike the hundreds of work skills that may exist, the number of needs is less. The Minnesota Importance Questionnaire (Rounds, Henly, Dawis, Lofquist, & Weiss, 1981) is a measure of needs. Although not encompassing all needs, the 20 need scales of the Minnesota Importance Questionnaire characterize important work-related concepts. The 20 need scales are listed in Table 4.1, together with the statement that represents each scale. In the questionnaire, each statement is paired in comparison with every other statement, to constitute 190 items.

TABLE 4.1 | VALUES, NEED SCALES, AND STATEMENTS FROM THE MINNESOTA IMPORTANCE QUESTIONNAIRE

Value	Need Scale	Statement
Achievement	Ability utilization	I could do something that makes use of my abilities.
	Achievement	The job could give me a feeling of accomplishment.
Comfort	Activity	I could be busy all the time.
	Independence	I could work alone on the job.
	Variety	I could do something different every day.
	Compensation	My pay would compare well with that of other workers.
	Security	The job would provide for steady employment.
	Working conditions	The job would have good working conditions.
Status	Advancement	The job would provide an opportunity for advancement.
	Recognition	I could get recognition for the work I do.
	Authority	I could tell people what to do.
	Social status	I could be "somebody" in the community.
Altruism	Coworkers	My coworkers would be easy to make friends with.
	Moral values	I could do the work without feeling it is morally wrong.
	Social service	I could do things for other people.
Safety	Company policies and practices	The company would administer its policies fairly.
	Supervision—Human relations	My boss would back up the workers (with top management).
	Supervision—Technical	My boss would train the workers well.
Autonomy	Creativity	I could try out some of my ideas.
	Responsibility	I could make decisions on my own.

Source: *A psychological theory of work adjustment* by R. V. Dawis and L. H. Lofquist, p. 29. Copyright © 1984, University of Minnesota Press. Reprinted by permission.

For example, an individual is asked whether he or she would rather "be busy all the time" (activity) or "do things for other people" (social service). By comparing the relative importance of each need, scores on each scale are determined. The disadvantage of this method is that it represents a narrower definition of the need than if several items were used for a particular scale. Choosing this method to define needs reflects Dawis and Lofquist's emphasis in their theory on the importance of rigorous measurement.

Using the statistical technique of factor analysis, Dawis and Lofquist (1984) derived 6 values from the 20 needs (see Table 4.1). Values are clustered with their opposites: achievement is negatively related to comfort, status is very different from altruism, and safety is negatively related to autonomy. The relationship of the needs to the values and the values to each other provides a way for a counselor to chunk and derive meaning from the need scales of the MIQ. The values are described as follows.

ACHIEVEMENT   Achievement is reflected in the need to make use of one's abilities (ability utilization) and to do things that give one a sense of accomplishment (achievement). For example, a carpenter who is proud of his or her abilities and the products he or she makes is likely to value achievement.

COMFORT   Included in the comfort value is a variety of needs dealing with specific aspects of work that make the job less stressful for the worker. These are quite diverse, including being busy all the time (activity), working alone (independence), doing different things (variety), and being paid well (compensation). Other aspects of comfort can be long range—for example, a desire for steady employment (security). Also, specific working conditions can be important. These may include lighting, heating, and amount of space. All of these have in common an emphasis on a nonstressful work environment; that is, one that will yield benefits to the employee, such as security and compensation.

STATUS   How one is perceived by others and the recognition one gets are the emphasis of the status value. Status can be attained by an opportunity for advancement; recognition for the work that one does; or, more generally, prestige (social status) that comes from being important in the community.

In addition, telling people what to do (authority) is another way of achieving status. Recognizing that status needs are important to some individuals can be particularly helpful both in career choice and in recognizing a problem with work dissatisfaction. For example, some people who have initially enjoyed a particular job may lose interest in it when they find that they are not advancing and are not being recognized for what they do.

ALTRUISM   Altruism is quite the opposite of status because it is concerned not with how one is perceived by others but with how one can help or work with others. Doing things for other people (social service) and, more specifically, getting along with colleagues at work (coworkers) can be an important aspect of work. In particular, being able to do work that feels morally correct (moral values) can be a need that is directly tied to work satisfaction. For example, people who are required to sell products that they feel are harmful or worthless may find that they must leave those jobs because their moral values are being violated.

SAFETY   Rather than being seen in the narrow sense of avoiding hazardous conditions, safety is broader in that it reflects the importance of orderliness and predictability. It includes the enforcement of policies in a fair manner (company policies and practices), as well as support from supervisors (supervision—human relations). Also, safety includes how coworkers are trained (supervision—technical), because it can affect how a person does his or her job. For example, an automobile assembly worker who could not count on coworkers to do their jobs well and who felt that management was lax in providing workers with training and materials would not have his or her safety needs met.

AUTONOMY   Some people are not concerned with how they are treated by their bosses (safety), rather they want the opportunity to work on their own. This may include trying out some of their own ideas (creativity) or making decisions on their own (responsibility). For example, an auto assembly worker who wants to try out new ideas to make his or her work easier or more efficient is concerned with autonomy rather than safety.

These values and needs provide a way for the counselor to understand a person's work experience. Without such a guideline, work experience can appear to be a series of unrelated events. The MIQ is a method of measuring the importance of needs that emerge from experience. For example, people who want to accomplish a lot in their work, help others, and make decisions on their own (achievement, altruism, and autonomy) will find satisfaction in different occupations from people who are concerned with pay and steady employment, getting recognition for the work they do, and being in a company with fair policies (comfort, status, and safety).

PERSONALITY STYLES

According to Dawis and Lofquist (1984), personality style is concerned with how an individual with particular abilities and values interacts with his or her work situation. They have identified four characteristics of personality style: celerity, pace, rhythm, and endurance. These describe ways in which people respond to their environment: how quickly, with how much intensity, in what particular pattern, and for how long. Celerity is concerned with the speed with which one approaches tasks. Pace is concerned with the effort one spends in working. Rhythm is the pattern of one's effort or pace. Endurance is concerned with how long one is likely to continue working at a task. Thus, someone who rates high on celerity, pace, rhythm, and endurance works quickly, is involved in a large number of activities, is consistent in his or her work, and can be relied on to complete projects. These work personality styles are an interesting addition to the ability and values concepts of Lofquist and Dawis. However, scales for the assessment of celerity, pace, rhythm, and endurance are not available (Lawson, 1993). Questions such as "Do individuals maintain the same work personality style (celerity, pace, rhythm, and endurance) in one work environment that they do in another?" remain to be answered.

INTERESTS

As stated earlier, interests are seen by Dawis and Lofquist (1984) as derived from values and abilities in that they are an expression of ability–value relationships. For these researchers, an interest in being an engineer or a bricklayer is derived from the abilities and values that one has. They believe that interest inventories can be helpful in counseling but do not feature them in their approach to work adjustment counseling. Rounds (1990) analyzed data that assessed the relative contribution of work values and vocational interests. His conclusion is that both are important, but that work values appear to be a slightly better predictor of job satisfaction than interests. Differences were also found for female and male individuals. This study lends support to the weight that Dawis and Lofquist put on values as an important aspect of prediction of job satisfaction.

A COUNSELING EXAMPLE

In the example below, the GATB and MIQ are used to assist a client with self-assessment. Later in this chapter, after a description of the work adjustment theory approach to occupational information, a continuing discussion with this client shows how work adjustment theory matches information about values and abilities with occupational information.

Winifred is a 45-year-old white farmer living with her husband in rural Missouri. Her husband is an auto mechanic in the local village, and Winifred runs the family farm. They have no children but cared for foster children until about 10 years ago. Winifred has been the principal farm manager and farm laborer for 20 years, raising feed corn and hogs. Winifred has been primarily responsible for planting, fertilizing, and harvesting the corn. She also takes the major responsibility for the constant activity of feeding the hogs. Winifred had no formal training in farming and learned most of it from her parents and from attending special agricultural extension programs. Recently, she sprained her back badly while harvesting. This came as an addition to chronic back pain that she had experienced over the last 3 years. After consulting with her physician, who has taken several X-rays of her spine, Winifred has come to the realization that she can no longer handle the heavy task of farming. Furthermore, she has become dissatisfied and bored with the work. Because Winifred is self-employed, she is both employee and employer. One measure of her satisfactoriness as a farmer is the productivity of the farm. Winifred has made the farm financially productive in good-weather conditions and has been able to maintain the farm's solvency in times of drought.

After briefly discussing her concerns with her vocational rehabilitation counselor, Winifred was asked to complete the GATB and the MIQ. Winifred's scores are summarized in Table 4.2. Her scores are highest in numerical ability, spatial ability, form perception, eye/hand coordination, and finger dexterity. Her greatest needs, as registered on the MIQ, are for ability utilization and achievement. Winifred and her counselor discuss the test results in the following dialogue:

CL: It was strange taking those tests. When I was in high school, I remember tests like that aptitude test I took [the GATB]. It's been 25 years. I never thought I'd see one of those again. But I was surprised to be playing with blocks and washers and things. [Winifred is referring to the finger and manual dexterity tests.]

TABLE 4.2 | TEST SCORES FOR WINIFRED

	High	Moderate	Low
GATB	Numerical ability		Verbal ability
	Spatial ability		Clerical ability
	Form perception		
	Eye/hand coordination		
	Finger dexterity		
MIQ	Ability utilization	Creativity	
	Achievement	Responsibility	
		Activity	
		Independence	
		Compensation	

Abbreviations: GATB, General Aptitude Test Battery; MIQ, Minnesota Importance Questionnaire.

CO: Well, you seemed to do fine. There's a lot of information for us to look at. [The counselor wants to explore Winifred's abilities, and the GATB seems to be a good place to start.]

CL: My husband always says that I can fix the tractor faster than he can. He says that my hands really whiz around when I get going.

CO: Well, you also have the abilities to visualize objects and to understand relationships of objects on paper. [The counselor wants to talk to Winifred about her spatial ability and her form perception.]

CL: When I was a girl in school 25 years ago, I couldn't take courses that I wanted to. Shop courses were for boys; home economics and business education were for girls. I know my mom wanted me to be a secretary. What a mess I would have been! I know that I don't have those kinds of skills. It drives me nuts even when I have to do some of that at the farm. I can't type lists, and I don't like it.

CO: Tell me more about what you're good at and not so good at on the farm. [So far, it seems that Winifred's perception of her own abilities matches that of the GATB; however, the counselor wants to check further.]

CL: Well, I'm good at fixing things. My husband has taught me a lot of mechanical stuff that he learned when he took courses in high school. I seem to pick it up real well. Later, I learned about electrical things. That's probably the most fun for me. My husband keeps telling me how good I am at it. I guess I am. That's the good part. The bad part is moving around and lifting. It really hurts. I used to do a lot more heavy work. Now I look for ways I can get other people to do it or get some machine to do it. You should see the way I use a tractor. I practically try to wash dishes with it. We've got all kinds of additions for the tractor, but sometimes it's real hard to hook them up.

CO: Seems like working on the farm has really given you a chance to see what you can do and what you can't do. [Winifred's own perception of her abilities confirms her scores on the GATB.]

Winifred and the counselor continue to discuss the GATB, and then move to a discussion of her work values, needs, and the MIQ. Even from the discussion so far, the counselor senses that achievement is important to Winifred. She seems proud of her abilities and of what she has done. The dialogue continues as follows:

CL: I like what I've done on the farm. A lot of my friends sit around and make pies. That's not me. At first, that bothered my husband. Now, he's OK with it. We figure it's OK to buy frozen foods, desserts, and such. He doesn't seem to mind that I don't cook. He doesn't want to, either.

CO: You've done a lot with the farm. What else have you done? [The counselor hears the achievement value and wants to inquire further.]

CL: I've done a lot of different things. I do so much on my own, particularly in the last few years. My husband seems to have lost some interest in the farm, too. I wish he hadn't. I kind of like it, but it gets to be a burden sometimes. I don't mind deciding what to do, but I guess I get tired of having to be there all the time. We can never leave the farm it seems. A few times we have; my folks come in. It's hard. You know pigs, you can't leave them for long.

CO: I would like to talk to you about the Minnesota Importance Questionnaire. Some of the scores fit in with what you're saying about what's important to you. You really do seem to like to be active and to work on your own. [Finding that Winifred's expressed values seem to fit with the MIQ makes things go smoothly.]

CL: I wondered how I did with the MIQ. That was easy. Not like the GATB.

CO: Well, your high scores show that you like to use your abilities and want to be able to get a sense of accomplishment in what you do.

CL: That's for sure. I can't imagine doing something that didn't matter. To do the same thing time after time that didn't matter would be awful. I want to feel like I'm getting somewhere, making progress.

CO: Well, we will consider that when we start to look at things that you might want to do. [The counselor makes a mental note that achievement is, again, important to Winifred. Its opposite, comfort, is not. Work conditions do not seem to be important to her.]

The counselor and Winifred continue to talk about Winifred's abilities, values, and interests. Later, they will discuss possible occupations and also matching occupations that fit the GATB.

STEP 2: MEASURING THE REQUIREMENTS AND CONDITIONS OF OCCUPATIONS

Just as there are methods to measure individuals' values and abilities, there are methods to measure the abilities and values needed for many occupations. Briefly, this is done by averaging scores on the GATB and the MIQ for people in various occupations. Such information is not available for the work personality styles of celerity, pace, rhythm, and endurance. Also, information about interest patterns of people in various occupations has not been used by Dawis and Lofquist in their psychometric application of work adjustment theory. This is because Lofquist and Dawis believe that interest is a secondary concept, as mentioned earlier, and that the information provided by the occupational patterns of abilities and values is sufficient. Ability and value patterns are discussed in more detail in this section.

ABILITY PATTERNS

Occupational Ability Patterns have been developed by the U.S. Department of Labor to describe the important abilities that are required for a vast variety of jobs. To do this, job analysts assessed an occupation at various sites. Furthermore, individuals employed in occupations took the GATB. From these two methods, a set of GATB ability requirements (three or four) was developed for each occupation. Furthermore, cutoff scores were selected. Those scoring greater than the cutoff point were people who had done their jobs successfully as determined by supervisor ratings or other means. This information enables an individual to assess whether he or she has abilities similar to those of successful people in a given occupation. However, in determining cutoff scores for occupations, it is important not to set the scores too high, which could possibly exclude adequate potential candidates.

VALUE PATTERNS

Work environments differ in the degree to which they meet the needs and values of an individual. Lofquist and Dawis developed a list of Occupational Reinforcer Patterns to assess how much an occupation reinforces the values of individuals. To do that, they developed the Minnesota Job Description Questionnaire (MJDQ; Borgen, Weiss, Tinsley, Dawis, & Lofquist, 1968a), which assesses how well an occupation reinforces or meets each of 20 needs. The MJDQ uses the same needs as the Minnesota Importance Questionnaire. Table 4.3 shows the wording of the items on the MJDQ. Comparing the items in Table 4.1 with those in Table 4.3 will illustrate the similarity. For example, on the MIQ, the need for activity is assessed by the item: "I would be busy all the time." Activity as a reinforcer is assessed through this MJDQ item: "Workers on this job are busy all the time." Thus, the needs of an individual are matched with the reinforcers provided by the job. Many occupations were assessed with the MJDQ so that reinforcer patterns could be established (Borgen et al., 1968b). Dawis, Dohm, and Jackson (1993) have described occupations as reinforcer systems, which can offer predictable versus unpredictable reinforcements, self-reinforcements versus non–self-reinforcements, and social versus nonsocial reinforcement. These ratings of reinforcement schedules are related to, but different from, occupational reinforcement patterns. Using information about value patterns helps counselors to see how the values of their clients match the values that are met or reinforced by a large number of occupations.

COMBINING ABILITY AND VALUE PATTERNS

Important information about occupations can be provided by combining information about Occupational Ability Patterns and Occupational Reinforcer Patterns. The combined data were used to create the Minnesota Occupational Classification System (MOCS). The original MOCS had 337 occupations. The third revision of the MOCS has 1,769 occupations. The relationship of instruments used to assess individual abilities and values and those found in occupations is shown in Table 4.4. The individual and occupational patterns are matched by using the MOCS, which is described in the next section.

TABLE 4.3	NEED SCALES AND STATEMENTS FROM THE MINNESOTA JOB DESCRIPTION QUESTIONNAIRE
Need Scale	**Statement (Workers on this job...)**
Ability utilization	Make use of their individual abilities
Achievement	Get a feeling of accomplishment
Activity	Are busy all the time
Advancement	Have opportunities for advancement
Authority	Tell other workers what to do
Company policies and practices	Have a company that administers its policies fairly
Compensation	Are paid well in comparison with other workers
Coworkers	Have coworkers who are easy to make friends with
Creativity	Try out their own ideas
Independence	Do their work alone
Moral values	Do work without feeling that it is morally wrong
Recognition	Receive recognition for the work they do
Responsibility	Make decisions on their own
Security	Have steady employment
Social service	Have work where they do things for other people
Social status	Have a position of "somebody" in the community
Supervision—Human relations	Have bosses who back up their workers (with top management)
Supervision—Technical	Have bosses who train the workers well
Variety	Have something different to do every day
Working conditions	Have good working conditions

Source: *Minnesota Job Description Questionnaire*, by F. H. Borgen, D. J. Weiss, H. E. Tinsley, R. V. Dawis, and L. H. Lofquist. Copyright © 1968, Vocational Psychology Research, Department of Psychology, University of Minnesota. Reprinted by permission.

STEP 3: MATCHING ABILITIES, VALUES, AND REINFORCERS

When matching values and abilities with the Occupational Ability Patterns and Occupational Reinforcer Patterns, counselors have three tools available to them: the Minnesota Importance Questionnaire report form, the GATB manual (U.S. Department of Labor, 1982), and the Minnesota Occupational Classification System (MOCS). All can be helpful in identifying occupations for clients to explore further. In addition, another useful concept is adjustment style that describes the degree of fit between the person and the environment. Four qualities describe this fit: flexibility, activeness, reactiveness, and perseverance. All of these tools can help the client and the counselor make use of a wealth of information and narrow the number of occupational alternatives so that the client has a manageable number of choices.

TABLE 4.4 | INSTRUMENTS USED IN WORK ADJUSTMENT THEORY

Assessment of Individuals	Assessment of Occupations
Abilities	Ability Patterns
General Aptitude Test Battery (GATB)	Occupational Ability Patterns
Values	Value Patterns
Minnesota Importance Questionnaire (MIQ)	Minnesota Job Description Questionnaire (MJDQ)
Personality Styles	Personality Styles
Instruments are being developed	Instruments are being developed

Matching Assessment of Individual and Occupation

Minnesota Occupational Classification System (MOCS)

Adjustment Styles (Instruments are not yet developed)

When clients take the Minnesota Importance Questionnaire, they receive scores on the 6 values and 20 needs described earlier and on 90 occupations. Table 4.5 provides an example of a report. It lists occupations whose reinforcer patterns match the client's identified needs. The strength of the correspondence (or relationship) between the individual's rating of the importance of a need on the MIQ and the importance attached to that need by a sample of people in an occupation is indicated by the C Index. Other indices such as the P Index, which is based on probability rather than correlation, also could be used (Eggerth, 2004). By using the C Index, a counselor can help the client locate occupations for future consideration. If the sample of 90 occupations is not sufficient, the counselor can request an extended report, which lists the scores of more than 183 occupations. The client and counselor also can match the client's ability scores and need patterns to occupations by using the Minnesota Occupational Classification System. Because the MOCS lists both Occupational Ability Patterns and Occupational Reinforcer Patterns for more than 1,700 occupations, it can be a particularly helpful resource. The counselor and client can examine occupations, perhaps taken from the Minnesota Importance Questionnaire report (see Table 4.5), and find matches between the client and the occupational group; this is a thorough matching process. However, this is not the only way of looking at the correspondence between the individual and the working environment.

Adjustment style refers to how an individual relates to the occupational environment (Dawis & Lofquist, 1984). The concepts of flexibility, activeness, reactiveness, and perseverance all concern the relationship of the individual to the occupation. *Flexibility* refers to the ability of an individual to tolerate unpleasant or difficult aspects of the job. For example, individuals differ in terms of their flexibility in working in a cramped working environment or with an unpleasant superior. When individuals are faced with unpleasant or difficult work situations, they may try to change the environment—*activeness*—or make a change in themselves—*reactiveness*. For example, a person who must deal with an unpleasant superior may choose to confront the superior and try to resolve the discomfort (activeness). In contrast, an individual

MIQ profile is compared with Occupational Reinforcer Patterns for 90 representative occupations. Correspondence is indicated by the C Index. A prediction of Satisfied (S) results from C values greater than .50, Likely Satisfied (L) for C values between .10 and .49, and Not Satisfied (N) for C values less than .10. Occupations are clustered by similarity of Occupational Reinforcer Pattern. Abbreviations after each cluster refer to the primary values (all capitals) and secondary values: For example, Achievement (ACH) is a primary value, and Comfort (Com) is a secondary value.

	C Index	Prediction Satisfied		C Index	Prediction Satisfied
Cluster A (ACH-AUT-Alt)			Cluster B (ACH-Com)		
Architect	.30	L	Bricklayer	.15	L
Dentist	.25	L	Carpenter	-.07	N
Family practitioner	.21	L	Cement mason	.24	L
Interior designer/decorator	.21	L	Elevator repairer	-.16	N
Lawyer	.43	L	Heavy equipment operator	.48	L
Minister	.35	L	Landscape gardener	.30	L
Nurse, occupational health	.13	L	Lather	.11	N
Occupational therapist	.12	L	Millwright	-.05	N
Optometrist	.33	L	Painter-paperhanger	.10	L
Psychologist, counseling	.39	L	Patternmaker, metal	.11	L
Recreation leader	.21	L	Pipefitter	.28	L
Speech pathologist	.15	L	Plasterer	.34	L
Teacher, elementary school	.28	L	Plumber	-.13	N
Teacher, secondary school	.23	L	Roofer	.37	L
Vocational evaluator	.28	L	Salesperson, automobile	-.04	N
	.36	L		.43	L

(continued)

113

TABLE 4.5 | CONTINUED

	C Index	Prediction Satisfied		C Index	Prediction Satisfied
Cluster C (ACH-Aut-Com)	.44	L	Cluster D (ACH-STA-Com)	.57	S
Alteration tailor	.27	L	Accountant, certified public	.43	L
Automobile mechanic	.25	L	Airplane copilot, commercial	.25	L
Barber	.46	L	Cook (hotel-restaurant)	.48	L
Beauty operator	.44	L	Department head, supermarket	.39	L
Caseworker	.28	L	Drafter, architectural	.41	L
Claim adjuster	.51	S	Electrician	.44	L
Commercial artist, illustrator	.56	S	Engineer, civil	.45	L
Electronics mechanic	.39	L	Engineer, time study	.59	S
Locksmith	.28	L	Farm equipment mechanic I	.52	S
Maintenance repairer, factory	.41	L	Line-installer-repairer (tel)	.13	L
Mechanical engineering tech	.40	L	Machinist	.54	S
Office-machine servicer	.53	S	Programmer (bus., eng., sci.)	.65	S
Photoengraver (stripper)	.54	S	Sheet metal worker	.50	S
Sales agent, real estate	.32	L	Statistical machine servicer	.56	S
Salesperson, general hardware	.15	L	Writer, technical publications	.61	S
Cluster E (COM)	.19	L	Cluster F (Alt-Com)	.21	L
Assembler, production	.05	N	Airplane flight attendant	.02	N
Baker	.16	L	Clerk (gen. ofc, civil svc.)	.03	N
Bookbinder	.28	L	Dietitian	.56	S

Occupation	C Index	Cluster		Occupation	C Index	Cluster
Bookkeeper I	.31	L		Firefighter	.16	L
Bus driver	.17	L		Librarian	.28	L
Keypunch operator	.10	L		Medical technologist	.21	L
Meat cutter	.16	L		Nurse, professional	.15	L
Post office clerk	.13	L		Orderly	−.08	N
Production helper (food)	.24	L		Physical therapist	.34	L
Sales, general (department store)	.20	L		Police officer	.13	L
Sewing machine operator, auto	.03	N		Receptionist, civil service	.29	L
Solderer (production line)	.16	L		Secretary (general office)	.26	L
Telephone operator	.17	L		Taxi driver	.12	L
Teller (banking)	.13	L		Telephone installer	.42	L
				Waiter/waitress	.18	L

Minnesota Importance Questionnaire profile is compared with Occupational Reinforcer Patterns for 90 representative occupations. Correspondence is indicated by the C Index. A prediction of Satisfied (S) results from C values greater than .50, Likely Satisfied (L) for C values between .10 and .49, and Not Satisfied (N) for C values less than .10. Occupations are clustered by similarity of Occupational Reinforcer Pattern. Abbreviations after each cluster refer to the primary values (all capital letters) and secondary values; for example, Achievement (ACH) is a primary value, and Comfort (Com) is a secondary value.

Source: From *A psychological theory of work adjustment* by R. V. Dawis and L. H. Lofquist. Copyright © 1984, University of Minnesota Press. Reprinted by permission.

may demonstrate reactiveness by trying to ignore the superior and by paying attention to other colleagues or the job itself. *Perseverance* refers to how long an individual can tolerate adverse conditions before changing jobs. For example, some people can persevere longer than others in cramped quarters or with an unpleasant superior. These concepts show how individuals deal with a conflict between themselves and their job. Lawson (1993) has had success in measuring three of these dimensions. She has developed an Inflexibility Scale, which measures the low end of the flexibility dimension; an Achievement Scale, which measures the high end of the activeness continuum; and a Reactiveness Scale, which measures some components of poor mental health. These dimensions may be helpful in conceptualizing different solutions to irritating job circumstances.

Another approach focuses on different variables: adaptive performance, satisfaction with change, and well-being while dealing with change (Griffin & Hesketh, 2005; Hesketh & Griffin, 2005). In general, these variables are related to how individuals cope with change in their working lives. Adaptive performance refers to three variables:

1. Proactive behavior—the actions individuals take to make changes in their work environment.
2. Reactive behavior—how individuals make changes in themselves to adjust to work.
3. Tolerant behavior—how individuals tolerate difficult work issues when proactive or reactive behavior do not work.

Satisfaction with changes refers to individuals being able to enjoy the challenge of dealing with change. Factors leading to well-being include personal factors such as cognitive ability, personality factors, and motivational factors, as well as issues in the workplace. Being able to manage stress is also important in individuals' well-being.

By matching the individual's abilities and values with Occupational Ability Patterns and Occupational Reinforcer Patterns, the counselor attempts to increase the likelihood of the client's future job satisfaction and satisfactoriness. This is a major focus of work adjustment theory. Thus, the counselor is trying to find not just an occupation that will be appealing to the client at the moment, but one that will lead to long-term satisfaction or job tenure.

By returning to our example of Winifred, the following dialogue between Winifred and her counselor further illustrates this concept:

CL: I'm wondering what other careers I can consider now that farming looks like it's going to be difficult for me.

CO: Let's look at your Minnesota Importance Questionnaire. [Winifred's scores are those reported in Table 4.5.] Note that it lists some occupations that it predicts would satisfy you (S) or are likely to satisfy you (L). Let's take a look at some of the S occupations. [The counselor wants to work with matches between the client's values as measured by the Minnesota Importance Questionnaire and the Occupational Reinforcer Patterns.]

CL: Oh, this is interesting. I don't think that I would want to be a claims adjuster. There isn't much call for that around here. Commercial artist—that's interesting. I guess that's a dream occupation. I don't think I have the ability to do that. Oh, look, farm equipment mechanic. I am doing that now, sort of. I know there is a demand for that around here. If I could do some light work, may be that would work out for me.

CO: Well, that is one that we can look into. We may need to find out about some specific employers and the kind of work they do. [The counselor's concern is that the client's physical condition will preclude her from being a farm equipment mechanic. However, some employers may have opportunities for work that requires little lifting or standing.]

CL: I see time study engineer on there, too. I don't know what that is.

CO: We can find out more about it. We can use the *Dictionary of Occupational Titles* or the *O*NET* to tell us more about it.

CL: Wow! Programmer—I think that I would like that. I just don't think that I could go back to school. Also, I'm not sure whether I have the mathematical ability that would be necessary.

CO: Well, let's look into that. Let us see how your GATB scores compare with those of programmers. [The counselor then consults the Minnesota Occupational Classification System.]

CL: But what kind of schooling would I need?

CO: Let's look in the *Occupational Outlook Handbook*. [The client and the counselor look at it together. They see that there are several ways of entering the occupation of programmer.]

The client and counselor continue in this manner to investigate possible occupations that the client may consider. The counselor will ask the client to do more reading to find out more about occupations that seem initially attractive. Using a method of matching the client with potential occupations, the counselor has narrowed the number of potential occupations to be considered to about 15. The client and counselor not only will explore occupational information, but they will also examine educational opportunities, physical limitations, salary, and other issues that will affect the client's eventual choice.

Work adjustment theory has produced more than 250 studies that lend support to its validity as an effective method of helping individuals with career choice and work adjustment problems. Research such as that done by Breeden (1993), which followed up 436 adults who had received career counseling, found that, after 2 years, those who had changed jobs and occupations were more satisfied after counseling than before counseling. Following up individuals 8 years after high school graduation, Bizot and Goldman (1993) found that the match between the aptitude of the individual and the aptitude required by the job was a good predictor of satisfactoriness and, to a somewhat smaller extent, job satisfaction. Work adjustment theory has also been found to predict satisfaction of 17 vocational needs for workers who are mentally challenged (Melchiori & Church, 1997). Also studying mentally challenged workers, Chiocchio and Frigon (2006) found that employee performance (satisfactoriness) is the main predictor of successful job placements, not employee satisfaction. Such studies are examples of those that support the value of work adjustment theory in career counseling.

JOB ADJUSTMENT COUNSELING

Work adjustment theory can also be used to assess the types of problems that individuals may have in adjusting to their job. An individual's skills may not yet have been developed sufficiently to meet the skill requirements of the job. Furthermore, the job may require skills that the individual is unable to develop because of lack of education or ability. A frequent problem is that an individual's values and needs are not met by the work environment. Another concern could be that the individual does not understand the reinforcer patterns of the work involved. Sometimes, dissatisfaction with the job is not caused by the job itself but by problems outside of work. For example, a person who is having difficulty at home may carry these problems into the workplace and become dissatisfied with the job as well.

When a client describes problems at work, the basic approach is to make an assessment of the client's work personality and the working environment. Assessing the work values and needs of a client can be done by using the MIQ or, if this is not possible, by using the conceptual schema of the MIQ. Thus, a counselor can determine the significance of each of the 6 values (achievement, comfort, status, altruism, safety, and autonomy) during the counseling session. Furthermore, the counselor can determine which of the 20 needs that make up the 6 values are most relevant for the client by discussing the work environment in terms of the reinforcers offered. The counselor need not ask about each reinforcer specifically, but using the 20 reinforcers as a conceptual system can determine the correspondence between the individual's most important needs and the reinforcers offered by the job.

Similarly, using the nine abilities described by the GATB as a guide, the counselor can assess, in a general sense, the abilities that the client has and the occupational ability patterns of the job itself. Correspondence between the abilities of the client and the abilities required by the job can then be assessed. Although it is possible to use tests such as the GATB, the counselor may choose not to do so, because they take several hours to complete.

Possible solutions for problems can come by assessing the discrepancies between the values and abilities of the individual and the ability and reinforcer patterns of the job. By further understanding the reinforcer patterns of work, the client may be able to improve his or her satisfaction level. Another possibility is to make changes in the work itself so that the reinforcer patterns are altered. For example, a person who values independence may discuss with his or her supervisor ways in which he or she can work alone on the job. When these solutions fail, individuals can look for reinforcers outside the work environment. These might include hobbies and part-time or volunteer work. If none of these suggestions is appropriate, then an individual may consider changing jobs.

The next example shows how a counselor can use work adjustment theory to assist a client with job adjustment counseling. Nick is a 37-year-old Russian American construction worker who is experiencing increasing job dissatisfaction. He works for a construction firm that builds new houses. Doing a variety of construction tasks, especially carpentry, he has worked with the same crew of construction workers for the last 5 years. However, there have been some changes as the crew has grown or shrunk in size and workers have left for other jobs. Recently, a new supervisor has been assigned to the crew. Nick is finding that he dislikes the new supervisor and is considering quitting his job. He seeks guidance from a Veterans Administration counselor whom he had talked to 4 years ago when he was having problems in his marriage. Following is an excerpt from their first session:

CL: My new supervisor, Wally, drives me nuts. I can't stand working with him. I never know where I stand. He never says anything. Other supervisors would give me direction. This guy just stands around like a two-by-four. I always knew where I stood with the other supervisors. With Wally I have no idea. I even ask him questions, and he doesn't give me much of an answer.

CO: Nick, tell me more about what you're doing at work. [The counselor hears that Nick values safety. He seems to feel that supervision, both human relations and technical, is lacking. The counselor wants to hear more before jumping to conclusions.]

CL: Well, we're building some real fancy homes now. We have to follow blueprints and make sure that everybody's doing what they're supposed to—that people aren't knocking into each other, getting in the way. It seems to be the same whether we're framing the house, putting up drywall, or whatever. All Wally does is stand around. Since I've been there a long time, some of the guys look to me for help. That is not my job.

CO: You don't want to be a supervisor? [Nick doesn't seem to want responsibility; he seems to place little value on autonomy, the opposite of safety. However, his supervisor seems to be reinforcing responsibility and not providing much supervision.]

CL: No, I just want to do my job. I want to get paid. I don't want to do the same thing all the time. I don't mind keeping busy, but I'd just as soon do what I'm told.

CO: It sounds as if before working for this supervisor you knew what to expect. You knew what to do and what you were going to do. Now you don't, and it's really frustrating. [Nick needs to be active, to do a variety of work, and to receive compensation. These needs indicate that Nick values comfort as opposed to achievement. A sense of achievement does not seem to be important to him.]

CL: I want to figure out some way to be more comfortable. It's terrible not knowing what to do.

Nick and the counselor will explore how Nick's values of safety and comfort can be met on the job. One solution that may emerge from counseling is discussing strategies to receive more direction from Wally. Another possibility is to determine if Nick can transfer to a different construction crew. The counselor may also wish to consider Nick's adjustment style. Nick does not appear to be flexible. He does not seem to be able to tolerate much discomfort in the work environment. The counselor, together with Nick, may try to decide whether Nick is likely to be able to actively change his environment by talking to his supervisor or to react to the problem by focusing on out-of-job activities and his relationship with his coworkers. In this way, work adjustment theory provides a conceptualization system for the counselor to use to help Nick improve his current work adjustment.

ADJUSTMENT TO RETIREMENT

When people face retirement, they may encounter some problems that have components of both job adjustment and career selection. Often, people have maintained a satisfactory correspondence with the work environment. That is, their work satisfaction is usually good, and their abilities and values match the abilities and reinforcers required and offered by the job. Now, the task is to find work in a "nonwork environment." If the person has found the reinforcers offered by his or her current work to be satisfactory, then the counselor should help the individual find similar reinforcers in a nonwork environment.

To help the client, the counselor will need to make some assessment of skills and ability, as well as of needs and values. This can be done by discussing in some detail the aspects of the current work that the individual finds particularly valuable.

Then, the counselor and client will try to identify environments that will match the individual's needs and abilities. One difficulty for the counselor is that there is relatively little organized information about retirement activities. There are many books and pamphlets on career options and there are several occupational classification systems; however, no comparable system exists for retirement activities. Ideally, a counselor could assess the abilities and needs of a client who was about to retire and match them by using a system similar to the Minnesota Occupational Classification System. However, there is no system for classifying volunteer or retirement activities.

In addition to this concern is the changing nature of the retiree in his or her situation. As people age, their physical abilities change. Assessing these changes is an important aspect of helping the retiring worker. In addition, the financial needs of an individual must be assessed, because the need for earning income may continue. Furthermore, retirees may not be able to move from their current location to take advantage of a variety of community activities, hobbies, and part-time or volunteer work. Thus, there are more constraining factors in retirement counseling than in career decision-making or job adjustment counseling. A case study will help to illustrate some of the factors involved in using work adjustment theory to counsel people on retirement issues.

Henrietta is a 64-year-old African American first-grade teacher living in New Orleans. She is a widow and lives alone. Her two children are married and live out of state. Henrietta has been depressed for several months, which has caused her to seek counseling. As the counselor and Henrietta have talked, it has become clear that her impending retirement is disturbing her very much.

Henrietta has always enjoyed working with small children. Helping others is important to her. One reason that she has enjoyed teaching so much is that most of her colleagues share her views. When her husband died 12 years ago, she became active in her church. This activity helped her deal with her husband's death. Henrietta's religious values are strong. She not only is involved in attending services weekly but also participates in social service projects that her church undertakes. Henrietta wants to be busy. She has enjoyed teaching so much because it has given her an extraordinary sense of accomplishment. She has never felt that her aging has distanced her from her young students. Each year, she has looked forward to a new class.

The counselor recognizes how much Henrietta values altruism. She sees that the reinforcers offered by teaching first-grade children clearly match Henrietta's moral values and social service needs. Furthermore, the counselor assesses how important achievement is to Henrietta. Their task is to discuss alternatives to teaching that will provide similar reinforcers. Because of the retirement plan of her school district, it is economically appropriate for Henrietta to retire at the age of 65 years. However, she feels a need to continue some work to supplement her income. Furthermore, she has many friends in her neighborhood and has strong ties with her church. She has no desire to move.

Many of the options that Henrietta and the counselor discuss have to do with part-time and volunteer activities that would satisfy her values of altruism and achievement. Some of these activities are working at, or possibly supervising, day care activities at a nearby church that is larger than her own. Other alternatives are to assist at a senior center in the neighborhood. Henrietta also considers work with the homeless but is concerned about transportation and safety. After talking with Henrietta for a little while, it is evident to the counselor why Henrietta has been rewarded by the school district for her teaching skills and her human relationship abilities. By concentrating on activities that would reinforce Henrietta's values of altruism and achievement, the counselor gets a sense of which activities are appropriate to consider and which are likely to be unattractive. Henrietta feels that the counselor has helped her, because the suggested alternatives appear to meet her social service and achievement needs.

NEW DEVELOPMENTS

Recently, work adjustment theory has been applied to young, gifted adolescents. Benbow and Lubinski have studied 13-year-old adolescents who scored greater than 370 on the College Board Scholastic Assessment Test (SAT) verbal and 390 on the SAT math for some studies and greater than 430 on the SAT verbal and 500 on the SAT math for other studies (Achter & Lubinski, 2005; Achter, Lubinski, Benbow, & Eftekhari-Sanjoni, 1999; Lubinski & Benbow, 2006; Lubinski, Webb, Morelock, & Benbow, 2001; Schmidt, Lubinski, & Benbow, 1998; Webb, Lubinski, & Benbow, 2002). Their research supports the view of Achter and Lubinski (2003), Lubinski (2000), and Lubinski and Benbow (2000, 2001) that the concepts of satisfaction and satisfactoriness, which are crucial to work adjustment theory, can be applied to the educational adjustment and achievement of 13-year-old gifted students. They examined educational reinforcer patterns of gifted adolescents and described how these youths are able to make educational and vocational decisions at an earlier age than their contemporaries by referring to concepts basic to work adjustment theory. Studying 13-year-old gifted adolescents over a 20-year period, Benbow, Lubinski, and their colleagues find the theory of work adjustment helpful in understanding the educational and vocational choices of these talented students. They believe this is because work adjustment theory considers abilities (satisfactoriness as measured by educational achievement measure) and preferences (satisfaction as measured by interest and values inventories). Lubinski and Benbow (2000) suggest counselors reinforce the effective behaviors of young adolescents rather than reinforce the feelings of these students, which may be more vague and diffuse.

THE ROLE OF ASSESSMENT INSTRUMENTS

Although the preceding examples show that work adjustment theory can be used in counseling without assessment instruments, they are an extremely important component of work adjustment theory. Particularly with regard to career selection, assessment is essential. Furthermore, the development of psychometric instruments has gone hand in hand with the development of work adjustment theory. Of all the instruments developed by the Work Adjustment Project, the Minnesota Importance Questionnaire is the one most likely to be used by counselors. Other instruments have been developed to test the theory: the Minnesota Job Description Questionnaire, the Minnesota Satisfaction Questionnaire (MSQ), the Minnesota

Satisfactoriness Scales, and a biographical information form. Described briefly by Dawis and Lofquist (1984), these instruments, as well as other research, are the subject of 30 monographs published by the University of Minnesota over a period of more than 35 years. Research on psychometric qualities of these instruments continues to be done (Eggerth, 2004), as does psychometric analysis of concepts such as tenure (Myors, 1996). This emphasis on the importance of testing in theory development carries over to Dawis and Lofquist's (1984) approach to counseling. More than other theorists, even other trait and factor theorists, Dawis and Lofquist emphasize the importance of measuring an individual's traits and matching them with information about occupations. Unlike most tests and inventories, their materials are not published commercially (however, they can be purchased from Vocational Psychology Research, Department of Psychology, University of Minnesota). Dawis (2005) points out that although these instruments can be used with work adjustment theory, other instruments may be used as well.

Assessment instruments can be used in combination with each other. For example, Thompson and Blain (1992) describe how a grid can be used to present information from the Minnesota Importance Questionnaire (MIQ). They suggest using a 3 × 3 grid that combines MIQ and MSQ data in low, moderate, and high categories (Figure 4.1). In this way, counselors can group the importance of the 20 client needs and the degree to which they are being satisfied into 9 areas.

Importance \ *Satisfaction*	Low	Moderate	High
Low			
Moderate		Creativity Responsibility Independence Compensation	Activity
High	Ability utilization Achievement		

FIGURE 4.1 | THE IMPORTANCE SATISFACTION GRID, INCLUDING WINIFRED'S DATA FOR SEVEN VOCATIONAL NEEDS.

Source: Adapted from Thompson and Blain, 1992.

The use of this grid can be illustrated by applying it to Winifred, discussed earlier. Winifred has studied computer programming and has worked at a grain company as a programmer for 5 months. She tells the counselor that she has enjoyed learning programming but does not find her current job fulfilling. The counselor asks her to take the MSQ, and then writes in seven of her highest MIQ needs (see Table 4.2, p. 108) in a 3 × 3 grid, placing them in boxes depending on Winifred's MSQ scores (see Figure 4.1). Winifred discusses these scores with her counselor. Her frustration with the lack of challenging work tasks in her current job becomes clearer. Although she enjoys keeping busy (activity), she feels she is basically rewriting programs used in the first few months of her job. She does not feel that she is accomplishing much (achievement) or using her new skills (ability utilization); these needs are important to her. Going over the grid helps Winifred decide that it is important that she get her supervisor to assign her more varied and challenging tasks.

THE ROLE OF OCCUPATIONAL INFORMATION

Occupational information presents a particular challenge for the counselor using work adjustment theory. Normally, a counselor using this theory would make use of the MIQ and the GATB. As shown earlier, each of these instruments provides a list of occupations that fit occupational patterns. In addition, the Minnesota Occupational Classification System lists Occupational Ability Patterns and Occupational Reinforcer Patterns for more than 1,700 occupations. Therefore, if the counselor is to use this system, it is important to have information available that explains these occupations. An important reference is the *Dictionary of Occupational Titles*, which lists definitions of 12,000 occupations. However, since the O*NET is more current, many counselors will use it as their source of information (Gore & Hitch, 2005). Furthermore, pamphlets and books that more fully explain occupations are necessary so that the client can learn more about any occupation that is suggested by the results of the MIQ and the GATB. Although it is certainly not necessary for counselors to know each of the 1,769 occupations in the Minnesota Occupational Classification System, the system is so specific in its recommendations of occupations for individual clients that a wide knowledge of occupational information is helpful to the counselor.

APPLYING THE THEORY TO WOMEN AND CULTURALLY DIVERSE POPULATIONS

Group differences have not been a focus of work adjustment theory. Dawis and Lofquist (1984) have focused on the large differences within groups, rather than the small differences that may exist between groups. For example, there is a wide range of scores on the achievement scale for men and for women (within groups), whereas there are very small differences between men and women on the achievement scale. Although Rounds, Dawis, and Lofquist (1979) report some differences between male and female individuals on various MIQ needs, Flint (1980) describes few differences. Gay, Weiss, Hendel, Dawis, and Lofquist (1971) report that women scored higher than men on the following needs: achievement, activity, company policies and practices, coworkers, independence, and working conditions; men scored higher than women on advancement, authority, creativity, responsibility, security, social status, and supervision. Fitzgerald and Rounds (1993) conclude that few gender differences are found in variables related to work adjustment theory.

The GATB manual (U.S. Department of Labor, 1982) shows that boys score higher than girls on spatial ability, but lower than girls on form perception, clerical ability, eye–hand coordination, and finger dexterity. A review of other research shows only minor differences in the cognitive abilities of men and women (Fitzgerald & Rounds, 1993). Gustafson (1997) suggests that cognitive factors can be helpful in predicting intrinsic job satisfaction. Although there are some differences between men and women in their abilities and preferences for needs, the implications for counseling are negligible. The information available from the Minnesota Occupational Classification System for women and men is identical.

Work adjustment theory can be applied to discrimination experienced by homosexual men and women as well as heterosexual women. Lyons, Brenner, and Fassinger (2005) have shown that work adjustment theory predicts the job satisfaction of lesbian, gay, and bisexual individuals, despite the discrimination that they may experience in their workplace. By attending to the reinforcement values and barriers to developing abilities, both important concepts in work adjustment theory, counselors can help lesbians deal with discrimination that they experience as they choose careers and adjust to problems at work (Degges-White & Shoffner, 2002). Fitzgerald and Rounds (1993) suggest how work adjustment theory can be expanded to encompass two issues related to women in general: integrating work and family and sexual harassment. For example, they suggest that "variables such as convenient and flexible hours of work, or benefits" (p. 343; e.g., leave for a sick child) could be added to the theory's list of needs. Further needs such as "compensation" could be broadened to include benefits such as parental leave for a sick child or child care at the workplace. Regarding sexual harassment, they suggest that the need for "company policies and practices" could include how clear organizations make guidelines on sexual harassment and how well they are implemented.

Dawis (1992) is clear in stating that work adjustment focuses on individual differences in needs, values, abilities, and skills. More specifically, Dawis (1994) says that "gender, ethnicity, national origin, religion, age, sexual orientation, and disability status are seen as inaccurate and unreliable bases for estimating the skills, abilities, needs, values, personality styles, and adjustment style of a particular person" (p. 41). Adding to this view, Rounds and Hesketh (1994) suggest ways in which work adjustment theory could address discrimination based on race or sex. They say that work needs and values could be broadened to include statements that address fairness issues, such as "supervisors create an environment of mutual respect," "my supervisors and coworkers treat me fairly," "promotions are based on merit," and "company policies concerning discriminatory practices are enforced" (p. 184). Such statements give counselors ideas on how work adjustment issues can be conceptualized when clients discuss problems at work related to discrimination by coworkers, supervisors, or customers. A recent investigation of African American employees shows that many indicated the following needs were important to them in predicting job satisfaction: staying busy, independence, compensation, and job security. Racial climate was infrequently mentioned as a predictor of job satisfaction (Lyons & O'Brien, 2006). Bowman (1998) gives a case example of how work adjustment theory can be useful in helping a woman who experienced racism at work. These writings provide suggestions on how work adjustment theory can be used with culturally diverse populations.

COUNSELOR ISSUES

In their book *Essentials of Person-Environment-Correspondence Counseling*, Lofquist and Dawis (1991) apply work adjustment theory to nonwork areas of life—called person-environment-correspondence theory. Dawis and Lofquist (1993) and Dawis (2005) show the value of expanding work adjustment theory in a broader approach to counseling and career development. Lofquist and Dawis (undated) suggest that it is helpful for counselors to see themselves, as well as their clients, as environments. Both the client and the counselor can serve as reinforcers for each other, just as a job environment can serve as a reinforcer for a worker. Lofquist and Dawis suggest that, in the course of training, counselors should identify their own needs and values. Awareness of their needs and values can help counselors understand the effect that they can have on a client. In a counseling session, a counselor should be able to identify the needs of a client. For example, if a counselor has a high need for social service (doing things for others) and the client has a high need for responsibility (deciding on one's own), the altruistic counselor may be frustrated. Realizing that there are differences between the values of the counselor (altruism) and the reinforcement pattern of the client (responsibility) will help the counselor to be less frustrated and more effective. Another example is a client with a strong safety value who may be frustrated by a counselor who uses an unstructured style. Lofquist and Dawis (undated) believe that it is necessary for the counselor to identify basic abilities and reinforcers within himself or herself and the client, so that effective counseling can take place. A key characteristic for a counselor is flexibility. It is important for the counselor to be able to adapt to the environment of the client so that the client's needs can be met. This can be done best when a counselor has knowledge about his or her needs and response requirements, so that the counselor can suspend, when necessary, his or her own needs to meet those of the client.

SUMMARY

The work adjustment theory of Lofquist and Dawis is notable because of its emphasis on specifying the traits of an individual and matching them with job requirements and reinforcers. Work adjustment theory is made up of 18 theoretical propositions that have been supported by research (Dawis & Lofquist, 1984; Lofquist & Dawis, 1991). The theory focuses on the prediction of adjustment to work. For Dawis and Lofquist, an individual's abilities and values can be predictive of work adjustment and length of time on a particular job, if the ability requirements and reinforcer pattern of the job are known. A major contribution of work adjustment theory is the development of the Minnesota Importance Questionnaire, which measures an individual's work needs. Combined with information about abilities, scores on the MIQ can be matched with Occupational Ability Patterns and Occupational Reinforcer Patterns. This matching yields specific occupations for an individual to consider in making a job choice. Broader than many career development theories, work adjustment theory has implications not only for career selection but also for a great variety of other counseling situations. Two that have been discussed in this chapter are job adjustment counseling and retirement counseling. More than any other theory, work adjustment theory represents a clear application of trait and factor theory.

REFERENCES

Achter, J. A., & Lubinski, D. (2003). Fostering exceptional development in intellectually talented populations. In W. B. Walsh (Ed.), *Counseling psychology and optimal human functioning* (pp. 25–54). Hillsdale, NJ: Erlbaum.

Achter, J. A., & Lubinski, D. (2005). *Blending promise with passion: Best practices for counseling intellectually talented youth*. Hoboken, NJ: John Wiley.

Achter, J. A., Lubinski, D., Benbow, C. P., & Eftekhari-Sanjoni, E. (1999). Assessing vocational preferences among gifted adolescents adds incremental validity to abilities. *Journal of Educational Psychology, 91*, 777–789.

Bizot, E. B., & Goldman, S. H. (1993). Prediction of satisfactoriness and satisfaction: An 8-year follow-up. *Journal of Vocational Behavior, 43*, 19–29.

Borgen, F. H., Weiss, D. J., Tinsley, H. E., Dawis, R. V., & Lofquist, L. H. (1968a). *Minnesota Job Description Questionnaire*. Minneapolis, MN: University of Minnesota, Psychology Department, Vocational Psychology Research.

Borgen, F. H., Weiss, D. J., Tinsley, H. E., Dawis, R. V., & Lofquist, L. H. (1968b). Occupational reinforcer patterns. *Minnesota Studies in Vocational Rehabilitation, 24*.

Bowman, S. L. (1998). Minority women and career adjustment. *Journal of Career Adjustment, 6*, 417–431.

Breeden, S. A. (1993). Job and occupational change as a function of occupational correspondence and job satisfaction. *Journal of Vocational Behavior, 43*, 30–45.

Chiocchio, F., & Frigon, J. (2006). Tenure, satisfaction, and work environment flexibility of people with mental retardation. *Journal of Vocational Behavior, 68*(1), 175–187.

Dawis, R. V. (1992). Individual differences tradition in counseling psychology. *Journal of Counseling Psychology, 9*, 7–19.

Dawis, R. V. (1994). The theory of work adjustment as convergent theory. In M. L. Savickas & R. W. Lent (Eds.), *Convergence in career development theories* (pp. 33–44). Palo Alto, CA: Consulting Psychologists Press.

Dawis, R. V. (2002). Person-environment-correspondence theory. In D. Brown & Associates (Eds.), *Career choice and development* (4th ed., pp. 465–509). San Francisco: Jossey-Bass.

Dawis, R. V. (2005). The Minnesota theory of work adjustment. In S. D. Brown & R. W. Lent (Eds.), *Career development and counseling: Putting theory and research to work* (pp. 3–23). Hoboken, NJ: Wiley.

Dawis, R. V., & Lofquist, L. H. (1984). *A psychological theory of work adjustment*. Minneapolis, MN: University of Minnesota Press.

Dawis, R. V., & Lofquist, L. H. (1993). From TWA to PEC. *Journal of Vocational Behavior, 43*, 113–121.

Dawis, R. V., Dohm, T. E., & Jackson, C. R. (1993). Describing work environments as reinforcer systems: Reinforcement schedules versus reinforcer classes. *Journal of Vocational Behavior, 43*, 5–18.

Dawis, R. V., England, G. W., & Lofquist, L. H. (1964). A theory of work adjustment. *Minnesota Studies in Vocational Rehabilitation, 15*, 1–27.

Dawis, R. V., Lofquist, L. H., & Weiss, D. J. (1968). A theory of work adjustment (a revision). *Minnesota Studies in Vocational Rehabilitation, 23*, 1–15.

Degges-White, S., & Shoffner, M. F. (2002). Career counseling with lesbian clients: Using the theory of work adjustment as a framework. *Career Development Quarterly, 51,* 87–96.

Eggerth, D. E. (2004). Applying the Bradley-Terry-Luce method to P-E fit. *Journal of Vocational Behavior, 64,* 92–107.

Farrell, J. N., & McDaniel, M. A. (2001). The stability of validity coefficients over time: Ackerman's (1988) model and the General Aptitude Test Battery. *Journal of Applied Psychology, 86,* 60–79.

Fitzgerald, L., & Rounds, J. (1993). Women and work: Theory encounters reality. In W. Walsh & S. Osipow (Eds.), *Career counseling for women* (pp. 327–354). Hillsdale, NJ: Erlbaum.

Flint, P. L. (1980). Sex differences in perceptions of occupational reinforcers (Unpublished doctoral dissertation, University of Minnesota, 1980).

Gay, E. G., Weiss, D. J., Hendel, D. D., Dawis, R. V., & Lofquist, L. H. (1971). Manual for the Minnesota Importance Questionnaire. *Minnesota Studies in Vocational Rehabilitation, 28,* 1–83.

Gore, P. A., Jr., & Hitch, J. L. (2005). Occupational classification and sources of occupational information. In S. D. Brown & R. W. Lent (Eds.), *Career development and counseling: Putting theory and research to work* (pp. 382–413). Hoboken, NJ: Wiley.

Griffin, B., & Hesketh, B. (2005). Counseling for work adjustment. In S. D. Brown & R. W. Lent (Eds.), *Career development and counseling: Putting theory and research to work* (pp. 483–505). Hoboken, NJ: Wiley.

Gustafson, S. A. (1997). Cognitive processes as dispositional factor in job satisfaction (Doctoral dissertation, University of Mississippi, 1997). *Dissertation Abstracts International: Section B: The Sciences and Engineering, 57/7-B,* 4760.

Hesketh, B., & Griffin, B. (2005). Work adjustment. In B. W. Walsh & M. L. Savickas (Eds.), *Handbook of vocational psychology: Theory, research, and practice* (3rd ed., pp. 245–266). Mahwah, NJ: Erlbaum.

Jeanneret, P. R., & Strong, M. H. (2003). Linking O*NET job analysis information to job requirement prediction: An O*NET application. *Personnel Psychology, 56,* 465–492.

Lawson, L. (1993). Theory of work adjustment personality constructs. *Journal of Vocational Behavior, 43,* 46–57.

Lofquist, L. H., & Dawis, R. V. (1969). *Adjustment to work.* New York: Appleton-Century-Crofts.

Lofquist, L. H., & Dawis, R. V. (1984). Research on work adjustment and satisfaction: Implications for career counseling. In S. Brown & R. Lent (Eds.), *Handbook of counseling psychology* (pp. 216–237). New York: Wiley.

Lofquist, L. H., & Dawis, R. V. (1991). *Essentials of person-environment-correspondence counseling.* Minneapolis, MN: University of Minnesota.

Lofquist, L. H., & Dawis, R. V. (undated). Client and counselor as environments: Implications for counseling (Unpublished manuscript, University of Minnesota, Psychology Department).

Lubinski, D. (2000). Assessing individual differences in human behavior: "Sinking shafts at a few critical points." *Annual Review of Psychology, 41,* 405–444.

Lubinski, D., & Benbow, C. P. (2000). States of excellence. *American Psychologist, 53,* 1–14.

Lubinski, D., & Benbow, C. P. (2001). Choosing excellence. *American Psychologist, 56,* 76–77.

Lubinski, D., & Benbow, C. P. (2006). Study of mathematically precocious youth after 35 years: Uncovering antecedents for the development of math-science expertise. *Perspectives on Psychological Science, 1*(4), 316–345.

Lubinski, D., Webb, R. M., Morelock, M. J., & Benbow, C. P. (2001). Top 1 in 10,000: A 10-year follow-up of the profoundly gifted. *Journal of Applied Psychology, 86,* 718–729.

Lyons, H. Z., Brenner, B. R., & Fassinger, R. E. (2005). A multicultural test of the theory of work adjustment: Investigating the role of heterosexism and fit perceptions in the job satisfaction of lesbian, gay, and bisexual employees. *Journal of Counseling Psychology,* 52(4), 537–548.

Lyons, H. Z., & O'Brien, K. M. (2006). The role of person-environment fit in the job satisfaction and tenure intentions of African American employees. *Journal of Counseling Psychology,* 53(4), 387–396.

Melchiori, L. G., & Church, A. T. (1997). Vocational needs and satisfaction of supported employees: The applicability of the theory of work adjustment. *Journal of Vocational Behavior,* 50, 401–417.

Myors, B. (1996). Utility analysis based on tenure (Doctoral dissertation, University of New South Wales, 1996). *Dissertation Abstracts International: Section B: The Sciences and Engineering,* 57/6-B, 4071.

Rounds, J. B. (1990). The comparative and combined utility of work value and interest data in career counseling with adults. *Journal of Vocational Behavior,* 37, 32–45.

Rounds, J. B., & Armstrong, P. I. (2005). Assessment of needs and values. In S. D. Brown & R. W. Lent (Eds.), *Career development and counseling: Putting theory and research to work* (pp. 305–329). Hoboken, NJ: Wiley.

Rounds, J. B., Dawis, R. V., & Lofquist, L. H. (1979). Life history correlates of vocational needs for a female adult sample. *Journal of Counseling Psychology,* 26, 487–496.

Rounds, J. B., Henly, G. A., Dawis, R. V., Lofquist, L. H., & Weiss, D. J. (1981). *Manual for the Minnesota Importance Questionnaire.* Minneapolis, MN: University of Minnesota, Psychology Department, Work Adjustment Project.

Rounds, J. B., & Hesketh, B. (1994). Emerging directions of person-environment fit. In M. L. Savickas & R. W. Lent (Eds.), *Convergence in career development theories* (pp. 177–186). Palo Alto, CA: Consulting Psychologists Press.

Schmidt, D. B., Lubinski, D., & Benbow, C. P. (1998). Validity of assessing educational-vocational preference dimensions among intellectually talented 13-year olds. *Journal of Counseling Psychology,* 45, 436–453.

Thompson, J. M., & Blain, M. D. (1992). Presenting feedback on the Minnesota Importance Questionnaire and the Minnesota Satisfaction Questionnaire. *The Career Development Quarterly,* 41, 62–66.

U.S. Department of Labor. (1982). *Manual for the USES General Aptitude Test Battery: Section II. Occupational aptitude pattern structure.* Washington, DC: U.S. Government Printing Office.

Webb, R. M., Lubinski, D., & Benbow, C. P. (2002). Mathematically facile adolescents with math/science aspirations: New perspectives on their educational and vocational development. *Journal of Educational Psychology,* 94, 785–794.

HOLLAND'S THEORY OF TYPES

CHAPTER 5

CHAPTER HIGHLIGHTS

The Six Types

Combinations of Types

Explanatory Constructs

Research on Holland's Constructs

The Role of Occupational Information

The Role of Assessment Instruments

Applying the Theory to Women

Applying the Theory to Culturally Diverse Populations

Counselor Issues

It is John Holland's view that career choice and career adjustment represent an extension of a person's personality. People express themselves, their interests, and values through their work choices and experience. In his theory, Holland assumes that people's impressions and generalizations about work, which he refers to as *stereotypes*, are generally accurate. By studying and refining these stereotypes, Holland assigns both people and work environments to specific categories.

Holland (1966, 1973, 1985a, 1992, 1997) has authored five books that explain his typological theory. Each book represents an updated and further refined version of earlier work in the development of his theory. The August 1999 issue of *The Journal of Vocational Behavior* contains 12 articles that describe John Holland's 40-year contribution to career development theory. Two psychological inventories were important in the development of his theory: the Vocational Preference Inventory

(VPI; Holland, 1985b) and the Self-Directed Search (SDS; Holland, Powell, & Fritzsche, 1994). These instruments, in different ways, measure self-perceived competencies and interests, which are an assessment of an individual's personality. Holland (1997) recognized that his theory could account for only a portion of the variables that underlie career selection. He was clear in stating that his theoretical model could be affected by age, gender, social class, intelligence, and education. With that understood, he specified how the individual and the environment interact with each other through the development of six types: Realistic, Investigative, Artistic, Social, Enterprising, and Conventional. Both individuals and environments consist of a combination of types.

THE SIX TYPES

The following sections describe each of the six work environments (Gottfredson & Richards, 1999), followed by a description of the personality type of the person who matches that environment (Low & Rounds, 2006; Spokane & Cruza-Guet, 2005). Next, behavior that can be expected from each type in the context of counseling is discussed. Other important concepts, such as congruence and differentiation, which are discussed later, describe the interaction between the person and the environment. When describing real people and work environments, which are never purely of one type, Holland uses a combination of three types, also discussed later. The relationships among the six types are illustrated in Figure 5.1. The placement of the types on the hexagon is purposeful. The arrangement is explained later in this chapter when the concept of consistency is described.

Realistic

The Realistic Environment   The Realistic (R) environment makes physical demands on the individual. Such work settings have tools, machines, or animals that the individual manipulates. In such a setting, individuals are required to have technical competencies that will allow them to do such things as fix machines, repair electronic equipment, drive cars or trucks, herd animals, or deal with other physical aspects of their environment. The ability to work with things is more important than the ability to interact with other people. Construction sites, factories, and auto garages are examples of environments that provide machinery or other things for Realistic people to master. Some Realistic environments require a great deal of physical agility or strength, such as roofing, outdoor painting, and pipe fitting. These environments may be hazardous and may produce more physical illness or accidents than other work environments.

The Realistic Personality Type   Realistic people are likely to enjoy using tools or machines in their hobbies or work. They tend to seek to develop competencies in such areas as plumbing, roofing, electrical and automotive repair, farming, and other technical disciplines. They are apt to like courses that are practical and teach the use of mechanical or physical skills. Realistic people are likely to have little tolerance of abstract and theoretical descriptions. Often, they approach problems, whether mechanical or personal, in a practical or problem-solving manner.

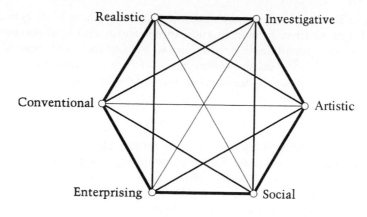

Degree of Consistency	Personality Patterns
———— High	RI, RC, IR, IA, AI, AS, SA, SE, ES, EC, CE
———— Medium	RA, RE, IS, IC, AR, AE, SI, SC, EA, ER, CS, CI
———— Low	RS, IE, AC, SR, EI, CA

FIGURE 5.1 | THE RELATIONSHIPS AMONG HOLLAND TYPES.

Source: Adapted from *Holland's hexagon, ACT research report no. 29* by J. L. Holland, D. R. Whitney, N. S. Cole, and J. M. Richards, Jr. Copyright © 1969. The American College Testing Program. Reprinted by permission.

They are likely to value money, power, and status, while placing a lesser value on human relationships.

BEHAVIOR OF REALISTIC CLIENTS   In the counseling situation, Realistic clients are likely to expect specific suggestions and advice to solve their career problems—a practical solution. Such clients may be somewhat resistant to expressing their feelings about their career choice and prefer to move directly to an answer to the problem of choosing a career. When discussing their activities, they are likely to enjoy talking about such activities as hunting, fishing, and fixing cars. They are apt to discuss things they have done that show an expertise in using tools. They may also talk about specific possessions, such as cars, radios, or other machinery, with which they like to tinker.

Women may encounter more resistance and harassment from men in a Realistic environment than in any of the other five types. Because many of the activities and participants in the Realistic environment tend to be traditionally masculine, Realistic women may encounter a considerable amount of sexism in trying to enter a Realistic occupation such as auto mechanics, coal mining, or roofing. Women who have received encouragement from their fathers and brothers in the development of Realistic competencies may become hurt and angry when they encounter resistance from men in a Realistic working environment. Dealing with such issues requires that the counselor be sensitive to women and support those with Realistic interests and competencies. Still, not all Realistic occupations present such problems. Many occupations have significant Realistic components, yet are not traditionally masculine. Examples include silversmith, dressmaker, floral designer, and inventory clerk.

INVESTIGATIVE

THE INVESTIGATIVE ENVIRONMENT   The Investigative (I) environment is one in which people search for solutions to problems through mathematical and scientific interests and competencies. In such a situation, people are encouraged to use complex and abstract thinking to solve problems creatively. Examples of occupations that offer the opportunity to use analytical thinking skills are computer programmer, physician, mathematician, biologist, science teacher, veterinarian, and research and development manager. In each of these environments, cautious and critical thinking is valued. Individuals are likely to need to use logic and precise methodical thinking to find solutions to problems in these fields. These jobs require that people use their intellect to work independently to solve problems. They are not required or encouraged to use human relations skills to solve problems; they also are not likely to need to use machines. For example, a computer programmer uses logic to figure out solutions to problems (an Investigative environment), whereas the computer technician works with machinery and may assemble or fix it (a Realistic environment).

THE INVESTIGATIVE PERSONALITY TYPE   The Investigative person is likely to enjoy puzzles and challenges that require the use of intellect. Such a person is apt to enjoy learning and to feel confident about his or her ability to solve mathematical and scientific problems. Such people often enjoy reading about science and discussing scientific issues. They seek to work independently to solve problems such as mathematical or scientific questions. They are likely to enjoy courses in math, physics, chemistry, biology, geology, and other physical or biological sciences. They are not likely to enjoy supervising other people or dealing directly with personal problems, but they may enjoy analyzing or searching for solutions to psychological problems.

BEHAVIOR OF INVESTIGATIVE CLIENTS   Clients who are primarily Investigative in their personality tend to enjoy the challenge of an unanswered question. They are often excited by a problem and want to work hard to find a solution, even though there may be relatively little financial or other reward. When it comes to solving a career problem, they may wish to solve it themselves and to approach it from a rational rather than emotional point of view. When the career problem itself is seen as a challenge, they may feel better if they view the counselor as a fellow investigator rather than as an expert who is telling them what to do.

ARTISTIC

THE ARTISTIC ENVIRONMENT   The Artistic (A) environment is one that is free and open, encouraging creativity and personal expression. Such an environment offers much freedom in developing products and answers. Examples of occupations in which people can use creative and unconventional ways to express themselves are musician, fine artist, and freelance writer. Such settings allow people to dress the way they wish, keep few appointments, and structure their own time. These work environments encourage personal and emotional expression rather than logical expression. If tools are used, they are used to express oneself (for example, a clarinet or a paintbrush) rather than as a means to complete a task (for example, an electric drill or a wrench).

THE ARTISTIC PERSONALITY TYPE   The Artistic person likes the opportunity to express himself or herself in a free and unsystematic way, creating music, art, or writing. Such people may use instruments to do this, such as a violin, their voice, sculpting tools, or a word processor. They are likely to want to improve their ability in language, art, music, or writing. Originality and creativity are particularly important in expression. To use a paint-by-numbers kit would be deeply offensive to an Artistic type, who needs and desires the opportunity to express herself or himself in a free and open manner. A pure Artistic type would dislike technical writing and would prefer writing fiction or poetry.

BEHAVIOR OF ARTISTIC CLIENTS   In a counseling session, Artistic clients often make clear how important art, music, or writing is in their lives. They may prefer a nonstructured counseling approach as opposed to one that uses worksheets and written materials. They may enjoy discussing the expression and development of an Artistic product. They may also like to comment on or criticize the products of others. When talking to Artistic people, it becomes clear that their excitement centers on their creative activity. They may enjoy using humor or other methods of expression to show that they are unique and not like other clients. Their expression may be unclear or appear disordered. Often, they discuss their own thinking and creative process. More than any other type, Artistic people are likely to rely on emotions in their discussion of career issues and to see the choice process as an affective rather than a logical one.

SOCIAL

THE SOCIAL ENVIRONMENT   The Social (S) environment is one that encourages people to be flexible and understanding of each other, where people can work with others through helping with personal or career problems, teaching others, affecting others spiritually, and being socially responsible. The Social environment emphasizes human values such as idealism, kindness, friendliness, and generosity. These ideals most commonly exist in the education, social service, and mental health professions. Examples of these occupations are elementary school teacher, special education teacher, high school teacher, marriage counselor, counseling psychologist, speech therapist, school superintendent, and psychiatrist.

THE SOCIAL PERSONALITY TYPE   The Social person is interested in helping people through teaching, helping with personal or vocational problems, or providing personal services. Social people enjoy solving problems through discussion and teamwork rather than through delegation. Preferring to talk and resolve complex problems that may be ethical or idealistic in nature, they often choose to avoid working with machines. They seek out environments where they can use verbal and social skills, such as in education, welfare, and mental health.

BEHAVIOR OF SOCIAL CLIENTS   In a counseling situation, Social people express their idealism, wanting to help others through religion, politics, or social service. Often altruistic, they are more concerned with contributing to a better world than with economic achievement for themselves. They are likely to value informal activities that they have done, such as teaching young children and helping friends with personal problems. When talking with a counselor, they may be interested in the counselor's profession (a Social environment) and appreciative of the counselor's help. Because it is in their nature to be helpful, they may wish to cooperate with their counselor's plans to assist them. Also, their Social nature may make them good candidates for career group counseling, where they may enjoy the opportunity to help others. However, they may be too verbal, because they value talking, making it difficult for the counselor to assist them and other career group members in dealing with questions of career planning.

ENTERPRISING

THE ENTERPRISING ENVIRONMENT   The Enterprising (E) environment is one where people manage and persuade others to attain organizational or personal goals. These are situations where finance and economic issues are of prime importance and risks may be taken to achieve rewards. In such an environment, people tend to be self-confident, sociable, and assertive. It is an environment where promotion and power are important, and persuasion and selling take place. Examples of Enterprising environments are sales work, buying, business management, restaurant management, politics, real estate, the stock market, insurance, and lobbying. All of these environments provide the opportunity for power, status, and wealth.

THE ENTERPRISING PERSONALITY TYPE   The acquisition of wealth is particularly important for Enterprising people. They enjoy being with others and like to use verbal skills to sell, persuade, or lead. They tend to be assertive and popular, trying to take on leadership positions. They enjoy working with people but prefer to persuade and manage rather than to help.

BEHAVIOR OF ENTERPRISING CLIENTS   Enterprising people may present themselves in a self-assured manner. They may appear to be more self-confident than they feel. Some Enterprising people may be quite open about their goal to accomplish wealth, whereas others may be reluctant to admit to a goal that they see as socially inappropriate. Like Social types, they may be very verbal with a counselor and willing to talk about past accomplishments. Unlike Social types, they value convincing and persuading others rather than helping others. In part, because of their self-confidence, Enterprising types may have difficulty seeing their competencies accurately, and thus overestimate their abilities. Enterprising types may be impatient with entry-level positions or occupations that do not lead quickly to the accumulation of wealth, power, or both. They are also likely to experience conflict with other Enterprising types who are competing for both power and money.

CONVENTIONAL

THE CONVENTIONAL ENVIRONMENT   Organization and planning best describe the Conventional (C) environment. Most Conventional environments are office environments, where one needs to keep records, file papers, copy materials, and organize reports. In addition to written material, the Conventional environment includes mathematical materials, such as bookkeeping and accounting records. Word processing, calculating, and copy machines are the type of equipment that is found in a Conventional environment. Competencies that are needed to work well in a Conventional environment are clerical skills, an ability to organize, dependability, and an ability to follow directions.

THE CONVENTIONAL PERSONALITY TYPE   The Conventional person is one who values money, being dependable, and the ability to follow rules and orders. Conventional people prefer being in control of situations and not dealing with ambiguous requests. They enjoy an office environment where their values of earning money and following rules, regulations, and guidelines can be met. Their strengths are their clerical and numerical ability, which they use to solve straightforward problems in their environment. Their relationships with people tend to be directed toward accomplishing tasks and establishing an organized approach to problems.

BEHAVIOR OF CONVENTIONAL CLIENTS   In a counseling situation, Conventional people are likely to present themselves as organized, yet dependent on others for direction. They may have difficulty being open to examining new occupations or career paths on their own initiative. However, they are often proud of their organizational ability in high school extracurricular activities and in business activities. If they have had work experience, they are likely to have had the opportunity to work in an office and enjoyed that experience. If they have worked in environments that were not Conventional, they are likely to have been frustrated by the lack of organization in these environments and probably tried to bring some type of order into their working world. When they explore occupational possibilities, they are most likely to be excited and interested in jobs in financial institutions, such as banks, or in occupations for which they can use counting skills, such as tax expert, inventory controller, and data processor. They are also likely to be interested in financial and accounting analysis. Other personality types are likely to see these jobs as routine or boring. Conventional types appreciate the opportunity to organize and regulate.

COMBINATIONS OF TYPES

Clearly, no real work environment is purely of one type. Rather, most working situations involve a combination of types. When describing occupational environments in *The Occupations Finder* (Holland, 2000) and training environments in *The Educational Opportunities Finder* (Rosen, Holmberg, & Holland, 1994), which accompanies his *Self-Directed Search Professional User's Guide* (Holland,

Powell, & Fritzsche, 1994), Holland uses a three-letter code to designate each of these environments. Holland's *The Occupations Finder* lists 3-letter codes for 1,156 occupations, and *The Educational Opportunities Finder* lists more than 750 programs of study. For example, a bookkeeping environment is not one that is strictly Conventional. It is primarily Conventional, secondarily Investigative, and thirdly Social; it is summarized as CIS. Environments differ in terms of how much they are dominated by one or two types. For example, the bookkeeper may work in a primarily Conventional environment, but a detective may work in an environment that is Social, Realistic, and Enterprising. It would be Social because of the need to help other people; Realistic because of the importance of driving cars, using guns and fingerprint material, and so forth; and Enterprising because of the persuasiveness and assertiveness that are required. Another book, the *Dictionary of Holland Occupational Codes* (Gottfredson & Holland, 1996), lists more than 12,000 occupations that have been coded by translating the U.S. Department of Labor system of *Dictionary of Occupational Titles* (DOT) codes into Holland codes. Thus, it is possible to look up any occupation and determine its three-letter code.

Just as no single environment can be described by one code, it is rare for a person to fit only one Holland psychological type. Through their experiences in school, with hobbies, and with parents, people are exposed to a large number of situations that help them become familiar with certain types of environments. For example, repairing a car exposes one to a Realistic environment, being involved in clubs at school is likely to involve one in a Social environment, and drawing and painting are examples of an Artistic environment. As people are exposed to these activities, they become more interested in certain environments and develop many specific abilities. They become better able to be successful in some environments than in others. As they do this, certain of the Holland types become stronger than others, and their personality type becomes more definite.

These types can be measured by instruments Holland has developed, such as the Vocational Preference Inventory (VPI) or the Self-Directed Search (SDS). In addition, other inventories, such as the Strong Interest Inventory (SII), use Holland's types and can be used to code the interests of individuals according to a three-letter Holland code.

When listening to a client describe his or her career history, it is helpful to think in terms of Holland's six types of people and environments. As a client describes a particular experience, a fit between personality type and interest and experience is likely to become apparent. As the client moves on to another topic, another type is likely to emerge. In this way, the counselor can keep a rough count or impression of the dominant personality types. For example, as a client describes her interest in military activities and parachuting, the counselor conceptualizes these activities in terms of Holland's Realistic type. When she talks about her interest in biology class in high school and her desire to take an advanced course in biology, the notion of interests and abilities in Investigative activities arises. As counselors become more familiar with Holland's theory, it is possible that the mention of activities will "ring a bell," and they will recall the appropriate type that describes the person at the moment. For the beginning counselor, it is often necessary to consciously memorize the Holland types and bring them into active memory to compare the type with the activity being discussed by the client. Sometimes, it is helpful to explain

Holland's system to clients, providing them with an opportunity to organize their thoughts about themselves and the world of work.

EXPLANATORY CONSTRUCTS

Four important constructs for conceptualizing and using Holland's types in counseling are congruence, differentiation, consistency, and identity. These refer to the relationship between the personality and the environment (congruence), the relationship between and the relative importance of types (differentiation), and the relationship of the types with each other (consistency). In addition, knowledge of the concept of identity, which is less directly tied to types, is important for counselors to have.

CONGRUENCE

The term *congruence* refers to the relationship of the personality to the environment. The more similar the personality is to the environment, the more congruent the relationship. Social types tend to enjoy working in a Social environment; Investigative types prefer the Investigative environment. Thus, a Social type working in a sales environment (Enterprising) might find the environment incongruent. An Investigative type working in an Artistic environment might also find that incongruent and would be frustrated by the ambiguity and flexibility that are required in the production of artistic or musical products. Using Holland's three-letter code, an SRA personality would be most congruent with an SRA environment and slightly less congruent with an SRC environment. Likewise, an SIC environment would be more incongruent, and an ICR environment would be quite incongruent with an SRA type of person. Thus, congruence decreases as the similarity between the three-letter code of the person and the environment decreases.

COUNSELING IMPLICATIONS   The concept of congruence is essential in counseling, where it can provide an important goal. A client wishing to make a career choice will want to find an environment that is congruent with his or her personality. It is the counselor's job to assess the client's personality and assist in finding environments that will fit the client according to the Holland type. Working toward the discovery of congruent occupations becomes the major purpose of career-counseling sessions. The counselor thinks about the client and possible career choices in terms of the six Holland types and the degree to which they match.

EXAMPLE OF CONGRUENCE   Jane, a white high school sophomore, has a counseling session with her guidance counselor that includes the following dialogue:

CL: Recently, I was working with a friend who was making a project for her high school science fair. It got kind of messy—we spent a lot of time sorting ants into different piles and developing different terrains—but it was a lot of fun. I was surprised how the time just went by so quickly. In fact, I got in trouble for getting home late. We worked on it Thursday night, and then most of last Saturday.

CO: Sounds like you were really intrigued by all of the different things that you could do. [The counselor encourages the client to keep talking about her interest in the science project to see if her interest in Investigative activities will sustain itself.]

CL: It was a lot of fun. I never knew that observing ants could be so interesting. It really got me thinking about what I might do. I wish that I had thought about doing a science project. But it's too late now.

CO: If you were to do a science project now, what do you think it might be? [The exploration of Investigative activities continues.]

CL: I'm not sure, really. But I think it might have something to do with mice and how they act. I'm taking biology now, and I really like it. I wish that I had room in my schedule next year for another biology course.

CO: You seem surprised that you have so much interest in biology. [The counselor tries to understand how important Investigative activities are to the client and if this is a recent awareness for the client.]

CL: I *am* surprised. I never thought I would like science so much. I've known all along that I enjoy art. My art teachers really like my work, and I enjoy painting. Last summer, I won first place in a contest with one of my paintings.

CO: That sounds exciting. It's great to have things that seem different from each other but are so enjoyable. [While reinforcing the client's enjoyment, the counselor acknowledges the existence of both Investigative and Artistic interests.]

CL: I've thought that it would be neat to do something with science and art after college. I've thought of doing something with biology, becoming a biologist or geneticist or something like that. But I'm not sure what I'd do with art. Sometimes I think that I might like to be an artist or an architect.

CO: These are occupations worth looking into. They certainly fit with the things that you've been telling me so far about yourself. [Without knowing the exact Holland codes for the occupations that the student mentions, the counselor can still tell that the occupations that have been described are congruent with the client's emerging personality type. The counselor is then in a position to find other occupations that may be congruent with the AI type. Furthermore, the counselor will have the opportunity to see if there are other Holland types that reflect the individual's personality. If so, this may help the counselor in finding other occupations to suggest that will be congruent with the client's type.]

DIFFERENTIATION

Both people and environments may differ in terms of how clearly they belong to one or two types. Some people may predominantly resemble one Holland type, whereas others may be quite undifferentiated and have interests and competencies across all six types. Most people are likely to have one, two, or three dominant types. For example, some people enjoy painting, writing, helping others, leading youth groups, and doing volunteer work in a hospital. They may dislike working with machinery, office work, science, and business. Such people would be readily identified as differentiated, because their interests (Social and Artistic) are clearly different from their dislikes (Investigative, Realistic, Conventional, and Enterprising). However, some people enjoy doing all kinds of activities and they do them well. These people are undifferentiated according to Holland's system. Holland determines *differentiation* by subtracting the lowest score of any type from the highest score of any type on the SDS or VPI. Any inventory that measures his six types can be used. A high result indicates a differentiated profile, and a low result indicates an undifferentiated profile.

Just as people vary in terms of differentiation, so do environments. Some environments allow for more freedom of movement to various Holland environments than do others. For example, assembly line work usually allows an individual only the opportunity to do Realistic work—a differentiated environment. In contrast, a teacher working in a university may have the opportunity to do research in his or her field (Investigative), teach students and help them select courses (Social), and possibly consult with industry (Enterprising)—an undifferentiated environment. Sometimes, environments are varied (undifferentiated) enough so that people who at first find that their personality and environment are not congruent can find a way to work within the environment that provides eventual congruence.

For example, a physician who is predominantly Enterprising rather than Investigative (the predominant type of physician) may find enough diversity in a hospital environment to work as a hospital administrator or fundraiser, thus meeting his or her Enterprising needs. To use another example, a secretary working in an office that requires typing, filing, and reception work will find an opportunity to meet both Conventional and Social needs, whereas a secretary in a typing pool will be able to meet only Conventional needs. Thus, environments differ in the degree to which they are differentiated.

COUNSELING IMPLICATIONS   Undifferentiated people are likely to have difficulty in making career decisions and may seek career counseling. One goal of counseling is to help clients to differentiate and broaden their knowledge of their interests, abilities, and values within each of the six types. Some clients who are trying to find a new career goal will find that they have interests and abilities in many different areas (undifferentiated). It is then the counselor's role to discuss more deeply their interests, values, and experiences, and to make explicit for the client the differing values of each of the six types. Other clients may find that they have few interests and low self-estimates of their abilities across all types. Such clients may need to address issues of depression or low self-esteem. The typology serves as a frame of reference for exploring areas of interest of which the client may not be aware. A discussion of a client's experiences with hobbies, part-time work, volunteer work, full-time work, extracurricular activities, and leisure time is apt to give the counselor an opportunity to conceptualize the client according to all six of Holland's personality types. Sometimes, it is not possible to provide further differentiation for a client without more work experience—whether part time, volunteer, or full time. The pursuit of differentiation can be a means of finding a congruent occupation for a client.

EXAMPLE OF DIFFERENTIATION   The client, Chester, is a young Chinese American man who dropped out of high school at the end of the 11th grade. For the last 3 years, he has been employed on an automobile assembly line. He has taken the Self-Directed Search (SDS) at a guidance program offered in the evening at his local high school. His highest score on the SDS was E, and it was considerably higher than R and I, the next highest scores. The following dialogue illustrates how his counselor uses this information, together with Chester's description of career-related experiences, to help Chester in career selection:

CL: When I was in school, there just wasn't very much that interested me. Now I have a job that gets more and more boring. When I first worked in auto-body assembly, I didn't mind it. Things were kind of fun then. Now I've done most of the jobs on the line, and there's never a challenge. It's the same thing all over again.

CO: The assembly work really sounds as if it is bothering you and making you rethink what you want to do. [Perhaps Realistic activities are not for this client. Do the client's R interests match his SDS scores?]

CL: Yes, there are a lot of things that I enjoy doing much more.

CO: Can you tell me about them? [More information about the client's personality, according to the six Holland personality types, is needed to compare with his scores on the SDS.]

CL: Well, on weekends, my friend and I work on cars to resell. It's fun and interesting, and I'm making a lot of extra cash.

CO: Sounds good; I'd like to hear more.

CL: Well, we get old cars from people who are about ready to junk them. We fix the mechanical problems, touch them up with paint, and list them in the newspaper.

CO: Which aspect of this work do you do most? [Realistic interests (in terms of working on cars) and Enterprising interests (for example, selling the cars) sound like possibilities. The counselor revises the original view that Realistic activities are not of interest to this client.]

CL: My friend really knows cars. I help him in some of the simple work. As I've worked with him, I've been able to help him when he takes an engine apart. But I couldn't do that myself. When it comes to people buying the car, I'm the one who sells it. It really is a challenge for me to take something that we've worked on and get someone to buy it. I feel as if we've got a good product, and I want them to know about it.

CO: Is selling something new for you? [The counselor is differentiating between the Realistic and Enterprising interests of the client, choosing to follow up and get more detail on the Enterprising aspect, Chester's highest score on the SDS.]

CL: No, I've sold before. When I was in high school I used to work in a tire store. I sold truck and auto tires, and then put them on. Although I didn't mind putting on new tires, it was more interesting to me to help the customer select tires and buy a real good set. I'd get a commission on what I sold, not a big one, but I liked it.

CO: It sounds as if there were a lot of things that you could take advantage of on that job. [The counselor continues to differentiate the interests in Realistic and Enterprising activities from each other, exploring the differentiation suggested by the disparity in the client's E and R scores on the SDS. This content reflection asks for further differentiation.]

CONSISTENCY

Consistency refers to the similarity or dissimilarity of types. Certain types, whether environment or personality, have more in common with some types than with others. For example, as shown in Figure 5.1 (page 131), Social and Artistic types are similar (close together). In contrast, Social types and Realistic types are quite different from each other, as are Enterprising types and Investigative types. The closer the types are to each other on the chart, the more consistent their characteristics are. For example, Social people tend to like to help others, work as a team, and value their interactions with people; Realistic types prefer not to work with people, but to work with machines and technical challenges. Social people may often have an aversion to machines; that is, Social people tend to have more in common with Artistic and Enterprising types than they do with Realistic individuals. Likewise, Realistic people are apt to have more in common with Investigative and Conventional individuals than with Social people.

Consistency also applies to environments. Some environments require skills and interests that are generally inconsistent. One example is an athletic trainer (SRE). The Social and Realistic environments are inconsistent, yet athletic trainers must help injured athletes who may be under emotional and physical stress. Furthermore, they use a variety of sophisticated medical equipment to remedy injuries. In general, there are few occupations that have codes that are inconsistent. For example, there are no occupations that could be labeled CA. When applied to a working environment, the term *inconsistent* means that the environment requires types of interests and abilities that rarely are required in the same job. Creative and artistic production (A) is seldom seen in conjunction with demands for numerical skill (C) in any occupation. However, individuals with inconsistent types may be able to identify a special niche for themselves. For example, an individual with a CA personality may enjoy organizing a music library for a symphony orchestra.

Consistency is not a goal of counseling, whereas differentiation and congruence can both be goals. Consistency is a more subtle concept than the others. Lack of consistency does not mean that a choice is poor. For example, a person who has inconsistent type (SIC) has not made a poorer career choice than a person who has a more consistent type (SAI). Perhaps the notion of consistency can best be used in counseling by making the counselor aware that it may be difficult to find an environment that will fit two or three inconsistent Holland codes. Often, the client may have to choose an occupation that fits one of the two inconsistent types, but not both. For example, a client with strong Artistic and Conventional interests and skills may choose to do accounting during the day and then moonlight as a musician. It would not be possible to find occupations that would easily incorporate both of these personality types.

Holland (1997) describes a second form of consistency: *consistency of aspirations*. Some clients may have a variety of aspirations or future dreams that vary in their degree of consistency. Some codes may be within one type or two adjoining types. Other codes may be found in types inconsistent with each other. A measure of consistency of aspirations can be obtained by examining the Daydreams section of the SDS. Aspirations or daydreams have always been an important concept to Holland (Spokane & Cruza-Guet, 2005). Knowing what clients daydream about, desire, or aspire to provides useful information to the career counselor in both assessing Holland type and the counseling process itself.

IDENTITY

Identity refers to the clarity and stability of a person's current and future goals. It also refers to the stability of the working environment. If an organization has identity, the tasks and goals of an occupation or employer do not vary widely. Identity is different from any of the other concepts relevant to Holland's system because it does not relate directly to his typology. It is measured not by the VPI or the SDS, but through a third instrument titled My Vocational Situation (MVS; Holland, Daiger, & Power, 1980).

Although the inventory My Vocational Situation will measure the concept of identity, the counselor's assessment of identity in a counseling interview can also prove to be helpful. A question for the counselor to consider is: Now that we are completing career counseling, does this client have a clear idea of career plans and contingency plans, as well as knowledge of how to implement those plans? For example, a man who decides to pursue acting should not only be aware of his interest in this profession but also be able to assess feedback he receives from directors and acting teachers. This man should be aware of the risks in obtaining work, alternative careers when unemployed, contacts for employment, and so on. To start looking for work without planning would be to have a diffuse sense of identity. To use another example, a young woman who wants to be a lawyer because lawyers make good salaries and work on exciting cases has not yet formed a sense of identity. Only when she has information about how to become a lawyer and whether she would like the duties of a lawyer will her sense of identity become clearer.

Identity can be an important goal of career counseling. Achievement of identity may occur when the goal of congruence has been accomplished. If a woman decides on the occupation of roofer, believing that laying new roofs would be something that she is able to do and would enjoy (congruence between person and environment), a sense of identity will develop. As she moves from one job site to another, her goals may stabilize, and she may grow more certain of her interests and abilities.

RESEARCH ON HOLLAND'S CONSTRUCTS

Holland's theory has produced more than 600 studies, which is more research than any other career development theory. Holland himself has been very influential in the production of research and the compilation of it. His five books (1966, 1973, 1985a, 1992, 1997) are indications of his continuing work to refine existing and develop additional theoretical constructs. Research on career development is reviewed periodically in the *Journal of Vocational Behavior*, the *Career Development Quarterly*, and the *Journal of Career Assessment*. These reviews devote a section to discussions of current research on Holland's theory.

Congruence is the most important of Holland's concepts and the one that is most widely researched. What seems like a straightforward concept is actually quite complex. For example, Brown and Gore (1994) evaluated 10 different methods of measuring congruence between personality type and employment, and Camp and Chartrand (1992) examined 13 methods. Many studies have related congruence to other important variables such as stress, job satisfaction, and personality variables. Using nine female and seven male samples to assess measures of complexity, Hoeglund and Hansen (1999) found small relationships between congruence and satisfaction across Holland types. In reviewing recent studies, the relationship between congruence measures and job satisfaction appears to differ widely depending on the way that congruence is measured and on the design of the study (Spokane, Luchetta, & Richwine, 2002). Recently, Eggerth & Andrew (2006) have proposed the C index to determine congruence when using Holland codes of unequal length. Some recent studies on congruence illustrate a variety of ways in which congruence can be studied. Examining 80,574 students attending 87 colleges, grade point average was predicted by the degree of congruence of interests and chosen major (Tracey & Robbins, 2006). In a smaller study at one college, there was a significant relationship between congruence of interest and major for Investigative, Social, and Conventional personality types, but not for the other types (Brown, 2006). Studying employed young adults, congruence of interest inventory scores and current job were related to satisfaction (Dik, 2006). However, congruence was more closely related to job satisfaction for individuals who placed less importance on their jobs than for individuals who placed more importance on their jobs. In Australia, adult career changers' Holland type as measured by the Self-Directed Search was more congruent with preliminary new career choices than with their current career choice (Donohue, 2006). Because of the different ways that congruence can be measured and the different variables, such as personality and achievement, that it can be related to, congruence is likely to be an important focus of research for some time.

Another area of research involves studying the relationship of Holland's personality types to various personality characteristics. The personality inventory that is most frequently paired with Holland's typology is the NEO Five-Factor Model (FFM). This inventory measures five broad factors known as the big five: Extraversion, Neuroticism, Agreeableness, Conscientiousness, and Openness to Experience. Two recent meta-analyses find relationships between the two instruments. Both Barrick, Mount, and Gupta (2003) and Larson, Rottinghaus, and Borgen (2002) find that Holland's Artistic type is related to an open style of personality, and Enterprising is related to Extraversion. In addition, Larson, Rottinghaus, and Borgen find that Holland's Social type is related to Extraversion and agreeableness, and the Investigative type is related to openness. Staggs, Larson, and Borgen (2003) note that when more specific measures of interest and personality are used, different relationships between personality and interest are found. DeFruyt (2002) reports that congruence across RIASEC type predicted job satisfaction. This prediction was enhanced when FFM traits were added. In comparing the Five-Factor Model of personality with Holland's typology, Hogan and Blake (1999) conclude that Holland's inventories measure identity, whereas the FFM personality inventory measures reputation—that is, an observer's view of an individual's personality. When the FFM was studied from the perspective of how it could be used as a supplement to the Self-Directed Search in assisting undecided students choose majors, the FFM added only marginal help, and the Self-Directed Search itself was only partially helpful (Crohan, 2006). Comparisons between Holland's typology and the FFM are a significant area of current research. In a study of individual differences used in career counseling, Armstrong, Day, McVay, and Rounds (2008) find that Holland's theory of six types is not sufficient to describe individual differences, but that personality factors as well as abilities should also be considered.

Although some studies have focused on redefining and developing consistency (Nauta & Kahn, 2007; Sanchez, 2002) and differentiation (Roberti, Fox, & Tunick, 2003), vocational identity has received the most recent attention. Leung, Conoley, Scheel, and Sonnenberg (1992) report no relationship between scores on the Vocational Identity Scale (VIS) of My Vocational Situation and consistency and differentiation. Analyzing the structure of the Vocational Identity Scale, Toporek and Pope-Davis (2001) show that identity is clearly measured by the VIS for both African American and white college students. Conneran and Hartman (1993) report that chronically career-undecided high school students showed lower levels of congruence and vocational identity than those students who were not chronically undecided. Nauta and Kahn (2007) found that higher identity status was associated with higher self-efficacy about one's career decision-making and a greater differentiation of interests. For male substance abusers, success in treatment was associated with a greater degree of identity, as measured by the My Vocational Situation (MVS) Hankinson (1998). On a theoretical level, Vondracek (2007) has criticized Holland's definition of identity as being oversimplified and less complex than "identity" as originally described by Erik Erikson.

Holland's theory has attracted researchers for several reasons. Holland defines his terms clearly and simply. His theory is directly related to the practice of vocational counseling. Most studies on Holland's concepts do not require longitudinal research or extensive follow-up studies. Also, John Holland has been very involved in research on his theory and helpful to those who wish to engage in research related to his work. In general, the research on Holland's theory offers counselors confidence that Holland's concepts have merit and can be used for counseling conceptualization.

THE ROLE OF OCCUPATIONAL INFORMATION

Holland's typological system is particularly useful to clients because it helps to integrate occupational information into the counseling process. By dividing all occupations (or environments) into six types, Holland gives the client an easy framework to use for conceptualizing all occupations. With this system, clients are less likely to ask, "Are there some occupations that I have never considered?" Using this system, counselors have a clear approach to explaining the world of work. Both client and counselor can use *The Occupations Finder* (Holland, 2000) to identify a thousand of the more common occupations and *The Educational Opportunities Finder* (Rosen, Holmberg, & Holland, 1994) to identify more than 750 programs of study. If more detail is wanted, Holland's *Dictionary of Holland Occupational Codes* (Gottfredson & Holland, 1996) lists 12,099 occupations sorted by Holland code.

For the counselor, Holland's typological system is a helpful way to group occupational information. Not only can Holland's system be used to classify items in an occupational library, but it can also be used by a counselor to classify the client's experiences with environments. For example, as a counselor talks to employers about their needs for employees, the environment that the employers describe can be classified mentally by the counselor. In a similar way, as a client describes work experience that he or she has enjoyed or disliked, the environment can also be classified according to Holland type. The knowledge gained from experiences such as visiting factories, reading occupational information, and talking to other counselors about work can be used to help in identifying occupations according to Holland type. By practicing with the Holland system, whether formally or informally, the counselor becomes increasingly familiar with it.

THE ROLE OF ASSESSMENT INSTRUMENTS

Inventories have had two purposes in Holland's system. The first use is in the development of the theory. For example, the Vocational Preference Inventory was initiated before Holland's theory and was partly responsible for the definition of his six types of people and environments. The VPI and the SDS then became research instruments to verify and validate Holland's theory. The second use of inventories is for individuals in need of career assistance. By using the SDS, the VPI, or another inventory that yields Holland types, the counselor can establish an objectively determined personality type for the client. By comparing the counselor's assessment of the client's Holland type with that of an objective inventory, the counselor can get confirmation or try to determine why there is a discrepancy, if one exists. By doing so, the counselor is likely to gain further insight into the client's interests, abilities, and values. Assessment is an important part of the development of Holland's theory. Making use of validated and reliable information can be a great help to counselors in working with clients.

Several inventories related to Holland's typology have been developed. Since the original version of the Self-Directed Search-R (regular), several other versions have been published, including an Internet version. There are Canadian and Spanish forms of the SDS, and a Chinese version has been tested (Yu & Alvi, 1996). Additionally, Wong's Career Interest Inventory is different than the Self-Directed Search and was developed for citizens of Hong Kong and other Chinese societies (Wong & Wong, 2006). Also, an easier form of the SDS, SDS-Form E, has been designed for adolescents and adults with limited (sixth-grade level) reading skills. The SDS-Career Planning has been developed for adults who aspire to greater levels of professional responsibility. It does not include Daydream or Self-Estimate sections. The SDS-Career Explorer focuses on helping middle school students with educational and vocational planning. Although the SDS was designed to be self-scoring, scan sheets and computer-based interpretive reports are available.

In addition to the SDS, Holland and colleagues have developed several other useful inventories. The Career Attitudes and Strategies Inventory (CASI) was designed to assess the views of adults toward work. Scales include Job Satisfaction, Work Involvement, Skill Development, Dominant Style, Career Worries, Interpersonal Abuse, Family Commitment, Risk-Taking Style, and Geographical Barriers (Holland & Gottfredson, 1994). The Position Classification Inventory (Gottfredson & Holland, 1991) was developed to classify positions according to Holland type. This 84-item inventory, which takes only 10 minutes to complete, can be given to large numbers of people who do the same type of work to determine the Holland code for a specific job. The Environmental Identity Scale (EIS; Gottfredson & Holland, unpublished data, 1996) assesses workers' views about the explicitness and consistency of employers' goals, work rules, and rewards. The RIASEC Activities List groups life activities of adults into the six Holland categories and was designed to clearly categorize activities that may offer cognitive benefits for adults (Parslow, Jorm, Christensen, & Mackinnon, 2006). These instruments show that Holland and his colleagues have been active in the development of measures to assess individuals, as well as their environments.

APPLYING THE THEORY TO WOMEN

Because Holland's system has six clearly defined types supplemented by explanatory constructs such as congruence, consistency, and differentiation, it has been the subject of a great deal of research. Much of the research has used both male and females, thus providing data on the appropriateness of Holland's theory for women. Holland (1997) has shown that men are more likely to score high on the Realistic, Investigative, or Enterprising scales, whereas women may score higher on the Social, Artistic, and Conventional scales. Holland's conclusion about summary codes is somewhat similar to that of Reardon, Bullock, and Meyer (2007), who analyzed 2000 census data that reflected the occupational choices of 120 million people in the United States. Men were employed predominately in the Realistic categories (44% vs. 15% for women) and Enterprising categories (31% vs. 28% for women), whereas women more often had Social careers (24% vs. 8% for men) and Conventional careers (26% vs. 6% for men). Murray and Hall (2001) and Roberti, Fox, and Tunick (2003) report somewhat similar findings. Some critics of Holland's theory have taken these differential preferences to mean that Holland's theory is biased against women. Holland points out that his system is a reflection of society and cultural expectations; it does not determine them.

Regarding Holland's concept of congruence, his review (1997) shows that the SDS or the VPI can predict occupational choice or entry about equally well for men and women. In general, Holland, Powell, and Fritzsche (1994) conclude that the predicted validities of aspirations and assessment tend to be greater for women than for men. Although there is less research on consistency and differentiation, there seems to be little difference in these two concepts when the gender variable is examined. In concluding their discussion of sex differences, Holland, Powell, and Fritzsche (1994) state that "women are most likely to have low scores on R and high scores on S" (p. 37). Thus, Holland points out those types that have been most influenced by cultural stereotyping.

Research on Holland's typology and theoretical constructs usually contains information that addresses the issue of male–female differences on relevant variables. Lent, Tracey, Brown, Soresi and Nota (2006) report that Holland's hexagon generally represented the interests of male and female Americans and Italian middle and high school students, but this adherence was more pronounced for Italian female than male students. In a sample of 69,987 eighth-, tenth-, and twelfth-grade American students, Darcy and Tracey (2007) found that Holland's model fit well across gender depending on the method used to analyze the structure of interests. Relating Millon's personality styles to Holland's typology, Rees (1999) reports that women's orientation to relationships was related to high scores on Social and, to a lesser extent, on Artistic. Women's orientation toward independence, separation, and autonomy was related to higher scores on Enterprising and Conventional scales. When studying self-efficacy, there were minimal differences between genders on the six Holland types (Betz, Borgen, Kaplan, & Harmon, 1998; Betz, Harmon, & Borgen, 1996). Both self-efficacy and the influence of role models had an effect on career choices for all six Holland types except for Investigative for college women (Quimby & DeSantis, 2006). For middle school students, participation in computer-assisted career interventions and exploration activities in small groups helped students to increase their interests in Holland types that are typically not associated with their gender, such as Realistic occupations for girls (Turner & Lapan, 2005). Studies such as these help to demonstrate how Holland's theory applies differently to men and women.

APPLYING THE THEORY TO CULTURALLY DIVERSE POPULATIONS

Holland's theory and instruments have been used internationally and with culturally diverse populations in the United States. Research (Spokane & Cruza-Guet, 2005) in countries such as China, Israel, France, Nigeria, New Zealand, and Australia gives some support to the use of Holland's six categories and the constructs of congruence, consistency, and differentiation (although there has been less work on the latter two concepts).

Recent studies have examined how well Holland's hexagon fits people from a variety of backgrounds and cultures. Comparing the interests of African Americans, Mexican Americans, Asian Americans, Latino/as, Native Americans, and Anglo individuals, Tracey and Robbins (2005) reported that Holland's circular structure of interests adequately represented the interest structure of these groups and did not vary by gender or ethnicity. Swanson (1992) reported that, in general, Holland's typology fit African American female college students somewhat better than African American males. Kaufman, Ford-Richards, and McLean (1998) report that African American adolescents and adults scored higher on Social, Enterprising, and Conventional scales on the Strong Interest Inventory, and white participants scored higher on Realistic and Investigative themes in their sample. Comparing poor inner-city middle school students with more affluent middle school adolescents, Turner and Lapan (2003) report that the two groups saw relationships between occupations in Enterprising and Social themes differently. In examining factors influencing career choices of Asian Americans, Tang, Fouad, and Smith (1999) reported that lower acculturated Asian Americans scored higher on Realistic and Investigative occupations than did more acculturated college students. In a study of Mexican American high school students, the RIASEC order was supported for female students but not male students (Flores, Spanierman, Armstrong, & Velez, 2006). However, information about the appropriateness of Holland's typological system for specific cultural groups is neither sufficient nor consistent enough to allow generalizations about its usefulness for specific groups.

Holland's typological system has also been studied in cultures outside of North America. Studies in China have typically not supported Holland's model of the structure of interests. Long and Tracey (2006) found that Holland's model did not fit Chinese individuals as well as it fit individuals in the United States. In Hong Kong and mainland China, Holland's model of the structure of interests was studied with individuals aged 18 to 50, yielding a misshapen RIASEC hexagon (Yang, Stokes, & Hui, 2005). In a study of Chinese high school students, Holland types tended to cluster into groups: Realistic and Investigative, Artistic, and Enterprising and Conventional, with Social interests found in the last two groupings (Leung & Hou, 2005). Using the Personal Globe Inventory rather than the Self-Directed Search, Long, Watanabe, and Tracey (2006), unlike the studies above, did find that Holland's typological model fit the students well. However, most studies in China have not supported Holland's model.

The structure of Holland's model has also been studied in many other areas of the world. Support for Holland's typological model has been found among Native Hawaiians (Oliver & Waehler, 2005). Support for the model was also found in a sample of Irish high school students (Darcy, 2005). For Italian middle and high school students, those who engaged in career exploration were more likely to fit the RIASEC model the following year than those who did not. This was especially true for middle school students (Tracey, Lent, Brown, Soresi, & Nota, 2006). In Croatia, Holland's RIASEC model was supported in a study of 1,866 adolescents (Šverko & Babarovic, 2006). However, in a study using the 16 PF Adolescent Personality Questionnaire that was translated into the Basque language, the RIASEC model was not supported, although a RASIEC model was found for adolescents living in the Basque Country region of Spain (Elosua, 2007). In South Africa, du Toit and de Bruin (2002) and Watson, Stead, and Schonegevel (1998) report that Holland's typology did not provide a good fit with the interests of disadvantaged black South African youths. For Chamorros and Filipino high school students living in Guam, interests were described better by a three-, four-, or five-type model than by Holland's typology (Sanchez, 2002). Studying university students in Iceland, Einarsdottir, Rounds, Aegisdottir, and Gerstein (2002) reported that Holland's RIASEC structure was a good fit for both men and women. These studies are typical of some of the more recent cross-cultural research that has tested Holland's theory.

Information about the distribution of the Holland types of different cultural groups working in the United States provides a useful perspective on the employment of culturally diverse populations. In her study of the distribution of workers by ethnic group, Arbona (1989) reports that more Hispanic (71%) and African American men (68%) than white men (54%) were employed in Realistic types of work. Furthermore, fewer African American (10%) and Hispanic men (6%) than white men (23%) were in Enterprising occupations. With regard to women, more African American (37%) and Hispanic women (41%) than white women (24%) were employed in Realistic jobs. More white women (15%) than African American (7%) and Hispanic women (10%) were employed in Enterprising occupations. In a further analysis of these data, Arbona reports that African American and Hispanic men were more often employed in low-level Realistic jobs. Arbona (1989) suggests that African American and Hispanic students may be exposed to role models working in relatively low-level jobs. Such data are not a critique of Holland's theory but rather show its use in identifying social inequities.

COUNSELOR ISSUES

Research on providing appropriate counseling techniques and approaches for different Holland types yields insights into how best to meet the career counseling needs of individuals who are predominantly of one Holland type. Boyd and Cramer (1995) report that Social and Enterprising college students preferred counseling with unlimited sessions, little structure in the sessions, a focus on self-awareness, and the opportunity for follow-up counseling. They preferred a less concrete focus than did Realistic or Conventional college students. Using a description of six counseling approaches that corresponded to each of Holland's six environments, Niles (1993) reports that students identified as a specific Holland type tended (but not strongly) to select a counseling approach similar to their type. This was particularly true of Realistic and Enterprising male students and was less true of Investigative, Artistic, and Conventional male students and of females in general. Holland's theory with clients of different Holland types are discussed next.

Although there are a number of counselor aids built into the Holland system, such as methods for conceptualizing client problems, classifying occupational information, and incorporating inventories, there are some problems that counselors are likely to encounter. A few potential problem issues can be described by using the concepts of congruence and differentiation.

In this chapter, the discussion has focused on the congruence between the client's personality and his or her working environment. Often, the client's and the counselor's personality types are incongruent. For counselors, the most common types are SE, SI, or SA. Most counselors are predominantly Social; many are secondarily Enterprising, Investigative, or Artistic. When counselors with these Holland codes encounter clients who are primarily Realistic and/or Conventional, they are dealing with a type quite opposite to and incongruent with their own. A major concern is that the values of the counselor, in terms of valuing personal interaction and helping, are likely to be different from those of the client. Being aware of this divergence of values can help counselors be more open toward and understanding of interests, abilities, and values that are different from their own. Many counselors may not respect hunting, fishing, being outdoors, fixing cars, and so on, but their Realistic clients will. Appreciating the differences among incongruent types can be helpful in providing good counseling.

Another problem concerns Holland's concept of differentiation. Counselors are likely to be differentiated according to their preference for types of environments. Because they have made a career choice, they are likely to have preferences for two or three types and lack interest in three or four types. For clients of any age who are having difficulty with career selection, there may be little differentiation among four, five, or all six types. For example, a client may enjoy and have abilities in Social, Realistic, Enterprising, Conventional, and Artistic activities. It then becomes the counselor's role to help further differentiate the client's experiences and desires, perhaps ascertaining that Realistic and Conventional activities are most satisfying. Counselors may become frustrated with the client's difficulty in differentiating when the counselor is not having that difficulty. Being aware of this divergence often helps the counselor become more patient.

There are times when Holland's personality theory will not suffice. For example, there are 53 RIE, 30 REI, and 17 SEA occupations listed in *The Occupations Finder* (Holland, 2000). Holland's theory does not provide enough information for the client to choose within a specific three-letter category, such as RIE. Other factors such as geographical location or non-Holland personality factors may also need to be considered. Arriving at a code for a client is an important step in counseling, not the end of the counseling process. For some clients, Holland's theory provides a start for differentiating interests and talents or for developing a sense of identity. Other factors such as education, ability, location, and/or personal responsibilities to family may be equally important, if not more so, than personality types. Holland's theory is a useful way of conceptualizing client concerns, but it does not provide a conceptualization system that will work with all clients, all problems, all of the time.

SUMMARY

John Holland's typological theory has been accepted widely by counselors and psychologists for several reasons. Conceptually, it is easy to use because the six personality types—Realistic, Investigative, Artistic, Social, Enterprising, and Conventional—can be matched with a corresponding environment. Usually, an individual and an environment are described by the most important, the second in importance, and the third in importance of the six categories. When the three letters of the code describing the person and the environment match or approximate a match, then congruence results. Congruence, the most important of Holland's constructs, is sought by assessing the type of the client and trying to match the type with appropriate occupations. Other constructs, such as consistency, consistency of aspirations, differentiation, and identity are also valuable in using Holland's theory conceptually. Because Holland's theoretical constructs are clearly defined, they have generated much research relevant to the applicability of his theory to all individuals, including women and culturally diverse populations. The occupational classification system that has been developed using the three-letter code is another practical aid for counselors. Several inventories besides Holland's Self-Directed Search and Vocational Preference Inventory are useful in identifying the client's type. Because of its wide acceptance by counselors and the abundance of supportive research, Holland's theory is likely to be used widely in the future.

REFERENCES

Arbona, C. (1989). Hispanic employment and the Holland typology of work. *Career Development Quarterly*, 37, 257–268.

Armstrong, P. I., Day, S. X., McVay, J. P., & Rounds, J. (2008). Holland's RIASEC model as an integrative framework for individual differences. *Journal of Counseling Psychology*, 35(1), 1–18.

Barrick, M. R., Mount, M. K., & Gupta, R. (2003). Meta-analysis of the relationship between the Five-Factor Model of personality and Holland's occupational types. *Personal Psychology*, 56, 45–74.

Betz, E., Borgen, F. H., Kaplan, A., & Harmon, L. W. (1998). Gender and Holland type as moderators of the validity and interpretive utility of the Skills Confidence Inventory. *Journal of Vocational Behavior*, 53, 281–299.

Betz, N., Harmon, L., & Borgen, F. H. (1996). The relationships of self-efficacy for the Holland themes to gender, occupational group membership, and vocational interests. *Journal of Counseling Psychology*, 43, 90–98.

Boyd, C. U., & Cramer, S. H. (1995). Relationship between Holland high-point code and client preference for selected vocational counseling strategies. *Journal of Career Development*, 21, 213–221.

Brown, M. P. (2006). The effect of person/environment congruence on academic achievement in college students: A test of Holland's theory. *Dissertation Abstracts International: Section A: Humanities and Social Sciences*, 67/4-A, 1239.

Brown, S. D., & Gore, R. A., Jr. (1994). An evaluation of interest congruence indices: Distribution, characteristics, and measurement properties. *Journal of Vocational Behavior*, 45, 310–327.

Camp, C. C., & Chartrand, J. M. (1992). A comparison and evaluation of interest congruence indices. *Journal of Vocational Behavior, 41,* 162–182.

Conneran, J. M., & Hartman, B. W. (1993). The concurrent validity of the Self-Directed Search in identifying chronic career indecision among vocational education students. *Journal of Career Development, 19,* 197–208.

Crohan, D. F. P. (2006). The utility of the Holland model with the Five-Factor Model to guide the undecided student toward academic major selection. *Dissertation Abstracts International: Section B: The Sciences and Engineering, 66/8-B,* 4527.

Darcy, M. U. A. (2005). Examination of the structure of Irish students' vocational interests and competence perceptions. *Journal of Vocational Behavior, 67(2),* 321–333.

Darcy, M. U. A., & Tracey, T. J. G. (2007). Circumplex structure of Holland's RIASEC interests across gender and time. *Journal of Counseling Psychology, 54(1),* 17–31.

Dik, B. J. (2006). Moderators of the Holland-type congruence-satisfaction and congruence-performance relations. *Dissertation Abstracts International: Section B: The Sciences and Engineering, 66/8-B,* 4520.

Donohue, R. (2006). Person-environment congruence in relation to career change and career persistence. *Journal of Vocational Behavior, 68(3),* 504–515.

du Toit, R., & de Bruin, G. P. (2002). The structural validity of Holland's RIASEC model of vocational personality types for young Black South African men and women. *Journal of Career Assessment, 10,* 12–77.

Eggerth, D. E., & Andrew, M. E. (2006). Modifying the C index for use with Holland codes of unequal length. *Journal of Career Assessment, 14(2),* 267–275.

Einarsdottir, S., Rounds, J., Aegisdottir, S., & Gerstein, L. H. (2002). The structure of vocational interests in Iceland: Examining Holland's and Gati's RIASEC models. *European Journal of Psychological Assessment, 18,* 85–95.

Elosua, P. (2007). Assessing vocational interests in the Basque Country using paired comparison design. *Journal of Vocational Behavior, 71(1),* 135–145.

Flores, L. Y., Spanierman, L. B., Armstrong, P. I., & Velez, A. D. (2006). Validity of the Strong Interest Inventory and Skills Confidence Inventory with Mexican American high school students. *Journal of Career Assessment, 14(2),* 183–202.

Gottfredson, G. D., & Holland, J. L. (1991). *Position Classification Inventory professional manual.* Odessa, FL: Psychological Assessment Resources.

Gottfredson, G. D., & Holland, J. L. (1996). *Dictionary of Holland occupational codes* (3rd ed.). Odessa, FL: Psychological Assessment Resources.

Gottfredson, L. S., & Richards, J. M., Jr. (1999). The meaning and measurement of environments in Holland's theory. *Journal of Vocational Behavior, 55,* 57–73.

Hankinson, G. L. (1998). The relationship of vocational identity and other mitigating variables to progress in substance dependence treatment in a therapeutic community (Doctoral dissertation, University of Michigan, 1998) *Dissertation Abstracts International: Section A: Humanities and Social Sciences, 59/1-A,* 0092.

Hoeglund, T. J., Hansen, J.-I. (1999). Holland-style measures of congruence: Are complex indices more effective predictors of satisfaction? *Journal of Vocational Behavior, 54,* 471–482.

Hogan, R., & Blake, R. (1999). John Holland's vocational typology and personality theory. *Journal of Vocational Behavior, 55,* 41–56.

Holland, J. L. (1966). *The psychology of vocational choice.* Waltham, MA: Blaisdell.

Holland, J. L. (1973). *Making vocational choices: A theory of careers.* Englewood Cliffs, NJ: Prentice Hall.

Holland, J. L. (1985a). *Making vocational choices: A theory of personalities and work environments* (2nd ed.). Englewood Cliffs, NJ: Prentice Hall.

Holland, J. L. (1985b). *Manual for the Vocational Preference Inventory.* Odessa, FL: Psychological Assessment Resources.

Holland, J. L. (1992). *Making vocational choices: A theory of vocational personalities and work environments.* Odessa, FL: Psychological Assessment Resources.

Holland, J. L. (1997). *Making vocational choices: A theory of vocational personalities and work environments* (3rd ed.). Odessa, FL: Psychological Assessment Resources.

Holland, J. L. (2000). *The Occupations Finder.* Odessa, FL: Psychological Assessment Resources.

Holland, J. L., Daiger, D. C., & Power, P. G. (1980). *My Vocational Situation: Description of an experimental diagnostic form for the selection of vocational assistance.* Palo Alto, CA: Consulting Psychologists Press.

Holland, J. L., & Gottfredson, G. D. (1994). *Career Attitudes and Strategies Inventory: An inventory for understanding adult careers.* Odessa, FL: Psychological Assessment Resources.

Holland, J. L., Powell, A. B., & Fritzsche, B. A. (1994). *The Self-Directed Search professional user's guide.* Odessa, FL: Psychological Assessment Resources.

Kaufman, A. S., Ford-Richards, J. M., & McLean, J. E. (1998). Black-White differences on the Strong Interest Inventory General Occupational Themes and Basic Interest Scales at ages 16 to 65. *Journal of Clinical Psychology, 54,* 19–33.

Larson, L. M., Rottinghaus, P. J., & Borgen, F. H. (2002). Meta-analyses of Big Six interests and Big Five personality factors. *Journal of Vocational Behavior, 61,* 214–239.

Lent, R. W., Tracey, T. J. G., Brown, S. D., Soresi, S., & Nota, L. (2006). Development of interests and competency beliefs in Italian adolescents: An exploration of circumplex structure and bidirectional relationships. *Journal of Counseling Psychology, 53*(2), 181–191.

Leung, S. A., Conoley, C. W., Scheel, M. J., & Sonnenberg, R. T. (1992). An examination of the relation between vocational identity, consistency, and differentiation. *Journal of Vocational Behavior, 40,* 95–107.

Leung, S. A., & Hou, Z. (2005). The structure of vocational interests among Chinese students. *Journal of Career Development, 32*(1), 74–90.

Long, L., & Tracey, T. J. G. (2006). Structure of RIASEC scores in China: A structural meta-analysis. *Journal of Vocational Behavior, 68*(1), 39–51.

Long, L., Watanabe, N., & Tracey, T. J. G. (2006). Structure of interests in Japan: Application of the Personal Globe Inventory occupational scales. *Measurement and Evaluation in Counseling and Development. Special Issue: Interest measurement, 38*(4), 222–235.

Low, K. S. D., & Rounds, J. (2006). Vocational interests. In J. C. Thomas, D. L. Segal, & M. Hersen (Eds.). *Comprehensive handbook of personality and psychopathology, Vol. 1: Personality and everyday functioning.* (pp. 251–267). Hoboken, NJ: John Wiley.

Murray, J. L., & Hall, P. M. (2001). Gender differences in undergraduate Holland personality types. Vocational and counselor implications. *NASPA Journal, 39,* 14–29.

Nauta, M. M., & Kahn, J. H. (2007). Identity status, consistency and differentiation of interests, and career decision self-efficacy. *Journal of Career Assessment, 15*(1), 55–65.

Niles, S. G. (1993). The relationship between Holland types preferences for career counseling. *Journal of Career Development, 19,* 209–220.

Oliver, K. E., & Waehler, C. A. (2005). Investigating the validity of Holland's RIASEC typology among Native Hawaiians. *Journal of Counseling Psychology, 52*(3), 448–452.

Parslow, R. A., Jorm, A. F., Christensen, H., & Mackinnon, A. (2006). An instrument to measure engagement in life: Factor analysis and associations with sociodemographic, health and cognition measures. *Gerontology, 52*(3), 188–198.

Quimby, J. L., & DeSantis, A. M. (2006). The influence of role models on women's career choices. *The Career Development Quarterly, 54*(4), 297–306.

Reardon, R. C., Bullock, E. E., & Meyer, K. E. (2007). A Holland perspective on the U.S. workforce from 1960 to 2000. *The Career Development Quarterly, 55*(3), 262–274.

Rees, A. M. (1999). Can relational personality theory provide a framework for differences on Holland typology for women? (Doctoral dissertation, Ball State University, 1999). *Dissertation Abstracts International: Section B: The Sciences and Engineering, 59/10-B,* 5610.

Roberti, J. W., Fox, D. J., & Tunick, R. H. (2003). Alternative personality variables and the relationship to Holland's personality types in college students. *Journal of Career Assessment, 11,* 308–327.

Rosen, D., Holmberg, K., & Holland, J. L. (1994). *The Educational Opportunities Finder.* Odessa, FL: Psychological Assessment Resources.

Sanchez, J. S. (2002). A cross-cultural study of Holland's vocational types with high school students in Guam (Doctoral dissertation, Washington State University, 2002). *Dissertation Abstracts International, Section A, 62/12-A,* 4060.

Spokane, A. R., & Cruza-Guet, M. C. (2005). Holland's theory of vocational personalities in work environments. In S. D. Brown, R. W. Lent (Eds.), *Career development and counseling: Putting theory and research to work.* (1st ed., pp. 24–41). Hoboken, NJ: John Wiley.

Spokane, A. R., Luchetta, E. J., & Richwine, M. H. (2002). Holland's theory of personalities in work environments. In D. Brown & Associates (Eds.), *Career choice and development* (4th ed., pp. 373–426). San Francisco: Jossey-Bass.

Staggs, G. D., Larson, L. M., & Borgen, F. H. (2003). Convergence of specific factors on vocational interest and personality. *Journal of Career Assessment, 11,* 243–261.

Šverko, I., & Babarovic, T. (2006). The validity of Holland's theory in Croatia. *Journal of Career Assessment, 14*(4), 490–507.

Swanson, J. L. (1992). The structure of vocational interests for African-American college students. *Journal of Vocational Behavior, 40,* 144–157.

Tang, M., Fouad, N. A., & Smith, P. L. (1999). Asian Americans' career choices: A path model to examine factors influencing their career choices. *Journal of Vocational Behavior, 54,* 142–157.

Toporek, R. L., & Pope-Davis, D. B. (2001). Comparison of vocational identity factor structures among African American and White American college students. *Journal of Career Assessment, 9,* 135–151.

Tracey, T. J. G., Lent, R. W., Brown, S. D., Soresi, S., & Nota, L. (2006). Adherence to RIASEC structure in relation to career exploration and parenting style: Longitudinal and idiothetic considerations. *Journal of Vocational Behavior, 69*(2), 248–261.

Tracey, T. J. G., & Robbins, S. B. (2005). Stability of interests across ethnicity and gender: A longitudinal examination of grades 8 through 12. *Journal of Vocational Behavior, 67*(3), 335–364.

Tracey, T. J. G., & Robbins, S. B. (2006). The interest-major congruence and college success relation: A longitudinal study. *Journal of Vocational Behavior, 69*(1), 64–89.

Turner, S. L., & Lapan, R. T. (2003). The measurement of career interests among at-risk inner-city and middle class suburban adolescents. *Journal of Career Assessment, 11,* 405–420.

Turner, S. L., & Lapan, R. T. (2005). Evaluation of an intervention to increase nontraditional career interests and career-related self-efficacy among middle-school adolescents. *Journal of Vocational Behavior, 66*(3), 516–531.

Vondracek, F. W., & Skorikov, V. R. (2007). Vocational identity. In V. B. Skorikov & W. Patton (Eds.) *Career development in childhood and adolescence* (pp. 143–168). Rotterdam: Sense Publishers.

Watson, J., Stead, G. B., & Schonegevel, C. (1998). Does Holland's hexagon travel well? *Australian Journal of Career Development*, 7(2), 22–26.

Wong, C., & Wong, P. (2006). Validation of Wong's career interest assessment questionnaire and Holland's revised hexagonal model of occupational interests in four Chinese societies. *Journal of Career Development*, 32(4), 378–393.

Yang, W., Stokes, G. S., & Hui, C. H. (2005). Cross-cultural validation of Holland's interest structure in Chinese population. *Journal of Vocational Behavior*, 67(3), 379–396.

Yu, J., & Alvi, S. A. (1996). A study of Holland's typology in China. *Journal of Career Assessment*, 4, 245–252.

MYERS–BRIGGS TYPE THEORY

CHAPTER 6

CHAPTER HIGHLIGHTS

Perceiving and Judging

Extraversion and Introversion

The Sixteen Type Combinations

Dominant and Auxiliary Processes

Using the Myers–Briggs Typology in Counseling

The Role of Occupational Information

The Role of Assessment Instruments

Applying the Theory to Women and Culturally Diverse Populations

Counselor Issues

Unlike most other theories in this book, the Myers–Briggs type theory was not designed to be a theory of career development. Why then is it included? The Myers–Briggs type theory has become popular with career counselors because many find that it is applicable to their work with clients. The Myers–Briggs type theory is a psychological theory based on the work of Carl Gustav Jung that was adapted by Katharine Briggs in the 1920s.

Because the development of the Myers–Briggs typology is unusual, it would be helpful to briefly describe its origins. Katharine Briggs was not a psychologist, but she was an acute observer of people. Before reading Jung's (1971; originally published in 1921) book *Psychological Types*, she had developed her own categories of human behavior. Becoming intrigued with Jung's work, she studied it extensively. During the next 20 years, she continued to observe people and to try to classify them into Jungian types. In the 1940s, she was joined by her only child, Isabel Myers, in the development of the Myers–Briggs Type Indicator (MBTI). They worked together sorting and analyzing responses to the MBTI. In 1956, she persuaded the Educational Testing Service to publish the MBTI. In 1962, a manual for the MBTI was published (Myers, 1962), and Isabel Myers spoke at the American Psychological Association meeting. Gradually, the MBTI attracted the attention of psychologists. In 1969, Isabel started to work with Mary McCaulley and began a typology laboratory at the University of Florida in Gainesville. In 1972, this laboratory became the Center for the Application of Psychological Type, sponsoring research on the MBTI and coordinating research efforts in the development of the Myers–Briggs typology. The Association for Psychological Type sponsors a research journal, *Journal of Psychological Type*, and a newsletter, *Bulletin of Psychological Type*. Although the Myers–Briggs typology has increased in popularity among psychologists and counselors over the years, it is not without its critics. Some psychologists have questioned both the theory and the methodology of the MBTI. This criticism is discussed in more detail later in this chapter.

In his book *Psychological Types* (1921), Jung wrote about different ways that individuals use perception and judgment. He was concerned with what people pay attention to and how they make decisions about what they see. Furthermore, he viewed some people as being primarily concerned with what is happening in the world outside them, whereas others are more concerned with their own views and ideas. This is a brief synopsis of the groundwork on which the Myers–Briggs typology is based. To put Jung's typology into perspective, it is only one of the many aspects of his theory of personality. Many Jungian psychotherapists are concerned with analysis of dreams and concepts other than personality type. However, many psychologists and counselors who use Jungian theory do so only within the limited confines of the Myers–Briggs typological system.

To put the Myers–Briggs type system within the context of career development, it will be helpful to think of it as a trait and factor theory. Chapter 2 lists the first step in selecting a career, according to trait and factor theory, as gaining a clear understanding of your aptitudes, achievements, interests, values, and personality. Within that context, the Myers–Briggs typology can be seen as a theory of personality. Those counselors who use the Myers–Briggs theory in helping clients with career choices use it as a personality theory. Rarely, if ever, would the Myers–Briggs theory be used without an assessment of aptitudes, achievements, or interests as well. Certainly, the Myers–Briggs theory can be used with theories other than trait and factor theory. However, it fits rather neatly into that model. Available in the MBTI manual (Myers, McCaulley, Quenk, & Hammer, 1998) are listings of environments (or occupations) in which various types of people work. This information, together with knowledge of a person's type, enables a counselor to help a client with the third step of trait and factor career selection: integrating information about one's self and the world of work. In addition, the Myers–Briggs typology can be used in assisting a client with career adjustment, applying type concepts to individuals and their current working conditions.

This chapter explains the four bipolar dimensions basic to Myers–Briggs theory: extraversion–introversion, sensing–intuition, thinking–feeling, and judgment–perception. Although the number of concepts in the Myers–Briggs typology is not great, the interrelationships among the types make for a complex and sometimes difficult theory to "chunk," or learn. Thus, to understand the theory, it is necessary to understand the four bipolar categories and how they work in conjunction with each other. Examples of counseling for career decision making and for work adjustment will illustrate the interrelationships among the constructs. Because the MBTI is such an important part of the use of the Myers–Briggs type theory, this chapter gives it considerable attention. The interaction between the counselor's and the client's MBTI type also has interesting ramifications. Because of its complexity, the information presented in this chapter is insufficient to enable readers to use the Myers–Briggs type theory in counseling without formal course work or attendance at workshops, as well as further reading.

The two most basic concepts within the Myers–Briggs typology are perception–judgment and extraversion–introversion. The next section deals with how individuals perceive their surroundings and then make judgments or decisions about their observations. This then can be related to an individual's view of the world—that is, focus on the outer world (extraversion) or on the inner world (introversion). These can be seen as "preference patterns," or different ways that individuals prefer to make decisions and choices.

PERCEIVING AND JUDGING

Myers–Briggs theory pertains to the way that individuals observe their world and make decisions based on their perceptions (Myers, 1993; McCaulley & Moody, 2001; Mitchell, 2001, 2006). In dealing with the world, the first step is perception. People form perceptions of events, people, objects, and ideas as they become aware of the information. Then, the individual must decide or make conclusions about the observed events, people, objects, or ideas. In doing so, the individual is judging the events and ideas that have been perceived. According to Myers, much of an individual's mental activity is devoted to *perceiving, judging,* or both. For example, when an adolescent watches a movie, he or she takes in information (perceives) and then makes decisions about the movie—whether it was liked, appreciated, informative, and so on (judges). Throughout school and work activities, individuals are constantly perceiving and judging. There are two modes of perceiving and two modes of judging.

THE TWO WAYS OF PERCEIVING

The two contrasting ways of perceiving are *sensing* and *intuition.* Sensing is taking in information by using visual and auditory processes, together with smell, taste, and touch. In contrast, intuition concerns the use of the unconscious, a concept of great importance in Jungian theory. Rather than direct perception, as in sensing, intuition is indirect and adds ideas to external perceptions. It was Jung's belief, which was incorporated into the Myers–Briggs theory, that a preference for perception (and other Myers–Briggs concepts) was innate and not learned through interaction with the environment.

People who favor sensing prefer to observe, primarily through hearing, vision, and touch. Their focus is on events that happen immediately around them. People who prefer sensing often have a good memory for details and are able to make clear observations. An adolescent who visits the dentist and makes use of the sensing perception may well be aware of the tools the dentist uses, the mannerisms of the dentist, and the location of the dental tools in the mouth. This common experience may eventually have some effect on occupational choice at a later time. At that point, the detailed information about the dental experience is stored in memory. This is in marked contrast to the opposite mode of perceiving: intuition.

Through use of insight, an individual may perceive meanings and relationships in events. This insight into observations and ideas can be called *intuition*. Intuition takes visible and auditory (and other) information as a base and goes beyond it. Often, the individual using intuition is focused not on the current event, but on a future event. Rather than being concrete, intuition is abstract, imaginative, and often creative. An adolescent who uses intuition while at the dentist's office is likely to imagine what the next dental appointment will be like (that it may be much worse than the current one) or to imagine himself or herself as a dentist (filling cavities and doing other dental work). This response to the dentist is in marked contrast to the practical, present-oriented, sensing response described above. After an idea is perceived, whether through sensing or intuition, a judgment often is made about it.

THE TWO WAYS OF JUDGING

Just as there are two kinds of perception (sensing and intuition), there are two types of judgment: *thinking* and *feeling*. After perceiving an event, an individual is likely to act primarily in one way, either thinking or feeling. Thinking refers to analyzing and being objective about an observed idea or event. Feeling is a subjective reaction, often related to one's own values.

When using thinking judgment, an individual may be concerned with logic or analysis. The person tries to be objective in making a judgment about a perceived event. He or she may be concerned with judging the event or idea fairly, and in the process may use objective criticism to analyze his or her perception. Returning to the adolescent in the dentist's chair, the individual may judge whether the experience will be similar next time, whether he or she would like to be a dentist and could perform dental functions, or what the dentist will do next.

A feeling judgment is deciding based on the values applied to observations or ideas. In making a feeling judgment, an individual is concerned with the impact of the judgment. Such individuals are more likely to be interested in human as opposed to technical problems. Again returning to the example of being in the dentist's chair, a feeling judgment may be concerned with wondering what it would be like to be a dentist who helps someone but creates physical pain in the process. This concern for others is in marked contrast to the previous example, which uses thinking judgment.

COMBINATIONS OF PERCEIVING AND JUDGING

Because perceiving precedes judging, these two functions are combined in individuals. Myers, McCaulley, Quenk, and Hammer (1998) describe the four combinations of perceiving and judging that can occur. They are as follows:

Sensing and Thinking	Intuition and Feeling
Sensing and Feeling	Intuition and Thinking

According to Myers (1993), individuals prefer one of these four categories. How people perceive and judge has an impact not only on their own way of life, but also on how they interact with others. People who use sensing and thinking abilities to perceive events and make judgments about events are very different from those who use primarily intuition and feeling.

SENSING AND THINKING   People who rely on sensing for perceiving and on thinking for judging are likely to focus on collecting facts that can be verified by their observations. They may want to see or hear what has happened. They may want to count the profits or assess the output of a machine. Such people are quite practical and pragmatic. They are likely to choose occupations that demand analysis of facts. Examples of such occupations are law, business management, accounting and auditing, and production and purchasing. When making a career decision for themselves, they are likely to use a rational decision-making process based on information they have acquired through occupational literature and talking with others.

SENSING AND FEELING   Although they do rely on vision, hearing, and other senses, people using sensing and feeling make decisions based on feeling. They are aware of the importance of feelings to themselves and others when making a decision. Because of their emphasis on others, they are more likely to be interested in observations about people than objects. Examples of occupations that they are likely to seek out are the medical profession, social work, teaching children, and providing customer services. In making a career decision, they focus on information about people and occupations, being aware of how they will feel doing a certain kind of work on a day-to-day basis.

INTUITION AND FEELING   Rather than focus on current observations or happenings, people who intuit are likely to be concerned about future possibilities. Their feeling involvement is likely to be personal, warm, and inspired. They are apt to take a creative approach to meeting human needs and to be less concerned about objects. Examples of occupations include clergy, teaching at the college or high school level, advertising, and social service occupations. When making a career decision, they are likely to use hunches based on what is best for them. Their emphasis is on feelings about observations rather than weighing the observations themselves.

INTUITION AND THINKING   People who use intuition and thinking are likely to make decisions based on analysis that uses hunches and projections about the future. They tend to enjoy solving problems, particularly those of a theoretical nature. Occupations that they tend to seek out include scientific research, computing, business (particularly financial) decision making, and development of new projects. In making their own career decisions, people using intuition and thinking are likely to project themselves into the future, thinking about what types of work would offer particular opportunities. Although based on projections about the future, their decision making is logical and clear to them.

TWO COUNSELING EXAMPLES

The following two brief counseling dialogues illustrate two different combinations of perception and judgment. The first example illustrates a counselor's assessment of sensing and thinking, and the second illustrates intuition and feeling.

Sharon is a college sophomore who has sought career counseling because she is thinking of entering a business occupation but is not sure which one to choose. The following dialogue is from one of Sharon's counseling sessions:

CL: Since we talked last week, I've been looking into a number of occupations. I went to the career library and started to read about careers such as stockbroker and banker. I only had time to read about six, but I intend to go back.

CO: It's good to hear that you got off to a quick start. [The concrete approach of the client sounds as if she perceives by using her sensing abilities.]

CL: There are several brochures on stockbroker and banker, not to mention other careers. I want to make sure that I have time to read them and weigh the information. Do you think it would be helpful for me to take notes?

CO: You seem to have a systematic way of doing things; notes seem to fit for you. [The counselor wants to reinforce the logical method that the client uses, which fits with people who use sensing and thinking.]

CL: I know that the occupational scales that I scored high on that interest inventory fit with these careers. But I do want to find out more about them. Maybe I'll talk with my father about it.

CO: That sounds like a good idea. You're really getting a lot of information to make a decision. [Getting and collecting information about occupations and then analyzing it seems to be the style of this client, which fits in well with the sensing and thinking modes of perceiving and judging.]

Harvey uses a different approach to career decision making. Also a sophomore in college, Harvey is exploring occupations in the social sciences and uses an approach that combines intuition with feeling. The following dialogue is from one of Harvey's counseling sessions:

CL: I'm so bored with school. I want to get out and do something, something that is going to mean something. I feel as if I'm just marking time. I'm not doing anything that's meaningful.

CO: You'd feel happier if you were doing something now that would make you feel worthwhile. [The client's feeling of frustration is strong, and there is an absence of observations about events in his statements.]

CL: Yes, I feel that I'd like to make a difference. I am working on an adult literacy project at the Literacy Center at school. That's probably the thing I get the most out of, even more than my courses. Helping an adult, like this man I'm working with, to learn to read really makes me feel good. I just wish that I could do more of it.

CO: You really want to have an impact on others. [Harvey's perceptions of what goes on at the Literacy Center are intuitive. The counselor hears how important feeling is to Harvey in making judgments about his work with the literacy project.]

CL: I know that I want to help people; that's why I've tried to keep my grades up. I figure I have to in order to get into clinical psychology or psychiatry.

CO: It sounds as if it's difficult, but you really seem to be putting a lot of effort into what you eventually might do, even though you're not sure. [Being aware of Harvey's commitment, the counselor wants to reinforce it, even though Harvey's exact choice about the future is not yet determined.]

Note the contrast between Harvey and Sharon. Sharon's approach is practical and systematic. In contrast, Harvey has a mission, about which he shows enthusiasm. He just has not yet clearly defined it. This contrast between a sensing–thinking and an intuitive–feeling approach is an illustration of how the Myers–Briggs theory can aid in understanding career decision making.

THE PREFERENCE FOR PERCEPTION OR JUDGMENT

When using the Myers–Briggs typology, it is important not only to understand how a client perceives and judges, but also to know which process is more important. People differ as to how important they consider perceiving objects and people around them compared with making judgments or decisions. Some people prefer to make decisions based on relatively few facts *(judgment)*, whereas others prefer to weigh many facts before reaching a judgment *(perception)*. To make a decision, people must stop perceiving, and then judge. People who have a perceiving attitude continue to take information in and do not decide. Those who have a judging attitude are apt to stop perceiving and make a judgment without including any more evidence. People who use judgment are apt to have a sense of order in their lives, whereas people who use perception just live their lives.

EXTRAVERSION AND INTROVERSION

Another factor that adds to the understanding of how individuals use perception and judgment is introversion versus extraversion. The common meanings of introvert and extravert are different from those used by Jung and Myers. In common terminology, introversion is generally associated with being shy and quiet, whereas extraversion refers to being louder and more outgoing. However, for Jung and Myers, the terms introversion and extraversion refer to how one relates to the world. *Introversion* refers to making perceptions and judgments based on one's interests in his or her inner world. In contrast, *extraversion* refers to using perceptions and judgments in the outer world. For the introvert, the inner world, consisting of concepts and ideas, is important. For the extravert, the outer world, concern with other people and objects, is important. Obviously, both introverts and extraverts live in the inner and outer world. The difference is that introverts prefer the inner world, whereas extraverts prefer the outer world.

Extraverts often like to take action. They want to work with people or things by talking and interacting. They prefer to speak directly to an individual rather than to write a memo. Being verbally and physically active is important to them. In contrast, introverts enjoy reflecting. They may like to work out problems or think for a long time before performing an action. They may be quieter than extroverts, but not necessarily due to shyness, but due to the need for time to process internally.

Introversion and extraversion are used in combination with judgment and perception in the Myers–Briggs system. Some people prefer to use judgment and perception in the outer world, whereas others prefer the inner world. Each of the four perceiving and judging types described earlier will have a preference for either the inner (introvert) or the outer world (extravert).

Regarding preference for work, extraverts tend to like activity that provides contact with people, whereas introverts tend to prefer activity that includes time for concentration. Thus, extraverts may prefer sales and business management occupations, as well as social service occupations. Conversely, introverts may prefer occupations such as science and accounting, where they spend time solving problems on their own.

When they do this, they are likely to be more careful in dealing with details than extraverts; that is, they exhibit more patience in that they can work on one project for a long time. Introverts do not need to work as part of a team; rather, they prefer to work alone without interruptions.

THE SIXTEEN TYPE COMBINATIONS

In the Myers–Briggs typology, the different ways of judging and perceiving, the preference for judgment or perception, and the preference for introversion or extraversion act in concert with each other to yield 16 different types. Type tables (for example, Table 6.1, pp. 163–164) are often used to describe the relationships among types. It is helpful to use abbreviations in examining the interrelations of the four basic bipolar dimensions. The following abbreviations are used throughout the rest of the chapter:

E—Extravert	I—Introvert
S—Sensing	N—Intuition
T—Thinking	F—Feeling
J—Judgment	P—Perception

Figure 6.1 illustrates the format of the type tables in terms of the four bipolar dimensions. At the top of the figure are the 16 combinations of 4 dimensions. The relationships of the dimensions can be seen more clearly by examining the diagrams directly below the 16 combinations. Note that introversion appears in the top half and extraversion in the bottom half of the 16 combinations. Sensing functions appear on the left side of the table, and intuition appears on the right side. Likewise, thinking and feeling dimensions, as well as judgment and perception dimensions, are distributed in a systematic manner. Figure 6.1 serves as an outline for the descriptions found in Table 6.1. These descriptions provide a brief overview of the characteristics of people who fit into each of the 16 categories. In their extensive manual, Myers, McCaulley, Quenk, and Hammer (1998) caution that type definitions are not to be taken literally; they describe general characteristics of individuals falling into 16 types. They see these types as gifts or attributes that people can make use of. They discourage the notion that there are only 16 types of people in the world, and that all people within a category are similar to each other. These types are described in far greater detail in the manual, together with various letter combinations. The Myers–Briggs Type Indicator yields scores on each of the four dimensions that point in the direction of sensing or intuiting, thinking or feeling, judging or perceiving, and extraversion or introversion. The MBTI, an important component when using the Myers–Briggs theory, is discussed in more detail later in this chapter. When using the Myers–Briggs typology, it is helpful to be aware that either the judging or the perceiving process may be more significant, an important consideration in how the categorization by type is to be interpreted.

TABLE 6.1 | CHARACTERISTICS FREQUENTLY ASSOCIATED WITH EACH TYPE

	Sensing Types		Intuitive Types	
	ISTJ	**ISFJ**	**INFJ**	**INTJ**
	Quiet, serious, earn success by thoroughness and dependability. Practical, matter-of-fact, realistic, and responsible. Decide logically what should be done and work toward it steadily, regardless of distractions. Take pleasure in making everything orderly and organized—their work, their home, their life. Value traditions and loyalty.	Quiet, friendly, responsible, and conscientious. Committed and steady in meeting their obligations. Thorough, painstaking, and accurate. Loyal, considerate, notice and remember specifics about people who are important to them, concerned with how others feel. Strive to create an orderly and harmonious environment at work and at home.	Seek meaning and connection in ideas, relationships, and material possessions. Want to understand what motivates people and are insightful about others. Conscientious and committed to their firm values. Develop a clear vision about how best to serve the common good. Organized and decisive in implementing their vision.	Have original minds and great drive for implementing their ideas and achieving their goals. Quickly see patterns in external events and develop long-range explanatory perspectives. When committed, organize a job and carry it through. Skeptical and independent, have high standards of competence and performance—for themselves and others.
	ISTP	**ISFP**	**INFP**	**INTP**
	Tolerant and flexible, quiet observers until a problem appears, then act quickly to find workable solutions. Analyze what makes things work and readily get through large amounts of data to isolate the core of practical problems. Interested in cause and effect, organize facts using logical principles, value efficiency.	Quiet, friendly, sensitive, and kind. Enjoy the present moment, what is going on around them. Like to have their own space and to work within their own time frame. Loyal and committed to their values and to people who are important to them. Dislike disagreements and conflicts, do not force their opinions or values on others.	Idealistic, loyal to their values and to people who are important to them. Want an external life that is congruent with their values. Curious, quick to see possibilities, can be catalysts for implementing ideas. Seek to understand people and to help them fulfill their potential. Adaptable, flexible, and accepting unless a value is threatened.	Seek to develop logical explanations for everything that interests them. Theoretical and abstract, interested more in ideas than in social interaction. Quiet, contained, flexible, and adaptable. Have unusual ability to focus in depth to solve problems in their area of interest. Skeptical, sometimes critical, always analytical.

Introverts

TABLE 6.1 | CONTINUED

Extraverts

ESTP	ESFP	ENFP	ENTP
Flexible and tolerant, they take a pragmatic approach focused on immediate results. Theories and conceptual explanations bore them—they want to act energetically to solve the problem. Focus on the here-and-now, spontaneous, enjoy each moment that they can be active with others. Enjoy material comforts and style. Learn best through doing.	Outgoing, friendly, and accepting. Exuberant lovers of life, people, and material comforts. Enjoy working with others to make things happen. Bring common sense and a realistic approach to their work, and make work fun. Flexible and spontaneous, adapt readily to new people and environments. Learn best by trying a new skill with other people.	Warmly enthusiastic and imaginative. See life as full of possibilities. Make connections between events and information very quickly, and confidently proceed based on the patterns they see. Want a lot of affirmation from others, and readily give appreciation and support. Spontaneous and flexible, often rely on their ability to improvise and their verbal fluency.	Quick, ingenious, stimulating, alert, and outspoken. Resourceful in solving new and challenging problems. Adept at generating conceptual possibilities and then analyzing them strategically. Good at reading other people. Bored by routine, will seldom do the same thing the same way, apt to turn to one new interest after another.

ESTJ	ESFJ	ENFJ	ENTJ
Practical, realistic, matter-of-fact. Decisive, quickly move to implement decisions. Organize projects and people to get things done, focus on getting results in most efficient way possible. Take care of routine details. Have a clear set of logical standards, systematically follow them and want others to also. Forceful in implementing their plans.	Warmhearted, conscientious, and cooperative. Want harmony in their environment; work with determination to establish it. Like to work with others to complete tasks accurately and on time. Loyal, follow through even in small matters. Notice what others need in their day-by-day lives and try to provide it. Want to be appreciated for who they are and for what they contribute.	Warm, empathetic, responsive, and responsible. Highly attuned to the emotions, needs, and motivations of others. Find potential in everyone, want to help others fulfill their potential. May act as catalysts for individual and group growth. Loyal, responsive to praise and criticism. Sociable, facilitate others in a group, and provide inspiring leadership.	Frank, decisive, assume leadership readily. Quickly see illogical and inefficient procedures and policies, develop and implement comprehensive systems to solve organizational problems. Enjoy long-term planning and goal setting. Usually well informed, well read, enjoy expanding their knowledge and passing it on to others. Forceful in presenting their ideas.

ISTJ	ISFJ	INFJ	INTJ
ISTP	ISFP	INFP	INTP
ESTP	ESFP	ENFP	ENTP
ESTJ	ESFJ	ENFJ	ENTJ

Extraversion–
Introversion

| I |
| E |

Sensing–Intuition

| S | N |

Thinking–Feeling

| T | F | F | T |

Judgment–Perception

| J |
| P |
| P |
| J |

FIGURE 6.1 | FORMAT OF THE TYPE TABLES.

Source: Modified and reproduced by special permission of the Publisher, CPP, Inc., Mountain View, CA 94043 from MBTI® Manual, Third Edition by Isabel Briggs Myers, Mary H. McCaulley, Naomi L. Quenk, Allen L. Hammer. Copyright 1998 by Peter B. Myers and Katharine D. Myers. All rights reserved. Further reproduction is prohibited without the Publisher's written consent. Myers-Briggs Type Indicator, MBTI, Myers-Briggs, and Introduction to Type are trademarks or registered trademarks of the Myers-Briggs Type Indicator Trust in the United States and other countries. Further information is available at www.cpp.com, where you will find the full range of Introduction to Type® titles along other products that allow you to expand your knowledge and applications of your MBTI® type. Modified and reproduced by special permission of the Publisher, CPP, Inc., Mountain View CA 94043 from *Introduction to Type®* 6th Edition, by Isabel Briggs Myers. Copyright 1998 by Peter B. Myers and Katharine D. Myers. All rights reserved. Further reproduction is prohibited without the Publisher's written consent.

DOMINANT AND AUXILIARY PROCESSES

Probably the most complex and confusing concept to those who are beginning to learn the Myers–Briggs type theory is dominant and auxiliary processes. Perhaps the easiest way to understand this concept is to think of the last letter of the type code as determining the dominant or auxiliary process. If the last letter is P, then the style of perceiving (either intuitive or sensing) is the key process. If the last letter is J, then the way of judging (either thinking or feeling) is the key process.

The dominant process is the guiding one; it is the general, and the auxiliary process is the lieutenant. What makes this particularly complex is that for extraverts, the last letter of the code (J or P) indicates the dominant process; for introverts, the last letter indicates the auxiliary function. The reason is that introverts function in the inner world, thus the dominant function is an inner-world function rather than an outer world function. For extraverts, the dominant process is in the outer world of people and things. For introverts, the dominant process is in the inner world of ideas and thoughts.

Another way of describing why the introvert's dominant process is the opposite of that indicated by the last letter of the Myers–Briggs code (J or P, judging or perceiving) is that introverts use their dominant process for the inner world and their auxiliary process for the outer world, whereas extraverts use their auxiliary process for the inner world and their dominant process for the outer world. The last letter of the code (J or P) thus refers to a preference for perceiving or judging in the outer world. Introverts whose dominant process is a judging process (thinking or feeling) show perceptiveness of their auxiliary process in dealing with the outer world and live their outer lives in this perceptive framework. The inner tendency to judge is not apparent to others. Also, introverts whose dominant process is perceptive (sensing or intuition) do not outwardly behave as if they were perceptive people. Rather, they show the judging strength of the auxiliary process. Others would see them as leading their outer lives in the judging attitude.

The preceding discussion is complex. Describing the auxiliary and dominant processes requires thorough familiarity with the Myers–Briggs typology. Critics of the Myers–Briggs theory may point to the dominant and auxiliary processes as having little research support (Healy, 1989). Conversely, some who find the Myers–Briggs theory to be useful in their counseling process claim that the concept of dominant and auxiliary processes is essential. Because not all counselors apply the concepts of dominant and auxiliary, the examples used in this chapter to illustrate Myers–Briggs conceptualization in counseling focus for the most part on the types themselves rather than on the dominant and auxiliary processes.

USING THE MYERS–BRIGGS TYPOLOGY IN COUNSELING

This section focuses on examples that illustrate two major career issues: career decision making and career adjustment. Over many years, researchers have accumulated a considerable amount of data that relate Myers–Briggs type to occupational choice. In their manual, Myers, McCaulley, Quenk, and Hammer (1985) describe the types of people in many different occupations. These types are listed primarily by four-letter codes. More data are available in the *Atlas of Type Tables* (1987), which includes more information about occupational groups and their codes. To summarize this information, Table 6.2 lists examples of frequent occupational choices that are made by people of each type. Some occupations occur in more than one category. Still, this table gives an idea of those occupations that are most commonly associated with certain Myers–Briggs types. This information that categorizes occupations by type can be useful in both career decision making and work adjustment counseling.

Tables 6.3 through 6.6 also can be useful in that they list the effects of each of the eight poles (Table 6.3: extravert–introvert; Table 6.4: sensing–intuition; Table 6.5: thinking–feeling; and Table 6.6: judgment–perception) on individuals' preferences

TABLE 6.2 | EXAMPLES OF FREQUENT OCCUPATIONAL CHOICES MADE BY EACH TYPE

ISTJ	ISFJ	INFJ	INTJ
Accountants	Health workers	Artists	Computer analysts
Auditors	Librarians	Clergy	Engineers
Engineers	Service workers	Musicians	Judges
Financial managers	Teachers	Psychiatrists	Lawyers
Police officers		Social workers	Operations researchers
Steelworkers		Teachers	Scientists
Technicians		Writers	Social scientists

ISTP	ISFP	INFP	INTP
Crafts workers	Clerical workers	Artists and entertainers	Artists
Construction workers	Construction workers	Editors	Computer analysts
Mechanics	Musicians	Psychiatrists	Engineers
Protective service workers	Outdoor workers	Psychologists	Scientists
Statisticians	Painters	Social workers	Writers
	Stock clerks	Writers	

ESTP	ESFP	ENFP	ENTP
Auditors	Child care workers	Actors	Actors
Carpenters	Mining engineers	Clergy	Journalists
Marketing personnel	Secretaries	Counselors	Marketing personnel
Police officers	Supervisors	Journalists	Photographers
Sales clerks		Musicians	Sales agents
Service workers		Public relations workers	

ESTJ	ESFJ	ENFJ	ENTJ
Administrators	Beauticians	Actors	Administrators
Financial managers	Health workers	Clergy	Credit managers
Managers	Office managers	Consultants	Lawyers
Salespeople	Secretaries	Counselors	Managers
Supervisors	Teachers	Home economists	Marketing personnel
		Musicians	Operations researchers
		Teachers	

TABLE 6.3 | EFFECTS OF EXTRAVERSION–INTROVERSION IN WORK SITUATIONS

Extraverts	Introverts
Like variety and action	Like quiet for concentration
Tend to be faster, dislike complicated procedures (especially ES types)	Tend to be careful with details, dislike sweeping statements (especially IS types)
Are often good at greeting people (especially EF types)	Have trouble remembering names and faces (especially IT types)
Are often impatient with long, slow jobs done alone	Tend not to mind working on one project for a long time alone and uninterrupted
Are interested in the activities of their job, in getting it done, and in how other people do it.	Are interested in the details and/or ideas behind their job
Often do not mind the interruption of answering the telephone (especially EF types)	Dislike telephone intrusions and interruptions (especially IT types)
Often act quickly, sometimes without thinking it through	Like to think a lot before they act, sometimes without acting
Like to have people around (especially EF types)	Work contentedly alone (especially IT types)
Usually communicate freely (especially EF types)	Have some problems communicating to others since it's all in their heads (especially IT types)

for work situations. For example, extraverts tend to prefer variety and action, whereas introverts prefer quiet and working alone. Sensing types like established ways of doing things, whereas intuitive types dislike doing the same thing repeatedly. Thinking types tend to respond to people's ideas rather than their feelings, whereas feeling types respond more to people's values than their thoughts. Judging types work best when they can follow a plan, whereas perceptive types do not mind last-minute changes. In the examples that follow, references are made to these tables.

EXAMPLE OF CAREER DECISION-MAKING COUNSELING

Edna is a 25-year-old African American woman who has just been discharged from the U.S. Army after spending 3 years of active duty on a large military base. Much of her work entailed keeping records of supplies and office management. Although

TABLE 6.4 | EFFECTS OF SENSING–INTUITION IN WORK SITUATIONS

Sensing Types	Intuitive Types
Like focusing on the here and now and reality	Like focusing on the future and what might be
Rely on standard ways to solve problems and dislike problems in which this approach doesn't work	Like solving new problems in unusual ways and dislike solving routine problems
Like an established order of doing things (especially SJ types)	Dislike doing the same thing repeatedly (especially NP types)
Enjoy using and perfecting skills already learned more than learning new ones	Enjoy learning a new skill more than using it
Work more steadily, with realistic idea of how long it will take (especially ISJ types)	Work in bursts of energy, powered by enthusiasm, with slack periods in between (especially ENP types)
Reach a conclusion step by step (especially ISJ types)	Reach an understanding quickly (especially ENP types)
Are patient with routine details (especially ISJ types)	Are impatient with routine details (especially ENP types)
Are impatient when the situation gets complicated (especially ES types)	Are patient with complex situations (especially IN types)
Are not often inspired and rarely trust the inspiration when they are	Follow their inspirations, good or bad, regardless of the data (especially with inadequate type development)
Seldom make factual errors	Frequently make errors of fact, preferring instead the big picture
Tend to be good at precise work (especially IS types)	Dislike taking time for precision (especially EN types)
Create something new by adapting something that exists	Create something new through a personal insight

she liked her military experience and enjoyed spending time with her colleagues, she did not want to reenlist. Rather, she has decided to take advantage of military financial support for higher education, which will finance much of her future education. Before entering the military, she had waited on tables in restaurants. She does not wish to return to this occupation. She is living in Pittsburgh in a small

| TABLE 6.5 | EFFECTS OF THINKING–FEELING IN WORK SITUATIONS |

Thinking Types	Feeling Types
Like analysis and putting things into logical order	Like harmony
Can get along without harmony	Efficiency may be badly disrupted by office feud
Tend to be firm minded	Tend to be sympathetic
Do not show emotion readily and are often uncomfortable dealing with people's feelings (especially IT types)	Tend to be very aware of other people and their feelings (especially EF types)
May hurt people's feelings without knowing it	Enjoy pleasing people, even in unimportant things
Tend to decide impersonally, sometimes paying insufficient attention to people's wishes	Often let decisions be influenced by their own or other people's personal likes and dislikes
Need to be treated fairly in accordance with the prevailing standards	Need praise and personal attention
Are able to reprimand people impersonally, although they may not like doing so	Dislike, even avoid, telling people unpleasant things
Are more analytically oriented—respond more easily to people's thoughts (especially IT types)	Are more people oriented—respond more easily to people's values

Source: Modified and reproduced by special permission of the Publisher, CPP, Inc., Mountain View, CA 94043 from MBTI® Manual, Third Edition by Isabel Briggs Myers, Mary H. McCaulley, Naomi L. Quenk, Allen L. Hammer. Copyright 1998 by Peter B. Myers and Katharine D. Myers. All rights reserved. Further reproduction is prohibited without the Publisher's written consent. Myers-Briggs Type Indicator, MBTI, Myers-Briggs, and Introduction to Type are trademarks or registered trademarks of the Myers-Briggs Type Indicator Trust in the United States and other countries. Further information is available at www.cpp.com, where you will find the full range of Introduction to Type® titles along other products that allow you to expand your knowledge and applications of your MBTI® type. Modified and reproduced by special permission of the Publisher, CPP, Inc., Mountain View CA 94043 from Introduction to Type® 6th Edition, by Isabel Briggs Myers. Copyright 1998 by Peter B. Myers and Katharine D. Myers. All rights reserved. Further reproduction is prohibited without the Publisher's written consent.

apartment with her sister and her sister's husband. Now she decides to seek counseling to help her decide on future plans.

The following segment is part of Edna's second interview with the counselor. During the first appointment, Edna went over her work experience, discussing activities that she had enjoyed. Immediately after finishing the session, she completed the Myers–Briggs Type Indicator as well as the Strong Interest Inventory. On the Myers–Briggs Type Indicator, she scored ESFJ, or extraverted feeling with sensing. The last letter, J, means that her dominant process is feeling, which is a judging process; therefore, her auxiliary process is one of perception, which is sensing. Thus, she uses her favorite process, feeling, in dealing with others, and the auxiliary function, sensing, in her inner world. The counselor has just gone over this information with

TABLE 6.6 | EFFECTS OF JUDGING–PERCEIVING IN WORK SITUATIONS

Judging Types	Perceiving Types
Work best when they can plan their work and follow the plan	Adapt well to changing situations
Like to get things settled and finished	Prefer leaving things open for alterations
May decide things too quickly (especially EJ types)	May unduly postpone decisions (especially IP types)
May dislike to interrupt the project they are on for a more urgent one (especially ISJ types)	May start too many projects and have difficulty finishing them (especially ENP types)
May not notice new things that need to be done in their desire to complete what they are doing	May postpone unpleasant jobs while finding other things more interesting in the moment
Want only the essentials needed to begin their work (especially ESJ types)	Want to know all about a new job (especially INP types)
Tend to be satisfied once they reach a judgment on a thing, situation, or person	Tend to be curious and welcome a new light on a thing, situation, or person

Edna and has reviewed the results of her Strong Interest Inventory. Her high scores were on the occupational theme S, Social, and on the basic interest scales for teaching and social service; she received many high scores on occupational scales. Examples of jobs matching her type include human resources director, public administrator, social worker, and elementary school teacher.

Edna is a soft-spoken young woman with a pleasant smile and a friendly presentation. The following portion of the dialogue focuses on the counselor's use of the Myers–Briggs typology in conceptualizing Edna's career decision-making concerns:

CL: It's helpful to look at these tests. I knew that I didn't like the work in the army. It really was boring for me to monitor inventory records and to keep track of purchase requisitions and things like that. It was funny: People thought I liked my work; I guess because I got along so well with the others. The other women that I worked with were real nice. Sure, there was turnover, but I seemed to be able to get along with everyone.

CO: Sounds as if getting along with others is very important to you in your work. [Feeling is an important process for Edna. It is not surprising that she emphasizes her feelings about others and wants to get along well with others.]

CL: Oh, yes, it is. I know some friends who worked in offices with people who were unfriendly, and I would have hated that. It seemed to me that the more my work had to do with people, the more I liked it. When I would have to fill in for the receptionist sometimes, I liked that more than my usual work, even though my usual work required more training. Often, when people would come into my office, they were looking for help, trying to find the right person, or trying to find a requisition. When I could help them, I really felt good, but I sometimes think I want to help in a different way.

CO: What kind of helping gives you a really good feeling? [The counselor speaks to Edna's emphasis on feeling. He wants to know what things are important to her. He suspects that it will be more difficult to get at her auxiliary process, sensing, which deals with her inner world, than to talk with her about her outer world, the dominant process of feeling.]

CL: I think I feel best when I'm helping children. It seems when I'm at home, not when I'm with my sister, I am always helping kids. I help them read; I help them when they're crying. All my mother's friends know I'm a soft touch. They can rely on me to help out.

CO: Yet you don't mind being a soft touch. [Again, the focus is on Edna's feeling type.]

CL: No, I don't. When we looked at the Strong Interest Inventory, I was glad to see teaching show up. I was afraid that maybe it would, and maybe it wouldn't.

CO: Can you tell me what you mean by would and wouldn't? [Because this is confusing, the counselor wants to hear what Edna seems to have mixed feelings about.]

CL: Well, sometimes I think deep down I've wanted to be a teacher.

CO: Tell me your thoughts about teaching. [Teaching is an occupation that ESFJ people often enter; see Table 6.2.]

CL: My father wanted me to work right away. We really didn't have any money. There were four children, all girls. I was the second youngest, and my oldest sister had gone to college. My father was pretty strict with me, and he didn't really let me do what I wanted. But I really admired him. He worked very hard, and I wanted to please him very much.

CO: But it seems as if now you want to please yourself. [Being compliant and wanting to be loyal to people that they respect can be characteristic of ESFJ people.]

CL: My father died two years ago, and I hate to say this, but somehow I feel relieved a little bit. Like now there are no blockades in my way.

CO: It's hard to be critical of your father now. [The counselor wants to be gentle with Edna, because her father is an important part of her.]

CL: I want to do something that I will enjoy. Now with money available, I think that I could go to school. It really seems like that would be a wonderful thing to do. Even my father wouldn't have objected if I had support from the government like I do.

CO: It really is nice to be able to be concerned about a decision that can be helpful for you. [The counselor is aware that Edna is starting to appreciate his confidence in her. Knowing that people who are ESFJ often appreciate support, he starts to offer more. He knows that Edna was disappointed by her father's lack of support.]

CL: I guess sometimes down inside I feel that teaching small children would be marvelous for me. I guess it scares me sometimes to think that. I used to hear that there weren't many jobs in teaching and things like that. I don't hear that much anymore. But I guess I never really had much confidence that I could do it.

CO: You seem to be excited when you think of it now, though. [Again, the counselor wants to reinforce feelings that Edna has inside that this is right. Her judgment about career choice is based on feeling. That her Myers–Briggs type code and her Strong Interest Inventory results are in agreement with her preference relates to the thinking aspect of judging, which Edna does not use often.]

In this example, the Myers–Briggs Type Indicator serves as a source for guiding the counselor in conceptualizing Edna's issues about her future career choices. He chooses not to introduce the terminology to her, but to use the conceptual framework of the Myers–Briggs theory as a basis for his own work. If it seems helpful to him to explain the concepts to Edna again, or to use them with her, then he will.

EXAMPLE OF CAREER ADJUSTMENT COUNSELING

Often, in counseling, a counselor finds it helpful to develop weaker components of an individual's perception and judgment. For example, a person whose Myers–Briggs type is INTP uses sensing and feeling less frequently than intuition and thinking. Myers and McCaulley (1985, p. 65) suggest that counselors should work on one process at a time; for example, they should work on judgment but not perception and judgment at the same time. Furthermore, the work should be conscious and purposeful, and counselors should not let other processes interfere. When working with people who are having difficulty on their job, counselors often find it helpful to make use of functions that are not a strong part of the individual's personality. These weaker functions are called *tertiary* and *inferior functions*. They are described in more detail in other publications (for example, Myers, McCaulley, Quenk, and Hammer, 1998; Quenk, 1996). An example of making use of weaker functions follows.

George is a 45-year-old Native American raised in New Mexico. He is married and has two teenage children. He has a doctorate in biology and has been employed at a large cancer research hospital to do basic research for the last 12 years. Two years ago, he was put in charge of a research team. Research progress has been frustrating. As a result, the five members of his team have become upset with each other. Two of the team members do not talk to each other any longer. George's supervisor has been concerned about this lack of progress. Members of George's team have talked to the supervisor about the increasing tension within the group.

George recently complained of chest pain. After being examined thoroughly by a physician, George was referred to a counselor for help with work-related issues. After talking with George, the physician believed that tension experienced at work might be the cause of the pain. Although somewhat reluctant to seek counseling, feeling that he should be able to handle the problems himself, George has come back for his second meeting with the counselor. After their first meeting, he completed the Myers–Briggs Type Indicator. His scores are summarized as INTP. The following dialogue is from George's second counseling session:

CL: I've been having a lot of trouble at work. I find myself distracted constantly. We're involved in much important research, and the people who work with me seem to spend more time bickering with each other and less time researching. I can't concentrate, and I don't like it. I find that I'm upset at the end of the day. I keep hoping things will work out, but they do not.

CO: This sounds very disturbing for you. You can't get your work done, and other people aren't getting their work done. [The counselor is aware that George's dominant process is thinking. He is thinking a lot about his research and the problems at work without the input of others. This process is an introverted one, thus it stays in his mind.]

CL: Yes, I am working often in my own head. I'm thinking constantly. I think at work; I can't stop thinking at home. I find that I'm distracted. My children notice this, too.

CO: What seems to be bothering you the most? [The counselor wishes to focus on a problem that she may be able to help with.]

CL: Part of it is we have some new doctoral-level people who have done good work before but haven't worked under my supervision. They don't say much to me, and I don't say much to them. I know I need to do something about it. Sometimes I can feel the tension; sometimes I can feel it in my chest.

CO: Tell me more about that feeling in the chest. [The counselor seizes the opportunity to talk about the least well-developed function, the inferior function, feeling, which is the opposite of George's dominant function, thinking.]

CL: I guess I feel tight. I usually feel upset, and I don't want to say anything.

CO: That's important information. [The counselor wants to deal with the feeling process, the least well developed of George's perception and judgment functions.]

CL: I guess it is important. It's hard for me sometimes to focus on things other than my research. These personal matters seem so trivial to me. But I'm starting to find that they are not. I remember what you said earlier when we were talking about the Myers–Briggs Type Indicator. You spoke of how important thinking is to me. It really is.

CO: I know, George. One of the things that we can work on is developing that other side of thinking—feeling. [The counselor avoids a long technical discussion of the Myers–Briggs Type Indicator and is eager to follow the lead-in that George has provided.]

CL: I know what happens at work is important. Sometimes I will tell myself its not.

CO: It's good that you recognize that, George. Perhaps we can work more on that—recognizing not only your own feelings, but the feelings of others also.

CL: It is just uncomfortable for me. Sometimes I find myself almost rushing to get through the laboratory and into my own little office, where I can work alone. I need to do more.

CO: What is it that you need to do more of, George?

CL: I need to talk to the people working at their desks and tables in the lab.

CO: That sounds good, George. How might you do it? [The counselor is pleased that George recognizes the need to develop his feeling side. She wants to see what he can do to develop his feeling function.]

CL: I think I need to stop and talk with them, see how things are going, maybe relax. I have some idea that my tension might be communicated to them.

CO: That sounds good, George. That could be happening. [George may be taking advantage of his intuitive process at this point. The counselor is pleased to hear that and yet can return to working on the feelings that are being discussed.]

CL: I know I need to slow down; I need to relax when I'm talking with someone in the lab and not pull away as quickly as I do. How can I do that?

CO: Being in a comfortable position, slowing your breathing, relaxing your hands. Anything to slow yourself down might help. [The counselor responds to this specific request for information, knowing that problem solving is something that is likely to appeal to George because of his emphasis on thinking.]

CL: It sounds simple.

CO: It's not so simple. Maybe we can work on some relaxation techniques later today. There are different ways of slowing down. [The counselor does not want to let relaxation be the only answer to dealing with the feeling function. She wants to return to ways that George can feel more and understand the feelings of others at his work site.]

In the above example, the counselor tries to strengthen and develop George's weakest function, the judging function of feeling. For the counselor, the Myers–Briggs Type

Indicator provides a way of conceptualizing George's work adjustment problem. Being well versed in the Myers–Briggs theory, she can think about George in terms of the concepts themselves. She can then relate George's type to her knowledge of the concepts, integrating this relationship into her counseling conceptualization. The counselor recognizes that the problem is a difficult one. Developing one's inferior function is not easy. In her continuing work with George, she may look at ways in which he can change his work environment to alleviate the situation, believing that it is easier for George to change his work environment to match his type than to change his type to match his work environment (Myers et al., 1985). Some examples of such changes would be getting others to assist him in supervision or changing his assignment to return to more research and less supervision. Certainly, George's choice of work, science, is a frequent choice of INTP individuals (Table 6.2). His difficulty with supervision is consistent with the description of thinking in Table 6.5. It is for the counselor and George to decide how much George can change and how much the environment can change.

The counseling dialogues used in this chapter give a small sample of the use of Myers–Briggs typological theory in counseling on career issues. Several books have been written that describe the 16 types in detail and include case studies that emphasize the conceptualization of the Myers–Briggs Indicator. Keirsey and Bates (1978) describe both temperaments and types in detail. A good overview of MBTI theory and its relationship to careers is *Introduction to Type and Careers* (Hammer, 1993). Particularly helpful for work adjustment counseling is *Introduction to Type in Organizations* (Hirsh & Kummerow, 1998). Specifically focusing on career counseling is *Do What You Are: Discover the Perfect Career for You through the Secrets of Personality Type* (Tieger & Barron-Tieger, 1992). How different types handle work tasks differently and how to adapt tasks to type is described in *WORK-Types* (Kummerow, Barger, & Kirby, 1997). A casebook approach, such as the one by Provost (1993), which has case illustrations for a variety of the 16 types, can be particularly helpful to counselors learning the Myers–Briggs typology. Possibly the single best overview of the Myers–Briggs topological theory is *Gifts Differing* (1993) by Isabel Myers. These books use numerous examples and cases to explore and explain the intricacies of the Myers–Briggs system of types.

THE ROLE OF OCCUPATIONAL INFORMATION

From a career development point of view, Myers–Briggs type theory can be conceived of as a matching version of trait and factor theory. Using the Myers–Briggs Type Indicator (or its conceptual system), the counselor can match the client's Myers–Briggs type with the Myers–Briggs types of occupations. By using information such as that in Tables 6.3 through 6.6 and in *Introduction to Type and Careers* (Hammer, 1993), the counselor can gain an idea of the preferred work setting of different Myers–Briggs types. Knowledge of an individual's type can be matched with knowledge of which types select which work settings most frequently (Table 6.2). However, Table 6.2 provides only some information. For each type, only five to seven occupations are listed. Also, some categories of occupations are very broad, such as scientists, health workers, and service workers; each of these categories includes many other occupations. Additionally, some occupations are listed in more than one type, such as actor (ENFP, ENTP, and ENFJ) and clergy (INFJ,

ENFP, and ENFJ). Information in the manual (Myers, McCaulley, Quenk, & Hammer, 1998) provides more information about other occupations and their types. As in Table 6.2, some occupations can be found in more than one type and some occupational categories are broad.

In their manual, Myers and McCaulley (1985) provide an example of a counselor giving occupational information to a client based on information known about various types. The following excerpt from their example will help to illustrate this*:

Q. I am an ISTJ and want to enter psychology. Where would I fit?

A. You are more likely to like the work of an experimental psychologist. In one study, more than twice the expected number of ISTJs chose experimental (I ratio 2.4, p .01). In fact, all the ISTJs in that study chose one of the experimental fields. Remember that most of your colleagues are likely to prefer intuition, but you will probably find more people who share your interest in the experimental fields.

Q. I know I want psychology, but I'm not sure which field to choose. What is the difference between clinical and experimental psychology?

A. Clinical psychology attracts more psychologists who are concerned with possibilities (N-intuition) for people (F-feeling) (NF 72%; ratio 1.6, p .01). Experimental psychology attracts more people interested in theory (N) and logical analysis (T-thinking), but there is also a sizable number of more practical people in experimental psychology (S ratio 1.8, p .001). You will find all types in each area, but these facts may help you think about how your interests relate to the psychological specialties.

This example shows how a counselor who is extremely knowledgeable about Myers–Briggs type theory can extrapolate knowledge from the *Atlas of Type Tables* (1987) and the *MBTI Manual* (Myers, McCaulley, Quenk, & Hammer, 1998) to give information to clients. There is no single source of occupational information that describes occupations solely in terms of Myers–Briggs types. Because many Myers–Briggs types can exist within a given occupation, counselors need to be careful not to give the impression that only certain Myers–Briggs types can work in specified occupations. People with different Myers–Briggs types who enjoy the same occupations are likely to approach their work in a way that allows them to express their type. In their manual, Myers, McCaulley, Quenk, & Hammer (1998) are careful to describe the advantages of different points of view of various Myers–Briggs types within any given occupation.

However, there are some general suggestions that can be gathered from research into the ways that people of different types process information (Myers et al., 1998).

In discussing occupational information with Sensing types, counselors may want to be concrete and specific, whereas with Intuitive types, counselors can be more abstract. For individuals whose thinking score is high, data about occupations should be objective; with those for whom feeling is strong, relating occupational information to the client's experiences may be most helpful. An introverted approach to learning career information is likely to focus on reading information and thinking about it. An extraverted approach may be to talk to others about occupations. Linnehan and Blau (1998) investigated job search behavior; they report that extraverted individuals preferred interactive job search behaviors, whereas introverted individuals preferred detached or less personal job search approaches. Counselors may want to help clients use both introverted and extraverted approaches.

THE ROLE OF ASSESSMENT INSTRUMENTS

The Myers–Briggs Type Indicator and the Myers–Briggs typological theory are closely wedded. Even counselors who are very familiar with the Myers–Briggs theory rarely use the theory with a client without administering the Myers–Briggs Type Indicator. More than for any other theory discussed in this book, the inventory is closely tied to the conceptualization process that a counselor uses with a client. The 420-page manual (Myers et al., 1998) is extensive in its description of research that supports the use of the four Myers–Briggs dimensions. Furthermore, Thorne and Gough (1991) have summarized 30 years of research on types done at the Institute of Personality and Social Research at the University of California at Berkeley, and Hammer (1996) has summarized a decade of research on the MBTI.

The manual describes the construction of Form M of the Myers–Briggs Type Indicator, as well as the construction of the earlier forms of the MBTI. The manual (Myers et al., 1998) refers to hundreds of studies that provide information about the reliability and validity of the MBTI. A few recent studies are mentioned here. Capraro and Capraro (2002) find that there is generally strong support for the test–retest reliability and internal consistency of MBTI scales. Tischler (1994) and Karesh, Pieper, and Holland (1994) find support for the bipolar scales of the MBTI, but Bess and Harvey (2002) question them. Some attempts have been made to develop short forms of the MBTI. Harvey, Murray, and Markham (1994) tested three different short forms and found that they provided less information than the long form, and that there were unacceptably high disagreement rates between the short forms and the long form.

The MBTI has been compared with other measures of personality. These studies provide construct validity for the MBTI and help counselors understand the eight constructs more clearly. Loffredo and Opt (2006) found that individuals scoring high on intuition and thinking (especially the ENTJ type) scored highest on a measure of argumentativeness. The NEO Personality Inventory Form (Big Five) Extraversion score was found to be related to extraversion on the MBTI. Neuroticism was not correlated with any of the MBTI scales (Furnham, 1996; Furnham, Moutafi, & Crump, 2003). Other comparisons between the MBTI and the NEO can be found in the *MBTI Manual*. The *MBTI Manual* also reports relationships to other personality constructs and inventories.

Some writers have specifically addressed the relevance of the MBTI to career counseling. Barrineau (2005) found that perceiving types, intuitive types with high scores on perceiving, and the ENFP type were found more frequently among students who withdrew from liberal arts colleges than were other types. When career indecision was studied, ISTJs and ISFTs were more frequently found to be decided about career choice than the average college freshman and ENFPs and ENFJs were more frequently found to be undecided (Kelly & Lee, 2005). McCaulley (2000) and McCaulley and Moody (2001) describe some ways that the MBTI can be used with career services. Kennedy and Kennedy (2004) explain how the MBTI can be useful in employment counseling in describing preferences as they relate to types of career choices. In studying the use of the MBTI by executive coaches who themselves received executive coaching, Bell (2006) suggests that executive coaches found that the use of the MBTI early in the coaching process may produce greater gains than if used later in the process. When used to help understand how clients deal with career obstacles, such as reluctance to change, or problems caused by anxiety or depression, the thinking and feeling scores were related to obstacles for male clients and the judgment–perception scores were related to obstacles for all clients (Healy & Woodward, 1998). Regarding résumé writing, the MBTI can help clients focus on strengths related to their psychological type in dealing with confidence in writing résumés (Peterson, 1998). Career counseling continues to be a significant research focus of the MBTI.

However, the Myers–Briggs Type Indicator is not above question, and several writers have challenged the findings presented previously. Although Bayne (2005) in evaluating evidence regarding the usefulness of the MBTI provides a positive view of the MBTI, he also suggests areas for further research. Healy (1989) argues against using the MBTI in counseling. He believes that there is limited evidence that classifying people into 16 types will enhance counseling, a view challenged by Murray (1990) and Tischler (1994). Furthermore, Healy questions whether the Myers–Briggs Type Indicator measures the constructs defined by Jung. He also finds that there is no evidence that using the MBTI in counseling will help clients with their concerns. However, Healy and Woodward (1998) show the value of the MBTI in dealing with obstacles to clients' career development. Pittenger (1993, 2005) provides evidence that the MBTI has limited counseling utility, reliability, and validity. Pittenger (2005) also suggests that it is not sufficient to use the client's MBTI type in counseling, but that counselors should make use of the client scores on each type, because type scores that fall near the middle of the bipolar scales may not fit clients as well as scores that fall closer to the extremes of the scales. In general, the research on the MBTI tends to focus on the four dimensions and not on the complex concepts that are used in counseling, such as the dominant and auxiliary processes. Despite these criticisms, researchers continue to develop and study the Myers–Briggs Type Indicator.

Several report forms and scoring systems are available for the MBTI. For the regular form of the MBTI, a special report is available called the *MBTI Career Report* (Hammer & MacDaid, 1994), which lists work behaviors and preferences that match the clients' type. Two instruments are available that provide more information, through more scales, for the four basic Myers–Briggs dimensions. The *MBTI Step II Profile Form Q* (Quenk & Kummerow, 2001) offers a detailed graphic profile of the MBTI. Also, the *Type Differentiation Indicator—Form J* (Saunders, Myers, & Briggs, 1989b) includes the same 20 subscales for the four dimensions as the *MBTI Expanded Analysis* (Saunders, Myers, & Briggs, 1989a), as well as 7 additional subscales. These instruments would appear to be useful to counselors because they help individuals explore MBTI concepts in depth and make a bridge to occupational choices that could be considered.

APPLYING THE THEORY TO WOMEN AND CULTURALLY DIVERSE POPULATIONS

In general, cultural and gender differences recently have become a greater focus of research in the study of the Myers–Briggs typology. The *MBTI Manual* (Myers et al., 1998) does report the percentage of male and female individuals at four levels of preference (slight, moderate, clear, or very clear) for each of the eight types. The sample sizes range between 15,000 and 25,000 for two different forms of the Myers–Briggs Type Indicator. By way of summary, the *MBTI Manual* estimates that about 75% of women in the United States prefer feeling to thinking, and about 56% of men in the United States prefer thinking to feeling. Laribee (1994), who studied accounting students, who would be expected to have a preference for thinking over feeling, provides another view into this difference. The male preference for thinking was 83% to 85%, and the female preference ranged from 44% to 63%. With regard to the gender distribution of type for the other scales, it appears that slightly more men (54%) prefer introversion to extraversion, and slightly more women (52%) prefer extraversion to introversion. Regarding sensing and intuition, both men (72%) and women (75%) prefer sensing to intuition. These gender differences represent U.S. national samples (Myers et al., 1998).

A new emphasis in the *MBTI Manual* is that of using type in multicultural settings (Kirby, Kendall, & Barger, 2007; McCaulley & Moody, 2001). Studying the use of the MBTI in many cultures, Kirby, Kendall, and Barger (2007) find that cultures have different preferred MBTI types for males and females. They also show how to consider values that are prominent in different cultures when interpreting and using the 8 MBTI types and their combinations with people of different cultures. The MBTI (Form G) has been translated into more than 20 languages including Anglicized English, Australian English, Bahasa Malay, Canadian French, Chinese, Danish, Dutch, European French, Finnish, German, Italian, Korean, Norwegian, Portuguese, Spanish, Spanish/Castellano, and Swedish. All of these translations are available commercially and have been deemed valid and reliable. Other translations currently are being tested for their validity and reliability. The *MBTI Manual* presents samples of the distribution of the 16 types combinations for high school, college, management, and other groups from many countries, such as Canada, Australia, New Zealand, Singapore, France, South Africa, Korea, Japan, Mexico, and several Latin American countries. Within the United States, samples of type distributions are also reported for African Americans and Hispanic Americans. McCaulley and Moody (2001) suggest that the MBTI can be used with clients of many cultures. They do suggest caution in using the MBTI with people from cultures that are group or collectivist in orientation such as black South Africans, the Maori of New Zealand, and certain Native American cultures. Kummerow (2001) offers another caution: Counselors who use psychological type in their work may prefer I, N, F, and P types to E, S, T, and J, and they may devalue characteristics important to clients from minority cultures.

Studies of differences in type for individuals from different cultures will provide examples of the worldwide interest in the Myers–Briggs theory. Comparisons were made between MBTI scores and college students' preferences for descriptions of specific types. African American female individuals tended to be overrepresented on the ISTJ categories on the MBTI (Posey, Thorne, & Carskadon, 1999). Contrasting the types of female middle school students and female counselors in Puerto Rico, Alvarado (1997) reports that both groups scored high in sensing and thinking, but the students scored higher on intuition. Comparing Canadian college students from a French-speaking background with those of an English-speaking background, Stalikas, Casas, and Carson (1996) report that more of the English-speaking students scored high on feeling, intuition, and perception than the French-speaking students. More of the French-speaking students scored high on introversion, sensation, thinking, and judging. Contrasting the MBTI types of Finnish Masters of Business Administration (MBA) students and American MBA students, Järlström (2005) reported that extraversion, intuition, and feeling were more prevalent in the Finnish sample than the American sample.

Comparing African American and Native American high school students, Nuby and Oxford (1998) report that African American students preferred judging much more than the Native American students. In characterizing the values of Native Americans, Little Soldier (1989) stresses the importance of cooperation, sharing, and the extended family. In a study of 210 non-reservation Native American college freshmen, Simmons and Barrineau (1994) report that sensing for male and sensing and feeling for female Native Americans were overrepresented compared with other freshmen, which are preferences that fit with the values described by Little Soldier. It is likely that in the future more studies similar to these will be reported.

An interesting concept of the Myers–Briggs typology that may be particularly appropriate to understanding populations that may be oppressed, such as women and people from different cultural backgrounds, is *falsification* of type. Because the development of type is assumed to be inborn, environmental influences can distort or falsify it. Individuals who are taught to respond in a certain way may learn and outwardly behave as one type, whereas inwardly their true type is being frustrated. This interesting clinical concept presents a difficult research problem: How can one separate the real type from the falsified type? Those who counsel using Myers–Briggs typology may find that they are able to do this. Whether some women and some individuals from minority cultures have been trained or expected by society to behave in a certain way that does not fit their true type remains to be proved.

COUNSELOR ISSUES

How do individuals communicate with each other? Luzader (2001), having observed individuals in communication laboratories, suggests that when talking, counselors and others are using extroversion to function in the outside world; when writing, they are functioning in the inside world (introversion); and when listening, they are using their auxiliary functions.

Myers, McCaulley, Quenk, & Hammer (1998) make several suggestions for dealing with clients of different types that are based on some of the research on how counselors communicate with their clients. These findings suggest that counselors need to adjust their style of communication for different Myers–Briggs types. In exploratory research, Yeakley (1982, 1983) suggests that it may be helpful for two people to be using the same communication style at the same time, whether it is in a business, a marriage, or a counseling relationship. Yeakley believes that listening to sensing types means listening at a pragmatic and literal level. Conversely, listening to an intuitive type requires listening to the underlying meaning. What does the speaker really mean, and what are the implications? When listening to a thinking type of person, the counselor should focus on the organization of the individual's comments, as in reading an essay: What are the main points, the less important points, and the overall concept? In contrast, listening to a feeling type would mean being aware of feelings about the client and the values or feelings projected by the client in the message. The implication is that counselors whose types are different from those of their clients will need to expend considerable effort to alter their style of interaction to fit with that of their clients. For example, a counselor whose perceiving style is sensing and whose judging style is feeling may have to adjust to a client whose perceiving style is intuitive and whose judging style is thinking.

SUMMARY

Although not generally considered a theory of career development, the Myers–Briggs type theory has been used as such by many counselors. Its broad focus is on how people perceive and judge the world. There are two different ways of perceiving (sensing and intuition), as well as two different ways of judging (thinking and feeling). Individuals must use the perceiving and judging functions many times during the course of a day. In addition, they deal with their inner world of ideas (introversion) and with the outer world of people and objects (extraversion). This chapter focuses on relating these styles to career decision making and work adjustment. The complex interactions between the eight Myers–Briggs types, which represent four bipolar dimensions, have been illustrated in several counseling situations. Because the Myers–Briggs Type Indicator is an essential part of the Myers–Briggs theory of types, a discussion of research on the Myers–Briggs Type Indicator, as well as criticism of it, has been presented. Readers will find that the presentation in this chapter is insufficient to enable them to use the Myers–Briggs Type Indicator in career counseling. Attendance at workshops that teach the use of the Myers–Briggs Type Indicator, as well as a thorough study of the *MBTI Manual* (Myers et al., 1998), is strongly recommended.

REFERENCES

Alvarado, I. Y. (1997). Psychological preference types of Puerto Rican school counselors and students using the Myers–Briggs Type Indicator (Doctoral dissertation, Walden University, 1997). *Dissertation Abstracts International: Section A: Humanities and Social Services, 57/9-A,* 3822.

Atlas of type tables. (1987). Gainesville, FL: Center for the Application of Psychological Type.

Barrineau, P. (2005). Personality types among undergraduates who withdraw from liberal arts colleges. *Journal of Psychological Type, 65*(4), 27–32.

Bayne, R. (2005). *Ideas and Evidence: Critical reflections on MBTI theory and practice.* Gainesville, FL: Center for Application of Psychological Type.

Bell, S. E. (2006). Myers–Briggs type indicator and executive coaching: Participants' self-perceptions about the effectiveness of the two when used together. *Dissertation Abstracts International: Section B: The Sciences and Engineering, 66(7-B)*, 3980.

Bess, T. L., & Harvey, R. J. (2002). Bimodal score distributions and the Myers–Briggs Type Indicator: Fact or artifact? *Journal of Assessment, 78*, 176–186.

Capraro, R. M., & Capraro, M. M. (2002). Myers–Briggs Type Indicator score reliability across studies: A meta-analytic reliability generalization study. *Education & Psychological Measurement, 62*, 590–602.

Furnham, A. (1996). The big five versus the big four: The relationship between the MBTI and NEO-PI Five Factor Model of Personality. *Personality and Individual Differences, 21*, 303–307.

Furnham, A., Moutafi, J., & Crump, J. (2003). The relationship between the revised NEO Personality Inventory and the Myers–Briggs Indicator. *Social Behavior & Personality, 31*, 577–584.

Hammer, A. L. (1993). *Introduction to type and careers.* Palo Alto, CA: Consulting Psychologists Press.

Hammer, A. L. (Ed.) (1996). *MBTI applications: A decade of research on the MBTI.* Palo Alto, CA: Consulting Psychologists Press.

Hammer, A. L., & MacDaid, G. P. (1994). *MBTI career report.* Palo Alto, CA: Consulting Psychologists Press.

Harvey, R. J., Murray, W. D., & Markham, S. E. (1994). Evaluation of three short form versions of the Myers–Briggs Type Indicator. *Journal of Personality Assessment, 63*, 181–184.

Healy, C. C. (1989). Negative: The MBTI: Not ready for routine use in counseling. *Journal of Counseling and Development, 67*, 487–488.

Healy, C. C., & Woodward, G. A. (1998). The Myers–Briggs Type Indicator and career obstacles. *Measurement and Evaluation in Counseling and Development, 31*, 74–86.

Hirsh, S. K., & Kummerow, J. M. (1998). *Introduction to type in organizations* (3rd ed.). Palo Alto, CA: Consulting Psychologists Press.

Järlström, M. (2005). Relationship between type profiles and desired work environments of business students in Finland. *Journal of Psychological Type, 64(5)*, 41–55.

Jung, C. G. (1971). *Psychological types: The collected works of C. G. Jung* (Vol. 6, H. B. Baynes, Trans., revised by R. F. Hull). Princeton, NJ: Princeton University Press. (Original work published 1921.)

Karesh, D., Pieper, W. A., & Holland, C. L. (1994). Comparing the MBTI, the Jungian Type Survey, and the Singer-Loomis Inventory of Personality. *Journal of Psychological Type, 30*, 30–38.

Keirsey, D., & Bates, M. (1978). *Please, understand me* (3rd ed.). Del Mar, CA: Prometheus Nemesis Books.

Kelly, K. R., & Lee, W. (2005). Relation of psychological type to career indecision among university students. *Journal of Psychological Type, 64(2)*, 11–20.

Kennedy, R. B., & Kennedy, D. A. (2004). Using the Myers–Briggs Type Indicator® in career counseling. *Journal of Employment Counseling, 41(1)*, 38–44.

Kirby, L. K., Kendall, E., & Barger, N. J. (2007). *Type and culture: Using the MBTI instrument in international applications.* Mountain View, CA: CPP, Inc.

Kummerow, J. M. (2001). Examining type bias and inclusivity: Lessons from ethnic identity viewpoints. *Journal of Psychological Type, 59*, 6–9.

Kummerow, J. M., Barger, N. J., & Kirby, L. K. (1997). *WORK-types.* New York: Warner Books.

Laribee, S. F. (1994). The psychological types of college accounting students. *Journal of Psychological Type, 28*, 37–38.

Linnehan, F., & Blau, G. (1998). Exploring the emotional side of job search behavior for younger workforce entrants. *Journal of Employment Counseling, 35,* 98–113.

Little Soldier, L. (1989). Cooperative learning and the Native American student. *Phi Delta Kappa, 71,* 161–163.

Loffredo, D. A., & Opt, S. K. (2006). Argumentativeness and Myers–Briggs Type Indicator® preferences. *Journal of Psychological Type, 66*(7), 59–68.

Luzader, M. (2001). Applying type to communication. *Journal of Psychological Type, 56,* 37–39.

McCaulley, M. H. (2000). The Myers–Briggs Type Indicator in counseling. In C. E. Watkins, Jr., & V. L. Campbell (Eds.), *Testing and assessment in counseling practice; Contemporary topics in vocational psychology* (2nd ed., pp. 111–173). Mahwah, NJ: Erlbaum.

McCaulley, M. H., & Moody, R. A. (2001). Multicultural applications of the Myers–Briggs Type Indicator. In L. A. Suzuki, J. G. Ponterotto, & P. J. Meller (Eds.), *Handbook of multicultural assessments in clinical, psychological, and educational applications* (2nd ed., pp. 279–305). San Francisco: Jossey-Bass.

Mitchell, W. D. (2001). A full dynamic model of type. *Journal of Psychological Type, 59,* 12–28.

Mitchell, W. D. (2006). Validation of the full dynamic model of type. *Journal of Psychological Type, 66*(5), 35–48.

Murray, J. B. (1990). Review of research on the Myers–Briggs Type Indicator. *Perceptual and Motor Skills, 70,* 1187–1202.

Myers, I. B. (1962). *Manual: The Myers–Briggs Type Indicator.* Princeton, NJ: Educational Testing Service.

Myers, I. B. (1993). *Gifts differing.* Palo Alto, CA: Consulting Psychologists Press.

Myers, I. B., & McCaulley, M. H. (1985). *Manual: A guide to the development and use of the Myers–Briggs Type Indicator.* Palo Alto, CA: Consulting Psychologists Press.

Myers, I. B., McCaulley, M. H., Quenk, N. L., & Hammer, A. L. (1998). *MBTI manual: A guide to the development and use of the Myers–Briggs Type Indicator* (3rd ed.). Palo Alto, CA: Consulting Psychologists Press.

Nuby, J. F., & Oxford, R. L. (1998). Learning style preferences of Native American and African-American secondary students. *Journal of Psychological Type, 44,* 5–19.

Peterson, A. C. (1998). Using psychological type to assist career clients with resume writing. *Journal of Psychological Type, 44,* 32–38.

Pittenger, D. J. (1993). The utility of the Myers–Briggs Type Indicator. *Review of Educational Research, 63,* 467–488.

Pittenger, D. J. (2005). Cautionary comments regarding the Myers–Briggs Type Indicator. *Consulting Psychology Journal: Practice and Research, 57*(3), 210–221.

Posey, A. M., Thorne, B. M., & Carskadon, T. G. (1999). Differential validity and comparative type distributions of blacks and whites in the Myers–Briggs Type Indicator. *Journal of Psychological Type, 48,* 6–21.

Provost, J. A. (1993). *Applications of the Myers–Briggs Type Indicator in counseling: A casebook.* Gainesville, FL: Center for the Application of the Psychological Type.

Quenk, N. L. (1996). *In the grip: Our hidden personality.* Palo Alto, CA: Consulting Psychologists Press.

Quenk, N. L., & Kummerow, J. M. (2001). *MBTI Step II Interpretation Report Form,* Palo Alto, CA: Consulting Psychologists Press.

Saunders, D., Myers, I. B., & Briggs, K. C. (1989a). *MBTI expanded analysis.* Palo Alto, CA: Consulting Psychologists Press.

Saunders, D., Myers, I. B., & Briggs, K. C. (1989b). *Type differentiation indicator.* Palo Alto, CA: Consulting Psychologists Press.

Simmons, G., & Barrineau, P. (1994). Learning style and the Native American. *Journal of Psychological Type, 28*, 3–10.

Stalikas, A., Casas, E., & Carson, A. D. (1996). In the shadow of the English: English and French Canadians differ by psychological type. *Journal of Psychological Type, 38*, 4–12.

Thorne, A., & Gough, H. (1991). *Portraits of type: An MBTI research compendium.* Palo Alto, CA: Consulting Psychologists Press.

Tieger, P. D., & Barron-Tieger, B. (1992). *Do what you are: Discover the perfect career for you through the secrets of personality type.* Boston: Little, Brown.

Tischler, L. (1994). The MBTI factor structure. *Journal of Psychological Type, 31*, 24–31.

Yeakley, F. R. (1982). Communication style preferences and adjustments as an approach to studying effects of similarity in psychological type. *Research in Psychological Type, 5*, 30–48.

Yeakley, F. R. (1983). Implications of communication style research for psychological type theory. *Research in Psychological Type, 6*, 5–23.

LIFE-SPAN THEORY

PART

Life-span theory, as it applies to career development, concerns the growing and changing ways that an individual deals with career issues over his or her entire life span. This approach is in marked contrast to the theories presented in Part One, which dealt with career issues at one point in time. Because life-span theory covers a long period, it tends to be more complex, in terms of the number of constructs that are used, than typological or trait and factor theories. Therefore, four chapters are needed to cover the entire life span. Chapter 7 discusses the development of career decision making in childhood. Included is the development of curiosity and exploration, which leads to obtaining information from role models and observed events. This approach leads to the development of interests and self-concept, resulting in the ability to plan and problem solve. The study of power, gender roles, and prestige provides another way of understanding the career development of children. Chapter 8 covers the development of interests, capacities, and values during adolescence. Related is the development of career maturity and vocational identity. Chapter 9 discusses career issues during late adolescence and adulthood. It focuses on life roles, as well as developmental stages. Chapter 10 emphasizes the career transitions and crises that often occur in adulthood. Each chapter addresses special problems related to women and culturally diverse populations that occur during each aspect of the life span. This part uses theoretical concepts to provide a conceptual framework for dealing with counseling issues that occur during childhood, adolescence, and adulthood.

The theoretical approach used in Part Two is based on the work of Donald Super and his colleagues, although other theories are used to augment their life-span concepts. There are several reasons for selecting Super's theory as the basis for the chapters on life-span theory. First, Super's developmental theory is one of only a few that cover the entire life span. Second, more than any other life-span theorist, Super developed inventories to validate the constructs of his theory, thus providing instruments to be used in counseling. Third, more research has been done in conjunction with the concepts of Super's developmental theory than with any other life-span theory. Fourth, unlike trait and factor and other career development theories, life-span theories are rather similar to each other. Discussing each life-span theory separately in terms of its implication for counseling would tend to produce similar suggestions for each theory. Therefore, other developmental theories are integrated into Part Two to supplement Super's life-span theory.

Several theorists have contributed to an understanding of career issues at various points during the life span. Gottfredson's developmental theory of occupational aspirations has significant insight about the development of gender-role stereotyping in childhood. Her theory, which is discussed in Chapter 7, provides an understanding of the development of women's, as well as men's, career choices. The work of Vondracek and colleagues, which is discussed in Chapter 8, shows the relevance of vocational identity in the study of adolescent development by emphasizing the social context in which adolescents make career choices. The model of minority identity development proposed by Atkinson, Morton, and Sue, although not a career development theory, helps in conceptualizing life-span issues that affect the career development of minorities. This theory, which is discussed in Chapter 9, focuses on the development of adults but is applicable to adolescents as well. Another theory that is not a career development theory is used as the basis for a discussion of adult career crises and transitions in Chapter 10. Hopson and Adams's theory for understanding adult transitions is integrated into the developmental stages of Super's theory. By combining these theories with work done by Super and colleagues, I describe a conceptual framework for counseling clients of all ages.

CAREER DEVELOPMENT IN CHILDHOOD

CHAPTER 7

CHAPTER HIGHLIGHTS

Super's Model of the Career Development of Children

Using Super's Model in Counseling Children

Gottfredson's Theory of Self-Creation, Circumscription, and Compromise

Career Development of Children from Culturally Diverse Backgrounds

The Role of Occupational Information

The Role of Assessment Instruments

Counselor Issues

This chapter covers career-related issues that affect the child until the age of 12 years. An emphasis of the chapter is the maturational activities in elementary school as described by Super's (1990) model of the bases of career maturity. This chapter also covers the development of gender role. However, Super's model of childhood career development deals only in general ways with gender issues. Gottfredson's (1981, 2002, 2005) theory makes hypotheses about the relationship of gender-role stereotyping to career choice and the role of prestige in career decisions. Gottfredson also explains the role of complex developmental and genetic contributions in career choice. The career development of children from different cultural backgrounds and presentation of occupational information to children are also discussed. This presentation includes ideas about classroom activities and the relationship between school and work (school-to-work). Research on children of culturally diverse backgrounds is more limited than is research on gender issues and children, but information does exist that can assist the counselor in conceptualizing career issues for children from culturally diverse backgrounds.

Research provides information to counselors who work with young children about vocational issues. Although there is less information on career development in childhood than any other part of the life-span, there are a number of studies. Many of these are not directly related to theory. Hartung, Porfeli, and Vondracek (2005) review research on the career development of children and put the research in the context of life-span development. Watson and McMahon (2005) describe how and what children learn about the world of work and their own role in the world. Taking a counseling point of view, Turner and Lapan (2005) examine both career development theory and research, suggesting ways that counselors and educators can support the career development and aspirations of children.

Often the focus of counseling young children is not career development. A major career task for counselors may be organizing an occupational information program for young children for or with teachers, as much career development takes place in the classroom. Counselors have an opportunity to influence the later career development of children in significant ways. However, the impact of counselors' interventions may not be recognizable until many years later. Implications of Super's and Gottfredson's career development theories for the communication of vocational information to children are discussed with suggestions. Super's theory also has implications for ways in which counselors can look at themselves in relationship to their clients. By using a developmental approach to occupations, assessment, and counselor issues, counselors can establish a consistent framework within which to view their young clients.

SUPER'S MODEL OF THE CAREER DEVELOPMENT OF CHILDREN

This chapter describes Super's (1990, 1994; Savickas, 2002) model of childhood career development as illustrated in Figure 7.1. Super developed a model of how children develop a concept of themselves that includes planfulness, career decision making, and time perspective. Included in the model is an explanation of the development of interests and self control. The model starts with recognizing that a basic drive in children is curiosity. Curiosity is often satisfied through exploration, an important career development activity that may never cease. This exploratory activity leads to the acquisition of information. This chapter gives several views of how children process information. One important source of information is the key figure—that is, a person who a child may choose to imitate. Interests are developed by using information derived from exploratory activities and impressions of role models. During the maturational process, children develop ways to control their own behavior by listening to themselves and others. To make career decisions, children need to develop a time perspective—that is, a sense of the future. This, together with the development of a self-concept, will eventually lead to planful career decision making. The development of a self-concept is an exceedingly important part of Super's life-span theory. The self-concept derives from the child's exploratory behavior, which leads to acquiring occupational information, imitating key figures, and developing interests. One study of 49 children from low socioeconomic status families analyzed written

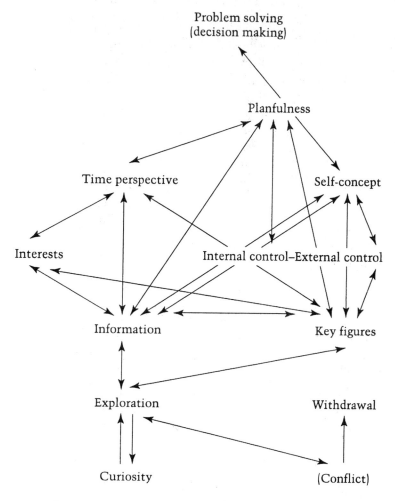

FIGURE 7.1 | A PERSON–ENVIRONMENT INTERACTIVE MODEL OF THE BASES
OF CAREER MATURITY.

Source: From *Career development in Britain* by A. G. Watts, D. E. Super, and J. M. Kidd, eds.
Copyright © 1981 by Hobson's Press. Reprinted by permission of Dr. Jennifer Kidd.

responses to questions about school and job goals, as well as skills and interests
(Schultheiss, Palma, & Manzi, 2005). Support for all of the concepts of Super's
model was found, except for curiosity, which was not assessed as directly as the other
concepts. Each of Super's concepts is illustrated through counseling examples.

CURIOSITY

Curiosity is among the most basic of all needs or drives; it has been observed in
animals, as well as infants. Using Berlyne's (1960) work as a starting point for his
discussion of exploratory behavior, Jordaan (1963) provides a useful approach to

the understanding of exploration and curiosity in children. According to Jordaan (1963), curiosity may develop when there are changes in an individual's physical or social needs. For a child, curiosity may be prompted by hunger, thirst, loneliness, and a variety of other stimuli. When a child is uncertain or confused, the child may decide to resolve his or her perplexity. Also, boredom, a wish for excitement, or a desire for stimulation may produce curiosity. In relating curiosity to vocational development, Jordaan emphasizes more complex stimuli than did Berlyne (1960) in his study of animal and infant behavior. Curiosity may be observed in very young children exposed to new objects, new people, or new concepts. Being exposed to puzzling new stimuli, the child must try to understand them or try out new behaviors. For example, a child seeing a toy horse in a playpen may try to ride it, fantasizing that he is riding a real horse. Another child may pick up a stick, pretending that it is a baseball bat and that he or she is a professional baseball player. Through curiosity, fantasized thinking may develop. Fantasy is the first stage of Ginzberg, Ginsburg, Axelrad, and Herma's (1951) theory of career development. Both Jordaan and Ginzberg and colleagues agree that curiosity and fantasy in the young child are important and should be encouraged, particularly in the early years of elementary school.

Although it is appropriate for elementary school counselors to encourage curiosity as an acceptable goal of career development for young children, doing so is often not simple. School counselors often see children because they are not doing what they are told to do by their teacher. A child who draws when he or she is expected to be reading or talks to another child when the teacher is talking may be expressing curiosity. In other words, being curious may often be disruptive. Reinforcing curiosity while discouraging disruptive behavior can be difficult. Encouraging the child to find ways to express curiosity in a positive sense may be one alternative to punishment as a means of dealing with disruptive behavior. Curiosity may lead to vocational exploration in later years; it is not important that curiosity have a career component at an early age.

EXPLORATION

In children, curiosity can lead to exploration of their environment, home, school, and peer and parental relationships. Curiosity refers to the desire for knowledge or for something new or unusual, whereas exploration is the act of searching or examining. Curiosity is a need; exploration is a behavior. For children, play and playful activities are an expression of exploratory behavior and help to meet curiosity needs. Jordaan (1963) lists ten dimensions of exploratory behavior. These are combined here to give examples of important activities that make up exploration. The behavior may be intentional and systematic, or it may be accidental. For example, children may want to find out how a clock works by carefully disassembling the pieces and putting them back together (intentional), or they may find a broken clock and just start to play with it (accidental). Exploratory behavior can occur because others ask a child to do it or because a child seeks it out. Sometimes, a teacher requests that a child put a puzzle together, or the child may take the initiative to do it. In exploring, a child can use either current or past experience. Having played with a puzzle 3 weeks ago, a child may decide to play with a similar one at that moment. Some exploratory behavior may benefit a child and help him or her to learn. Other behavior may be just for the enjoyment of the activity, such as writing one's name backward. Some exploratory behavior that is required can later turn out to be enjoyable. For example, being required to read does not mean that reading will always be a chore. Once the skill is partially mastered, children are likely to read on their own initiative. All these play behaviors are vocationally relevant only in an indirect sense. However, as the behaviors become more complex, they are likely to be more related to tasks required by various jobs.

When exploration is thwarted, the child may experience conflict and have less to do with peers, adults, and school subjects. (Note the arrow leading away from exploratory and planful behavior at the bottom of Figure 7.1.) Chak (2002) describes how parents can hinder their children's exploratory behavior. When exploration is stifled, a child is likely to lose the motivation to study. His or her work may become less imaginative. The child is less likely to respond to teachers' questions or to initiate activities in the classroom, obtaining information only because of external factors. A truly withdrawn child will have difficulty developing vocational maturity, because interests and information about career-related activities will be missing. Naturally, most children are not at one end or the other of the exploration–withdrawal continuum. Rather, they choose to explore some activities and not others.

Exploratory behavior builds on other exploratory behavior. To encourage exploratory behavior of any type (that is, behavior that is not damaging to oneself or others) can have eventual positive consequences in terms of career development. Trusting the exploration process without forcing it can be a useful goal for counselors and teachers. For example, a third-grade student may learn, in general terms, how a phone works. Such learning will develop in sophistication, both at a teacher's request and also perhaps through the child's own initiative in later years. As a fifth-grade student, the child may draw on past experience with the phone, as he or she learns more about the details of its operation. When counselors are talking to children about problems at school or at home, exploratory activity may play a minor role. However, there are times when reinforcement of this activity is helpful. For example, a young girl who is unhappy about her unmarried mother's new boyfriend may feel some satisfaction and control in her life when she can talk about the new things she has learned while reading stories at home.

Exploratory behavior is not a panacea for family or school problems. Rather, it is an activity that is likely to produce more exploratory behavior, leading eventually to an increased likelihood of successful vocational planning. In the process of exploratory activity, the child obtains much information about the environment. How this information is learned and processed is the subject of the next section.

INFORMATION

Clearly, the learning of information is essential to a child's development and success as an adolescent and as an adult. This section focuses on how theories of learning can be applied to occupational information for elementary school children. A point that is repeatedly stressed in the work of Jean Piaget is that children are not merely uninformed adults; rather, there are differences in how children process information throughout their development. A brief synopsis of the work of Piaget and Erikson follows, so that different theoretical approaches to the acquisition of knowledge by elementary school children can be compared.

Piaget (1977) describes four major periods of cognitive development: sensorimotor, pre-operational, concrete operational, and formal operational. The sensorimotor stage occurs from birth to age 2 years, when infants attend to objects and events around them, and then respond to these objects or events. *Attending* refers to the sensory acts of touching, seeing, smelling, and so on. *Responding* refers to such motor acts as biting, hitting, and screaming.

The pre-operational thought period occurs from approximately ages 2 to 7 years. In this period, the child can learn to add and subtract and perform similar operations. Children younger than 7 years are characterized as being egocentric. If a teacher announces that one child in a classroom will be selected to do a highly regarded task, each child is apt to think that he or she will be chosen. Furthermore, it is difficult for young children to distinguish fantasy from reality. When war scenes are shown on the evening news, it may be difficult for young children to have an idea of how far this occurrence is from their home. Another example of the egocentricity of the young child is the "internalization of action" that occurs when young children describe what they are doing out loud, apparently talking to no one.

The third stage of cognitive development, and the one of most relevance in this chapter, is concrete operations. In this stage, which occurs between the ages of about 7 and 11 years, children think in concrete terms. They do not have to see an object to imagine manipulating it, but they must be aware that it exists. They can imagine adding three elephants to five elephants, but they cannot add $3y$ to $5y$. The ability to think abstractly takes place in the final period, called *formal operations*, beginning about the age of 12 years. It is easier for children between the ages of 7 and 11 years to learn what a dentist does—how he or she uses equipment, examines teeth, and so forth—than it is for them to sense how long 8 years of post–high school training really is, or what a $75,000 income means. It is hard, for example, for an 8-year-old child to grasp what it means to "help others feel better about themselves," as a social worker does. This idea is more likely to be understood by adolescents.

A different view, but one with somewhat similar conclusions, is that of Erik Erikson (1963). In his eight stages of psychosocial development, he lists as the fourth stage that of industry versus inferiority. This occurs between the ages of 6 and 11 years. Children at this age have the freedom to make things and to organize them. This can give them a sense of industriousness if they are successful and inferiority if they are unsuccessful. In this stage, children develop a sense of achievement by organizing, developing, and applying information, or they have a sense of failure if they do not master these skills. From an occupational information perspective, if elementary school students have an opportunity to make signs or drawings for an occupation or to use tools, such as an electrician's pliers, they may be able to experience a sense of success. The concrete completion of an activity will be appreciated. The emphasis on the concrete is not unlike that of Piaget's third stage of learning. As shown in the next section, having role models to imitate and observe is consistent with the emphasis on concrete thinking and industriousness.

KEY FIGURES

Adults are important role models for children in learning about the world of work and in developing their own self-concept. Key figures for children are parents, teachers, public figures such as athletes and television personalities, and people with whom they come in contact in their own community, such as police officers or mail carriers. Parents' impact on children's view of occupations is illustrated by Trice and Tillapaugh's (1991) finding that children's aspirations to their parents' occupations are influenced by their perception of how satisfied their parents are with their own work. For seventh- and eighth-grade girls, mothers can be extremely important key figures, with maternal education and mothers' attitudes toward women having strong influences on girls' career orientation (Rainey & Borders, 1997). The findings that emphasize the importance of parental influence are consistent with Bandura's (1997) view that a significant method of learning for children is imitation. Rich's (1979) study shows that children know best those occupations that are in their own communities. Trice, Hughes, Odom, Woods, and McClellan (1995) support this conclusion. They report that, among boys, 42% of students in kindergarten, 40% in second grade, 47% in fourth grade, and 36% in sixth grade knew someone holding a job similar to their current career choice. Because of population density, rural children may be exposed to fewer occupations than urban children. People who work in occupations that children can observe have the potential of becoming key figures. As children imitate the behavior of important others, they may choose to adopt or discard those aspects of the individual that seem to fit themselves. This process is one aspect of the development of the child's self-concept.

Super's emphasis on key figures in the development of children's self-concept can be a useful reminder to the counselor to listen carefully to what a child learns from his or her observations of role models. Gibson (2004) suggests that role models can be seen as representing the child's needs, wants, and ambitions. For example, a child whose father is a long-distance truck driver may be impressed by the father's mastery of such a huge vehicle, entranced by the father's visits to distant places, or amazed by the father's ability to lift heavy objects. These thoughts may reflect the child's needs and ambitions. Depending on the parent–child interaction, any one of these impressions may have an impact on the child. If the person modeling truck driving is not the father, but an uncle or neighbor, the impact of the role model is likely to be different. Sometimes children's observations of role models are inaccurate. If there is an occasion to correct the misinformation, counselors can take advantage of that opportunity by describing the behavior of other key figures or different behaviors of the misperceived key figure. Key figures are likely to make a greater impact on children as they are more able to observe others, thus developing a greater amount of control over their own behavior.

INTERNAL VERSUS EXTERNAL CONTROL

Gradually, children begin to experience a feeling of control over their own surroundings. Children are often used to doing what they are told to do by their teachers and parents. Rules are to be followed. Even in games that elementary school children devise, following the rules is often quite important.

As children are successful in completing tasks and projects, they develop a feeling of autonomy and of being in control of future events. For counselors, children's "out-of-control" behavior is a frequent source of concern. The notion that self-control can have a direct impact on one's concept of oneself and also on one's ability to make career decisions (see Figure 7.1) is an interesting one. Often, the counselor who is dealing with a child who has hit another child in the classroom or talked back to a teacher is concerned with controlling the situation. Helping to develop a balance between self-control and external control may be a counseling goal. Relating this goal to career maturity may never be in the counselor's thoughts. The notion that self-control has an eventual impact on career planning, however, is an important one, regardless of whether it is a conscious element of the counselor's thinking when working with a child. Being able to control their behavior can help children become more aware of their likes and dislikes.

DEVELOPMENT OF INTERESTS

In time, children's fantasies of occupations are affected by information about the world, and they become interests. The child who wants to become a professional athlete may enjoy the activity, for example, playing ball or gymnastics, and not just imagine himself or herself receiving the adulation of an audience. In the development of interests, the capacity of a child to actually become an athlete is immaterial. Young children often do not see any barriers to what they may want to do in their future. Tracey (2001) has studied the structure of interests in children. In a study of fifth- and seventh-grade students, Tracey (2002) reports that just as interests led to the development of a sense of competence, the development of a sense of self-competence fostered interests. As children grew older, there was a gradual decline in the ratings of interests and competencies. With few exceptions, these declines were seen across all Holland types. This finding suggests that with age, students' views of themselves (self-concept) are affected by how they view themselves in relation to their environment. The development of interests is related to exploration. As the child tries new behaviors, some become attractive and some do not. The development of interests in activities inside and outside of school becomes an important facet of decision making in adolescence.

Encouraging children's emerging interests is helpful in the development of their career maturity. Talking about those aspects of their life that are exciting can eventually be helpful in career planning. Because counselors of elementary school children are rarely concerned with career issues, it may seem unimportant to focus on interests. Furthermore, the impact that counselors and other significant role models have may not be seen for many years. Talking to a child about an interest in baseball, an excitement about helping an injured animal, or the pleasure of a recent trip to a zoo may help the child to feel more important. This feeling of importance can contribute to the child's ability to develop a sense of what he or she is like, and how he or she is different from others. This development of self-concept is essential to the later career selection process.

TIME PERSPECTIVE

To develop a time perspective is to develop a sense of the future, to have a real appreciation that 6 months is different from 6 years. For children younger than 9 years, this is difficult, if not impossible. For example, the child who says, "I want to be a boat captain so I can steer a boat now," has a sense only of the present. The notion of how long "later" is develops over time (Ginzberg et al., 1951). Friedman's (2002) study of 92 children between the ages of 4 to 8 years shows that children's sense of future events depended on the way events were described to them. The implication of time perspective for counseling is that it is unrealistic to expect young children, particularly those below fourth grade, to think about planning future vocational or higher education. Rather, it is more important to examine jobs and job tasks now, to start to develop interests, and to reinforce exploratory behavior. As a future orientation develops, children are able to construct a sense of planfulness that will allow them to start making educational choices in middle school that will have an impact on their eventual career choices. Developing a time perspective is an issue that is also important for adolescents. A career program designed to develop a future orientation in 15- to 17-year-old teenagers and adults was effective in developing optimism about the future and a sense of continuity between the past and the future (Marko & Savickas, 1998).

SELF-CONCEPT AND PLANFULNESS

Self-concept has been at the core of Super's developmental theory. Super (1953) describes vocational development as the process of developing and implementing a self-concept. He saw self-concept as a combination of biological characteristics, the social roles individuals play, and evaluations of the reactions other individuals have to the person. *Self-concept* refers to how individuals view themselves and their situation. Figure 7.2 shows Super's arch, which illustrates his segmental theory (Chapters 8 and 9). Note that the self, at the top of the arch, is the keystone and center of Super's model. How individuals perceive themselves and interact is a reflection of personality, needs, values, and interests (Figure 7.2, left side). These perceptions change over the life span. Discussed in *Career Development: Self-Concept Theory* (Super, Starishevsky, Matlin, & Jordaan, 1963), the developing nature of the self-concept is of particular importance. Super et al. (1963) describe processes such as self-differentiation, role playing, exploration, and reality testing, which lead to the development of the self-concept. Interaction with society (Figure 7.2, right side) brings about the development of the self-concept as the individual interacts with family, school, peers, and coworkers. The self-concept refers to individuals' views of themselves and society and is subjective. This is in contrast to trait and factor theory, which emphasizes objective or outside measures of the self, for example, interest inventories and aptitude tests. Super's emphasis on the self-concept can be seen in his development of inventories that focus on evaluating roles and values that are important in the different stages of life.

Slightly different from the self-concept is the term *image norms*, which provides another way of viewing an organizing concept of the self. Image norms (Giannantonio & Hurley-Hanson, 2006) can be used in understanding Super's developmental stages. The term image norms includes three aspects of images of one's self: perceptions of occupational stereotypes, perceptions of one's physical self-image, and organizational images. Perceptions of occupational stereotypes refer to a belief that one must have a certain image in order to enter a particular occupation. Perception of one's self-image includes views of one's physical appearance

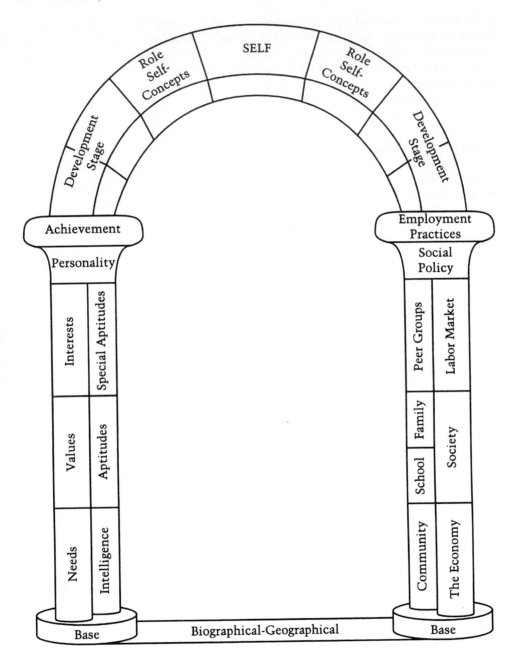

FIGURE 7.2 | THE ARCHWAY OF CAREER DETERMINANTS.

Source: From "A Life-Span, Life-Space Approach to Career Development" by Donald E. Super (1990). In D. Brown, L. Brooks, and Associates, *Career choice and development: Applying contemporary theories to practice* (2nd ed., p. 200). Copyright © 1990 by Jossey-Bass. Reprinted by permission of John Wiley & Sons, Inc.

as well as characteristics such as age, gender, race, desirability, and so forth. Organizational images refer to images about a specific company or work. Image norms are created as children develop views of themselves and workers as well as places of work. Giannantonio and Hurley-Hanson (2006) relate image norms to Super's view of the career development of children and how one's self-concept or image norms develops with age. They suggest that children perceive images from comments that family, teachers, peers, and others make about occupations as well as comments about the children themselves. Also, image norms develop from television, magazines, and other media. Recognizing this, counselors can help children to challenge these images to see if they apply to the child.

A sense of self begins to emerge in late childhood or early adolescence. By following through on the need to discover more about the environment and to explore objects and people in the environment, the child learns information that will be one basis for the development of a self-concept. The child learns how he or she is different from or similar to other people. Furthermore, by observing important people in their lives, children learn occupational and other roles. Also, exploratory behavior leads to information and experience with key figures that will eventually help the child develop interests in some activities and a lack of interest in others. The child starts to have a clear profile in terms of interest and experience that separates him or her from others. As a sense of self develops, the drama and excitement of activity become less important and the accomplishment of goals becomes more significant. Children now are in a position where they can plan and make decisions. Naturally, not all children have the same experiences, and not all are able to develop a strong sense of self and an ability to plan. Differences in career maturity among individuals and the elements of career maturity are the focus of Chapter 8, "Adolescent Career Development."

The point of the preceding discussion is to emphasize the importance of those concepts that lead to a sense of self and a feeling of planfulness as shown at the top of Figure 7.2. To plan, children must have sufficient information, motivation in terms of interests and activities, a sense of control over their own future, and an idea of what that future will be (a time perspective), which is described in Figure 7.1. Although the development of interests, the acquisition of information, and the development of a time perspective are goals that can be achieved in counseling, they are not ends in themselves. They are important because they lead to the development of planfulness and a sense of self. As these important concepts are developing, it is not possible for children to make career choices that are planful. Rather, they may express an interest in an occupation because of information they may have or because of their experience with role models. Therefore, career counseling as it is done with adolescents and adults is inappropriate for children. An awareness of Super's model of career development in childhood can be helpful when discussing other issues with children in counseling.

USING SUPER'S MODEL IN COUNSELING CHILDREN

Common topics in counseling young children deal with school and family. The National Model of the American School Counselors Association [www.schoolcouns elor.org] suggests ways that counselors can work to help elementary school children with career and other problems. Thomas (1989) describes the following as typical elementary school problems: lack of academic progress; dyslexia; lack of reading achievement; problems having to do with intellectual ability, sight, or hearing; and disruptive behavior. Typical family problems that Thomas (1989) cites are child abuse, child neglect, and issues arising from single-parent families, divorce, unwed parents, stepfamilies, and working parents. Occasionally, in dealing with these issues, counselors have the opportunity to make comments that fit with Super's model of childhood career development. This might mean a discussion of the child's exploratory behavior, the reaction the child is having to experiences with school, or a positive or negative reaction to key figures. An awareness of a limited time perspective in children can help the counselor in not expecting planful behavior from them. Another area where Super's view can be useful is in the attention that the counselor pays to the development of interests. The following example shows how a counselor can incorporate knowledge of Super's concepts while working with a child on a topic seemingly not related to career choice.

Arthur is a white fourth-grade student in a predominantly wealthy suburban school system. Both of his parents were raised in Toronto, Canada. Previously a C-level student, Arthur is starting to fall behind the other children in his class in reading, and he senses it. He seems to have few social contacts with his peers and cries rather easily when frustrated by reading assignments. His teacher has referred Arthur to the counselor because the teacher is concerned about his behavior and suspects that Arthur may have a learning disability. The following dialogue between Arthur and the counselor is from rather late in their discussion:

CL: I hate reading! It's too hard.

CO: What do you like to do? [The counselor very much feels Arthur's frustration with reading and wishes to move to a topic where Arthur does not have a sense of failure. Later, they will return to the topic of reading.]

CL: I like baseball. My friends and I play after school. We trade cards, too.

CO: What teams do you collect? [The counselor, almost randomly, chooses to follow up on collecting baseball cards rather than playing baseball. Mainly, the counselor wants to follow up on an area of interest that Arthur has.]

CL: All kinds. I like the American League. I like new players' and pitchers' stats.

CO: You really seem to enjoy collecting cards. [The counselor notes that Arthur is starting to relax and sound more enthusiastic. Furthermore, the counselor notes that Arthur is interested in an activity that requires reading but chooses not to comment about it; rather, the counselor follows Arthur's exploratory behavior.]

CL: Oh, yes. It's really great. I buy cards when my parents will give me money, and I trade with whatever kids I can find. People know I am a good trader and sometimes it's hard to find kids to trade with. I've got a box full of cards.

CO: Seems like that's something that you do well. [The counselor is concerned about Arthur's sense of failure, coming from his difficulty with reading, and wishes to reinforce his areas of interests and strength. Arthur's self-concept is important. The collecting of baseball cards itself does not need to have direct occupational relevance.]

CL: Yeah, I know the cards, and I know the players. I like to watch them on TV. It's fun to see a player whose card I have. Sometimes, when I'm playing baseball, I pretend that I'm a player.

CO: Who would you like to be like? [In his fantasy, Arthur is influenced by a key figure. The counselor wants to hear more about it.]

CL: The center fielder for the Red Sox. He can really hit. I like to watch him. I want to hit just like him. I want to be a ballplayer like him. I want to hit home runs and have a high batting average. I want to play for the Boston Red Sox. I love to hit the baseball hard. I love to catch the balls.

CO: Sounds like great things to do. [The counselor is aware that Arthur's time perspective is vague. Arthur seems to see himself in a short time being a professional baseball player. Not wanting to push Arthur into developing a time perspective when he is unable to do so, the counselor reinforces Arthur's interest in and exploration of baseball. The counselor is aware that they are moving away from the reading issue, but the counselor feels it is important to spend some time on areas that will strengthen Arthur's concept of himself.]

In this example, the counselor has used Super's concepts to encourage exploratory behavior in Arthur and to help him feel better about himself. Although the goal of counseling is to help Arthur with his reading problem, and this discourse seems unrelated, it is likely that helping Arthur have a sense of success will make him feel less frustrated in general. At a later point in the interview, the counselor may be able to draw a parallel between reading baseball cards and reading schoolwork. The counselor does not introduce career issues in a forced sense but uses knowledge of Super's theory to respond helpfully in the context of the situation. This example uses a gender-stereotyped situation. It is one in which a boy is choosing a traditionally masculine activity. The issue of gender-role stereotyping is important in the development of occupational selection. The next section extensively deals with this issue along with a different view of cognitive and career development.

GOTTFREDSON'S THEORY OF SELF-CREATION, CIRCUMSCRIPTION, AND COMPROMISE

Like Donald Super, Linda Gottfredson has been concerned with the development of an individual's self-concept. Her theory of career development helps to explain how people see themselves in terms of society and in terms of their individuality (their values, their feelings, and interests). Gottfredson (1981, 2002, 2005) has articulated a developmental theory of career choice, focusing on childhood and adolescence. Her theory describes how individuals create themselves as their psychological selves interact with environmental factors, including gender and prestige. She describes this theory as a theory of self-creation. Basic to the theory is the role that cognitive development plays in vocational choice; individual differences in intellectual growth can play a strong role in one's career path in adulthood. Influencing cognitive growth as well as personality and interests is the relationship between genetics and the environment. Gottfredson integrates this complex relationship into her theory of career development, explaining the different roles that genetic factors will play in the development of intellect, personality, and interests. Her theory addresses not only individuals' concepts of themselves but also how they view their world and, in her terms, develop a cognitive map of occupations. To navigate this map, people develop an ever-growing internal compass, which guides them as they make choices in their daily lives and is developed by the many choices they make each day. The internal compass reflects the interaction between one's biological self and the experiences that one encounters in the world. It serves as a guide for many developmental processes, including career development.

The process of choosing a career includes the development of a cognitive map of occupations that is integrated into an individual's self-concept. Thus, people must determine which occupations are compatible with how they see themselves. However, the occupations must not only be compatible with their view of themselves, but they must be accessible or attainable. If they are not, the individuals are not likely to pursue these occupations. Related to the notions of compatibility and accessibility are Gottfredson's concepts of circumscription and compromise. *Circumscription* is a process in which young people eliminate alternatives that they feel will not be appropriate to them. *Compromise* is a process in which young people give up alternatives that they may like for ones that may be more accessible to them. In these two concepts, Gottfredson acknowledges that individuals must not only make choices about occupations (circumscription) but must also deal with the influence of the outside world, which includes culture, discrimination, the job market, and competition with others. In her theory, Gottfredson demonstrates how biological factors play a role in the processes of circumscription and compromise.

In the following sections, I will first describe Gottfredson's views of cognitive growth as they provide a way of understanding how individuals create themselves. People develop an internal compass that guides them through life by interacting with their intellect, traits, interests, and other factors. In this way, they are creating their own unique self. Part of the process of self-creation and development of an internal compass is the impact of social and biological factors on occupational choice (circumscription) and how individuals make compromises based on what they know about themselves in relation to the world of work. Then, by using a case example, I will describe how Gottfredson's theory has implications for career counseling.

COGNITIVE GROWTH

In order to match occupations with their view of themselves, children must learn both about themselves and about the world of work. In learning about the world of work, children develop a *cognitive map of occupations*. This map is similar for children living in the same area or country. For example, children living in France are exposed to information about similar occupations. These occupations will be similar in some ways, but not in every way, to those that children in Nigeria learn about. On the other hand, the *self-concept* that children develop is unique to each child. In order to develop a cognitive map of occupations and a concept of themselves, children must develop in their capacity to learn.

Gottfredson (2005) uses Bloom's taxonomy of cognitive tasks to describe the characteristics of the learning process. The six levels of Bloom's taxonomy (Anderson & Krathwol, 2001; Moseley et al., 2005) are described here to give an overview of learning tasks that children master as they grow older. The tasks are listed in order from the most basic to the most complex.

1. *Remember*—Learning specific facts, not necessarily related to others
2. *Understand*—Identifying and understanding similarities and differences among objects or ideas

3. *Apply*—Making inferences from information and deciding about the value of this information
4. *Analyze*—Drawing from information to weigh advantages and disadvantages of a decision
5. *Evaluate*—Using various criteria to make judgments about which decisions would be best
6. *Create*—Making a plan to obtain a goal

Using Bloom's taxonomy can be helpful in understanding the capacity of a child to deal with career or vocationally related issues. As children learn about occupations, acquire skills leading to occupational requirements, and analyze and evaluate experiences as they develop interests, they are using these cognitive tasks.

Gottfredson (2005) makes use of Blooms' taxonomy, but also makes reference to children being able to move from concrete thinking to more abstract thinking as they get older. This process, described earlier on page 192, is part of Piaget's (1977) four major periods of cognitive development: sensorimotor, pre-operational, concrete operational, and formal operational. Both Bloom's taxonomy and Piaget's periods of cognitive development help to understand the development of children's capacity to learn both in general and when applied to career development.

Gottfredson (2005) also points out that children of the same age vary greatly in terms of their ability to learn. Reviewing research on cognitive development, Gottfredson (2005) shows that genetic factors have an important influence on how children develop intellectually. Children may go through the tasks of Bloom's taxonomy or Piaget's cognitive development stages at different ages. Children who have highly developed intellectual skills are better able to make use of information in their environment and information given to them by teachers than children with less developed intellectual skills. From the point of view of career development, the more intellectually able children are to take information from their environment, the more likely they are to have developed *career maturity*, a concept discussed in detail in Chapter 8, Adolescent Career Development.

Self-Creation

In her most recent explanation of her theory, Gottfredson (2005) describes in detail how hereditary or biological factors influence the choices that individuals make as they deal with a complex world. Although almost all other theorists say that environmental factors are important, only Gottfredson describes a view, based on her thorough research and study, of how biological factors and environmental factors interact with each other as a child grows. Gottfredson explains that the individual enters a very complex world with a simple and incomplete cognitive map of the world. The remainder of this section describes the complex way in which nature and nurture (genetics and environment) interact with each other as the child develops into an adult.

Gottfredson (2005) points out that we are active participants in our relationships between our biological selves and our environment, which are constantly changing. Even the environment that we share with our siblings may look very different from the environment that we are in as we become adults. Where our parents live, how much schooling they have, and how wealthy they are seem to have little impact on our personality traits at any age. In addition, the impact of our parents on our intellectual abilities wanes as we become adolescents.

However, other factors such as interests, attitudes, and skills are more influenced by environments that we share with others. Vocational interests are affected by the relationship between genetics and the environment. Interests are particularly influenced by our world, whereas temperaments and intellect are influenced less by one's environment and more by our genetic makeup. One reason for this is that interests deal with objects, such as sports equipment, musical instruments, money, and so forth. Objects are not as important a component of temperament and intelligence as they are in the development of interests, attitudes, and skills (Gottfredson, personal communication, April 17, 2008). Interests emerge as they fit with human traits that people in specific cultures develop to meet their needs. Very specific tasks meet the needs for different cultures. For example, many cultures require medical personnel or teachers, but only certain cultures require sailors or atomic physicists. Many adolescents do not have enough experience to bring out certain interests or abilities or values. For example, someone may have the ability to navigate large ships but never encounter large ships in their interaction with their culture, except in books or movies. Certain events that are not shared by others can have a large impact on our development and in turn contribute to our uniqueness. For example, if a young person is driving with friends and the car breaks down and the young person fixes it when none of the other people can, it may be an important event in that person's life, leading toward the exploration of mechanics or engineering as a career. Gottfredson highlights the importance of such *nonshared* events. Such events are likely to become more common as we grow older.

As we interact with our environment our genetically based temperaments become more stable, or *traited*. As we repeat experiences, traits develop. This does not mean that we are born to be extraverted or introverted and that's how we will be. Rather, traits gradually become a more stable expression of who we are. In this way, over time a person with a personality trait of introversion will experience and enjoy more activities that allow expression of that introversion.

Also, individuals will gradually choose more events that help to define various traits. For example, as we interact with others, we will seek out situations that allow us to be some combination of extraverted or introverted, ranging from very introverted to very extraverted. In this way, *traits* develop, and the effect of genetics on individuals becomes stronger rather than weaker as they age. Regarding intelligence, adopted children become more and more like biological relatives they have not met rather than more like their adoptive parents (Plomin, DeFries, McClearn, & McGuffin, 2001).

The concept that one becomes more like one's biological family rather than one's adoptive family may at first seem incorrect. Gottfredson (2005) explains children's learning process by describing the *genes-drives-experience theory*. As children get older, they take a more active role in choosing, directing, and understanding their environment. However, when they make their choices about what to do and how to understand their role, they are influenced by what Gottfredson refers to as an *internal genetic compass*. This "compass" is an internal guide as to what they are generally likely to prefer. It does not determine exactly what they will be like, as that is influenced by their environment. For example, children with a compass that includes drawing ability are likely to choose more artistic activities, whereas those with a proclivity towards sports will choose more sports activities. If skills in these activities are reinforced by others, this support will add to choosing more of such activities. Individuals, as they grow older, are likely to have more positive experiences and more support for their traits, thus developing those that they were born with. Gottfredson states that "The partly genetic origin of environments is confirmed by research showing that the occupations and educational credentials that people obtain, the major life events they experience, the social support they receive, and other important aspects of their lives are often moderately heritable" (Gottfredson, 2005, p. 76). As mentioned previously, interests, because they require being active, doing tasks, and dealing with objects, are less heritable than intellect or temperament.

Individuals are influenced by two factors as they grow. Genes (the genetic compass) are a guide moving individuals toward some choices rather than others throughout life. However, individuals also must deal with environmental factors affecting their choices. For example, wanting to go to medical school while raising a family does not make attending medical school impossible, but does make it more difficult. Or having a parent be unemployed for 2 years may have an impact on the colleges that one may be able to afford. As individuals grow they make observations about themselves, their personalities, their skills, their interests, and values. Gottfredson refers to this process as the development of one's *self-concept*. In the interaction between their self-concept and the environment individuals are seeking *niches*, throughout their lives. *Niches* are the life settings and roles that individuals occupy. The process of choosing careers is one type of niche seeking. Cultures, families, and societies provide a limited amount of niches, but still there are many for individuals to develop. Thus, the process of self-creation leads to the development of one's unique pattern of niche seeking. How environmental or social factors contribute to an individual's self-creation is the subject of the next section.

CIRCUMSCRIPTION

There are several factors that influence circumscription, that is, the process by which young people eliminate occupational alternatives that do not fit their self-concept. Gottfredson believes that children's increasing ability to deal with abstraction has a great influence on how they understand and organize their views of the world. How they view themselves influences their occupational choices, and their early occupational choices likewise influence how they view themselves. Children consider their social selves first, so they begin eliminating occupations that do not fit into their perceived *social space* (occupations that seem suitable or compatible). They do this by rejecting occupations that they do not consider acceptable in terms of gender roles and prestige level. For example, a young girl who does not feel that being a truck driver is an appropriate occupation for a girl is likely to eliminate it. Likewise, a young boy who believes that men should not enter the nursing profession may eliminate this occupation from his potential choices. Although children are eliminating occupational choices based on ideas about gender and social class, they are not aware that they are doing this. They are rarely aware that they are even making choices as they progressively narrow the range of options they even think about when later searching for occupations that match their personal abilities and interests. Gottfredson describes four stages of circumscription that are based on the ways that children develop as described in this paragraph. Both boys and girls move through these stages at different ages depending on their cognitive abilities. Ages given for each stage described here and illustrated in Figure 7.3 are approximate.

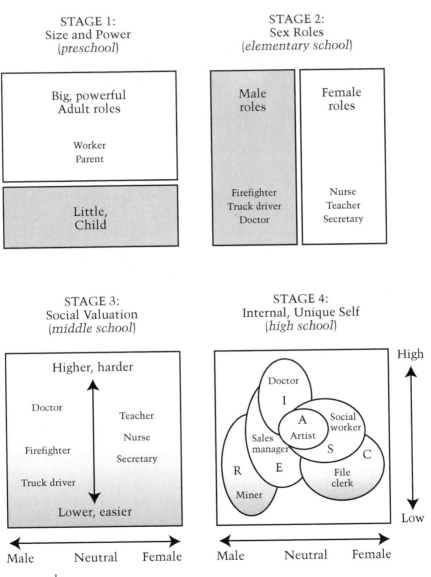

FIGURE 7.3 | GOTTFREDSON'S FOUR STAGES OF CIRCUMSCRIPTION.

Source: From "Applying Gottredson's Theory of Circumscription and Compromise in Career Guidance and Counseling," pp. 71–100 in *Career development and counseling*, Steven D. Brown and Robert W. Lent, eds. Copyright © 2005 John Wiley & Sons, Inc. Reprinted with permission of the publisher.

STAGE 1: ORIENTATION TO SIZE AND POWER (3–5 YEARS OLD) Children tend to view things concretely. They begin to classify others in terms of simple terms such as large–small or old–young. When they view occupations, they may be aware of things that are used in an occupation: bulldozers, shovels, blackboards, saws, baseballs, and so forth. For example, Alice, at age 4, sees the wires, pliers, and other tools that her father, an electrician, brings home at the end of the day. She may be aware that her big father can use these tools, and that she, little Alice, cannot. At this point, she may have little awareness of concepts such as male–female or prestigious–not prestigious.

STAGE 2: ORIENTATION TO SEX ROLES (6–8 YEARS OLD) When children are in the early grades of elementary school, they are likely to think in concrete terms and make simple distinctions. For example, they may see things as good–bad or easy–hard. It is at this age when they become aware of gender roles and are likely to see occupations as ones that are or are not appropriate for their gender. Children aged 6 to 8 years may believe that their own gender is superior. At this point they develop a *tolerable-sex type boundary*, which refers to the idea that certain occupations are acceptable or tolerable for boys only or for girls only. For example, Alice at age 7 believes that being an electrician is a boy's job and is therefore out of bounds for her. At this point, she will not consider electrician as a possible occupation for herself as her culture has limited options available to her because of gender stereotyping. If Ray at age 8 decides that being a secretary is not appropriate for him because it is girls' work, then he has removed an option for himself in his future working life.

STAGE 3: ORIENTATION TO SOCIAL VALUATION (9–13 YEARS OLD) As students enter the fourth grade, they tend to become more and more aware of their peers, including what they think of their peers and what their peers think of them. At this point, they become more conscious of social class. For example, they may pay attention to what clothes their friends wear, what cars their friends' parents drive, and the types of houses or neighborhoods that their friends live in. Children now are recognizing the relationships among education, income, and occupations. Gottfredson (2002) states that by the eighth grade, most students are able to rank the prestige of occupations similar to the way adults do. In general, there is good agreement across gender, cultural group, and occupational group as to which occupations have the most and least prestige. Children at this age have a good idea of the types of occupations that their family would reject. In Alice's case, at age 10 she is aware that occupations such as farm worker, factory worker, and custodian are not jobs that her parents would consider desirable. These occupations, therefore, are outside her *tolerable level boundary*. She will not consider them as occupations that are appropriate for her. However, when Alice was younger than 9 years, she might have considered these as appropriate. Alice may differ from her friends in the number of occupations that she considers within her social space. For example, her friend, Karen, who has a wealthy family, may have learned that there are relatively few occupations that are prestigious enough for her to consider. Alice may not view some very high prestige occupations as fitting into her tolerable level boundary. Stage 3 in Figure 7.3 (bottom left) gives an example of how a few occupations rate on social valuation and difficulty level as they are perceived by middle school students.

STAGE 4: ORIENTATION TO THE INTERNAL UNIQUE SELF (14 YEARS AND OLDER)   At this stage, adolescents now have an idea, similar to adults, of which occupations are acceptable to them. They have become keenly aware of sexual attractiveness to others, how they look, and notions of status; they are also concerned with how others view them. Fitting into the right crowd becomes important in adolescence. Individuals are not only concerned about how they see themselves, but also how others see them. Teenagers are likely to see obligations that they will have toward others, the notion that they will have families to provide for, and the importance of providing for themselves. In the first three stages, children are rejecting occupational possibilities that would not be appropriate to them (outside their social space). In this stage, teenagers are trying to identify which of the acceptable alternatives are most preferred and accessible. As they learn about their values, their abilities, the needs of their family, and their own personality, they are likely to prefer choices that will meet all of these criteria. They are also becoming more aware of different work environments, and their own interests, and abilities as illustrated by the plotting of Holland types by gender and prestige in the Stage 4 diagram in Figure 7.3. For example, Alice, now 15, considers her love for music (Artistic), her enjoyment and success in biology and physics (Investigative), and her enjoyment and success in writing when she thinks about choices. These choices are influenced by her view of gender role and prestige. Furthermore, they are influenced by her biologically based abilities, which include an aptitude for music, high general intelligence, and mathematical ability. These biologically based abilities have been reinforced by her teachers and chorus director. She has been given solos in her church choir; she has earned A grades in biology and physics, and she assisted her Advanced Biology instructor in preparing laboratory materials for the initial biology course. She has also earned A grades in English and writes for her school paper. She continues to develop these abilities throughout school. Now that she has gone through the four stages of circumscription, she encounters a process of compromise.

COMPROMISE

Throughout the circumscription process, individuals put aside occupations that do not fit for them. In compromise, they must let go of some highly preferred alternatives. An aspect of compromise is how available or accessible individuals think an occupation is. Occupations that are most preferred are likely to get the individual's attention. Also, when it becomes close to the decision-making time, such as graduation, individuals are more willing to lower their aspirations. To make decisions about which occupations to let go of, young people may seek advice from teachers, parents, friends, and others. This advice may also shape their view of which occupations are suitable and which ones are not. When individuals are ready to make occupational choices, they are ready to consider compromising. There are situations in which they will not need to compromise at all. However, many people will need to compromise their choices and to give up career choices that they feel are highly desirable.

Gottfredson (2005) describes three factors of the compromise process that can create difficulties for young people making career decisions by answering these questions: (1) Why do young people know so little about how to enter or get education for work they prefer? (2) How does the behavior of individuals affect their access to educational or occupational information? (3) Which factors in the process of selecting an occupation are young people most and least willing to give up when they can not obtain their first choice of occupation or work?

1. *Why do young people know so little about how to enter or get education for work they prefer?* As they go through adolescence, individuals become aware of social and psychological factors that they use to judge the suitability of occupations for themselves. However, Gottfredson believes that young people tend to know only a modest amount about occupations that are not their preferred choice(s), commonly seeking occupational information mainly from their social circle (friends, family, or part-time work). They often lack information about how to enter occupations and where and how education or training is available. Such information can be difficult to find and goes out of date. Getting this information can be very time consuming, and adolescents may not bother to look for such information on secondary choices.

2. *How does the behavior of individuals affect their access to educational or occupational information or work?* Information rarely comes to individuals; they must actively seek it. Information about jobs and training programs can be difficult to locate and individuals must use sources such as school counselors or libraries to get information. To become a competitive applicant for a college or a job, individuals must participate in activities or work to make themselves desirable to the educational institution or employer. Some occupations may exist far from the place where an individual lives or be very different from jobs that friends or family are likely to know about. Getting such information can require considerable effort on the part of adolescents. However, there are some adolescents who may grow up in a situation where access to information and individuals working in a variety of prestigious occupations is readily available.

Although Gottfredson values a variety of ways of obtaining occupational information, she particularly values occupational work experience (L. Gottfredson, personal communication, April 17, 2008.) There are many methods of experiencing occupations such as shadowing someone at his or her workplace; doing volunteer or part-time work; taking experiential courses, like welding or sewing; and other ways in which individuals can do a portion of work similar to that done in the occupation. This experience provides a way for individuals to further develop their cognitive maps of occupations. Put another way, by dealing with samples of the actual work, one's inner compass has significant material to work with that reading, watching, or hearing about occupations does not provide. In their interactions with individuals and activities, people create themselves (their interests, abilities, and values) in ever-changing ways.

3. *Which factors in the process of selecting an occupation are young people most and least willing to give up when they cannot obtain their first choice of occupation or work?* According to Gottfredson (2005), adolescents look for jobs

that are compatible with their self-concept, giving up those factors that are least critical to their self-concept while letting go of other factors. They tend to select from ones that they know about (in their social space). For an occupation to be compatible with an individual's self-concept, it must fit with their view of sex type of the job, the prestige level, and the field of work he or she finds acceptable. Individuals seek matches that are "good enough" because they are easier to determine and easier to locate than the best possible occupations.

Often, individuals have no alternative than to settle for a "good enough" job. According to Gottfredson's theory, in that case they will select a job in their chosen field only if the sex type and prestige level of the job are acceptable. The sex type of an occupation is closest to the self-concept, because it develops before prestige level and desire for a specific field. To be acceptable, it is important that a job fit the appropriate gender type that the individual requires. If that requirement is satisfied, then it must fit within tolerable prestige-level boundaries. If it meets that requirement, the job must fit the appropriate field that the person desires.

Alice has many skills and interests. As she approaches spring of her senior year in high school, she thinks about what she would like to do in college. She had considered being a surgeon or an engineer (Figure 7.4). However, these occupations do not

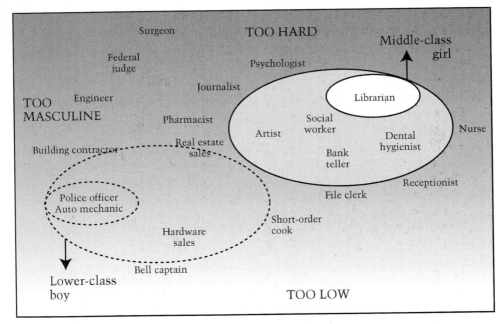

FIGURE 7.4 | AN OUTLINE OF ALICE'S CAREER CHOICES AS INFLUENCED BY GENDER TYPE AND ACADEMIC DIFFICULTY ACCORDING TO GOTTFREDSON.

Source: From "Applying Gottredson's Theory of Circumscription and Compromise in Career Guidance and Counseling," pp. 71–100. In *Career development and counseling*, Steven D. Brown and Robert W. Lent, eds. Copyright © 2005 John Wiley & Sons, Inc. Reprinted with permission of the publisher.

seem right to her because they do not seem to be the kinds of occupations that she feels women should enter. Although she is probably not aware of this, Alice is less likely to enter a job that she feels is masculine than one which does not fit her tolerable boundary for prestige level or field of interest. She has, because of her interest in music, considered becoming a musician; however, she lets go of this alternative because she does not feel that she would be able to attain that position. She considers bank teller, but that does not seem to challenge her intellectually. Instead, she decides to go to a college where she can major in library science. Thus, Alice gives up the more prestigious and masculine jobs of surgeon and engineer for the job of librarian, in part because they may be too difficult to attain, but also because they seem too masculine to her. Not all people in Alice's position would make the same choice. Some girls might choose to be a surgeon and go against the societal stereotype that it is a male occupation. Counselors, parents, and teachers may provide encouragement to students who wish to choose an occupation that does not fit with societal stereotypes of appropriateness for a specific gender. As Alice goes through these experiences, her cognitive map (view of herself and her choices) grows. Her previous experiences lead her forward, and in this way she is guided by her internal compass.

Most vocational research on Gottfredson's theory has focused on circumscription and compromise rather than cognitive development and the role of environment and genetics. Although there is much research on cognitive development and the role of environment and genetics in the field of psychology, it has not been related specifically to career development or work adjustment. Also, many of the changes that Gottfredson has made in her theory reflect recent findings in research in cognitive development and the role of environmental or genetic factors. Circumscription and compromise were concepts that made specific predictions about vocational choice. These concepts have drawn the most attention of vocational researchers.

As mentioned above, individuals will sacrifice interests and prestige before they will sacrifice sex type. That is, for many individuals, it is important that the sex type of the occupation fit their view of their own self-concept and their view of what occupation is appropriate for them. Gottfredson (2002) makes different predictions based on the degree of compromise and how severe it is. Examples of predictions from her theory about how individuals will compromise their choices are included below. Compromise refers to having to make tradeoffs between sex type, prestige, and interests.

> When compromises are relatively small (that is, all options are still within their social space), individuals are likely to give their greatest priority to maximizing fit with their interests.

> When compromises are moderate (that is, all options are somewhat outside their social space), individuals will likely sacrifice interest in a job before they will sacrifice acceptability in either prestige or sex type.

> When compromises are severe (that is, all options are far outside their social space), individuals will likely sacrifice both interests and prestige to maintain an acceptable sex type.

Although vocational interests are important to almost all individuals, they may be overshadowed by their concern for prestige or sex type, unless the prestige and sex type of available alternatives are close to acceptable.

There are many types of compromise, and compromise issues are different for older individuals than for younger individuals. Predictions in Gottfredson's theory are rather complex. This has made tests of her theory rather difficult. However, a number of researchers have attempted to test her concepts of circumscription and compromise. The next section summarizes some research to illustrate the types of studies that have been conducted to validate Gottfredson's theory.

Although studies in circumscription do not always test predictions as outlined by Gottfredson (2002, 2005), they tend to support her predictions. Henderson, Hesketh, and Tuffin (1988) found that gender type had more of an effect at ages 6 to 8 years than did prestige when career choices were examined. After the age of 8 years, prestige had more of an effect on occupational choice than did gender. Studying second-, fourth-, and sixth-grade students, Helwig (1998, 2000) reports that children chose more socially valued occupations in the latter grades, supporting Gottfredson's view that prestige becomes more important for children 9 years and older. Helwig (2001) studied older children as well. As Gottfredson suggests, Helwig (2001) reports that the emphasis on the prestige of children's occupational aspirations increased as children reached 13 or 14 years of age. Also in keeping with Gottfredson's predictions, he found that as students approached the age of 17 years, their occupational choices reflected an increased concern with interests more than social values.

A few studies have dealt specifically with the concept of compromise. Some hypotheses deal directly with why it seems so difficult to encourage girls and women to consider nontraditional careers. Hesketh and colleagues (Hesketh, Durant, & Pryor, 1990; Hesketh, Elmslie, & Kaldor, 1990) state that interests are most important in career decision making, followed by prestige, and then by gender type. Studying 119 university students, Blanchard and Lichtenberg (2003) report that students with little career compromise placed more emphasis on interests than prestige, followed by sex type. For students categorized as being in moderate-to-high compromise conditions, prestige and sex type were not significantly different from each other, but they were stronger than interests. Their findings are generally supportive of Gottfredson's predictions. Hall, Kelly, and Van Buren (1995) report that the degree to which the interests of students in the 8th and 11th grade were compromised, if any, depended on the area of interest (for example, scientific- or business-oriented). Asian American college students were more likely to compromise gender type for prestige than prestige for gender type, as Gottfredson (2002) hypothesizes. In college students, the larger the career compromise that individuals made, the greater the emotional impact on the individuals was and the less reported satisfaction with work (Tsaousides, 2007).

Gottfredson (2002) comments that the reasons for the variation in support for the compromise aspect of her theory may be explained, in part, by whether the compromises under investigation are major or minor or are real or artificial. As a way of making the issue of compromise less artificial and more practical, a workbook (*Mapping Vocational Challenges* [MVC]) has been designed to help middle school students understand factors that can limit (compromise) their career options (Lapan, Loehr-Lapan, & Tupper, 1993; Turner & Lapan, 2005).

IMPLICATIONS OF GOTTFREDSON'S THEORY FOR SUPER'S THEORY

Super's (1990) model of early career development (Figure 7.1) does not deal with gender bias. Gottfredson's (1981, 2002, 2005) theory is relevant to several of Super's important concepts. Consistent with both theories is the importance of career exploration unrestricted by gender-role stereotyping. Thus, children of both genders should be able to explore activities such as knitting, sewing, sports, and science. Furthermore, information made available in the schools should not reinforce gender-role stereotypes. In general, publishers of textbooks have made strides in showing adults and children in pictures that do not reinforce traditional gender-role models. By providing information free of gender-role bias, educational systems are more likely to provide an atmosphere in which wide varieties of interests can develop, regardless of gender. If exploration and information are not gender biased, the selection of key figures by children is also more likely to be unbiased. These concepts will ultimately affect the child's self-concept and ability to make career decisions.

USE OF GOTTFREDSON'S AND SUPER'S CONCEPTS IN COUNSELING

When counseling children, counselors may introduce alternative information about occupational gender roles when discussing exploration, key figures, information, and interest. If a young girl enjoys studying and watching insects but has been told by someone that little girls do not do that kind of thing, the counselor can indicate that this may be a view of one individual and emphasize the young girl's pleasure in learning about insects. By doing this, the counselor is providing alternative information to the young girl about activities that may lead to an interest in biology. Dealing with key figures, particularly parents, who provide gender-stereotyped examples or information is more difficult. In a direct challenge to an important key figure, the counselor is likely to lose, and the child is likely to believe or identify with the key figure. In the following example, a counselor deals with this issue.

Lucy is a white fifth-grade student in a small city in Texas. She has recently turned 11 years old and has done well in her schoolwork. She has been referred to the counselor by one of her teachers, who talked briefly with Lucy about why she seemed to be less interested in her English, history, and science work. Lucy just shrugged and said that things weren't fun anymore. In talking with Lucy, the counselor learns that Lucy's mother, a practical nurse at a local hospital, has asked Lucy's father to move out of their house. Lucy's father is a self-employed accountant. Lucy says that he yells a lot at her mother and throws things around the room. In talking with Lucy, the counselor is trying to decide how best to intervene to help Lucy—that is, whether to talk to one or both parents, to make suggestions to Lucy, or to help Lucy express her feelings about the events at home. The following dialogue takes place in the middle of the initial counseling session:

CL: My mom usually gets home right after I do because she works from seven in the morning 'til three. She doesn't talk to me the way she used to. I usually go to the refrigerator, and she may go to her room. It's not like it used to be.

CO: How did it used to be? [The counselor wants to learn more about what is happening to Lucy and how things have changed in the family.]

CL: She used to come home and talk with me. Sometimes she'd ask me about school, and sometimes she'd talk about her work.

CO: That felt good, to talk with her. [The counselor, in an attempt to learn more about the situation, is encouraging Lucy to talk about her relationship with her mother.]

CL: Yeah! Like sometimes she'd tell me funny things that happened at work. She doesn't like being a nurse. She tells me it's awful being told what to do all the time and taking care of sick people who yell at her. I wouldn't want to do that.

CO: What seems so bad about that? [Not wanting to reinforce nursing as an occupation for women and not wanting to reinforce Lucy's biased view of nursing, the counselor feels caught. Furthermore, Lucy's mother is an obvious key figure. Challenging her is not likely to work. Thus, the counselor asks for Lucy's view.]

CL: I don't know. I like doing things for other people. I like to baby sit my little sister. She's only three and kind of fun sometimes—a brat at other times—and likes to play with me, too.

CO: What do you like to do with her? [Wanting to follow Lucy's lead, the counselor asks Lucy about her work.]

CL: I like to pretend that I'm her mother, and I make her do things, like behave right or read her a story. I'd like to be a mother sometime. Mom says that's what she wishes she could be all the time and not have to work. I don't want to work.

CO: Why not? [The counselor is concerned about Lucy's attitude toward work, which is learned from a key figure, her mother, as well as the gender-role stereotyping Lucy may be learning that suggests the woman's place is in the home.]

CL: You have to do what everybody tells you to, and you get tired.

CO: Babysitting is work, and you seem to like that. [Hearing Lucy voice some of her mother's objections to work, the counselor gently confronts Lucy with her own positive experience of work, which is different from her mother's experience. The counselor wants Lucy to learn from her own exploratory behavior. Although babysitting is something that Lucy is required to do, the ways in which she does it are of her own choosing, and she seems to like them. The response, "Not everyone has to take orders in their work. Some people enjoy helping and taking care of others," might be effective, but the counselor is afraid that it would be challenging the view of Lucy's mother, and therefore Lucy might reject it.]

CL: Yes, it's fun to do different things with my baby sister. Sometimes we try to fix things like my father. We broke a lamp that way. I was in lots of trouble for a while.

CO: What do you like to fix? [Seizing the opportunity to move away from traditional female occupational roles, the counselor is pleased that Lucy brings up a more traditionally male activity, fixing things, so that the counselor can explore this. The counselor wants to minimize the effect of gender stereotyping as gender stereotyping would limit or further circumscribe Lucy's field of possible occupational alternatives.]

Clearly, the career issue is secondary to the more pressing problem of helping Lucy with the crisis that has happened in her home. However, although the career issue may be subtle, it is far-reaching. This brief career intervention may have an impact on Lucy, allowing her to broaden her occupational possibilities, to have a more positive attitude toward work, and to continue in exploratory activities. Hopefully, when she enters high school, she will conceive of herself as someone who can listen to the input of others and will also be able to start making her own decisions. Notably, the counselor was aware of Lucy's developmental stage in terms of processing information. Thus, the conversation stayed on a concrete level and did not deal with abstract concepts. When she enters high school, Lucy will be better able to deal with intangible issues.

CAREER DEVELOPMENT OF CHILDREN FROM CULTURALLY DIVERSE BACKGROUNDS

Within the field of the career development of children, little research has been done on issues that confront children of culturally diverse backgrounds in their career development. Some recent studies have focused on children from cultures that are different than those of children in industrialized societies. One study (Torimiro, Dionco-Adetayo, & Okorie, 2003) describes the importance of animal rearing in nomadic families, because animal rearing is important to children if they are to continue to be involved in their culture. The authors studied 100 children aged 4 to 15 years and found the children to be highly involved in animal-rearing activities; the children also viewed these activities positively. Another study (Morelli, Rogoff, & Angelillo, 2003) examines how children aged 2 and 3 years respond differently to work depending on their access to adult work or their access to activities that are especially for children. The authors studied 12 children in each of 4 communities: 2 middle-class European American communities, Efe individuals from the Democratic Republic of the Congo (who are primarily foragers of food), and Maya individuals from Guatemala. Children in European American communities were found to have more activities that were especially designed for children, whereas the Efe and Guatemalan children had more exposure to adult work. The authors suggest that Efe and Guatemalan children may not need to participate in special child-focused activities because they are already participating in situations where they observe adults at work. In her research on Mexican and Central American immigrant children who live in California, Orellana (2001) describes the work that immigrant children do to help their families and their households. Orellana suggests that these children's work can be seen in positive ways as volunteerism, as an opportunity to learn, and as ways of learning how to go back and forth between the culture and language of their home and the culture and language of the outside world. In the United States, one study showed how teaching career-related skills to Native American middle school students could help them in their career planning (Turner et al., 2006). These studies are useful because they provide a broad cultural perspective of how children's views of work can be different depending on the place of work or occupations in their culture.

Stereotyping occupations by race is an important issue because it can impact the occupational aspirations of children from different cultures. Bigler, Averhart, and Liben (2003) studied the perceptions about the workforce of African American first and sixth grade students. In this study, children rated both familiar and novel or unfamiliar jobs that had been illustrated with African Americans, European Americans, or both African and European Americans. African American students rated those jobs (both familiar and unfamiliar) that featured high concentrations of African Americans as lower in prestige than those that featured European Americans. This finding held true for both first and sixth grade students. However, when children were asked which racial groups should perform the familiar occupations, the students responded both whites and blacks (Bigler, Averhart, & Liben, 2003, p. 577). This research finds that occupations in which African Americans are seen as participants are viewed as lower in status than those in which European Americans participate. This study shows that children's perception of race can influence their perception of the desirability of an occupation. Counselors may have a challenging job to help students avoid stereotyping occupations by race. Counselors can do this by talking with the child about parents and relatives and the work they do. The following section makes suggestions about how occupational information can be used with children of all racial and ethnic groups to put them in a better position to make career decisions when they reach adolescence.

THE ROLE OF OCCUPATIONAL INFORMATION

Both Super's and Gottfredson's theories have implications for the delivery of occupational information to elementary school children. Most occupational information is provided not in the counseling office but in the classroom. The provision of occupational information through the educational system is called *school-to-work*. Rather than review the many programs for educating students about the world of work, this section deals with theoretical implications for the use of occupational information in elementary school counseling and career education.

OCCUPATIONAL INFORMATION IN COUNSELING

Suggestions for giving information to children about occupations can be taken from developmental theorists. Piaget's view of learning suggests that information given to children younger than 12 years should be concrete and clear. Erikson focuses on the importance of success and achievement for the young child. Learning about an occupation should not be overwhelming, so it should be done in small pieces. Because of the limited time perspective that younger children have, counselors should focus on what adults do now rather than on future occupational entry. Gottfredson's emphasis on the cognitive development of children is useful in reminding the counselor that information about occupations should be without gender bias and should seek to broaden gender tolerance boundaries. The actual discussion of occupational information between a school counselor and a child may be infrequent. However, when such a dialogue occurs, these suggestions may be helpful. More common is the provision of occupational information in classroom activities.

SCHOOL-TO-WORK PROGRAMS DESIGNED FOR CHILDREN

Because school-to-work programs are a curricular rather than an individual or group counseling function, full treatment is beyond the scope of this book. However, one activity of counselors is the development of, or consultation on, programs that integrate work and school activities. Because school-to-work is such an important part of the precareer decision-making process in the United States, discussion is warranted. This is partially because of the signing of the School-to-Work Opportunities Act in 1994. School-to-work programs have been developed at all educational levels including elementary. In the United States, funding for such programs exists mainly at state and local levels, because the funding for the School-to-Work Opportunities Act ceased in 2001.

Much attention has been focused on school-to-work programs. Business Publishers releases a monthly School-to-Work Report that describes legislation and programming that deals with activities that incorporate work in the classroom or education in the work setting. School-to-work is also the subject of research. For example, the transition from school to work can be studied by examining different roles (such as the role of family member) that affect how individuals move from school to work (Ng & Feldman, 2007). Others have examined how mastery of basic skills affects the transition from school to work (Cieslik & Simpson, 2006). School-to-work is not only a subject of interest in the United States, but in other countries as well, such as South Africa (Nel, van der Westhuyzen, & Uys, 2007) and Taiwan (Chan & Chadsey, 2006). The school-to-work initiative has been particularly effective in creating programs for those students who do not go on to 4-year college programs (Blustein, 2006; Joyce & Neumark, 2001; Solberg, Howard, Blustein, & Close, 2002).

Implementing school-to-work, formerly referred to as career education, in the elementary school can be done in three basic ways (Herr, Cramer, & Niles, 2004). The first type is the infusion of occupational information into the classroom in the form of films, oral reports on occupations, or the development of interest centers in the classroom. A second and less formal approach in the classroom involves group activities such as writing a skit using terms from the world of work; completing crossword puzzles that use occupational terms; and comparing lists of interests, abilities, and achievements with requirements of occupations. The third type is community involvement, which can mean taking students out of the classroom or bringing the community into the classroom. Examples include going to a factory and observing each aspect of a manufacturing process or having students follow workers on the job as they go through their daily activities. Herr, Cramer, and Niles (2004) list 80 of these activities that can be helpful to counselors in designing programs in collaboration with teachers. In addition, comprehensive programs have been developed for young children (Zunker, 2006).

Super's theory of the career development of children can be applied to activity programming for young children to relate work to school. The Experiential Career Guidance Model (Kyle & Hennis, 2000) includes activities designed for preschool children. The program is sensitive to children's limited time perspective. Activities focus on the family and home and include a play store and library in which children learn by playing roles as customers, librarian, storekeeper, and so forth. Field trips to a children's museum can help children learn about communication, transportation, and other activities through hands-on play or observation. For 8- to 11-year-old children, Smith (2000) proposes a model called FOCUS (Finding Out the Child's Underlying Self), which emphasizes exploratory behavior and the development of the self-concept. FOCUS includes materials that assess children's interests, personality, and behaviors. Gamelike activities and age-appropriate questionnaires and books help children develop a sense of self. The Experiential Career Guidance Model and FOCUS are two examples of activities that consider the developmental progress and needs of children in career exploration. Developmental needs of children and issues that they may encounter can be applied to counseling children when career issues may be a part of the process.

Exercises can be structured in such a way that they are consistent with the learning stage of children and with their ability to process information. In general, the successful activities focus on concrete functions, not abstract ones. They are often visual; for example, using films of an occupation or using tools brought into class. Exposure to people in occupations gives an increased opportunity for modeling behavior, as well as an opportunity for the child to have more exposure to key figures. Being able to explore equipment in a factory or to explore dental tools can be helpful to a child in acquiring information about the world of work. Having a veterinarian show animals and how he or she helps them is more useful and

concrete than just talking about his or her daily work. Gottfredson's theory suggests the importance of being careful to avoid gender-role stereotyping in factory
visits or choice of outside speakers. This is often difficult, because the counselor or
teacher may have less control over these activities than over ones that they direct in
the classroom.

THE ROLE OF ASSESSMENT INSTRUMENTS

Because interests, capacities, and values are not sufficiently developed in elementary
school children, assessment of them should be done carefully. Rather, the emphasis
is on acquiring information about oneself, others, and occupations and the development of a self-concept. Children need to be able to see a future and to have a sense of
how far away college or work is with regard to time. The appropriate timing of career
assessment is a difficult issue (see Chapter 8, "Adolescent Career Development," for a
more detailed discussion). Various career maturity inventories serve as a means of
assessing this readiness.

However, some inventories have been changed so that they are appropriate for
children, whereas others have been developed specifically for children. For example,
Holland's Self-Directed Search has a form (Form E) that can be used for middle
school students. The Murphy–Meisgeier Type Indicator assesses Myers–Briggs
types and can be used for children 7 to 13 years old. Personality inventories such
as the Children's Personality Questionnaire have been designed to be used with
preadolescents.

COUNSELOR ISSUES

Career counseling with young children can be challenging because children are at
the beginning of the career choice process, and counselors are usually in an establishment or maintenance phase. Counselors have gone through the process of making career decisions; assessing their abilities, capacities, and values; and acting on
them. Children are far from this stage. They need to experience and acquire information long before they are able to make decisions. This gap in developmental
stage makes patience on the part of the counselor particularly important. Piaget's
(1977) reminder that children are not adults without information is quite helpful.
Being aware of Super's explanation of the career development of children can aid
the counselor in dealing with them.

SUMMARY

Counseling children on career issues is rarely thought of as a duty of counselors.
The purpose of this chapter has not been to show that it should be an important
activity, but rather that, when it does occur, there are effective ways of talking
about career development with children. Super's model of the bases of career maturity is helpful in stressing how curiosity leads to exploration, which can lead to the
acquisition of information and the development of interests. Furthermore, Super

emphasizes the importance of key figures in the development of the self-concept, together with the development of a sense of internal control and respect for parental and educational authorities. As the young child develops a sense of the future and a sense of self, he or she becomes ready to plan and decide. Gottfredson's model includes the role of gender and prestige in examining career development of young children. Like Super, Gottfredson attends to the child's cognitive development and ability to learn. The complex interaction of genetic and environmental factors plays a role in career development and in narrowing (circumscribing) choices. As adolescents, individuals may make compromises and give up factors that affect career choices, such as amount of schooling. Recently, school-to-work has become an important initiative in the schools. Suggestions were described for school activities that are consistent with Super's and Gottfredson's theories.

REFERENCES

Anderson, L. W., & Krathwohl, D. R. (Eds.). *A taxonomy for learning, teaching, and assessing: A revision of Bloom's taxonomy of educational objectives.* New York: Longman.

Bandura, A. (1997). *Self-efficacy: The exercise of control.* San Francisco: W. H. Freeman.

Berlyne, D. E. (1960). *Conflict, arousal, and curiosity.* New York: McGraw-Hill.

Bigler, R. S., Averhart, C. J., & Liben, L. S. (2003). Race and the workforce: Occupational status, aspirations, and stereotyping among African American children. *Developmental Psychology, 39,* 572–580.

Blanchard, C. A., & Lichtenberg, J. W. (2003). Compromise in career decision making: A test of Gottfredson's theory. *Journal of Vocational Behavior, 62,* 250–271.

Blustein, D. (2006). *The psychology of working: A new perspective for career development, counseling, and public policy.* Mahwah, NJ: Erlbaum.

Chak, A. (2002). Understanding children's curiosity and exploration through the lenses of Lewin's field theory: On developing an appraisal framework. *Early Child Development & Care, 172,* 77–87.

Chan, M., & Chadsey, J. G. (2006). High school teachers' perceptions of school-to-work transition practices in Taiwan. *Education and Training in Developmental Disabilities, 41*(3), 280–289.

Cieslik, M., & Simpson, D. (2006). Skills for life? Basic skills and marginal transitions from school to work. *Journal of Youth Studies, 9*(2), 213–229.

Erikson, E. H. (1963). *Childhood and society* (2nd ed.). New York: Norton.

Friedman, W. J. (2002). Children's knowledge of the future distances of daily activities and annual events. *Journal of Cognition and Development, 3,* 333–356.

Giannantonio, C. M., & Hurley-Hanson, A. E. (2006). Applying image norms across Super's career development stages. *The Career Development Quarterly, 54*(4), 318–330.

Gibson, D. E. (2004). Role models in career development: New directions for theory and research. *Journal of Vocational Behavior, 65,* 134–156.

Ginzberg, E., Ginsburg, S. W., Axelrad, S., & Herma, J. (1951). *Occupational choice: An approach to a general theory.* New York: Columbia University Press.

Gottfredson, L. S. (1981). Circumscription and compromise: A developmental theory of occupational aspirations. *Journal of Counseling Psychology, 28,* 545–579.

Gottfredson, L. S. (2002). Gottfredson's theory of circumscription, compromise, and self-creation. In D. Brown & Associates (Eds.), *Career choice and development* (4th ed., pp. 85–148). San Francisco: Jossey-Bass.

Gottfredson, L. S. (2005). Applying Gottfredson's theory of circumscription and compromise in career guidance and counseling. In S. D. Brown & R. W. Lent (Eds.). *Career development and counseling: Putting theory and research to work.* (pp. 71–100). Hoboken, NJ: Wiley.

Gottfredson, L. S., & Lapan, R. T. (1997). Assessing gender-based circumscription of occupational aspirations. *Journal of Career Assessment, 5,* 419–441.

Hall, A. S., Kelly, K. R., & Van Buren, J. B. (1995). Effects of grade level, community of residence, and sex on adolescent career interests in the zone of acceptable alternatives. *Journal of Career Development, 21,* 223–232.

Hartung, P. J., Porfeli, E. J., & Vondracek, F. W. (2005). Child vocational development: A review and reconsideration. *Journal of Vocational Behavior, 66*(3), 385–419.

Helwig, A. A. (1998). Developmental and sex differences in workers' functions of occupational aspirations of a longitudinal sample of elementary school children. *Psychological Reports, 82,* 915–921.

Helwig, A. A. (2000, April). Career development of a longitudinal sample of school children. Paper presented at the American Counseling Association World Conference, Washington, DC.

Helwig, A. A. (2001). A test of Gottfredson's theory using a ten-year longitudinal study. *Journal of Career Development, 28,* 77–95.

Henderson, S., Hesketh, B., & Tuffin, K. (1988). A test of Gottfredson's theory of circumscription. *Journal of Vocational Behavior, 32,* 37–48.

Herr, E. L., Cramer, S. H., & Niles, S. G. (2004). *Career guidance and counseling through the life span* (6th ed.). Boston: Allyn & Bacon.

Hesketh, B., Durant, C., & Pryor, R. (1990). Career compromise: A test of Gottfredson's (1981) theory using a policy capturing procedure. *Journal of Vocational Behavior, 36,* 97–108.

Hesketh, B., Elmslie, S., & Kaldor, W. (1990). Career compromise: Alternative account to Gottfredson's theory. *Journal of Counseling Psychology, 37,* 49–56.

Jordaan, J. P. (1963). Exploratory behavior: The formation of self and occupational concepts. In D. Super, R. Starishevsky, N. Matlin, & J. P. Jordaan (Eds.), *Career development: Self-concept theory* (pp. 42–78). New York: College Entrance Examination Board.

Joyce, M., & Neumark, D. (2001). School-to-work programs: Information from two surveys. *Monthly Labor Review, 124,* 38–50.

Kyle, M. T., & Hennis, M. (2000). Experiential model for career guidance in early childhood education. In N. Peterson & R. C. Gonzalez (Eds.), *Career counseling models for diverse populations* (pp. 1–7). Pacific Grove, CA: Brooks/Cole.

Lapan, R. T., Loehr-Lapan, S. J., & Tupper, T. W. (1993). *Tech-prep careers workbook: Counselor's manual.* Columbia, MO: Columbia Department of Educational and Counseling Psychology, University of Missouri–Columbia.

Marko, K. W., & Savickas, M. L. (1998). Effectiveness of a career time perspective intervention. *Journal of Vocational Behavior, 52,* 106–119.

Morelli, G. A., Rogoff, B., & Angelillo, C. (2003). Cultural variation in young children's access to work or involvement in specialized child-focused activities. *International Journal of Behavioral Development, 27,* 264–274.

Moseley, D., Baumfield, V., Elliot, J., Gregson, M., Higgins, S., Miller, J., et al. (2005). *Frameworks for thinking: A handbook for teaching and learning.* New York: Cambridge University Press.

Nel, L., van der Westhuyzen, C., & Uys, K. (2007). Introducing a school-to-work transition model for youth with disabilities in South Africa. *Work: Journal of Prevention, Assessment & Rehabilitation, 29*(1), 13–18.

Ng, T. W. H., & Feldman, D. C. (2007). The school-to-work transition: A role identity perspective. *Journal of Vocational Behavior, 71*(1), 114–134.

Orellana, M. F. (2001). The work kids do: Mexican and Central American immigrant children's contributions to households and schools in California. *Howard Educational Review, 71,* 366–389.

Piaget, J. (1977). *The development of thought: Equilibration of cognitive structures.* New York: Viking Press.

Plomin, R., DeFries J. D., McClearn, J. E., & McGuffin, P. (2001). *Behavioral genetics* (4th ed.). New York: Worth.

Rainey, L. M., & Borders, L. D. (1997). Influential factors in career orientation and career aspirations of early adolescent girls. *Journal of Counseling Psychology, 44,* 160–172.

Rich, N. S. (1979). Occupational knowledge: To what extent is rural youth handicapped? *Vocational Guidance Quarterly, 27,* 320–325.

Savickas, M. L. (2002). Career construction: A developmental theory of vocational behavior. In D. Brown & Associates (Eds.), *Career choice and development* (4th ed., pp. 149–205). San Francisco: Jossey-Bass.

Schultheiss, D. E. P., Palma, T. V., & Manzi, A. J. (2005). Career development in middle childhood: A qualitative inquiry. *The Career Development Quarterly, 53*(3), 246–262.

Smith, T. L. (2000). FOCUS: Finding Out the Child's Underlying Self: A career awareness model for children. In N. Peterson & R. C. Gonzalez (Eds.), *Career counseling models for diverse populations* (pp. 8–21). Pacific Grove, CA: Brooks/Cole Publishing.

Solberg, V. S., Howard, K. A., Blustein, D. L., & Close, W. (2002). Career development in the schools: Connecting school-to-work-to-life. *Counseling Psychologist, 30,* 705–725.

Super, D. E. (1953). A theory of vocational development. *American Psychologist, 8,* 185–190.

Super, D. E. (1990). A life-span, life-space approach to career development. In D. Brown, L. Brooks, & Associates (Eds.), *Career choice and development: Applying contemporary theories to practice* (2nd ed., pp. 197–261). San Francisco: Jossey-Bass.

Super, D. E. (1994). A life-span, life-space perspective on convergence. In M. L. Savickas & R. W. Lent (Eds.), *Convergence in career development theories* (pp. 63–74). Palo Alto, CA: Consulting Psychologists Press.

Super, D., Starishevsky, R., Matlin, N., & Jordaan, J. P. (Eds.) (1963). *Career development: Self-concept theory.* New York: College Entrance Examination Board.

Thomas, R. M. (1989). *Counseling and life-span development.* Newbury Park, CA: Sage.

Torimiro, D. O., Dionco-Adetayo, E., & Okorie, V. O. (2003). Children and involvement in animal rearing: A traditional occupation for sustainability of nomadic culture? *Early Child Development & Care, 173,* 185–191.

Tracey, T. J. (2001). The development of structure of interests in children: Setting the stage. *Journal of Vocational Behavior, 59,* 89–104.

Tracey, T. J. (2002). Development of interests and competency beliefs: A 1-year longitudinal study of fifth to eighth-grade students using the ICA-R and structural equation modeling. *Journal of Counseling Psychology, 49,* 148–163.

Trice, A. D., & Tillapaugh, P. (1991). Children's estimates of their parents' job satisfaction. *Psychological Reports, 69,* 63–66.

Trice, A. D., Hughes, M. A., Odom, K. W., Woods, K., & McClellen, N. C. (1995). The origins of children's career aspirations: IV. Testing hypotheses from four theories. *The Career Development Quarterly, 43,* 307–322.

Tsaousides, T. (2007). The effects of perceived career compromise on expected emotional states and work-related satisfaction in college students. *Dissertation Abstracts International: Section B: The Sciences and Engineering, 67*(9-B), 5427.

Turner, S. L., & Lapan, R. T. (2005). *Promoting career development and aspirations in school-age youth.* Hoboken, NJ: Wiley.

Turner, S. L., Trotter, M. J., Lapan, R. T., Czajka, K. A., Yang, P., & Brissett, A. E. A. (2006). Vocational skills and outcomes among Native American adolescents: A test of the integrative contextual model of career development. *The Career Development Quarterly, 54*(3), 216–226.

Watson, M., & McMahon, M. (2005). Children's career development: A research review from a learning perspective. *Journal of Vocational Behavior, 67*(2), 119–132.

Zunker, V. G. (2006). *Career counseling: A holistic approach*. (7th ed.). Belmont, CA: Thomson.

ADOLESCENT CAREER DEVELOPMENT

CHAPTER **8**

CHAPTER HIGHLIGHTS

Factors Influencing Adolescent Career Development

Super's Growth Stage of Adolescent Career Development

Career Maturity

Identity and Context

The Role of Occupational Information

The Role of Assessment Instruments

Gender Issues in Adolescence

Career Development of Adolescents from Diverse Cultural Backgrounds

Counselor Issues

Some career development theorists have focused their attention on adolescence, because it is the time when educational commitment to career choices is made. Life-stage theorists have been helpful in identifying developmental tasks that are important for individuals in the career selection process. This chapter first describes cognitive and emotional factors that impact career decision making. Then, the emergence of interests, capacities, and values are discussed in terms of Super's theory of the stages of adolescent career development. This chapter gives examples of how counselors can recognize the emergence of interests, capacities, and values through the use of the concept of career maturity. A similar area of research is related to Erikson's writings on identity formation, called vocational identity. In this chapter, Super's research on the Career Development Inventory (Super, Bohn, Forrest, Jordaan, Lindeman, &

Thompson, 1971; Thompson & Lindeman, 1981) is used as a formulation for a conceptual understanding of career maturity, and James Marcia's and Fred Vondracek's work is used as a basis for understanding vocational identity. Although there are no theories that specifically address the career development of adolescent girls or adolescents from diverse cultural backgrounds, there is a wide body of research that explores this topic. As in other areas of career life-span theory, there has been much more research on the career development of white adolescents than on other adolescents. However, that trend is changing. Counseling examples in this chapter demonstrate how Super's theory and vocational identity theory can be used with different groups.

FACTORS INFLUENCING ADOLESCENT CAREER DEVELOPMENT

Abstract thinking is a process that greatly facilitates career planning. According to Piaget (1977) a gradual process of developing the ability to solve problems and to plan begins during adolescence. With age, planning becomes more ordered, permitting adolescents to introspect and think about themselves in a variety of situations. At this point, adolescents can more accurately picture themselves working in occupations than they could a few years earlier. This ability, which occurs in the last of Piaget's (1977) four stages of cognitive development, is called *formal thought*. There are individual differences regarding when an adolescent develops the ability to think abstractly. Furthermore, there are differences across courses in the requirement to think abstractly. For example, a high school sophomore may be able to think abstractly in algebra class but not in biology. Ability to use logic develops gradually. As formal thought emerges, the egocentrism of the concrete operational thinking of childhood does not disappear quickly. Because adolescents have developed the ability to think logically, they are apt to be quite idealistic, expecting their world to be logical when it is not. The process of job entry and job selection can help young people become more realistic in their thinking (Inhelder & Piaget, 1958). Cognitively, the period of formal thought is likely to bring the adolescent into conflict with parents and teachers, because students are likely to think that they are right and others are wrong. Although overstated, this suggests that adolescent thinking is a more tumultuous process than the thinking that takes place in elementary school children.

Just as Piaget identified adolescence as a time of mild turmoil, Erikson (1963) believed that, in terms of psychosocial development, adolescence is a time of identity and role confusion. No longer concerned with following rules and being productive, as in Erikson's (1963) earlier stage focusing on industry and accomplishment, adolescents question their world. Together with their physical development and their exposure to difficult sexual decisions (premarital sex, pregnancy, AIDS) come career decisions that may affect the rest of their lives. As early as middle school, adolescents need to decide whether they want a "vocational track," a "college track," or something else. The ability to deal with these decisions varies greatly among adolescents. Career theorists have studied those aspects of adolescent development that are pertinent to the career choice process, such as interests, capacities, and values.

SUPER'S GROWTH STAGE OF ADOLESCENT CAREER DEVELOPMENT

Super's (1955) stages of adolescent career development arise from the stages of curiosity and fantasies in childhood (Figure 8.1). Starting around the age of 8 years old, development of interest begins to replace occupational fantasies. At the age of 11, children develop a sense of their capacities, a view of their own ability to master certain skills. The age of the development of interests and capacities varies from child to child and the age ranges are only approximate. During adolescence, children develop a system of values. Different values develop at different times for

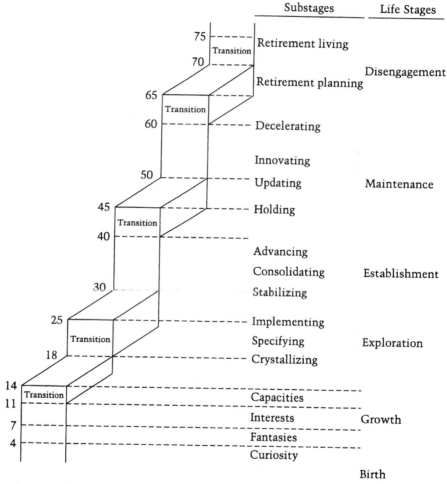

FIGURE 8.1 | SUPER'S LIFE STAGES AND SUBSTAGES BASED ON THE TYPICAL DEVELOPMENTAL TASKS.

Source: From *Career choice and development* by D. Brown, L. Brooks, and Associates. Copyright © 1984 by Jossey-Bass, Inc. Reprinted by permission.

different children. This period of growth evolves into the transition phase (about the age of 18) as it prepares adolescents for starting the crystallizing substage of adulthood that begins around the age of 18.

DEVELOPMENT OF INTERESTS

Super (1955) believed that, at about 7 years old, children ceased to make fantasy choices and instead tend to base their choices on interests. In particular, Super observed that many choices of young boys are related in some way to their fathers' careers. Based on their current interests, 10-year-old boys would comment about whether they would like to be in an occupation like their father's. The children were quite aware that their interests might change and that they might make different choices. However, they were vague about and not concerned with alternative choices, because they knew that there was a lot of time to make choices. At 11 years old, the ability to judge their competencies was limited but beginning to become more important to them.

When talking with students who are ready to enter middle school, counselors may notice that the students can speak more clearly about what they like than about what they are able to do. Children may have some exposure through their community to a number of occupations. They may be interested in being a detective or a doctor after seeing these occupations portrayed on television. They may observe the roles of their parents and their friends' parents. They are able to ask themselves: Is this something I may like to do? Participating in sports and childhood jobs such as mowing lawns and babysitting also permits them to test their interests. Children who have not yet developed the ability to judge their capacities may want to be, for example, professional athletes, but they are not yet able to consider the quality of their performance.

DEVELOPMENT OF CAPACITIES

According to Super, the capacity period covers the ages of 11 to 14 years. In their discussions with counselors, adolescents are more likely to accurately assess their own abilities than they would have been able to 2 years before. They may be able to say, "Two years ago, I wanted to be a basketball player, but now I realize I will never be good enough," or "I'm not sure that I could ever be an engineer like my father; you have to know so much difficult math." For 11- to 14-year-olds, the educational process becomes more important in their preparation for work. Two years before, they may have been less concerned about that process. It is at this point that their time perspective improves and they are able to have a more realistic view of themselves and their future.

Recognizing an adolescent's ability to assess his or her own capacities can be useful to the counselor. It is difficult for children to make decisions about curricular choice in eighth grade if they are not able to assess their capacities. Their choices at this point are likely to be based on interests or what their parents have told them. Often, parents make decisions for their young adolescent children, partially because the children have not yet developed the ability to assess their own capacities.

DEVELOPMENT OF VALUES

According to Super (Super, Thompson, & Lindeman, 1988), different values may emerge and become more important at various times in the life span. At the ages of 15 and 16 years, some adolescents are able to take their goals and values into consideration when making a career decision. They may not know how to weigh their interests, capacities, and values, but they have the necessary building blocks for making choices. They are becoming aware that they must make choices so that they can fit into a complex world. With their developed cognitive abilities, they may start to consider such abstract questions as: Is it better to make money or to help others? Weighing the satisfaction of helping others or contributing to environmental protection may be issues they had not thought about 2 years before. Making a contribution to the world and being a credit to society are factors that now may be considered. The issue of marriage and life plans may emerge, even though there is no marriage partner in mind. Such abstract conceptualization allows adolescents to continue to the next period.

TRANSITION TO THE CRYSTALLIZING SUBSTAGE

During the transition period, reality conditions start to play an important role in career choice. This period usually occurs in the last year of high school, at 17 or 18 years of age. Decisions about whether to go to college and, if college is the choice, what to major in are real, immediate questions. Adolescents are aware that they need to pay attention to issues such as job availability. They know that they may not be able to get into the college or the field of their choice. Often, 17- or 18-year-old teenagers are aware that they may not have to make a decision, such as one about medical school, for a few years, but they are aware of the imminence of the decision. They know that they can determine their own future and must take action to do so, even if they cannot do it immediately. Considering salary, the education required, and working conditions becomes more important in this period than it was 2 years before. This period directly precedes Super's exploration stage, which is discussed in Chapter 9.

Career guidance for 17- and 18-year-olds usually includes an assessment of their interests, capacities, and values. When hearing a student discussing the world of work and her or his own abilities and desires, counselors can feel that assessment and counseling may be helpful. Super and colleagues deal with this topic in great detail in their discussion of career maturity.

Of interest is the research that describes when adolescents and children pursue the tasks of developing interests, capacities, and values. In a study of 9-year-old children, Miller (1977) reports that many were able to state interests in activities and occupations. In eighth, tenth, and twelfth grade, adolescents' interests became more differentiated as the adolescents moved on to the next grade, but also interests were generally quite stable (Tracey, Robbins, & Hofsess, 2005). Aubrey (1977) reports that many children were able to say what they could and could not do, although girls were better able to do this than boys. However, Tierney and Herman (1973) note the difficulty in making accurate self-estimates. This is consistent with O'Hara and Tiedeman (1959), who observe that, during the high school years, adolescents have difficulty in accurately seeing their capacities. Westbrook, Buck, Wynne, and Sanford (1994) state that adolescents were most accurate in rating their scholastic aptitude and least accurate in rating specific or special aptitudes, which they tended to overrate. Regarding values, Kapes and Strickler (1975) describe little consistency in the work values of high school students. They suggest that different high school curricula may bring about different changes in work values. Porfeli (2007) reported that high school students who did not plan to earn an advanced degree, valued their part-time work more than they valued anticipated later full-time work. Those students who were seeking advanced degrees tended to develop their value system later in life than students not seeking advanced degrees, as they were working on issues related to their career goals when in their advanced training programs. These studies do not support the use of age guidelines in expecting consistent patterns in development of interests, capacities, and values in adolescents. Rather, they reaffirm the importance of assessing the individual student. The theorists and the research, however, are consistent in predicting that, in most adolescents, the development of interests precedes that of capacities.

A COUNSELING EXAMPLE

To show the usefulness of assessing the relative development of interests, capacities, and values, this chapter uses a 14-year-old ninth-grade student as an example. Joan is an African American girl from an affluent Chicago suburb. Both of her parents work in the advertising field. Her father is an account executive with a Chicago firm, and her mother is a market researcher in another firm. Although Joan's grades through her first two quarters of school have been As and Bs, her parents are concerned by her lack of motivation for college and have asked that she talk with her guidance counselor. The following section of the interview takes place toward the beginning of Joan's session with her counselor:

CO: Do you have any idea what you want to do when you finish high school? [This question is designed to get Joan started talking about her plans.]

CL: Well, I'm not sure, but I have some ideas.

CO: Go ahead. I'd like to hear them.

CL: Well, I think I'd like to go into advertising like my parents. They seem to know lots of people and have fun with the products. Sometimes they talk about the products on TV that they've worked with. Sometimes my father will show me a magazine ad that he worked on. But sometimes I think I might like to be an actress or a model, or an aeronautical engineer, like my friend's mother. Sometimes I think I would like to be a teacher like Mrs. Morgan. I have her for English now, and she's great. Then, I've thought of writing, too. It would be fun to write for a magazine.

CO: Can you tell me more of what appeals to you about advertising? [Feeling bombarded, the counselor decides to concentrate on depth rather than on breadth. Returning to the first topic, because it was talked about in detail, the counselor inquires about advertising, wanting to hear more about Joan's interest.]

CL: I think that I'd like to write ads. It would be fun to do. Sometimes my dad talks about them at dinner. I'm not sure I'd like to do research on toilet paper, the way my mother does.

CO: You seem to enjoy English. [Wanting to follow up on Joan's interest in advertising, the counselor further explores the topic.]

CL: Writing seems so much fun, especially with Mrs. Morgan. She's given us great assignments to do. For her, I like to do my homework.

CO: How is your work going? [This question may get at Joan's perception of her performance in English.]

CL: Oh, I'm doing OK; Mrs. Morgan likes me and my work, I think. But I don't know how I'm *really* doing.

CO: I'm not quite sure what you mean. [The counselor has an idea that Joan is making some distinction between school and occupational ability but is not sure.]

CL: Maybe I could do schoolwork OK, but doing what my father does seems really hard. You really have to be smart to get people to work with your company and give them good ads.

CO: It seems difficult for you to make plans about what you want to do. [Joan seems able to differentiate between ability needed at school and in an occupation. She seems to be aware that she does not know yet whether she has the ability needed to be successful in advertising.]

CL: Sometimes it seems too hard. I wish I were a psychiatrist.

CO: Tell me more about that, please. [The counselor wonders where this came from. Joan's interests are varied and seem to have no end.]

CL: I really like to help people. I have seen psychiatrists on television programs and how they do it. It seems great.

CO: To help people? [Wanting to learn more about Joan's motivation, the counselor inquires further.]

CL: Yes, it's just so easy to sit there and talk and make a lot of money.

CO: Seems like fun to you. [What had started out as a possible value for Joan has turned into a rather naive interest.]

Joan's difficulty in establishing her capacities and values suggests that career counseling using assessment instruments may be premature. Although the use of a career maturity inventory (described in the next section) may be helpful, the counselor wishes to continue discussing Joan's interests, because they are varied and confused. This may lead to more suggestions as to how to proceed. Currently, the counselor's goal for counseling is to assess career maturity, rather than to work on career selection, and to continue to conceptualize Joan's interests, capacities, and values.

CAREER MATURITY

Super (1955) describes vocational maturity as having the following five major components:

1. Orientation to vocational choice, which deals with concern about career choice and using occupational information
2. Information and planning about a preferred occupation—that is, the specific information that the individual has about the occupation he or she intends to enter
3. Consistency of vocational preference, concerned not only with stability of an occupational choice over time, but also with its consistency within occupational fields and levels
4. Crystallization of traits, including seven indices of attitudes toward work
5. The wisdom of vocational preference, which refers to the relationship between choice and abilities, activities, and interests

This work of Super's was a major focus of the early monographs published by the Career Pattern Study, an in-depth study of a sample of adolescents followed into adulthood. Super and colleagues further refined the concept of vocational maturity (Super, Crites, Hummel, Moser, Overstreet, & Warnath, 1957; Super & Overstreet, 1960). This extensive work led to the development of the original Career Development Inventory (Super et al., 1971) and culminated in a revised edition of the Career Development Inventory (Thompson & Lindeman, 1981). The concepts that make up Super's definition of career maturity have been developed by studying the responses of boys and girls, and men and women, to various versions of the Career Development Inventory (Patton & Lokan, 2001). These concepts are described in detail in this section.

SUPER'S CONCEPTION OF CAREER MATURITY

Throughout the extensive research that Super and colleagues have done with adolescents, they have been concerned with readiness of individuals to make good choices. They do not assume that just because a student reaches ninth grade, he or she is ready to plan his or her future career. Not only do they see differences in career maturity among individuals, but they are also able to identify different components of career maturity. To understand Super's model, it is helpful to use the structure of the Career Development Inventory (Thompson & Lindeman, 1981). With Figure 8.2 as a guide, this section explains the five subscales that make up the Career Development Inventory: Career Planning, Career Exploration, Decision Making, World-of-Work Information, and Knowledge of the Preferred Occupational Group. Also, the Career Orientation Total, which is a combination of subscales, is described. Another concept that is part of Super's definition of career maturity, but that is not tested by the Career Development Inventory, is realism. The concepts described in the following paragraphs can be used to guide client discussion, with or without the use of the Career Development Inventory.

CAREER PLANNING   The Career Planning scale (and therefore the concept of planning) measures how much thought individuals have given to a variety of information-seeking activities and how much they feel they know about various aspects of work. The

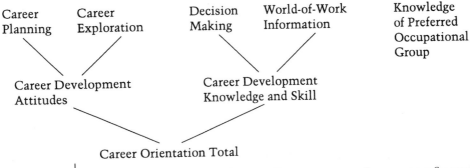

FIGURE 8.2 | RELATIONSHIP OF THE CAREER DEVELOPMENT INVENTORY SCALES.

amount of planning that an individual has done is critical to this concept. Some of the activities that are included are learning about occupational information, talking with adults about plans, taking courses that would help one make career decisions, participating in extracurricular activities or part-time or summer jobs, and obtaining training or education for a job. In addition, this concept deals with knowledge of working conditions, required education, job outlook, different approaches to job entry, and chances of advancement. *Career planning* refers to how much a student *feels* that he or she knows about these activities, not how much he or she actually knows. The latter is covered by the World-of-Work Information and Knowledge of the Preferred Occupational Group scales.

When talking with a student about career planning activities, it is helpful to know not only what the student has done, but also what the student *thinks* he or she has done. Discussion of future plans, including courses to be taken the following year, college selection, or ideas about a potential college major or postsecondary education, all contribute to career planning. Either a low score on the Career Planning scale of the Career Development Inventory or the counselor's assessment that the student has not given much thought to career plans suggests that it is necessary to move to the next step in counseling. This step is to give more thought to experiences that may provide more information that could serve as a basis for planning.

CAREER EXPLORATION   Willingness to explore or look for information is the concept basic to the Career Exploration scale. In this subscale (and concept), students' willingness to use resources such as parents, other relatives, friends, teachers, counselors, books, and movies is investigated. In addition to willingness, career exploration deals with how much information the student has already acquired from the source. Career exploration differs from career planning in that the latter concerns thinking and planning about the future, whereas the former deals with use of resources, but both focus on attitudes toward work. Combined, Super refers to them as career development attitudes, and a score for this concept is given on the Career Development Inventory.

Counselors may often find that students are reluctant, for various reasons, to use resources to get occupational information, sometimes because of a student's attitude that he or she does not need information. In such a case, the counselor can explore reasons for this thinking. Sometimes, students are hostile to authority figures and rule out certain valuable resources such as parents, teachers, or coaches. Other students may be afraid to use resources because they are apprehensive that teachers or relatives will not take them seriously. Encouraging career exploration can be an important activity before assisting a student with career selection. Giving the student 1 week, 3 months, or some specified period to talk to teachers and use books containing occupational information or some other resource and then return for counseling is often a useful strategy. By focusing on attitudes toward work, the counselor can determine the next step in assisting the student with career development. However, a positive attitude toward work may not be sufficient to start career planning. Knowledge of how to make a career decision and some knowledge of occupational information is also important.

DECISION MAKING   The idea that a student must know how to make career decisions is important in Super's concept of vocational maturity. This concept concerns the ability to use knowledge and thought to make career plans. In the Decision-Making scale, students are given situations in which others must make career decisions and are asked to decide which decision would be best. An assumption is that, if students know how others should make career decisions, they will be able to make good career decisions for themselves.

Asking students how they plan to go about making a career decision can be useful. Some students will be unable to answer the question, or to say anything more than "I don't know; it will come to me." This is an opportunity for the counselor to explain portions of the career decision process. The counselor can focus on what the next steps may be for career decision making. If the counselor uses the Career Development Inventory, it would be helpful to review that section of the inventory with the student, explaining why some of the student's answers were correct and others were wrong.

WORLD-OF-WORK INFORMATION   The World-of-Work Information concept has two basic components. The first deals with knowledge of important developmental tasks, such as when others should explore their interests and abilities, how others learn about their jobs, and why people change jobs. The other portion of this concept (and subscale) covers knowledge of job duties in a few selected occupations, as well as job application behaviors. Super believes that it is important for individuals to have some knowledge about the world of work before effective career decision-making counseling can be done.

For the counselor, knowledge of the accuracy of the information that students have about work is helpful. Some students have misinformation about how to obtain a job and how to behave when they get a job. Others have little idea of the work that people such as doctors, lawyers, stockbrokers, and secretaries do. Often, some information is inaccurately gathered from television or films. Correcting students' inaccurate perceptions of the world of work may be a part of predecision-making counseling.

KNOWLEDGE OF THE PREFERRED OCCUPATIONAL GROUP   In the Career Development Inventory, students are asked to choose which of 20 occupational groups they prefer. Then, they are asked questions about their preferred occupational group. They are asked about duties of the job, tools and equipment, and physical requirements of the job. In addition, they are asked to judge their own ability (or capacities) in nine different areas: verbal ability, nonverbal reasoning, numerical ability, clerical ability, mechanical ability, spatial ability, motor coordination, English skills, and reading ability. They are also asked to identify the interests of the people in the preferred occupation. The interest categories that they choose from are verbal, numerical, clerical, mechanical, scientific, artistic/musical, promotional, social, and outdoor. This, then, constitutes a thorough inquiry into students' knowledge of their preferred occupational group.

Information about students' knowledge of the occupation that they want to enter can be extremely helpful in determining what type of counseling should be offered. In talking to students about their knowledge of occupations, counselors can learn about their progress in career planning. For example, some students may have misinformation about their career choice. Some students may be quite naive, thinking that to be a veterinarian does not require more than an Associate's degree. Others may believe that, to enter a business career, one needs a Bachelor's degree in Business. The assessment of knowledge of a preferred occupation is often a key aspect of counseling. If a counselor is not aware of a student's assumptions about his or her preferred occupation, the counselor may assume the student has made a good decision, when, in fact, that is not true. Assessing good decision making is related to another of Super's concepts: realism.

REALISM   Realism, a concept that is part of Super's view of career maturity (Super, 1990), is not assessed in the Career Development Inventory. Rather, Super describes it as a "mixed affective and cognitive entity best assessed by combining personal, self-report, and objective data as in comparing the aptitudes of the individual with the aptitudes typical of people in the occupation" (p. 213). Thus, to measure whether a choice of an individual is realistic, a counselor would need knowledge of the ability required in the occupation, together with aptitude or grade information about the student.

The use of realism in career counseling has some dangers. It requires that the counselor be an accurate judge of the student's aptitudes and the aptitudes required by the job. Inappropriate use of judging realistic choices can lead to the following statements: "My high school guidance counselor told me I could never make it to medical school, but I am in medical school now"; "My high school guidance counselor said I could never make it through college, and I graduated last year"; "My high school guidance counselor said I don't have the ability to go to college, so I guess I won't." Because students can misinterpret or misuse aptitude information, the concept of realism has to be used quite carefully. Inaccurate predictions can have a significant effect on an individual's later choice of occupation.

CAREER ORIENTATION   Career orientation is a general term encompassing the concepts described previously. The Career Orientation Total score gives a single summary of the following scales: Career Planning, Career Exploration, Career Decision Making, and World-of-Work Information. It does not include the Knowledge of the Preferred Occupational Group score or the unmeasured concept, realism. Having a general sense of students' career maturity before looking at the specific subscales may be useful for the counselor. It may provide a summary of what to expect from the student in terms of orientation toward careers. However, the five subscales are likely to have more relevance for the counselor in deciding which areas of career maturity to explore with a student. Probably, the counselor will want to talk most about those in which the student scores low. The following example explores how a counselor used both career maturity concepts derived from the Career Development Inventory and the inventory itself.

USING THE CONCEPT OF CAREER MATURITY IN COUNSELING   Ralph is a white 10th-grade student attending a high school in Providence, Rhode Island. His parents are second-generation Italian Americans. His father is a mail carrier, and his mother is a waitress. Ralph took the Career Development Inventory, together with the rest of his 10th-grade class, in the early fall. He is talking about his schedule with his career guidance counselor and is trying to decide what courses to take next year. Ralph has earned C grades in science and math and A grades in English and social studies. He works after school in a fast-food restaurant and spends much of his weekends working with his older brother on his brother's car. Compared with other 10th-grade students, Ralph's Career Planning and Career Exploration scores are at about the 15th percentile. His Decision Making score on the Career Development Inventory is at the 50th percentile, and his World-of-Work Information score is at about the 45th percentile. His scores on Knowledge of the Preferred Occupational Group and the Career Orientation Total are at about the 25th percentile. The following transcript begins after the counselor and client have exchanged some introductory remarks:

CL: I know I need to think about next year and beyond, but I just haven't had time.

CO: Been very busy? [The counselor wants to learn more about Ralph's career maturity by discussing how Ralph spends his time.]

CL: After school, I work at that fast-food place down the street, and then at night, I go out with my friends.

CO: Does it give you any time to think about what you want to do? [The counselor wants to inquire about career planning that Ralph may have done. The counselor has Ralph's Career Development Inventory results. He has not shared these results directly with Ralph at this point.]

CL: I really haven't thought about it much. It doesn't sound like fun. After work, I'm kind of tired, and I like to go home and have dinner. Then I like to go out. Sometimes I do some homework, but not too much.

CO: Have you had a chance to talk to anyone about what you might do? [The counselor, aware of Ralph's low scores on Career Planning and Career Exploration, wants to see if there is a possibility for Ralph to make progress in this area.]

CL: Not really. My parents don't seem to know much about what is available. They just think I should work hard and get a good, secure job that pays well. My friends don't seem to know anything serious anyway.

CO: Would you like to know more about what's available? [Possibly, Ralph's friends and relatives are limited sources of information. There may be other sources that can help Ralph.]

CL: Yes, I know I should do more than I am doing. Where can I learn?

CO: Your teachers, the Career Center here at school, maybe friends of your parents.

CL: I know that our math teacher brought in an accountant, and I learned a little bit that way. But I certainly don't want to be an accountant.

CO: Sounds as if you've given some thought to possible occupations. [The counselor wants to reinforce the little career exploration that Ralph has done.]

CL: Actually, what seems more interesting to me—and it surprises me—is doing what my social studies teacher does.

CO: Surprises you? [Ralph is starting to think a bit about world-of-work information and is using a key figure—the importance of which is described in the previous chapter—in that exploration.]

CL: Yes, I never thought about doing anything like teaching. I always just thought that work was work, a real pain.

CO: Now it seems maybe work could be fun. You seem to be interested in teaching. Wanting to note this change in attitude, the counselor emphasizes it.]

CL: Yes, I think I would like to help people learn things. My social studies teacher seems to really like what he's doing, and that's great. All I ever do at home is hear my parents complain about their work.

CO: You seem to be picking up some ideas about what teachers do, more than you have in past years. [Perhaps Ralph is starting to learn more world-of-work information because of a growing maturity. Even though he has been exposed to teachers for the last 11 years, he is just now starting to think about teaching as an occupation.]

By exploring ideas about career choice, the counselor is helping Ralph become more vocationally mature. As their counseling progresses, the counselor will make some decisions, as will Ralph. The counselor will decide when to share the Career Development Inventory scores with Ralph and how to help him learn from them. Furthermore, the counselor will decide whether to do interest, aptitude, or values assessment with Ralph. For Ralph, decisions about whether to continue thinking about career planning and the world of work will have to be made. By making use of Super's career maturity concepts, the counselor is able to make some assessment of Ralph's readiness for career decision making. Vocational maturity is one way of viewing adolescent career development; vocational identity is yet another. Erikson's view of identity formation has been modified by Marcia and has been applied to career development by Vondracek and others.

IDENTITY AND CONTEXT

Erik Erikson's (1963, 1968, 1982; Kroger, 2007) theory of human development is broad, with several implications for career development. Influencing more career theorists than any other single developmental theory, Erikson's life-stage approach is frequently cited by Super as influential in his own theory. Of particular interest are his conceptualizations about adolescent identity issues. His identity stage is the fifth of eight stages and serves as a bridge between the four stages occurring in childhood and the three stages that arise in adulthood. This section focuses on the identity stage and its relationship to other stages as they affect career development.

Compared with the attraction of career development theorists to Erikson's model, the direct application of Erikson's theory to career development issues has been minimal. Munley (1977) has made an effort to apply Erikson's theoretical constructs to career development. Some research by Munley (1975) and others (Lewis, 2003; Powers & Griffith, 1993; Savickas, 1985) has focused on the identity crisis. Fred Vondracek and colleagues have done the most consistent research on vocational identity. These writers have attempted to define the concept of identity and to explain it through research and case studies. Although Erikson has written frequently on issues concerning the identity crisis, his work does not provide clear prescriptions for the counselor or psychotherapist. It could be said that Erikson presents an artistic rather than a scientific view of the identity crisis. Describing identity issues in the lives of clients sometimes can be difficult.

A significant effort has been devoted to studying Erikson's stages. For example, Zuschlag and Whitbourne (1994) studied three groups of college students, who were surveyed in 1967, 1977, and 1988. The authors concluded that college seniors had more advanced emotional and cognitive development than younger students. Marcia, Waterman, Matteson, Archer, and Orlofsky (1993) provide a handbook for investigating Erikson's psychosocial stages, especially identity and intimacy. Marcia (1989, 1998, 1999, 2003) has modified Erikson's work so that research can be done on important aspects of identity development. Marcia refers to these aspects as statuses, and they include diffusion, moratorium, foreclosure, and achievement.

Vondracek and colleagues (Vondracek, 2003; Vondracek & Porfeli, 2003; Vondracek & Skorikov, 2007) prefer to use Marcia's diffusion, moratorium, foreclosure, and achievement statuses rather than vocational maturity because they believe that Marcia's statuses helps to identify four levels of vocational identity development. Consistent with their developmental-contextual conceptual framework they believe that identity development is best understood when studied within a specific context. These statuses can be measured through interviews or self-report questionnaires, including the Extended Objective Measure of Ego Identity Status (Adams, Bennion, & Huh, 1987), or survey questions such as those from the Shell Youth Study (*Jugendwerk der Deutschen Shell*, 1992). In their work, Vondracek and colleagues examined political and social issues that affect adolescents, as well as individual issues.

In the course of developing a firm vocational identity, adolescents can be viewed as occupying one of the four identity statuses at any given time (diffusion, moratorium, foreclosure, and achievement).

Diffusion refers to having few clear ideas of what one wants and not being concerned about the future. Living in the present rather than thinking about more schooling or the type of work one might like to do are examples of diffusion.

A *moratorium* is a time, often more than several months, in which one explores options while wanting a direction, but not having one. This is often a time between high school and college or a time-out from college. A moratorium is most effective when it is spent in an activity that has meaning to the individual. Volunteering to improve the environment is likely to have more meaning than earning money by washing dishes.

Foreclosure refers to making a choice, often based on family tradition, without exploring other options. Entering the family business without considering whether or not it fits one's interests, values, and abilities would be an example of foreclosure.

Achievement refers to knowing what one wants and making plans to attain an occupational goal. Considering experiences one has had to decide what future activities or jobs to participate in, would be an example of achievement.

In some of their studies, Vondracek and colleagues use single items to identify the vocational identity statuses. Each of the following statements, taken from *Jugendwerk der Deutschen Shell* (1992), is used as a single-item measure of each status (due to limitations in the available data):

Diffusion—I don't know what I want; what happens, happens.

Moratorium—I don't know what I want, but I want to find out.

Foreclosure—I know what I want and I follow established paths.

Achievement—I know what I want and have made plans already.

Several factors lead to the development of vocational identity in childhood and adolescence (Vondracek & Skorikov, 2007). Children remember vocational events of family members. Such events may include parents or grandparents changing jobs being laid off, or retiring from work. Also, family members may have views of what a child should do when he or she grows up. Sometimes children may commit to an occupation early in their lives, an example of the foreclosure status. Examples of occupations that children may commit to that they have a poor chance of being able to enter are professional singer or professional athlete. If in adolescence young people do not have positive career role models or expectations from family members or others about their career choice, they may have little sense of what may happen next—an example of the diffusion status. If they have parental pressure to choose an occupation, they may go into the foreclosure status. This can lead to confusion, which can bring about a delay in seeking a career, and adolescents may try activities that, at first, may only be indirectly related to their career development—a moratorium. However, active and system-atic seeking of vocational information during a moratorium can bring an adoles-cent into the achievement status in which they make plans for their career. The route to a formation of vocational identity can be confused and have obstacles along the way. But, typically, adolescents would not go through all the statuses of diffusion, foreclosure, moratorium, and achievement. However, they may par-ticipate in statuses in a different order than is described above and may also repeat them.

Vondracek and colleagues have examined identity development from several points of view. As individuals advance in their vocational identity development, they tend to have positive attitudes and an openness to a variety of occupations. In college students, higher identity status was related to a greater sense of self-efficacy in decision making and more differentiation of interests than lower identity status (Nauta & Kahn, 2007). In Latino high school students, when students had more obstacles (such as lack of finance or family support), their vocational identity as measured by Holland's My Vocational Situation was less well defined than when there were fewer obstacles (Gushue, Clarke, Pantzer, & Scanlan, 2006). Adoles-cents with a strong sense of vocational identity were also more willing to explore occupations and feel more confident about being successful in their work (Vondracek & Skorikov, 1997). In studying occupational exploration of 13- to 19-year-olds, Schmitt-Rodermund and Vondracek (1999) report that those in the identity diffusion status explored activities in leisure, school, technology, and music areas the least, whereas those in the achievement phase explored these activities the most. They also report that doing activities with parents predicted more explor-atory behavior. Environmental exploration also predicts vocational identity achievement in college students (Robitschek & Cook, 1999). Identity development also has been studied in domains other than the vocational domain, such as reli-gion, politics, lifestyle, and interpersonal relations. Vocational identity tends to pre-cede the development of identity in the other domains, setting a tone for how the other aspects of identity will develop (Skorikov & Vondracek, 1998; Vondracek, 2003). The authors suggest that vocational development in early adolescence is par-ticularly important because it influences other areas of identity development. Vocational identity is important in late adolescence, as well as in early adolescence, and it is related to the age of the individual for all adolescents (Johnson, Buboltz, & Nichols, 1999). However, Reitzle (2007) did find that older adolescents' views of themselves as being adults was related more to their perception of their romantic and family situations and relationships than their career situations.

Whereas most work on career maturity does not attend to the importance of environmental factors, Vondracek and colleagues are concerned with the effect of social, political, and historical factors on individuals that influence them and their vocational identity. Examples of some of these factors are changes in the economy, local and federal social and educational policy, advances in technology affecting job performance, and job availability. This focus on the broader context of development is referred to as *developmental–contextual theory.*

Vocational identity develops in both an educational context and a broader social context (Vondracek & Skorikov, 2007). Adolescents develop their interests and occupational choices through participation in school and leisure activities. Community service and participation in religious activities is an important aspect of developing vocational identity. Countries such as Germany that have many educational programs that focus on vocational training provide more work-related experience to develop vocational identity than do countries such as the United States that typically focus on academic programs more than on vocational training programs. Vondracek and Skorikov (2007) believe that apprenticeship programs can be an excellent means of increasing vocational identity. In the United States, many adolescents work part time after school; this is less true in many other countries. However, part-time work is often limited to unskilled jobs such as landscaping or food service. Such work does not provide much opportunity to advance one's vocational identity.

There are many broad social factors that affect the vocational choices of adolescents that they are typically not aware of. Globalization of work affects the types of work that are offered in different countries. With the development of technology, new occupations emerge. Changes in the demand for different products and services also affect the jobs that are available to individuals. Being flexible with regard to their vocational identity helps individuals adapt to the social and economic aspect of a world that is in constant change. In this way, the adolescent's vocational identity must interact within the context of a changing society.

General support was found for the developmental contextual model on explaining occupational choice for over 20,000 young adults in England who were studied as young adolescents and again 12 years later (Schoon, Martin, & Ross, 2007). Vondracek (Vondracek, Reitzle, & Silbereisen, 1999; Vondracek & Porfeli, 2003; Vondracek & Skorikov, 2007) stresses the importance of the timing of career choices within their specific contexts, because it can retard or advance vocational identity development. For example, adolescents in East Germany who grew up under a communist regime had fewer career choices available to them than those in West Germany, where there was a strong economy and many more choices. West German youth were slower to develop their vocational identity because they had many more choices; thus, it was more difficult for them to choose than for East German youths (Reitzle, Vondracek, & Silbereisen, 1998; Vondracek & Reitzle, 1998). Comparisons of majority group and minority group high school students in Quebec also show the effect of context on vocational maturity (Perron, Vondracek, Skorikov, Tremblay, & Corbiere, 1998), with advancement in maturity depending on group membership, the participants' ages, and the time of measurement. Schoon and Parsons (2002) studied more than 17,000 individuals born 12 years apart. They report that educational qualifications were more important for the group born later than for the group born earlier. This demand for educational qualifications had an influence on occupational aspirations of teenagers and in predicting occupations they would enter later. Identity develops not in isolation from cultural events, but in the context of the development of society.

A COUNSELING EXAMPLE

The following case illustrates how an identity issue may arise in counseling, creating both personal and career strains for an adolescent. Erikson's and Marcia's conception of status development helps us to understand issues and difficulties that arise from a crisis at a particular point in time.

Frank is a white college sophomore who has not yet declared his major. He is attending a large university in Boston. His father is a lawyer in New York City, and his mother is vice president of a large bank. His two younger sisters are still in high school. Frank has been wondering for some time what he is going to do with his future. He is confused about his career goals and feels that he is wasting time in college because he does not know what to major in or what career to prepare for. Returning from winter vacation, he decides to talk to a counselor about his dilemma. The following dialogue occurs in the first session with the counselor:

CL: My friends seem to know what they are doing—they seem to have goals, ideas. My girlfriend is premed, studies a lot, and knows where she is going.

CO: And you?

CL: I don't know. Sometimes I feel real lost. I wonder if I belong here at school. Sometimes with my courses, I just do the work, but the courses don't seem to matter.

CO: There's no feeling of being there, of being a part of things. [The counselor notices immediately a lack of an overall feeling of identity.]

CL: I think I used to like to do things more than I do now.

CO: What kinds of things, Frank?

CL: Well, when I first got here, I played in the marching band—trumpet. I used to like that, but it didn't seem to matter after a while, so I didn't join the band this year. The excitement of it seemed to wear off fast last year.

CO: Now things are just blah. [Again, Frank's lack of clarity seems apparent. This issue is similar to that of Marcia's diffusion status.]

CL: Yeah, *blah* is a good word for it. I don't know what I'm doing, and whatever it is I'm doing, I can't seem to do it right.

CO: That statement covers a lot of territory. Let me ask you about it. What can't you do right, Frank? [Frank seems to be talking about a lack of feeling of competency, leading the counselor to think that Frank may be advancing to the moratorium status where he can explore a variety of areas.]

CL: I did OK in high school, particularly music. I played in every band or orchestra that we had at school. I really liked the trumpet. I was always first chair and that felt good.

CO: Something happened?

CL: Yes, I auditioned for a national competition between my junior and senior years in high school. I didn't get offered a position. At first I was very disappointed. Then, it was after that like nothing seemed to matter very much. I didn't care much about things after that.

CO: That seems to have been an important event for you. [The counselor hears that this disappointment is a threat to Frank's sense of identity and wonders if this alone could cause the feeling of depression that he seems to be experiencing.]

CL: Well, I guess I didn't care, and no one else seemed to care, either.

CO: Go on.

CL: Well, I think that my father always thought that the music was kid stuff—fluff. You know?

CO: How did he react? [The counselor observes Frank's anger at his father, something that is not unexpected when there is a sense of a lack of identity.]

CL: It was like, "Well, so what else is new?" He has always seemed real caught up in his work. He brings work home from the office. When I was a kid I used to think that all he ever did was work.

CO: And work seemed unpleasant? [Thoughts about identification with his father and views of work occur to the counselor.]

CL: Nothing seemed fun at all. Actually, I guess fun was being at school. That always seemed funny to me because most of my friends couldn't wait to get out of school.

CO: It certainly had an effect on you. [Frank's father's commitment to work seems to be having a negative effect on Frank. He doesn't want that same feeling. Perhaps he sees that work can only be unpleasant.]

CL: It seemed that when I couldn't play the trumpet better than anybody else, I was nobody. In college, the novelty of playing in a college band lasted a while, but it wore off.

CO: Real strong feelings, Frank. [Frank has experimented with exploration but may need encouragement to make good use of a moratorium period.]

Frank and the counselor spend four sessions discussing his problems. Frank is seeking a moratorium. He feels that he needs time to solve his problems. Each semester, school seems to become more futile to him. He is trying to look for meaning in his life, with school and with friends. He does not plan to continue school in the fall, preferring to work so that he can continue his search for meaning in his life. At appropriate points, the counselor will introduce occupational information into the counseling process. When to introduce occupational information and more testing is a future consideration. Occupational information and assessment, as they pertain to Super's theory and vocational identity theory, are the subjects of the following sections.

THE ROLE OF OCCUPATIONAL INFORMATION

As may be apparent from the description of the Career Development Inventory, occupational information is critical to Super's theory. The Career Planning subtest asks students how much thinking and planning they have done about various educational and occupational opportunities. The Career Exploration scale asks students who they have gone to, or would go to, for occupational information. Implicit in the Decision-Making scale is the integration of occupational information with career decision making. The World-of-Work Information and the Knowledge of the Preferred Occupational Group scales are measures of occupational knowledge. Clearly, Super's theory depends on the integration of self-concept and information about the world of work.

A concept described by two of Super's colleagues (Starishevsky & Matlin, 1963) provides another view of the relationship between self-concept and the world of work. Concepts of psychtalk and occtalk emphasize the relationship between occupation and self. *Psychtalk* refers to statements used to describe aptitudes, interests, and other characteristics of one's self. *Occtalk* refers to statements about occupations. Starishevsky and Matlin (1963) believed that occtalk and psychtalk statements can be translated from one to the other. For example, they state (p. 34) that wanting to be a lawyer may translate as being socially minded or being aggressive. A person who says that she will be a physician may also be saying, "I am intelligent, healthy, and concerned about others." Likewise, a person may say, "I am intelligent, healthy, and concerned about others" (psychtalk); "I could be a physician" (occtalk). The notion that discussion about occupations implies beliefs about self, and that beliefs about self can have implications for occupations, can be useful for counselors. The concepts of occtalk and psychtalk provide a convenient bridge in Super's theory between what could appear to be two vastly different concepts.

In the development of vocational identity, individuals gradually incorporate information from their environment into their sense of themselves. In the diffusion status, individuals are likely to learn about their interests and abilities, but they do not incorporate this information into a sense of themselves. In the moratorium status, adolescents experience leisure and work and start to develop a sense of self. In foreclosure, individuals may have information about an occupation, but they have not fully incorporated this information into a sense of themselves. In the achievement status, adolescents make plans based on incorporating information about themselves and the world of work. Vondracek and Skorikov (2007) stress the importance of the changing context of work. Different cultures have different occupational changes. Furthermore, changes in technology, environmental conditions, and demand for new goods and services suggest that it is important for counselors to be aware of occupational changes on a global level.

THE ROLE OF ASSESSMENT INSTRUMENTS

Assessment is an important part of Super's developmental model. Assessing career maturity through the use of the Career Development Inventory has been discussed in detail in this chapter. An Australian version is also available (Hughes & Thomas, 2006). Inventories measuring the importance of work roles, as well as the stages of late adolescent and adult development, are discussed in Chapter 9. These inventories stem directly from Super's life-span theory. In addition to these inventories, Super also advocates the use of inventories and tests that measure interests, capacities or abilities, and values. His Values Scale (Nevill & Super, 1989) and a revised version (Zytowski, 2004) are an example of measures of values.

Super and others (1990; Osborne, Brown, Niles, & Miner, 1997; Niles, 2001; Herr, Cramer, & Niles, 2004) provide a detailed and extensive model for career assessment, called the Career Development Assessment and Counseling (CDAC) model. Typical instruments that they recommend are the Adult Career Concerns, the Values Scale, the Salience Inventory described in Chapter 9, the Strong Interest Inventory, and the Career Development Inventory, which is explained on pages 228–231. Hartung, Vandiver, Leong, Pope, Niles, and Farrow (1998) suggest that a measure of cultural identity should also be used as a part of this assessment. This model can be used for work-bound youth (Herr & Niles, 1997), as well as college-bound youth. Clients are not always ready for or open to an in-depth assessment, and counselors often do not have the time necessary. Sometimes, assessment in counseling can be done in groups; sometimes, it can occur over a period of months or even years. Super has developed a multitude of assessment techniques, and he advocates the use of many others. It is up to the counselor to decide how best to use these tests and inventories.

Assessment of vocational identity has received less attention than vocational maturity. Adams's (Adams, Bennion, & Huh, 1987) Extended Objective Measure of Ego Identity Status can be used to measure statuses of diffusion, moratorium, foreclosure, and achievement, as well as the four items used in the Shell Youth Study (p. 234). Frequently, counselors assess vocational identity by talking with their adolescent clients about the issues that are affecting their lives. Additional information about male and female adolescents and adolescents from diverse cultural backgrounds can influence the use of developmental assessment and theoretical concepts.

GENDER ISSUES IN ADOLESCENCE

Just as gender-role stereotyping has a limiting effect on the selection of occupations by children, it also does for adolescents. This section cites research studies to give some idea of the effect that gender-role stereotyping has on occupational choice and aspirations for occupational success. Rojewski (1997) reported that female adolescents were more likely to aspire to lower or higher levels of occupations compared with males who aspired to mid-level occupations as determined by a measure of prestige. For about a third of the 10th- and 12th-grade girls whom they studied, Davey and Stoppard (1993) report that desired occupations were significantly less traditional than the occupations the girls actually expected to enter. Comparing career aspirations of 95 boys and 132 girls 11 to 14 years of age who were identified as gifted, Mendez and Crawford (2002) state that girls were interested in more careers than boys. Also, girls had interests in traditionally male careers compared with boys, who were not as interested in traditionally female careers. Boys also had aspirations for occupations that were more prestigious and required more education than those to which girls aspired. Lease (2003) examined traditional and nontraditional career choices of 354 male college students. Men with liberal social attitudes were more likely to choose traditionally female occupations compared with men with more conservative social attitudes. Studying older adolescent girls and young women (ages 18 to 25), those who did not maintain their occupational aspirations in male dominated fields most frequently gave the following reasons for their change in aspirations: wanted a more flexible job, the occupation demanded too much time, or they viewed physical science as having a low intrinsic value (Frome, Alfeld, Eccles, & Barber, 2006). Lease also reports that men in gender nontraditional occupations may be influenced by educational aspirations not socioeconomic status (SES). In general, men with higher occupational aspirations and higher SES selected more nontraditional occupations than other men. As these studies show, stereotyping occupations according to gender continues to be an issue for adolescents.

Some studies have used less direct approaches to examine the effect of gender-role stereotyping on adolescents. If high school girls were led to believe that the gender ratios in certain occupations would be balanced in the future, they expressed more interest in traditionally male occupations (Heilman, 1979). However, high school boys expressed less interest when they were told that the gender ratio would be more balanced in the future. These findings suggest that male adolescents prefer the dominant gender ratio and female adolescents are put off by occupations if they felt that other women were not going to be in them. Studying seventh-grade adolescents, Robison-Awana, Kehle, and Jenson (1986) asked their subjects to take a self-esteem inventory, both as themselves and as someone of the opposite gender. Their results show that both boys and girls believed that girls had lower self-esteem. Using Crites's Career Maturity Inventory as a measure of career maturity, Powell and Luzzo (1998) report that male teenagers between the ages of 15 and 19 years believed that they had more control over their career decision making than did women of comparable ages. To educate 8th- and 11th-grade students about choosing non-traditional occupations, Van Buren, Kelly, and Hall (1993) used videotape to model various occupations. They report that the boys' interest in social occupations increased. Van Buren, Kelly, and Hall's (1993) work represents an effort to make career information free of gender bias. For lesbian, gay, and bisexual youth there is evidence that dealing with sexual identity issues can have a negative effect on career maturity, as some youths focus their attention on sexual identity rather than career concerns (Schmidt & Nilsson, 2006).

In reviewing gender differences on the Career Development Inventory, Super (1990) states that girls tend to score slightly higher than boys on measures of career maturity, a finding that is supported by Busacca and Taber (2002), D'Achiardi (2006), Hartung (1997), Patton and Creed (2002), Patton, Creed, and Muller (2002), and Taveira, Silva, Rodriguez, and Maia (1998). However, Flouri and Buchanan (2002) report that boys tended to score higher than girls on career maturity. In a study of Australian adolescents, Patton and Creed (2001) report that at the age of 13 years, boys scored higher than girls on career maturity attitude scales, but girls scored higher than boys at ages 15 and 17 years. Girls scored higher than boys on knowledge scales of career maturity at all age levels. Career maturity inventories continue to be used with adolescents. Studies on gender differences tend to, with exceptions, suggest that girls develop maturity with regard to career choice earlier than boys do.

A COUNSELING EXAMPLE

Lucy is a high school sophomore. Her situation also was discussed in Chapter 7. In Chapter 7, she was 11 years old and talking to a counselor about problems at home that were having an effect on her schoolwork. Now she is 15 years old. Her current counselor does not have the benefit of information from the Career Development Inventory, but is able to use Super's concepts of career development. The following dialogue is from one of Lucy's sessions with her guidance counselor:

CL: I wanted to talk to you because I'm not sure what to do next year. I'm thinking of applying to a bunch of different schools in two years. Maybe I can get a scholarship. I'm not sure.

CO: What have you been thinking about?

CL: Well, I really would like to go to medical school, but I'm not sure I can afford it, and I'm not sure I can get into it.

CO: What makes you hesitant? [The counselor wants to know more about Lucy's uncertainty in questioning her career plans.]

CL: Well, my father would like me to go to work soon. He says to me that he doesn't want to support me forever. And my boyfriend says if I go to med school we'll never get married until we're fifty-five.

CO: It's hard to separate out what you might want from what others want for you. [The counselor wants to relieve Lucy of some of the burdens put on her by others.]

CL: I know. I've given a lot of thought to this. Most people might think it's only a dream, but I've got As and Bs in my courses. I think I might be able to do it. I know you need Bs in science, at least, and As, too, to get into medical school. I know that it takes a lot of training. There are scholarships in college, and it is possible to get money for medical school. I could work for a while to earn money to go to medical school.

CO: You seem to have found out a lot about college. [Lucy certainly seems to have some knowledge of her preferred occupation and some information about the abilities required. Furthermore, she seems to have some world-of-work information.]

CL: Yes, I've talked to my family doctor about medicine, and my cousin works for another doctor. He was really nice and took some time to talk to me. I think it seems fine, but I'm not sure. There are other medical occupations that don't take so long to get into and are easier to get into. Maybe I should just go into nursing like my mother. I know there's a nursing shortage. It would be easier.

CO: You seem to be questioning yourself. [The counselor is impressed again that Lucy has done considerable initial career exploration and has some knowledge of decision making. The counselor is aware that Lucy's self-concept is fragile but growing.]

CL: It seems that I am in this all alone. *(Lucy starts to cry.)* Nobody seems to think I know what I'm doing. Sometimes, I think others want me to do things their way.

CO: You seem scared about doing it your way. [Lucy's lack of self-confidence seems to be quite strong.]

CL: I am scared. Do you think I'm making the right decision?

CO: It's hard to know what the right decision is. I really am impressed that you've talked to so many people and seem to have such good information about your future. It is just hard to do things when there's not a lot of support. [The counselor does not know the "right" decision for Lucy but does want to support her career exploration and information seeking.]

Being knowledgeable about the career maturity concepts of Super and being aware of gender biases in the culture, the counselor is able to understand Lucy's struggle with her career choice. Even though Lucy is asking for limited help in career selection (not being sure about the right area of health science), counseling serves a valuable purpose. Lucy's decision making is being supported in part by the knowledge the counselor has of the important components of career maturity. The goal of counseling in this particular portion of the interview is to help Lucy increase her confidence in her career planning, career exploration, decision making, and learning about the world of work. This goal certainly is consistent with Super's theoretical propositions regarding career maturity.

CAREER DEVELOPMENT OF ADOLESCENTS FROM DIVERSE CULTURAL BACKGROUNDS

One area of research with adolescents of diverse cultural backgrounds has been the study of the applicability of the concept of career maturity. In a study of African American high school students, Brown (1997) reports that African American female students scored higher on career maturity indices than male students. Asian American students scored lower in career maturity and indicated a stronger preference for a dependent style of decision making than did white students (Leong, 1991). Discussing the career maturity of Asian Americans, Leong and Serifica (1995) question the applicability of Super's concept to Asian Americans, pointing out the effect of differing cultural values on developmental tasks. In one study in India, Mathur and Sharma (2001) found that male 12th-grade students had more favorable attitudes about their career possibilities and more knowledge about career development than did female 12th-grade students. In the United States, Mexican American ninth-grade students scored lower on the Decision-Making and World-of-Work Information scales of the Career Development Inventory than Anglo American ninth-grade students; both are scales that focus on knowledge and skill rather than attitude (Lundberg, Osborne, & Miner, 1997). Because of variations in their findings, these studies suggest the need for more research on the use of Super's concept of career maturity with adolescents of diverse cultural backgrounds.

Another focus of research has been the vocational aspirations of adolescents from different cultural backgrounds (Rojewski, 2005). Most studies have focused on aspirations of adolescents in the United States. However, Tlhabano & Schweitzer (2007) interviewed adolescent Sudanese and Somali refugees about their career aspirations. Despite the disruption in their schooling and difficulties in resettlement, the young people expressed high aspirations. Aspirations depended somewhat on their education and social skills in their country of origin. Difficulties with the English language were their greatest concern about their ambitions. In the remainder of this section, I will discuss the aspirations of Mexican American and African American students.

Arbona (1990) has pointed out that Hispanic/Latino, including Mexican Americans, and African American students often have aspirations that are more prestigious or desirable than the occupations that they actually enter. It may be that this gap results from expectations that do not match the availability of jobs, especially gender-stereotyped jobs (Arbona & Novy, 1991). Caldera, Robitschek, Frame, and Pannell (2003) studied two groups of Mexican American college women. They highlight the importance of attending to parent's education, because Mexican American women may be first-generation college students. They suggest that counselors pay attention to whether Mexican American women look to their mothers as occupational role models, or if they want to surpass their mother's career attainments. Related to this is consideration of support that Mexican American college women are likely to receive from their families. In her study of white and Mexican American 11th- and 12th-grade students, McWhirter (1997) reports that Mexican American students anticipated that there would be more barriers to attaining future goals than did white students. Developing a model for understanding the career choices of Mexican American girls of high school age, McWhirter, Hackett, and Bandalos (1998) found that culture had a greater influence on career choice than gender. They report that families' lack of support for pursuing prestigious occupations occurred more frequently in families that held traditional Mexican American values. Rivera and Gallimore (2006) emphasize the importance of having useful resources to help Latina adolescents work towards their career goals.

Aspirations and expectations of African American high school youths have also been explored. The top three occupational preferences for African American male youths were professional careers, professional sports, and business management; for African American female youths, there was a greater preference for social careers such as teaching and social work (Brown, 1997). Studying the career aspirations of

11th- and 12th-grade African American inner-city male students, Parmer (1993) reports that 32% thought they were likely or very likely to become professional athletes in 10 years. The chances of becoming a professional athlete are about 1 in 50,000 (Parmer, 1993). In a study of poor, urban, African-American adolescent mothers, Hellenga, Aber, and Rhodes (2002) report that those adolescent mothers who lived with their biological parents, had high grades, and had a career mentor were more likely to have occupational aspirations that matched expectations for what they would attain than African American adolescent mothers who did not meet these conditions. These studies provide detailed information for counselors to consider when discussing vocational aspirations with African American or Mexican American adolescents from diverse cultural backgrounds.

CASE EXAMPLE

Chad is a 15-year-old student whose parents left Vietnam about 15 years after the Vietnam War. Chad lives near Los Angeles with his parents, two younger brothers, and an older sister. His mother is currently unemployed, and his father is a rental car clerk. Chad has been sent to talk to the counselor because he has been absent from school sporadically throughout the year and recently has missed a week of school. As Chad enters the office, the counselor sees an attractive, average-size young man wearing jeans, a black T-shirt, and expensive sneakers. The counselor, to use the terms of Vondracek and colleagues, is well aware of the context of the situation. The counselor has walked by Chad's home several times, and many of the neighborhood children attend the school where she works. The major sources of income for adolescents on Chad's street are working in fast-food restaurants, working in grocery stores, and selling illegal drugs. The counselor resists making hypotheses based only on Chad's appearance and wants to listen to him. The following dialogue occurs between Chad and the counselor:

CL: *(Smiling)* Sorry I haven't been in school as much as I should. I've been sick a lot.

CO: What's happening with you, Chad? [The counselor does not want to get into an argument with Chad, but she also does not want to show that she will take his story at face value.]

CL: Times are tough.

CO: Yes, can you tell me what's been happening?

CL: I've needed to make some extra money. My parents just don't have enough money for the kids.

CO: It's been hard for you. [The counselor doesn't want to challenge Chad immediately. Rather, she prefers to take his side.]

CL: Yes, my little brother broke his leg and my father doesn't make much money anyway. I've had to pick some up on the side.

CO: Selling drugs? [The counselor decides to get to the point. She believes that Chad knows that she can guess this anyway.]

CL: Yes. *(Defensively)* Not too much—just enough.

CO: What are you going to do? [The counselor asks a very broad, open question about Chad's future to see in what direction he will take it.]

CL: I don't know. Maybe get a job. I'm not sure.

CO: Some thoughts about what you'd like to do? [The counselor wants to know how developed Chad's interests are.]

CL: I like cars—fixing them, riding in them, racing them, anything to do with them. And I like TV and movies.

CO: Have you thought about doing more with working on cars? [The counselor picks the activity that has the most vocational relevance and asks about it.]

CL: I've thought about the voc-tech school, but I don't know. I don't think that mechanics make enough money.

CO: Do you know how much they make? [Not having access to the Career Development Inventory or other maturity inventories, the counselor asks about Super's concept of World-of-Work Information.]

CL: No.

CO: Let's find out.

As the counselor goes with Chad to look at information about auto mechanics, she has several questions running through her mind. Will she be able to help Chad in his career planning and exploration? How much has he done so far? How accurate is his knowledge about the world of work? His role as worker has barely begun. Although she has not stated it at this point, the counselor believes that she is working with a potential life-or-death issue. If Chad continues to sell drugs, there is a chance that he may be killed or may kill someone. To Chad, being an auto mechanic may not be as attractive as selling drugs because of the excitement and the income. The counselor does not want to argue directly with Chad, feeling that she will lose. She is trying to find a way for Chad to look into his future, so that his life will give him a sense of pride and accomplishment. Chad currently is not making decisions that are giving him much satisfaction. The counselor hopes that she will be able to develop a relationship with Chad so that he will return, and so that she will gradually be able to make an impact. Chad's self-awareness and occupational awareness are limited. The counselor can look to the future, and she is scared for Chad. Super's theory of life-span development for adolescents is not a panacea. It does provide guidelines for what to look for in career decision making. Sometimes, the context of a situation is so overwhelming that a theoretical conceptualization makes little difference. It is possible in the case of Chad that the application of Super's concepts of career decision making will be just enough to keep him looking into a legitimate form of work. If the counselor is able to help Chad develop his interests in auto mechanics, find an auto mechanics program that he likes, and support his efforts, there may be a chance of his success. Or, possibly, Chad and the counselor will arrive at some entirely different vocational goal. If Chad believes that the counselor is just some other adult who has a good income and for whom life is wonderful, then the counselor is likely to be discounted.

COUNSELOR ISSUES

A number of issues make counseling adolescents difficult. Earlier in this chapter, the notion (Piaget, 1977) that formal thinking brings with it a certain amount of egocentrism suggests that the client may think that he or she is right and the counselor is wrong. Furthermore, Erikson's point that adolescents may be in an uncomfortable search for identity suggests that they need to separate themselves from adults and may be less likely to listen to them. In contrast, the counselor may have a strong sense of vocational identity. Because the counselor has decided on a career, and has information about that occupation and other occupations as well, the counselor's life situation is in marked contrast to that of the adolescent. These factors make it important for the counselor to be empathic toward the client's decision-making issues. One of the frustrations of a counselor is that he or she can look ahead in terms of a client's occupational direction. Often, adolescents still have a limited time perspective and find it difficult to envision their lives in 5 or 10 years. Super's life-stage theory makes it possible to see how vastly different the goals of the counselor can be from those of the client. This knowledge enables the counselor to structure limited goals that are consistent with the student's vocational maturity. Vondracek's theory of vocational identity also provides a view that contrasts the client, who could be in a status of diffusion, foreclosure, or moratorium, with the counselor, who is in the achievement status.

SUMMARY

Super and colleagues offer concepts and inventories that can assist the counselor in working with adolescents. Being able to assess the development of interests, capacities, and values in a teenage client is quite helpful. Also helpful to the counselor are Super's concepts of career planning, career exploration, decision making, world-of-work information, and knowledge of the preferred occupational group.

Vocational identity and the context in which it emerges is yet another useful view of adolescent career development. Attending to career development in terms of the statuses of diffusion, foreclosure, moratorium, and achievement within Vondracek's developmental-contextual theory can be useful to counselors. These concepts, used in combination, help the counselor assess the student's career orientation. Gender-role stereotyping and the obstacles confronting adolescents of culturally diverse backgrounds present additional problems. Knowledge of the context of the situation serves as a useful adjunct to Super's theory because it deals with conditions external to the individual. Because adolescence is such a critical time in the career decision-making process, applying both Super's and Vondracek's theories can be helpful.

REFERENCES

Adams, G. R., Bennion, L., & Huh, K. (1987). *Objective measure of ego identity status: A reference manual* (Unpublished manuscript). Salt Lake City, UT: Laboratory for Research on Adolescence, Utah State University.

Arbona, C. (1990). Career counseling research with Hispanics: A review of the literature. *The Counseling Psychologist, 18,* 300–323.

Arbona, C., & Novy, D. M. (1991). Career aspirations and expectations among Black, Mexican American, and White college students. *Career Development Quarterly, 39,* 231–239.

Aubrey, R. G. (1977). *Career development needs of thirteen-year-olds: How to improve career development programs.* Washington, DC: National Advisory Council for Career Education.

Brown, C. (1997). Sex differences in the career development of urban African American adolescents. *Journal of Career Development, 23,* 295–304.

Busacca, L. A., & Taber, B. J. (2002). The Career Maturity Inventory—Revised: A preliminary psychometric investigation. *Journal of Career Assessment, 10,* 441–453.

Caldera, Y. M., Robitschek, C., Frame, M., & Pannell, M. (2003). Interpersonal, familial, and cultural factors in the commitment to a career choice of Mexican American and non-Hispanic White college women. *Journal of Counseling Psychology, 50,* 309–323.

Cardoza, D. (1991). College attendance and persistence among Hispanic women: An examination of some contributing factors. *Sex Roles, 24,* 133–147.

D'Achiardi, C. (2006). A new approach to measuring adolescents' career maturity: Evaluating a career exploration intervention. *Dissertation Abstracts International: Section B: The Sciences and Engineering, 66 (11-B),* 6311.

Davey, F. H., & Stoppard, J. M. (1993). Some factors affecting the occupational expectations of female adolescents. *Journal of Vocational Behavior, 43,* 235–330.

Erikson, E. H. (1963). *Childhood and society* (2nd ed.). New York: Norton.

Erikson, E. H. (1968). *Identity: Youth and crisis.* New York: Norton.

Erikson, E. H. (1982). *The life cycle completed.* New York: Norton.

Flouri, E., & Buchanan, A. (2002). The role of work-related skills and career role models in adolescent career maturity. *The Career Development Quarterly, 51,* 36–43.

Frome, P. M., Alfeld, C. J., Eccles, J. S., & Barber, B. L. (2006). Why don't they want a male-dominated job? An investigation of young women who changed their occupational aspirations. *Educational Research and Evaluation, 12*(4), 359–372.

Gushue, G. V., Clarke, C. P., Pantzer, K. M., & Scanlan, K. R. L. (2006). Self-efficacy, perceptions of barriers, vocational identity, and the career exploration behavior of Latino/a high school students. *The Career Development Quarterly, 54*(4), 307–317.

Hartung, P. J., Vandiver, B. J., Leong, F. T., Pope, M., Niles, S. G., & Farrow, B. (1998). Appraising cultural identity in career-development assessment and counseling. *Career Development Quarterly, 46,* 276–293.

Heilman, M. E. (1979). Perception of male models of femininity related to career choice. *Journal of Counseling Psychology, 19,* 308–313.

Hellenga, K., Aber, M. S., & Rhodes, J. G. (2002). African American adolescent mother's vocational aspiration-expectation gap: Individual, social and environmental influence. *Psychology of Women Quarterly, 26,* 200–212.

Herr, E. L., Cramer, S. H., & Niles, S. G., (2004). *Career guidance and counseling through the life span* (6th ed.). Boston: Allyn & Bacon.

Herr, E. L., & Niles, S. (1997). Perspectives on career assessment of work-bound youth. *Journal of Career Assessment, 5,* 137–150.

Hughes, C., & Thomas, T. (2006). Adapting the Career Development Inventory-Australia for cross-cultural research. *Journal of Vocational Behavior, 69*(2), 276–288.

Inhelder, B., & Piaget, J. (1958). *The growth of logical thinking from childhood to adolescence.* New York: Basic Books.

Johnson, P., Buboltz, W. C., & Nichols, C. N. (1999). Parental divorce, family functioning, and vocational identity of college students. *Journal of Career Development, 26,* 137–146.

Jugendwerk der Deutschen Shell. (1992). Jugend 1992. Band 4. Methodenberichte-Tabellen-Fragebogen (Youth 1992, Vol. 4: Methods, Tables, Questionnaires). Opladen: Leske & Budrich.

Kapes, J. T., & Strickler, R. T. (1975). A longitudinal study of change in work values between ninth and twelfth grade as related to high school curriculums. *Journal of Vocational Behavior, 6,* 81–93.

Kroger, J. (2007). *Identity development: Adolescence through adulthood* (2nd ed.). Thousand Oaks, CA: Sage.

Lease, S. H. (2003). Testing a model of men's nontraditional occupational choices. *Career Development Quarterly, 51,* 244–258.

Leong, F. T. (1991). Career development attributes and occupational values of Asian American and White American college students. *Career Development Quarterly, 39,* 221–230.

Leong, F. T., & Serifica, F. C. (1995). Career development of Asian Americans: A research area in need of a good theory. In F. T. Leong (Ed.), *Career development and vocational behavior of racial and ethnic minorities* (pp. 67–102). Mahwah, NJ: Erlbaum.

Lewis, H. L. (2003). Differences in ego identity among college students across age, ethnicity, and gender. *Identity, 3,* 159–189.

Lundberg, D. J., Osborne, W. L., & Miner, C. U. (1997). Career maturity and personality preferences of Mexican-American and Anglo-American adolescents. *Journal of Career Development, 23,* 203–213.

Marcia, J. E. (1989). Identity and intervention. *Journal of Adolescence, 12,* 401–410.

Marcia, J. E. (1998). Peer Gynt's life cycle. In E. E. Skoe & A. L. von der Lippe (Eds.), *Personality development in adolescence: A cross national and life span perspective: Adolescence and society* (pp. 193–209). New York: Routledge.

Marcia, J. E. (1999). Representational thought in ego identity, psychotherapy, and psychosocial developmental theory. In I. E. Sigel (Ed.), *Development of mental representation: Theories and applications* (pp. 391–414). Mahwah, NJ: Erlbaum.

Marcia, J. E. (2003). Treading fearlessly: A commentary on personal persistence, identity development, and suicide. *Monograph of the Society for Research in Child Development, 68,* 131–138.

Marcia J. E., Waterman, A. S., Matteson, D. R., Archer, S. L., & Orlofsky, J. (1993). *Ego identity: A handbook for psychosocial research.* New York: Springer-Verlag.

Mathur, G., & Sharma, P. (2001). A study of career maturity among adolescents. *Psycho-Lingua, 31,* 85–88.

McWhirter, E. H. (1997). Perceived barriers to education and career: Ethnic and gender differences. *Journal of Vocational Behavior, 50,* 124–140.

McWhirter, E. H., Hackett, G., & Bandalos, D. L. (1998). A causal model of the educational plans and career expectations of Mexican-American high school girls. *Journal of Counseling Psychology, 45,* 166–181.

Mendez, L. M., & Crawford, K. M. (2002). Gender-role stereotyping and career aspirations: A comparison of gifted early adolescent boys and girls. *Journal of Secondary Gifted Education, 13,* 96–107.

Miller, J. (1977). *Career development needs of 9-year-olds: How to improve career development programs.* Washington, DC: National Advisory Council for Career Education.

Munley, P. H. (1975). Erik Erikson's theory of psychosocial development and vocational behavior. *Journal of Counseling Psychology, 22,* 314–319.

Munley, P. H. (1977). Erikson's theory of psychosocial development and career development. *Journal of Vocational Behavior, 10,* 261–269.

Nauta, M. M., & Kahn, J. H. (2007). Identity status, consistency and differentiation of interests, and career decision self-efficacy. *Journal of Career Assessment, 15*(1), 55–65.

Nevill, D. D., & Super, D. E. (1989). *The Values Scale: Theory, application, and research* (2nd ed.). Palo Alto, CA: Consulting Psychologists Press.

Niles, S. G. (2001). Using Super's Career Development Assessment and Counseling (C-DAC) Model to link theory to practice. *International Journal for Educational Vocational Guidance, 1,* 131–139.

O'Hara, R. P., & Tiedeman, D. V. (1959). Vocational self-concept in adolescence. *Journal of Counseling Psychology, 6,* 292–301.

Osborne, W. L., Brown, S., Niles, S., & Miner, C. U. (1997). *Career development, assessment, and counseling: Applications of the Donald E. Super C-DAC approach.* Alexandria, VA: American Counseling Association.

Parmer, T. (1993). The athletic dream—but what are the career dreams of other African American urban high school students? *Journal of Career Development, 20,* 131–145.

Patton, W., & Creed, P. A. (2001). Developmental issues in career maturity and career decision status. *The Career Development Quarterly, 49,* 336–351.

Patton, W., & Creed, P. A. (2002). The relationship between career maturity and work commitment in a sample of Australian high school students. *Journal of Career Development, 29,* 69–85.

Patton, W., Creed, P. A., & Muller, J. (2002). Career maturity and well-being as determinants of occupational status of recent school leavers: A brief report of an Australian study. *Journal of Adolescent Research, 17,* 425–435.

Patton, W., & Lokan, J. (2001). Perspectives on Donald Super's construct of career maturity. *International Journal for Educational and Vocational Guidance, 1,* 31–48.

Perron, J., Vondracek, F. W., Skorikov, V. B., Tremblay, C., & Corbiere, M. (1998). A longitudinal study of vocational maturity and ethnic identity development. *Journal of Vocational Behavior, 52,* 409–424.

Piaget, J. (1977). *The development of thought: Equilibration of cognitive structure.* New York: Viking Press.

Porfeli, E. J. (2007). Work values system development during adolescence. *Journal of Vocational Behavior, 70*(1), 42–60.

Powell, D. F., & Luzzo, D. A. (1998). Evaluating factors associated with the career maturity of high school students. *Career Development Quarterly, 47,* 145–158.

Powers, R. L., & Griffith, J. (1993). The case of Rosie: Adlerian response. *The Career Development Quarterly, 42,* 69–75.

Reitzle, M. (2007). The effects of work- and family-related transitions on young people's perception of being adult. *Journal of Vocational Behavior, 70*(1), 25–41.

Reitzle, M., Vondracek, F. W., & Silbereisen, R. K. (1998). Timing of school-to-work transitions: A developmental-contextual perspective. *International Journal of Behavioral Development, 22,* 7–28.

Rivera, W. & Gallimore, R. (2006). Latina adolescents' career goals: Resources for overcoming obstacles. In J. Denner, & B. L. Guzman (Eds.) *Latina girls: Voices of adolescent strength in the United States* (pp. 109–122). New York: New York University Press.

Robison-Awana, P., Kehle, T. J., & Jenson, W. R. (1986). But what about smart girls? Adolescent self-esteem and sex role perceptions as a function of academic achievement. *Journal of Educational Psychology, 78,* 179–183.

Robitschek, C., & Cook, S. W. (1999). The influence of personal growth initiative and coping styles on career exploration and vocational identity. *Journal of Vocational Behavior, 54,* 127–141.

Rojewski, J. W. (1997). Characteristics of students who express stable or underrated occupational expectations during early adolescence. *Journal of Career Assessment, 5,* 1–20.

Rojewski, J. W. (2005). Occupational aspirations: Constructs, meanings, and application. In S. D. Brown & R. W. Lent (Eds.) *Career development and counseling: Putting theory and research to* work (pp. 131–154). Hoboken, NJ: John Wiley.

Savickas, M. L. (1985). Identity in vocational development. *Journal of Vocational Behavior, 27,* 329–337.

Schmidt, C. K., & Nilsson, J. E. (2006). The effects of simultaneous developmental processes: Factors relating to the career development of lesbian, gay, and bisexual youth. *The Career Development Quarterly, 55*(1), 22–37.

Schmitt-Rodermund, E., & Vondracek, F. W. (1999). Breadth of interests, exploration, and identity development in adolescence. *Journal of Vocational Behavior, 55,* 298–317.

Schoon, I., Martin, P., & Ross, A. (2007). Career transitions in times of social change. His and her story. *Journal of Vocational Behavior, 70*(1), 78–96.

Schoon, I., & Parsons, S. (2002). Teenage aspirations for future careers and occupational outcomes. *Journal of Vocational Behavior, 60,* 262–288.

Skorikov, V., & Vondracek, F. W. (1998). Vocational identity development: Its relationship to other identity domains and to overall identity development. *Journal of Career Assessment, 6,* 13–15.

Starishevsky, R., & Matlin, N. A. (1963). A model for the translation of self-concept into vocational terms. In D. E. Super, R. Starishevsky, N. Matlin, & J. P. Jordaan (Eds.), *Career development: Self-concept theory* (pp. 33–41; Research Monograph No. 4). New York: College Entrance Examination Board.

Super, D. E. (1955). Personality integration through vocational counseling. *Journal of Counseling Psychology, 2,* 217–226.

Super, D. E. (1990). A life-span, life-space approach to career development. In D. Brown, L. Brooks, & Associates (Eds.), *Career choice and development: Applying contemporary theories to practice* (2nd ed., pp. 197–261). San Francisco: Jossey-Bass.

Super, D. E., Bohn, M. J., Forrest, D. J., Jordaan, J. P., Lindeman, R. H., & Thompson, A. S. (1971). *Career Development Inventory.* New York: Teachers College Press, Columbia University.

Super, D. E., Crites, J. O., Hummel, R. C., Moser, H. P., Overstreet, P. L., & Warnath, C. F. (1957). *Vocational development: A framework for research.* New York: Teachers College Press, Columbia University.

Super, D. E., & Overstreet, P. L. (1960). *The vocational maturity of ninth-grade boys.* New York: Teachers College Press, Columbia University.

Super, D. E., Thompson, A. S., & Lindeman, R. H. (1988). *Adult Career Concerns Inventory.* Palo Alto, CA: Consulting Psychologists Press.

Taveira, M.-D.-C., Silva, M. C., Rodriguez, M.-L., & Maia, J. (1998). Individual characteristics and career exploration in adolescence. *British Journal of Guidance and Counselling, 26,* 89–104.

Thompson, A. S., & Lindeman, R. H. (1981). *Career Development Inventory: User's manual* (Vol. 1). Palo Alto, CA: Consulting Psychologists Press.

Tierney, R. J., & Herman, A. (1973). Self-estimates of ability in adolescence. *Journal of Counseling Psychology, 20,* 298–302.

Tlhabano, K. N., & Schweitzer, R. (2007). A qualitative study of the career aspirations of resettled young Sudanese and Somali refugees. *Journal of Psychology in Africa. Special Issue: Community psychology, 17*(1-2), 13–22.

Tracey, T. J. G., Robbins, S. B., & Hofsess, C. D. (2005). Stability and change in interests: A longitudinal study of adolescents from grades 8 through 12. *Journal of Vocational Behavior, 66*(1), 1–25.

Van Buren, J. B., Kelly, K. R., & Hall, A. S. (1993). Modeling nontraditional career choices: Effects of gender and school location on response to a brief videotape. *Journal of Counseling Psychology, 20,* 298–302.

Vondracek, F. W. (2003). Career development from childhood to young adulthood: Industry to identity. Paper presented at the Tenth Annual Society for Research on Identity Formation Meeting, May 15–18, 2003, Vancouver, British Columbia, Canada.

Vondracek, F. W., & Porfeli, E. J. (2003). The world of work and careers. In G. R. Adams & M. D. Berzonsky (Eds.), *Blackwell handbook of adolescence* (pp. 100–108). New York: Blackwell.

Vondracek, F. W., & Reitzle, M. (1998). The viability of career maturity theory: A developmental-contextual perspective. *Career Development Quarterly, 47,* 6–15.

Vondracek, F. W., & Skorikov, V. B. (1997). Leisure, school, and work activity preferences and their role in vocational identity development. *Career Development Quarterly, 45,* 322–340.

Vondracek, F. W., & Skorikov, V. B. (2007). Vocational identity. In V. B. Skorikov & W. Patton (Eds.) *Career development in childhood and adolescence* (pp. 143–168). Rotterdam: Sense Publishers.

Vondracek, F. W., Reitzle, M., & Silbereisen, R. K. (1999). The influence of changing contexts and historical time on the timing of initial vocational choices. In R. K. Silbereisen & A. von Eye (Eds.), *Growing up in times of social change* (pp. 151–169). New York: de Gruyter.

Westbrook, B. W., Buck, R. W., Jr., Wynne, D. C., & Sanford, E. E. (1994). Career maturity in adolescence: Reliability and validity of self-ratings of ability by gender and ethnicity. *Journal of Career Assessment, 2,* 125–161.

Zuschlag, M. K., & Whitbourne, S. K. (1994). Psychosocial development in three generations of college students. *Journal of Youth and Adolescence, 23,* 567–577.

Zytowski, D. G. (2004). Super's Work Values Inventory-Revised user manual. Adel, IA: National Career Assessment Services.

9 | LATE ADOLESCENT AND ADULT CAREER DEVELOPMENT

CHAPTER HIGHLIGHTS

Role Salience

Adult Life Stages

Life Stages of Women

Life Stages of Culturally Diverse Adults

Counselor Issues

Super's life-span theory of late adolescent and adult career development makes use of two major concepts: life role and life stage. For Super, important roles for an individual are studying, working, community service, home and family, and leisure activities. The importance, or salience, of these roles can be seen by a person's participation in an activity, commitment to the activity, or how much that activity is valued. Values are also significant in Super's theory, as can be seen by the development of several values inventories (Super, 1970; Super & Nevill, 1986, 1989; Zytowski, 2004).

In Super's theory, roles form the context within which to view the basic stages of career development: exploration, establishment, maintenance, and disengagement. The exploration stage includes the substages of crystallization, specification, and implementation. Next follows the establishment stage, which includes the tasks of stabilizing, consolidating, and advancing. The substages of holding, updating, and innovating make up the maintenance stage. Finally, the disengagement stage includes deceleration, retirement planning, and retirement living. A key aspect of Super's theory is that these stages are not entirely related to age. Individuals may recycle, or go through these stages, at many different times in life. This chapter provides explanations and examples of counseling conceptualizations that can be useful in these stages. Theorists and researchers have questioned whether these stages apply to women and to people from different cultures. Research on women suggests several factors to be considered. Atkinson, Morten, and Sue (1998) offer a series of developmental stages that people from diverse cultures may experience. This provides another dimension to Super's view of the life span. Exploration of the developmental issues that arise for the counselor in dealing with people in various life stages will help to explain some of the issues that counselors face in counseling adults.

ROLE SALIENCE

Super (1990) believed that people differ in terms of the importance they assign to work in their lives. Work can vary in importance to an individual at different points in that person's life. In fact, Nevill and Super (1986) provide normative data for the Salience Inventory that show that people at different ages and across different cultures value work differentially. For example, high school students in the United States tend to value work, home, and leisure more than study and community service. In general, this is also true for college students. However, adults in the United States tend to value work and family life more than study, community service, or leisure. Not surprisingly, there are great individual differences across all age ranges. A constant concept throughout Super's career development theory is the concept of role (Hartung, 2002). Super describes six major roles: homemaker, worker, citizen, leisurite, student, and child. His Salience Inventory (Nevill & Super, 1986) measures the importance of all the roles, except that of child. In childhood, the roles of leisurite, student, and child are particularly important, whereas the roles of worker, citizen, and homemaker (in the sense of responsibility for these roles) are minimal. In adolescence, citizen and worker may become more important roles, but they are generally limited. In adolescence, work is not often directly related to one's eventual career. It is in adulthood that one has more choice in life roles.

Super's rainbow (Figure 9.1) shows how the roles may vary within the lifetime of an individual. In this figure, each arc represents a role in life. The thicker the shaded area in each arc, the more important the role is. As Super and Nevill (1986) explain, "The person portrayed in this rainbow finished college at the age of 22, went at once to work, married at age 26, became a parent at age 27, intermittently attended school part time until returning full time at age 47, suffered the loss of parents at age 57, retired at 67, was widowed at 78, and died at age 81" (p. 3). In conjunction with developmental stages, the concept of life roles may be useful in many career counseling situations.

In the Salience Inventory, Nevill and Super (1986) measure three aspects of life roles: commitment, participation, and values expectations. Another important aspect of work salience, but one not measured by the Salience Inventory, is knowledge of roles. The following sections describe first the life roles measured by the

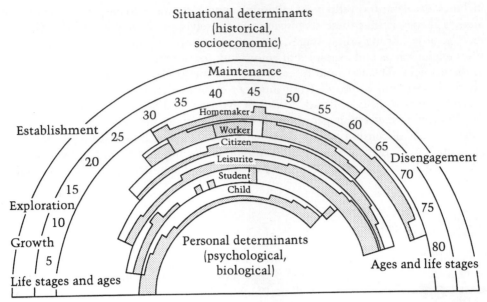

FIGURE 9.1 | THE LIFE—CAREER RAINBOW: SIX LIFE ROLES IN SCHEMATIC
LIFE SPACE.

Source: Adapted from *Career choice and development*, by D. Brown, L. Brooks, and Associates.
Copyright © 1984 by Jossey-Bass, Inc. Reprinted by permission.

Salience Inventory (studying, working, community service, home and family, and
leisure activities) and then different indicators of the salience of these life roles.

LIFE ROLES

STUDYING   Studying includes a number of activities that may take place throughout the life span. During the school years, these activities include taking courses,
going to school, and studying in a library or at home. People may choose to continue education at any point during their lifetime. Newspapers show pictures of
80-year-old men and women receiving their high school diplomas or college degrees. Many people continue their education on a part-time basis at some stage
during their lives for pleasure or to enhance their job advancement or success.

WORKING   Working may start in childhood, when children help their parents
around the home, mow the lawn, or take jobs such as babysitting and delivering
newspapers. It is common for adolescents to take a part-time job after school, during the summer, or both. Many adults work at one or more jobs at various times
during their lives. During retirement, jobs for pay or profit may be for fewer hours
than they were during a person's younger years.

COMMUNITY SERVICE   Community service includes a broad range of voluntary service groups that may be social, political, or religious. Young people often participate

in Boy or Girl Scouts, Indian Guides, or boys' or girls' clubs, which have as a part of their purpose either direct service to others or indirect service through the collection of money or goods. These groups, together with service fraternities and sororities, are available to adolescents in various forms. Activities may include literacy projects, environmental cleanup, or assistance in hospitals. Activity in these service groups, together with participation in political parties and trade unions, is available to adults throughout the entire life span.

HOME AND FAMILY   The role of home and family can vary greatly depending on the age of the individual. A child may help out at home by taking care of his or her room, doing the dishes, or mowing the lawn. Adolescents may take on more responsibility by doing more complex tasks and ones with more responsibility, such as babysitting. For adults, responsibility for children and a home becomes much more important than it was in earlier years. Adults may have to take care not only of their own children but also of their aging parents. As adults enter their later years, their responsibility for home and family may increase or markedly decrease. For example, grandparents may live with their children and/or grandchildren, live in adult communities, or live alone.

LEISURE ACTIVITIES   The nature and importance of leisure are likely to vary considerably throughout one's lifetime. Leisure is a particularly important and valued activity of children and adolescents. Often, this includes active participation in sports, as well as more sedentary activities such as watching television and reading. The term *lifetime sports* refers to sports that are less physically demanding and require fewer participants; therefore, they are easier for adults to participate in at various points in their lifetime. Contrast football and basketball with golf, tennis, and bowling. For adults, leisure activities may become more sophisticated and intellectual, such as attending the theater and museums or joining groups that discuss books, stocks and bonds, or religious issues.

Liptak (2000) considers leisure so important that he has outlined a leisure theory of career development. Often, leisure serves as a substitute for work and as a way of trying out new activities. Liptak's theory is based partly on the importance of play throughout the life span. His theory shows the significance of leisure in a variety of life stages. In early childhood, parents are an important influence in the development of play and curiosity. At ages 6 to 12 years, school and after-school activities provide an opportunity to develop cognitive and motor skills through play or leisure activity. In adolescence, team and individual activities such as sports, clubs, and hobbies help individuals refine their interests and abilities. Between the ages of 19 and 25 years, individuals can develop leisure opportunities that may be related to work or educational pursuits. In adulthood, leisure may focus on work- or family-related activities. In retirement, leisure often becomes much more important than work as an outlet for interests and skills. From Liptak's perspective, leisure can play a more important role in career development than work, especially in the beginning and end of the life span. Another view of leisure describes the benefits of two types: active/challenging and passive or recuperative leisure (Trenberth & Dewe, 2002) Research also demonstrates the role of leisure in reducing stress at work and shows that different types of stress could be reduced by different leisure activities (Trenberth & Dewe, 2005).

INDICATORS OF THE SALIENCE OF LIFE ROLES

Not only does the importance of life roles change during a person's lifetime, but the nature of the involvement also changes. This involvement can be measured in terms of participation, commitment, knowledge, and values expectations.

PARTICIPATION   Participation in a role can take a number of different forms. It can include spending time on something, improving a performance, accomplishing something, being active in an organization concerned with an activity, or just being active. A slightly less direct way of participating is through talking to people or reading about an activity. The concept of participation is particularly useful because it measures the actual behavior of an individual, not just what he or she says is important. For example, a person may say that he is committed to his religion but may in reality never pray or go to church (participate).

COMMITMENT   Commitment often concerns future plans. It may deal with a desire to be involved or to be active. It also concerns the present—that is, feeling proud of doing well or being personally committed. A less direct way of being committed is to admire people who are good at something.

KNOWLEDGE   Acquiring information about a role by experiencing the role either directly or observing it brings about knowledge, a cognitive aspect of role importance. A child's knowledge may be limited to leisure and study. Knowledge of parental roles is gained by observation; only much later will the experience be direct. Knowledge of the worker role may be very different for a food service worker in high school compared with that same individual employed as an engineer or physician 15 years later. The Salience Inventory does not measure knowledge. A measurement of knowledge is available only for the worker role in the Career Development Inventory and in the Decision Making, World-of-Work Information, and Knowledge of the Preferred Occupational Group subscales (see Chapter 8). However, when talking with clients about their study, leisure, or community service roles, the counselor may find assessing the client's knowledge to be helpful. For example, new college students often have little knowledge of the changing studying role that they will soon encounter. However, they are likely to be committed to the role and will soon participate in it. Knowledge, commitment, and participation, together with values expectations, are components of role salience.

VALUES EXPECTATIONS   Similar theoretically to the concept of commitment, values expectations concern the opportunity for various roles to meet a variety of value needs. Many values are related to career issues. Values are measured by two of Super's instruments: the Values Scale (Super & Nevill, 1989; Zytowski, 2004) and the Salience Inventory (Nevill & Super, 1986). The Values Scale lists 21 different values; 14 of these are used in the Value Expectation Scale of the Salience Inventory. These 14 values expectations are described below in terms of how they can be met in the five life roles. Zytowski (2004) has made some changes in the Values Scale and in the names of the scales. However, since his revision is new and available only through National Assessment Services, I will use Super's original scales. Reading through this list of values, the counselor can determine the relevance of the values for his or her clients, and thus decide which of the many values to focus on when conceptualizing client issues. The 14 values expectations are as follows:

- *Ability utilization:* For some, an important value, regardless of the role performed, is using one's skills and knowledge. This may mean doing work or studying to develop one's ability. It also refers to applying one's skills in community service or being a good parent.
- *Achievement:* Regardless of the role, achievement refers to the feeling that one has produced good results. Individuals with this value set high standards for their work or study. If the role is leisure, achievement may mean a feeling of accomplishing something significant in sports or music.
- *Aesthetics:* Aesthetics deals with finding beauty in the role that one chooses. It is often associated with artistic values, which are satisfied by creating a picture, a musical composition, or a poem.
- *Altruism:* Referring to helping others with problems, the need for altruism can be met clearly in several roles. One can help people with personal problems in one's family and in one's career (social work). Also, there are many community organizations, such as the Red Cross, that are devoted to helping others. Athletic coaching is a way of helping others in the pursuit of leisure.
- *Autonomy:* Some individuals value the opportunity to be independent and work on their own. They may want to make their own decisions about studying, about sports, and about how to run their family.
- *Creativity:* To be able to discover or design new things can be important in a variety of situations. Being able to try out new ideas in a hobby or in a community organization can be as important to some people as creating a new product at work.
- *Economic rewards:* To have a high standard of living and desired material possessions, one requires income derived from the working role. Although study may eventually lead to high income, and a wealthy family serves as a source of high income for some people, the primary role for obtaining economic rewards is as a worker.
- *Lifestyle:* To plan one's own activities—that is, to live the way one wants to live—can be an overriding issue for some people. Because studying is a solitary activity, studying the way one wants can sometimes be done rather easily. Some leisure activities can be chosen without regard to other people's needs. However, working is most often a role done with others, and certainly community service and family life make it difficult to live life the way one wants, unless individuals can find people who feel the same way they do.
- *Physical activity:* Although being physically active in studying is quite difficult, the other roles allow opportunity for physical activity. One can do community service, for example, by helping repair church or community center buildings. With one's family, one can choose to be active, for example, in taking trips, boating, or making things.
- *Prestige:* Many roles provide the opportunity for individuals to be acknowledged for what they accomplish. Although prestige is ordinarily associated with the work role, teachers recognize good students, and local communities recognize the contributions that citizens have made to them. A wife, husband, or child can acknowledge the contributions of a parent or a spouse.

• *Risk:* Some people like to have dangerous or exciting challenges in their lives. Leisure can provide that opportunity. Activities such as mountain climbing, wind surfing, and parachute jumping provide such an occasion. In work, logging, high-rise steel construction, and race car driving may provide another outlet for excitement. Risks taken in community service, studying, or home and family may be more psychological and less physical. In studying, taking risks could include trying a challenging course, procrastinating until the night before an examination to study, or waiting until the last minute to write a paper. For home and family, taking risks may mean surprising someone with a gift or, to be more negative, having an affair.

• *Social interaction:* Being with other people and working in a group can be accomplished in all roles. Some people prefer to study in a group, and some enjoy working as part of a team on a project. Certainly, community service provides that opportunity. Working with one's children and spouse to have a pleasant vacation or to paint a room can be enjoyable for some people. Leisure activity provides the opportunity for many types of social interaction, for example, parties, sports, and visiting friends.

• *Variety:* Being able to change work activities pleases some people. Variety in other roles may mean changing the subject that one is studying or moving from one type of task at work to another. Being involved in many different sports or community organizations can also meet these needs. At home, one can spend time with children or various relatives, cook, clean, and socialize.

• *Working conditions:* Having the proper light to study, a pleasing home, or the right equipment for sports activities are necessary conditions for some people. Also, working conditions, which would include lighting, pleasant temperature, and good equipment, can be important in work with community organizations or in the workplace itself.

When applying Super's theory in counseling, counselors will sometimes have the Salience Inventory available to them; at other times, they will not. Assessing which roles are important to a client and which values expectations are met by the roles can be extremely helpful. To do this, the counselor may want to make use of the Values Scale. Although the Minnesota Importance Questionnaire (Chapter 4) could be used, Hackbarth and Mathay (1991) report only low to moderate correlations between similar scales of the two inventories. In addition to those listed above, which are contained in but not measured by the Salience Inventory, the Values Scale includes the following concepts: authority (telling others what to do); personal development (developing as a person); social relations (being with friends); cultural identity (being with people of the same race and religion); physical prowess (working hard physically); and economic security (having secure and regular employment). Values have also been related to Holland themes (Chapter 5) to help counselors in discussing interests and values with clients (Rottinghaus & Zytowski, 2006). Results of this study suggest that clients with similar interests that participate in the same activity can satisfy their different needs and values. Reviews of the Salience Inventory (Niles & Goodnough, 1996; Nevill & Calvert, 1996) and the Values Scale (Niles & Goodnough, 1996; Nevill & Kruse, 1996) provide more evidence for the validity of these instruments, especially as applied to culturally diverse populations. The authors also suggest counseling applications.

A counselor working with Super's concepts for the first time may wish to become comfortable with the five roles measured in the Salience Inventory. Also, incorporating values into the career stages described in the next section may be useful. Later, the counselor can memorize the values in the Values Scale for use in counseling sessions. This chapter integrates the Salience Inventory's and the Values Scale's constructs into examples demonstrating counseling issues in each of the four major adult life stages described in the next section to help you understand how these constructs can be useful.

ADULT LIFE STAGES

The idea of stages and substages is essential to Super's life-span theory. Figure 9.2 depicts the stages and substages associated with various ages. Chapter 7, "Career Development in Childhood," describes those tasks that take place during the growth stage. Chapter 8, "Adolescent Career Development," focuses on the development of interests, capacities, and values that takes place during the exploration stage. How and when interests and capacities emerge in career decision making is an aspect of career maturity that is a part of Super's theory. This chapter describes the further exploration that may occur during late adolescence or early adulthood. The exploration stage includes crystallizing—that is, making an occupational choice, becoming more specific in the choice, and implementing it by finding and choosing a job. The other stages discussed here are establishing oneself in one's career, maintaining one's position, and disengaging from the world of work.

Super's (1990) concepts of life stages and substages can be confusing because they are both age-related and not age-related. They are age-related in the sense that there are typical times when people go through stages of exploration, establishment, maintenance, and decline or disengagement. However, it is also possible for an individual to experience a stage at almost any time during his or her lifetime. Furthermore, one can be involved in several stages at one time. Super (1990) uses the term *maxicycle* to describe the five major life stages. *Minicyle* is a term that describes the growth, exploration, establishment, maintenance, and disengagement that can occur within any of the stages in the maxicycle. For example, a 42-year-old dentist could be in the establishment stage. She may be becoming less concerned with stabilizing and advancing in her practice, explore ways to maintain herself in her practice, gradually disengage from the establishment stage, and grow into the maintenance stage. Or more dramatically, she could start to explore other career options and discover that she wants to become an artist and disengage from dentistry. Each of these is an example of a minicycle within a maxicycle. The concept of the minicycle highlights the dynamic nature of Super's theory. Throughout their lives, individuals are constantly trying out new ideas and activities as they make transitions to a new stage. For consistency and clarity, the stages and substages of the maxicycle are first presented in the typical order in which the average person encounters them. Then, the concept of *recycling*, which refers to going through aspects of the stages at various times in one's life, is discussed.

Super's life-stage theory has a long history. Beginning in 1951 with the Career Pattern Study (Super, Crites, Hummel, Moser, Overstreet, & Warnath, 1957), the study of life-stage theory is described. Super's book, *The Psychology of Careers* (1957), presents a more general exposition of his ideas, whereas the work of

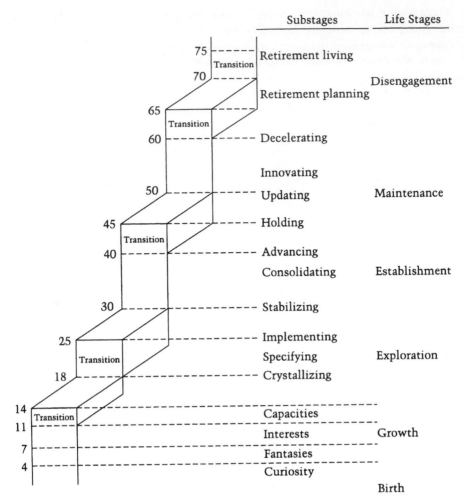

FIGURE 9.2 | LIFE STAGES AND SUBSTAGES BASED ON THE TYPICAL
DEVELOPMENT TASKS.

Source: Described by D. Brown, L. Brooks, and Associates in *Career choice and development.*
Copyright © 1984 by Jossey-Bass, Inc., Reprinted by permission.

Gribbons and Lohnes (1968), Crites (1979), and Super (Thompson & Lindeman, 1981) presents a vast array of studies on vocational maturity and measures that were developed to describe the concepts of maturity and life stages. After studying adolescents, Super focused considerable attention on developing instruments with which to measure and define adult development (Super & Kidd, 1979; Super & Knasel, 1979).

From this work, Super, Thompson, and Lindeman (1988) developed the Adult Career Concerns Inventory (ACCI), which assists in conceptualizing life stages. Confirmation of the validity of these stages can be seen in studies such as that of Smart and Peterson (1994), who report that the ACCI accurately classified 219 male and 238 female Australian adults. Patterns of maintenance in an occupation, recycling, and innovating are important exploratory behaviors in adults and are a focus of the ACCI (Herr, Cramer, & Niles, 2004; Niles, Anderson, Hartung, & Staton, 1999). Niles and colleagues' research (Niles, Anderson, & Goodnough, 1998) has focused on using the ACCI as a basis for studying exploratory behavior, and its use has led to the development of a version of the ACCI that is a behavioral response scale (Niles, Lewis, & Hartung, 1997), consistent with Super's stage concepts. One study found that for individuals who did not have to search for a job because they got unsolicited information about job openings, there were different pathways of nonsearchers depending on the stage they were in (McDonald, 2005). Those in the exploration stage often acquired jobs while still in school. Those in the establishment or maintenance stage who changed jobs using unsolicited information were often women with little work experience who had been taking care of their families, or highly experienced men who may have been well-known in their field. Comparing workers in companies that experienced layoffs with workers in companies that did not experience layoffs, Lahner (2005) found that many workers who were in the exploration stage at companies that had layoffs reported feelings of less job satisfaction and less security than workers whose companies did not lay off workers. Super's stages and their substages are described in more detail in the following sections.

EXPLORATION

According to Super (1957), the exploration stage ranges from about 15 to 25 years of age. This stage includes the efforts that individuals make to get a better idea of occupational information, choose career alternatives, decide on occupations, and start to work. This stage includes three substages: crystallizing, specifying, and implementing.

CRYSTALLIZING Crystallizing is the stage in which people clarify what they want to do. They learn about entry-level jobs that may be appropriate for them, and they learn what skills are required by the jobs that interest them. Many high school students go through this stage. Much of what was described in Chapter 8 in terms of the realization of abilities, interests, and values is applicable to this stage. Work experience and work knowledge help the person narrow his or her choices. When a person changes fields, as an adult may do at any time, he or she is likely to recycle through this stage to reexamine interests, abilities, and values.

SPECIFYING For college graduates, specification occurs in their early 20s; for those who seek employment directly after high school graduation, specification occurs earlier. As these young people must choose their first full-time job, they are required to *specify* their preferences so they may find an employer. For those who go on to graduate school or specialized education, such as pediatric nursing or advanced electrical engineering, preferences must also be specified. Whereas some must specify an occupation, others must specify a job within an occupation. They may wish to have part-time work or summer work in the occupation of their choice. For example, a student may work as a part-time nursing assistant in a hospital so that he or she may reaffirm that the choice is appropriate.

IMPLEMENTING Implementing is the last phase before working. At this point, people are making plans to fulfill their career objectives. They may be starting to network by meeting people who can help them get a job. Talking to a counselor in a university career-planning and placement office would be part of this phase. People may be writing résumés, having job interviews, or deciding between potential employers.

EXAMPLE   The following example illustrates the exploration stage. Incorporated into the example is the use of the Salience Inventory, the Values Scale, the Adult Career Concerns Inventory, and the Strong Interest Inventory. The Adult Career Concerns Inventory (Super, Thompson, & Lindeman, 1988) gives scores for each stage and substage. The counselor will use the scores from these inventories, as well as the concepts, to think about clients' issues using a counseling model similar to the Career Development Assessment and Counseling (C-DAC) method (Hartung, Vandiver, Leong, Pope, Niles, & Farrow, 1998; Herr, Cramer, & Niles, 2004; Super, Osborne, Walsh, Brown, & Niles, 1992).

Ben is a white college student currently in the second semester of his junior year. His father is a stockbroker, and his mother is an airline ticket agent. He lives about 50 miles from the large city where he is enrolled in a major university as a business major. He has come to the counseling center because he is not sure which career direction to take within the business field, or whether to seek a business career at all. In their first meeting, the counselor assigns Ben to take the Adult Career Concerns Inventory, the Values Scale, the Salience Inventory, and the Strong Interest Inventory. The results, summarized in Table 9.1, show that Ben has considerable concern about the crystallization substage, the specification substage, and the implementation substage. He has little or no concern about the other stages (establishment, maintenance, and disengagement). Regarding his scores on the Salience Inventory, Ben has high scores on leisure activities for participation, commitment, and values expectations. His scores for studying indicate moderate participation in commitment and low values expectations. Working also has moderate participation, commitment, and values expectations. The scores on the Community Service and the Home and Family scales are low to moderate, except for a high score on values expectations for home and family. On the Values Scale, Ben scores high on economic rewards, advancement, prestige, and risk. Briefly, his Strong Interest Inventory reveals high interest in athletics, sales, and law and politics. He has high scores on several business occupations in the Occupational Scales. He has interests that are similar to those of marketing executives, human resources directors, and credit managers. After having talked with the counselor once and having taken these inventories, Ben returns to talk about the results. Several segments of the discussion are used below to illustrate a number of Super's concepts:

CL: Those were a lot of tests. I'm curious how I did.

CO: We'll go over as much as we can today, but we may not finish—in fact, we probably won't. [There is a lot of material to discuss and the counselor does not want to rush, because he realizes that Ben is at a critical point in his career decision making.]

CL: Well, OK. Those inventory results really got me thinking.

CO: What about?

CL: I really started to think about what I'm going to do. I graduate in another year, and I really haven't thought a lot about it. My friends and I talk some, but mainly we throw names of companies around and talk about who's going to have the nicest car—things like that.

CO: But you're concerned. [The counselor wonders about Ben's motivation for career counseling. However, he remembers Ben's high scores on the Adult Career Concerns Inventory, which would probably indicate that Ben is indeed concerned.]

| TABLE 9.1 | SUMMARY OF BEN'S SCORES ON FOUR INVENTORIES |

Inventory	High Scores
Adult Career Concerns Inventory	Crystallizing Specifying Implementing
Salience Inventory	*Leisure* Participation Commitment Values expectations *Home and Family* Values expectations
Values Scale	Economic rewards Advancement Prestige Risk
Strong Interest Inventory	*Basic Interests* Athletics Sales Law and politics *Occupational Scales* Human resources director Credit manager Marketing executive

CL: We joke about it, but sometimes it makes me nervous thinking about what happens in a year. It seems as if things will just end, and it's blank from there.

CO: Well, let's take a look at one of the inventories that you finished. [The counselor shows Ben his scores on the Adult Career Concerns Inventory.]

CL: High scores on all the exploration stages. What does that mean?

CO: You seem to be unsure of what you want to do, quite concerned about a job, and maybe wondering how to get one.

CL: Yes, all of those things, but I always thought of them as a big jumble, not as three different steps.

CO: Yes, it's hard to decide what you want to do and find a job all at once. [The counselor is pleased that Ben seems to be taking the process seriously and understands the need to take things one at a time.]

Ben and the counselor go on to talk further about the results of the Adult Career Concerns Inventory and its meaning for Ben. The following dialogue is from this point in the discussion:

CO: I also wanted to talk to you about the role of work in your life.

CL: I know that I have to work hard to make a lot of money.

CO: What would you like to do with your money if you made $100,000 your first year? [Wanting to see if Ben's role values are the same as those in the Salience Inventory, the counselor tries to find out what areas Ben would participate in and where his commitment is.]

CL: I'd put a down payment on a boat and a sports car and get the best stereo you ever saw. I would really like to race motorcycles, so I would get a new one. I'd find as much time as I could to mess around.

CO: You certainly want to have fun. [Leisure activities come through loud and clear in terms of participation, commitment, and values expectations. The counselor is interested in Ben's commitment to studying and working.]

CL: Yes, school is a bore. I like summertime, when I can just work and take it easy. I'm a lifeguard at a hotel pool. It's a busy hotel, but the pool isn't very busy most times, so I get to relax, chat with people, and have a good time. It's not much of a job, but the pay is OK.

CO: Pay seems important to you. [The counselor starts to explore Ben's work values.]

CL: Yes, it really is. I would like to have a nice home someday and to be able to have some free time to be with my family to do things. I'm not sure I want a family for a while. But someday I would.

CO: Sounds like you're starting to think more and more about the future. [The counselor notes that, for home and family, values expectations come out high on the Salience Inventory, whereas participation and commitment do not. That seems to fit with Ben's statement, because home and family are not an immediate commitment for him but may be in future years.]

Ben and the counselor continue to discuss his plans and goals. They are getting ready to talk about the Strong Interest Inventory. Wanting to put the Strong Interest Inventory in context, the counselor talks to Ben about its purpose:

CO: Let's look at your interest inventory results. It's helpful to talk about interests and careers in terms of the importance to you of working. [Not wanting to overstate the value of the Strong Interest Inventory, the counselor wants to establish a context for it.]

CL: Well, I'm curious about what it has to say.

CO: When we look at it, it may be helpful to remember that work seems to be a means to an end for you. You certainly want to get the things that work provides for you. This inventory will help you to understand how similar your interests are to those of people in different occupations.

CL: As you talk, it does sound important. I've been thinking so much about what I want to do with what I will make that I've been less concerned about what I will do.

CO: Some of your basic areas of interest seem to be in athletics and sales. [The counselor starts with the two highest scores on the Basic Interests scales.]

CL: Yes, I really like to do fun things like play tennis, basketball, and volleyball and race boats and cars.

CO: It would seem that way. The values inventory that you took seems to emphasize risk as well. [The counselor wants to integrate the inventory scores with each other to form a clearer impression of Ben.]

CL: Sales is interesting to me. I never thought about that. I think I would like it. It's a real challenge. One summer I spent trying to sell as much as I could in an appliance store. They gave me commissions. I really did a good job.

CO: You really seem to have gotten a lot of satisfaction from that accomplishment. [The counselor hears how important achievement is to Ben and reinforces it. At this point, the counselor is aware that Ben's values are quite different from his own values. The counselor's values are more altruistic and creative, whereas Ben's tend more toward achievement and economic rewards. The counselor does not want to devalue Ben just because their values are so different.]

In a counseling situation that uses four different inventories, it is impossible to give a good overview of the process of discussing the inventories. However, the purpose of this illustration has been to show how the counselor can make use of Super's developmental concepts and inventories to help someone who is in the exploration stage. The issues that are important in the exploration stage are quite different from those in the establishment stage.

ESTABLISHMENT

The establishment stage generally ranges from the age of 25 to about 45 years. In general, establishment refers to getting established in one's work by starting in a job that is likely to mean the start of working life. In skilled, management, and professional occupations, this means work in an occupation that will probably be steady for many years. For those in semiskilled and unskilled occupations, establishment does not mean that a person will be established in a particular job or organization. Instead, it suggests that the person will be working for much of his or her lifetime (Super, Thompson, & Lindeman, 1988). The substages of *stabilizing, consolidating*, and *advancing* refer to career behaviors that take place once working life has started.

Within the establishment stage, values are important (as in other stages as well). In studying changes of values between when people are seniors in high school and when they are in the establishment stage (about 31 or 32 years old), Johnson (2001) notes how values vary in importance over time for each individual as he or she moves out of adolescence. Johnson shows how certain values become stronger as individuals have their values reinforced through successful experiences that occur during the ages covered by the exploration and establishment stages.

STABILIZING   Getting started in a job requires a minimum amount of permanence. The individual needs to know that he or she will be in this job for more than a few months. Stabilization is concerned with settling down in a job and being able to meet those job requirements that will ensure that a person can stay in the field in which he or she has started. At this point, an individual may be apprehensive about whether he or she has the skills necessary to stay with the work in the long-term. As individuals become more comfortable, they start to consolidate their position.

CONSOLIDATING   Once a person has stabilized his or her position, which often occurs when people reach their late 20s and early 30s, consolidation can take place. The person starts to become more comfortable with her or his job or work and wishes to be known as a dependable producer, one who is competent and can be relied on by others. In this stage, individuals want bosses and coworkers to know that they can do their job well. Once they consolidate their position and feel secure, then they can consider advancement to higher positions.

ADVANCING   Occurring any time in the establishment stage, but usually after stabilizing and consolidating have taken place, advancing refers to moving ahead into a position of more responsibility with higher pay. Particularly in business, there is a concern with advancing to positions of higher authority. To do so, individuals often plan how to get ahead and how to improve their chances of being promoted.

They want their superiors to know that they do their work well and are capable of handling more responsibility.

EXAMPLE   Lucy, whose case was discussed in Chapters 7 and 8, is now a 28-year-old physical therapist working with people who have spinal cord injuries. She lives in a large city, is unmarried, and works in a nationally known hospital on a staff with many physical therapists. Lucy has sought counseling because she has not been happy with her personal life or her work. She recently ended a 3-year relationship with a man and now finds that she is lonely, having not attended to friendships when she was romantically involved. Though she had intended to go to medical school, she had been afraid that she could not finance her education and worried that she could not stay in school and study for another four years after college; she also had needed income immediately. Now she is questioning that decision and is trying to decide whether to apply to medical school. She is clear that her career choice is within the field of health but is hesitant to apply to medical school. She feels frustrated in her work because she questions her supervisor's competence and feels limited by the job duties of a physical therapist. She wonders if she would be happier if she had more responsibility for patients, like the physicians do who work with her patients.

Lucy's counselor has decided to use the Salience Inventory, the Values Scale, and the Adult Career Concerns Inventory. The counselor hopes that these instruments will help Lucy understand the importance of work in her life, the values that are important to her, and the developmental concerns that matter most to her. There are differences between Lucy's participation scores on the Salience Inventory and her commitment and values expectations scores (Table 9.2). Lucy's participation is in working, then leisure activities, followed by home and family. Her high scores on the Values Scales are for autonomy, lifestyle, social interaction, and achievement. The Adult Career Concerns Inventory shows that Lucy has considerable concern about crystallization and great concern about stabilizing. Other stages of development are of little or some concern to her. Having talked about her loneliness and worries about her social isolation during the first session, Lucy brings up her career concerns with the counselor at the beginning of their second session. The counselor has just shared the results of the Salience Inventory and the Adult Career Concerns Inventory with Lucy. The following dialogue recounts their discussion of Lucy's results:

CL: Work really is very important to me. I feel that I have accomplished some things just by being able to get a job in the hospital. I've shown others that I can take care of myself.

CO: Getting set and on your feet sounds important. [The counselor hears Lucy talking about stabilizing and sees the parallel between this discussion and her high score on the Stabilizing Scale.]

CL: Really, it is important to me. I think now it's even more important to me because Max and I have broken up. There were times when I thought that we really would get married. When he continued to back off from me, and finally when I found out that he had cheated on me, that did it. It seemed then as if work was all I had.

CO: It's scary now to think that being married and having a family seems so unknown. [Being aware of the salience of home and family, the counselor is aware of how deeply Lucy is affected. That role seems to be hard for her to imagine now.]

TABLE 9.2	SUMMARY OF LUCY'S SCORES ON THREE INVENTORIES

Inventory	High Scores
Salience Inventory	*Working* Participation Commitment Values expectations *Leisure* Participation *Home and Family* Commitment Values expectations
Values Scale	Autonomy Lifestyle Social interaction Achievement
Adult Career Concerns Inventory	Crystallizing Stabilizing

CL: It's been so hard. I seem so much more aware of what other people are doing at work now. I don't mean just with patients, but sometimes I think about what they do when they go home. When Max and I were living together, I never thought about that.

CO: A lot more thought about you, too, and what you're going to do. [Disruption in the participation in one salient role, a relationship leading to home and family, seems to have had the effect of causing questioning of other salient roles.]

CL: Even though I really like the people I work with and still enjoy being with them, I feel more removed from them. I look at where they're going and I look at where I'm going. I wonder if I'm going in the right direction.

CO: Sounds like we ought to talk more about medical school—you brought that up last time. [Lucy seems to want to recycle, in the sense that she wants to question her choices and return to the crystallizing stage. Furthermore, Lucy values social interaction; her statement is confirmed by her high score on the Values Scale.]

CL: Yes, now that I'm learning a lot about physical therapists and physicians, much more than I ever knew before, I am questioning it.

CO: Sounds like you have a lot more practical experience than you got just from your internship. [The counselor hears how Lucy's world-of-work information has increased (a concept discussed in Chapter 8) and how Lucy may wish to return to the question of occupational selection with new information.]

CL: I really don't want to have to depend on anyone. I want to do what I want to do.

CO: What is that? [Lucy's autonomy is apparent. She seems to have a strong sense of who she is and what she wants.]

CL: Being a physician, working with people who are badly hurt, has a great appeal to me. I think I can do it.

CO: You seem to want it but seem scared. [Understanding the wavering between the stabilizing and the crystallizing stages, the counselor sees Lucy as embarking on one career and starting to like it but also seeing another career with more potential. In some ways, a change from physical therapist to physician can be seen as advancing, rather than career change. If seen that way, it may be less traumatic. However, returning to school for several years is more than advancing.]

The use of Super's instruments and concepts to help Lucy deal with her relationship and career issues provides an organizing format for the counselor. Being able to identify the life stage and the movement back and forth within it can be quite helpful in making sense of changes in a person's life. Furthermore, knowing that the role of work can change in one's life and seeing it in terms of other roles—home and family, leisure, community service, and studying—can be quite helpful. Lucy's values are important in her decision making. Super's value concepts provide a way to label the important issues with which Lucy is struggling.

MAINTENANCE

Individuals from about the age of 45 to 65 years may be in a situation where they are not advancing but are maintaining their status in their work. This can vary from individual to individual, depending on physical abilities, company policies, personal financial situation, and motivation. Examining work in the 21st century, Power and Rothausen (2003) note the importance for individuals to find out about changes that might affect their jobs from sources other than their employers. They suggest that individuals in the maintenance (and establishment) stages ask themselves questions such as: Will the work I am doing still be available to do in a few years? How will automation or computerization affect my work? What topics concern the people who do my type of work? What types of problems are people who do my type of work trying to solve? These questions can be asked in the substages of holding, updating, and innovating. The substages are useful to the counselor because they help expand on the meaning of the maintenance stage.

HOLDING   When some level of success has been attained, the individual is concerned with holding onto the position that he or she has. This may mean learning new things to adapt to changes that take place in the position and being aware of activities that coworkers are involved in. In some companies, individuals may see forced early retirement or potential mass layoffs as a threat. This is enough motivation for an individual to hold his or her own in the workplace.

UPDATING   In many fields, holding one's own is not enough. For example, health and education occupations often require that workers attend continuing education programs to maintain their status in that occupation. Attendance at these programs updates workers on changes in the field. Less formal activities than continuing education seminars include attending professional meetings, visiting with colleagues or customers to see new developments in the field, and meeting people who can update one's knowledge.

INNOVATING   Somewhat similar to updating, innovating refers to making progress in one's profession. It may not be enough to learn new things (updating); it may be important to make new contributions to the field. To do so, an individual might need to develop new skills as a field changes. Sometimes, there are new ways to improve one's work or to find new areas of work to learn. Innovating may sound as if it contradicts

the idea of maintenance. However, in most occupations, particularly higher level occupations, if workers stop learning new things, they will not maintain themselves;
rather, they will decline and will be in danger of losing their position.

EXAMPLE   Having knowledge of Super's stages can be useful to counselors with or
without Super's inventories. The following case describes Richard, a 57-year-old insurance salesperson. He is talking to a psychiatrist about the general fatigue, together with
occasional low-back pain, that he is experiencing. The psychiatrist, although not familiar with Super's instruments, is familiar with Super's life-stage theory.

CL: I seem to be tired much more than I used to be.
CO: None of the tests, as we've discussed, has shown anything to be wrong. How is your
    life going? [The psychiatrist decides to take the time to listen to Richard and see if she
    can help out. Perhaps she will make a referral to a counselor, a psychologist, or a psy-
    chiatrist, or perhaps she will be able to help Richard herself.]
CL: My twin boys are doing well in their new jobs and my wife likes hers, so things are
    going well with them.
CO: But how are things going with you?
CL: At home things are fine—we have two new grandchildren, and that's great—but work
    is the same as it's always been.
CO: And how is that? [The psychiatrist wants to learn more about Richard's working role,
    because he seems content with home and family.]
CL: It's pretty drab. I have the same customers. I get some commissions for renewing their
    accounts. Customers refer friends to me, so I get new accounts that way. My business
    is pretty much established now, so I don't have to work the way I used to.
CO: Richard, the way you describe it, it doesn't sound very interesting to you. [Questioning
    how Richard is dealing with the maintenance stage, the psychiatrist wonders whether
    Richard is even holding his own in the field, let alone updating knowledge or
    innovating.]
CL: Yes, it is rather boring. They have seminars and I get materials all the time, but they
    seem like the same old stuff. I don't read half of them.
CO: What keeps you from reading them? [The psychiatrist knows the value of updating
    knowledge and innovating. She is hopeful that she will be able to get this across to
    Richard.]
CL: I don't know. There are all these people who seem brand new to the company, telling
    me what I ought to do and how I ought to do it. I've worked for them for 20 years.
CO: You really seem to resent their telling you what to do, almost as if you don't feel respected.
    [The psychiatrist wants to explore the resentment that Richard feels, believing that it may
    hold back his progress in his work and contribute to his overall feeling of tiredness.]

In this example, by having some idea of life stages, the psychiatrist is able to be
sensitive to her patient and start to explore issues of concern. Later, she may decide
to refer Richard elsewhere for counseling. For now, she has used her knowledge of
adult career development and the importance of various life roles to diagnose a significant psychological issue for the client.

DISENGAGEMENT

In the maintenance stage, if individuals do not update their knowledge of the field
and make some effort to innovate, they are in danger of losing their job. In the previous example, Richard may be in that position. He may be starting to disengage from

his work. Sometimes, the need to disengage comes from physical limitations. People in their 50s and 60s who have been involved in some kind of physical labor—for example, construction, painting, or assembly line work—may find that they are no longer able to work as long or as fast as they once were. Super (1957) originally referred to this stage as "decline" but changed his label because of its negative connotations for many people. Although people in this age group may be slowing down in their physical abilities and their ability to remember, this age is also associated with wisdom. People can continue to use their mental capacities for growth and at the same time disengage from various activities. The substages of disengagement—decelerating, retirement planning, and retirement living—can be seen as tasks that older adults often, but not always, consider.

DECELERATING   Slowing down one's work responsibility is what is meant by decelerating. For some people, this may mean finding easier ways of doing work or spending less time doing work. Others may find that it is difficult to concentrate on things for as long as they did when they were younger. Drawing away from difficult problems at work and wanting to avoid deadline pressure are signs of decelerating.

RETIREMENT PLANNING   Although some individuals begin their retirement planning early, almost all individuals must deal directly with retirement plans during their later years. This task includes activities such as financial planning and planning activities to do in retirement. Talking to friends, retirement counselors at work, and others will aid in this process. Some individuals may choose a new part-time job or volunteer work. In a sense, when they do this, individuals are returning to the crystallization stage and reassessing their interests, capacities (both physical and mental), and values.

RETIREMENT LIVING   Retirement living is common for people in their late 60s, who often experience changes in life roles. Leisure, home and family, and community service may become more important, whereas work may become less significant. Important aspects of retirement living are the place in which one lives, one's friends, and use of the free time that may come with retirement.

As aging populations become larger (as of 2000, more than half the U.S. population was older than 50 years), there is a greater need to address the issues of individuals facing retirement. Suggestions for counseling retirees are provided by Sterns and Subich (2005) that include ideas for educating retirees, methods for preventing problems in retirement, as well as remediation strategies. Suggestions for retirees for approaching retirement are given in *Retire Smart, Retire Happy* (Schlossberg, 2004). Good health is often the key factor in satisfactory retirement (Goldberg & Beitz, 2007). How individuals about to retire anticipated upcoming events in their lives affected the outcome of these events (Jonsson, Josephsson, Kielhofner, 2001). Promoting an optimistic view, Atchley (2003) believes most people have learned how to adapt to life's challenge and cope well with retirement. Recently, investigators have studied retirement issues in populations that traditionally have not been studied, such as lesbian, gay, bisexual, and transgendered individuals (Kimmel, Rose, & David, 2006) and adults with an intellectual disability (Cordes & Howard, 2005).

RECYCLING

Super recognizes that not everyone follows these stages in the neat order outlined here. In fact, most do not. Many reassess their career plans at various points during their lifetime and recycle through various stages. When they do this, they reenter the exploration stage and may reassess their values, interests, and capacities. When people enter a stage that they have been through before, they are said to recycle through it. In a study of Australian men, Smart and Peterson (1997) confirm the concept of recycling, finding that men who were in the process of changing careers did show more concern with Super's exploration stage than men who did not change careers. On the Adult Career Concerns Inventory, Super (Super, Thompson, & Lindeman, 1990) uses one item to determine a person's recycling status. Because it so clearly describes the concept of recycling, the item is reprinted as follows, together with five choices (Super, Thompson, & Lindeman, 1990):

> After working in the field for a while, many persons shift to another job for any of a variety of reasons: pay, satisfaction, opportunity for growth, shut-down, etc. When the shift is a change in field, not just working for another employer in the same field, it is commonly called a "career change." Following are five statements which represent various stages in career change. Choose the one statement that best describes your current status.
>
> 1. I am not considering making a career change.
> 2. I am considering whether to make a career change.
> 3. I plan to make a career change and I am choosing a field to change to.
> 4. I have selected a new field and I am trying to get started in it.
> 5. I have recently made a change and I am settling down in the new field.

The following dialogue is part of an initial interview between Matthew, a 64-year-old journalist working for a newspaper in a midsize southwestern city, and the retirement counselor who is on the staff in the newspaper's personnel office. Matthew, a Mexican American who moved to Texas at the age of 12 years, has been on the staff of the paper for 37 years. For 25 years, the newspaper has had a pension plan that he has participated in. Matthew's job requires him to be mobile, interviewing politicians and police officers throughout the county. In the last 15 years, Matthew has gained considerable weight, and he had a heart bypass operation 3 years ago. He is finding that he does not have the stamina that he used to have and is extremely tired at the end of the day. He has been looking forward to retirement. The counselor and Matthew have been going over the financial aspects of his retirement plan. The following dialogue occurs when the counselor asks Matthew what his plans are for retirement:

CL: I've really been looking forward to relaxing and sitting around taking it easy. This job is getting to me now. My health isn't what it once was. I just want to be able to take it easy. I'm planning to work a thirty-hour workweek for the next nine months. My editor says that's fine and not to worry about it.

CO: And after that? [Using his knowledge of Super's life-stage theory, but not Super's inventories, the counselor recognizes that Matthew is discussing the deceleration substage of disengagement. His focus seems to be mainly on that stage and not on retirement planning or retirement living.]

CL: My home is all paid for, and my wife will be working for another few years. I'll just sit around and watch television.

CO: Does that seem enjoyable to you? [Expecting to go from an active work role to a very passive role with little activity may be unrealistic.]

CL: Well, that's not all that I'll do.

CO: And what else?

CL: Something that I've always wanted to do is work in the literacy program with adults who can't read and those who are having a hard time learning English. It really helped me when I was a boy to be able to learn English as quickly as I did. I remember, in high school, I got better grades in English than the Anglo kids, and it wasn't even my native language. I've seen so many people suffer here because they can't read or speak English.

CO: Sounds as if you've thought about it for a while. [Moving from an active work role to an active community service role seems to be a comfortable shift.]

CL: I think about it quite a bit when I have to interview someone for an article and they can't speak well or their English is lousy. I find myself more and more giving tips to the young guys coming up in the office.

CO: You seem to like teaching. [Identifying an interest that is different from those in Matthew's current work may be helpful as Matthew and the counselor recycle to the crystallization stage. It is not a dramatic recycling, because Matthew has had some opportunity to do a little bit of teaching and has given it some thought.]

CL: Well, I never have had much opportunity to teach, but I do it informally. I try not to be obnoxious about it. Most reporters have their own style, and they don't like being told what to do. You know I think I'd like to do something for other Mexican Americans who have not had it as good as I have.

CO: Helping them sounds as if it will be very meaningful to you. [The values of altruism and cultural identity underlie Matthew's desire to change his role in a positive sense to community service.]

From this brief example, the utility of Super's life-stage and role salience concepts can be seen. Without them, the counselor would just be using his own intuitions as to what to look for in helping Matthew. He would not be taking advantage of the wide array of research and concept development that has been a part of the work of Super and colleagues. It is not that Super's theory is the only theory; there are others, such as those of Levinson, Darrow, Klein, Levinson, and McKye (1978) and Erikson (1963), but they have not generated as much research as Super's theory, and they are not related directly to career development. However, the use of any of the theories would probably be better than relying solely on hunches.

LIFE STAGES OF WOMEN

Although the original sample for Super's theory was white middle-class male adolescents, Super was concerned about the career patterns of women. He proposed the following seven career patterns for women (Super, 1957, pp. 76–78):

1. *Stable homemaking career pattern:* Women marry shortly after they finish their education and have no significant work experience afterward.
2. *Conventional career pattern:* Women enter work after high school or college; however, after marriage, they cease work to enter full-time homemaking.

3. *Stable working career pattern:* After high school or college, women work continuously throughout their life span.
4. *Double-track career pattern:* This pattern characterizes those women who combine career and homemaking roles throughout their life span.
5. *Interrupted career pattern:* Women enter into work, then marriage and full-time homemaking, and later return to a career, often after children can care for themselves.
6. *Unstable career pattern:* In this pattern, women drop out of the workforce, return to it, drop out, and return—repeating the cycle over and over again.
7. *Multiple-trial career pattern:* In such a pattern, a woman works but never really establishes a career. She may have a number of different unrelated jobs during her lifetime.

In 1990, Super pointed out that the career patterns for women that he described more than 40 years ago would be different now. Many changes in society have taken place to allow women to enter a much broader spectrum of careers. In her review of women's career development, Fassinger (2005) examines the career development of women from different theoretical points of view and describes how society's impact on women has affected their career development. Examining Super's life-span theory, Coogan and Chen (2007) make suggestions for counselors in helping women with career issues. They discuss concerns that women have in dealing with multiple roles and the influences of others. In a study of 105 women over a 14-year span, Vincent, Peplau, and Hill (1998) report that women's career behavior was predicted by their gender-role views and their views of the preferences that their boyfriends and parents had for them 14 years earlier. When considering combining work and being a mother, adolescent girls may have difficulty dealing with pressures they see to be a mother and to give up work to raise children (Marks & Houston, 2002). Research shows that women see themselves in many roles and that there are several reasons for these perceptions.

Dual incomes of couples have been a focus of research due in part to changing patterns of working couples. In the United States in 1970, the husband was the sole provider in 56% of couples, whereas in 2001 the husband was the provider in 25% of couples. In 1970, 4% of women were the sole provider compared to 12% in 2001 (Raley, Mattingly, & Bianchi, 2006). With so many more women in the workforce than in previous years, it is important to examine the impact of work on women's lives.

One investigation has focused on dual career women by studying factors that women find helpful in managing a career and work (Jackson & Scharman, 2002). Focusing on women with children who worked less than 30 hours a week, Jackson and Scharman describe six general themes that help women to integrate raising children and working. These themes are as follows:

1. Joint decision making with their partner about work and family
2. Developing creative alternative work schedules
3. Enjoying their work
4. Feeling good about being able to juggle work and family
5. Being uncertain how work and family desires and obligations would evolve
6. Giving up some things (money, promotion) in exchange for other things (time with children, personal time)

Jackson and Scharman's study (2002) examines what is successful for working mothers. Cron (2001) reports that the most problematic job satisfaction issue for young working mothers is not problems at work but problems in the marital relationship. Cron suggests that when women are not satisfied with their jobs, they may find it helpful to improve communication with their partner by negotiating what tasks need to be done at home and who should do them and by planning shared child care and other factors that will help to improve the marriage. Attention has also been paid to same-sex dual earner couples and the many roles individuals play, such as worker, parent, step-parent, partner, and caregiver (Perrone, 2005).

Several investigators have reviewed women's choices to enter or not enter science or technology careers. Comparing women who entered engineering (a traditionally closed area) with those entering math education (a traditionally open area), Brown, Eisenberg, & Sawilowsky (1997) report that the expectations that these women had of their success played an important role in their career choices. Helen Farmer performed several longitudinal studies of women and their career development. Farmer (1997a) reports that women experienced sexual harassment and discrimination in math and science courses, whereas men did not. Another study (Farmer, 1997b) gives several reasons for women changing their career aspirations from science to other fields: selecting a popular career without much thought, finding a career that better fit their interests and personality, having to overcome too many career obstacles, and experiencing one or more critical events that changed their career goals. Another longitudinal study follows up 1,100 13-year-old adolescents who did very well in math Webb, Lubinski, & Benbow, C. P., 2002). At 33 years old, more women than men had completed degrees in non-science fields. However, many individuals in non-science majors eventually chose math/science jobs. Also, a number of individuals in math/science majors eventually chose other types of jobs.

Bardwick (1980) examined the typical experiences of women at various points in their adult lives. It is useful to compare these observations with Super's life stages. Whereas Super characterized the establishment stage as a time to stabilize oneself in a career, consolidate one's gains, and prepare to advance in the profession, Bardwick suggested that many women between the ages of 30 and 40 years who had been involved in a career were concerned with not wanting to delay having children any longer. Bardwick believed that many women were concerned about balancing their professional role with their feminine role. For some women, professional success at midlife did not seem to bring about independence, but rather increased dependence. Whereas Super described the maintenance stage as a time to hold one's gains and to update and innovate one's career skills, Bardwick believed that many women between the ages of 40 and 50 years (the late establishment and early maintenance stages) were starting to develop more autonomy and to become more independent. That is the time when those women who gave up careers so they could raise children may return to a career. For women older than 50 years, Bardwick described a time not of maintenance, but of career accomplishments. For some women, their husband's retirement or death may open up more opportunities for a creative and autonomous lifestyle. Cron (2001) reported a similar observation in older women, referring to the importance of adaptability in job satisfaction. Bardwick's observations of women's working patterns focused on women's concerns about marriage and family and were based mainly on middle-class and upper-middle-class women. In contrast, a very different model of women's career patterns describes jobs of Swedish women: upwardly mobile, stable, and downwardly mobile career patterns (Huang & Sverke, 2007). Bardwick's stages are contrasted with Super's stages to remind counselors of the different ways of viewing the impact of marriage and family on women's career choice.

Using Super's theory with women is made easier by the use of Super's five roles: study, work, community service, home and family, and leisure. When examining participation in different roles, men were found to participate more in work and leisure activities, whereas women participated more in leisure and family (Perrone, Webb, & Blalock, 2005). To explore life roles with clients, Brott (2005) mentions techniques such as using genograms (described in Chapter 11) and life lines (described in Chapter 12). These techniques help clients creatively explore how they view their various life roles.

The issue of the applicability of life-stage theory to women will probably continue to be a difficulty for some time. Pavalko and Gong (2005) emphasize the difficulty of using stage models in this context because of the wide variation in experience that women have at midlife, some of which is affected by race and social class variables. Drawing from several studies of graduates from Radcliffe College, Vandewater and Stewart (1997) describe three different approaches to careers. Women with continuous career commitments pursued stable and prestigious careers. They were as likely to be married as women in the other groups but had fewer children. Their lives were devoted to work and family. Women with alternative commitments took on traditional roles and pursued social values. Their occupations were traditional (for example, artists, nurses, and social workers). Women with midlife career commitments took on traditional roles when they left college but pursued high-level careers as their children grew older. These patterns provide another view of women's ways of integrating family and work and are somewhat similar to those of Bardwick (1980) and Super et al. (1992). Clearly, differences in men's and women's perceptions of the importance of life roles suggest that counselors need to recognize the complexity of life-span theory. The counseling examples given in this chapter all show counselors listening to the client and not trying to force life-span theory into their conceptualization of a client.

Another view of career development that has been applied to women is the ecological perspective (Betz, 2002; Cook, Heppner, & O'Brien, 2002a, 2002b, 2005; Heppner, Davidson, & Scott, 2003). The ecological perspective examines the relationship between the person and the environment, with particular emphasis on the role of the environment. The ecological perspective focuses on broad sociocultural factors that affect individuals, such as cultural, political, educational, and other systems. Most other career development theories focus more on interests, abilities, and values rather than these sociocultural factors. In this approach, counselors not only help women clarify their options, but they help support their decisions and help them deal with the various roles (mother, worker, and so forth) that they have. In addition, counselors who use this perspective may help women obtain good child care, deal with problems in the workplace (such as sexual harassment), and obtain equal pay. In the following example, a counselor using the ecological perspective would attend to issues such as child care, as well as provide support for the client's choices.

Jill is a 38-year-old white woman who is married to a truck driver. She has three teenage children who are in school. For the past four years, Jill has been attending classes at a local community college. She now wishes to go to a four-year college but is unsure whether she wants to enroll in a teaching or a business curriculum. She has a slight preference for teaching but is afraid that this curriculum will be longer, because some of her credits will not transfer, and that she will have more difficulty finding a job near home. Her husband tolerates her pursuit of higher education but complains about her lack of attention to the children, because he has to spend more time with them. Jill is tired of his pressure and cannot wait until she finishes school so he will not pester her. However, she really enjoys the studying that she is doing, and her view of herself as a competent individual has grown.

From the points of view of several life-span theories, several comments can be made about Jill. First, Super's theory can explain that Jill is juggling her participation in studying and in home and family because she is committed to work and to home and family. She values autonomy, personal development, prestige, and achievement. From a life-stage point of view, she is recycling through the crystallization phase. She has greater family commitment and responsibilities than students who are 18 years younger. She would benefit from some help in crystallizing her abilities, interests, and values. She does not fit Bardwick's (1980) description of 30- to 40-year-old women because her children are teenagers. However, she somewhat resembles Bardwick's description of 40- to 50-year-old women. An ecological point of view would emphasize the importance of Jill's educational desires and the stress caused by her husbands gender-role values regarding child care and related issues. Each of these perspectives provides a useful way of understanding the problems that Jill faces.

LIFE STAGES OF CULTURALLY DIVERSE ADULTS

Recent research on college students and adults has focused on the career development of individuals from different cultural groups, especially African Americans. Valuing work was related to career maturity for African American university students. In general, these students valued home and family roles more strongly than work or study roles (Naidoo, Bowman, & Gerstein, 1998). Using a case study approach, Chung, Baskin, and Case (1999) show the importance of financial support and role modeling of fathers on the career development of male African Americans. Even when fathers were not available as role models, other African American males provided positive role models for the sample of adult African American men. In a study of 14 African American women, averaging 40 years of age, several types of family experiences tended to influence their career development (Pearson & Bieschke, 2001). Women reported that family members, especially the primary caregiver, provided considerable support. Getting approval for successfully completing tasks was important, as was the valuing of education in the family. Not only have researchers been concerned with how the career development of African Americans may be different from other groups, practitioners have devoted effort to career counseling for African Americans, as illustrated by the book *Career Counseling for African Americans* (Walsh & Bingham, 2001).

Research on Latino/Latina and American Indian populations has also added to the knowledge of career development of culturally diverse populations. Comparing the attitudes of Mexican American men and women with regard to attitudes toward the role of women in the workplace and views of responsibility for child care for working parents, Gowan and Trevine (1998) report Mexican American men were more likely to have traditional views than were Mexican American women. A study of 20 successful Latinas reports the need to bridge two cultures (Gomez, Fassinger, Prosser, Cooke, Mejia, & Luna, 2001). Because of the importance of family in Latina culture, reliance on family support was important, but nontraditional role models such as teachers also were important. Women in the study also said that their career paths were unplanned, but researchers report that optimism, passion, and persistence helped them achieve career goals.

Using a different population, researchers claim family and community support to be important to 18 North American Plains Indians with varied educational backgrounds (Juntunen, Barraclough, Broneck, Seibel, Winrow, & Morin, 2001). Examining the life-roles of Native American college students, Brown and Lavish (2006) reported that indicators of life role salience (participation, commitment, and values) were more important for the role of worker than for the role of community service. However, participation in and commitment to home and family were stronger than they were to work. Maintaining ties to home and dealing with the different value systems of home versus the broader culture were important factors in successful career development. Studies such as these provide information that can be used to test existing theories of adult career development as they apply to individuals from different cultural backgrounds, or they can be used to develop new theories.

Together with research studies, there have been efforts to apply theory, assessment techniques, and new approaches to culturally diverse populations. Super's Career Development Assessment and Counseling (C-DAC) system has been expanded to include culturally sensitive interventions (Hartung et al., 1998; Herr, Cramer, & Niles, 2004). The C-DAC system includes attention to the interplay of universal, group (cross-cultural), and individual factors for clients. Also, the C-DAC model can include attention to the degree to which clients integrate their cultural background with the majority culture (acculturation). The C-DAC model also discusses collectivism, which is found in many nonwhite cultures that value the group more than the individual. Other authors (McCollum, 1998; Walsh & Bingham, 2001) have taken a broader view of strategies for counseling African Americans, discussing social, political, and cultural issues, as well as specific issues such as the accessibility of career counseling to African American clients. The Perceived Occupational Opportunity Scale and the Perceived Occupational Discrimination Scale were developed out of an awareness of barriers that African Americans encounter when trying to enter the job market (Chung & Harmon, 1999; Burkard, Boticki, & Madson, 2002). All of these approaches are innovative in their application to culturally diverse populations. Of these applications, the C-DAC model is most closely related to Super's theory.

For each cultural group, it can be argued that there are aspects of that culture that make the application of career theory—in this case, life-stage theory—inappropriate. A good example of this line of thinking is that of Cheatham (1990), who contrasts "Africentrism" with "Eurocentrism." Cheatham argues that African American culture differs from majority American culture in that interdependence, communalism, and concern about others in the group are valued over autonomy and competitiveness. These concepts are similar to "collectivism," which was described previously in the C-DAC culturally sensitive model (Hartung et al., 1998). This difference may manifest itself in that African Americans are overrepresented in the social and behavioral sciences, including many of the helping professions. Cheatham also states that Africentrism may explain differences in management styles of African Americans and their relationships with coworkers. Since Cheatham's work, several different measures of Africentrism have been developed, such as a projective measure of African racial identity (Azibo, 2006) and the Africentrism Scale and the Racial Identity Scale (Cokley, 2005). The work of Vondracek and colleagues, as described in Chapter 8, emphasizes the social and historical context of individual development that can be considered when using Super's life-stage theory. Another approach is to look at developmental issues that affect all groups that are not in the majority culture.

Use of the minority identity development model (Atkinson, Morten, & Sue, 1998; Diller, 2007) may help in the conceptual application of Super's theory to different populations. There has been little research on the theory, yet it is included because of the balance that it provides to life-stage theory. Not being a career- or age-related theory, the minority identity development model is less specific in its use than other models or theories described in this book. Outlined in Table 9.3, the minority identity development model emphasizes the attitude toward self, toward others of the same minority, toward others of different minorities, and toward the dominant culture for an individual in a minority group (Diller, 2007). Atkinson, Morten, and Sue (1998) describe five stages that individuals go through in dealing with their attitude toward self and others. In the conformity stage, minority individuals generally prefer the values of the majority culture to the values of their own culture. In the second stage, the dissonance stage, the minority individual, through information and experience, encounters conflict and confusion between the values of his or her minority culture and those of the dominant culture. In the third stage, the resistance and immersion stage, an individual rejects the dominant culture and embraces the minority culture. In the fourth stage, the introspection stage, the minority individual begins to question his or her total acceptance of the minority culture. In the last stage, the synergetic articulation and awareness stage, minority individuals incorporate the cultural values of both the dominant group and other minorities; they develop a desire to abolish all forms of oppression.

When discussing this model, Atkinson, Morten, and Sue (1998) are clear that not all minorities start in with the first stage or finish in the fifth stage. Furthermore, not all stages are experienced in the order in which they are described in Table 9.3. However, being aware that these issues can take place among minority group members at virtually any time during their lifetime can add to the effectiveness of using Super's developmental theory with minority group members.

To demonstrate integrating the minority identity development model with Super's life-span theory, some examples are given for each of Super's basic career development stages. In the exploration stage, counselors not only need to consider assessment of abilities, interests, and values, together with career information, but they must also be aware of the attitudes of the individual toward himself or herself and others. For example, an individual in the conformity stage may have a self-deprecating attitude, which may make it difficult to appropriately assess abilities, interests, and values. Other individuals in the conformity stage may not attend to the existence of real discrimination that may be operating in the workplace and

TABLE 9.3 | SUMMARY OF MINORITY IDENTITY DEVELOPMENT MODEL

Stages of Minority Development Model	Attitude Toward Self	Attitude Toward Others of the Same Minority	Attitude Toward Others of Different Minority	Attitude Toward Dominant Group
Stage 1—Conformity	Self-depreciating	Group-depreciating	Discriminatory	Group-appreciating
Stage 2—Dissonance	Conflict between self-depreciating and self-appreciating	Conflict between group-depreciating and group-appreciating	Conflict between dominant views held by minority hierarchy and feelings of shared experience	Conflict between group-appreciating and group-depreciating
Stage 3—Resistance and immersion	Self-appreciating	Group-appreciating	Conflict between feelings of empathy for other minority experiences and feelings of culturo-centrism	Group-depreciating
Stage 4—Introspection	Concern with basis of self-appreciation	Concern with nature of unequivocal appreciation	Concern with ethnocentric basis for judging others	Concern with the basis of group depreciation
Stage 5—Synergetic articulation and awareness	Self-appreciating	Group-appreciating	Group-appreciating	Selective appreciation

Source: From *Counseling American Minorities* (6th ed.) by Donald R. Atkinson, George Morten, and Derald Wing Sue. Copyright © 1997. Reprinted by permission of the McGraw-Hill Companies.

may instead blame themselves for the problems that they encounter. Someone in the resistance and immersion stage may be unduly suspicious of the counselor's advice and information about the world of work. Also, implementing a career choice can be difficult if an individual has to deal with employers who are in the dominant group. Making a place for oneself in an organization when one resists or is angry at colleagues and supervisors can be extremely difficult. Likewise, in the maintenance stage, when an individual has to update knowledge and innovate, not respecting the values of the organization with which one is working can create identity confusion. If an individual is in the dissonance stage or the resistance and immersion stage and is going through Super's disengagement phase, this can be a traumatic process. One can feel quite isolated and not valued at the end of one's career. At any of Super's stages, an individual from a minority group who experiences dissonance will have more problems to contend with in terms of adjustment to his or her job and the majority culture values it supports than will a majority group member. Atkinson, Morten, and Sue (1998) provide a model that can add dimensionality to career issues for people from diverse cultures.

COUNSELOR ISSUES

By focusing on the comparative life-span development of the counselor and the client, we can identify potential difficulties for counselors. For example, a counselor who has just completed graduate school and is in Super's implementation substage may be confronted with a client who is planning retirement. Both the counselor and the client may worry about the gap in age. The client may feel, "How can the counselor help me? He hasn't worked; he hasn't raised a family into adulthood. How can he possibly know what it's like to retire?" A beginning counselor may share those feelings. An answer to these concerns is the counselor's ability to understand the unique situation by listening to the content and the feeling of the client's concerns. Also, by having knowledge of the context of the situation, such as retirement benefits, pension plan information, and other concrete information, the counselor can react to this criticism. Furthermore, knowledge of the life-span issues of people in the disengagement phase is likely to make the counselor feel more comfortable.

A different type of issue may arise when the counselor is in the disengagement stage and the client is in the exploration stage. Young clients may question whether a 65-year-old counselor can help them, because the client is just at the start of his or her career. Again, the counselor's understanding of the client's knowledge of career development issues and occupational information will help to cross the age barrier. Although the counselor may be in the disengagement phase in terms of life span, that does not mean that she or he will disengage from the client in counseling. One of the indications of a good counselor is the ability to put one's own life issues aside so that one's counseling can be effective. If life-role or life-stage issues impede the counselor's ability to listen to and help the client, then that counselor should seek counseling for himself or herself and consider temporarily or permanently removing himself or herself from the role of counselor.

SUMMARY

Career development issues for adults may be exceedingly complex. Commitment to, participation in, and value of the roles of studying, working, community service, home and family, and leisure may be much more difficult than in adolescence and childhood, when individuals spend the majority of their time doing study and leisure activities. Throughout the life span, the importance of roles may change, varying with the stages. When one is first exploring the type of work that he or she would enjoy and trying to choose among occupations, the career concerns are different from when one is trying to establish oneself in a job, trying to become a dependable worker, and learning how to advance in the profession. Likewise, maintaining a position in an organization, which includes updating knowledge and innovating new processes or ideas, may create a different type of stress and conflict from when one is exploring or establishing oneself. Also, the process of disengagement or retiring from a career forces individuals to look at their life roles differently than they did before. At any point, individuals may wish to, or may be forced to, consider change in their career or lifestyle. This may mean recycling through previous stages. For some people, this is traumatic and may be quite difficult. The career crisis or transition that occurs is the subject of Chapter 10.

REFERENCES

Atchley, R. C. (2003). Why most people cope well with retirement. In J. L. Ronch & J. A. Goldfield (Eds.), *Mental wellness in aging: Strengths-based approaches* (pp. 123–138). Baltimore, MD: Health Professions Press.

Atkinson, D. R., Morten, G., & Sue, D. W. (1998). *Counseling American minorities: A cross-cultural perspective* (5th ed.). New York: McGraw-Hill.

Azibo, D. A. (2006). An African-centered rudimentary model of racial identity in African descent people and the validation of projective techniques for its measurement. *Humboldt Journal of Social Relations, 30*(1), 145–176.

Bardwick, J. (1980). The seasons of a woman's life. In D. McGuigan (Ed.), *Women's lives: New theory, research, and policy* (pp. 35–57). Ann Arbor, MI: University of Michigan, Center for Continuing Education of Women.

Betz, N. E. (2002). Explicating an ecological approach to the career development of women. *Career Development Quarterly, 50,* 335–338.

Brott, P. E. (2005). A constructivist look at life roles. *The Career Development Quarterly, 54*(2), 138–149.

Brown, C., & Lavish, L. A. (2006). Career assessment with Native Americans: Role salience and career decision-making self-efficacy. *Journal of Career Assessment, 14*(1), 116–129.

Brown, M. T., Eisenberg, A. I., & Sawilowsky, S. S. (1997). Traditionality and the discriminating effect of expectations of occupational success and occupational values for women within math-oriented fields. *Journal of Vocational Behavior, 50,* 418–431.

Burkard, A. W., Boticki, M. A., & Madson, M. B. (2002). Workplace discrimination, prejudice, and diversity measurement: A review of instrumentation. *Journal of Career Assessment, 10,* 343–366.

Cheatham, H. E. (1990). Africentricity and career development of African Americans. *Career Development Quarterly, 38,* 334–346.

Chung, Y. B., Baskin, M. L., & Case, A. B. (1999). Career development of Black males: Case studies. *Journal of Career Development, 25,* 161–171.

Chung, Y. B., & Harmon, L. W. (1999). Assessment of perceived occupational opportunity for Black Americans. *Journal of Career Assessment*, 7, 45–62.

Cokley, K. O. (2005). Racial(ized) identity, ethnic identity, and Afrocentric values: Conceptual and methodological challenges in understanding African American identity. *Journal of Counseling Psychology*, 52(4), 517–526.

Coogan, P. A., & Chen, C. P. (2007). Career development and counselling for women: Connecting theories to practice. *Counselling Psychology Quarterly*, 20(2), 191–204.

Cook, E. P., Heppner, M. J., & O'Brien, K. M. (2002a). Career development of women of color and white women: Assumptions, conceptualizations, and interventions from an ecological perspective. *Career Development Quarterly*, 50, 291–305.

Cook, E. P., Heppner, M. J., & O'Brien, K. M. (2002b). Feminism and women's career development: An ecological perspective. In S. G. Niles (Ed.), *Adult career development: Concepts, issues, and practices* (3rd ed., pp. 168–189). Columbus, OH: National Career Development Association.

Cook, E. P., Heppner, M. J., & O'Brien, K. M. (2005). Multicultural and gender influences in women's career development: An ecological perspective. *Journal of Multicultural Counseling and Development. Special Issue: Multicultural career counseling*, 33(3), 165–179.

Cordes, T. L., & Howard, R. W. (2005). Concepts of work, leisure and retirement in adults with an intellectual disability. *Education and Training in Developmental Disabilities*, 40(2), 99–108.

Crites, J. O. (1979). *Career adjustment and development inventory*. College Park, MD: Gumpert.

Cron, E. A. (2001). Job satisfaction in dual-career women at three family life cycle stages. *Journal of Career Development*, 28, 17–29.

Diller, J. V. (2007). *Cultural diversity* (3rd ed.). Belmont, CA: Thomson-Brooks/Cole.

Erikson, E. H. (1963). *Childhood and society* (2nd ed.). New York: Norton.

Farmer, H. S. (1997a). Gender differences in career development. In H. S. Farmer (Ed.). *Diversity and women's career development: From adolescence to adulthood. Women's mental health and development* (Vol. 2., pp. 127–158). Thousand Oaks, CA: Sage.

Farmer, H. S. (1997b). Why women don't persist in their high school aspirations. In H. S. Farmer (Ed.), *Diversity and women's career development: From adolescence to adulthood. Women's mental health and development* (Vol. 2., pp. 62–80). Thousand Oaks, CA: Sage.

Fassinger, R. E. (2005). Theoretical issues in the study of women's career development: Building bridges in a brave new world. In B. W. Walsh & M. L. Savickas (Eds.). *Handbook of vocational psychology: Theory, research, and practice* (3rd ed., pp. 85–124). Mahwah, NJ: Lawrence Erlbaum.

Goldberg, E., & Beitz, J. M. (2007). Aging after retirement: A social psychological process. *Activities, Adaptation & Aging*, 31(1), 41–54.

Gomez, M. J., Fassinger, R. E., Prosser, J., Cooke, K., Mejia, B., & Luna, J. (2001). Voces abriend caminos (voices forging paths): A qualitative study of the career development of notable Latinas. *Journal of Counseling Psychology*, 48, 286–300.

Gowan, M., & Trevine, M. (1998). An examination of gender differences in Mexican American attitudes toward family and career roles. *Sex Roles*, 38, 1079–1093.

Gribbons, W. D., & Lohnes, P. R. (1968). *Emerging careers*. New York: Teachers College Press.

Hackbarth, J., & Mathay, G. (1991). An evaluation of two work values assessment instruments for use with hearing impaired college students. *Journal of the American Deafness and Rehabilitation Association*, 24, 88–97.

Hartung, P. J. (2002). Cultural context in career theory and practice: Role salience and values. *Career Development Quarterly*, 51, 12–25.

Hartung, P. J., Vandiver, B. J., Leong, F. T., Pope, M., Niles, S. G., & Farrow, B. (1998). Appraising cultural identity in career-development assessment and counseling. *Career Development Quarterly, 46,* 276–293.

Heppner, M. J., Davidson, M. M., & Scott, A. B. (2003). The ecology of women's career barriers: Creating social justice through systematic intervention. In M. Kopala & M. A. Keitel (Eds.), *Handbook of counseling women* (pp. 173–184). Thousand Oaks, CA: Sage.

Herr, E. L., Cramer, S. H., & Niles, S. G. (2004). *Career guidance and counseling through the lifespan: Systematic approaches* (6th ed). Boston: Allyn & Bacon.

Huang, Q., & Sverke, M. (2007). Women's occupational career patterns over 27 years: Relations to family of origin, life careers, and wellness. *Journal of Vocational Behavior, 70*(2), 369–397.

Jackson, A. P., & Scharman, J. S. (2002). Constructing family friendly careers: Mother's experience. *Journal of Counseling and Development, 80,* 180–187.

Johnson, M. K. (2001). Change in job values during the transition to adulthood. *Work &Occupations, 28,* 315–345.

Jonsson, H., Josephsson, S., & Kielhofner, G. (2001). Narratives and experience in an occupational transition: A longitudinal study of the retirement process. *American Journal of Occupational Therapy, 55,* 424–434.

Juntunen, C. L., Barraclough, D. J., Broneck, C. L., Seibel, G. A., Winrow, S. A., & Morin, P. M. (2001). American Indian perspectives on the career journey. *Journal of Counseling Psychology, 48,* 274–285.

Kimmel, D., Rose, T., & David, S. (Eds.). (2006). *Lesbian, gay, bisexual, and transgender aging: Research and clinical perspectives.* New York: Columbia University Press.

Lahner, J. M. (2005). The impact of downsizing on survivors' career development: A test of Super's theory. *Dissertation Abstracts International: Section B: The Sciences and Engineering, 65*(8-B), 4293.

Levinson, D. J., Darrow, C. N., Klein, E. B., Levinson, M. H., & McKye, B. (1978). *The seasons of a man's life.* New York: Knopf.

Liptak, J. J. (2000). *Treatment planning in career counseling.* Pacific Grove, CA: Brooks/Cole.

Marks, G., & Houston, D. M. (2002). The determinants of young women's intentions about education, career development and family life. *Journal of Education & Work, 15,* 321–336.

McCollum, V. J. C. (1998). Career development issues and strategies for counseling African Americans. *Journal of Career Development, 25,* 41–52.

McDonald, S. (2005). Patterns of informal job matching across the life course: Entry-level, reentry-level, and elite non-searching. *Sociological Inquiry, 75*(3), 403–428.

Naidoo, A. V., Bowman, S. L., & Gerstein, L. H. (1998). Demographics, causality, work salience, and the career maturity of African American students: A causal model. *Journal of Vocational Behavior, 53,* 15–27.

Nevill, D. D., & Calvert, P. D. (1996). Career assessment and the Salience Inventory. *Journal of Career Assessment, 4,* 399–412.

Nevill, D. D., & Kruse, S. J. (1996). Career assessment and the Values Scale. *Journal of Career Assessment, 4,* 383–397.

Nevill, D. D., & Super, D. E. (1986). *The Salience Inventory: Theory, application and research.* Palo Alto, CA: Consulting Psychologists Press.

Niles, S. G., Anderson, W. P., Jr., & Goodnough, G. (1998). Exploration to foster career development. *Career Development Quarterly, 46,* 262–275.

Niles, S. G., Anderson, W. P., Jr., Hartung, P. J., & Staton, A. R. (1999). Identifying client types from Adult Career Concerns Inventory scores. *Journal of Career Development, 25,* 173–185.

Niles, S. G., & Goodnough, G. E. (1996). Life-role salience and values: A review of recent research. *Career Development Quarterly, 45,* 65–86.

Niles, S. G., Lewis, D. M., & Hartung, P. J. (1997). Using the Adult Career Concerns Inventory to measure task involvement. *Career Development Quarterly, 46,* 87–97.

Pavalko, E. K., & Gong, F. (2005). Work and family issues for midlife women. In S. M. Bianchi, L. M. Casper, & King, B. R. (Eds.), *Work, family, health, and well-being* (pp. 379–393). Mahwah, NJ: Lawrence Erlbaum.

Pearson, S. M., & Bieschke, K. J. (2001). Succeeding against the odds: An examination of familial influences on the career development of professional African American women. *Journal of Counseling Psychology, 48,* 301–309.

Perrone, K. M. (2005). Work-family interface for same-sex, dual-earner couples: Implications for counselors. *The Career Development Quarterly, 53*(4), 317–324.

Perrone, K. M., Webb, L. K., & Blalock, R. H. (2005). The effects of role congruence and role conflict on work, marital, and life satisfaction. *Journal of Career Development, 31*(4), 225–238.

Power, S. J., & Rothausen, T. J. (2003). The work-oriented midcareer development model: An extension of Super's maintenance stage. *The Counseling Psychologist, 31,* 157–197.

Raley, S. B., Mattingly, M. J., & Bianchi, S. M. (2006). How dual are dual-income couples? Documenting change from 1970 to 2001. *Journal of Marriage and Family, 68*(1), 11–28.

Rottinghaus, P. J., & Zytowski, D. G. (2006). Commonalities between adolescents' work values and interests. *Measurement and Evaluation in Counseling and Development. Special Issue: Interest measurement, 38*(4), 211–221.

Schlossberg, N. K. (2004). *Retire smart, retire happy: Finding your true path in life.* Washington, DC: American Psychological Association.

Smart, R. M., & Peterson, C. C. (1994). Super's stages and four-factor structure of the Adult Career Concerns Inventory in an Australian sample. *Measurement and Evaluation in Counseling and Development, 26,* 243–257.

Smart, R. M., & Peterson, C. C. (1997). Super's career stages and the decision to change careers. *Journal of Vocational Behavior, 51,* 358–374.

Sterns, H. L., & Subich, L. M. (2005). Counseling for retirement. In S. D. Brown & R. W. Lent (Eds.), *Career Development and counseling: Putting theory and research to work* (pp. 506–521). Hoboken, NJ: John Wiley.

Super, D. E. (1957). *The psychology of careers.* New York: Harper & Row.

Super, D. E. (1970). *Work Values Inventory.* Boston: Houghton Mifflin.

Super, D. E. (1990). A life-span, life-space approach to career development. In D. Brown, & L. Brooks (Eds.), *Career choice and development: Applying contemporary theories to practice* (2nd ed., pp. 197–261). San Francisco: Jossey-Bass.

Super, D. E., Crites, J. O., Hummel, R. C., Moser, H. P., Overstreet, P. L., & Warnath, C. F. (1957). *Vocational development: A framework for research.* New York: Teachers College Press, Columbia University.

Super, D. E., & Kidd, J. M. (1979). Vocational maturity in adulthood: Toward turning a model into a measure. *Journal of Vocational Behavior, 14,* 255–270.

Super, D. E., & Knasel, E. G. (1979). *Specifications for a measure of career adaptability in young adults.* Cambridge and Hertford, UK: National Institute for Careers Education and Counseling.

Super, D. E., & Nevill, D. D. (1986). *The Salience Inventory.* Palo Alto, CA: Consulting Psychologists Press.

Super, D. E., & Nevill, D. D. (1989). *The Values Scale: Theory, research, and application.* Palo Alto, CA: Consulting Psychologists Press.

Super, D. E., Osborne, W. L., Walsh, D. J., Brown, S. D., & Niles, S. G. (1992). Developmental career assessment and counseling: The C-DAC. *Journal of Counseling and Development, 71*, 74–80.

Super, D. E., Thompson, A. S., & Lindeman, R. H. (1990). *The Adult Career Concerns Inventory*. Palo Alto, CA: Consulting Psychologists Press.

Thompson, A. S., & Lindeman, R. H. (1981). *Career Development Inventory: User's manual* (Vol.1). Palo Alto, CA: Consulting Psychologists Press.

Trenberth, L., & Dewe, P. (2002). The importance of leisure as a means of coping with work related stress: An exploratory study. *Counseling Psychology Quarterly, 15*, 159–172.

Trenberth, L., & Dewe, P. (2005). An exploration of the role of leisure in coping with work related stress using sequential tree analysis. *British Journal of Guidance & Counselling, 33*(1), 101–116.

Vandewater, E. A., & Stewart, A. J. (1997). Women's career commitment patterns and personality development. In M. E. Lachman & J. B. James (Eds.), *Multiple paths of midlife development* (pp. 375–410). Chicago: University of Chicago Press.

Vincent, P. C., Peplau, L. A., & Hill, C. T. (1998). A longitudinal application of the theory of reasoned action to women's career behavior. *Journal of Applied Social Psychology, 28*, 761–778.

Walsh, W. B., & Bingham, R. P. (Eds.). (2001). *Career counseling for African Americans*. Mahwah, NJ: Erlbaum.

Webb, R. M., Lubinski, D., & Benbow, B. P. (2002). Mathematically facile adolescents with math science aspirations: New perspectives on their educational and vocational development. *Journal of Educational Psychology, 94*, 785–794.

Zytowski, D. G. (2004). Super's Work Values Inventory-Revised user manual. Adel, IA: National Career Assessment Services.

ADULT CAREER CRISES AND TRANSITIONS

CHAPTER HIGHLIGHTS

Types of Transitions

Categories of Career Transitions

Models of Transitions and Crises

Hopson and Adams's Model of Adult Transitions

Career Crises Affecting Women

Career Crises Affecting Culturally Diverse Populations

Counselor Issues

This chapter is concerned with developmental issues of adults that include crises and transitions affecting men, women, and culturally diverse populations. From a stage theory point of view, *transition* refers to movement from one stage to another. Transitions may be quite smooth, such as the transition from the establishment to the maintenance stage, provided an individual experiences relatively few abrupt changes in his or her career pattern. *Crisis* is a more negative term and refers to a situation in which a person has to develop new methods of dealing with a problem that has arisen rather suddenly. Definitions by Moos and Schaefer (1986) and Hill (1949) emphasize the suddenness and disorienting aspects of a crisis. This chapter focuses on career crises—that is, disruptive situations that are likely to cause considerable consternation for the individual and may cause the person to seek counseling. Less dramatic transitions also are covered in this chapter. These crises and transitions are described in the context of Super's life-span stages.

There are several models of how individuals cope with crises or transitions (Fouad & Bynner, 2008). Although some are described in this chapter, the model of Hopson and Adams (1977) is used for conceptualizing reactions of clients to career crises and transitions. Examples are used to identify clients in various stages of transition. Certain career crises tend to occur mainly with women and members of minority groups who experience discrimination. These special situations also are examined in the context of Hopson and Adams's theory of transitions.

TYPES OF TRANSITIONS

Reviewing the literature, Schlossberg (1984) identifies four types of transitions: anticipated, unanticipated, "chronic hassles," and events that do not happen (nonevents). Anticipated events are ones that will happen in the life span of most individuals. Examples of these would be graduating high school, getting married, starting a job, and retiring. Unanticipated transitions are those that are not expected. Examples of these would be the sudden death of a family member or being fired from a job or transferred. Hopson and Adams (1977) refer to anticipated crises as predictable and unanticipated crises as not predictable. "Chronic hassles" are situations such as a long commute to work, an unreasonable supervisor, concern with deadline pressures, or unsatisfactory physical conditions. A nonevent is something that an individual wishes to happen but that never occurs. For some, this may be a promotion that does not happen or a transfer to a desired community that does not take place. A common nonevent for women is the ability to enter or leave the workforce. Some women wish to leave the workforce and spend more time with family or other pursuits but do not do so because of financial conditions. Others may wish to enter the workforce as their children grow but hesitate to do so because of continuing responsibilities at home or lack of confidence.

Another class of transitions mentioned by Hopson and Adams (1977) is voluntary and involuntary transitions. An example of a voluntary transition would be the decision to quit one's job as an accountant and become an actor. An involuntary transition would be being fired or laid off from one's job. An anticipated transition can be involuntary. For example, being given a new sales territory may not be voluntary, but the individual may know about it for 6 months in advance. An unanticipated event can be voluntary. For example, making oneself available for an assignment without knowing whether it will occur can lead to uncertainty about how such an assignment would affect one's life in the next few months. Fouad and Bynner (2008) believe that voluntary transitions are often a predictor of successful adjustment to work. In general, crises tend to be unanticipated and involuntary. Examples would be being fired from a job, being given a radical shift in an assignment, or encountering a flood at work. These types of transitions can be sorted into useful categories, as described in the following section.

CATEGORIES OF CAREER TRANSITIONS

In categorizing a variety of different strains on an individual's life roles, Schlossberg (1984) lists common life strains on a person's career, marriage, and parenthood. The career events are classified into three areas: nonnormative events, normative role transitions, and persistent occupational problems. Normative transitions tend to be anticipated and voluntary. Situations such as starting one's first full-time job or reentering the labor market after giving birth can be predicted weeks or months in advance. Many of these examples occur in Super's exploration stage. Another normative role transition is the loss of role. This may mean movement from an occupation to retirement. In terms of Super's theory, this could be construed as the movement (in terms of retirement) from the maintenance stage into the disengagement stage. Normative transitions tend to become crises only when they are not anticipated. For example, a person who ignores impending retirement and does not plan may be shocked by the change of roles forced by retirement. How counselors can help their clients deal with a variety of transitions may include a variety of different work issues such as developing an effective assessment of their skills, handling finances, losing a sense of career identity due to job loss, and interacting with a youth-oriented culture (Bobek & Robbins, 2005).

Louis (1980a, 1980b) has created five categories of normative transitions that individuals experience in work roles: entering or reentering a labor pool, taking on a different role within the same organization, moving from one organization to another, changing professions, and leaving the labor pool. A prime example of entering the labor pool is the school-to-work transition, where understanding the transition process itself is helpful. A second transition may be less formal as individuals move within a company, changing tasks, technologies, coworkers, and/or the actual physical surroundings. The third type of transition may cause greater stress as individuals change to a new employer, encountering new styles of work, tasks, and coworkers. A more dramatic change occurs when one leaves one profession for another; for example, an engineer becomes an entrepreneur, a lawyer, or a farmer. The fifth type of transition is the exit from the workforce: leaving for retirement, pregnancy, a sabbatical, or being laid off or fired. Using a sample of 742 U.S. Navy officers, Bruce and Scott (1994) validated the applicability of Louis's typology as a useful way of categorizing career transitions.

Events and transitions that Louis describes are likely to be experienced in non-traditional ways. Several investigators, (Briscoe & Hall, 2006; Mirvis and Hall, 1994; Sullivan, 1999; Sullivan & Arthur, 2006) describe the *boundaryless* career, in which there may be frequent job rotations, temporary assignments, and transfers from one part of a company to another, making the experience of transitions more frequent than in the past and occurring in more configurations than those that Louis describes. A part of the evolution of the "boundaryless" career is the increase in complexity, both in the nature of the work done and in relationships with coworkers (Lissack & Roos, 1999). Included in the idea of boundaryless careers are those individuals who work on their own but are consultants to a company (Cohen & Mallon, 1999). Such individuals may work at home, communicate with colleagues through the Internet, and work on several tasks with different colleagues. To be successful in pursuing a boundaryless career, individuals should "know why," "know when," and "know how" as they develop competence in their area of work (Eby, Butts, & Lockwood, 2003). However, reliance on self may produce a sense of isolation, resulting in heightened feelings of job insecurity. More involvement with family, community, and religious organizations may reduce the tensions that result from more frequent job transitions.

Briscoe and Hall (2006) describe the *protean* career path that is related to the boundaryless career. The word *protean* is a term derived from an ancient Greek god of the sea, Proteus, who was known for being able to change shape; thus, protean has become an adjective associated with characteristics of flexibility, adaptability, and versatility. Individuals who have a protean attitude about their career are self-directed and make choices based on their personal values. Similar to a boundaryless career, in a protean career individuals are likely to be mobile both within a company and to move from company to company. Scales have been developed to separately measure boundaryless and protean careers (Briscoe, Hall, & Frautschy DeMuth, 2006). The scales measuring the concept of "boundarylessness" measure attitudes towards a boundaryless environment and a preference for being mobile within an organization and between organizations. The scales measuring protean career attitudes include being self-directed in managing one's own career and being values driven in one's career choices. Both protean and boundaryless careers are career paths that have developed as organizations become more flexible, use more temporary and contract workers, and have more opportunities for individuals to work at home. Lips-Wiersma and McMorland (2006) express concern that it can be difficult for individuals to find meaning and purpose in career choices that are influenced by labor demands.

To assess how well individuals believe they have made career transitions, Heppner, Multon, and Johnston (1994) developed the Career Transitions Inventory. Its five subscales measure readiness, confidence, control, perceived support, and decision independence (Heppner, 1998). *Readiness* refers to how motivated an individual is to make a career transition. *Confidence* refers to an individual's sense of self-efficacy in being able to make a successful transition. *Control* refers to the degree to which individuals feel that they can make their own decisions. *Perceived support* refers to how much support individuals feel they get from family and friends. *Decision independence* refers to the extent to which individuals make the decisions based primarily on their own needs or whether they are considering the needs and desires of others. The Career Transitions Inventory may help counselors identify significant aspects of their clients' transitions that trouble or concern them. Specific variables, neuroticism and openness to experience, are both related to scores on the Career Transitions Inventory (Heppner, Fuller, & Multon, 1998), setting the stage for discussion and exploration of these issues. The subscales would seem to apply well to Louis's five categories of normative transitions. However, nonnormative transitions create special problems.

Nonnormative career events are far more likely to become crises than normative transitions. Perhaps the most common, as well as one of the most deeply disturbing, is loss of job. Being fired or laid off is a devastating experience for many people. However, if the work role is not a salient one, it is less likely to be devastating. If a person does not value work and relies on others or savings for income, then the family, leisure, or community service role is likely to fulfill that person's needs. However, for many people during the establishment and maintenance stage, the work role is highly valued. Stability is implied by the terms *establishment* and *maintenance*. When the essence of one's career is disrupted through job termination, this stability can turn into instability. If a person is fired at the beginning of his or her career (the exploration stage) or 6 months before planned retirement (the disengagement stage), the disruptions may be easier to handle. Other nonnormative events are promotion, transfer, or demotion to another job. Although less dramatic than termination, these changes are likely to be most powerful in the establishment and maintenance stages. When these events are unanticipated, as they often are, the experience can be traumatic, more so than both normative and persistent occupational problems.

Persistent occupational problems are career problems that persist for a long period, causing a cumulative effect that can lead to a transition crisis. One example is an unpleasant physical working environment. This might include working in an uncomfortably hot or cold building, in cramped quarters, or in hazardous conditions. Loggers, farm workers, and chemical workers, for example, are people who may have to continually face an unpleasant working environment. Another type of career problem that may persist is pressures on the job. These pressures may take the form of work deadlines such as those that journalists must meet, or there may be pressures to produce, for example, having to increase one's sales year after year. When rewards of the job decrease—in the form of a pay decrease, a smaller commission rate, fewer vacation days, a lack of recognition for performance by superiors, or being given less interesting work tasks—worrisome problems may arise. Another significant work problem that can start out small but fester to create a major problem is work relations with colleagues and superiors. Not being able to get along with people that one must work with daily can create an emotional strain. If it continues, a worker must decide how to change the situation. If attempts at change fail, then the worker must decide whether to live with the stress or change to another job. Although longer in duration than nonnormative events, such as getting a termination notice, these persistent problems are most significant when the work role is extremely important to the individual. Furthermore, similar to nonnormative transitions, persistent problems are most disruptive during the establishment and maintenance stages. How people react to persistent, nonnormative, and normative transitions is the focus of the next section (adapted from Schlossberg, 1984).

MODELS OF TRANSITIONS AND CRISES

Reaction to a crisis or a transition takes place over time. In their study of transition, Moos and Tsu (1976) identify two basic phases: the first phase is directed toward dealing with and decreasing the stress that comes with the crisis, and the second is directed toward attending to details of the crisis so that one can return to normal life. These observations would seem to summarize the general reaction of individuals to a crisis. A closer look at reactions of individuals to a career crisis will help to illustrate these reactions.

Researchers report that individuals often respond to loss of a job with depression, anxiety, and reduced self-esteem (Guindon & Smith, 2002). Furthermore, job loss can affect the entire family, especially in situations where both husbands and wives lose their jobs (Root, 2006). In a study of 756 individuals who experienced job loss, Price, Choi, and Vinokur (2002) reported that individuals may experience a lack of personal control in their lives, a lack of finances, and as a result, poor health and problems in emotional functioning. Falba, Teng, Sindelar, and Gallo (2005) found that the stress of job loss tended to result in increased smoking behavior, especially among older workers. Even though the cost of cigarettes was a difficult financial burden at a time when workers were making minimal, if any, income, the value of stress reduction from smoking was apparently worth the expense.

Loss of a job can result in reduced commitment to seeking employment, more difficulty managing time, less support from others, and decreased coping skills (Wanberg, Kammeyer-Mueller, & Shi, 2002). Job loss can have the effect of increased alcohol use both for those who drank alcohol before losing their job as well as for those who did not (Gallo, Bradley, Siegel, & Kasl, 2001). As bleak as these results appear to be, however, not all individuals respond negatively to job loss.

Often, positive change and growth occur with involuntary work changes. Observing 515 professionals who had been displaced involuntarily, Eby and Buch (1995) note different reactions to this change in men and women. For women, family flexibility in dealing with family, work, and other roles increased the chances that positive changes would occur with the involuntary change. For men, positive growth was more likely to occur if they could avoid financial hardship and emotionally accept the job transition, as well as receive support from friends and family. Malen and Stroh (1998) observe that in their study of involuntarily unemployed managers, women seemed to have less confidence in their ability to seek and get a new job than did men. Being able to positively appraise oneself was an important factor in coping well with job loss, as were problem-focused strategies such as searching for a job, seeking training, and relocating, rather than focusing on symptom-focused strategies such as getting social support and finding financial help (Leana, Feldman, & Tan, 1998; Zikic & Klehe, 2006). Although positive growth may occur after involuntary work changes, severe reactions often take place, and individuals may seek the help of an outplacement counselor.

Outplacement counselors often have several functions. They help individuals deal with the shock and negative emotional impact of the career disruption. They also help individuals assess their current situation, abilities, values, and interests. From this information, they help their clients set career goals and develop strategies for a constructive job search. Depending on the client's needs, the search may be for a job similar to the one that was lost, or it may lead to new training and education. Common skills that are taught by outplacement counselors are résumé writing, interviewing techniques, and locating job or educational opportunities. In some situations, outplacement counselors work directly for a firm or may be hired on a consulting basis by a firm. Less frequently, individuals may seek out the private services of an outplacement counselor to help them deal with involuntary transitions.

Studies of outplacement counseling have found the work of outplacement counselors with professionals to be effective. Earnings of those professionals receiving outplacement counseling have been found to be related to previous earnings, gender, and years working for the previous employer (Edwards, Rudisill, Champney, Hershberger, Polaine, & Archambault, 1998). A program designed to resolve emotions about job loss, enhance self-esteem, and increase a sense of control and competence has been found to be successful with unemployed individuals who had previously worked in business fields (Joseph & Greenberg, 2001). Individuals in this program had higher employment rates than did a comparison sample not participating in the program.

Most approaches to outplacement counseling do not follow a theoretical approach, although some have been influenced by Super's stages of adult career development (Aquilanti & Leroux, 1999). Studies about the content of outplacement counseling, as well as racial attitudes, provide more information on the service provided by outplacement counselors. Addressing the emotional needs of clients who have lost a job is an aspect of outplacement counseling that many clients find helpful, but do not always receive (Butterfield & Borgen, 2005). Examining racial attitudes of outplacement counselors, Likier (2005) found that counselors who were younger and had more multicultural and more professional training were better able to integrate racial identity and cultural variables into their assessment of outplacement clients than other counselors. For individuals who have lost their job for a variety of reasons, outplacement counseling continues to be used as a means of helping with the transition to future employment.

HOPSON AND ADAMS'S MODEL OF ADULT TRANSITIONS

No one model of coping with adult transitions fits every individual. One model that has been used by a number of psychologists is that of Hopson and Adams (1977). Brammer and Abrego (1981) adopt this model in their strategies for coping with transitions. In terms of career transitions, Perosa and Perosa (1983, 1985, 1987, 1997) find this model appropriate to the understanding of adult career crises. Hopson (1981) has slightly revised the earlier model of Hopson and Adams (1977). This revision, together with examples of its use as a conceptualization system in adult career crises and transitions, is described in this section.

Figure 10.1 presents the seven stages of the model by showing the relationship of each stage or phase to mood and to time. Whether one is initially depressed or excited depends on the nature of the transition. Other phases are associated with varying degrees of depression or positive feeling. When describing each of the seven

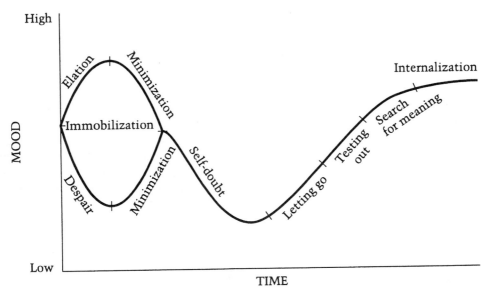

FIGURE 10.1 | A SEVEN-PHASE MODEL OF STAGES ACCOMPANYING TRANSITION.

Source: From *Transition: Understanding and managing personal change* by J. Adams, I. Hayes, and B. Hopson, p. 38. Copyright © 1997 by Sage Publications, Inc. Reprinted by permission.

stages, I use as a continuing example a man who has sought help from his minister because the company that he has been with for 23 years has gone bankrupt and closed its doors. A 55-year-old white man, John has worked hard as an inside sales-person, taking orders from people in the United States for bicycle parts.

IMMOBILIZATION

The initial shock that occurs when one finds out that one has been fired or laid off is an example of immobilization. The person is overwhelmed, unable to make plans, and perhaps even unable to respond verbally. The period of immobilization could be a few moments or a few months. How long the period lasts depends on the nature of the event and the psychological makeup of the individual.

When John first heard from his supervisor that the company was closing in 2 weeks, he was speechless. He kept repeating to himself, "I can't believe it; I can't believe it." He went back to his desk at 3:30 that afternoon. For the rest of the day, he answered the phones as usual, but he was just barely able to hear the customers. His voice was hollow; he did not engage in casual talk with some customers whom he had known for many years, and he did not ask them about their inventory of bike accessories or hardware, something that he would often do. After work, he went home and sat down on the sofa. This was uncharacteristic of him. His wife, who had come home from work earlier, was surprised by the look on his face. Had the event been a happy one, such as being given a promotion or a coveted assignment, the feel-ing would have been elation, rather than despair (see Figure 10.1).

MINIMIZATION

Minimization refers to the desire to make the change appear smaller than it is. Often, an individual will deny that the change is even taking place or will tell himself or her-self that the event really does not matter, that things will be perfectly fine anyway.

When John returned to work the next day, things were, in a physical sense, as usual. The building was standing there; his desk was in the same place. He talked to the salespeople whose desks were near his, but before they had a chance to talk about the news, the phones started to ring. It was a busy day, and although John's job ordinarily provided little time to talk to his coworkers, that morning he had no time at all to talk to them. At noon, half the salespeople went to lunch, while the others covered the phones. John went with them, and they talked about the closing. Most expressed surprise and said that the company was in good financial shape, that there seemed to be plenty of inventory. They could not understand why the company would be closing. A few said that perhaps they would hear in a few days that the company was going to make it after all. John's spirits were boosted; he felt a little bit better that others saw the situation the way he did. Not only was John denying the plant's closing, but so were some of his coworkers.

About 7:00 that evening, John received a call from his minister. Knowing that his wife had called their minister during the day, John was not surprised. The following dialogue is a portion of their conversation:

CL: I was shocked like everyone else yesterday. The company had done so well for so many years, I couldn't believe it.

CO: I'm sorry to hear it. That's terrible news for you. [Although the minister has several people in his congregation who have experienced the same layoff, the minister wants to focus on John's experience, noticing how the event has immobilized him.]

CL: Well, it may not be so bad. Maybe there's a chance that the company will be able to continue and someone will buy it out.

CO: Yes, that would feel a lot better to you. [Knowing that a company does not give two weeks' notice to employees without being very certain, the minister is not hopeful, as John is. He recognizes the denial, because he has experienced this many times with parishioners who have lost jobs or loved ones or have had other significant losses. He knows that this is not the time to argue with John about the likelihood of the plant's reopening.]

CL: I hope it will work. It would be a terrible disaster for me if things don't work out.

CO: I know, John, you put so much of yourself into your work. [The tragedy of this crisis is dramatically clear.]

CL: I have another 12 years to go before retirement, if only the company could hold on.

CO: You feel you need the company so much. [Staying with John's feelings of desperation seems really important to the minister now.]

SELF-DOUBT

Many different feelings can occur at this stage. A common feeling is doubting oneself and one's ability to provide for oneself and for one's dependents. Other common reactions are anxiety caused by not knowing what will happen, fear of the future, sadness, and anger.

For John, after a few days, the principal emotion was anger. When John realized that plans were being made to liquidate inventory, the chances of the company's continuing began to appear small to him. When John came home that night, he called his minister. Having known the minister for 15 years, he felt comfortable with him and had been encouraged by him to call at any time. Their conversation was as follows:

CL: The company never gave me a chance. After all the hours I've put in for them, I didn't get a chance to even find out what was happening. They never told me until the last minute—what a bunch of jerks they are! I can't understand how they could do such a thing.

CO: You're so angry at them. I can hear it in your voice. [John is furious, yet he is toning down his language so as not to offend the minister.]

CL: I can't understand why they would do it. Such fools! It's like they don't care about anybody who has given them service and made them rich. I'm not the only one. A lot of others have been with the company a long time. It's a rotten thing to do.

CO: It feels as if they've betrayed you after all you've done for them. [The minister just wants to stay with the anger and not challenge it. He senses that John doesn't want to hear anything else.]

LETTING GO

As can be seen in Figure 10.1, the individual next starts to let go of the anger, tension, frustration, or other feelings. This is the time when the person accepts what is really happening to him or her. The individual detaches himself or herself from the original situation and starts to look toward the future.

With each passing day, it becomes clearer that the company is going to close. John starts to think about what will happen to him next. He knows that a few of the workers in the plant are being kept on to close down the plant. There is no news that anyone will buy the plant. The company is giving each person 2 extra weeks of severance pay, but no other assistance. The money that John has accumulated in his pension will not be affected by the closing. As he goes home on Friday night, he starts to think about the future. In the evening, he goes through the want ads in his local paper. The next day, he goes out to buy newspapers from nearby cities. He plans to look for work on Monday. At home, he starts to think about what he can do and what he is good at. From Super's lifespan point of view, John now recycles from the maintenance stage to the exploration stage. Although this was an involuntary, unpredictable event, John is letting go of his angry feelings and his desperate denial of the impending plant closing. John has hobbies that he has worked on from time to time. They now become potential career directions. Also, John thinks of the church work that he has done with poor families in his city. His leisure and community service pursuits can now become career possibilities.

TESTING OUT

At this point individuals may develop a burst of energy, a sense of "now I can handle it." In fact, sometimes they will describe the way things should be. They may have advice for others in the same situation. In a career situation, an individual may have thoughts about how he or she is going to network (that is, talk to other significant people in the field) and move forward.

Sunday, after church services, John talks briefly with his minister, who inquires how John is adjusting:

CL: Things are looking up now. I have a number of avenues that I plan to explore this week. I am going to take a couple of days off and talk to some old friends. I have some ideas about opening up an auto garage or working as a salesman for machine parts. I haven't talked to anybody yet.

CO: Nice to hear your enthusiasm, John. [It is a relief to hear that John has moved away from his preoccupation with the company's closing. Some people stay in the denial stage or are extremely angry at the company for weeks. Yet, John's newfound confidence does not sound real. It may fade quickly, but it is a start.]

CL: I do hope that I'll find something. It's been such a long time since I've thought about what I might do. I guess I never thought about being in this situation. When I think of new possibilities, it isn't so bad.

CO: It's good to hear you thinking about new possibilities. It's good to see that spark. [Encouragement is given for exploring new activities that will help John move on in his search not only for a job, but also for his own peace of mind.]

SEARCH FOR MEANING

In the search-for-meaning stage, an individual seeks to understand how events are different and why. This is a cognitive process in which people try to understand not only the feelings of others, but also their own.

Having finished his work with the company and having spent a week looking for work, John is busy following prospects. He has contacted auto supply stores and hardware manufacturers for job leads. He had started out looking at the possibility of opening a gas station or car repair shop. As he learned more about this option, he felt he did not have the necessary experience or capital. He also was not prepared to work in someone else's shop, believing it would be a step down, not only in financial reward, but also in prestige. He is more comfortable using the skills that he has developed in his 23 years of experience as a bicycle parts salesperson. As John recycles through Super's exploration stage, he reconsiders his interests, capacities, and values. This is something that he had not done for many years. As he does this, he sees his job loss as a challenge and an opportunity to improve himself. His understanding of the reasons for the company's collapse is more apparent. Not only does he have more information now about the financial situation of the company, but he is also able to be more objective and less angry in his view of the actions that have taken place in the last 3 weeks.

INTERNALIZATION

The final phase of dealing with transitions, internalization, implies a change in values and lifestyle. The individual may have developed new coping skills and has grown emotionally, spiritually, or cognitively as a result of going through a difficult crisis.

Three months after being terminated from his job, John calls his minister to tell him of the progress that he has made:

CL: It took me over two months, but I finally got a job that I think will be an improvement, a step up for me. I started working a week ago for a very large auto parts distributorship. My work will be sales, like before, but also managing some other employees. That's something that I only did informally in my old job. I really want that opportunity now. Things are looking up.

CO: Sounds very much as if they are. It's great to hear such good news from you, John.

CL: It's been a rough few months. The second month that I was out of work was pretty depressing. I started to lose confidence in my ability to get a job. I wondered who would hire an old guy like me, but I really kept going at it, even though times got discouraging. My wife was really helpful, really encouraging.

CO: The ups and downs sound pretty tough. [John sounds quite different than from a few months ago. The panic, anger, and tension are gone from his voice. He seems to have been fortunate in his resolution of the crisis.]

CL: Some days, I would be really excited about possibilities; others, I wasn't. But I was able to think about what I was able to do and what I couldn't. I had dreamed of owning my own business, but it took a while for me to realize that I just couldn't handle it financially and maybe I really wasn't able to commit the energy that I think it needs.

CO: You really have done a lot of thinking about yourself and your future. [John's *search for meaning* has not been an easy one, nor has that search been one that moved steadily upward; it has been full of fits and starts.]

CL: It's been rough, but when I think where I am now, I am a lot better off than I was three months ago. I feel more sure of myself. If this were to happen to me again, I think it would be easier the next time. Things that I was so afraid of before—like losing my job, and then having to get a new one—don't scare me as much. I think I know more now what I can do than I did before.

CO: You sound terrific. [Hearing John talk this way feels very good. John has *integrated* this transformation into his life. As a result, he is feeling better about himself than he did before the crisis. He has moved past his fears and anxieties to an excellent resolution of his transition.]

Not all crises follow Hopson and Adams's (1977) seven-phase transition model as closely as this example does. John's case was presented to illustrate the sequence of the phases. Many people's situations, as shown by the examples in the following sections, do not fit the model so neatly. Clearly, not everyone is able to resolve a job crisis by finding a better job. Some people facing job crises have become physically ill, committed suicide, found only temporary and inferior work, or never found work again. The advantage of Hopson and Adams's model of transition is that the counselor has an idea of what to expect. For example, if during the second phase a client denies that his job is really important, Hopson and Adams's model is useful in helping the counselor accept this, without believing the client's statement to be one that will be true for a long period. Rather, the counselor accepts the denial as a phase. If a client's experience does not fit Hopson and Adams's model, there is no need to attempt to force it. The career-related crises that are especially applicable to women and to culturally diverse populations, which are described in the next sections, often do not fit smoothly into this model.

CAREER CRISES AFFECTING WOMEN

Three general types of career crises are far more likely to affect women than men. Women are much more likely than men to experience discrimination, to make decisions based on child-raising and family issues, and to face sexual harassment (Fassinger, 2008). Discrimination, when it occurs, is usually unanticipated and involuntary. The effects of discrimination are described in more detail in the example later in this section and in Chapter 3, which addresses sociological and economic theories of career development. The transitions out of and into the workforce or out of full-time and into part-time work are decisions that many women make at various times in their lives because of children and family considerations. Chapter 9 describes Bardwick's (1980) views of child-raising and family issues at various points in a woman's life as they relate to Super's life-span theory. Such transitions tend to be anticipated and voluntary. However, this is not always the case, and regardless of the type of transition, it can be a difficult crisis. An example of a dramatic, unanticipated, and involuntary transition is sexual harassment. Having both severe personal and career consequences, this can be an extremely devastating experience. Betz (2005) and Roscigno (2007) describe research on discrimination, the effects of child-raising on workforce participation, and sexual harassment. The following sections describe the relationship between career and family and the effects of sexual harassment in the context of Hopson and Adams's (1977) theory.

TEMPORARY REENTRY INTO AND LEAVE-TAKING FROM THE LABOR FORCE

Women may follow a large variety of patterns in going into and out of the labor force. For many women, leaving the workforce may be relatively easy. Some may participate in maternity leave programs that allow them to reenter their position. In contrast, others may wish to stay out for a longer period than their position can be held for them. They may have to go through the process of job hunting all over again. For some, a career that was satisfactory before leaving the workforce may no longer be fulfilling. Managing both marriage and career may mean limiting social relationships, increasing organization and delegation of home and other activities, and developing flexible jobs that allow part-time work and time at home.

One solution for women is self-employment. However, working for oneself does not always provide a good means for combining family with work (Taniguchi, 2002). For 25- to 28-year-old women, choices to stay in the labor force were influenced by the amount of their work experience, when they worked, and the positive impression of their work experience (Alon, Donahoe, & Tienda, 2001). In contrast, older women who had decided to retire but then returned to the labor market usually did so out of financial necessity (Choi, 2001).

When examining women's reentry into the labor force, it is also important to consider cultural factors. In the United States, African American and Latina women leave and reenter the workforce more quickly than white women. This happens even though previous job rewards have been less for African American women than for white women (Taniguchi & Rosenfeld, 2002). Yu (2006) reported that women living in Taiwan are much more likely to leave the labor force for longer periods of time because of marriage or pregnancy than women living in Japan. Woman in Japan leave the labor force for short periods of time, often returning to their previous job. The difference in patterns of reentry may be due in part to men's and women's salaries being closer to each other in Taiwan as opposed to Japan, where men generally earn significantly more than women.

The phases that are discussed by Hopson and Adams (1977) may be experienced by women leaving or reentering the labor force. However, for some women, entry or reentry into the workforce can be traumatic. Particularly if reentry is because of divorce or the death of a husband, a woman can find herself in an uncomfortable and unfamiliar position with sole responsibility for her income and survival, as well as the survival of her family. A decision to return to school may bring about a crisis. With the possibility of increased income in the distant future, school can become a financial burden. Deciding on a new career, new training, or a return to school also means returning to Super's exploration stage. When talking with a woman who is reentering the labor force, counselors may determine whether there are changes in self-esteem during the transition.

For example, Mary had been an elementary school teacher for 7 years before having children; she had decided to raise her family and stay at home with two young children for a 6-year period. When her children were 4 and 6 years old, she decided to return to the school system. In February, she contacted the principal of the school she had worked at and made arrangements to teach again in September of that year. Excited about returning to work, she made arrangements for her children to go to school and attend an after-school program.

Rachel, in contrast, had worked as a teacher for 6 years before raising a family of four children. After 20 years of marriage, her husband died suddenly, leaving her with few financial resources and two children in high school and two in college. She had disliked teaching and had not planned to return to the workforce. Rachel now was dealing with two crises: the death of her husband and the requirement that she return to work. Rachel's period of immobilization lasted 4 weeks. She was in shock over the sudden death of her husband. She did not experience a period of denial or minimization; rather, she became depressed, seeing no reason for living. Relatives helped with her children, but some grew impatient. Finally, Rachel let go of her grief somewhat and started to plan for her children. She made some attempts to get work and finally settled for a job as a grocery cashier. At this point, she had no energy to use her interests, abilities, or values. After a year as a cashier, she sought career counseling to help her decide what jobs might interest her. A year and a half after her husband's death, she was moving back and forth between the stages of letting go and testing out, until she finally began to search for what might be most appropriate for her. The above two examples illustrate the wide range of reactions possible when women reenter the labor force.

Sexual Harassment

When it occurs, depending on its nature, sexual harassment may be an unanticipated, involuntary crisis that threatens one's career and psychological health. This section defines sexual harassment and discusses the different perceptions that people have of it. This section also examines who the victims are, how sexual harassment affects them, and what the stages of reacting to sexual harassment are. Also, an example of dealing with sexual harassment in the workplace is provided below.

Sexual harassment is a form of sexual discrimination that includes sexual threats, sexual bribery, sexual jokes or comments, and touching that interfere with a person doing her job (Betz, 2005; DeFour, David, Diaz, & Thompkins, 2003; Roscigno, 2007). Are sexual innuendoes or sexual jokes harassment? Till (1980) describes five levels of harassment, which Fitzgerald and Shullman (1985) built on in developing the Sexual Experience Questionnaire. Listed in order of increasing severity, these levels are helpful in defining the different types of sexual harassment that women may experience (DeSouza & Solberg, 2003). The levels are as follows:

Level 1—Gender Harassment: Gender harassment refers to verbal remarks or nontouching behavior that is sexist in nature. Examples include being told suggestive stories or being required to listen to rude, sexist remarks.

Level 2—Seductive Behavior: Included in seductive behavior are inappropriate sexual advances. The individual may attempt to discuss a woman's sex life or may express sexual interest in the woman.

Level 3—Sexual Bribery: Sexual bribery refers to the request for sexual activity in return for some kind of reward. Often offered by a superior, the bribe may be a higher grade in a course, an increase in pay, or a promotion.

Level 4—Sexual Coercion: Sexual coercion is the opposite of sexual bribery in that an individual is coerced into sexual activity by threat of punishment. For example, if a woman is told that, if she does not engage in sexual activity, she will fail a course, lose a job, or be demoted, she is being coerced. All outcomes are potentially threatening to a woman's career.

Level 5—Sexual Assault: Such behavior includes forceful attempts to touch, grab, fondle, or kiss.

These definitions provide a useful way of viewing the different ways in which individuals perceive sexual harassment. Not surprisingly, males and females are likely to view sexual harassment quite differently (DeFour, David, Diaz, & Thompkins, 2003; Levy, 2002; and Roscigno, 2007). Variables that influence attitudes towards sexual harassment include the sex of the perpetrator and the victim, as well as the degree of physical contact (Gordon, Cohen, Grauer, & Rogelberg, 2005). Men and supervisors, whether male or female, tend to blame the victim for sexual harassment more than do women coworkers or female victims. However, when sexual harassment is severe, both men and women are likely to agree that the behavior is harassment. When the behaviors are shown as being romantic or seductive, then both men and women may have difficulty determining if the activity is sexual harassment. Examining employee responses to sexual harassment allegations, Plater & Thomas (1998) note that men and women did not respond differently to the definitions of sexual harassment, but women were more likely to attribute company responsibility for it than were men. O'Hare and O'Donohue (1998) report that sexual harassment was more likely to occur in a work setting that was unprofessional, had a sexist atmosphere, and where there was little knowledge of formal grievance policies than in a more professional and regulated environment. Interviews with working professionals suggest that some individuals were worried about developing friendships with people of the other gender because they were concerned that this behavior might be interpreted as sexual harassment (Elsesser & Peplau, 2006). How questions are asked about sexual harassment can have an effect on the outcome. Individuals answered questions about sexual harassment differently if the sponsoring organization was said to be a feminist organization than if it was described as a neutral research institute (Galesic & Tourangeau, 2007).

Given the different factors influencing the variety of perceptions of the definition of sexual harassment, it is difficult to determine the incidence of sexual harassment. In a sample of union workers in Boston, Massachusetts, 26% of women and 22% of men reported experiencing sexual harassment (Krieger et al., 2006). In a meta-analysis of 55 samples (of 86,000 total participants) of women in the United States, 58% reported behaviors that they believed had the potential for being called sexual harassment (Ilies, Hauserman, Schwochau, & Stibal, 2003). Of the entire sample, 24% reported having experienced sexual harassment in their work environments. The evidence of sexual harassment varies depending on the country where it occurs (DeSouza & Solberg, 2003). In a study of female secretaries and college students, about one-third of each group reported some level of sexual harassment (Chan, Tang, & Chan, 1999). Those who reported harassment also stated that they had less satisfaction with studies or college work. As demonstrated by this research sample, reports of sexual harassment may vary widely depending on where and how it is studied.

Given the frequency of sexual harassment, who is most likely to be harassed? DeFour, David, Diaz, and Thompkins (2003) report that sexual harassment is rarely reported by male individuals, except at the least severe level. The incidence of same-sex sexual harassment is also relatively uncommon. After women have experienced sexual harassment, they are more likely to label as a form of sexual harassment behavior that they may not have previously classified as sexual harassment (Fitzgerald & Ormerod, 1993).

Regarding age and cultural background, women of all ages and cultural affiliations report sexual harassment (Roscigno, 2007). Relatively little information is available regarding the differences in the incidence of harassment for women of color and homosexual women. Both groups may be harassed for their color or their sexual preference, as well as for their gender. African American female college students report receiving sexual attention based on racial stereotypes or racially based physical features (Mecca & Rubin, 1999). Based on a sample of adult African American women, Buchanan and Ormerod (2002) reported that harassment was frequently both social and sexual, and it was often difficult to separate the two types of harassment. Latinas who have been sexually harassed report more job dissatisfaction, less involvement with work, and more physiological symptoms than those Latinas who have not been harassed (Cortina, Fitzgerald, & Drasgow, 2002). Mexican farmworking women employed in California farms experienced high rates of sexual harassment, including sexual coercion and sexual harassment combined with racial discrimination (Waugh, 2006).

A variety of studies have examined differences in the incidence of sexual harassment in different occupational groups. In a sample of female lawyers, 66% working in private practice and 50% in corporate or public agency settings reported experiencing or observing sexual harassment within a 2-year period (Laband & Lentz, 1998). In a survey of 144 female clothing and textile students who had worked full or part time in the fashion retail industry, 73.6% had experienced at least one incident of sexual harassment (Leslie & Hauck, 2005). Examining teachers of students with disabilities, 40% experienced sexual harassment on the job, with 74% of the harassment cases being perpetrated by students. Most of the sexual harassment was verbal (Heath, Young, Ashbaker, & Smith, 2005). Women working for a large grocery store chain as well as women working in professional service jobs in the health industry and business reported sexual harassment from clients and customers, which lead to lower job satisfaction (Gettman & Gelfand, 2007). Gold (1987) reported that blue-collar tradeswomen were much more likely to report sexual harassment than were women who worked as secretaries, lawyers, or accountants. Interviewing 22 African American female firefighters, Yoder and Aniakudo (1995) stated that 20 reported sexual harassment; of these women, 16 reported unwanted sexual touching. Researchers report that it is not the number of male workers at a job site that is related to the incidence of sexual harassment, but rather the degree to which the work group is male dominated (Gruber, 2003). Sexual harassment has been a significant problem in the United States military, prompting action at all levels of leadership. In a study of more than 28,000 military personnel, it was found that sexual harassment occurred less frequently when men were aware that sexual harassment would not be tolerated by superior officers (Fitzgerald, Drasgow, & Magley, 1999). Examining a sample of 11,521 female enlisted personnel and officers over a 4-year period, sexual harassment was a significant factor for women in the military deciding not to reenlist (Sims, Drasgow, & Fitzgerald, 2005).

How do victims of sexual harassment respond to the event? Fitzgerald and Ormerod (1993) summarize reactions and divide them into two major categories: internally and externally focused strategies. Internally focused strategies include those that Hopson and Adams observed, such as minimizing a behavior or denying that it is really offensive. Other internal strategies include putting up with the harassment, excusing the offender ("He didn't really mean it"), or taking responsibility for the incident ("I should have been wearing different clothes"). Externally focused strategies include avoiding or placating the person doing the harassing. Other approaches are more assertive, such as confronting the person doing the harassing and telling him that the behavior is unwanted. Yoder and Aniakudo (1995) reported that about half of their sample of firefighters responded to sexual harassment with aggressive verbal remarks, and a few responded physically, such as pushing the harasser up against a wall. Other external responses include getting support from the institution, such as an appropriate supervisor, and getting social support from friends or family. Such events tend to affect other work-related attitudes, including relationships with supervisors and coworkers, and general work satisfaction (Lundberg-Love & Marmion, 2003).

Gutek and Koss (1993) document how sexual harassment affects women's careers, as well as their physical and psychological well-being. In a sample of over 1,500 university employees, sexual harassment was related to the incidence of illness, injury, or being assaulted (Roscigno, 2007). A study by the U.S. Merit Systems Protection Board (1981) shows that more than 36,000 federal employees quit their jobs or were transferred, reassigned, or fired after they reported sexual harassment. A large meta-analysis including over 17,000 individuals showed that sexual harassment was related to psychological illness, including posttraumatic stress disorder (Willness, Steel, & Lee, 2007). Other studies show negative effects on relationships with coworkers and company loyalty. Lundberg-Love and Marmion (2003) summarize studies that show that self-esteem and life satisfaction are negatively affected. Physical symptoms that were reported included stomach ailments, teeth grinding, nausea, and sleeplessness. In addition, sexual harassment may play a role in eating disorders (Harned & Fitzgerald, 2002).

Sexual harassment usually is not a single event, but a series of events occurring over a period of weeks or months. Gutek and Koss (1993) describe four stages of reacting to sexual harassment that can occur over time: confusion and self-blame, fear and anxiety, depression and anger, and disillusionment. Wright & Fitzgerald (2007), in a study of 72 women who had brought litigation because of sexual harassment, also found four distinct emotional clusters that are similar to the following four categories described by Gutek and Koss:

Confusion and self-blame: Individuals may assume the responsibility for being harassed. They may be upset by their inability to stop the harassment, which may begin to worsen.

Fear and anxiety: Fear for her career or safety may cause a woman to be afraid to drive home or to answer the phone and may affect her work performance. Her attendance at work and her ability to concentrate on her work may suffer.

Depression and anger: When a woman recognizes that she is not responsible for the harassment, she may become less anxious and more angry. If charges are filed, the work situation may get worse, and the individual may feel despair over her progress on her job.

Disillusionment: The process of bringing charges against a harasser may be long and arduous and may not always have a successful outcome. Many organizations are not supportive of women who choose to follow through on harassment charges.

These stages bear some resemblance to those proposed by Hopson and Adams. They differ in that they do not assume the organizational or social support that Hopson and Adams do. Women often feel powerless when harassed by a supervisor or coworker and may feel little support from other coworkers or superiors in their organization. Women may not report sexual harassment because they feel the organization minimizes it or may retaliate against them (Bergman, Langhout, Palmieri, Cortina, & Fitzgerald, 2002). For individuals wishing to prevent and deal with sexual harassment in the workplace, *Investigating Sexual Harassment in Law Enforcement and Nontraditional Fields for Women* (Harrington & Lonsway, 2007) *and The Face of Discrimination: How Race and Gender Impact Work and Home Lives* (Roscigno, 2007) may prove helpful. In the following example, the client reacts to a sexual harassment situation assertively and with power. Because she negotiates the situation well, her process of working through the incident pertains more to the model of Hopson and Adams than to the more model of Gutek and Koss.

Roberta is a 30-year-old lawyer working in a large New York City law firm. One of five children from a poor Puerto Rican family in New York, Roberta has worked her way through college and law school with the help of scholarships that she has earned. Specializing in tax matters, Roberta has been pleased with her training and is looking forward to the opportunity to advance in this firm, which she joined 6 months ago. She worked for a smaller law firm for 3 years after graduation but felt limited. She was offered a substantial pay increase to join her new firm. One day, as she is bending over to pick up a pencil that fell off her desk, her immediate supervisor, the head of the tax law department, pats her buttocks. She is shocked by what has happened and continues with her work, growing angrier and angrier as the day goes on. When she is leaving at the end of the day, her superior says to her, "Let me help you on with your coat." Before she has a chance to respond, he helps her with her coat, brushing his hand against her breast. She says to him coldly, "Don't do that. Get your hands away from me." He responds, "Don't complain. I didn't mean anything." Shaking as she leaves work, she goes home to her apartment and calls a respected friend who is an affirmative action officer at the university that she attended as an undergraduate. The following dialogue is from part of their phone conversation:

CL: I can't believe what happened today. I've got to talk to you about it. My boss, who has said hardly anything to me since I've been here, touched me twice today—on my backside and on my breast. Can you believe that!? Then the stupid jerk has the nerve to say to me, "Don't complain!" Who does he think he is?

CO: What a terrible thing! Absolutely awful. [Having dealt with situations like this before, her friend realizes that although she knows methods of dealing with such situations, this is not the time to make suggestions. Recognizing that Roberta has gotten over the shock, is not minimizing what has happened, and is very angry, not depressed, she wants to listen. That Roberta's reaction does not fit neatly into Hopson and Adams's theory of transition is unimportant.]

CL: I never expected that to happen. That fool—who does he think he is, that he can touch me like that!

CO: I've never heard you so angry—really, really furious. [Being aware of Roberta's anger, the counselor listens to her, knowing that when it is time to move from this phase, Roberta will determine it.]

At the end of the 45-minute conversation, Roberta finally says, "I know I've got to do something about this. Can I call you back later tonight? I just need to sit down." Her friend agrees, and later that night, they do discuss possible actions. They talk about how to confront the supervisor, who else to talk to in the law firm, and how to proceed. By doing this, Roberta is letting go of her reaction to the situation so that she can deal with it. Being strongly committed to the role of working and being at the beginning of the establishment stage, Roberta, rather than starting to stabilize her career, now has to deal with an extremely destabilizing event. Ideally, she will be able to deal with it in such a way that her superior will be punished and his behavior will desist. However, the possibility exists that Roberta could lose her job and face a lengthy suit against her law firm. The potential ramifications of such an incident may affect not only her career mobility, but also her self-esteem. Being fired could lead to much self-questioning on her part, even though the situation was not of her making.

CAREER CRISES AFFECTING CULTURALLY DIVERSE POPULATIONS

Discrimination is well documented as a major problem in career development for members of minority groups. Roscigno (2007) and Fassinger (2008) describe how racial (and gender) inequalities affect discrimination of culturally diverse adults in the United States. Discrimination is also discussed in Chapter 3 in terms of the social structure of the U.S. labor market. Discrimination is particularly damaging when one is in the establishment or maintenance phase of one's career and work is important to one's self-esteem. Burlew and Johnson (1992) have taken an interesting approach to this concern; they contrast barriers to movement toward career success among African American women. They report that African American women in traditional occupations such as counseling and teaching experienced fewer barriers to success, such as race and gender discrimination, marital discord, and colleagues' doubt about their competence, than did African American women who were in nontraditional occupations such as law, engineering, and medicine. Phelps and Constantine (2001) report that African Americans continue to experience barriers to career advancement in most major occupational settings. Not only has discrimination at work presented barriers for African Americans, but it has also resulted in long-lasting psychiatric symptoms, including paranoia (Palmer, 2006). To deal with these barriers, both workplaces that recognize family needs and families that recognize educational needs to enter the workplace can provide help in making the transition to work (Thompson, 2005). Barriers to choice can present a variety of crises that are affected by diverse cultural issues.

Discrimination takes many forms. Overhearing a customer in a department store make a derogatory racial remark to another customer, even though it is not directed at the salesperson, is offensive. Immigrants may face discrimination when they move to a new culture and are treated more poorly than other members of the society. Being denied promotion, attractive assignments, raises, or other advantages because of racism can be devastating to an individual. When discrimination occurs, a person is likely to experience a crisis, as described by Hopson and Adams. How the individual deals with that crisis will depend partly on the situation, the supervisor, and the individual's own temperament. The model proposed by Atkinson, Morten, and Sue (1998) (see Table 9.3) may describe how an individual deals with a job-related crisis caused by discrimination. For example, an individual in Stage 1, conformity, may blame himself or herself when faced with discrimination by a white superior, whereas someone in

Stage 3, resistance and immersion, may lose self-control and respond angrily in dealing with a white superior. In Stage 5, synergetic articulation and awareness, an individual may be able to effectively confront his or her superior—and others, if necessary—to remedy the discriminatory situation.

These same individuals may go through Hopson and Adams's stages differently. The person in Atkinson, Morten, and Sue's Stage 1 may be stuck in Hopson and Adams's first and second phases for some time: being shocked by the discrimination, and then minimizing it—in essence, denying its importance. The person in Atkinson, Morten, and Sue's Stage 3 may move quickly to Hopson and Adams's third phase, self-doubt, and may experience a great deal of anger. He or she may not move beyond that stage. In contrast, individuals in Stage 5 may move rather quickly through, or may skip entirely, Hopson and Adams's phases of immobilization, minimization, and self-doubt and may proceed to letting go and testing out. Ultimately, they may have a better sense of themselves for having handled the discriminatory situation positively. However, the nature of discrimination is such that, no matter how articulate and aware people from minority groups may be, the "dominant group" may exert its power destructively.

For an example of discrimination as a crisis, let us return to Roberta. If we use Roberta as an example, the notion of "double jeopardy" can be illustrated. *Double jeopardy* in this context refers to the fact that women from minority groups may face occupational barriers both because they are women and because they are culturally different from the dominant culture.

Roberta was able to handle the situation with her sexually inappropriate superior in a positive way. She discussed her experience with one of the law partners who had hired her. Three weeks after the incident, the supervisor left the firm. Roberta had heard rumors that similar incidents had happened to two other women in the firm, but no forthright explanation was ever given.

Roberta continued to work for the firm, was given more and more responsible tasks, and was put in charge of the tax portion of large corporate accounts and wealthy clients. When a senior member of the tax department left to join another firm, his accounts were divided among the members of the department. Two weeks after being put in charge of the tax aspect of one of the firm's largest accounts, the Doe Corporation, Roberta was told that it would be given to someone else. When she asked her new superior why she would no longer be working on that account, he became embarrassed and talked about how another member of the department had expertise that she lacked. Roberta knew that the individual mentioned did not, in fact, have more expertise and that the Doe Corporation had a reputation of being conservative and discriminatory.

Her immediate reaction was shock when she realized what was happening. Having experienced racism several times during her life because she was Puerto Rican, she was surprised that it would occur among people whom she believed to be humanitarian and intelligent. Having gone through the stages described by Atkinson, Morten, and Sue (1998) and arriving at Stage 5, synergetic articulation and awareness, Roberta did not minimize the situation, nor would she take responsibility for it by doubting herself or being depressed. She had observed hypocrisy before in large corporations that stated that they had an affirmative action policy but did not act as if they did. Roberta was able to talk with her superior about different strategies for handling the situation. She talked with him about not making the switch, and leaving the account in her hands. He accepted her advice and returned to a representative of the Doe Corporation to discuss it. She felt empowered by how she had handled the situation and by her superior's appreciation of her advice.

COUNSELOR ISSUES

Two major issues confront counselors when dealing with clients in a career crisis or transition. The first issue concerns the counselor's own experience with his or her own past transitions. The second issue concerns counseling when one is in a crisis oneself. Regarding the first issue, counselors need to remember that each individual experiences a crisis differently. Even though a counselor may have experienced being laid off from work at one time, the counselor may have been in a different life-span stage from the client's. Experiencing different phases of the transition and valuing different life roles would make the counselor's response different from the client's. One helpful idea that counselors can learn from their experiences with transitions is that no one can move a person through phases; a person in crisis works through phases at his or her own pace.

The second issue deals with how counselors respond when they are themselves in crisis. Crises and transformations can consume much energy and time. A counselor going through a divorce or job loss may be able to think of little else. Seeking counseling is often extremely helpful. Sometimes, that is not sufficient, and the counselor temporarily or permanently removes himself or herself from the counseling situation. It is particularly the first three phases of Hopson and Adams's model that require much self-preoccupation. The phases of letting go, testing out, search for meaning, and internalization lend themselves to less preoccupation than do the first three phases.

SUMMARY

Career crises and transitions tend to be most difficult to handle when they are unanticipated and involuntary. Furthermore, if they are experienced at a time when work-role salience is high for an individual and that person is in the establishment and maintenance stages as described by Super, then considerable trauma may occur. Hopson and Adams (1977) offer a seven-phase model for understanding crises that can be applied to career transitions.

Women and people from different cultures may experience discrimination as a type of adult life transition or crisis that white male individuals do not experience. Furthermore, women may encounter difficult situations in terms of reentering or leaving the world of work because of child-raising issues. Also, sexual harassment can be devastating to a woman's career development and sense of self at whatever time in the life span it occurs. Responding to a wide variety of career-related transitions is a fairly common occurrence for counselors or therapists who counsel working adults.

References

Alon, S., Donahoe, D., & Tienda, M. (2001). The effects of early work experience on young women's labor force attachment. *Social Forces, 79,* 1005–1034.

Aquilanti, T. M., & Leroux, J. (1999). An integrated model of outplacement counseling. *Journal of Employment Counseling, 4,* 177–191.

Atkinson, D. R., Morten, G., & Sue, D. W. (1998). *Counseling American minorities: A cross-cultural perspective* (5th ed.). New York: McGraw-Hill.

Bardwick, J. (1980). The seasons of a woman's life. In D. McGuigan (Ed.), *Women's lives: New theory, research, and policy* (pp. 35–57). Ann Arbor, MI: University of Michigan, Center for Continuing Education of Women.

Bergman, M. E., Langhout, R. D., Palmieri, P. A., Cortina, L. M., & Fitzgerald, L. F. (2002). The (un)reasonableness of reporting: Antecedents and consequences of reporting sexual harassment. *Journal of Applied Psychology, 87,* 230–242.

Betz, N. E. (2005). Women's career development. In J. Worell & C. C. Goodheart (Eds.), *Handbook of girl's and women's psychological health* (pp. 312–320). Hoboken, NJ: Wiley.

Bobek, B. L., & Robbins, S. B. (2005). Counseling for career transition: Career pathing, job loss, and reentry. In S. D. Brown & R. W. Lent (Eds.), *Career development and counseling: Putting theory and research to work.* (pp. 625–650). Hoboken, NJ: Wiley.

Brammer, L. M., & Abrego, P. J. (1981). Intervention strategies for coping with transitions. *The Counseling Psychologist, 9*(2), 19–35.

Briscoe, J. P., & Hall, D. T. (2006). The interplay of boundaryless and protean careers: Combinations and implications. *Journal of Vocational Behavior, 69*(1), 4–18.

Briscoe, J. P., Hall, D. T., & Frautschy DeMuth, R. L. (2006). Protean and boundaryless careers: An empirical exploration. *Journal of Vocational Behavior, 69*(1), 30–47.

Bruce, R. A., & Scott, S. G. (1994). Varieties and commonalities of career transitions: Louis' typology revisited. *Journal of Vocational Behavior, 45,* 17–40.

Buchanan, A. T., & Ormerod, A. J. (2002). Racialized sexual harassment of lives of African American women. *International Journal of Aging and Human Development, 52,* 45–70.

Burlew, A. K., & Johnson, J. C. (1992). Role conflict and career advancement among African American women in nontraditional professions. *Career Development Quarterly, 40,* 291–301.

Butterfield, L. D., & Borgen, W. A. (2005). Outplacement counseling from the client's perspective. *The Career Development Quarterly, 53*(4), 306–316.

Chan, D. K., Tang, C. S., & Chan, W. (1999). Sexual harassment: A preliminary analysis of its effects on Hong Kong Chinese women in the workplace and academia. *Psychology of Women Quarterly, 4,* 661–672.

Choi, N. G. (2001). Relationship between life satisfaction and post-retirement employment among older women. *International Journal of Aging and Human Development, 52,* 45–70.

Cohen, L., & Mallon, M. (1999). The transition from organizational employment to portfolio working: Perceptions of "Boundaryless." *Work, Employment and Society, 13,* 329–352.

Cortina, L. M., Fitzgerald, L. F., & Drasgow, F. (2002). Contextualizing Latina experiences of sexual harassment. Preliminary tests of a structural model. *Basic and Applied Social Psychology, 24,* 295–311.

DeFour, D. C., David, G., Diaz, F. J., & Thompkins, S. (2003). The interface of race, sex, sexual orientation, and ethnicity in understanding sexual harassment. In M. Paludi & C. A. Paludi, Jr. (Eds.), *Academic and workplace sexual harassment: A handbook of cultural, social science, management, and legal perspectives* (pp. 31–45). Westport, CT: Praeger.

DeSouza, E. R., & Solberg, J. (2003). Incidence and dimensions of sexual harassment across cultures. In M. Paludi & C. A. Paludi, Jr. (Eds.), *Academic and workplace sexual harassment: A handbook of cultural, social science, management, and legal perspectives* (pp. 3–30). Westport, CT: Praeger.

Eby, L. T., & Buch, K. (1995). Job loss as career growth: Responses to involuntary career transitions. *Career Development Quarterly, 44,* 26–42.

Eby, L. T., Butts, M., & Lockwood, A. (2003). Predictors of success in the eras of the boundaryless career. *Journal of Organizational Behavior, 24,* 689–708.

Edwards, J. M., Rudisill, J. R., Champney, T. F., Hershberger, P. J., Polaine, V. H., & Archambault, D. L. (1998). Outplacement: Client characteristics and outcomes. *Consulting Psychology Journal: Practice and Research, 50,* 173–180.

Elsesser, K., & Peplau, L. A. (2006). The glass partition: Obstacles to cross-sex friendships at work. *Human Relations, 59*(8), 1077–1100.

Falba, T., Teng, H., Sindelar, J. L., & Gallo, W. T. (2005). The effect of involuntary job loss on smoking intensity and relapse. *Addiction, 100*(9), 1330–1339.

Fassinger, R. E. (2008) Workplace diversity and public policy : Challenges and opportunities for psychology. *American Psychologist, 63*(4), 252–268.

Fitzgerald, L. F., Drasgow, F., & Magley, V. J. (1999). Sexual harassment in the armed forces: A test of an integrated model. *Military Psychology, 11,* 329–343.

Fitzgerald, L. F., & Ormerod, A. J. (1993). Breaking silence: The sexual harassment of women in academia and the workplace. In F. L. Denmark & M. A. Paludi (Eds.), *Psychology of women: A handbook of issues and theories* (pp. 553–581). Westport, CT: Greenwood.

Fitzgerald, L. F., & Shullman, S. L. (1985). *The development and validation of an objectively scored measure of sexual harassment.* Paper presented at the 93rd Annual Conference of the American Psychological Association, New York.

Fouad, N.A., & Bynner, J. (2008). Work transitions. *American Psychologist, 63*(4), 241–251.

Galesic, M., & Tourangeau, R. (2007). What is sexual harassment? It depends on who asks! Framing effects on survey responses. *Applied Cognitive Psychology, 21*(2), 189–202.

Gallo, W. T., Bradley, E. H., Siegel, M., & Kasl, S. V. (2001). The impact of involuntary job loss on subsequent alcohol consumption by older workers: Findings from the Health and Retirement Survey. *Journal of Gerontology: Series B, 56B,* S3–S9.

Gettman, H. J., & Gelfand, M. J. (2007). When the customer shouldn't be king: Antecedents and consequences of sexual harassment by clients and customers. *Journal of Applied Psychology, 92*(3), 757–770.

Gold, Y. (1987). *The sexualization of the workplace: Sexual harassment of pink-, white-, and blue-collar workers.* Paper presented at the 95th Annual Conference of the American Psychological Association, New York.

Gordon, A. K., Cohen, M. A., Grauer, E., & Rogelberg, S. (2005). Innocent flirting or sexual harassment? Perceptions of ambiguous work-place situations. *Representative Research in Social Psychology, 28,* 47–58.

Gruber, J. (2003). Sexual harassment in the public sector. In Paludi M. & C. A. Paludi, Jr. (Eds.), *Academic and workplace sexual harassment: A handbook of cultural, social science, management, and legal perspectives* (pp. 49–76), Westport, CT: Praeger.

Guindon, M. H., & Smith, B. (2002). Emotional barriers to successful reemployment: Implications for counselors. *Journal Employment Counseling, 39,* 78–82.

Gutek, B. A., & Koss, M. P. (1993). Changed women and changed organizations: Consequences of and coping with sexual harassment. *Journal of Vocational Behavior, 42,* 28–48.

Harned, M. A., & Fitzgerald, L. F. (2002). Understanding a link between sexual harassment and eating disorder symptoms: A mediational analysis. *Journal of Consulting and Clinical Psychology, 70,* 1170–1181.

Harrington, P. E., & Lonsway, K. A. (2007). *Investigating sexual harassment in law enforcement and nontraditional fields for women.* Upper Saddle River, NJ: Pearson Education.

Heath, M. A., Young, E. L., Ashbaker, B. Y., & Smith, B. (2005). Sexual harassment of teachers serving students with disabilities. *Research in the Schools, 12*(2), 12–21.

Heppner, M. J. (1998). The Career Transitions Inventory: Measuring internal resources in adulthood. *Journal of Career Assessment, 6,* 135–145.

Heppner, M. J., Fuller, B. E., & Multon, K. D. (1998). Adults in involuntary career transition: An analysis of the relationship between the psychological and career domains. *Journal of Career Assessment, 6,* 329–346.

Heppner, M. J., Multon, K. D., & Johnston, J. A. (1994). Assessing psychological resources during career change: Development of the Career Transitions Inventory. *Journal of Vocational Behavior, 44,* 55–74.

Hill, R. (1949). *Families under stress.* New York: Harpers.

Hopson, B. (1981). Response to papers by Schlossberg, Brammer, and Abrego. *The Counseling Psychologist, 9*(2), 36–39.

Hopson, B., & Adams, J. D. (1977). Towards an understanding of transitions: Defining some boundaries of transition. In J. Adams, J. Hayes, & B. Hopson (Eds.), *Transition: Understanding and managing personal change* (pp. 1–19). Montclair, NJ: Allenheld & Osmun.

Ilies, R., Hauserman, N., Schwochau, S., & Stibal, J. (2003). Reported incidence rates of work- related sexual harassment in the United States: Using meta-analysis to explain reported rate disparities. *Personnel Psychology, 56,* 607–631.

Joseph, L. M., & Greenberg, M. A. (2001). The effects of a career transition program on reemployment success in laid off professionals. *Consulting Psychology Journal, 53,* 169–181.

Krieger, N., Waterman, P. D., Hartman, C., Bates, L. M., Stoddard, A. M., Quinn, M. M., et al. (2006). Social hazards on the job: workplace abuse, sexual harassment, and racial discrimination–a study of Black, Latino, and White low-income women and men workers in the United States. *International Journal of Health Services, 36*(1), 51–85.

Laband, D. N., & Lentz, B. F. (1998). The effects of sexual harassment on job satisfaction, earnings, and turnover among female lawyers. *Industrial and Labor Relations Review, 51,* 594–607.

Leana, C. R., Feldman, D. C., & Tan, G. Y. (1998). Predictors of coping behavior after a layoff. *Journal of Organizational Behavior, 19,* 85–97.

Leslie, C. A., & Hauck, W. E. (2005). Extent and nature of sexual harassment in the fashion retail workplace: 10 years later. *Family and Consumer Sciences Research Journal, 34*(1), 7–33.

Levy, A. (2002). *Workplace sexual harassment.* Upper Saddle River, NJ: Prentice Hall.

Likier, M. S. (2005). Outplacement counselors: A study of racial attitudes and multicultural competence. *Dissertation Abstracts International Section A: Humanities and Social Sciences, 66/6-A,* p. 2113.

Lips-Wiersma, M., & McMorland, J. (2006). Finding meaning and purpose in boundaryless careers: A framework for study and practice. *Journal of Humanistic Psychology, 46*(2), 147–167.

Lissack, M., & Roos, J. (1999). *The next common sense: Mastering corporate complexity through coherence.* London: Nicholas Brealey.

Louis, M. (1980a). Career transitions: Varieties and commonalities. *Academy of Management Review, 5,* 329–340.

Louis, M. (1980b). Surprise and sense-making: What newcomers experience in entering unfamiliar organizational settings. *Administrative Science Quarterly, 25,* 226–251.

Lundberg-Love, P., & Marmion, S. (2003). Sexual harassment in the private sector. In M. Paludi & C. A. Paludi, Jr. (Eds.), *Academic and workplace sexual harassment: A handbook of cultural, social science, management and legal perspectives* (pp. 77–101). Westport, CT: Praeger.

Malen, E. A., & Stroh, L. K. (1998). The influence of gender on job loss coping behavior among unemployed managers. *Journal of Employment Counseling, 35*, 26–39.

Mecca, S. J., & Rubin, L. J. (1999). Definitional research on African American students and sexual harassment. *Psychology of Women Quarterly, 23*, 813–817.

Mirvis, P. H., & Hall, D. T. (1994). Psychological success and the boundaryless career. *Journal of Organizational Behavior, 15*, 365–380.

Moos, R. H., & Schaefer, I. A. (1986). Life transitions and crises: A conceptual overview. In R. H. Moos (Ed.), *Coping with life crises: An integrated approach* (pp. 3–28). New York: Plenum Press.

Moos, R. H., & Tsu, V. (1976). Human competence and coping: An overview. In R. H. Moos (Ed.), *Human adaptation: Coping with life crises* (pp. 3–16). Lexington, MA: Heath.

O'Hare, E. A., & O'Donohue, W. (1998). Sexual harassment: Identifying risk factors. *Archives of Sexual Behavior, 27*, 561–580.

Palmer, M. V. (2006). The effects of workplace discrimination on African Americans and their developing psychiatric symptoms. *Dissertation Abstracts International: Section B: The Sciences and Engineering, 67/1-B*, p. 555.

Perosa, S., & Perosa, L. (1983). The mid-career crisis: A description of the psychological dynamics of transition and adaptation. *Vocational Guidance Quarterly, 32*, 60–79.

Perosa, S., & Perosa, L. (1985). The mid-career crisis in relation to Super's career and Erikson's adult development theory. *International Journal of Aging and Human Development, 20*(1), 53–68.

Perosa, S., & Perosa, L. (1987). Strategies for counseling mid-career changers: A conceptual framework. *Journal of Counseling and Development, 65*, 558–561.

Perosa, L. M., & Perosa, S. L. (1997). Assessments for use with mid-career changers. *Journal of Career Assessment, 5*, 151–165.

Phelps, R. E., & Constantine, M. G. (2001). Hitting the roof: The impact of the glass ceiling effect on the career development of African Americans. In W. B. Walsh & R. P. Bingham (Eds.), *Career counseling for African Americans* (pp. 161–175). Mahwah, NJ: Erlbaum.

Plater, M. A., & Thomas, R. E. (1998). The impact of job performance, gender, and ethnicity on the managerial review of sexual harassment allegations. *Journal of Applied Social Psychology, 28*, 52–70.

Price, R. H., Choi, J. N., & Vinokur, A. D. (2002). Links in the chain of adversity following job loss. How financial strain and loss of control lead to depression, impaired functioning, and poor health. *Journal of Occupational Health Psychology, 7*, 302–312.

Root, K. A. (2006). Job loss, the family, and public policy. *Marriage & Family Review, 39*(1–2), 11–26.

Roscigno, V. J. (2007). *The face of discrimination: How race and gender impact work and home lives*. Lanham, MD: Rowman & Littlefield.

Schlossberg, N. K. (1984). *Counseling adults in transition*. New York: Springer.

Sims, C. S., Drasgow, F., & Fitzgerald, L. F. (2005). The effects of sexual harassment on turnover in the military: Time-dependent modeling. *Journal of Applied Psychology. 90*(6), 1141–1152.

Sullivan, S. E. (1999). The changing nature of careers: A review and research agenda. *Journal of Management, 25*, 457–484.

Sullivan, S. E., & Arthur, M. B. (2006). The evolution of the boundaryless career concept: Examining physical and psychological mobility. *Journal of Vocational Behavior, 69*(1), 19–29.

Taniguchi, H. (2002). Determinants of women's entry into self-employment. *Social Science Quarterly, 83*, 875–893.

Taniguchi, H., & Rosenfeld, R. (2002). Women's employment exit and reentry: Differences among Whites, Blacks, and Hispanics. *Social Sciences Research, 31*, 432–471.

Thompson, G. L. (2005). Home to school to work–transitions for African Americans: Eliminating barriers to success. In D. F. Halpern & S. E. Murphy (Eds.). *From work-family balance to work-family inclusion: Changing the metaphor* (pp. 117–133). Mahwah, NJ, US: Lawrence Erlbaum.

Till, F. (1980). *Sexual harassment: A report on the sexual harassment of students.* Washington, DC: National Advisory Council on Women's Educational Programs.

U.S. Merit Systems Protection Board. (1981). *Sexual harassment of federal workers: Is it a problem?* Washington, DC: U.S. Government Printing Office.

Wanberg, C. R., Kammeyer-Mueller, J. D., & Shi, K. (2002). In N. Anderson & D. S. Ones (Eds.), *Handbook of industrial, work, and organizational psychology, V2. Organizational Psychology* (pp. 253–269). Thousand Oaks, CA: Sage.

Waugh, I. M. (2006). Latinas negotiating "traffic": Examining the sexual harassment experiences of Mexican immigrant farm working women. *Dissertation Abstracts International: Section B: The Sciences and Engineering, 67/5-B*, p. 2868.

Willness, C. R., Steel, P., & Lee, K. (2007). A meta-analysis of the antecedents and consequences of workplace sexual harassment. *Personnel Psychology, 60*(1), 127–162.

Wright, C. V., & Fitzgerald, L. F. (2007). Angry and afraid: Women's appraisal of sexual harassment during litigation. *Psychology of Women Quarterly, 31*(1), 73–84.

Yoder, J. D., & Aniakudo, P. (1995). The responses of African American women firefighters to gender harassment at work. *Sex Roles, 32*, 125–137.

Yu, W. (2006). National contexts and dynamics of married women's employment reentry: The cases of Japan and Taiwan. *The Sociological Quarterly, 47*(2), 215–243.

Zikic, J., & Klehe, U. (2006). Job loss as a blessing in disguise: The role of career exploration and career planning in predicting reemployment quality. *Journal of Vocational Behavior, 69*(3), 391–409.

SPECIAL FOCUS THEORIES

Several theories have been developed that represent different ways of viewing the career selection process. Many of these theories have taken psychological theory and applied it to career development. Chapter 11 applies Cochran's narrative approach and Savickas's career construction theory to career development. Both are constructivist approaches that emphasize understanding clients' perceptions of the world. Chapter 12 describes the importance of relationships (parental, family, teachers, friends, and others) in career choice. The work of Susan Phillips and her colleagues addresses how individuals are influenced by others in career decision making. Attending to the impact of people in clients' lives can be helpful in career counseling. Learning theory and behavioral approaches in psychology have also had an impact on career development theory. In Chapter 13, Krumboltz's social learning theory of career development focuses on making good use of chance events. In Chapter 14, social cognitive career theory shows the importance of self-efficacy as individuals deal with supports and barriers to career choice. Chapter 15 describes two different career decision-making theories. Counselors who take a spiritual approach emphasize personal values and beliefs in making career decisions. In contrast, cognitive information processing theory examines how individuals can improve their career decision making by understanding and changing their thought processes. Each of these chapters provides important perspectives that may be useful in counseling.

(postmodern philosophy)
constructivism-individuals
percieve their own reality & truth
*create own views of relationships &
events
in life

CONSTRUCTIVIST AND NARRATIVE APPROACHES TO CAREER DEVELOPMENT

CHAPTER II

CHAPTER HIGHLIGHTS

Narrative Counseling

Cochran's Narrative Career Counseling

Savickas's Career Construction Theory

The Role of Assessment Instruments

The Role of Occupational Information

Applying the Theories to Women and Culturally Diverse Populations

Counselor Issues

Narrative approaches have been derived from constructivism. *Constructivism* is a psychological approach that has developed out of a philosophical position, *postmodernism*. Followers of the postmodern philosophy believe that individuals construct or perceive their own reality or truth, and that there is no fixed truth (Neimeyer & Stewart, 2002). Postmodernism is a reaction to *modernism*, which takes a *rationalist* approach that emphasizes scientific proof and is a reflection of advances in technology and science. Postmodernism reflects a multiculturally diverse world in which psychologists, counselors, philosophers, and others have recognized that different individuals can have their own construct or view of what is real for them.

Related to postmodernism is constructivism. Constructivists view individuals as creating their own views of events and relationships in their lives. Constructivist counselors attend not only to the meanings that their clients give to their own problems, but they also help clients see problems as meaningful options that are no longer helpful. Constructivist counselors deal with the ways in which their clients impose their own order on their problems and how they derive meanings from their experiences with others.

There are two somewhat different views on constructing one's view of the world: constructivism and social construction. Constructivist theories of counseling and therapy owe their origins to the work of George Kelly (1955; Fransella, Dalton, & Weselby, 2007). Kelly believed that personal constructs are ways that individuals interpret and view their lives and that individuals' careers are a major means of giving their lives role clarity and meaning. This focus on how individuals think and how they process what they learn is referred to as *constructivism. Social construction* focuses on how interactions with others affect people's views of the world and the actions that they take as a result of their views (Young & Collin, 2004). Thus, social constructionists examine how people fit into the world of work and how people fit the world of work into their lives (Brott, 2005; Chen, 2006; Savickas, 2002, 2005a, b).

Much of the work on constructivist approaches to career counseling has been done since the 1980s. One reason for this is that the structure of occupations has changed since the 1970s. There was a time when individuals might spend their whole life in one occupation and job. Now, there is less loyalty by companies to employees, more "downsizing," and more workers who are hired in a part-time capacity or as consultants. As Savickas (1997, 2005b) points out, the notion of matching people with positions is no longer as attractive as it once was, because individuals are changing occupations more frequently. Rather than corporations being managers of people's careers, individuals themselves must manage their careers. Counselors can be helpful to clients by helping them draw meaning from their own lives, not just by understanding an organization. In the postmodern age, careers now take twists and turns that did not occur before the 1970s. The career counselor then focuses on careers not as lifetime employment, but as a way of providing meaning to individuals.

This chapter describes two different constructivist approaches to career counseling: narrative counseling and career construction theory. Each of these approaches shares an emphasis on understanding clients' values or constructs (the way they see the world). In the narrative approach, the client is seen as an active player in a story. Cochran's (1997) seven-episode counseling method shows how clients can actively understand their own career story and apply this understanding to actively constructing the future of their careers. Career construction theory (Savickas 2002, 2005a, 2005b) draws from Super, Holland, and other theories to develop an integrative therapy that relies on a narrative approach to career counseling that influences both the assessment of the client and the way in which career counseling takes place. Savickas describes a structured approach that is influenced by the psychotherapeutic theory of Alfred Adler, a contemporary of Sigmund Freud. Cochran's and Savickas's approaches are quite different from each other in that Cochran uses no other theories than narrative in his method of career counseling. Savickas, on the other hand, integrates narrative counseling with other career development theories. Savickas has been criticized by narrative therapists as allowing theoretical ideas to get in the way of understanding the client's story and history. Savickas counters that criticism by showing how listening to the client's story is the first priority in his theory and that he uses theory to provide more ways of thinking about the client both to the counselor and to the client. Therefore, both Cochran and Savickas provide a way of understanding the client as well as suggestions for counseling the client.

NARRATIVE COUNSELING

In narrative counseling, clients narrate, or tell about, their past and present career development and construct their future career. Listening to clients describe their lives and how they enact the work role helps the counselor assist the clients in future career decision making. This is an active approach that attends to how clients intentionally interact with their world and learn about it through these interactions (Young, Marshall, & Valach, 2007; Young, Valach, & Collin, 2002). The narrative model is similar to that of a play or psychodrama, in which individuals enact their lives. The career is seen as a story.

Seeing a career as a story, Brott (2001, 2005) and Cochran (1991, 1994, 1997) suggest that the metaphor of viewing a client's career as a story is an excellent metaphor for counseling. Meaning can be derived from these stories by attending to what clients feel is important or unimportant in their description of their life or career. Like stories, careers contain two important elements: action and time. The client acts or interacts with his or her environment within a time frame.

Viewing the client's career as a story, or possibly even a novel, allows the application of concepts from literary criticism (Jepsen, 1992). The narrator or author of the story (the client) is referred to as the *agent*. There is a *setting* in which the story occurs, much like the background or scenery in a play. However, the setting also includes important people such as family, friends, and colleagues at work. Like a play or a story, there is *action* that is designed to reach a goal that will satisfy the needs of the agent (client). The agent then uses an *instrument* to reach the goal. Instruments can include one's abilities, friends, family, or employers. This is similar to a novel where characters interact with each other to achieve a goal, and action takes place as the protagonist (major character) interacts with others in the environment (the setting) to achieve a goal. From Jepsen's point of view, problems arise when the instruments and goals do not match, the actions and goals do not match, or the client (agent) and the goals do not match.

When there are problems in the career story, difficulties in decision making, such as career indecision, often occur. From a narrative perspective, indecision can be seen positively; that is, as a sign that the client is in the process of making change. Clients are losing a sense of where they are in their story of their life, but they do not have a clear idea of where they are going and their goals. By examining the indecision and sensing the meaning that takes place before acting (choosing an occupation), clients can get a fuller sense of their career pattern. Career indecision is seen as an active process, not as something that happens to the client in a passive manner. Cochran (1991) uses the term *wavering*. When clients waver back and forth they are moving toward finding meaning in their career path. This presents an opportunity for counselors to help clients clarify their needs, values, and aspirations. That is, there is a pause in the story and the counselor's role is to help clients determine the future direction of their story and to clarify the plots within the story. This may mean a change in setting (for example, another career or job, a move to another location) and a plan of how to reach this setting or situation.

STORYTELLING

In narrative counseling, both client and counselor learn from the client's narration of the story. Like a story, the client's narration has a beginning, middle, and end. In the beginning, the difficult or troubling situation is described. This provides the motivation for the middle and end of the story. In the middle of the story, the client describes the obstacles and instruments that may be used in working toward reaching a personal goal. In the end, the counselor and client work together to develop solutions that will help to provide contentment and to reach a goal that will satisfy the client. In using this approach, there are some goals that are implicit in the narrative approach.

GOALS OF ASSESSMENT IN NARRATIVE COUNSELING

The counselor listens through much of the story, sorting out significant data. A guideline is needed for the counselor to know what data are important and what data are of less importance. In a sense, the counselor is like an editor, putting together the significant parts of the story in order, emphasizing some and deleting others. This story will include an emphasis on the client's past life, the current way the client sees himself or herself, and future plans or desires. As an editor, the counselor has several goals in assessing the client's life patterns.

One goal in listening to a narrative is to identify a pattern in the clients' lives. The counselor focuses not on a chronology of events, but on the meaning of those events. For example, a chronology might read, "Started work in a hardware store November 3, 2000. Left job April 17, 2001." In contrast, a story might read, "Started job in hardware store November 3, 2000. Liked my coworkers but not my boss. Was fired for stealing ammunition from the ammo locker on April 17, 2001." In the brief story, much more information is told than is implied in the chronology. The stealing and not liking the boss connect having the job with being fired from the job. Still, there is a need for more information. Thus, stories explain the meaning and events. This brief story would be one of many that the counselor would listen to in attempting to identify the pattern in an individual's life. There are likely to be many plots besides the brief one described here.

Another goal of assessment is for the client and counselor to form a sense of the client's identity. The client's identity consists of both the story that the client tells and the client's approach to telling the story. The client is active in the story, and the client is the protagonist, or focus, of the story. The counselor learns about the client by the way the client tells the story: Is it brief and choppy? Does the client put herself down? Does she make excuses for herself? Listening to clients describe their stories and listening to the unfolding of the story helps the counselor to get a sense of who the client is—that is, the client's identity.

Another goal in listening to the narrative and assessing it is to learn about the client's goals for the future. When counseling is ending, the plot line should be extended beyond the past and present into the future. To do this, counselors need to help clarify the choices that are available to clients. Tasks are likely to include generating alternative choices and explaining decisions to be made. Tools that may be helpful in this process are describing occupational daydreams, writing one's future biography, and writing one's own obituary (Savickas, 1991). At this point, the focus on assessment changes to that of counseling. Certainly, some aspects of counseling occur during the assessment phase, as clients are learning more about themselves, their skills, interests, abilities, and desires through the assessment phase.

COCHRAN'S NARRATIVE CAREER COUNSELING

To understand the application of narrative counseling to career counseling, I will explain Cochran's (1997) approach, which is described in his book, *Career Counseling: A Narrative Approach*. In his book, Cochran describes seven "episodes" or phases in career counseling using a narrative point of view. The first three episodes emphasize making meaning out of the career narrative: elaborating a career problem, composing a life history, and founding a future narrative. Episodes four through six focus on enactment or being active: constructing a reality, changing a life structure, and enacting a role. The seventh episode refers to the crystallization of a decision. The seven episodes are listed here:

Elaborating a Career Problem

Composing a Life History

Eliciting a Future Narrative

Reality Construction

Changing a Life Structure

Enacting a Role

Crystallizing a Decision

Dennis's situation is used below as an example to illustrate Cochran's narrative career counseling approach.

A 25-year-old white man, Dennis has sought career counseling because he is dissatisfied with his current employment. He is an assistant manager in a grocery store where he has worked on and off since high school. When he graduated high school at 18 years old, Dennis entered the Navy, where he worked in radio communications. He left the Navy at the age of 22 years. At first, Dennis thought joining the Navy would be fun and he would get a chance to see the world. However, he was not prepared for what he believed was much routine work as a communications technician. He had some regrets about not entering an officer's training program, but then decided he wanted to leave the Navy. After leaving the Navy and returning to his home in Iowa City, Dennis went back to the supermarket where he had been employed when he was a high school student. He spends most of his spare time racing cars and preparing them for races in the local area. He has thought that he might want to go to college so that he can enter into a management position in the supermarket or retail field, but he is not sure. Because narrative counseling is a thorough approach, only parts of his interaction with the counselor can be illustrated here.

ELABORATING A CAREER PROBLEM   The first step in narrative counseling is to clarify the client's concerns. The gap between what the current situation is and what the client wants it to be is the start of counseling (Cochran, 1985). Not only must there be a gap between the ideal and the actual, but the client must also want to do something about this discrepancy. Also, the client should be uncertain about how to bridge the gap. If the client were certain, then there would be no need for counseling. To elaborate a career problem, the counselor and client work to fill in the middle between the current reality and the future ideal.

There are a number of ways to elaborate on the problem and fill in the middle. The counselor's interest in the client's story shows that he or she cares about the client and the problem that the client is sharing with the counselor. Although ordinary conversation is a primary way of elaborating the career problem, there are other ways. The vocational card sort, described next, helps the counselor and client understand the constructs that the client uses in viewing his own life.

The Vocational Card Sort (VCS) was developed by Tyler (1961), and then refined by Dolliver (1967). Basically, the VCS is a group of 100 cards with the name of an occupation on one side and information about the occupation, such as a description and entry requirements, on the other side. Some counselors have developed their own card sorts using just occupational titles or other information. Typically, these card sorts include 60 to 100 cards. Clients are asked to sort the cards into three piles: occupations one would consider or find acceptable, those that one would not choose, and those about which the client is uncertain. Some counselors may use the card sort technique to choose from a group of occupations to consider for a possible career. However, Cochran (1997) uses the card sort to derive constructs or values for the client and counselor to consider.

In using a constructivist approach to the card sort, the counselor asks the client to first divide the pile into accept, maybe, and reject. Then, working either with the accept or reject pile, the counselor asks the client to divide that pile into as many piles as he or she wants, which reflects a common reason for rejection (or acceptance). When the client has divided the cards into piles, he or she is asked what the jobs in each pile have in common. Then the clients are asked, "What is it about these jobs that you reject (or accept)?"

When the client describes the reason for rejecting or accepting a pile of occupations, the counselor may ask more questions or summarize what the client has said. The counselor is attempting to determine the values or constructs that are important to the client. This procedure is followed for the accept and reject piles. Cochran (1997, p. 45) gives some examples of constructs that he has obtained as a result of using this process, including:

Be your own person, more individualistic
>   *versus*
Too much conformity, too controlling

Confident in practical work with mechanics and electricity
>   *versus*
Lack talent in artistic work

Authority and prestige, being looked up to
>   *versus*
Restricted, being looked down on

Being able to take credit for good results

versus

Fear of being held accountable for bad results

Using the card sort this way, the counselor and client can discuss the constructs that were developed as a result of using this procedure. They may also wish to discuss the occupations in the accept or reject pile and how they fit with the constructs. Thus, the client learns about jobs and also learns about himself or herself.

Another technique is that of drawing. This is an intuitive approach that usually starts with having the individual relax or use guided meditation (Dail, 1989). The client can be instructed to draw pictures or symbols that represent "What I am," that is, a representation of the actual situation currently facing the client. Two other pictures, "What I'd like to be" and "What hinders me," represent the middle of the story. The fourth picture, "What will overcome the obstacle," can be used to see the ending of the story—that is, how the client would like to be in the future. This approach fits closely with Cochran's (1997) narrative approach to assessment.

A technique that fits in well with the narrative approach is that of *anecdotes*. These are short stories that individuals tell that help the counselor understand aspects of clients' lives. The client may tell an anecdote, followed by the counselor and client working together to see its importance and how it fits into a career pattern. In interpreting this story, the counselor wants to be as precise as possible and not just make a generalization.

The following is an example of Dennis telling an anecdote to his counselor:

CL: When I get home from work at the store, my father always has some wise guy thing to say.

CO: Oh, tell me more about that. [The counselor wants to hear this story, even though it is short.]

CL: Well, a few days ago after I came home from work, he says to me, "How are all the rotten apples."

CO: Sounds like that had several meanings for you.

CL: Yeah. He doesn't think much of the people I work with. He hears me talk about these 40-year-old men and women who are still working in the produce or other sections, and he doesn't think that they did much with their lives. He is also talking about one guy, I think, who was in prison for a while and now is working at the store. On top of all that, he likes to tease me about the quality of the vegetables and fruits themselves. He can really be a pain.

CO: You get tired of hearing his negative comments about your work and your colleagues.

CL: I sure do. It's happened again and again. It makes me think that he has no confidence in me, no confidence in my ability to do well in life.

CO: That really hits home for you, a real sore spot. [The counselor is aware that Dennis has some of the same feelings himself and it bothers him to have that theme touched on by his father.]

CL: Yes, you know I am concerned that I am not advancing, that I am not doing more with my life. To hear my father make comments about what I am doing sometimes distracts me by getting me angry at him instead of working on what I need to do with myself.

Dennis shares many other similar anecdotes with his counselor. Together, Dennis and the counselor work to see how such incidents are woven together and fit in with a theme.

Using techniques such as the vocational card sort, drawing, testing, and anecdotes, the counselor helps clients elaborate their career problems. Cochran (1997) also suggests that interest inventories, value inventories, and ability tests may be useful in providing information about the client that can be integrated with information gathered from other sources. This all helps the client prepare for the next step, which is putting together a life history.

COMPOSING A LIFE HISTORY   Exploring a client's life history has two basic intentions. The first intention, which is similar to the first stage of trait and factor theory, is to gather information about clients' interests, values, abilities, and motives. The second intention is different from that of most other theories. It is to attend to the way individuals select and organize their life stories. Counselors listen to the way in which individuals describe their previous activities and the kind of people they are. Perhaps the most common way to obtain a life history is to ask individuals to describe important events in their lives and to discuss their meaning. Often, the counselor might ask the client to present his or her history from a third-person perspective, as if he or she is talking about someone else. However, if this is done, it is important also to use a first-person approach, because it may add more meaning to the story.

Cochran (1997) suggests several ways in which counselors can help clients add more meaning to their stories. In telling a story, counselors can point out, when appropriate, either positive or negative meanings for the client. This is done to help put together a pattern of experiences. Cochran also suggests that counselors emphasize strengths, because clients too often dwell on their weaknesses. When clients express desires that they have for the future, it is particularly helpful for counselors to comment on them. A method that is effective and stimulates finding meaning in a story is that of dramatization. In this method, the counselor becomes the narrator of the story and may refer to the client in the third person. The counselor may do that with Dennis, for example:

There is this eight-year-old boy walking home from school. The neighborhood bully, Wally, is looking for him and beats him up about a block from his house. Going home should feel like a safe haven; it doesn't. He's worried what will happen when his father comes home. Will he get mad or criticize him? So he watches television; he fantasizes about the cartoons and the programs he watches. He forgets himself, but not totally. When the commercials come on the child worries about what will happen with Wally tomorrow and what his father will say when he comes home tonight.

By talking about Dennis in the third person, the counselor is emphasizing the emotional aspect of this event and sets it up to be related to other events so that a pattern can be determined. Other aspects of composing a life history deal with the continuity of the character and the story. The counselor attends to qualities of the individual that are likely to be found in most events. This provides a pattern or a theme for the client and counselor to attend to. The client is the protagonist responsible for events, rather than a passive victim.

In addition to asking clients to describe their life histories, there are several techniques that counselors can use in composing a life history. Four of these techniques are success experiences, lifelines, the Career-O-Gram, and life chapters.

1. *Success Experience*: To develop a list of strengths, or success experiences, a counselor asks a client to make a list of activities that were enjoyable and in which the client felt a sense of accomplishment. Strengths could include basic abilities, skills, special knowledge, or character traits such as being honest. In using the list of strengths, a counselor may wish to keep a chart to see if the strengths are similar to or different from each other and to find a pattern in them.

2. *Lifeline*: In the lifeline, an individual draws a line lengthwise across a piece of paper. The client then is asked to record important life experiences and put them in chronological order on the paper. Each dot is labeled to represent a particular event. This lifeline may include not only the events, but thoughts and emotions related to the events. Mayo (2001) has developed an extended version of this that he calls "life story narratives." It is a thorough analysis of past, current, and possibly future events that are critically analyzed by the individual. Mayo uses these as a part of a course in life-span developmental psychology.

3. *Career-O-Gram*: Rather than a single line (like the lifeline), the Career-O-Gram groups important factors in a person's development into categories, and then draws lines from one to another to indicate where connections exist (Thorngren & Feit, 2001). The important categories include: major goal or actual job, interpersonal relationships, significant experiences, and prevalent themes. In using the Career-O-Gram, counselors integrate information about the individual's life experiences, and then help to clarify the decision process to take action in reaching career goals.

4. *Life Chapters*: In life chapters, the client can be told to imagine that his or her life is a book, and that he or she is to come up with titles for important chapters in his or her life. The client is told not to use common terms such as *preschool, elementary school*, and *military training*. Rather, these should be titles that are distinctive to the client. For Dennis, the titles may be "Wally the Bully," "Running to Escape," "My First Love," and other titles that have meaning to the client and to the counselor. Then the counselor can ask questions about each chapter or period of the client's life having to do with conflict, goals, significant influences, interests, and skills.

All of these exercises focus on the past and, to a limited extent, on current events. Each provides a different method to help clients tell their story to gather meaning from their life experiences.

ELICITING A FUTURE NARRATIVE   In constructing a future narrative, clients consider their strengths, interests, and values as they may appear in the future. This stage focuses on evaluation of one's strengths, interests, and values. Several of the techniques that are used are an extension of those needed when composing a life history. These include success experiences, lifeline, Career-O-Gram, and life chapters. In the success experience exercise, clients can project what would constitute success in their future lives. They can also examine strengths in past events and project activities that they may best use these strengths in. For the lifeline exercise, individuals can extend their lifeline into the future and identify experiences that they would like to have that would make their life complete. For the Career-O-Gram, individuals can try to predict future jobs or significant events they would like to have happen. These experiences would be a reflection of current desires, strengths, and resolution of conflict.

A similar approach can be taken with the life chapters exercise. Clients develop chapter titles that represent important accomplishments for them. If clients use negative chapter titles, they can be reworded in a positive way. For example, if Dennis has a chapter entitled "Not Experienced Enough to Be Promoted," this could be rephrased as "Learning Enough to Be Promoted." For Dennis, chapter titles might include "Managing the Department," "Managing the Store," "Managing My Father's Tantrums," and "Having a Home." These titles provide an opportunity for the counselor and client to explore them and to attach meaning to them.

A technique that often is used in eliciting a future narrative is that of guided fantasy. Guided fantasies can be descriptive, evaluative, or some combination of each. Often, guided fantasies represent an end point. For example, the counselor may present a fantasy of an award ceremony, a retirement ceremony, or going to one's funeral. The purpose of the fantasy is, in part, to help the client reflect on accomplishments that he or she would like to achieve. When using this procedure (Cochran, 1997, p. 88), counselors are likely to help clients relax first, then narrate a fantasy as the client imagines the narration, filling in parts of the fantasy. The fantasy can also be interpreted.

In addition to guided fantasy and other exercises, Cochran (1997) recommends a written and narrative outline. The written report is constructed in collaboration with the client. There are five sections: mission, strengths, work needs, vulnerabilities, and possibilities. The mission statement encapsulates the client's goals for the future. This is followed by a list of strengths, usually in clusters reflecting the clients own expressions of accomplishments. The work needs section reflects the client's work values and focuses on what clients need to facilitate their performance. This section is followed by one that focuses on client vulnerabilities—that is, what is likely to sidetrack the client from meeting goals. Finally, the client is presented with a list of occupational possibilities or descriptions of relevant fields.

When the client receives the report, he is given an opportunity to read it and to ask questions about it or comment on it. This can be followed by the counselor's verbal description of the report. When doing this, counselors ask questions such as, "Did I portray your values accurately?" "Do you think I was accurate in discussing your vulnerabilities?" "Are there any vulnerabilities that you might add?" In this way, the process is collaborative and not limited to the counselor's impressions or views.

When a written and a narrative report are concluded, then the counselor and client can move into a more active process, called *actualizing the narrative*. To end counseling with the written report would be to describe goals, values, interests, abilities, strengths, and weaknesses and not proceed further. In the three types of enactment, clients construct reality, change a life structure, and enact a role.

REALITY CONSTRUCTION   Action is a significant component of narrative career counseling. Whether the problem is work adjustment or making a career decision, individuals need to enact a script; that is, they need to try out a variety of actions. The more active the exploration, the better the chances are for a successful outcome. Reading a description of a job is a good beginning, but it is not as rich as talking to people within a field or interviewing them to get work information. More active than reading is volunteer work, job visitations, discussions with friends, spending a day on a job with a friend, and so on. There are three major purposes to active exploration. First, it immerses the client in the real world. The client has to get things done and check things out. Second, individuals get information from a variety of sources and are able to evaluate the information as they talk to many sources. Third, as individuals talk to people in a variety of occupations about those occupations, they can imagine themselves in an occupation. They now have a clearer idea about possible occupational choices than they did when they started interviewing and talking to people.

For Dennis, reality construction meant going beyond familiar people he knew in his store. A friend of his worked at a large home improvement store and had arranged for him to talk with the manager there. Banking had also been a consideration, and he wanted to learn about customer service and being a loan officer. He arranged to talk to the assistant manager and manager at the branch office where he had an account. Also, he talked to his father's accountant about his work and his relationships with customers. What was new to Dennis was the amount of activity in which he participated. Previously, he would just go home after work and watch television; occasionally, he would call a few friends. By talking to so many different people, he developed a sense that he had more control over the direction of his life.

CHANGING A LIFE STRUCTURE   When seeking career counseling, clients expect some type of change. Usually there is change to the situation, oneself, or both. For work adjustment counseling, clients often expect to make a positive change in the way they work or with whom they work. For career decision-making counseling, clients expect to be in a new setting unlike one that they are in currently. With change come new opportunities, such as training, salary increase, or being appreciated. However, change also can bring more negative aspects, such as fear of failing, anxiety about doing a poor job, and so forth.

When changing a life structure, a theme often emerges. Cochran (1992) calls the theme a *career project*. Individuals perform many different tasks that are indirectly or directly related to their career. They make friends, take exams, pay bills, and so forth. These can be seen as unrelated tasks. However, there may be themes that emerge in the way that individuals go about these tasks. If individuals feel good about the ways they interact with others, manage their finances, and so on, then they are likely to have a positive sense of meaning about what they do.

For Dennis, there was a certain amount of caution in which he approached activities. He wanted to make sure that he understood what he was supposed to do at his job before he did it. More cautious than most, he might ask more questions than his coworkers. With friends, he wanted to have a sense that they were interested in him, and that he could depend on them. With his finances, Dennis was careful to pay his bills on time and not to overspend. His career project could be tentatively summarized as a caution that suggests concern about vocational adequacy. Eliciting more events and more information would help to clarify or alter what may be his personal theme or career project (Young, Valach, & Collin, 2002).

ENACTING A ROLE   Trying things out, or enacting a role, is a way of trying to make one's desired goal possible. In doing so, individuals try out activities that are meaningful and enjoyable. Sometimes it is not clear which activity would be best, so several activities are tried. Also, some activities may not be immediately attainable. Individuals cannot start out as successful athletes. People work toward achieving a role and may or may not meet with success.

Often, individuals start with a small role, and that role develops into other opportunities for more enactment. For example, Dennis used to work out at the YMCA after work in the evenings. He had become friendly with the director, as they had helped some children learn how to use equipment. The director asked him if he wanted to help organize activities for 9- to 12-year-old boys. Dennis liked the idea and did some part-time volunteer work organizing some sports events for the boys. One evening, he was talking to the father of one of the boys about the activities in which the boys were involved. The father asked Dennis if he would like to help with soccer coaching on some weekends. Dennis thought that would be fun and tried it out for a season. By enacting one role, going to the YMCA, Dennis put himself in a position to enact other roles. He uncovered possibilities that existed through his actions that he could not plan. This may or may not have a direct impact on Dennis's later career development.

CRYSTALLIZING A DECISION   Crystallization occurs when a gap between a client's career problem and the ideal or possible solutions diminishes. Sometimes crystallization takes place when clients experience the previous six episodes. Choosing among occupations may not be a deliberate process, but rather one that comes from being active in ways described in the six previous episodes.

Not all decisions need to focus on making a specific choice. For some individuals, exploring occupational possibilities is sufficient. For example, freshmen at college may be in the position of exploring opportunities rather than deciding immediately on majors or occupational alternatives. Other problems may be related to work adjustment, such as finding ways to get along with a boss.

Cochran (1997) believes that crystallization can be facilitated in three ways: identifying and eliminating obstructions, actualizing opportunities, and reflecting on career decisions. Sometimes, there are internal obstructions to crystallizing a choice, such as lack of confidence in being able to obtain a job. Other times, there are external factors, such as pressures from parents to enter a certain occupation. Obstructions such as these represent an opportunity to start a new story and remove oneself from the old story. By actualizing a choice, individuals are taking advantage of new roles and new opportunities. Counselors can encourage clients to accept new challenges in their work. Clients often can reflect on their experience of choosing occupations. Discussing the narrative career counseling process is an excellent way to put career choice issues in perspective.

In crystallizing a career choice, Dennis addressed both internal and external obstructions. An external barrier for Dennis was his father's comments about the unlikelihood of Dennis succeeding in an occupation other than his current one. Dennis also had similar feelings, when presenting internal obstructions, which brought him to consider whether he could handle higher level administrative abilities. When Dennis thought of his ability in managing others at work and the types of management responsibilities that he encountered in his interviews, he believed that he could be successful in accomplishing such administrative tasks. By discussing this with a counselor, Dennis could see that much of his self-doubt came from his father's criticism, and that when he was actually in a management position, he could handle the responsibilities well. Review of the six previous episodes involved in narrative counseling helped Dennis to have a new perspective on his career choices. He was now excited about taking college courses that would lead to a business degree and was looking for new work that would lead to more administrative responsibility.

Cochran's (1997) approach to narrative career counseling focuses on the client's active role in telling his or her story. For Cochran, the counseling process includes seven "episodes." In the first three episodes, clients see meaning in their lives by actively elaborating their career problems, telling stories about their lives (composing a life), and looking into their future (constructing a future narrative). After telling a story about their past and constructing stories about their future, clients then can move into the three enactment episodes: constructing reality, changing a life structure, and enacting a role. With these three episodes completed, individuals then can move toward crystallizing a decision.

SAVICKAS'S CAREER CONSTRUCTION THEORY

While Cochran's view originates in psychological constructivism, Savickas views career theory from a social constructionist point of view. He sees Holland's hexagon and Super's stages as social constructions, and is less concerned about viewing them from a scientific point of view than from the point of view of the client. Individuals construct their careers by giving meaning to career-related behavior. Important for Savickas (2005a, 2005b) is the adaptation to the environment and events that individuals face. It is this adaptation rather than stages of life or maturity itself that are important. One's career enfolds as one makes choices and develops a narrative or story of one's life. Career is a construction that an individual makes. One's career is not made up of scores on inventories or tests, or opinions of employers or family. The construction of one's career changes throughout life and is constantly developing. When individuals tell their career stories, they are producing a narrative, which is essentially their own view of their career. It is this narrative that counselors listen for as they talk to their clients. In his theory, Savickas examines four areas of client narratives. Career construction theory is a meta-theory of these areas. A meta-theory is a comprehensive theory derived from existing theories. The sections below describe the four areas of client narratives: vocational personality, developmental tasks, dimensions of career adaptability, and life themes.

VOCATIONAL PERSONALITY—HOLLAND'S THEORY

Holland's personality theory includes traits of an individual's abilities, needs, values, and interests, which are described in Chapter 5. Savickas (2005a, 2005b) believes that Holland's theory is very useful for conducting vocational appraisals and summarizing aspects of an individual that describe their uniqueness and their subjective self. As Holland does, Savickas makes use of the three-letter code (p. 135). According to current career construction theory, interests or personality types are clusters of socially constructed attitudes, interests, and abilities. In essence, they represent a person's social reputation and his or her own self-concept. From Savickas's point of view, Holland's theory is dynamic and changing; it does not represent stable traits. In his theory, Savickas is not interested in how an individual's personality compares to others, but in how Holland's theory helps both the client and counselor to understand the client's story. The Holland types can be used to generate possibilities to consider and to explore. They are not used to predict the client's future. Counselors may also use Holland's theory to explain the world of occupations to the client (p. 144). The types become an organizing method for categorizing information about the world of work. Not only does Holland's theory help individuals understand the world of work but it also helps them to connect the world of work to the individual's own vocational personality (interests, attitudes, abilities, and values). Holland's six types are summarized briefly below from the point of view of career construction theory.

Realistic: In a client's story, talking about using tools or machines in hobbies or work or doing construction work such as plumbing or roofing would be a common theme for this type. Being practical and using mechanical or physical skills such as repairing or farming may also be found in the stories.

Investigative: The narrative of the investigative person is likely to include enjoying intellectual challenges or puzzles, liking to solve problems that are scientific or mechanical, and reading or talking about science. In their stories, clients are likely to be interested in solving scientific problems independently.

Artistic: Creative activity is an important aspect of an artistic individual's story. The creative expression may include art, music, writing, cooking, or similar types of creative expression. Artistic individuals may have enjoyed and have shown skill in playing music, painting, and cooking. As they tell their story, their excitement about creating artistic products is likely to be evident.

Social: In a social person's narrative, individuals are likely to discuss teaching others or helping others with personal problems. They may also enjoy providing personal services such as assisting others with medical problems. When faced with problems in their stories, they are likely to enjoy talking and resolving complex or idealistic problems.

Enterprising: Making money is likely to be an important aspect of the narrative for an enterprising person. Selling, persuading, or managing others is also likely to be a part of his or her story.

Conventional: Since conventional people prefer organizing and planning in their work, they are likely to discuss this in their narratives as they talk about doing office work, organizing reports, or working with numbers, such as accounting records.

    In understanding career construction theory, it is helpful to note the difference, sometimes subtle, between Savickas's view of Holland's types as they relate to individual narratives and Holland's view of his personality types, which he describes as a trait and factor theory. From Holland's perspective, his concepts should be measured and should be related to each other using statistical analysis. Savickas concentrates on using Holland's types to understand the clients' narratives about how they have constructed themselves and built their careers.

DEVELOPMENTAL TASKS OF CAREER ADAPTABILITY

Throughout life, individuals must adapt to changes as they grow older, moving from school to jobs and eventually toward retirement. Career adaptability is concerned with how individuals construct and manage their careers. Career personality discussed in the previous section is concerned with which career they will choose. The question that is most likely to bring about a discussion of career adaptability is "How did you decide on that occupation?" (Savickas, 2005b, p. 48). The discussion of how one deals with difficulties at school or at work concern career adaptability. Career adaptability can refer both to dealing with issues within oneself and with issues related to society or the world of work. In dealing with career adaptability there are several developmental tasks that individuals must face. In organizing developmental tasks, Savickas draws from Super's life stages (p. 260). The stages in the life cycle include growth, exploration, establishment, management, and disengagement. In Super's theory, Savickas's management task is referred to as the maintenance stage. As individuals grow older, they move up the occupational ladder. Their stories are likely to show evidence of progress to bring about success, both financially and in other ways. However, some individuals encounter barriers that force them to drift or stagnate. Counselors often help individuals deal with these barriers by working with stories that are relevant to these developmental tasks. The sections below describe the developmental tasks from the point of view of career construction theory.

Growth: Before the age of 15, individuals are dealing with stories having to do with the school system and their families and friends. Their interests, capacities, and values are changing. Stories often reflect these changes as interests can be more fully developed than fantasies. Children later develop the ability to judge their own capacities. Their stories reflect their growth in relationship to issues that concern dealing with teachers, peers, parents, and siblings.

Exploration: From about 15 to 25 years of age, individuals are exploring a number of career possibilities. Their stories concern clarification of what they may want to do, how they learn about entry level jobs, how they did in their part-time positions, and whether they want more education. This turns into specifying their career direction. Talking about their first full-time job and the type of encounters they have with superiors and coworkers often make up stories in this developmental task.

Establishment: Occurring generally between the ages of 25 and about 45 years, stories about establishment refer to advancing in one's work. Stories are likely to concern feeling a sense of stability on the job, knowing the basic requirements of the job, and thinking about the job on a long-term basis. Usually as individuals move through this developmental task they may become more comfortable with their job and wish to be regarded by others as an effective worker who can be relied upon. Stories toward the end of this developmental task are likely to reflect promotion and increases in pay.

Management: Stories between the ages of 45 to 65 often include holding onto one's job, while at the same time learning more about what is required in the job and dealing with new technological advancements. Individuals in this developmental task are making innovative changes and showing others how they can improve their performance.

Disengagement: Around the age of 65, but often earlier or later, individuals think about the possibility of losing their job due to health or physical limitations. They may also slow down their work or work part time. Thoughts of planning for their retirement and actually retiring are tasks that individuals may discuss with a counselor at this point in their life.

Although these are common developmental tasks that individuals adapt to, not all individuals encounter these tasks at the same age, nor do they encounter all tasks. Some individuals may choose to recycle and look for a new career, thus entering these developmental tasks at a different age than described above. Also, as the job market no longer provides the type of security that it once did for individuals, they are often focusing more on their own career story than that of a company that they may be working for at the present time. Although the descriptions above are similar to those given in Chapter 9, Late Adolescent and Adult Career Development, the emphasis here is on the narrative or story that the individual tells and not comparison with other individuals.

DIMENSIONS OF CAREER ADAPTABILITY

Savickas is concerned not only with developmental tasks of career adaptability but also the process of adapting. Whereas Donald Super developed the psychological concept of career maturity for adolescents (p. 227), Savickas uses adaptability as a similar psychosocial concept that can be used throughout the lifecycle whenever an individual makes an occupational transition, rather than just during the adolescent's school-to-work transition. Psychosocial adaptability refers to the individual, whereas psychological (such as career) maturity involves comparison with other individuals. For Savickas, psychosocial career development is a process that is unique for each person and does not necessarily move in an orderly way. This is particularly true for relatively high-turnover jobs as well as changes in jobs as a result of technological advances and global changes in supply and demand. For Savickas, career adaptability is a construct that shows how an individual can deal with current developmental tasks and job crises. Career adaptability helps individuals implement their self-concept as they deal with current work and other demands. Savickas describes the dimensions of career adaptability, which are explained in more detail below: concern, control, curiosity, and confidence. These dimensions represent the individuals' readiness to cope with current work demands and to manage their developmental tasks.

CONCERN   When individuals become concerned about their indifference or lack of action on an issue dealing with career choice or work adjustment, they may ask themselves if they feel that they have a future. When they are dealing with *concern*, they are likely to plan for their future and to become aware of the necessary preparation for dealing with a concern. Counselors can be helpful by assisting individuals in becoming more optimistic about their future, seeing their future in some detail, reinforcing positive attitudes toward planning, and looking at the relationship between plans and actions for the future. Practicing planning skills can be helpful as individuals cope with concerns about the future.

CONTROL Individuals, at various times in their lives, may feel they have relatively little control over their own actions and may be unaware of the need to become more decisive and to make decisions. They may ask themselves the question, Can I control my future? At other times they may be able to be assertive and disciplined as they take control of their future. Counselors can help with this control by teaching assertiveness skills, helping clients develop a method to make decisions, and to support clients in taking responsibility for their own actions. Self-management strategies and time-management techniques may also help in dealing with career indecision and taking control over one's own issues.

CURIOSITY People may become curious about their future. They may start to question their choices and wonder if what they are choosing is correct for them. This inquisitiveness can lead to exploration and action in making change. If individuals are willing to explore, they may be willing to experiment with new possibilities, to inquire about new occupational alternatives, to take risks, or to do different types of volunteer work or part-time work. Counselors can help in dealing with the uncertainty of change by helping individuals to clarify their values, take interest inventories, discuss possibilities for changing majors or jobs, and to urge exploration. This exploration can include trying out a job, shadowing workers, reading occupational pamphlets or researching on the Internet, volunteering, or taking part-time jobs. When discussing occupational possibilities, using Holland's hexagon can be helpful in organizing job exploration.

CONFIDENCE Although individuals may be willing to explore and take steps to do so, they sometimes lack the confidence to fully explore possibilities. They might ask themselves the question, Can I do it? They may want to address and try to solve their problem, but can be fearful of doing so because they may be lacking in self-esteem or self-efficacy. As individuals become able to solve problems in their daily lives, they usually develop more self-confidence. By addressing small daily problems, individuals begin to experience confidence and success and the belief in their ability to address larger issues. Mistaken beliefs may also result in lack of confidence. Counselors can be helpful by developing a supportive relationship with their clients so that the clients may develop self-efficacy, self-acceptance, and self-regard. Support, encouragement, and anxiety-reduction training may also be helpful. Clients may develop confidence not only in dealing with their current problem but in developing coping attitudes that they can use in addressing future problems.

As clients relate their stories, the counselor is able to assess if issues such as lack of concern, indecisiveness, lack of curiosity, or lack of confidence are interfering with career exploration and other career issues. Some counselors may choose to use inventories such as Super's Career Development Inventory (Chapter 8) or Krumboltz's Career Beliefs Inventory (Chapter 13). Many counselors will try to understand the meaning of the stories that clients tell by using the concepts of adaptability discussed in this section. The concept of adaptability helps counselors decide if clients have sufficient concern, control, curiosity, or confidence to continue to explore career choice or work adjustment. If the client is not ready, the counselor can address the issue before continuing counseling. Adaptability is a factor when listening for the life theme or themes that individuals express in their stories. The interaction of self (psychological personality) and society (psychological adaptability) produces a story. Savickas uses the glue of a coherent and continuous story to integrate personality type and transitional tasks by focusing on the story's theme.

LIFE THEMES

A major component of career construction theory is the concept of life themes, which is derived from Adler's lifestyle concept (Savickas, 1988, 1989; Sharf, 2008). Adlerian theory is an important aspect of career construction theory. Alfred Adler was a contemporary of Sigmund Freud. Born in 1870, like Freud he lived near Vienna, Austria. He was influenced by Freud's psychoanalytical ideas, but broke off from Freud and developed practical ideas that are still in use in counseling and psychotherapy today. His concept of lifestyle (sometimes referred to as style of life) helps to explain why individuals make the career choices that they do. Savickas draws on several Adlerian concepts, explained below. Knowing a person's lifestyle provides a means of understanding the basic themes in that person's life. Lifestyles are significant concepts that are different for each person, and examples help to illustrate them. In determining lifestyles, early recollections can be used to help discover the important theme or themes for individuals in their lives.

LIFESTYLE   According to Alfred Adler, the lifestyle is typically developed by the ages of four to six. Adler observed children interacting with each other and believed that their behavior at that age influenced them in later life. He saw children compensating for their feelings of inferiority and believed that the theme of inferiority and superiority was an important concept that would play a significant role in their lifestyle. For Adler, the way individuals live their lives now is often a reflection of their earlier lifestyles that may have already been evident in childhood. For example, if an adult is manipulative in dealing with people in a work situation, this is probably a style that developed in childhood.

Adlerian theory does not use a specific list of lifestyles; rather, Adlerians observe the lifestyle in an individual by listening to their life stories, including their childhood. Mwita (2004) gives an example of how early experiences affected Martin Luther King's personality and leadership style as he sought racial and social justice. One memory that Martin Luther King describes took place when he was very young. He remembered his father being angry and refusing to buy Martin shoes at a shoe store when the clerk asked him and his father to sit in the seats for "colored people." The theme of this story is an example of an early recollection that became an important theme to Martin Luther King throughout his life. The role of early recollections in developing life themes is described next.

EARLY RECOLLECTIONS   For Adlerians, early recollections are a significant aspect of determining the person's lifestyle. Early recollections are the memories of the incidents that clients recall. They are different from reports, which are incidents that other people recall about the client when the client was young. Early recollections are important because they have had an influence on clients' lives. When obtaining early memories, counselors often ask: "Would you try to recall your earliest memories for me? Start with your earliest specific memory, something that happened to you that you can remember, not something that was told to you." After that memory is recalled, the client is asked to try to recall another specific memory that happened when he or she was very young. Some counselors may ask for three or four memories, others more. Adlerians believe that early memories of events that occurred at the age of 4 or 5 are often the most helpful, because they occurred when the lifestyle was being crystallized. When the lifestyle is being determined, early recollections are a part of the process, not the entire process. They represent memories of the client, which may be different than what other individuals remember about the same incident. In essence, they are part of the story of an individual's life.

Another concept of importance to Savickas is that of the five major interrelated life tasks described by Adler, of which work is one of the tasks.

FIVE MAJOR LIFE TASKS   In determining lifestyle, Adlerians attend to five major interrelated tasks: self-development, spiritual development, occupation, society, and love (Mosak & Maniacci, 1999). Adler stated, "The person who performs useful work lives in the midst of the developing human society and helps to advance it." (Ansbacher & Ansbacher, 1956, p. 32). For Adler, work was a significant life task that often reflected social interest. *Social interest*, another important Adlerian concept, was a significant aspect of lifestyle, because to have a complete life, one should interact positively and successfully with others. Occupations or work are tasks that are done for other people. Adler felt that wanting to help other people, not just manipulate them or make money from them, was an important factor in a healthy lifestyle. The five tasks are interrelated in that one's self-development is related to one's love relationships, to one's work, and to the way in which one deals with society. More than most psychotherapists, Adler was interested in work, because he saw it as a reflection of both personality and life satisfaction.

Savickas focuses on the Adlerian task of work, but not to the exclusion of the other tasks. He sees the process of career counseling as helping individuals turn thoughts or preoccupations into an occupation that they will do, or participate in, within society. Rather than just assess interest with inventories, Savickas believes that counselors should help create interest by assisting clients in seeing how various occupations can be a means to express their thoughts or preoccupations. This way, the development of interest can lead to a resolution of career choice issues. In essence, Savickas wants to help clients find what matters to them. The concept of *mattering* is an important component of an individual's life story. The counselor tries to help clients give meaning and purpose to what they do in life. Much of this meaning comes through discussion of work and other life tasks. This meaning and purpose is a reflection of life themes or life style.

CAREER COUNSELING USING THE CAREER CONSTRUCTION MODEL

Unlike most career counseling, the career construction model uses a structured assessment process. Called the *Career Style Interview* (Savickas, 1989), it provides questions to ask clients that will help the counselor identify the lifestyle of the individual. The counselor will look for a unity of themes. Savickas believes that the career counseling process is one of turning a preoccupation into an occupation, as illustrated by the story of Martin Luther King. The *Career Style Interview* provides a means for doing this. In the case that follows, the counselor assesses the vocational personality type, career adaptability, and the life theme of the client. First, I will present the results of an abbreviated career style interview with Tiffany. Then I will illustrate the types of questions that a counselor using career construction theory is likely to ask. Finally, I will show how counseling proceeds using the career construction model to help the client take action on the problem.

Tiffany is a 25-year-old female who graduated from college four years ago with a degree in English. Her father is African American and her mother is Caucasian. She has a younger brother who is a senior in college in Chicago. She currently works as an assistant editor for a book publishing company in Chicago. She has been dissatisfied with her career for about two years. Because she has been reluctant to make changes, she has been slightly depressed and is procrastinating about going to graduate school and changing her career direction. As she became more and more bored with her work, she felt the need to seek out counseling. She has considered several career possibilities including teaching, social work, sales, and management. Although she has reasons for considering each, she also has reasons for rejecting them and she feels like she is at a standstill. The counselor conducted a Career Style Interview with Tiffany. Some of the results of this interview are described below.

CAREER STYLE INTERVIEW WITH TIFFANY

Three role models:

Angela Lansbury—She is a wonderful actress who really puts life into her roles. She also seems to have a wonderful effect on the other actors and actresses she works with.

Martin Luther King—He was really concerned about other people. He was so effective in making change. I admire him so much.

My Aunt Rita—She is a psychologist who works with young children. She seems to have so much energy and really cares about the kids that she works with. I like to talk to her about her work.

Magazines:

Wired—I am really interested in technology and what you can do with it to help people communicate better.

Psychology Today—I've always had an interest in psychology since high school. I guess I got interested in this from my Aunt Rita. It really helps me understand human behavior in an easy to understand way.

The New Yorker—The cartoons and the stories are really creative. I wish I could draw or write to the way these people do.

Favorite television show:

Star Trek—I keep watching the reruns. I like the idea of different races and cultures that are explored. I prefer the old *Star Treks*, which weren't so violent.

Favorite book:

The *Harry Potter* series—I've read the whole series. I really admire the creative approach to Harry and his friends. The stories are fun and exciting; even though I'm older than a lot of the readers I continued to read all the books in the series.

Hobbies:

Reading—I love to read fiction. Not just *Harry Potter*, but all kinds of stories. I like romance, science fiction, and stories with travel in them.

Being in the Big Sister Program—I have been assigned two Little Sisters in Chicago. I have enjoyed taking them places and talking to them about their problems. We have fun together and they seem to respect me.

Favorite sayings:

"If it is worth doing, it is worth doing well." My mother used to say that to me. I think it makes me scared of change because I'm afraid sometimes of doing something new that may not work out well.

What were your favorite subjects in school?

History and English—I like to hear about what happened to people in different countries and how countries developed the way they did. I liked the English courses because I love the stories. I like to read and to write reports about what I read. I think I liked English in high school better than in college, maybe because it was not as demanding.

Four early recollections with headlines:

1. Making a color collage
    When I was about three years old, I remember being in preschool and painting with my fingers on very large pieces of paper. I would paint big yellow swirls, wash my hands; paint big red swirls, wash my hands; paint green swirls. I loved it. The colors were so meaningful to me. They were so bright.

2. Being aware of skin color
    I think that it was at Thanksgiving when my mother's family and my father's family came over for dinner. It had never occurred to me before that my mother's family was white and my father's family was black. I noticed that my mother's family talked to each other and my father's family talked to each other, but there was not a lot of mixing, although everyone was friendly. I may have been aware of skin color and racial differences before then, but this memory stands out to me.

3. Helping dad
    When I was about four, I would follow my father around the yard with my little toy lawnmower. I really wanted to help him. I didn't know that the lawnmower didn't work. My father would always tell me how well I was doing and how he liked mowing the lawn with me. He would do that at other times too; he encouraged me to do things he did.

4. Feeling sorry for the girl who did not mix in
    I remember a time when I was in kindergarten. I think I must have been about
    five. We were out in the schoolyard, and the schoolyard had a red brick wall
    around it. There was a large grassy area with some of the cemented part of the
    playground being near the school. Anyway, I remember there was a group of
    maybe 10 or 15 kids playing with a ball or something in the middle of the
    field. Way off, in a corner under some trees, was a little girl—I guess one of my
    classmates, but I don't remember her as a friend. Anyway, she was standing
    under the tree crying or looking very sad. I wanted to do something about her
    sadness.

After Tiffany completed the Career Style Interview, the counselor asked her questions having to do with her career concerns. These questions follow Savickas (2005a).

CO: What were the circumstances during which your procrastination was labeled for the first time?

CL: My mother gets frustrated because I never seemed to do anything about my dissatisfaction with my publishing work.

CO: How does it feel to be undecided about future career plans?

CL: I feel nervous. And dissatisfied with myself that I'm not getting anywhere and I think I should get somewhere.

CO: What does this feeling remind you of?

CL: Like I am on a treadmill. Like I am not getting anywhere, and I don't like it.

CO: Please tell me about an incident in which you had the same feeling.

CL: When I am at work I feel like I file, I photocopy, and I read manuscripts, over and over again. It seems endlessly boring.

CO: What haunts you about this?

CL: Sometimes I have this idea that I will be doing this forever and ever until I finally die. It's really an empty feeling. I dislike it very much.

CO: Tell me part of your life story that is important to your career choice.

CL: In high school I'd procrastinate. I would do math on the school bus going to school. I would write my English papers late at night and always at the last minute. But when it came to friends, I never procrastinated. I would talk to them on the phone, sometimes go over to their house, anything to help. My schoolwork always came last. My mother didn't like this.

CAREER COUNSELING USING CAREER CONSTRUCTION THEORY

In both career assessment and career counseling, career construction theory focuses on the stories that clients tell. Sometimes these are very brief stories about parts of clients' lives, and sometimes they are longer. Career construction theory states that the person's real self comes out during the narration of the stories. People will talk about things that matter and have meaning to them. Savickas (2005a, 2005b) suggests that counselors use the same language as clients, such as favorite words or metaphors that the client uses. Savickas views career construction theory as having the advantage of being able to deal with personality types, such as in Holland's model; developmental tasks (Super's stages); and adaptability as they relate to the clients' expressions of their narratives. Savickas uses a seven-step interpretive routine that emphasizes a career construction framework. I will illustrate these steps by showing how a counselor would talk to Tiffany about her Career Style Interview. The steps do not need to be sequential, but this is a structure suggested by Savickas (2005a).

REVIEWING COUNSELING GOALS   The first step is to review the client's goals. When the client expresses what she would like to get from counseling, this gives the counselor a perspective on how to view the client's narrative. In Tiffany's case, she would like to make a new career choice. However, she is also concerned about her tendency to procrastinate and worried that she may not follow up on her choice. This alerts the counselor to attend to two issues of adaptability. Tiffany may be lacking in confidence in making her decision and may have concerns about her ability to control herself when it comes to being decisive and making a choice. The counselor may also attend to stories that Tiffany tells about past decision-making.

ATTENDING TO VERBS   Verbs are action words. In a story, they suggest a movement or direction or a lack of movement. Savickas attends to the first verb in the first early recollection. Then he proceeds to listen to other verbs in the first recollection, moving on to other recollections. If there is a theme, he makes note of it. The verbs will help to give a clue as to a life theme or themes. By attending to verbs, the counselor may observe the client telling a story that he or she may need to hear. In the first recollection, Tiffany uses the word "remember." This suggests thoughtfulness. The second verb is "paint." This suggests a desire to create and that she has an artistic interest. In the second recollection, the three verbs are "think, noticed, and occurred." All of these suggest thoughtfulness and observation. In the third recollection, the verbs "follow" and "help" suggest connections to others and helping relationships. The helping theme is seen again in the fourth recollection in which "sad" for others is the most significant verb.

EXAMINING HEADLINES OF THE RECOLLECTIONS   The counselor asked Tiffany to come up with a catchy headline that includes a verb for each of the recollections. These headlines compress the story. They suggest ideas for a theme that may fit the client. The first headline includes the verb "making," which suggests productivity. The second headline uses the verb "aware" and suggests attention to surroundings. The last two recollections use the terms "helping" and "feeling sorry." Both suggest concern for others.

MOVING FROM PREOCCUPATION TO OCCUPATION   The counselor wants to understand how Tiffany solves problems in constructing a career and how occupations will help her master her problems. Savickas suggests that counselors focus on movement from preoccupation to occupation in the analysis of stories, which will be the essence of the life theme. The counselor then will compare Tiffany's early recollections to her role models. Her first recollection suggests creating. Her first role model is Angela Lansbury, a famous actress, who Tiffany associates with being creative and productive. Martin Luther King and Aunt Rita are both people that observe others, want to help others who are experiencing personal or social problems, and who do something to help them—the themes that are related to Tiffany's last three early recollections. There is a suggestion that Tiffany wants to move forward in her life and help others, a clear example of the Adlerian concept of social interest.

ROLE MODELS AS A SUGGESTION FOR A PLAN   The choice of role models can indicate that these are people who the client wants to be like. Thus the client would like to lead her life as the role models have. In essence, they suggest a plan for a life or career. Tiffany's comments about the three role models suggest that she wants to be productive in her life, to make a difference. She admires her aunt's energy and Martin Luther King's effectiveness. Both are seen as really caring for people, a theme important to Tiffany. These are attributes she is not feeling in her life now, but wants to move toward. Feeling effective for Tiffany can come from helping others with their personal or social problems.

PROFILING ADAPTABILITY   In career construction theory, counselors look for how clients cope in the stories that are told to the counselor. Career adaptability concepts are useful in understanding coping strategies. Clients' adaptability may not be clear at first, but may be revealed in early recollections or other parts of the Career Style Interview or in discussion with the counselor. Tiffany has a desire to increase her confidence. She has sought out the counselor for help because she is undecided about her life, feeling relatively little control. The counselor is aware of this and sees her indecision as a positive sign. She is dealing with the fear of making a change, and needs encouragement. The counselor will help her to examine her life story and to take action. Indecision is seen here not as a weakness, but as a strength. The counselor sees both current issues and social interest represented in the role models that Tiffany has chosen. This suggests Tiffany's willingness to gain control over her life and to work toward increasing her confidence.

APPRAISING VOCATIONAL PERSONALITY   In career construction theory, Holland's six personality types are seen as a way of looking at the client's view of the story. Information that comes from the Career Style Interview can be used to determine which types the client most closely resembles. More questions may be asked in order to get information about the six personality types. Using the Self-Directed Search or the Strong Interest Inventory would also be a way to get information about the client's vocational personality. For Tiffany, Holland's social personality seems to be the most prominent of Holland's six types. There seems to be a clear interest in helping others with personal problems and making a difference in people's lives. Perhaps Tiffany's second Holland type would be Artistic. There is little material that Tiffany presents at this point that suggests interest in any of the other four types. More discussion may reveal that other types are represented in her vocational personality.

CRAFTING A SUCCESS FORMULA   The steps that were outlined above provide the information needed to make a success formula. Savickas suggests that the counselor develop a success formula so that the counselor and the client can go over the draft together. In his development of the success formula, Savickas draws on the work of Haldane (1975). The focus of Haldane's work is on specifying and articulating dependable strengths. Thus, the success formula will focus on Tiffany's strengths, which are determined by an analysis of information provided in the Career Style Interview with an emphasis on vocational personality. Table 11.1 lists Tiffany's strengths for each of the six Holland types.

For Tiffany, the first draft of the success formula was derived by focusing on her Social and Artistic Holland types. The counselor writes: *You feel happy and successful*

TABLE 11.1	SUCCESS FORMULA COMPONENTS	

Realistic	Investigative	Artistic
Work with tools	Solve the problems	Be independent
Think with my hands	Work with science	Share feelings
Use mechanical ability	Work with math	Be sensitive
Apply physical skill	Use logic	Paint
Work outdoors	Research ideas	Play an instrument
Work with animals	Figure out how things work	Write
Work with nature	Read	Apply artistic flair
Demonstrate skill	Analyze situations	Decorate
	Discover	Design

Social	Enterprising	Conventional
Help others	Make decisions	Be part of a team
Work with people	Convince others	Record data
Provide a service	Lead a group	Type
Be outgoing and pleasant	Use power	Organize materials
Help children	Act with enthusiasm	Have a set routine
Assist the elderly	Sell things	Know what is expected
Teach	Be the center of attention	Carry out orders
Counsel	Be dynamic	Work with a partner
Advise	Have a lot of variety	

Source: Savickas, M. L. (1989). Career-style assessment and counseling. In T. Sweeney (Ed.), *Adlerian counseling: A practical approach for a new decade*, (3rd ed.) (pp. 289–320). Muncie, IN: Accelerated Development Press. Reprinted by permission of Mark Savickas.

when you help others with personal problems and provide a service to improve their lives. In doing this you try to be sensitive and design programs that may help people improve their lives. After reading this, Tiffany indicates that it fits her, but she wants to figure out which people she wants to help and how she wants to help them.

THE LIFE PORTRAIT   The success formula is a start in drawing a more comprehensive portrait of the client. Savickas suggests thinking about the client using the information that has come from the Career Style Interview. In addition to thinking, the counselor's own reactions and feelings about the client can help in writing the life portrait. This portrait aims to highlight emotional realities and themes of the client. It will try to answer questions such as "Who am I?" "What is my quest?" and "How can I grow and flourish?" In the life portrait, the life theme is repeated and emphasized to make sure it fits the client well. The life theme will bring together the very different career stories that the client has told. Sometimes career stories have conflicting information or views. The life portrait will try to bridge these different views and present a theme rather than a set of disjointed ideas. The life portrait should represent the ruling passion of the client's life (Savickas 2005a). The client wishes to make choices, and the life portrait will help the client to decide among choices. When this is done, the client and the counselor go over the life portrait. In the life portrait there is a movement from symptoms to strength. This should help clients feel that they can master past problems and do something about them. The counselor is the storyteller and the client is the editor. The client will design a story to fit as accurately as possible. Restating the obvious can be helpful because it is important to acknowledge all aspects of the client's life portrait. The counselor is curious about the client, never certain. The counselor will ask "What am I missing?" The portrait is a tentative sketch, not the counselor telling the client what he or she thinks the life portrait is. It should represent a portrait that that client feels is accurate.

The counselor might discuss Tiffany's life portrait in this way. In this example, the life portrait is based on the limited information provided in Tiffany's Career Style Interview that focuses on her early recollections.

CO: Tiffany I want to present this portrait of your life that I have come up with. It certainly is not final. I very much want your input in it, and please disagree with me if you like.

You are very concerned about others, especially people who are not allowed or are unable to mix in with others. You want to help them when they experience distress. If you can use your creativity as well as your concern, it will be pleasing to you. The desire to help others and to be involved in the lives of others comes out of the wish to observe them when they interact with you or in other situations. Even though you question your abilities, and this can interfere in doing things that you really want to do, you have the desire to make these changes in your life so that you can help others. You are depressed now because as a book editor you are out of the mix. You are not using your passion and feelings to put life into your work. You feel like a little girl sitting under a tree watching others engage in life.

CL: I think you have captured what is important to me. You also talk about how I am scared. I'm scared of leaving a secure job and going back to graduate school or to consider losing some income if I were to become a psychologist or social worker. I guess what I would also add is an emphasis on creativity. I like to create and still like to paint, something I have always liked. However, that is probably less important to me than what you have put in your life portrait of me.

CO: You seem to be giving a lot of thought into what you are going to do next.

CL: Yes. As we examine my life and what's important to me, I become even more motivated to find what I want to do. Although I am still scared.

CO: I can understand the scare. You hesitate to get up and walk out from the shadow of the tree into the full mix of life. However, now as you narrate your story you are developing your own strengths and resources so that you can take actions to help you. [Savickas (2005a) uses the metaphor of the girl sitting under the tree. It is a way for the counselor to make clear that a struggle is going on as the client tries to move in a new direction. It is also a way of telling the client that she began to move away from the security of the tree when she sought career counseling.]

CL: That's an interesting way of putting it. I do feel like I'm making some movements to free myself.

CO: To help you to move on, we have looked at your resources. You have the determination to figure out what you want to do. You also have demonstrated ability to work with people and have them appreciate your efforts. Your hard work is also another one of your abilities. [In career construction theory, Savickas emphasizes the importance of encouraging and supporting client strengths.]

CL: That is a help to me to feel more motivated to change and to take the risks that are involved in looking at the helping professions as a possible alternative for me.

CO: Your initial reluctance to move and your lack of certainty about direction have now turned to thinking about first steps. In fact, you may be quite skilled at helping people in pain learn to take steps to paint their lives a brighter color. [In his work, Savickas sees the problem as being part of the solution. It is a very positive way to view what the client is doing and not to criticize her for being indecisive; rather, it encourages her to take action.]

At this point, the counselor and Tiffany have come to the conclusion that staying in her current assistant editor position is not a good solution for her and does not fit her plot or story. She makes clear also that she has made progress in dealing with her procrastination and is more excited about change. Now she wants to clarify more specifically what type of career she wants to consider within the helping professions. She also needs to address how much schooling she is willing to undertake to reach her objectives.

The counselor shows Tiffany two resources that she can use. First, she can use the Occupation Finder that Holland developed to find a list of occupations that would match different Holland codes. The other is the *Occupational Outlook Handbook (2008)*, which is available in print or online. The counselor asks Tiffany to look at these before their next meeting in order to get an idea as to which would occupations might best fit into her life story.

At their next meeting, Tiffany explained to the counselor that she had looked at the Occupation Finder to get some ideas of careers, but found the *Occupational Outlook Handbook (2008)* to be most helpful. As she talked about social work, psychiatry, clinical psychology, occupational therapy, and vocational rehabilitation occupations, she was quite excited. She was able to articulate how all of these related to her vocational personality, which was primarily social. As she compared the five occupations that most interested her, she was able to identify aspects of occupations that did not fit her life plan as well as those that did. For Tiffany, psychiatry and clinical psychology would require over six years of training in graduate school. The increased income that these fields would offer her did not seem to be worth the investment both financially and in terms of eagerness to get started working. Also, Tiffany had less interest in the medical settings that are part of occupational therapy and vocational rehabilitation counseling. Social work was becoming more and more attractive to her. She had taken action on her own to talk to a friend of her mother's who was a social worker in the school system. Tiffany was interested in the work that was described and the opportunity to work with children from diverse cultural backgrounds. She and her mother's friend made a date for Tiffany to visit her at work. The counselor was impressed with how Tiffany had overcome her procrastination and how Tiffany was excited by possible changes. The counselor encouraged and reinforced Tiffany's actions to fill out her narrative in a way that felt very satisfying to Tiffany.

In this case, I have tried to illustrate the importance of the client's role in career construction theory. Although the counselor may have guesses about what the next chapter will be in the client's life, that is not important. Being able to predict the client's next action or ultimate choice does not matter. What is important is that the counselor should help the client to further the story in a way that is satisfying to the client and helps the client become more in control of and confident about his or her ability to manage the future. Knowing one's vocational personality and preferred work environments can help the client take satisfying action. The success formula and the life portrait are means for clarifying and encouraging the client to look into ways to change his or her life so that life tasks become more meaningful and satisfying.

THE ROLE OF ASSESSMENT INSTRUMENTS

Standard interest inventories, values inventories, and tests of ability and achievement play a minor role in constructivist career counseling. Because constructivist counselors are interested in how their clients see reality, applying inventories or tests that are used for all individuals may not help in understanding the perceptual world of the client. In narrative career counseling, Cochran (1997) shows how traditional tests and inventories can be integrated with constructivist methods, such as the vocational card sort, drawing, and anecdotes, in the first episode of his model, elaborating a career problem. Savickas (2005b) uses the Self-Directed Search or the Strong Interest Inventory if the client wishes to use an inventory. His Career Style Interview is the major assessment instrument that he uses to understand client stories. In their overview of qualitative career assessments, Whiston and Rahardja (2005) discuss the advantages of using a constructivist approach. They emphasize that a constructivist approach acknowledges that one's view of the world is constantly changing and is influenced by historical and cultural events. Additionally, a constructivist approach is an excellent way to understand the impact of cultural issues on clients. This last point is also made by Guichard and Lenz (2005) in their suggestions that constructivist approaches can be used with populations from many different countries because of the constructivist emphasis on how each client sees the world. There are several constructivist assessment methods that are not mentioned in this chapter, but have been used by constructivist counselors (Schultheiss, 2005). These include a retrospective construction of parental influence to try to understand influences on the development of client career narratives. Making a videotape of a parent and adolescent discussing a career issue and then having the parent and adolescent comment on career goals and other career issues of the adolescent can be helpful (Young, Valach, & Collin, 2002; Young, Valach, & Domene, 2005). The Thematic Apperception Test that asks individuals to tell stories of pictures of people and different settings has been studied as a means for assessing Savickas's career-related adaptability dimensions (Hartung & Borges, 2005).

Because constructivist and narrative career counselors are focused on understanding the client's perception of their career problems and the constructs that they use to see their world, constructivist counselors are cautious about using instruments that impose a test or inventory developer's set of constructs on the client.

THE ROLE OF OCCUPATIONAL INFORMATION

Constructivist and narrative career counselors are concerned not only with the constructs that individuals use to see themselves, but also with the constructs that they use in viewing the world around them. Each of the two approaches discussed in this chapter has similar but slightly different perspectives on integrating occupational information into career counseling.

Cochran (1997) emphasizes the importance of action on the part of the client. After clients tell their stories, they are involved in three enactment episodes. All three involve active exploration and occupational research. It is not enough for the client to just read about occupations. In the reality construction episode, clients may do volunteer work, visit people at work, interview workers, or discuss occupations with relatives or friends. In the changing a life structure episode, clients focus on the work that they do, studying the effects on their lives. As clients try out new activities, their lives change, and they can examine how they react to different occupational tasks. When enacting a role, clients live out roles that they are interested in exploring. On page 326, an example was given of how Dennis tried different supervisory assignments and tasks. This increased his knowledge of relevant occupational information.

In career construction theory, Savickas (2005b) integrates occupational information into the career counseling process after the Career Style Interview has been completed. Using Holland's theory, he has clients make use of the Occupational Finder as a bridge to occupational information. In the example of Tiffany, reference is made to the *Occupational Outlook Handbook (2008)* as a source of information. However, career construction counselors might also make use of the O*NET, the Guide for Occupational Exploration, career brochures and pamphlets, and other occupational information. To construct a full story about one's career it is necessary to take action to find out more about occupations. This could include networking with friends, parents' friends, former employers, and others who would be able to help individuals find enough information about occupations so that they could see if the occupation fits into the plot of their narrative.

APPLYING THE THEORIES TO WOMEN AND CULTURALLY DIVERSE POPULATIONS

From a constructivist point of view, culture and gender interact within the context of client actions (Young et al., 2007). Thus, stories or histories exist within a cultural context. How one views an action can have varying cultural interpretations. For example, putting an arm around a coworker can be seen as friendly encouragement or sexual harassment. One's cultural background may influence how one interprets such an event.

Both gender and culture guide how individuals develop attitudes, skills, and values (Cochran, 1997). For example, in North America, there are cultural stereotypes that suggest that women are not as skilled as men in math. Other cultural narratives may guide certain views, such as Asian individuals prefer science to all other fields. Cochran cautions that cultural narratives are only one aspect of what individuals learn. Some cultural systems are closely related to vocational expectations. For example, caste systems in India often were linked with certain types of occupations, whether they be custodial, small business, or other occupations.

Constructivist approaches to career counseling provide an open way of viewing the client. The focus is on how the client sees the world. Thus the counselor is careful to observe that his or her own cultural views do not obstruct the understanding of the client's narrative. In examining career theory from an international perspective, Guichard and Lenz (2005) show how a constructivist viewpoint can be an asset in dealing with many diverse cultural attitudes and traditions regarding work by valuing individual narratives. In working with gifted female adolescents, the use of constructivist techniques such as the Vocational Card Sort, life lines, and similar techniques are suggested as a way to help gifted female adolescents examine their life stories and to consider new actions (Maxwell, 2007). Studying aboriginal people in Canada, Young et al. (2007) focus on the action of families as they construct projects about their adolescents. For example, they observed the effectiveness of the "talking circle," a group of people whom the adolescent and his or her family have selected to help with development into adulthood.

Young and colleagues have studied the career project in adolescents. They see *career project* as a series of actions that adolescents and their parents take that is related to the adolescents' choice of career (Young et al., 2007; Young et al., 2006; Young, Valach, Ball, Paseluikho, Wong, DeVries, McLean, & Turkel, 2001). Young et al. (2001) studied 20 pairs (each pair included one adolescent and one parent) for 6 months by videotaping two parent–adolescent conversations for each pair. They found that the career projects were related to four other significant projects: the relationship, identity, parenting, and culture. Young, Valach, Ball, Turkel, and Wong (2003) then studied six of the parent–adolescent pairs who were Chinese Canadian. They found that the career project of these pairs was closely related to other projects, especially the cultural project. The career project of the Chinese Canadian pairs were mainly determined by the parent and accepted by the adolescent, both in terms of the adolescent's interests and future goals. Typically, Chinese Canadian parents saw the need to structure career goals and to take actions that would help to achieve these goals. In another study of pairs of 19 parents and adolescents, career development goals and actions were found to vary as to how important they were in the parent–adolescent relationships (Young et al., 2006). Projects involving career exploration were common with mother-son groups, whereas conflict and avoiding conflict was more common in mother-daughter projects (Domene, Arim, & Young, 2007). These findings emphasize the importance of culture and family relationships in the development of career goals as well as the role of parents in the construction of career projects.

Constructivist and narrative career counselors attend to cultural components of stories, as well as stories about culture. Such constructs can help counselors understand their clients' value systems. Each client's story, whether referring to gender, culture, or some other topic, provides a way of perceiving that client's construction of reality.

COUNSELOR ISSUES

Because the focus of constructivist and narrative approaches to career counseling is on understanding the way clients view reality, it is important for counselors to be aware of their own construction of reality and its relationship to significant constructs of clients. For example, if the prestige of an occupation is irrelevant to the counselor but is relevant to the client, it is important that the counselor's values do not interfere with the client's valuing of prestige.

There are some differences in counselor issues between the two approaches discussed in this chapter. When using the narrative approach to career counseling, counselors are focused on the client's story. When listening to the client's history, counselors may be reminded of their own history and see differences between the two. Seeing these differences can be advantageous or disadvantageous to the counselor depending on how they affect the counselor's perception of the clients' stories. In Savickas's career construction theory, there is a specific structure for dealing with clients. This can put the counselor in a directive role in which the counselor asks questions that fit a structure. Therefore, it is helpful, as Savickas does, to be a respectful audience by continually asking for the client to comment on counselor understandings and story summaries, such as the counselor's presentation of the success formula and life portrait that has been developed for the client. By seeing the client as the author of the narrative plot, the counselor as audience tries to avoid adding pieces to the client's story that do not fit the client.

SUMMARY

This chapter has focused on two different approaches to constructivist career counseling. Both narrative career counseling and career construction theory have in common their attention to clients' perceptions of reality.

The narrative approach to career counseling views the client's story as the focus of career counseling. In this approach, the client is seen as an active player, someone responsible for making changes in his or her environment. Cochran describes seven "episodes" that counselors use in working with clients. The first three episodes involve the construction of career narratives: elaborating a career problem, composing a life, and founding a future narrative. The next three episodes emphasize enactment: constructing a reality, changing a life structure, and enacting a role. The final episode is crystallizing a career decision.

Career construction theory is a meta-theory that makes use of other theories in understanding the client. Holland's theory is used in listening to the client's vocational personality. Super's stage theory (p. 259) is used as a basis for Savickas's transitional tasks, which include career adaptability. The dimensions of career (psychosocial) adaptability for dealing with transitions are a significant modification of Super's view of career maturity. Adler's theory of counseling and psychotherapy is the source of the concept of life themes. The assessment method that is used is called the Career Style Interview. It includes questions about role models, favorite magazines and television shows, books, hobbies, favorite sayings, and school subjects. Early recollections about past events are also important aspects of the Career Style Interview. Seven techniques for discussing vocational personality, career adaptability, and life themes are described in the chapter. All are based on understanding the client's narrative, or story, and on helping the client act on a career choice.

Both approaches provide different ways of viewing the career counseling process. A significant feature of these approaches is specific assessment and career counseling techniques for counselors to use to help clients construct their reality. Differences between the two approaches tend to focus on ways of assessing clients' perceptions of their value or construct systems and whether or not to integrate other career theories into the counseling process. Cochran's narrative approach does not make use of other theories, but Savickas's career construction theory does integrate concepts from other theories.

References

Ansbacher, H. L., & Ansbacher, R. R. (Eds.). (1956). *The individual psychology of Alfred Adler*. Evanston, IL: Northwestern University Press.

Brott, P. E. (2001). The storied approach: A postmodern perspective for career counseling. *Career Development Quarterly, 49*, 304–313.

Brott, P. E. (2005). A constructivist look at life roles. *The Career Development Quarterly,* *54*(2), 138–149.

Chen, C. P. (2006). Strengthening career human agency. *Journal of Counseling & Development,* *84*(2), 131–138.

Cochran, L. (1985). *Position and nature of personhood.* Westport, CT: Greenwood Press.

Cochran, L. (1991). *Life-shaping decisions.* New York: Lang.

Cochran, L. (1992). The career project. *Journal of Career Development, 18,* 187–197.

Cochran, L. (1994). What is a career problem? *Career Development Quarterly, 42,* 204–215.

Cochran, L. (1997). *Career counseling: A narrative approach.* Newbury Park, CA: Sage Publications.

Dail, H. (1989). *The lotus and the pool.* Boston: Shambhala.

Dolliver, R. (1967). An adaptation of the Tyler Vocational Card Sort. *Personnel and Guidance Journal, 45,* 916–920.

Domene, J. F., Arim, R. G., & Young, R. A. (2007). Gender and career development projects in early adolescence: Similarities and differences between mother-daughter and mother-son dyads. *Qualitative Research in Psychology,* *4*(1–2), 107–126.

Fransella, F., Dalton, P., & Weselby, G. (2007). Personal construct therapy. In W. Dryden (Ed.), *Dryden's handbook of individual therapy* (5th ed., pp. 173–194). Thousand Oaks, CA: Sage.

Guichard, J., & Lenz, J. (2005). Career theory from an international perspective. *The Career Development Quarterly.* *54*(1), 17–28.

Haldane, B. (1975). *How to make a habit of success.* Washington, DC: Acropolis Books.

Hartung, P. J., & Borges, N. J. (2005). Toward integrated career assessment: Using story to appraise career dispositions and adaptability. *Journal of Career Assessment,* *13*(4), 439–451.

Jepsen, D. A. (1992). Understanding careers as stories. In M. L. Savickas (Chair), *Career as story.* Symposium conducted at the American Association for Counseling and Development. March 1992.

Maxwell, M. (2007). Career counseling is personal counseling: A constructivist approach to nurturing the development of gifted female adolescents. *The Career Development Quarterly,* *55*(3), 206–224.

Mayo, J. A. (2001). Life analysis: Using life-story narratives in teaching life-span developmental psychology. *Journal of Constructivist Psychology, 14,* 25–41.

Mosak, H. H., & Maniacci, M. (1999). *A primer on Adlerian psychology.* Philadelphia: Brunner/Mazel.

Mwita, M. (2004). Martin Luther King Jr.'s lifestyle and social interest in his autobiographical early memories. *Journal of Individual Psychology.* *60*(2), 191–203.

Neimeyer, R. A., & Stewart, A. E. (2002). Constructivist and narrative psychotherapies. In C. R. Snyder & R. E. Ingram (Eds.), *Handbook of psychological change* (pp. 337–357). New York: Wiley.

Occupational Outlook Handbook (2008). Washington, DC: U. S. Department of Labor.

Savickas, M. L. (1988). An Adlerian view of the Publican's pilgrimage. *Career Development Quarterly, 36,* 211–217.

Savickas, M. L. (1989). Career style assessment and counseling. In T. Sweeney (Ed.), *Adlerian counseling: A practical approach for a new decade* (3rd ed., pp. 289–320). Muncie, IN: Accelerated Development Press.

Savickas, M. L. (1991). Improving career time perspective. In D. Brown & L. Brooks (Eds.), *Techniques of career counseling* (pp. 236–249). Boston: Allyn & Bacon.

Savickas, M. L. (1997). Constructivist career counseling: Models and methods. *Advances in Personal Construct Psychology, 4,* 149–182.

Savickas, M. L. (2002). Career construction: A developmental theory of vocational behavior. In D. Brown & Associates (Eds.), *Career choice and development* (4th ed., pp. 149–205). San Francisco: Jossey-Bass.

Savickas, M. L. (2005a). Career construction theory and practice. Presented at the American Counseling Association meeting. April 2005. Atlanta, GA.

Savickas, M. L. (2005b). The theory and practice of career construction. In S. D. Brown & R. W. Lent (Eds.), *Career development and counseling: Putting theory and research to work* (pp. 42–70). Hoboken, NJ: John Wiley.

Schultheiss, D. E. P. (2005). Qualitative relational career assessment: A constructivist paradigm. *Journal of Career Assessment, 13*(4), 381–394.

Sharf, R. S. (2008). *Theories of psychotherapy and counseling: Concepts and cases* (4th ed.). Belmont, CA: Thomson Brooks/Cole.

Super, D. E. (1957). *The psychology of careers.* New York: Harper.

Thorngren, J. M., & Feit, S. S. (2001). The Career-O-Gram: A postmodern career intervention. *Career Development Quarterly, 49,* 291–303.

Tyler, L. (1961). Research explorations in the realm of choice. *Journal of Counseling Psychology, 8,* 195–201.

Whiston, S. C., & Rahardja, D. (2005). Qualitative career assessment: An overview and analysis. *Journal of Career Assessment, 13*(4), 371–380.

Young, R. A., & Collin, A. (2004). Introduction: Constructivism and social constructionism in the career field. *Journal of Vocational Behavior, 64*(3), 373–388.

Young, R. A., Marshall, S., Domene, J. F., Arato-Bolivar, J., Hayoun, R., Marshall, E., et al. (2006). Relationships, communication, and career in the parent-adolescent projects of families with and without challenges. *Journal of Vocational Behavior, 68*(1), 1–23.

Young, R. A., Marshall, S. K., & Valach, L. (2007). Making career theories more culturally sensitive: Implications for counseling. *The Career Development Quarterly, 56*(1), 4–18.

Young, R. A., Valach, L., Ball, J., Paseluikho, M. A., Wong, Y. S., DeVries, R. J., McLean, H., & Turkel, H. (2001). Career development as a family project. *Journal of Counseling Psychology, 48,* 190–202.

Young, R. A., Valach, L., Ball, J., Turkel, H., & Wong, Y. S. (2003). The family career development project in Chinese Canadian families. *Journal of Vocational Behavior, 62,* 287–304.

Young, R. A., Valach, L., & Collin, A. (2002). A contextual explanation of career. In D. Brown & Associates (Eds.), *Career choice and development* (4th ed., pp. 206–252). San Francisco: Jossey-Bass.

Young, R. A., Valach, L., & Domene, J. F. (2005). The action-project method in counseling psychology. *Journal of Counseling Psychology, 52*(2), 215–223.

CHAPTER 12

RELATIONAL
APPROACHES TO
CAREER DEVELOPMENT

CHAPTER HIGHLIGHTS

Roe's Personality Development Theory

Attachment Theory

Parent–Child Career Interactions

Family Systems Therapy

Phillips's Developmental–Relational Model

Applying the Theories to Women and Culturally Diverse Populations

Career development researchers have been interested in the questions: What impact do parents and others have on the occupational choice of children? And what impact does the child-raising experience and the family have on the career choices and decision-making styles of children? Most theorists who have studied influences that others have on the career development of children have focused on parental influence, but others have examined the effect of siblings, other family members, friends, teachers, and others on career choice and development. The impetus for the study of parental impact on career development comes from the work of Sigmund Freud and his influence on psychodynamic explanations of personal development. Influenced by Freud, Anne Roe was the first researcher to develop a theory of career development that focused, similar to Freud's psychoanalysis, on the importance of parents' influence on childhood development. Roe proposed a theory that tried to predict the influence of parental child-raising styles on individual occupational choices. Her theory had received considerable attention for more than 50 years, but has received little attention since the 1980s and will be briefly summarized in this chapter.

Also growing out of the influence of Freud and psychoanalysis has been attachment theory that examines children's attachments to parents. Receiving much attention from developmental psychologists, attachment theory has also been used to predict how individuals make career choices. Psychologists who study families and therapists who treat families have examined how interactions among family members affect career choices of children. This has been a particular focus of Richard Young and his colleagues. A comprehensive review of the research of the role of parenting, in a broad sense, on the career development of adolescents and children examines issues such as activities parents do with their children, parents as a source of career information, parents' responsiveness to children's career issues, and availability of parents to children (Bryant, Zvonkovic, & Reynolds, 2006).

Whereas these approaches have attended to the involvement of parents and families in career decision-making of children and adolescents, Susan Phillips and her colleagues have taken a broader approach. They have examined how siblings, friends, extended family, and many others affect the career decision-making process of adolescents and adults. They believe that relationships of many types are important to consider in understanding the career choice process. They have identified two themes. The first concerns how individuals involve themselves in the decision making of others. The second theme describes the ways in which individuals seek out others when trying to make career decisions.

This chapter discusses all of these approaches. First, I give an overview of attachment theory as it relates to career development. Then, I describe how family systems theory and the study of parent–child interactions helps to further the understanding of career development. A major focus of this chapter is on the developmental–relational model of Susan Phillips and her colleagues. This chapter describes their categories of relational decision making in detail and gives an example of how their theory can be applied to career counseling.

ROE'S PERSONALITY DEVELOPMENT THEORY

Roe developed a theory to predict occupational selection based on individual differences, which are biological, sociological, and psychological. More specifically, she focused on predicting occupational selection based on the psychological needs that develop from the interaction between children and their parents. She wanted to show that people in certain occupations have a common background in terms of the way they were raised. To build this theory, she developed an occupational classification system so that she could relate parent–child relationships to specific occupational groupings.

Roe (Roe, 1957; Roe & Lunneborg, 1990) also classified early parent–child relationships into three types, each with two subclassifications. Roe was more interested in the attitudes of parents toward their children than in the specific ways in which parents behaved toward their children. Her classification system deals with the attitude toward (or away from) the child. The six attitudes are briefly described here.

Concentration on the Child: Roe describes two types of emotional concentration on the child: Parents can be overprotective or overdemanding.

An *overprotective* parent encourages dependence in the child and restricts curiosity and exploration. An *overdemanding* parent may request perfection from the child, asking for excellent performance and setting high standards of behavior.

Avoidance of the Child: Roe suggests two different methods of avoidance: rejection and neglect. An *emotionally rejected* child may be criticized or punished by his or her parents and not given love and affection. A *neglected* child may be ignored for many reasons, such as parents' concern with their own problems, other children, and work.

Acceptance of the Child: Parents encourage independence rather than dependence and do not ignore or reject their child, creating a relatively tension-free environment. *Casual acceptance* refers to a low-key attitude of the parent, offering a minimum of love. *Loving acceptance*, in contrast, shows a warmer attitude of the parent toward the child, while not interfering with the child's resources by fostering dependency.

Roe's theory, together with views of children's attachment to parents, provides interesting perspectives of parental influence on the career choice of children. However, there is little research support for this theory. The lack of support has lead to lack of interest in doing further research or applying it to counseling.

ATTACHMENT THEORY

Just as Roe has tried to make predictions based on parent–child interactions, attachment theorists have similar intentions. Briefly, attachment theory studies the role that attachments (primarily parental) play in shaping the life of an individual (Erdman & Caffrey, 2003). Attachment theory grew out of object relations theory, a development of psychoanalysis (Sharf, 2008), which emphasizes the relationship that the infant has with others, particularly the mother. Bowlby (1973, 1980, 1982), the most well-known attachment theorist, studied the importance of attachment, separation, and loss in human development. Unlike object relations theorists, who are interested in mother–child relationships in early childhood and their effect on psychiatric illness, some attachment theorists have studied the effect that attachment has on children without diagnosed psychiatric problems. Other attachment theorists have focused on the entire life span. Bowlby was particularly interested in how individuals' sense of being worthwhile and views of their own competence develop, together with their views of others. Of great importance in this development, according to Bowlby, is the role of "attachment figures," such as the mother and the father. To study attachment, Ainsworth (Ainsworth, Blehar, Waters, & Wall, 1978) used the "strange situation" method to observe the attachment behavior of young children. This involves making unobtrusive observations of children when the mother comes and goes, when a stranger enters, and when the child is alone. From these observations, three types of responding were found: the secure pattern, the anxious–ambivalent pattern, and the avoidant pattern.

Secure pattern: The infant responds to the caregiver easily and is able to continue exploratory behavior (an important feature for career development, as described in Chapter 7). The security experienced by infants allows them to interact well with people and things in their world.

Anxious–Ambivalent pattern: Because the infant experiences the caregiver as being inconsistent, the child becomes anxious. Also, the child's view of herself or himself is one of uncertainty, as is the child's view of others. Such anxiety and uncertainty often result in decreased exploratory behavior.

Avoidant pattern: The infant ignores or rejects care that is offered by an adult. Ainsworth, Blehar, Waters, and Wall (1978) observed that such children would develop a sense of being alone in the world and of being unable to trust others.

A large amount of research has shown that these patterns are stable during the first 6 years of life and are different from infant moods or temperament (Erdman & Caffrey, 2003). Attachment patterns are less consistent in families with high stress than in those with low stress. Other researchers have modified these attachment patterns and added one or two others. Suggested by patterns of attachment is the idea that children who have a secure pattern of attachment in their first 6 years of life are more willing to explore relationships with others and more willing to play with objects or animals, activities leading eventually to greater familiarity with their world and the world of work. However, there is no direct evidence to support this conjecture because, like Roe's theory, attachment theory has the difficult task of trying to predict behavior over a long period. Longitudinal studies of this type are rare.

Reviewing nonlongitudinal studies, Blustein, Prezioso, and Palladino Schultheiss (1995) show how attachment theory can be useful in understanding career development. Of particular importance is the relationship between attachment and exploration that is related to learning. Being secure, the adolescent and adult can more freely explore his or her world, and thus develop social competence throughout life that is related to job satisfaction (Lucas, 1999). Two studies illustrate the role of strong attachment to parents in career development. College students who had a strong attachment to parents together with movement toward becoming more responsible and independent were more likely than students without these characteristics to involve others in a positive way to make helpful career decisions (Gravino, 2002). Puffer (1999) reports that when female college students were attached to parents who were committed to encouraging independence, the students had a stable sense of vocational identity and minimal anxiety or indecision about career choice. In written responses to open-ended questions, adults between the ages of 32 and 34 indicated that their attachment to parents had an impact on career issues (Perrone, Webb, & Jackson, 2007).

Research adds information about the relevance of separation from and attachment to both fathers and mothers to vocational development. O'Brien (1996) reports that attachment and emotional closeness to the mother and attitudes that were similar to those of both parents were predictive of confidence in career decision making and in being realistic about career choices. Career indecision was related to attachment security, attachment anxiety, paternal and maternal separation, and paternal and maternal conflictual independence (Tokar, Withrow, Hall, & Moradi, 2003). In this study of college students, those who felt separated (in a positive sense) from their mothers were less undecided and more clear in their career choice than those who were anxious about separating from their mothers or who felt separated in a negative sense. However, appropriate separation from fathers was related to increased career indecision. This study shows the complexity of parental attachment relationships as they relate to career indecision. Scott and Church (2001) report that college students with divorced parents reported that they were more on their own emotionally and less attached to their parents than those students from intact families. In studying attachment, attachment to the mother, but not the father, appeared to contribute to fuller career exploration (Felsman & Blustein, 1999). Not only was attachment to the mother important, but also attachment to peers was related to increased exploration of one's environment and greater progress in committing to career choices. Tyson (1999) reports that ratings of attachment to the mother and father were related to different styles of career indecision that included anxiety about career choice, general indecisiveness, need for career information, and need for more knowledge about one's self. These studies suggest that the concepts of separation and attachment can add to knowledge of the career development process, but the findings are not specific enough to make concrete suggestions to counselors.

When applied to career development, attachment theory does not make specific predictions about career choices, but it does have some implications about how people may go about making their decisions and pursuing their careers. Because the research is limited and predictions are only partially related to career development, the suggestions for counseling application are general. Blustein, Prezioso, and Palladino Schultheiss (1995) and Tokar, Withrow, Hall, and Moradi (2003) believe that understanding individuals' relationships with others in terms of separation and attachment is useful in working with career choice and career adjustment concerns. Particularly, discussing issues of separation from and attachment to parents that are causing problems in an adolescent's life may help individuals develop a sense of security so that they can deal with career exploration and choice issues that are causing anxiety. When working with clients who are anxious about their career choice, counselors may find it helpful to ask about current or past strains in parental relationships. In such cases, the counselor can be a person with whom the client can feel secure and be less anxious in exploring career decisions. For example, if her or his parents are in the process of getting a divorce or were divorced earlier, the client may feel unsure of herself or himself in deciding about how to deal with parents, siblings, and educational or career decision making. In the *Father Factor: How Your Father's Legacy Impacts on Your Career*, Poulter (2006) gives examples of how attachment to one's father impacts career issues by examining fathers' attachment styles. Studies of the role of parental relationships in career decision making by observing or investigating the ways in which parents and their adolescent children talk about career choices have focused not on attachment but on interactions between parent and child.

PARENT–CHILD CAREER INTERACTIONS

A relatively recent focus of research has been the work of Richard Young and colleagues on the influence of parents on the career development of young people (Young, Valach, & Collin, 2002; Young, Valach, & Marshall, 2007). They refer to this research, which studies conversations between parent(s) and child, as an Action Project Method (Young, Valach, & Domene, 2005). When describing how parents and children perceive career decision making and their areas of agreement and disagreement, they use the term *contextual action theory*, which is particularly useful in developing culturally sensitive explanations (Young, Marshall, & Valach, 2007). This emphasis on the perceptions of parents and children reflects the constructivist point of view described in Chapter 11. In studies of videotaped parent–adolescent career conversations, Young and his colleagues (Domene, Arim, & Young, 2007; Young et al., 2006; Young, Valach, Ball, Paseluikho, Wong, DeVries, McLean, & Turkel, 2001; Young, Valach, Paseluikho, Dover, Matthes, Paproski, & Sankey, 1997) focus on the feelings and emotions that arose from parent–adolescent conversations. Young et al. (1997) show how parents and children try to establish a common ground or area of agreement in their conversations. In a later study, Young et al. (2001) identify four important goal-directed actions (projects) that families used. These covered issues such as relationships in the family, identity issues, reporting objectives, and attention to cultural goals.

As families talk, they may establish closeness or a sense of separateness depending on the nature of the agreements and disagreements (Young, Valach, & Marshall, 2007). Young and colleagues identify the importance of exploration, struggle, and negotiation as parents and their children in high school address the career choice of the students. The investigators studied short-term goals, such as continuing an open discussion between parent and child, and long-term goals, such as selecting a career direction. In another study of the conversations of adolescents and their parents, Young, Antal, Bassett, Post, DeVries, and Valach (1999) examined the way adolescents talked to their parents about reaching goals such as educational planning, career selection, and their future. Processes that take place in these conversations included exploring ideas, formulating plans, validating plans, and challenging ideas. When asked about the role of parental influence, adolescents saw that parental influence was appropriate in developing short-term goals, especially if the adolescents' decisions may have negative moral consequences (Bregman & Killen, 1999). Studying 19 pairs of adolescents and their mothers for 6 months, three types of projects were used to describe the parent–child interaction: projects focused mainly on the parent–adolescent relationship, projects shifting from career goals and actions to dealing with the parent–adolescent relationship, and projects used to help with career and related goals (Young et al., 2006). Another study examined differences between mother–son and mother–daughter pairs (Domene et al., 2007). There were many similarities, but mother–son pairs focused more on explicit career goals than mother–daughter pairs. Also, mother–daughter pairs experienced more conflict and avoidance following the conflict than the mother–son pairs. Unlike the work of attachment theorists who study career development, Young and colleagues analyze actual parent–child conversations. This work has helped in the development of a specific approach to involving parents in the career counseling process.

Amundson and Penner (1998) designed a five-step method of including parents and children in career counseling: Parent Involved Career Exploration (PICE) Counseling Process. This method includes an introduction, pattern identification exercises, discussion of school preferences and performance, a perspective on education and labor market possibilities, and planning the next step. In this process, which is designed for students between the ages of 14 and 18 years, two students and their parents are involved in the counseling sessions. In the first step, the process is introduced so that students and parents can understand how counseling can be helpful to them. In the second step, the Pattern Identification Exercise (PIE) is used so that students may identify their strengths and weaknesses that are related to their career development. They are asked to talk about a leisure activity that went well and to discuss a time when it did not work out so well. By doing this, students can see some patterns of weaknesses and strengths. Students consider the patterns that are suggested by this information and how these patterns can affect their career choice. Then parents are asked for additional comments. In the third step, School Preferences and Performance, the students talk about what they like about their courses and how well they are doing. After the students illustrate their views with examples, the parents are asked for feedback. In the fourth step, Perspectives on Educational and Labor Market Opportunities, they discuss labor market trends, the need to be flexible in choices, how school and work activities relate, the need to talk with others for information, admissions standards, and so forth. Their parents are asked to contribute to this discussion and provide their own information about the labor market strategies that they might find useful. The fifth step, Setting the Next Step, occurs at the end of the session and includes time for the counselor to give students and parents information about resources in the school and the community.

Typically, PICE is done in one session. Amundson and Penner (1998) suggest that PICE is an adjunct counseling approach that will work best when both student and parent are interested and motivated to explore careers. This innovative approach highlights the importance of the role of parents in the career exploration of their children.

FAMILY SYSTEMS THERAPY

In general, family therapists and marriage counselors have paid little attention to career counseling. But some scholars have examined ways to deal with the assessment of career issues within the family (Chope, 2006). Also, a few studies have described the effect of family relationships on career development. Of particular interest to researchers on family processes have been the enmeshed and the disengaged family (Goldenberg & Goldenberg, 2008). Basically, an enmeshed family is one in which the responsibilities in the family are unclear. For example, the mother and the father may give an 11th-grade student different advice about choosing a career. Her younger sister may tease her about being stupid because she has no career plans. In contrast, in a disengaged family, an 11th-grade student may be told by his father to make plans to study engineering because there are well-paid jobs in that field. The relationship between father and son is authoritarian, with the father telling the son and not listening to him. Penick and Jepsen (1992) find that family relationships, such as enmeshment or disengagement, were stronger predictors of career development than gender, socioeconomic status, or educational achievement. The extent to which family members are encouraged to express their feeling and discuss their problems had a small relationship to having positive career planning attitudes (Hargrove, Inman, & Crane, 2005). In a study of learning disabled adolescents, three types of parental interaction relevant to career development were identified: advocate for the adolescent, protector of the adolescent, and removed from the adolescent (Lindstrom, Doren, Metheny, Johnson, & Zane, 2007). In a study comparing college students whose parents were divorced with those who were not, students from intact families shared more about the decision making and were more decided than those whose parents were divorced, especially when parents were recently divorced (Scott & Church, 2001). These studies help to explain how methods of relating within the family can affect the career development of children and adolescents.

One approach that family therapists use with their clients can be applied to career counseling. When working with clients who are trying to choose an occupation, it may be helpful to discuss family career patterns. Shellenberger (2007) describes the use of the genogram as a way to determine therapeutic options for a family or couple. Sueyoshi, Rivera, and Ponterotto (2001) describe how genograms can be used in career counseling. Genograms encourage client self-disclosure, organize relevant information about the attitudes of the family toward work, and reveal how the work patterns of family members affect the client. To construct a genogram, Sueyoshi, Rivera, and Ponterotto (2001) suggest gathering relevant information about the family and writing important parts of the information on the genogram. An outline of a genogram is illustrated in Figure 12.1; this figure shows the client, Carlotta, in relationship to her family. Female individuals are represented by circles, and male individuals are represented by squares. The female client is indicated by a double circle, and the male client is indicated by a double square. In this abridged version of the genogram, the occupations of Carlotta's brothers, her parents, and her parents' brothers and sisters are also listed. In a larger genogram, cousins, spouses of parents' brothers and sisters, and grandparents would be included. When occupational information about the family is included, many issues of the client's view of himself or herself,

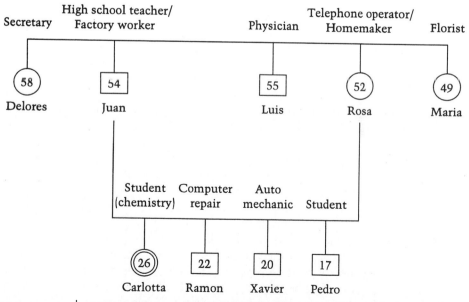

FIGURE 12.1 | GENOGRAM OF CARLOTTA'S FAMILY, INCLUDING AGES AND OCCUPATIONS.

others, and the world of work can be explored. Counselors can find out from their clients how different family members served as role models for attitudes toward work and further education. For example, did certain relatives stereotype careers by gender, or did they especially value certain occupations, such as medicine or the ministry? Did the family members have different attitudes toward obtaining more education after high school? Discussing such topics helps clients better understand the origin and the content of their own attitudes toward career decision making.

PHILLIPS'S DEVELOPMENTAL–RELATIONAL MODEL

Whereas attachment theorists have focused attention on the effect of parents on their children's career choices, other writers have focused more broadly on relationships that include friends, siblings, and teachers as they affect the career choices of individuals (Blustein, Schultheiss, & Flum, 2004; Phillips, Carlson, Christopher-Sisk, & Gravino, 2001; Phillips & Jome, 2005; Schultheiss, 2003). The following studies show how researchers have examined the ways that people help others as they struggle with career decisions. How schools and parents helped poor, non-white 12th-graders had effects on vocational expectations and valuing work (Diemer, 2007). Parents' relational support included doing activities with the student, discussing troubling issues with the student, and talking relatively frequently with the student. Parents' instrumental support included contacting the school about the student's career plans, attending programs about potential student employment, discussing their student's career plans with parents of their teenager's friends, and discussing job plans with their own teenager. School instrumental support included providing interest inventories, job fairs, and career readiness workshops. In a study of urban high school students, support from family, teachers, peers, and close friends helped students be more adaptable in their career choice, improve their expectations of their career outcomes, and helped in career planning (Kenny & Bledsoe, 2005). Bosley, Arnold, and Cohen (2007) examined the factors that make people helpful to others in their career development by interviewing 28 English working adults. Being credible by having information about employment-related factors was a major criterion. Also, being able to provide access to opportunities or influence others who could do so was important in being a valued career helper. Being supportive, genuine, willing to give time, being empathic, and being "on my side" were also valued.

Some other investigators have developed categories of relational responding that they have observed when interviewing students (primarily college students) about their career-selection process and their interaction with other people. Schultheiss, Kress, Manzi, A. J. and Glassock (2001) categorized types of responses of interactions that 14 college students had with parents, siblings, and significant others. Kenny, Blustein, Chaves, Grossman, and Gallagher (2003) categorized types of social support (and the lack of it) in the career decision making of high school students. Although each of these studies identifies different themes or issues, there is general agreement that studying the types of relationships in career development is useful. However, none of the investigators has been as thorough as Phillips and her colleagues in their development of categories of relational responding as it relates to career choices.

Philips and her colleagues have done a series of studies using 10 to 20 individuals to develop and refine categories of relational responding (Carlson & Phillips, 2001;

Jome, Phillips, Page, Donovan, Surething, Podchaski, & Sheehy, 2003; Lisi, Phillips, Christopher, Groat, & Carlson, 1999; Phillips, Carlson, Christopher-Sisk, & Gravino, 2001; Phillips, Christopher-Sisk, & Gravino, 2001; Phillips, Groat, Jome, Stramenga, Gravino, Christopher-Sisk, & Carlson, 2000; Phillips, Jome, Stramenga, Merrigan, Page, Tully, Groat, Koehler, & Mowry, 2002). The developmental–relational model has been applied to a variety of life decisions with career decision making receiving considerable attention. There are two major themes represented in the model: Actions of Others and Self-Directedness. Actions of Others includes seven ways in which the people in an individual's life involve themselves in career decision making. Self-Directedness includes eight ways in which an individual may participate in finding other people to help in career decision making. Each theme is described below using Phillips, Carlson, Christopher-Sisk, and Gravino's (2001) explanation as a basis for the overview.

ACTIONS OF OTHERS

When we make decisions, others often involve themselves in a variety of ways. The Actions of Others theme includes seven ways that others may involve themselves in our decision-making process. As Figure 12.2 indicates, the seven different Actions of Others range on a continuum from low involvement or little action of others to high involvement or action of others. The following sections describe these seven categories in order of involvement, starting with the least involved, Nonactive Support. Also given is an example of the type of comment or statement a person making a decision would likely make that represents the category.

NONACTIVE SUPPORT   Reflecting the least involvement of others, a nonactive support statement generally is not involved with the decision maker's choice process. It may be somewhat supportive, but no guidance is given to the person making the

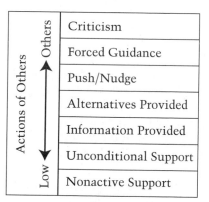

FIGURE 12.2 | ACTIONS OF OTHERS CATEGORIES LISTED IN ORDER OF INVOLVEMENT OF OTHERS.

Source: Reproduced from Phillips, S. D., Jome, L. M., Stramenga, M. S., Merrigan, B. A., Page, J. C., Tully, A. W., Gorat, M., Koehler, J., and Mowry, M. (2002). Relational influences in career decision making. Paper presented at the American Psychological Annual Convention. August 2002. Chicago, IL.

decision. For example, "Although my brother and I are close, he never gets involved in what I will do after I graduate college."

UNCONDITIONAL SUPPORT   In this category, the other person is actively supportive of the decision maker. That person listens to and supports the decision maker. Generally, the other person expresses his or her view that the individual making the decision is making one that they think is good, regardless of what the decision is. For example, "I've told my dad at different times that I want to be a doctor, a football player, and a funeral director. He has always supported my choice, whatever it was."

INFORMATION PROVIDED   In this category, a person provides information to the individual making the decision. The information is related to the options that the person making the decision has. Information is provided without suggestions of what decision would be best. For example, "I was able to go back to see my pediatrician, who I hadn't seen in years. She let me watch her with a few children and told me what a typical day was like."

ALTERNATIVES PROVIDED   This category goes beyond providing information to a person making a decision. Individuals provide the person making a decision with career-related opportunities. They may provide information about a possible job or an activity that will further a person's career development. For example, "Rose knew that I was interested in acting, and when an opportunity came to audition for this new play, she let me know."

PUSH/NUDGE   This category is different from the preceding ones in that an individual tries to guide the person making the decision to make a particular choice. The other person has a point of view about what is right for the decision maker and suggests it. Compared with providing alternatives, this is a significant increase in involvement or activity in another's decision-making process. For example, "My biology teacher in high school said that I should consider majoring in biology, even though I wasn't sure."

FORCED GUIDANCE   Unlike Push/Nudge, Forced Guidance is a category in which an individual may offer suggestions and guidance without considering the interests or desires of the decision maker. Essentially, in this category, individuals are telling others what they think would be best for them. For example, "My mom said I have to go to a school in the state because the tuition was so much lower. That meant I couldn't go to some other schools that I had been considering."

CRITICISM   This category goes beyond the previous one by telling a person what he or she can do, and also criticizes the individual in the process. The criticism may be of the individual's abilities, interests, values, or goals. Example: "My dad said that I shouldn't choose engineering. He said I'm not good enough in math, and besides, engineering does not seem right for a woman."

These seven categories of Actions of Others represent a broad range of involvement of others. Not surprisingly, more involved statements are likely to come from individuals who know the decision makers well, such as parents. Being aware of influences on a client's decision can be helpful to a career counselor as the counselor helps the client consider alternatives and options. The theme of Actions of Others focuses on how people influence a decision maker. In contrast, the theme of Self-Directedness focuses on ways in which an individual makes a career-related decision.

SELF-DIRECTEDNESS

In the theme of Self-Directedness, there is an increasing effectiveness of making good use of other people in career decision making. Figure 12.3 indicates an increasing level of self-directedness among the eight categories. These categories range from not using others at all to using them in a planful way. The first category reflects little self-direction or use of others in decision making.

CONFIDENT INDEPENDENCE (FALSE CONFIDENCE)   Individuals in this category do not appear to be planful or to be in the process of exploring what they would like to do. They may appear to be confident but do not really know what they plan to do in the future or what their interests, abilities, and values are. For example, "I just live one day at a time. I just do what I want. Things will work out."

UNSUCCESSFUL RECRUITMENT   Although individuals making a decision know that they need help, they have not been able to get it in a way that has been useful to them. They may have tried to get help previously, but those previous attempts may not have helped them make career decisions. For example, "When I ask my parents or my friends what I should do, they just say, 'Well, you'll know when the time comes.' That doesn't help at all."

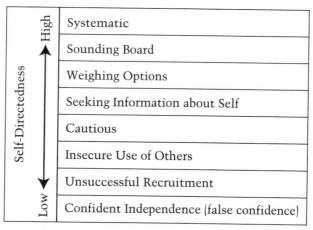

Self-Directedness		
High ↑	Systematic	
	Sounding Board	
	Weighing Options	
	Seeking Information about Self	
	Cautious	
	Insecure Use of Others	
	Unsuccessful Recruitment	
Low ↓	Confident Independence (false confidence)	

FIGURE 12.3 | SELF-DIRECTEDNESS CATEGORIES LISTED IN ORDER OF DEGREE FROM HIGHEST TO LOWEST.

Source: Reproduced from Phillips, S. D., Jome, L. M., Stramenga, M. S., Merrigan, B. A., Page, J. C., Tully, A. W., Gorat, M., Koehler, J., and Mowry, M. (2002). Relational influences in career decision making. Paper presented at the American Psychological Annual Convention. August 2002. Chicago, IL.

INSECURE USE OF OTHERS   Although individuals may seek out the advice of others and think about the advice, they tend to be unsure of their own ability to make decisions. They hope that by talking to others, they will be better able to make a decision. For example, "It is really hard for me to make career decisions, but if I talk to enough people, I may be able to trust their view and go with it."

CAUTIOUS   Cautious decision makers are those who are careful not to make mistakes when they are making decisions. They move toward making decisions more quickly than those in the Insecure Use of Others category, but consider the views of others carefully. For example, "I've made mistakes in the past. I've had several majors, and I'm not sure, now that I need a new one, that I'm going to pick the right one. I really want to hear what other people think before I choose what to do."

SEEKING INFORMATION ABOUT SELF   In this category, individuals may be unsure of their interests, abilities, or values. They actively seek out others to give them perspectives about what they may be good at or what they may like. They may be likely to seek out information from those who know them well. For example, "Roz seems to really know me very well. She's a great friend. She can tell me whether she thinks I could do well in medical school, or if maybe I should consider another health profession."

WEIGHING OPTIONS   When making decisions, those individuals in this category find it useful to ask others to help them with one or more parts of the decision-making process. They take responsibility for making the decision but find others' opinions to be important in figuring out what to do. For example, "My parents and I will sit down to talk about what college I should go to next year."

SOUNDING BOARD   Some individuals like to have others listen to their decision-making process. They like to talk out their point of view with other people but do not expect them to help in making any decision. For example, "Just talking to my girlfriend about different jobs that I may take after I leave my current one is really helpful to me."

SYSTEMATIC   When individuals make career decisions thoughtfully and in a planful manner, they are said to be systematic in their approach. This approach is similar to a rational approach to decision making. Individuals consider the input of others, but they take responsibility for making their decision. For example, "I've looked at career information, talked to a lot of people, and made a list of options that I have when looking for work."

Paying attention to the level of self-directedness that individuals have can help them in their approach to assisting clients in career decision making. Knowing ways in which individuals involve other people can help counselors decide on how to progress in discussing abilities, interests, values, and occupational information. Phillips and her colleagues, through their developmental–relational model, show the importance of others in the decision-making process. Individuals make different decisions in different ways. Some individuals may be in one category of self-directedness in making romantic decisions, but in another category in making career decisions. Also, individuals may move back and forth on the continuum of self-directedness depending on the nature of their decision and other people involved in their life.

Counseling Example of the Developmental–Relational Model

Counselors may find the developmental–relational model useful in counseling clients. Frequently, issues arise in the counseling interview about the involvement of others in career decision making. Counselors can attend to both the Actions of Others and Self-Directedness when talking with their clients. In the following example, Maria is a junior in high school. Her mother is the manager of the produce department in a large supermarket. Her father divorced her mother when she was 6 years old and rarely visits Maria. Her mother has a live-in boyfriend of 2 years who is a self-employed painter. Maria comes to the counselor to discuss what she should do after high school. Following is an excerpt from their conversation:

CL: I'm not sure what's gonna happen to me when I graduate. I'm thinking about things but, gee, I don't know.

CO: What things are you thinking about?

CL: Just things. I'm thinking of maybe being a paralegal or maybe an occupational therapist. I don't know.

CO: It's hard to be sure right now. There are several different options that you're considering. [Maria certainly does sound unsure. Maybe she fits the Insecure Use of Others or Cautious category. The counselor needs to hear more.]

CL: My mom has this friend who's a paralegal, Ms. Witherell. She really seems to like it. I talked to her about it one day.

CO: Oh, what did you learn? [Does the information from her mother's friend fit with the Information Provided category of the Actions of Others?]

CL: She told me that she liked working with lawyers, that it was fun for her. That she has been given more and more responsibility since she's had the job. She likes searching titles and working on wills and stuff.

CO: How does that sound to you?

CL: It started to sound good, but then she started to misunderstand me, I think.

CO: How did she misunderstand you?

CL: Well, she started to talk to me as if I'd already decided what I wanted to do. That I was going to be a paralegal. She starts to tell me what schools to apply to and where I should go, and who would be good employers when I finish.

CO: It bothered you, like she didn't seem to consider your opinion. [Maria is describing a situation that fits with the Forced Guidance category of Actions of Others. This seems to disturb Maria. It is disruptive to Maria's sense of Self-Directedness, where she seems to be mainly dealing with Insecure Use of Others or Cautious categories.]

CL: Yes, I'm just deciding. I get different input from others, although my father, my real father, says everything I do is okay. He never shows up at school or events or anything like that, I guess he's too busy.

CO: It hurts to be involved in a lot of activities and not have him show up. [The counselor hears about Maria's dad's Nonactive Support and her reaction to it.]

Although many counselors would not use the developmental–relational model as literally as the counselor in the example above, counselors may find it helpful to use the categories within Actions of Others and Self-Directedness that Phillips and her colleagues suggest. Maria's counselor uses the developmental model to understand how Maria's current career decision making tends to fit in the Cautious and Insecure Use of Others categories of Self-Directedness. When Maria describes Ms. Witherell's Forced Guidance approach to being a paralegal, the counselor can understand how disruptive it is to Maria's cautious approach to career decision making. Phillips, Carlson, Christopher-Sisk, and Gravino (2001) provide a more elaborate model of combining Self-Directedness and Actions of Others. They suggest a model that has four quadrants that include varying levels of Self-Directedness and Actions of Others. This method can be used both for assessing and counseling individuals.

The developmental–relational model is specific in identifying categories of decision making. It is consistent with a more general relational approach to career counseling (Schultheiss, 2003). Without being specific as to categories of relatedness, Schultheiss makes several suggestions about attending to relationships in career counseling. She suggests that in assessing career choice concerns, it is helpful to learn about important relationships that the client has with parents, siblings, and significant others. Discussing how specific aspects of the relationship have been important or influential to the client can be useful. These may be in positive, negative, or neutral ways. Learning about how clients have made career decisions in the past and how others have influenced them can also be helpful. Attending to ways individuals who are close to the client have already influenced the client's academic and work life can be helpful. Understanding attitudes about work within the family and how family members have affected each others' career progress can be useful. Some interactions with family members are not helpful, and examining how those relationships affect career development may lead toward better career decision making.

APPLYING THE THEORIES TO WOMEN AND CULTURALLY DIVERSE POPULATIONS

With regard to attachment theory, there are few, if any, consistent gender differences reported in early childhood in attachment styles, and few differences have been found in studies relating attachment to career development (Blustein, Prezioso, & Palladino Schultheiss, 1995). Investigations on attachment have been performed in England, Uganda, the United States, and other countries, providing a multicultural approach to this work. Studying 488 African American, 661 European American, and 434 Mexican American high school students, Arbona and Power (2003) report few differences in patterns of attachment among the three groups. In a study of French high school students, secure attachment and a fear of failure were related to career exploration for girls (Vignoli, Croity-Belz, Chapeland, de Fillipis, & Garcia, 2005). For boys, fear of disappointing parents was significantly related to exploring careers. In a study of 46 adults who had immigrated from Holland and Belgium to California, van Ecke (2007) showed that attachment anxiety and avoidance were related to having dysfunctional career thoughts such as confusion about making a career decision and anxiety about committing to a career choice. From a broader perspective, psychoanalytic writers such as Chodorow (1999, 2004) discuss the impact of different social roles of men and women on raising children. However, Chodorow and other writers provide observations that are more speculative than research that investigates attachment theory. Chodorow has not focused on career development, or on issues related to cultural diversity.

Recently, much attention has been paid to gender and multicultural issues in family therapy, as shown by Goldenberg and Goldenberg (2008) and Sharf (2008). These authors provide an overview of how genders and different cultural groups vary in their child-raising strategies. Chope and Consoli (2006) describe how cultural factors affect families and how these factors can have an impact on career decision making. Song (2001) reports that career aspirations of 428 Korean college women were related to nontraditional gender role attributes of women and close relationships with their mothers. Sinacore, Healy, and Hassan (1999) note that parents' advice to children about career concerns often differs depending on the child's gender. The sense of connectedness of college women with their parents predicted young women's anticipated distress about their future career choices (Li & Kerpelman, 2007). Although family therapists do not focus on career development issues, their observations of the role of culture and gender in career adjustment and decision making would appear to be consistent with the research on women and culturally diverse populations discussed in Chapters 7, 8, and 9.

The developmental–relational model of Phillips and colleagues is a recent approach that focuses on finding ways that individuals involve themselves in the career decisions of others and how individuals look for others to help in decision-making tasks. Their approach to research is to use in-depth interviews with small groups of individuals. They do not yet have sufficient information to address differences in gender and among cultural groups. In general, compared with other theories described in this book, investigators have done a limited amount of research on all of the relational approaches described in this chapter as applied to career development. Diversity issues are likely to be addressed in the future.

SUMMARY

Insights into parental roles in career development come from attachment theory and family systems theory. Although Roe's theory provides little information about parental roles in career development, attachment theory does have some information on how patterns of attachment to parents (secure, anxious–ambivalent, and avoidant) influence career development. Family systems therapy attends to relationships within the family and their impact on career development. This work is recent, presenting interesting questions about family influences on career choice, as well as some issues to be considered in counseling, such as discussing parental relationships as they affect confidence and exploration regarding career decision making and involving parents in the career counseling session. A practical application of the importance of parental influence is a counseling approach that includes two students and their parents.

Phillips's developmental–relational model goes beyond parental relationships and includes siblings, other family members, friends, teachers, and others. This model examines Actions of Others—that is, ways in which people involve themselves in the career decision making of others. Actions of Others is a theme with seven categories: nonactive support, unconditional support, information provided, alternatives provided, push/nudge, forced guidance, and criticism. The second theme that Phillips and colleagues have identified is Self-Directedness—that is, the degree to which people seek out others to help in their career decision-making process. They describe eight categories within this theme: confident independence (false confidence), unsuccessful recruitment, insecure use of others, cautious, seeking information about self, weighing options, sounding board, and systematic. The developmental–relational model, together with attachment theory and family systems theory approaches, is relatively new and offers much opportunity to further the study of career development.

References

Ainsworth, M. D., Blehar, M. C., Waters, E., & Wall, S. (1978). *Patterns of attachment: A psychological study of the strange situation*. Hillsdale, NJ: Erlbaum.

Amundson, N. E., & Penner, K. (1998). Parent involved career exploration. *Career Development Quarterly, 47*, 135–144.

Arbona, C., & Power, T. G. (2003). Parental attachment, self-esteem, and antisocial behaviors among African American, European American, and Mexican American adolescents. *Journal of Counseling Psychology, 50*, 40–51.

Blustein, D. L., Prezioso, M. S., & Palladino Schultheiss, D. P. (1995). Attachment theory and career development: Current status and future directions. *The Counseling Psychologist, 23*, 416–432.

Blustein, D. L., Schultheiss, D. E., & Flum, H. (2004). Toward a relational perspective of the psychology of career and working: A social constructivist analysis. *Journal of Vocational Behavior, 64*, 423–440.

Bosley, S., Arnold, J., & Cohen, L. (2007). The anatomy of credibility: A conceptual framework of valued career helper attributes. *Journal of Vocational Behavior, 70*(1), 116–134.

Bowlby, J. (1973). *Attachment and loss: Separation* (Vol. II). New York: Basic Books.

Bowlby, J. (1980). *Attachment and loss: Loss* (Vol. III). New York: Basic Books.

Bowlby, J. (1982). *Attachment and loss: Attachment* (Vol. I). London: Tavistock. (Original work published 1969.)

Bregman, G., & Killen, M. (1999). Adolescents' and young adults' reasoning about career choice and the role of parental influence. *Journal of Research on Adolescence, 9*, 253–275.

Bryant, B. K., Zvonkovic, A. M., & Reynolds, P. (2006). Parenting in relation to child and adolescent vocational development. *Journal of Vocational Behavior, 69*(1), 149–175.

Carlson, C., & Phillips, S. D. (2001). Relational perspectives on the college choice decision making process. Paper presented at the American Psychological Association Annual Convention. August 2001. San Francisco, CA.

Chodorow, N. J. (1999). *The power of feelings: Personal meaning in psychoanalysis, gender, and culture*. New Haven, CT: Yale University Press.

Chodorow, N. J. (2004). Psychoanalysis and women: A personal thirty-five-year retrospect. *The Annual of Psychoanalysis, 32*, 101–129.

Chope, R. C. (2006). Assessing family influence in career decision making. In G. R. Walz, J. C. Bleuer, & R.K. Yep (Eds.), *Vistas: Compelling perspectives on counseling* (pp. 183–186). Alexandria, VA: American Counseling Association.

Chope, R. C., & Consoli, A. J. (2006). Multicultural family influence in career decision making. In G. R. Walz, J. C. Bleuer, & R. K. Yep (Eds.), *Vistas: Compelling perspectives on counseling* (pp. 85–88). Alexandria, VA: American Counseling Association.

Diemer, M. A. (2007). Parental and school influences upon the career development of poor youth of color. *Journal of Vocational Behavior, 70*(3), 502–524.

Domene, J. F., Arim, R. G., & Young, R. A. (2007). Gender and career development projects in early adolescence: Similarities and differences between mother–daughter and mother–son dyads. *Qualitative Research in Psychology, 4*(1–2), 107–126.

Erdman, P., & Caffrey, T. (Eds.) (2003). *Attachment and family systems: Conceptual, empirical, and therapeutic relatedness*. New York: Brunner-Routledge.

Felsman, D. E., & Blustein, D. L. (1999). The role of peer relatedness in late adolescent career development. *Journal of Vocational Behavior, 54*, 279–295.

Goldenberg, H., & Goldenberg, I. (2008). *Family therapy: An overview* (7th ed.). Belmont, CA: Brooks/Cole.

Gravino, K. L. (2002). The role of parental attachment and psychological separation in the career decision-making process (Doctoral dissertation, State University of New York at Albany, December 2002). *Dissertation Abstracts International: Section B, 63/5-B*, 2650.

Hargrove, B. K., Inman, A. G., & Crane, R. L. (2005). Family interaction patterns, career planning attitudes, and vocational identity of high school adolescents. *Journal of Career Development, 31*(4), 263–278.

Jome, L. M., Phillips, S. D., Page, J. C., Donovan, B., Surething, N., Podchaski, E. J., & Sheehy, J. (2003). Relational influences in career and life decision making: A qualitative analysis of "good" and "bad" decisions of college students. Paper presented at the American Psychological Association Annual Convention. August 2003. Toronto, Ontario, Canada.

Kenny, M. E., & Bledsoe, M. (2005). Contributions of the relational context to career adaptability among urban adolescents. *Journal of Vocational Behavior, 66*(2), 257–272.

Kenny, M. E., Blustein, D. L., Chaves, A., Grossman, J. M., & Gallagher, L. A. (2003). The role of perceived barriers and relational support in the educational and vocational lives of urban high school students. *Journal of Counseling Psychology, 50*, 142–155.

Li, C., & Kerpelman, J. (2007). Parental influences on young women's certainty about their career aspirations. *Sex Roles, 56*(1–2), 105–115.

Lindstrom, L., Doren, B., Metheny, J., Johnson, P., & Zane, C. (2007). Transition to employment: Role of the family in career development. *Exceptional children, 73*(3), 348–366.

Lisi, K. L., Phillips, S. D., Christopher, E. K., Groat, M., & Carlson, C. (1999). Understanding the role of others in career decision making. Paper presented at the meeting of the American Psychological Association. August 1999. Boston, MA.

Lucas, C. (1999). Predicting at-risk adolescent work adjustment: An application and extension of attachment theory (Doctoral dissertation, University of Missouri–Columbia, 1999). *Dissertation Abstracts International, 59*/7B, 3747.

O'Brien, K. M. (1996). The influence of psychological separation and parental attachment on the career development of adolescent women. *Journal of Vocational Behavior, 48*, 257–274.

Penick, N. I., & Jepsen, D. A. (1992). Family functioning and adolescent career development. *Career Development Quarterly, 40*, 208–222.

Perrone, K. M., Webb, L. K., & Jackson, Z. V. (2007). Relationships between parental attachment, work and family roles, and life satisfaction. *The Career Development Quarterly, 55*(3), 237–248.

Phillips, S. D., Carlson, C., Christopher-Sisk, E., & Gravino, K. L. (2001). Treating clients with decision making problems: A developmental-relational model. In L. VandeCreek & T. L. Jackson (Eds.), *Innovations in clinical practice: A source book* (Vol. 19, pp. 129–140). Sarasota, FL: Professional Resource Press.

Phillips, S. D., Christopher-Sisk, E., & Gravino, K. L. (2001). Making career decisions in a relational context. *The Counseling Psychologist, 29*, 193–213.

Phillips, S. D., Groat, M., Jome, L., Stramenga, M., Gravino, K. L., Christopher-Sisk, E., & Carlson, C. (2000). Relationships and career decision making: Actions of Others and Self Directedness. Paper presented at the American Psychological Association Annual Convention. August 2000. Washington, DC.

Phillips, S. D., & Jome, L. M. (2005). Vocational choices: What do we know? What do we need to know? In W. B. Walsh & M. L. Savickas (Eds.), *Handbook of vocational psychology: Theory, research and practice* (3rd ed., pp. 127–154). Mahwah, NJ: Lawrence Erlbaum.

Phillips, S. D., Jome, L. M., Stramenga, M. S., Merrigan, B. A., Page, J. C., Tully, A. W., Gorat, M., Koehler, J., & Mowry, M. (2002). Relational influences in career decision making. Paper presented at the American Psychological Annual Convention. August 2002. Chicago, IL.

Poulter, S. B. (2006). *The father factor: How your father's legacy impacts your career.* Amherst, NY: Prometheus Books.

Puffer, K. A. (1999). A study of collegians' family activities, roles, and interpersonal relations and their vocational identity, career choice commitment and decision making: An application of the development contextual framework (Doctoral dissertation, Purdue University, 1999). *Dissertation Abstracts International, 59/12-A,* 4370.

Roe, A. (1957). Early determinants of vocational choice. *Journal of Counseling Psychology, 4,* 212–217.

Roe, A., & Lunneborg, P. W. (1990). Personality development and career choice. In D. Brown, L. Brooks, & Associates (Eds.), *Career choice and development: Applying contemporary theories to practice* (2nd ed., pp. 68–101). San Francisco: Jossey-Bass.

Schultheiss, D. E. (2003). A relational approach to career counseling: Theoretical integration and practical application. *Journal of Counseling & Development, 81,* 301–310.

Schultheiss, D. E., Kress, H., Manzi, A. J., & Glassock, J. (2001). Relational influences in career development: A qualitative inquiry. *The Counseling Psychologist, 29,* 214–239.

Scott, D. J., & Church, A. T. (2001). Separation/attachment theory and career decidedness and commitment: Effects of parental divorce. *Journal of Vocational Behavior, 58,* 328–347.

Sharf, R. S. (2008). *Theories of psychotherapy and counseling: Concepts and cases* (4th ed.). Thomson Higher Education: Belmont, CA.

Shellenberger, S. (2007). *Use of the genogram with families for assessment and treatment.* Hoboken, NJ: Wiley.

Sinacore, A. L., Healy, P., & Hassan, S. (1999). Parent connection: Enlisting parents in career counseling. *Canadian Journal of Counseling, 33,* 317–335.

Song, H. (2001). The mother-daughter relationship as a resource for Korean women's career aspirations. *Sex Roles, 44,* 79–97.

Sueyoshi, L. A., Rivera, L., & Ponterotto, J. G. (2001). The family genogram as a tool in multicultural career counseling. In J. G. Ponterotto, J. M. Casas, L. A. Suzuki, & C. M. Alexander (Eds.), *Handbook of multicultural counseling* (2nd ed., pp. 655–671). Thousand Oaks, CA: Sage Publications.

Tokar, D. M., Withrow, J. R., Hall, R. J., & Moradi, B. (2003). Psychological separation, attachment security, vocational self-concept, crystallization, and career indecision: A structural equation analysis. *Journal of Counseling Psychology, 50,* 3–19.

Tyson, T. S. (1999). The relation of parental attachment to career indecision subtypes of college students (Doctoral dissertation, New York University, 1999). *Dissertation Abstracts International: Section B: The Sciences and Engineering, 59/9-B,* 5115.

van Ecke, Y. (2007). Attachment style and dysfunctional career thoughts: How attachment style can affect the career counseling process. *The Career Development Quarterly, 55*(4), 339–350.

Vignoli, E., Croity-Belz, S., Chapeland, V., de Fillipis, A., & Garcia, M. (2005). Career exploration in adolescents: The role of anxiety, attachment, and parenting style. *Journal of Vocational Behavior, 67*(2), 153–168.

Young, R. A., Antal, S., Bassett, M. E., Post, A., DeVries, N., & Valach, L. (1999). The joint actions of adolescents in peer conversations about career. *Journal of Adolescence, 22,* 527–538.

Young, R. A., Marshall, S., Domene, J. F., Arato-Bolivar, J., Hayoun, R., Marshall, E., et al. (2006). Relationships, communication, and career in the parent-adolescent projects of families with and without challenges. *Journal of Vocational Behavior, 68*(1), 1–23.

Young, R. A., Marshall, S. K., & Valach, L. (2007). Making career theories more culturally sensitive: Implications for counseling. *The Career Development Quarterly, 56*(1), 4–18.

Young, R. A., Valach, L., Ball, J., Paseluikho, M. A., Wong, Y. A., DeVries, R. J., McLean, H., & Turkel, H. (2001). Career development in adolescence as a family project. *Journal of Counseling Psychology, 48,* 190–202.

Young, R. A., Valach, L., & Collin, A. (2002). A contextualist explanation of career. In D. Brown & Associates (Eds.), *Career choice and development* (4th ed., pp. 206–252). San Francisco: Jossey-Bass.

Young, R. A., Valach, L., & Domene, J. F. (2005). The action-project method in counseling psychology. *Journal of Counseling Psychology, 52*(2), 215–223.

Young, R. A., Valach, L., & Marshall, S. K. (2007). Parents and adolescents co-constructing career. In V. Shorikov & W. Patton (Eds.), *Career development in childhood and adolescence* (277–294). Rotterdam, The Netherlands: Sense Publishers.

Young, R. A., Valach, L., Paseluikho, M. A., Dover, C., Matthes, G. E., Paproski, D. L., & Sankey, A. M. (1997). The joint action of parents and adolescents in conversation about career. *Career Development Quarterly, 46*, 72–86.

13 | # KRUMBOLTZ'S SOCIAL
LEARNING THEORY

CHAPTER HIGHLIGHTS

Genetic Endowment

Environmental Conditions and Events

Learning Experiences

Task-Approach Skills

Client Cognitive and Behavioral Skills

Counselor Behavioral Strategies

Cognitive Strategies for Counseling

Social Learning Theory Goals for Career Counseling

Applying Planned Happenstance Theory to Career Counseling

The Role of Occupational Information

The Role of Assessment Instruments

Applying Social Learning Theory to Women

Applying Social Learning Theory to Culturally Diverse Populations

Counselor Issues

The study of human learning makes up a significant portion of research in theoretical, experimental, and educational psychology. Bandura (1969, 1977, 1986, 1997, 2000, 2002, 2006, 2007) has reviewed and compiled research that supports a social learning view of human behavior based on both reinforcement theory and observational learning. Bandura believes that individuals' personalities grow from their learning experiences more than from their genetic or intrapsychic processes.

Bandura (1986) acknowledges the role of behavior in learning but also recognizes the importance of thoughts and images in psychological functioning. He refers to the interaction of the environment, personal factors (such as memories, beliefs, preferences, and self-perceptions), and actual behavior as a *triadic reciprocal interaction system*. In this system, each of the three factors affects the other two. As this chapter shows, Bandura values the importance of learning by observation and by doing. Regulating these three factors is a self-system of cognitive structures and perceptions that determines individual behavior.

John Krumboltz and his colleagues have developed a theory of how individuals make career decisions that emphasizes the importance of behavior (action) and cognitions (knowing or thinking) in making career decisions (Krumboltz, 1994b; Mitchell & Krumboltz, 1996). It differs from most other theories in this book in that it focuses on teaching clients career decision-making techniques and helping them use these techniques effectively in selecting career alternatives and dealing with unexpected events. The theory also focuses on helping the counselor conceptualize issues. This chapter presents a general overview of this theory that considers genetic endowment, environmental conditions, learning experiences, and task-approach skills. With this background, important client cognitive and behavioral skills that are needed to make career decisions are explained. Behavioral counseling skills, such as reinforcement and modeling, are important tools that counselors are likely to find helpful for determining and correcting problematic beliefs about the career decision-making process. Cognitive and behavioral techniques and skills can be used by the client and the counselor in dealing with many career concerns and in encountering unplanned situations.

Why do people choose the occupations they do? Why do they choose one major rather than another? Why choose one college and not another college? Krumboltz's social learning theory attempts to answer these questions by examining four basic factors: genetic endowment, environmental conditions and events, learning experiences, and task-approach skills. Each of these factors plays an important part in the eventual selection of a specific career alternative; all four factors are diagrammed in Figure 13.1. The way they interact with each other is shown here. Although many other theories of career development focus on inherited abilities and environmental events, social learning theory emphasizes the importance of learning experiences and task-approach skills as no other theory does. Each of the four components of career decision making are described in the following paragraphs, but learning experiences and task-approach skills receive the most attention in this section. These are described in more detail in Mitchell and Krumboltz (1996) and Krumboltz and Henderson (2002).

GENETIC ENDOWMENT

Genetic endowment refers to those aspects of the individual that are inherited or innate rather than learned. These include physical appearance (such as height, hair color, and skin color), a predisposition to certain physical illnesses, and other characteristics. In addition, some individuals are born with special abilities in the arts, music, writing, athletics, and so on. In general, the greater an individual's innate genetic abilities, the more likely he or she is to respond to learning and teaching. For example,

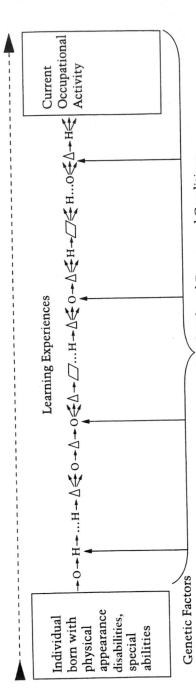

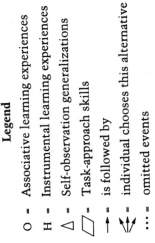

Time

Learning Experiences

Current Occupational Activity

Individual born with physical appearance disabilities, special abilities

Genetic Factors

Environmental, Economic, Social, and Cultural Events and Conditions

Legend

O = Associative learning experiences

H = Instrumental learning experiences

△ = Self-observation generalizations

▱ = Task-approach skills

→ = is followed by

⥸ = individual chooses this alternative

… = omitted events

FIGURE 13.1 │ General Model of Factors Affecting Occupational Selection.

Source: From "A social learning theory of career decision making," by J. D. Krumboltz, p. 32. In A. M. Mitchell, G. B. Jones, & J. D. Krumboltz (Eds.), *Social learning and career decision making*. Copyright © 1979 by Carroll Press. Reprinted by permission.

an individual with limited musical ability (for example, tone deafness) is unlikely to respond well to musical instruction no matter how long and how well it is done. The individual may improve but is not likely to become a skilled musician. The issue of how much of a particular ability is inherited and how much is learned is a difficult one. Social learning theory does not deal directly with this issue; rather, it focuses on learning and enhancing skills and abilities, where appropriate, as well as considering them in the career decision-making process.

ENVIRONMENTAL CONDITIONS AND EVENTS

A vast array of conditions affects individuals. These factors generally are outside the control of the individual and include social, cultural, political, and economic considerations. Factors such as climate and geography also affect an individual in significant ways. Living in a polluted environment or an environment subject to earthquakes or extremely cold weather certainly has an impact on an individual's career choices. Mitchell and Krumboltz (1996) and Krumboltz and Henderson (2002) describe several conditions and events—categorized as social, educational, and occupational— that affect an individual's career decision making. Such factors may be planned or unplanned, but they usually are beyond the control of the individual.

SOCIAL FACTORS

Changes in society have had a great effect on the available career options. For example, technological developments such as improved medicine and changes in transportation (for example, faster cars and planes) create new jobs. The use of computers to process and store information in a wide variety of fields has also had great impact on the labor market. Abuses of technology, which lead to jobs in environmental engineering and waste management, are also important. Related to the abuse of the environment is the continuing demand for natural resources, such as oil, that requires new techniques to find and remove from the earth. Social organizations, such as the Social Security system, programs for military personnel, and welfare programs, affect how people finance or seek careers and also require a staff to manage them, thus creating jobs. On another level, communities vary greatly in the occupations that they require. For example, a plains region may require ranchers and farmers, whereas a city requires merchants and salespeople. Social conditions also affect the availability of and the demand for educational resources.

EDUCATIONAL CONDITIONS

The availability of education is influenced by both social and personal factors—for example, the degree to which a person's parents value higher education and have the ability to lend financial assistance. Related to that is the school system that an individual attends and the effect of the teachers and the resources in that system on the development of the individual's interests and abilities. Furthermore, training opportunities vary. Universities, technical schools, military service, and apprenticeship programs provide a variety of opportunities. Financial assistance also varies greatly among these institutions. The ability to acquire the necessary education to undertake a career is just one of several occupational considerations.

OCCUPATIONAL CONDITIONS

There are a number of factors affecting jobs and the job market over which individuals have little control. One of the most important is the number and nature of job opportunities. Jobs may be seasonal—that is, limited by geographical considerations, such as logging and fishing—or may be affected by changing economic conditions. Educational requirements vary; some jobs require certification, licensure, a college degree, or other prerequisites to entry. Some jobs may require a college degree or other training that may not really be necessary for performance of the job. Furthermore, the salary and the prestige of jobs differ, depending on supply, demand, and cultural value. Also, labor laws or union rules may limit the number of people in a given occupation. Safety and other requirements may also affect the availability of certain occupations.

LEARNING EXPERIENCES

One's career preferences are a result of her or his prior learning experiences. An individual may have millions of prior learning experiences that eventually will influence his or her career decisions. Hundreds of times during a day, a child in school is exposed to bits of information that he or she responds to and may feel good about, confused by, discouraged by, and so on. Because the variety of experience is so great, each individual's learning experience is different from another's experience. Two basic types of learning experiences—instrumental (H) and associative (O)—are important in career choice (see Figure 13.1).

INSTRUMENTAL LEARNING EXPERIENCES (H)

An instrumental learning experience has three components: antecedents, behaviors, and consequences. *Antecedents* refers to almost any type of condition, including genetic endowment, special abilities and skills, environmental conditions or events, and tasks or problems. People then respond to the antecedent with behaviors. The *behavior* may be quite obvious or it may be subtle. Likewise, the *consequences* of the behavior may be obvious or subtle. Furthermore, the behavior may or may not have an impact on others. Perhaps the key to understanding the instrumental learning experience is the focus on the behavior of the individual. Examples of an instrumental learning experience include taking an exam, studying for an exam, reading about an occupation, or talking to someone about his or her work. If the consequences of the behavior are positive, the individual is more likely to repeat it or similar behaviors. For example, if an individual receives an A grade on an exam, he or she is more likely to continue studying in that field and to take more courses in the same subject area than if he or she does poorly.

ASSOCIATIVE LEARNING EXPERIENCES (O)

When an individual pairs a situation that was previously neutral with one that is positive or negative, an associative learning experience occurs. Two types of associative learning experiences are observation and classical conditioning. Classical conditioning is an associative learning experience that occurs when an event is generalized to a category of experiences. For example, an individual who gets caught between floors for half an hour in an elevator may develop a fear of all elevators. Future uneventful elevator rides will help to change the fear, and it is likely that the individual will return to former neutral associations with elevators. Less dramatic associative learning may occur through observing others, for example, watching a mail carrier or teacher perform his or her occupation. More passive associative experiences come about through reading and hearing. Reading occupational information and hearing a discussion about occupations are frequent ways of learning occupational information. Occupational stereotypes may develop from powerful associative experiences. For example, if a child hears that "dentists like to hurt people" or "bankers want to steal your money," inaccurate information may be learned.

TASK-APPROACH SKILLS

Understanding how an individual approaches a task is critical to career decision making. For the purpose of this chapter, task-approach skills include goal setting, values clarification, generating alternatives, and obtaining occupational information. Interactions among genetic endowment, environmental conditions, and learning experiences lead to skills in doing a variety of tasks. One's study skills, work habits, ways of learning, and ways of responding emotionally are a result of genetic characteristics, special abilities, environmental conditions, and instrumental and associative learning experiences. How an individual approaches a task depends on previous experience and influences the outcome of the task. For example, how an individual studies a French assignment depends on her innate ability, how she was taught French, and how much she has already learned. These factors, combined with how she prepares for the French exam, will affect the outcome (her grade). Certain task skills are particularly important in career decision making. These skills include setting goals, clarifying values, predicting future events, generating alternatives, and seeking occupational information. The development of these task-approach skills is a major emphasis of Krumboltz's social learning approach to career decision making.

Thoughts and beliefs arise from the four influencing factors just discussed. Thoughts and beliefs about the self and the environment arise from genetic endowment, environmental conditions, learning experiences, and task-approach skills. The ways in which individuals develop beliefs and act on them is the subject of the following section.

CLIENT COGNITIVE AND BEHAVIORAL SKILLS

How individuals apply their prior learning experience and innate abilities has a direct effect on career choice and other career issues. Individuals may make observations about themselves and their environment that they will then use to make career decisions. Observations about self include observations about capacities or abilities, interests, and work values. Generalizations about the world include the world of work, as well as other events outside oneself. Task-approach skills are related to the manner in which individuals approach the career decision-making process. Implicit in social learning theory is the idea that more experience provides an opportunity to make better career decisions.

SELF-OBSERVATION GENERALIZATIONS ABOUT ABILITIES

People make observations about their ability to perform tasks adequately based on prior experience and information that they may have acquired about themselves. Students may observe that they are good in math but poor in music, or they may observe that they are skillful in dealing with young children but awkward in dealing with elderly people. For many people, making accurate generalizations about their own competencies is quite difficult. People may tend to understate or overstate their abilities. Furthermore, some students would regard a B as a high grade, where others would view it as a failure. Similarly, students who receive scores on the SAT or ACT that put them at the 50th percentile compared with other students may possibly be disappointed or overjoyed. A person's view of his or her singing abilities may be quite different from the view of the audience. Thus, the accuracy of generalizations about one's own abilities often is derived from comparing one's view of one's capacities with others' views.

SELF-OBSERVATION GENERALIZATIONS ABOUT INTERESTS

Just as individuals make observations about what they are good at, they also generalize about what they like or do not like. If a student in a biology class does not like dissecting animals, is bored by studying anatomy, and dislikes learning about plants, he may generalize that he does not like biology. Interests can be very general or very specific. For example, an individual may enjoy 18th-century European history but may not be as interested in other aspects of history. Interest inventories are helpful in assessing generalizations that individuals have about interests derived from learning experiences. However, interest inventories do not assess specific interests, such as an interest in 18th-century European history. Furthermore, interest inventories are not likely to separate an interest in chemical engineering from an interest in electrical engineering. However, they are of particular use when an individual has difficulty in identifying interests that have arisen from a large number of prior learning experiences.

SELF-OBSERVATION GENERALIZATIONS ABOUT VALUES

People make judgments about the desirability of certain behaviors or events. From these judgments, they develop both personal and work values. Personal values may include a desire to be politically active or a desire to be involved in religious activity. Other personal values may include a deep love of art, music, or the natural beauty of the environment. Work values may include the desire to achieve or advance in one's profession. Other common work values include security, prestige, and high income. Some work values may be more difficult to state because they may be different from the work values that others hold. For example, a desire to persuade others by selling them a product may be more difficult to observe in oneself than the wish to help small children. Views of one's capacities, interests, and values contrast with perceptions of the world outside oneself.

GENERALIZATIONS ABOUT THE WORLD

As people make observations about themselves, they also make observations about the world in which they live and the people around them. Generalizations about occupations may come from both instrumental and associative learning experiences. Some generalizations may come from a great deal of actual experience. For example, a student who has worked in many retail businesses after school and during the summer may be able to make generalizations about retail sales work based on her experience. However, if that experience has not included training and management experience or exposure to managers, she may not be able to make accurate generalizations about the work of retail store managers. Some students may make generalizations based on few associative learning experiences. For example, it is common to hear people stereotype the career of funeral director based on jokes or movies. Frequently, they have little accurate information about the job duties of a funeral director. The purpose of occupational information and experience is to provide an opportunity for people to make generalizations about the world.

TASK-APPROACH SKILLS USED IN CAREER DECISION-MAKING

Often, individuals apply to career decision making the task-approach skills that they have learned in studying or working. Because career decision making requires one to make many generalizations about oneself and the world, previous task-approach skills may not be sufficient. Furthermore, the accuracy of an individual's worldview and self-observation generalizations may need to be questioned. The accuracy of these observations may be determined by a combination of the quantity of experiences, the representativeness of the experiences, and the task-approach skills that an individual uses in evaluating these experiences. Mitchell, Levin, and Krumboltz (1999) describe an approach to planned happenstance that emphasizes using learning strategies to cope with unexpected events. The following sections describe behavioral and cognitive techniques to assist clients in learning new skills and challenging troublesome beliefs.

COUNSELOR BEHAVIORAL STRATEGIES

Many behavioral techniques have been developed by psychologists to deal with a vast variety of problems. This section explains four procedures that follow from social learning theory and are directly related to career issues in counseling: reinforcement, the use of role models, role-playing, and the use of simulation in counseling. Reinforcement is the most important technique, with the broadest use, having an application in all phases of career decision-making counseling. In addition, the use of role models and simulation (trying out an occupation) can be particularly helpful when assisting clients in expanding their worldview generalizations.

REINFORCEMENT

Individuals are positively reinforced for their actions many times throughout the day. Positive reinforcement increases the occurrence of a response. For example, a student may be thanked for helping with the breakfast dishes, taking out the trash, and doing well on a history exam. Having been rewarded (thanked), the student is more likely to continue the behavior than if the student had not been rewarded. These experiences of positive reinforcement are cumulative. As suggested earlier, they influence an individual's observations of his or her capacities, interests, and values.

By reinforcing various aspects of a client's behavior, the counselor can assist in the accomplishment of career counseling goals, such as selecting an appropriate occupational alternative or dealing with difficult problems on the job. To reinforce a client's skills, the counselor needs to be viewed as a reinforcer. In most cases, this is automatic. Clients seek out counselors for help because they value their expertise. Thus, a counselor's positive reinforcement of an activity may have greater value than that of a client's friend or acquaintance. Positive reinforcement can include expressions of approval, positive excitement, and appreciation by the counselor. The following brief example further illustrates the benefits of reinforcement:

CL: Last week after we talked, I read about what sales managers do in the *Occupational Outlook Handbook*. It really gave me a pretty good idea. Then I went out and talked to my uncle's friend, who is a sales manager at a local paint distributorship.

CO: That's great! You really made progress in finding out about an important career possibility for you.

CL: Both the article and my uncle's friend helped me to get a better idea of the difference between being a salesperson and being a sales manager.

CO: That puts you in a better position to make an informed decision.

Both of the counselor's statements positively reinforce the client. The second statement is more subtle and less exuberant than the first. Sometimes, it is helpful for a counselor to reinforce an activity that has already been reinforced. For example:

CL: I just got an A on my Latin exam.

CO: That's terrific! I know how important it was to you.

CL: It makes me feel as if I can go on to college, and to a real good one.

CO: It makes you feel good about what you can accomplish academically.

The counselor reinforces an important event for the client, even though the A on the Latin exam is in itself reinforcing. By doing this, the counselor is assisting the client in developing accurate self-observation generalizations about her ability. Positive reinforcement can be given for both self-observation and worldview generalizations.

ROLE MODELS

Through the use of role models, clients can have a valuable associative learning experience. Counselors can assist clients by acting as role models and by providing role models for them. By describing appropriate ways to deal with career issues, counselors become role models for the client. It is likely that a client will think of the counselor's strategies when approaching future career concerns. Furthermore, a counselor who follows a social learning framework is likely to act in an organized and decisive manner, thus providing a role model for the client. Counselors can provide other role models for clients by making available videotapes or CDs, of people describing their decision-making process. For group career counseling, the counselor can invite employed individuals or recent graduates to discuss their career development with the group. In addition to being role models for dealing with career concerns, individuals can be role models for specific occupations. Videotapes or CDs of individuals who describe their occupation can be useful, as can referrals to job sites. There a client can watch and/or talk to a worker in a particular field.

ROLE-PLAYING

In role-playing, several strategies can be used to help clients learn new behaviors. Sometimes the counselor can play the role of the client and the client can play the role of another person. For example, the counselor may model an information-seeking interview by asking the client about something with which he or she is familiar, such as writing computer programs. The counselor can also model job interviewing skills by playing the role of the client, where the client plays a manager wishing to hire a computer programmer. After playing the role, the counselor may ask the client for feedback on strategies the counselor used to effectively request information or answer questions. By identifying strategies, the client can then try them out with a counselor.

By changing roles, the counselor can play the part of the person who has information the client wants, the role of a job interviewer, or a number of other roles. The client can play herself and practice new strategies. Sometimes it is helpful for the client to practice a portion of an interview several times. After each role-play, the client can discuss aspects of her behavior that seemed effective and others that needed improvement. The counselor may positively reinforce assertive and other effective behavior that the client demonstrates. Role-playing may continue until the client and counselor believe that new skills have been learned.

Audiotaping or videotaping the role-playing sessions can be an effective technique. Rather than recalling behavior from memory, the client and counselor can observe the behavior and discuss the client's strengths. Counselors are likely to use positive reinforcement as often as appropriate and to use criticism or point out problems as infrequently as possible. Reinforcement is likely to increase the chances that clients will use the behavior in actual situations. Counselors who use taping are likely to stop the tape and discuss a situation when behavior seems to warrant discussion. In some instances, the counselor may suggest that the client role-play a situation with a friend.

SIMULATION

By doing some of the tasks that an individual in a particular occupation must perform, a client can simulate a career experience. Several investigations researched kits designed to help high school students experience jobs (Krumboltz, 1970; Krumboltz, Baker, & Johnson, 1968; Krumboltz, Sheppard, Jones, Johnson, & Baker, 1967). The purpose of the job experience kits (Krumboltz, 1970) was to give students a chance to experience success in tasks that are common in a specific occupation. Care was taken to ensure that the initial task would not be frustrating to the client. Research done by the investigators listed above indicates that students who used the job experience kits expressed more interest in that occupation than students who received written or filmed occupational information.

To some extent, job simulation is provided by high schools and vocational technical schools when they offer introductory courses to various craft and trade professions, such as carpentry, metalworking, or welding. However, such courses often do not describe an occupation to a student; rather, they just provide the student an opportunity to learn simple tasks associated with that occupation. For counselors who do not have access to job experience kits, suggestions of volunteer, part-time, or summer jobs for clients sometimes provide a simulated job experience. However, there is often the danger that an individual who seeks such work will end up doing menial tasks. For example, a student who desires to find out what it is like to be a chef could end up in a part-time job washing dishes.

COGNITIVE STRATEGIES FOR COUNSELING

There is a greater variety of cognitive than behavioral strategies for career decision-making counseling. Many of these strategies are adaptations of cognitive psycho-therapeutic approaches. However, they are mentioned only briefly here, because a full description is beyond the scope of this book.

Mitchell and Krumboltz (1996) and Krumboltz (1996) describe several strategies for determining and changing inaccurate thoughts and generalizations regarding career issues. These suggestions are concrete and are excellent illustrations of a cognitive approach to career concerns. An interesting point that Mitchell and Krumboltz make is that, although many beliefs may be erroneous, some will be quite unimportant and not worth changing. The counselor must decide which of the client's faulty beliefs are interfering with the career decision-making process. The following sections discuss methods for assessing and changing inaccurate beliefs and generalizations.

GOAL CLARIFICATION

According to Krumboltz (1996), for individuals to learn necessary skills to apply to a variety of career issues, it is important that goals be clear and identifiable. Often, the counselor makes goals explicit so that the client and the counselor agree on what issues are to be explored, what choices may be made, and/or what skills may be learned. Sometimes, clients expect that the counselor will tell them what to do, or that a test will tell them what occupation to seek. Counselors may wish to restate goals so that the counselor and the client can arrive at mutually agreeable goals. For example, the counselor may say, "I want to work with you to help you explore occupational alternatives. This may or may not lead to an actual choice on your part at the conclusion of our work." The counselor and client can then explore the acceptability of this proposed goal.

Often, it is helpful to break down goals into smaller goals so that the client does not feel overwhelmed. For example, the counselor may say, "One of the first steps that we will take in trying to find possible future occupations is to examine activities and aspects of jobs you have enjoyed." This makes the problem of examining occupational alternatives seem more attainable, because steps are taken one at a time.

In clarifying goals it is helpful to reinforce open-mindedness. When a client says, "There is so much to do, so many occupations to choose from, I don't know where to start," the counselor can view this as open-mindedness. Open-mindedness means that the client is willing to explore options and is open to suggestions and learning new information. Such an attitude helps in seeing goals as attainable and something that the client can implement in the not too distant future.

Counter a Troublesome Belief

Clients may often make generalizations that are inaccurate or that may inhibit them from career exploration; for example, "You have to know someone to get a job in that field." This statement can be challenged; there are other ways of getting jobs besides having a friend in the occupation. Furthermore, there are ways to get to know people. The client's statement illustrates an inaccurate assumption. Another example of a troublesome belief may be a belief about oneself. For example, a client may say, "I am not smart enough to go to medical school." Instead of accepting that assumption, a counselor can ask for evidence for that belief. A freshman in college may not have sufficient course grades to support that belief. Furthermore, a senior with all C grades may not be able to compete well with other applicants to medical school, because candidates often need better than a B average to be selected to medical school. That is different from saying, "I am not smart enough." This method of dealing with a troublesome belief is referred to as *reframing*. The counselor may make the following response to the senior: "Just because you may not be able to compete with other applicants for medical school now does not necessarily mean you are 'not smart enough.' There may be other explanations for your C grades."

Look for Inconsistencies Between Words and Actions

Clients may say that they realize they need to spend time talking to people in different fields, but they may spend their time doing something else. Pointing out the difference between the behavior of a client and the intention may be helpful. In general, when clients state that they will do something, such as look at occupational information on given occupations, but then fail to follow through, there is an inconsistency between words and actions.

Cognitive Rehearsal

Sometimes, it is not sufficient to counter a troublesome belief. Individuals may need to practice or rehearse statements that are positive, which replace negative thoughts that they have about themselves. Individuals often are prone to focus on negative criticism rather than positive feedback. Sometimes, the negative criticisms of others turn into negative beliefs about oneself. Counselors may encounter beliefs about which clients seem to be quite persistent. Having clients mentally rehearse positive statements that dispute the negative statement often is quite helpful. The following dialogue illustrates a counselor's attempt to shift the focus from negative to positive statements:

CL: Throughout my life, my parents have either implied or told me that maybe college is not for me. Now that I'm a sophomore at Washington High School, I keep running into teachers who knew my older brother, who's now a freshman in college. They all tell me how well he did in school, and I know I didn't do so well last year.

CO: These comments from your parents and teachers make it hard for you to believe that you can actually go to college. We have talked about courses that you have done well in before, and there is plenty of evidence to show that you are capable of going to college. Furthermore, you told me how much you want to learn.

CL: I know I do want to learn, and I know that we have talked about my good grades in English and in math.

CO: When you find yourself feeling like you won't be able to go to college, you can say to yourself, "I have done well in English and math, and I really do want to go to college."

CL: Do you think that will help?

CO: Yes I do. In fact, I want you to say those words to yourself silently now five times.

CL: OK, I did that.

CO: How do you feel when you say that to yourself?

CL: Much better. Repeating that makes me feel I can do it. I'm not so discouraged.

Cognitive rehearsal helps strengthen clients' positive beliefs. When used in career counseling, it helps clients expand on options that they have. It also helps to ensure that when clients encounter opportunities in the future, they will not automatically dismiss them. In the previous example, the client would be encouraged to use this positive self-statement throughout the week. At the next meeting, the counselor may ask the client how often she used the positive self-statement and how well it worked. If the client did not use it, the counselor again may encourage the client to do so.

In their writings, Krumboltz and his colleagues (Krumboltz, 1996; Mitchell & Krumboltz, 1996) suggest many behavioral and cognitive techniques that counselors may use in helping their clients. These methods focus on coping with assumptions that they make about themselves or their world that interfere with their career goals. This section describes how reinforcement, role models, role-playing, and simulation are techniques that assist clients in exploring their interests, abilities, and values, as well as their world around them. These techniques focus on activities that clients can do rather than the way they think about themselves. Cognitive strategies are designed to help clients change their thinking about themselves and their environment. One strategy is related to the goal of career counseling: goal clarification. Other methods focus on dealing with beliefs that interfere with career goals. These include countering a troublesome belief and looking for inconsistencies between words and actions. Cognitive rehearsal is a method for actively dealing with interfering beliefs. There are many more cognitive and behavioral techniques that can be used in career counseling. I have presented only techniques that appear to arise more commonly when using behavioral and cognitive strategies for assisting clients with career issues.

SOCIAL LEARNING THEORY GOALS
FOR CAREER COUNSELING

The factor that distinguishes the goals of Krumboltz's social learning theory from other theories described in this book is the emphasis on learning. Krumboltz (1996) states that "The goal of career counseling is to facilitate the learning of skills, interests, beliefs, values, work habits, and personal qualities that enable each client to create a satisfying life within a constantly changing work environment" (p. 61). This statement emphasizes learning about self and the environment rather than making a choice. It is not that choosing is unimportant, it is that learning is the focus of social learning theory.

When applying principles of learning to career counseling, Krumboltz does not limit goals of career counseling to the selection of an occupation. Career counseling includes work adjustment, as well as career choice issues. For example, Krumboltz (1993) suggests that clients often are concerned about obstacles, such as finances and family responsibilities that interfere with achieving career goals. Often, discouragement and motivation are concerns of clients when they have lost a job or are seeking a job and feel they are being rejected by potential employers. Job dissatisfaction may result from problems with supervisors and colleagues or other aspects of the job, such as a commute or problems in one's company. For many individuals, planning a family and planning a career are interrelated issues. Both men and women often need to decide when and if they will work part time, full time, or devote full time to child care responsibilities. For older workers, retirement planning is an issue requiring the consideration of abilities, interests, values, financial responsibilities, and physical condition. Krumboltz (1993) believes that social learning theory has much to offer clients who have concerns in any of these areas.

A theme that emerges out of Krumboltz's recent work (Krumboltz, 1996; Mitchell & Krumboltz, 1996; Mitchell, Levin, & Krumboltz, 1999; Krumboltz & Henderson, 2002; Krumboltz & Levin, 2004) is an emphasis on change within the individual and the individual's environment. Krumboltz and his colleagues believe that individuals need to be prepared to make adjustments as their abilities and interests and the social, educational, and occupational environments change. Krumboltz (1996) describes three criteria that influence goals of career counseling.

1. *People need to expand their capabilities and interests, and not base decisions on existing characteristics only.* Krumboltz states that self-observation generalizations about abilities, interests, and values are subject to change. Also, some individuals have limited knowledge on which to base these self-observations. Thus, answers to an interest inventory may be based on an individual's lack of knowledge of certain aspects of the working world. This may make the interest inventory of limited use, because it may discourage an individual's development of new interests. Encouraging individuals to explore new hobbies and occupations is an important part of career counseling. Trying new educational, occupational, or other experiences is likely to help the client make better judgments about career selection, as well as deal with new events that the client encounters in his or her life.

2. *People need to prepare for changing work tasks, and not assume that occupations will remain stable.* In his theory of social learning, Krumboltz emphasizes the

importance of social, educational, and occupational conditions as they affect individuals' learning experiences. In particular, Krumboltz (1996) and Krumboltz and Henderson (2002) note how there are many factors that are moving rapidly in the change from an industrial to an informational society. Because of this, people's generalizations about the world need to be based on rapidly changing information. Workers often need to be flexible to complete several tasks rather than follow a written job description that may remain in place for several years.

Chapter 10 describes the concept of "boundaryless" work. There are fewer and fewer task specifications. Individuals are expected to deal with tasks that were not originally described to them when they applied for a job. An example of rapid changes in the environment is the Internet and the new approaches to commerce that have developed as a result of easier access to the Internet. As individuals see the need to improve their own abilities to cope with new occupational demands, they are likely to experience more stress.

3. *People need to be empowered to take action, not merely given a diagnosis.* From Krumboltz's (1996) point of view, trait and factor theory focuses on giving individuals a diagnosis. He believes that trait and factor theory helps individuals to make decisions based on their interests, values, and abilities, but it does not help them deal with changes that they may encounter as they look for work, experience work, or deal with others in relation to work. Because of changes that are occurring both in the individual and in the world of work, Krumboltz believes that it is the counselor's role to help the individual take action, as well as decide on a course of action.

According to Krumboltz (1996), career counseling should not end when a person has decided on a course of action. Rather, the person will need to look for a job, perhaps experience rejection, deal with positive and negative aspects of a job, and have to deal with new unforeseen problems and possible crises that may arise in following through on a plan of action. Krumboltz believes that counselors should follow up with their clients as they implement their job hunting or changing.

In our current society, individuals need to be able to respond to new and unexpected events that occur in their lives. Individuals should be able to respond in a positive way that will help them improve their lives when unexpected events occur. Mitchell, Levin, and Krumboltz (1999) and Krumboltz and Levin (2004) refer to this positive approach as planned happenstance. This recent work focuses on how counselors can help their clients deal with unplanned events.

APPLYING PLANNED HAPPENSTANCE THEORY TO CAREER COUNSELING

Krumboltz (Mitchell, Levin, & Krumboltz, 1999; Krumboltz & Henderson, 2002; Krumboltz & Levin, 2004) recognizes the importance of chance events in people's lives. Chance events in career decision making can be studied from many theoretical points of view (Chen, 2005), but Krumboltz has probably provided the most systematic suggestions for helping clients with career issues. As described on pages 371 and 372, unpredictable social factors, educational conditions, occupational conditions, as well as one's genetic endowment influence one's life. From Krumboltz's point of view, individuals need to capitalize on the events that occur in their lives. Bright, Pryor, and Harpham (2005) surveyed 772 Australian high school and university students about the role of chance events in their career decision making; 69.1% reported their career decisions were influenced by chance events. Taking advantage of chance events is called *planned happenstance*, an idea first put forth and developed by Kathleen Mitchell. In using this theory, the counselor helps clients recognize and incorporate chance events into their lives. Counselors also help clients generate such events so that they may work with them. In many ways, the more chance events that clients have in their lives, the more opportunities there are to take advantage of them. Of course, not all such events are likely to lead to positive outcomes. Illnesses and deaths of loved ones are examples of events that may require coping skills but do not typically lead to positive career development.

Planned happenstance theory is positive and encouraging. It replaces *indecision* with *open-mindedness*. When clients have difficulty making a choice, this then becomes an opportunity to look at a number of different paths and chances that they can take. Rather than help a client make a decision quickly, the counselor can help the client see that this is an opportunity to explore alternatives. The client may say, "I'm not sure what I'm going to do when I graduate high school. I'm really worried about it." Then the counselor may respond, "One thing we can do now is help you to become more comfortable with being undecided."

In planned happenstance theory, five skills are helpful in dealing with chance career opportunities. These skills are curiosity, persistence, flexibility, optimism, and risk taking (Mitchell, Levin, & Krumboltz, 1999).

- *Curiosity* is used to explore new learning opportunities and to follow up on options that result from chance events.
- *Persistence* is learned when there are setbacks in one's experience. For example, if a client is not offered a job but keeps trying, and finally a job interview results in an offer, the client may learn persistence.
- *Flexibility* is learned when dealing with many chance events. Individuals often are flexible in changing their attitudes when dealing with different circumstances such as different employers in different job interviews.
- *Optimism* comes from pursuing new opportunities and finding that actions can pay off.
- *Risk taking* occurs when there are unexpected new events. Clients learn that taking risks (for example, having an interview for a job in which the client does not feel sufficiently qualified) can result in a positive outcome. The outcome may not be a job offer, but rather another job lead.

According to Mitchell, Levin, and Krumboltz (1999), a model of planned happenstance should be integrated into career counseling. By doing this, clients can be prepared for a counseling process in which a discussion of unplanned events is a part of the process. This process deals with clients' anxiety about their future and problems they may encounter. It also helps clients understand that they may need to make many decisions when faced with unexpected events. The goal of counseling in dealing with planned happenstance is to initiate a learning process that encourages curiosity and helps clients take advantage of unplanned events. Mitchell, Levin, and Krumboltz (1999) describe the following four steps:

Step 1: Normalize planned happenstance in the client's history.

Step 2: Assist clients to transform curiosity into opportunities for learning and exploration.

Step 3: Teach clients to produce desirable chance events.

Step 4: Teach clients to overcome blocks to action.

In the following example, Xavier's career concerns are used to illustrate the application of planned happenstance theory. Xavier is a high school senior whose father repairs kitchen appliances. His mother is an assembly line worker at a local car manufacturing company near Tucson, Arizona. Xavier was a star linebacker on his high school football team and was having an excellent year when he broke his leg in the fourth game. Aspiring to be a professional football player, he has not let go of these aspirations, but he is frustrated by not being able to finish his senior year on the football team. Although Xavier would really like a career in football, he is aware that he would need to do well in college for four years and that the competition is extremely stiff. Now he has the time to consider other options, although unwillingly. He discusses possibilities with his guidance counselor, who makes use of planned happenstance theory.

STEP 1: NORMALIZE PLANNED HAPPENSTANCE IN THE CLIENT'S HISTORY

Using planned happenstance theory, the counselor integrates finding out about Xavier's background with happenstance-related questions. The counselor wants to know about Xavier's interests both in and out of school, as well as how well he has done in courses. The counselor also inquires about Xavier's experience in both part-time and volunteer work. Knowing Xavier's parents' aspirations for themselves and Xavier is also helpful.

However, in addition to these questions, the counselor wants to know how the client has dealt with chance experiences in his life. The counselor will try to make the client aware of how the client's own choices or actions have contributed to educational and career opportunities. In this first step, the counselor will try to help Xavier identify examples of happenstance and how he has taken advantage of happenstance through actions that he has taken. As the following dialogue illustrates, the counselor's goal is to help Xavier realize how he has been able to benefit from events that occurred by chance:

CL: Since I broke my leg in that football game a month ago, things haven't been the same.

CO: How has breaking your leg affected you and what you might do now? [The counselor wants to find out how Xavier is responding to having broken his leg and being out of football—a chance event.]

CL: It's been really tough. Especially the first few weeks were bad. There was a lot of pain. Now that my leg is better, it's not so bad.

CO: You have a lot more time now than you used to. [The counselor is setting up an opportunity for Xavier to talk about how he has used his time and what other events may have occurred in his life.]

CL: Yes, I have. In a way it turned out to be good timing.

CO: What do you mean?

CL: Well, my brother, who is in the eighth grade, got in trouble. He was caught about three weeks ago breaking windows at his school. That really turned things around at home. Were my parents ever angry!

CO: It sounds like your brother's trouble has had an impact on you, too.

CL: It sure has. My brother isn't allowed out of the house, and my parents are really concerned about his poor grades. So that means that I have to help him.

CO: Help him with his studies? [Xavier's brother's problem becomes an opportunity for Xavier.]

CL: Yes, I have to help him on his English and math. It really isn't something I've ever done before. I kind of like it.

CO: What is it that you like?

CL: I like the tutoring and teaching. I'd never really thought about teaching, but maybe the idea of coaching or teaching might be something that I could do.

CO: Xavier, this is great. You've taken two real difficult situations that happened beyond your control, your broken leg and your brother's trouble, and turned them into something positive. You've learned that maybe teaching could be something that you will do later on. Chance events can be something that you learn from and take advantage of. It seems you've really been able to benefit from these unplanned events. [The counselor reinforces and normalizes random events in Xavier's recent history.]

The counselor and Xavier can continue to discuss Xavier's history and other chance events that have occurred in his life. As they discuss these events, the counselor can point out how Xavier can learn about himself and the world of work from events that occur in his life.

STEP 2: ASSIST CLIENTS TO TRANSFORM CURIOSITY INTO OPPORTUNITIES FOR LEARNING AND EXPLORATION

Chance events become an opportunity for the client to indulge his curiosity. Future possibilities can be thought of and explored. Sometimes, the learning may be self-observations about abilities, interests, values, or the world. These unexpected events give clients a larger platform from which to make decisions and to deal with new unexpected events.

In the following example, Xavier and the counselor discuss how helping his brother, Raoul, has helped Xavier learn. Following is an excerpt from Xavier's counseling session:

CO: Xavier, can you tell me more about your thoughts about considering teaching after you worked with your brother?

CL: Sure. I really liked showing him how to do things. It really made me think about how I could help others by teaching. It was a really good feeling.

CO: Sounds like it made you want to learn more about teaching. [The counselor notes that Xavier is curious and excited about teaching. He wants to help Xavier take advantage of his curiosity.]

CL: But there's this problem with teaching. Teachers don't make any money. I mean their salaries are really low.

CO: How do you know that? [The counselor is trying to counter a troublesome belief. She believes that Xavier may not have accurate information about teaching.]

CL: Well, I don't exactly. I just hear teachers grumble about not making money.

CO: Here. Let's look at information in this booklet about teaching.

The counselor and Xavier take a few minutes to look at salary information about teachers and discuss benefits that come with teaching.

CL: Teachers make more money than I thought. Plus, they have the summers off. I think I can live with that.

CO: It seems now that we've addressed that issue you can continue thinking about teaching. It's not that teaching has to be definite now, but you're curious about it, and it's great to take advantage of that now.

The counselor finds out how Xavier's curiosity is increased by his learning experience. She helps him to deal with a troublesome belief that interferes with his curiosity. Two unfortunate events, his brother's troubles and Xavier's broken leg, have become opportunities for learning and exploration.

STEP 3: TEACH CLIENTS TO PRODUCE DESIRABLE CHANCE EVENTS

Clients not only can respond positively to chance events, they can plan to respond positively if they encounter chance events in the future. In Xavier's case, he did not plan to respond positively to these two incidents; he just did so. When unplanned events occur, there are many things that individuals can do to take advantage of them. For example, Xavier may wish to talk to his teachers about their teaching experiences. He may do some volunteer tutoring or literacy work. Because he is a senior, he may wish to explore opportunities for elementary and secondary teaching by reading college catalogs. So far, the example has focused on teaching to clearly describe the application of happenstance theory. However, the counselor is likely to use many other examples. The following dialogue is from later in Xavier's counseling session:

CO: Xavier, we've been talking a lot about teaching your brother, but I'm also wondering what kind of chance event you would like to happen to you?

CL: Well, I guess I would like to win two million dollars in the lottery.

CO: OK, let's say that does happen. [The counselor is hoping for a more realistic example, but this will do.]

CL: I guess I'd want to pay for my college education and my brother's. I think I'd like to get a new house for my parents, too.

CO: I understand how this would change your life financially, but how else would it change your life? [The counselor is interested in finding out how Xavier would respond to new opportunities and deal with fewer financial restrictions.]

CL: I would like to have more opportunity to watch sports and to read.

CO: What kind of reading would you do? [The counselor wants to know how Xavier might produce desirable chance events.]

CL: I read the newspaper now. But I'd have much more time to learn about local politics. I'd like to be more involved in that; it seems fun.

CO: It seems like you would be able to make a lot of opportunities for yourself. That seems important to you. Can you do that if you don't get two million dollars? [Since winning two million dollars is not likely, the counselor wants to follow up on Xavier's curiosity.]

CL: You know, I could. My uncle works in the office of a councilman. I think I'll talk to him and ask him about what he does. I know he is coming over to help my father with some stuff this weekend.

CO: Sounds like a great idea. Here your uncle is coming over and you're going to make it something that will be helpful to you. You would enjoy his visit anyway, but this will help you learn more. [By talking to his uncle, Xavier may generate unexpected information, which then may lead to other opportunities, such as visiting his uncle at work.]

The counselor uses positive reinforcement to encourage Xavier to explore opportunities related to Xavier's career development. Talking about what he would do with two million dollars leads Xavier to talking about his uncle, and then sets up the possibility of learning more about politics from his uncle. Furthermore, that may lead to visiting his uncle at his office or going with his uncle to a political event. In this way, clients can be taught to produce chance events that are likely to have desirable consequences.

Step 4: Teach Clients to Overcome Blocks to Action

Encouraging clients to engage in positive actions is important. It is not sufficient to just discuss possible actions. Sometimes, there are blocks to beliefs. A small example of a block was Xavier's inaccurate information about teaching. The counselor wants to take opportunities to promote curiosity, persistence, flexibility, optimism, and risk taking discussed earlier on page 383. Clients sometimes become overwhelmed or discouraged in pursuing career-related issues. They may be afraid of what other people think, and therefore not wish to pursue new skills or ideas. In the following example, Xavier talks about politics as a possible career:

CL: I know that my uncle is pretty good with words. He has lots of friends and they really respect him. I think he may run for political office sometime soon. I hope he does. I'd like to see him get elected. He deserves it.

CO: You really seem to admire him. You like what he is doing.

CL: I really do. I think he has really helped other people in his community a lot in the last few years. I think I would like to do that, but I could never do it.

CO: You seem to think you would be blocked from ever becoming a politician because of your skills. [Xavier's beliefs are being directly challenged.]

CL: I just don't think I could talk to people as well as my uncle.

CO: You seem to think you wouldn't be able to develop the skills that your uncle has. [The counselor challenges some of Xavier's self-observation generalizations about his skills.]

CL: Well, I guess I could. If I had four years of college like my uncle does, I would know a lot more.

CO: So you think it would be possible to develop those skills?

CL: Yes, I guess I could. I know I get along with people now. It's just that I don't know enough about how to work with people in a political way. I guess I could learn that from people like my uncle.

CO: As you talk about how you can learn from talking to people, from going to college, from being with your uncle, I can see that you are learning how to overcome obstacles that get in the way of your taking advantage of events that you may encounter in your life that can help you do things that you may enjoy, such as politics.

In this case, the counselor's challenge to Xavier helps him to overcome a block to action. The counselor lets Xavier reflect on different options he has to learn new skills that can take advantage of opportunities that may occur should he choose to become more involved in local politics.

The four steps described above may overlap at times, but they are designed to help clients take advantage of many events that happen in their lives over which they have little control (such as a broken leg). Because unexpected events continue to happen in an individual's life, Krumboltz and his colleagues want to assist clients in making the most of these opportunities through their description of planned happenstance theory. Within this theory, interests, abilities, values, and personal styles can be discussed, but they are done in an active way to promote the client's curiosity, persistence, flexibility, optimism, and risk taking. In working with planned happenstance, attending to clients' beliefs is important.

Krumboltz and Levin (2004) have written a book for adolescents and adults who wish to learn about making career decisions. *Luck is No Accident: Making the Most of Happenstance in Your Life and Career* helps individuals apply planned happenstance theory to their lives. This book includes many examples of individuals who have made the most of unplanned events. Many suggestions help individuals to create their own luck and not be sidetracked by mistakes. The exercises at the end of each chapter are helpful in applying Krumboltz and Levin's (2004) ideas to life situations.

Krumboltz (1988) has developed the Career Beliefs Inventory, which assesses many of the career beliefs that are potential problems for clients. The Career Beliefs Inventory contains 25 scales that measure a wide variety of beliefs, relating to such issues as experimenting with jobs, self-improvement, and learning to overcome obstacles. These 25 scales have been organized into five categories (Krumboltz, 1994a): my current career situation, what seems necessary for my happiness, factors that influence my decision, chances I am willing to make, and effort I'm willing to initiate. Many of these groups of scales emphasize empowering clients to take advantage of unexpected events that may occur in their lives. In social learning theory, there is an emphasis on learning about one's interests, skills, and values, as well as taking advantage of unpredictable events.

THE ROLE OF OCCUPATIONAL INFORMATION

Accurate occupational information is essential to the application of social learning theory. Rather than just saying that occupational information is important, Krumboltz (1970) designed job experience kits to be used to simulate occupations, providing exercises that are similar to tasks done by people working in the occupations. Additionally, Krumboltz (personal communication, November 23, 1999) has developed computer simulations of occupations, such as advertising, in which the client plays the role of an employee in the profession, interacts with simulated colleagues, and learns about the profession. Furthermore, in research that he and colleagues have done on career decision making, they use occupational information seeking as a criterion for effective career planning. More than most theorists, Krumboltz emphasizes the importance of learning occupational information in the career decision-making process.

THE ROLE OF ASSESSMENT INSTRUMENTS

Although tests and inventories are not featured in social learning theory as they are in some other career development theories, they are still useful. Values inventories may be particularly helpful in clarifying values when dealing with planned happenstance. Interest inventories and ability and aptitude tests may be useful in the application of social learning theories with regard to expanding self-observations about interests and abilities. In using Krumboltz's theory, counselors provide information from outside the individual, so that clients can make accurate self-observation generalizations. Because client beliefs are an integral part of Krumboltz's model, the Career Beliefs Inventory (Krumboltz, 1994a) may be of considerable help in most stages of career decision making.

APPLYING SOCIAL LEARNING THEORY TO WOMEN

Mitchell and Krumboltz (1996) discuss the application of their social learning theory to women in the context of four basic components of their theory: genetic endowment and special abilities, environmental conditions and events, learning experiences, and task-approach skills. They note that, although women do not have control over their gender, they do have some (limited) control over environmental forces, and more control over their learning experiences and task-approach skills. Mitchell and Krumboltz comment on the gender stereotyping that creates traditional and nontraditional occupations for men and for women. Relatively little research has been done on Krumboltz's social learning theory as it applies to women. Almquist (1974) reported that women who selected nontraditional careers were likely to have been influenced by female role models. When women were shown a videotape of other women who were being reinforced for making nontraditional career choices, those who viewed the videotape subsequently made more nontraditional career choices than did women who had not seen the videotape (Little & Roach, 1974). More recently, Williams, Soeprapto, Like, Touradji, Hess, and Hill (1998) have shown the importance of unplanned events in the lives of prominent women in counseling psychology. Williams et al. (1998) showed that the five skills (curiosity, persistence, flexibility, optimism, and risk taking) that Mitchell, Levin, and Krumboltz (1999) identify as important factors in dealing with chance events were helpful to the women in their study in taking advantage of unplanned events in their lives. By calling attention to the importance of learning experiences in career issues for women, Mitchell and Krumboltz and colleagues hoped that their emphasis would alert counselors to the need for enhancing opportunities for women who have been denied these opportunities because of discrimination.

APPLYING SOCIAL LEARNING THEORY TO CULTURALLY DIVERSE POPULATIONS

Although some studies have shown the importance of role models for culturally diverse clients, little research has applied Krumboltz's social learning theory to culturally diverse groups. In one study of Taiwanese college students, participants were trained in using Krumboltz's approach to planned happenstance in a 12-session workshop and scored higher on affective and behavioral inventories than did control groups (Chien, Fischer, & Biller, 2006). Mitchell and Krumboltz (1996) suggest several ways to apply social learning theory to culturally diverse populations. They comment that some cultures glamorize one occupation, whereas other cultures may favor another. Furthermore, some cultures may value income as opposed to spirituality or educational success. Such values may reinforce certain occupations for people from different cultures. Racial discrimination is another environmental barrier to culturally diverse people, who may encounter obstructions in trying to follow through on a career choice. Although it is difficult to do so, the environment can be changed through collective action that leads to the passing of laws such as those dealing with racial discrimination and affirmative action. By emphasizing the importance of social learning, Krumboltz and Henderson (2002) point out that counselors can assist in developing a proactive approach to career concerns and can help culturally diverse clients deal with discrimination that might otherwise limit their career opportunities.

COUNSELOR ISSUES

Krumboltz views the counselor's role from a social learning point of view. He believes it is important that the skills, interests, and values of the counselor be appropriate to the client. The counselor may have his or her own ways of dealing with unexpected events. Such social learning strategies may or may not be appropriate for the client. Listening to the client's description of how he or she deals with unexpected events allows the counselor to apply appropriate cognitive or behavioral techniques to the client's learning system without depending on the counselor's personal social learning system.

In determining whether to work with a client, a counselor must decide whether the client's problem fits within the interests, competencies, and ethical standards of the counselor (Krumboltz, 1964). If counselors specialize in a type of population (for example, older adults or college students) or a specific counseling technique (such as behavioral counseling), it is important that they be certain that the needs of the client are within their areas of expertise. Furthermore, if the client has a goal that seems unethical or inappropriate to the counselor, the counselor is bound to tell the client, and then either not work with the client or help the client to redefine his or her goal. For example, if a client says to a counselor, "I want you to guarantee me that I can get a job in business," the counselor must decline working with the client or must change the client's goal. When applying the planned happenstance approach to clients, it is particularly important for counselors to listen to concerns that may not necessarily fit in with the planned happenstance steps. For example, if a client is grieving over the death of a parent, the counseling should be flexible enough so that the counselor can assist the client with his or her grief. Because the concept of self-observed generalizations of abilities, interests, and values is quite broad, the counselor should be open to a discussion of experiences that may at first appear to be unrelated to career concerns.

SUMMARY

Krumboltz's social learning theory presents a model that emphasizes a behavioral orientation, with some cognitive components. The theory stresses the importance of genetic endowment, environmental conditions, learning experiences, and task-approach skills. Krumboltz and his colleagues provide both conceptualization skills and counseling techniques to help clients deal with future unexpected events. The behavioral and cognitive counseling techniques that they suggest include reinforcement, role modeling, role-playing, and simulation. Their cognitive strategies include goal clarification, countering troublesome beliefs, and cognitive rehearsal. These techniques are used at various points throughout career counseling. This chapter also illustrates a four-step approach to dealing with planned happenstance.

REFERENCES

Almquist, E. M. (1974). Sex stereotypes in occupational choice: The case for college women. *Journal of Vocational Behavior, 5,* 13–21.

Bandura, A. (1969). *Principles of behavior modification.* New York: Holt, Rinehart & Winston.

Bandura, A. (1977). *Social learning theory.* Englewood Cliffs, NJ: Prentice Hall.

Bandura, A. (1986). *Social foundations of thought and action: A social cognitive theory.* Englewood Cliffs, NJ: Prentice Hall.

Bandura, A. (1997). *Self-efficacy: The exercise of control.* San Francisco: W. H. Freeman.

Bandura, A. (2000). Social cognitive theory: An agentic perspective. *Annual Review of Psychology, 52,* 1–26.

Bandura, A. (2002). Social cognitive theory in cultural context. *Applied Psychology: An International Review, 51,* 269–290.

Bandura, A. (2006). Toward a psychology of human agency. *Perspectives on Psychological Science, 1*(2), 164–180.

Bandura, A. (2007). Much ado over a faulty conception of perceived self-efficacy grounded in faulty experimentation. *Journal of Social & Clinical Psychology, 26*(6), 641–658.

Bright, J. E. H., Pryor, R. G. L., & Harpham, L. (2005). The role of chance events in career decision making. *Journal of Vocational Behavior, 66*(3), 561–576.

Chen, C. P. (2005). Understanding career chance. *International Journal for Educational and Vocational Guidance, 5*(3), 251–270.

Chien, J., Fischer, J. M., & Biller, E. (2006). Evaluating a metacognitive and planned happenstance career training course for Taiwanese college students. *Journal of Employment Counseling, 43*(4), 146–153.

Krumboltz, J. D. (1964). Parable of the good counselor. *Personnel and Guidance Journal, 43,* 118–124.

Krumboltz, J. D. (Ed.). (1970). *Job experience kits.* Chicago: Science Research Associates.

Krumboltz, J. D. (1988). *Career Beliefs Inventory.* Palo Alto, CA: Consulting Psychologists Press.

Krumboltz, J. D. (1993). Integrating career and personal counseling. *Career Development Quarterly, 42,* 143–148.

Krumboltz, J. D. (1994a). The Career Beliefs Inventory. *Journal of Counseling and Development, 72,* 424–428.

Krumboltz, J. D. (1994b). Improving career development theory from a social learning perspective. In M. L. Savickas & R. W. Lent (Eds.), *Convergence in career development theories* (pp. 9–32). Palo Alto, CA: Consulting Psychologists Press.

Krumboltz, J. D. (1996). A learning theory of career counseling. In M. L. Savickas & W. B. Walsh (Eds.), *Handbook of career counseling theory and practice* (pp. 55–80). Palo Alto, CA: Consulting Psychologists Press.

Krumboltz, J. D., Baker, R. D., & Johnson, R. G. (1968). *Vocational problem-solving experiences for stimulating career exploration and interests: Phase II.* Washington, DC: U.S. Office of Education.

Krumboltz, J. D., & Henderson, S. J. (2002). A learning theory for career counselors. In S. G. Niles (Ed.), *Adult career development: Concepts, issues, and practices* (3rd ed., pp. 39–56). Columbus, OH: National Career Development Association.

Krumboltz, J. D., & Levin, A. S. (2004). *Luck is no accident: Making the most of happenstance in your life and career.* Atascadero, CA: Impact.

Krumboltz, J. D., Sheppard, L. E., Jones, G. B., Johnson, R. G., & Baker, R. D. (1967). *Vocational problem-solving experiences for stimulating career exploration and interest.* Washington, DC: U.S. Office of Education.

Little, D. M., & Roach, A. J. (1974). Videotape modeling of interest in nontraditional occupations for women. *Journal of Vocational Behavior, 5,* 133–138.

Mitchell, K. E., Levin, A. S., & Krumboltz, J. D. (1999). Planned happenstance: Constructing unexpected career opportunities. *Journal of Counseling and Development, 77,* 115–124.

Mitchell, L. K., & Krumboltz, J. D. (1996). Krumboltz's learning theory of career choice and counseling. In D. Brown, L. Brooks, & Associates (Eds.), *Career choice and development* (3rd ed., pp. 233–280). San Francisco: Jossey-Bass.

Williams, E. N., Soeprapto, E., Like, K., Touradji, P., Hess, S., & Hill C. E. (1998). Perceptions of serendipity: Career paths of prominent women in counseling psychology. *Journal of Counseling Psychology, 45,* 379–389.

SOCIAL COGNITIVE CAREER THEORY

CHAPTER HIGHLIGHTS

Self-Efficacy

Outcome Expectations

Goals

Contextual Factors: Barriers and Supports

Social Cognitive Model of Career Choice

Social Cognitive Model of the Development of Interests

Social Cognitive Model of Performance

Social Cognitive Model of Work and Life Satisfaction

The Role of Occupational Information

The Role of Assessment Instruments

Applying Social Cognitive Career Theory to Women

Applying Social Cognitive Theory to Culturally Diverse Populations

Counselor Issues

Started about 1980 and first known as career self-efficacy theory, social cognitive career theory focuses on the strength of individuals' beliefs that they can success-fully accomplish something. This belief in oneself has been viewed as playing a cen-tral role in career choice–directing interests, values, or abilities. Like Krumboltz's social learning theory (Chapter 13), social cognitive career theory is based on Bandura's social cognitive theory (Bandura, 1986, 1997, 2000, 2002, 2006, 2007). Social cognitive theory studies the interaction of the environment; "personal factors such as memories, beliefs, preferences, and self-perceptions"; and actual behavior. Known as a *triadic reciprocal interaction* system, because one factor affects the other two, this system is regulated by cognitive structures. A key concept is *self-efficacy*, which refers to individuals' views of their ability to organize and take action to attain the results they want (Bandura, 1986).

Generating many research studies that have investigated the role of self-efficacy in the career choices of women, the developers of social cognitive career theory, Steven Brown, Gail Hackett, and Robert Lent, expanded the original concepts into a detailed theory of career and academic interests, choice, and performance for both men and women. The cognitive concepts of self-efficacy, outcome expectation, and goal selection are significant factors in academic and career decision making. They affect how individuals view their capabilities and what they believe they are able to achieve. Brown, Hackett, and Lent also recognize that individuals vary in the barriers they face and the support they receive. Some individuals must deal with barriers such as racial and gender discrimination or lack of financial support. Others may receive emotional and financial support that helps them in attaining their choice. Social cognitive career theory attends closely to gender and cultural issues that have an impact on people's career choices and eventual attainments. Although focusing on theory development and research, this approach gives suggestions for helping clients make academic and career choices by helping them raise the level of their belief in their own effectiveness and their expectations of potential outcomes and goals.

Similar to Krumboltz's theory of career development, social cognitive career theory (Brown & Lent, 1996; Lent, 2005; Lent & Brown, 1996; Lent, Brown, & Hackett, 1994, 2000, 2002; Lent & Hackett, 1987, 1994) is based on Bandura's social learning theory. Although both Krumboltz's theory and social cognitive career theory make use of Bandura's concepts, they emphasize different aspects of his theory in their work. Both theories make use of Bandura's triadic reciprocal interaction system, focusing on the environment, personal factors, and behaviors. These theories emphasize the role of instrumental and associative learning experiences in career decision making and development. Both also view thoughts and cognitions, which include memories, beliefs, preferences, and self-perceptions, as a part of the career decision-making and development process.

However, social cognitive career theory and Krumboltz's theory differ in several important respects. Social cognitive career theory emphasizes cognitive processes (such as self-efficacy) that moderate or regulate actions more than does Krumboltz, who focuses on learning behaviors related to a variety of career concerns. Social cognitive career theorists have developed a model of career development that is more specific and complex than Krumboltz's theory (Figure 14.1), which focuses primarily on how prior learning experiences affect later learning experiences, and ultimately career choices. Social cognitive career theorists emphasize different individuals' belief systems that affect their behaviors more than does Krumboltz.

Because social cognitive career theory is relatively recent (starting in the early 1980s), Hackett and Betz (1981) have focused on the development of a theory and providing research evidence to support it. However, the theory has application for counselors; this chapter illustrates some applications after describing the theory itself (Brown & Lent, 1996; Lent, 2005; Lent, Brown, & Hackett, 2000, 2002). First, this chapter examines three important cognitive concepts that regulate the

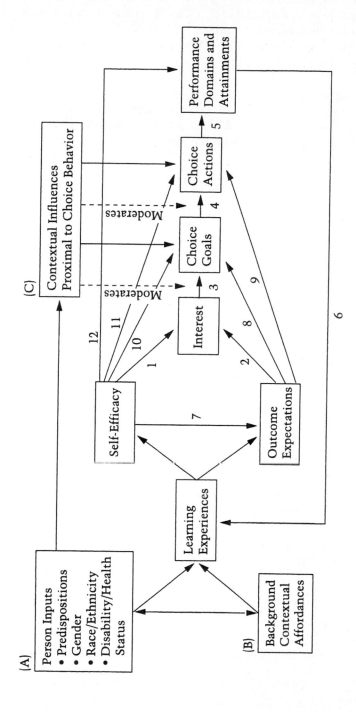

FIGURE 14.1 | MODEL OF PERSONAL, CONTEXTUAL, AND EXPERIENTIAL FACTORS AFFECTING CAREER-RELATED CHOICE BEHAVIOR.

Source: From, "Toward a unified social cognitive theory of career and academic interest, choice, and performance" by R. W. Lent, S. D. Brown, and G. Hackett, *Journal of Vocational Behavior,* 1993, 45, 79–122. Copyright © 1993 by Academic Press, Inc. Reprinted by permission of Elsevier.

career decision-making process and are essential to social cognitive career theory: self-efficacy, outcome expectations, and personal goals. Then this chapter describes factors outside the individual (contextual factors) that may present barriers to career choices or provide support for them. Social cognitive career theory has four different models: career choice, development of interests, predicting educational and occupational performance, and predicting work and life satisfaction. These models are generally similar to each other. In this chapter, I will describe the model of career choice in detail, while summarizing the other models. To illustrate the concepts of self-efficacy, outcome expectations, and personal goals, Sharon's career decision-making behavior is examined. Sharon is a 16-year-old African American girl who attends a large high school in San Francisco, where she is in the spring of her junior year.

SELF-EFFICACY

Bandura (1986) describes self-efficacy as "people's judgments of their capabilities to organize and execute courses of action required to attain designated types of performances" (p. 391). How individuals view their abilities and capacities affects academic, career, and other choices. Individuals with a low sense of self-efficacy may not persist in a difficult task; they may have thoughts that they will be unable to do the task well, and they may feel discouraged or overwhelmed by the task. Self-efficacy is a changing set of beliefs about oneself that varies, depending on the context of the situation. Some of the factors include the nature of the task, the people and surroundings with which an individual has contact, and feelings of competence on similar tasks. Brown, Lent, and Gore (2000) show that estimates of self-efficacy beliefs are related more closely to vocational interests and possible career choices than are individuals' estimates of their own abilities.

Sharon is worried about school. She does not like her math class and feels stupid when she is in class. Although she has earned a B-minus grade for the year so far, Sharon believes that she cannot do the algebra assignments well enough: "I never will be able to know what I'm doing in math, and the teacher seems to make it seem as if this is so easy." Some of her friends share her views, and they talk about how hard math is and how glad they will be when they are done with it. Her friends' beliefs reinforce Sharon's own low sense of self-efficacy as it applies to math. There is clearly a difference between Sharon's grades in math and her sense of self-efficacy regarding math. Sharon's sense of self-efficacy about math refers to the concept of academic self-efficacy, which is different from, but related to, the concept of career self-efficacy (Lent, Brown, & Hackett, 2002, Lent, 2005). Sharon's view that she is not very good at math is likely to affect her plans for future education and the career alternatives that she will consider.

OUTCOME EXPECTATIONS

When individuals estimate what the probability of an outcome would be, this is referred to as outcome expectations. Examples are: "If I play basketball, what will happen?" "If I play well, what will happen?" "If I apply to Harvard University, what will happen?" and "If I ask Mrs. Brown for a reference, what will happen?" In contrast, self-efficacy beliefs are concerned with "Can I do this activity?" Examples of self-efficacy beliefs are: "How well can I play basketball?" "Can I get good grades?"

and "Will I perform my job effectively?" Thus, outcome expectations refer to what may happen, and self-efficacy is concerned with estimates of the ability to accomplish something. Bandura (1986, 1997, 2002) has written about several types of outcome expectations, including the anticipation of physical, social, and self-evaluative outcomes. An example of a physical outcome expectation would be getting paid for working; a social outcome might be approval from your father for having done well in school; and a self-evaluative outcome might be being satisfied with your own performance in a class. In making judgments, individuals combine outcome expectations ("If I do this activity, what can happen?") and self-efficacy ("Can I do this activity?"). In general, Bandura finds that self-efficacy often is more important in determining a behavior than outcome expectations. Depending on the situation, either self-efficacy or outcome expectations may be more important than other expectations. Examples from Sharon's situation will help to illustrate the importance of outcome expectations and self-efficacy.

Sharon is considering the possible outcome of her next math exam. She wonders, if she does the homework and discusses her questions with the teacher, perhaps her math grade will be an A or A-minus. However, her sense of self-efficacy with regard to math is low, causing her to doubt her ability to do these activities; therefore, her sense of self-efficacy may be a more powerful determinant of her eventual math performance than is her outcome expectation. Thus, it is possible that she will not do her homework or ask questions of the teacher or other students; consequently, her math performance will be poor. Another factor that may influence her performance is her goals.

GOALS

Individuals do more than just respond to the events and the environment around them. They set goals that help them to organize their behavior and to guide their actions over various periods. They may ask the question, "How much and how well do I want to do this?" (Lent, 2005). This contrasts with outcome expectations, where they might ask themselves, "If I try doing this, what will happen?" For example, a freshman in college who decides to be a lawyer must set subgoals and choose behaviors that will help in reaching the goal. The reinforcement of being a lawyer will not occur for another 7 years. Goals are self-motivating, and the satisfaction that comes with meeting goals, such as graduation, is highly significant. Goals, self-efficacy, and outcome expectations are related to each other and affect each other in a variety of ways.

Sharon has a goal to be a store manager. Her outcome expectation is that, if she goes to college, works part-time in the mall, and enters a training program with a department store, she can reach this goal. Her self-efficacy beliefs cause her to think that she is a poor math student, will not be able to do math in high school, and therefore cannot do math in college. These beliefs will directly affect her outcome expectations and may cause her to revise her goal.

CONTEXTUAL FACTORS: BARRIERS AND SUPPORTS

Lent and colleagues recognize that individuals interact with others and that many factors affect self-efficacy, outcome expectations, and goals. Individuals' experiences exist within a context of various events and circumstances. Lent, Brown, and Hackett (2000, 2002) and Lent (2005) describe two basic types of contextual factors: background contextual factors and contextual influences proximal to choice behavior. *Background contextual factors* are ones that occur as individuals learn about and interact with their own culture and learn gender role expectations. These factors are also absorbed as people learn social and academic skills. In contrast, *contextual influences proximal to choice behavior* refer to environmental factors that come into play at particular academic and career choice points. Referred to as *proximal influences*, they tend to be current and directly related to career choice concerns. Examples are current role models in a specific occupation, part-time or full-time job opportunities in a desired field, and financial support for education.

Contextual factors can support an individual's choice or may be a barrier to obtaining a desired career objective. Most supports and barriers refer to proximal (recent) influences rather than background contextual factors. Proximal influences are ones that can be dealt with directly. For example, it is easier to try to overcome a financial barrier by searching for financial aid than it is to overcome being raised in a family where there was not enough food available to eat. Even when severe background contextual factor limitations (such as not enough food) exist, there can be supports, such as parents encouraging their children to study.

Contextual factors are a current area of research. In addition to personal factors such as interests, abilities, and values, barriers (such as limited financial circumstances) and support (such as encouragement from teachers) also are important career choice considerations (Lent, Brown, Talleyrand, McPartland, Davis, Chopra, Alexander, Suthakaran, & Chai, 2002). Both support and barriers can affect self-efficacy, which has an impact on career choice goals and actions (Lent, Brown, Schmidt, Brenner, Lyons, & Treistman, 2003). This finding was supported in an investigation of college students who intended to enter the sport and leisure industry (Cunningham, Bruening, Sartore, Sagas, & Fink, 2005). In a study of math and science options, perceptions of support were more highly related to outcome expectations than perceptions of barriers (Lent, Brown, Brenner, Chopra, Davis, Talleyrand, & Suthakaran, 2001). These findings are a few examples of the research that is being performed to examine the role of contextual factors in the social cognitive career model.

To illustrate the role of contextual factors on an individual's career choice, let us return to Sharon. Sharon worries about being limited in her choice of college because her parents have considerable debt (barrier). She feels she must first go to her local community college and is worried that she may not be able to get into the university of her choice (barrier). She has been getting some additional help in math from her teacher, Mr. Aldo, who is helping her feel more able to be successful academically. This support is having an impact on her sense of self-efficacy and her outcome expectations.

SOCIAL COGNITIVE MODEL OF CAREER CHOICE

The social cognitive model of career choice is quite complex, involving interactions among self-efficacy, outcome expectations, goals, choice, outcome, and contextual factors. Related to the model of career choice are the models of interest development, academic and occupational performance, and work and life satisfaction that will be described after the model of social cognitive career theory is explained (Lent, Brown, & Hackett, 1994, 2000, 2002; Lent 2005). All of these models are circular in that concepts indirectly or directly affect each other and continue to do so throughout most of the life span. Figure 14.1 is a diagram of the model of career choice behavior, and this section describes the paths of interaction among the concepts.

To illustrate the social cognitive model of career choice, I continue our example of Sharon's academic and career concerns. The following paragraphs explain and illustrate the paths that are a part of this model. The factors described here are those that social cognitive career theorists consider the most significant (but not the only) factors in career selection. The model starts out with those concepts that are significant in career choice and the selection of occupations.

Self-Efficacy   1 ⟶ Interest

Outcome Expectations ── 2 ⟶ Interest

Bandura (1986) believes that interests that are likely to persist across time arise from activities that people feel they can effectively complete and in which their participation would lead to success. As individuals try out activities, such as sports, they may feel that they are not good at them and subsequently lose interest. Likewise, when they feel that the outcome of the activity, such as sports, will not be successful, they tend to lose interest. Sharon believes that she cannot learn math well; furthermore, she expects that the outcome on her math exam will be poor. Both of these factors contribute to her lack of interest in math.

Interest   3 ⟶ Choice Goals

Individuals' interests affect their intent to do certain activities and affect their goals that relate to activities. Sharon has lost interest in math; she intends not to study, and she chooses goals other than math. Because she believes that she is an excellent soprano and her expectations that she will do well are strong, based in part on being asked to be a soloist in church several times, her interest in singing (Paths 1 and 2) has grown. Therefore, Sharon's goals for singing become much stronger than her goals for math.

Goals ── 4 ⟶ Choice Actions

The goals that individuals choose affect the actions that they take to achieve the goals. Sharon chooses to improve her singing and takes actions, such as singing lessons and more practice, to enhance her expertise as a singer. Math becomes a relatively unimportant goal, and she spends only 10 minutes a day on math homework.

Choice Actions ── 5 ⟶ Performance Outcomes

The actions that individuals choose greatly affect the outcome of their performance. Sharon's singing improves, whereas her math performance decreases.

Performance Outcomes ——— 6 ——➤ Learning Experiences ——— 7 ——➤
Self-Efficacy/Outcome Expectations

The outcome of the performance that individuals experience affects their learning experiences in general, which, in turn, affect beliefs in self-efficacy and outcome expectations. Sharon has positive learning experiences in her chorus and as a soloist. Her beliefs about her singing ability increase, as does her expectation regarding her ability to get offers to sing. In contrast, her negative performance on math exams affects her experience of learning, and thus she believes that she is not a good math student (self-efficacy) and will do poorly on future math tests (outcome expectations).

Outcome Expectations ——— 8 ——➤ Choice Goals ——— 9 ——➤ Choice Actions

Outcome expectations may have a direct effect on the way individuals perceive goals. If Sharon can find no opportunities to sing professionally, this will affect her goal to be a professional singer and influence future career choice actions. Although Sharon values the goal of professional singer, her expectation of a positive outcome is not great.

                        1 ——➤ Interest

Self-Efficacy ——— 11 ——➤ Choice Actions

                       12 ——➤ Performance Outcomes

One's belief in oneself is a major force that directly affects one's career goals, choice actions, and performance outcomes. For example, Sharon's lack of belief in her math ability not only affects her interests, her goals, and her choices related to occupations, but also her eventual occupational choice.

Social cognitive theorists make clear that there are other factors that affect learning and performance. Box A in Figure 14.1 (*person inputs*) shows the importance of personal and background factors. Biological predisposition, gender, ethnicity, disabilities, and other factors such as parental background have an impact. For example, Sharon has a strong, excellent voice, which contributes to her positive performance outcomes and positive learning experiences, and thus to her sense of self-efficacy as a singer. With regard to math, Sharon has heard that women are not good at math (a background contextual affordance), which negatively affects her learning experience and sense of math self-efficacy.

Contextual influences, or factors outside an individual's control, also moderate or have an impact on career choices (see boxes B and C in Figure 14.1). For example, that there are few jobs for singers and Sharon has few financial resources for further singing training are likely to be barriers to her choice to be a singer.

Sharon's older brother, Martin, is a senior at a prestigious college. His success is often talked about by Sharon's parents in a way that motivates Sharon to do better. That Martin went to a respected college (and does well) is a *background contextual affordance* (box B in Figure 14.1). Sharon's parents' discussion of his success is a current activity and is a *contextual influence proximal to choice behavior* (box C in Figure 14.1) because it has an impact on her choice goals and actions. Sharon also looks forward to her talks with Martin when he comes home from college. This is a supportive contextual influence proximal to choice behaviors (box C in Figure 14.1) because it motivates her to study harder, even in math.

Figure 14.1 diagrams important factors in an individual's career choice. Although self-efficacy and outcome expectations are significant factors in this process, Lent, Brown, and Hackett (1994, 2002) and Lent (2005) do not ignore either past biological, social, or environmental influences (box A) or current contextual factors (boxes B and C). These authors note that as individuals get older, it becomes more difficult (but not impossible) to change interests, goals, and performance outcomes, because these are affected by past behaviors. This conceptualization of the choice process gives counselors a useful perspective from which to view their clients.

COUNSELING EXAMPLE

Although there has been relatively little research on the application of social cognitive career theory to counseling, Betz (1992, 2006), Brown and Lent (1996), Lent (2005), and Lent, Brown, and Hackett (2002) make several suggestions that are of use to counselors. As she did in her earlier work, Betz (2006; Hackett & Betz, 1981) focuses on counseling women. She recognizes the importance of environmental forces that affect women's beliefs about both their ability to master particular content areas, such as math and science, and their ability to enter particular career areas. Betz suggests that counselors help women to understand that low self-efficacy with regard to math and other areas is part of their socialization as women. Such suggestions can also be applied to people from a variety of cultures, who may be the victims of discrimination or stereotyping. Exploring how feelings of low self-efficacy negatively affect the development of certain interests can be useful to clients. Observing nontraditional role models may also help to encourage the client to pursue nontraditional academic courses or work. Providing a support rather than a barrier by reinforcing clients' beliefs in their underused capabilities may be quite helpful. For example, encouraging women to persist with difficult math assignments supports their efforts to finish assignments. Sometimes, it may also be useful to reduce the anxiety that surrounds the notion of taking math or science courses. Social cognitive career theorists recognize the negative impact of social biases and discrimination on women and culturally diverse people. Thus, they have been particularly interested in developing a theory that would explain the career choices of all people, especially women and minorities.

Brown and Lent (1996); Lent and Brown (2002); and Lent (2005) examine self-efficacy and barriers and supports as they apply social cognitive career theory to both men and women. They suggest that counselors help clients identify instances when they foreclose on options because of low or inaccurate self-efficacy beliefs or low outcome expectations. In Sharon's case, the counselor would attend to Sharon's beliefs about her ability to learn math and her goals for math. These beliefs may become barriers for Sharon as she proceeds through high school. Even if Sharon did not have low self-efficacy beliefs about math, she might see barriers to pursuing a goal for a math or science career because of finances or other reasons. The counselor could help Sharon to remove or reduce these barriers. Helping Sharon have new positive experiences related to math (and science) may become a goal of counseling.

The following example shows how her counselor helps Sharon with both academic and career choice issues by using social cognitive career theory as a conceptual basis. Sharon has come to see her high school guidance counselor about picking courses for her senior year of high school. She is unsure about her future career goals and the specific courses she will take. Furthermore, she is unsure about whether to apply to colleges. The following dialogue is from Sharon's counseling session:

CL: I am not sure what to take next year, or what I'm going to do. Math is really getting to me. It stinks.

CO: Tell me more about math, Sharon.

CL: I just can't do it. It's getting too hard and too much boring stuff. I don't see why I should have to do it. It's a real pain.

CO: It's really frustrating. Sounds as if you try hard to do the work, but it doesn't come. [The counselor believes that Sharon is frustrated by not getting results from her work.]

CL: Well, I guess I could have tried harder to do my homework, but I guess I kind of gave up.

CO: Gave up?

CL: Yeah, I just don't think math is for me. After all, the guys in class seem to do well in it, but not the girls.

CO: Sharon, you might be surprised by how many women are able to do well in science and in engineering. Many of them do very well in math. In fact, there have been a number of women who have left our school to go to college in math. [The counselor gives Sharon information that contradicts her perception of how others have done, so as to prevent Sharon from foreclosing on a goal too quickly.]

Lent (2005) believes that it is important to attend to social cognitive processes that are a part of career choice problems. Particular attention is paid to inaccurate self-efficacy and outcome expectations. Lent suggests that counselors revisit options that clients have discarded or are discarding. Clients may have inaccurate outcome expectations or low self-efficacy beliefs. In this example, the counselor gives Sharon new information about math that may help to challenge her low self-efficacy beliefs about math. In her comment below, Sharon thinks again about her performance in math.

CL: Well, I guess I have done pretty well in math, but sometimes I get tired of it.

CO: Yes, I see that you've earned Bs in math. You really have done well in math before. That's great. [The counselor supports Sharon's math performance, hoping to influence both her math self-efficacy and outcome expectations.]

CL: Well, now it seems that the teacher is just going too fast. I've been busy with singing, which is going great, but neither the math teacher nor I seem to have time to work on this.

CO: I'm sure that Mr. Aldo would be glad to help you with some of your algebra. Continuing with math really increases your options. You seem to have done well and liked it before. It would be great if it doesn't slip away. [The counselor is working to help Sharon boost her sense of math self-efficacy, knowing that it can affect her interest, and ultimate goals, both for academic subjects and for her career choice.]

CL: *(not convinced)* Well, I could do that, but I'd really like to be a singer. Things are going great at church. I was asked to sing at a wedding, and I can't wait.

CO: Singing seems like it could lead to an occupation that you like.

CL: I'd love to do it, but I just know how difficult it is. There're some people in our neighborhood who have been singing in a group for years, and they never went anywhere.

CO: Having several skills, including math and music, can really increase your options. [The counselor is well aware of the job market for singers and wants to help Sharon develop her abilities and competencies as much as possible. By doing so, Sharon can develop and broaden her goals, which, in turn, will give her more choices and will increase her chances of good performance. By reinforcing Sharon's interest in math, the counselor helps her to expand her career options.]

In future sessions, the counselor may help Sharon to learn more about the importance of math. If Sharon is anxious, she might show her ways to use relaxation techniques and positive self-talk to improve her confidence. The counselor may also introduce her to women who are using math in their careers. Books and pamphlets on minority mathematicians and scientists may also prove helpful as a way to reduce barriers to considering new career goals.

Lent (2005) suggests several ways to help clients deal with barriers and build supports. First, counselors can help clients to identify and anticipate possible barriers to achieving career goals. When the barriers are identified, the counselor and client can examine the likelihood that the client will have to deal with the barriers. Then, counselors and clients can develop strategies to prevent or deal with the barriers if they occur. A strategy that Lent suggests is the *decisional balance sheet* in which clients list positive and negative consequences for each career option. Next, the client estimates the chances that each barrier might be encountered. Then the client writes down strategies for preventing or managing the barriers. Addressing supports, Lent (2005) suggests that clients identify ways in which families, friends, teachers and others can provide support in achieving career goals. Because the counselor recognizes the negative effect of biases about math for women, she uses many techniques to help Sharon increase her sense of self-efficacy and deal with anticipated barriers to achieving her career goal.

SOCIAL COGNITIVE MODEL OF THE DEVELOPMENT OF INTERESTS

The social cognitive career development model of interest is very similar to the model of career choice (Lent, 2005). The diagram of the model of the development of interest is similar to that outlined in Figure 14.1. The major difference is that the focus is on interest rather than on career choice. Social cognitive career theory views interests as developing as individuals see themselves as effective in activities and anticipate that there will be positive outcome expectations in continuing the activities. In contrast, disinterest develops when individuals doubt their ability and do not expect positive outcomes. Interests emerge along with the development of self-efficacy and outcome expectations. The goals that individuals develop increase the likelihood of practice in an activity, which then serves to develop self-efficacy and increased outcome expectations. As in Figure 14.1, this is a process that continues again and again. In social cognitive career theory, interests are seen as being subject to change depending on whether availability of certain activities is restricted and whether individuals are able to find appropriate learning experiences. These experiences enable individuals to develop self-efficacy and positive expectations into new areas. For example, babysitting or volunteering in an elementary school may turn into a goal of teaching. In social cognitive career theory, changes in interest are seen largely as being brought about by changes in self-efficacy beliefs and outcome expectations.

In social cognitive career theory, the development of abilities and values is seen as similar to that of developing interest. One's ability is viewed as influencing, positively or negatively, one's self-efficacy beliefs. One's career-related values are a part of and influence outcome expectations. For example, one's preference for comfortable working conditions is a value that also impacts one's outcome expectations of working in a comfortable situation.

In social cognitive career theory, culture and gender are variables that influence and affect self-efficacy and outcome expectations. In general, society views gender and culture in many different ways. Depending on the views of individuals and institutions with whom a person has contact, the different social and cultural environments can have a variety of impacts on an individual's view of self-efficacy and outcome expectations. To use gender as an example, if society views nursing as an occupation that is for females, males are less likely to have outcome expectations about nursing or to have it as a career goal. They are also less likely to develop interests or abilities in nursing-related activities.

The social cognitive career theory model of the development of interest can be applied to Sharon. She has started to do more of her math homework. Her teacher has told her that her work is improving, indicating how pleased he is with that. Her grades (ability in math) also reflect her improvement. Additionally, Martin, her brother, has told her about the accounting courses that he has taken for his business major in college, and how he thinks they are helping him prepare for a business career. Sharon believes that she may also want to major in business at college, and that math could be a possible outcome expectation for her. Her improved math performance has led to more activity in math. This has increased her sense of math self-efficacy, as well as her ability. Already having a strong interest in music and singing, her sense of music self-efficacy remains strong. Her view of singing as an interest continues even though social (workforce) factors affect her view of singing as a career choice. Thus self-advocacy and outcome expectations play an important role in the development of interest in social cognitive career theory.

SOCIAL COGNITIVE MODEL OF PERFORMANCE

One's ability to perform, both academically and on a job, is predicted by the social cognitive model of performance. Social cognitive career theory recognizes both the importance of the development of interest and the ability to perform, both at school and at work. As in other social-cognitive career models, the model of performance is one that continues to build for each individual. Thus, it is circular in nature. As Figure 14.2 illustrates, individuals' ability in schoolwork or at their job affects self-efficacy and outcome expectations. These then affect the academic or career goals that individuals will have, which in turn affects their levels of academic or

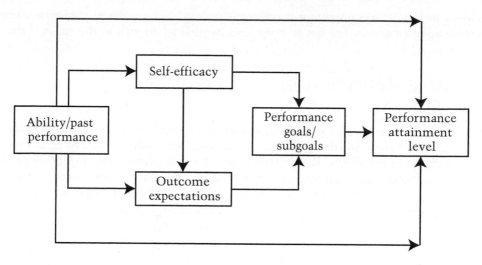

FIGURE 14.2 | MODEL OF TASK PERFORMANCE.

Source: From "Toward a unified social cognitive theory of career and academic interest, choice, and performance" by R. W. Lent, S. D. Brown, and G. Hackett, *Journal of Vocational Behavior*, 1993, *45*, 79–122. Copyright © 1993 by Academic Press, Inc. Reprinted by permission of Elsevier.

work performance. Additionally, one's performance will affect one's ability, which again will affect one's self-efficacy and outcome expectations. Important in this model is that many different environmental features influence people's learning experiences, which in turn influence their performance. Examples of these environmental features include the quality of the school work or training they receive, the helpfulness of teachers or instructors, support from parents, and support from friends, teachers, and others.

In this model, self-efficacy complements ability; it is not a substitute for it. For example, one's performance on a test in college is helped by a belief that one knows the subject well, but it is not a substitue for effort and ability. Having an appropriate degree of self-efficacy is helpful, but not sufficient. Lent (2005) suggests that if individuals overestimate their current abilities in a specific area, this may lead to failure and discouragement. Lent suggests that self-efficacy that is slightly greater than one's current abilities may be useful in further skill development and further motivation. However, if one's sense of self-efficacy is too high or too low, it can negatively affect one's performance.

The social cognitive career model of performance can be applied to Sharon's struggle with math. Her ability is increasing, which is affecting both her math self-efficacy and her outcome expectations. Her A-minus grade on her math test has helped her believe that she can do better in math than she used to believe (increased self-efficacy) and that she may be able to get an A on math tests in the future (increased outcome expectations). This leads to developing goals to get high grades on math and to continue to do well in math in this course and in future courses. This leads her to believe that she could take accounting (a future outcome expectation) and do well in it. It is important that Sharon not only have a career choice that she feels is appropriate for her but that she also be able to do well in the subjects that she chooses.

SOCIAL COGNITIVE MODEL OF WORK AND LIFE SATISFACTION

The most recent model of social cognitive career theory examines how the basic concepts of social cognitive theory predict work and life satisfaction (Lent & Brown, 2005, 2008; Lent et al., 2005). Lent and Brown have been interested in studying not only the development of career choice and ways of predicting career choice, but also in extending their model to be able to predict satisfaction with one's current work as well as a more general measure of satisfaction with life. As Lent and Brown (2008) and Lent et al. (2005) show, many studies have found a moderate relationship between satisfaction with one's work and satisfaction in life. There continues to be much research on the relationship of satisfaction with life with a number of different specific areas of life satisfaction, such as satisfaction with one's job.

The social cognitive model of work and life satisfaction is somewhat similar to that of the models of interest development and career choice. At the core of the model of work and life satisfaction is one's self-efficacy. However, rather than outcome expectations about one's career choice, this model examines individuals' expectations about work that they will do and the conditions under which they will do it. These variables are used to predict participation and progress in goal-directed activity, which is used to predict work satisfaction and overall life satisfaction. One aspect of this model that is different from other models is that personality traits such as extroversion, anxiety, and conscientiousness are studied to examine what affect they have on work satisfaction and overall life satisfaction. This model is a complex one that looks at relationships among personality or affective, cognitive, behavioral, and environmental variables. Because this model is relatively recent, research on it is less definitive. Brown and Lent (2008) describe possible research that is needed to show that it can be used to predict work and life satisfaction.

To apply this model to Sharon, it is necessary to look into her future. Although this model is meant to be studied by analyzing groups, not an individual, it is easiest to illustrate it by using a case example. If Sharon were to act in a way that is consistent with this model, we might predict that after 10 years she will have finished high school and gone to college to finish a business degree. At that point, Sharon would have self-efficacious beliefs about her academic abilities, specifically math, and have expectations about work conditions and potential outcomes in her job in retail management. If she realizes these expectations and moves forward in developing her managerial skills, this model would predict not only satisfaction with her work, but satisfaction with her life in general. If Sharon is conscientious and somewhat extroverted, while lacking anxiety, this model is particularly likely to hold true. However, this is a model, and it is imperfect in its predictions. Sharon may have had support and skill to attain an alternate goal of becoming a successful singer rather than a store manager. If she chooses this goal, she may also achieve work and life satisfaction. Because this model predicts both job and life satisfaction, it is more comprehensive than the other models described in this chapter. Future research will determine the accuracy of these predictions.

THE ROLE OF OCCUPATIONAL INFORMATION

Not having accurate and sufficient occupational information can be a barrier to achieving choice goals and choice actions. Betz (1992) describes the importance of having career information that is accurate and unbiased, featuring women and culturally diverse people in nontraditional occupations. Lent (2001, 2005), Lent, Brown and Hackett (2002), and Lent, Brown, Talleyrand, McPartland, Davis, Chopra, Alexander, Suthakaran, and Chai (2002) recognize societal and workforce changes that individuals may encounter. Krumboltz (see Chapter 13) uses the concept of *planned happenstance* to help individuals deal with new or difficult workforce changes. Social cognitive career theory (Lent, 2005) describes how individuals are able to regulate their lives, develop their abilities, and make good career choices. By using the education that is available to them (for example, training programs, community colleges, and universities), individuals can increase their skill levels and their information about occupations. By doing this, their interests and abilities develop more fully. They may change choice goals and choice actions to reach new levels of career attainments. In social cognitive career theory, career information is especially essential in developing realistic outcome expectations (that is, beliefs about the working conditions and reinforcers available in different occupations, and how they compare with one's work values). Learning occupational information is one of many learning experiences that interact with the development of self-efficacy and outcome experiences leading to new choice actions.

THE ROLE OF ASSESSMENT INSTRUMENTS

In social cognitive career theory, interest, values, and performance are important aspects of a model of career choice. Tests and inventories provide information for the client to use in making career decisions. Furthermore, the instruments give the counselor information, so that he or she may support and strengthen self-efficacy beliefs and discuss outcome expectations. Brown and Lent (1996) believe that discrepancies between measured interests and abilities in a specific area, such as biology, may point to low self-efficacy beliefs about biology. When there are discrepancies between work-related needs or values and interest measures, clients may be experiencing faulty outcome expectations. The Career Decision-Making Self-Efficacy Scale (Betz & Luzzo, 1996; Taylor & Popma, 1990) has been used primarily for research purposes. More recently, this 50-item form has been complemented by a 25-item inventory called the Career Decision Self-Efficacy Scale–Short Form (CDSES). The CDSES has five subscales that are aspects of career decision self-efficacy: goal selection, gathering occupational information, problem solving, planning for the future, and accurate self-appraisal. Betz, Hammond, and Multon, (2005); Betz and Taylor, (2000); Chaney, Hammond, Betz, and Multon (2007), and O'Brien (2003) provide information about the reliability and validity of the

CDSES. A measure of outcome expectations, the Educational Outcome Expectancy Scale has also been developed and revised (Springer, Larson, Tilley, Gasser, & Quinn, 2001; Tilley, 2006).

APPLYING SOCIAL COGNITIVE CAREER THEORY TO WOMEN

Whereas career development issues for women have played a minor role in Krumboltz's social learning theory, they have been a major focus in the development of social cognitive career theory. In their original article on career self-efficacy, Hackett and Betz (1981) proposed that career self-efficacy beliefs would play a stronger role than interests, values, or abilities in restricting women's career choices. Since this article was written, more than 40 investigations have been performed to test their propositions. Almost all of these studies have addressed self-efficacy as it relates to women's academic, career, and other choices. Because this research is so extensive, only general findings arising from the results of these studies are presented here. Lent (2005) summarizes research evidence that relates to propositions that are a part of social cognitive career theory. Betz (2007), Betz and Hackett (1997, 2006), and Solberg (1998) have summarized much of the research that relates to career self-efficacy issues as they relate to women. The information that is presented here is drawn from these sources, as well as more recent research.

A number of studies have examined the general topic of the relationship of self-efficacy to career-related choices (Hackett, 1995). Early research (Betz & Hackett, 1981) showed that college men's occupational self-efficacy was relatively constant across occupations, but that women scored significantly lower on occupational self-efficacy for nontraditional occupations and significantly higher for traditionally female occupations. Other studies have shown that occupational self-efficacy predicts interests and career choice. Furthermore, there are gender differences in occupational self-efficacy in different groups of college students for different occupational choices, job tasks, and work activities. However, gender differences in self-efficacy usually are not found in samples that are quite similar to each other, such as high-achieving students. When adults were studied across all six Holland types (21 occupations were included), minimal gender differences were found for self-efficacy (Betz, Borgen, Kaplan, & Harmon, 1998). When tasks are particularly gender-stereotyped, differences in self-efficacy between men and women may be found. Stereotypes about how women should behave are likely to undermine women's self-efficacy regarding the choice of a nontraditional career. A conclusion reached about this research is that, if women eliminate nontraditional career opportunities because of low self-efficacy beliefs, they are limiting their opportunities to find satisfying and well-paid jobs after college. Although most studies have been done on college students, research on high school students also shows gender differences in occupational self-efficacy.

Besides studying the relationship of career self-efficacy to career-related choices, researchers have found relationships between self-efficacy and the choice of a college major, career interests, and career decision-making processes. Few gender differences have been found in these studies. When women are engineering majors and presumably have confidence in their math ability, few differences are found between male and female engineering majors in levels of math self-efficacy, as well as persistence in engineering (Schaefers, Epperson, & Nauta, 1997, Lent et al., 2005). The social cognitive career model is not limited to predictions about math and science; the model has also been predictive in areas of study in art, English, and social studies in college students (Fouad, Smith, & Zao, 2002). However, no gender differences were found in this study.

A number of studies have been concerned with career barriers that women encounter. Luzzo and McWhirter (2001) report that women perceived more barriers to occupational success than did men. However, in another study women (but not men) viewed barriers as being positively related to their outcome expectations (Lindley, 2005). In another study, women tended to see personal finances as barriers to career goals, whereas men saw time management issues as barriers (Perrone, Sedlacek, & Alexander, 2001). Concerned about barriers that battered women face, Chronister and McWhirter (2003) make use of social cognitive career theory as a means to help women overcome career barriers. In part, their model helps women become aware of power dynamics that affect them in domestic violence situations, as well as job-related issues. Coogan and Chen (2007) suggest ways that counselors could help women develop skills to overcome barriers such as early gender-role orientation, family responsibilities, and discrimination in the work place.

Social cognitive career theory is the most active area of current career-related research. Although the research has broadened since its original focus on women's lack of self-efficacy in their academic and career choices, attention to gender issues continues to be a focus of research. The large number of research studies has been important in developing and confirming models of academic and career interest, choice, and performance (Lent, 2005; Lent, Brown, & Hackett, 2002). As research has expanded in this area, more attention has been given to understanding the role of self-efficacy in individuals from diverse cultural groups.

APPLYING SOCIAL COGNITIVE THEORY TO CULTURALLY DIVERSE POPULATIONS

Several studies have examined hypotheses that are based on social cognitive career theory for a variety of cultural groups. In Japan, Adachi (2001) found support for social cognitive career theory, reporting that self-efficacy and outcome expectations had an impact on college students' intentions to explore occupations. Chang (2006) found similar results for Korean American college students, especially among Korean American women, in predicting career choices in both science and non-science areas. Studying the career choices of 109 African American and Latina ninth-grade girls, evidence showed that the better able the girls were in integrating their views of their own ethnicity and egalitarian gender roles as a part of their self-understanding, the better able they were to deal with career decision making (Gushue & Whitson, 2006b). In a sample of 128 Latino/a ninth graders, ethnic identity was directly related to career decision-making self-efficacy (Gushue, 2006). Flores and O'Brien (2002) studied the applicability of social cognitive career theory to Mexican American women who were seniors in high school. They found that self-efficacy expectations regarding nontraditional careers were predicted by how well the women felt they were assimilated into United States culture. Feminist attitudes were a factor in predicting the students' career aspirations. In a study of 590 high school students in Southern Turkey, preferences for math were not predicted by math self-efficacy or interests. Özyürek (2005) suggests that this may be due to the nature of entrance exams and placement in the university system in Turkey. Using a workshop approach, a career program was developed for Israeli Arab adolescents to increase their self-efficacy to better manage work and family roles (Cinamon, 2006). In Italy, self-efficacy and outcome expectations predicted interests across all Holland types in Italian high school students (Lent, Brown, Nota, & Soresi, 2003). These studies are examples of research that is being done with a variety of cultural groups on variables such as self-efficacy that are key concepts in social cognitive career theory.

Researchers have been concerned that members of different cultural groups may experience more barriers to career attainment and fewer supports than European Americans. Luzzo and McWhirter (2001) reported that ethnic minorities believed they had lower levels of self-efficacy for coping with career-related barriers than did European Americans. Weiss (2001) reported that the greater the perceived likelihood of career barriers, the lower the career decision-making self-efficacy among African American, Asian American, and white college students. Studying African American adolescents, perceived occupational barriers predicted career indecision, whereas perceived parental support was related to career certainty (Constantine, Wallace, & Kindaichi, 2005). Examining supports for math/science self-efficacy, Navarro, Flores, and Worthington, (2007) reported that both past performance in math/science and perceived parental support predicted math/science self-efficacy for Mexican American youth. A study of African American college students showed that math self-efficacy was the strongest factor in predicting interest in math and in predicting math as a choice of further study (Waller, 2006). Parental support was also found to predict self-efficacy beliefs for nontraditional careers for Mexican American adolescent males (Flores, Navarro, Smith, & Ploszaj, 2006). Studying rural Appalachian youth in the southeastern United States, parental support and self-efficacy beliefs independently predicted intentions to attend college (Ali & Saunders, 2006). For ninth-grade African American students, parental support was positively related to career decision self-efficacy (Gushue & Whitson, 2006a). These studies provide more information about the role of barriers to occupational attainment of different cultural groups, and the role of support in career decision-making.

Just as women must deal with myths about their abilities that negatively affect their sense of self-efficacy, so must people of different cultures. Individuals from cultures that have been negatively stereotyped in a society may find it difficult to believe that they, as members of that culture, can achieve high levels of academic or occupational success. Furthermore, some individuals may be isolated from other members of society, as are many Native Americans who live on reservations, which limits educational and occupational skill development opportunities and information that may enable them to develop stronger self-efficacy beliefs and more realistic outcome expectations regarding a wide range of options.

COUNSELOR ISSUES

Social cognitive career theorists focus on cognitive processes that interact with behaviors. Self-efficacy, outcome expectations, and goals are important aspects of social cognitive career theory. It is important that counselors be aware of their own issues or stereotypes that may interfere with helping their clients. Unrecognized biases about race and gender directly interfere with helping clients develop career self-efficacy beliefs. Being aware that clients may face more barriers, as well as ones that are more severe than the counselor has faced, can help the counselor be more empathic with clients as they develop a sense of career self-efficacy. As counseling evolves, counselors may become aware of the differences between their clients' outcome expectations and their own views of educational and career possibilities for their clients. Similarly, as counselors help their clients to develop self-efficacy beliefs, they may find that they are developing goals for their clients that are different from the goals their clients develop for themselves. When they are aware of their own values and views of their clients, counselors can help clients to make their own career decisions without interfering in the decision-making process.

SUMMARY

Starting with the work of Hackett and Betz (1981), who proposed that career self-efficacy plays a more important role than interests, values, and abilities in restricting women's choices, social cognitive career theory has developed into a widely researched theory of career development. This theory includes four related but different models. In this chapter, most attention has been paid to the social cognitive career model of career choice. Models of the development of interests, the prediction of educational and job performance, and work and life satisfaction are discussed more briefly. Emphasizing cognitive concepts in addition to behavioral ones, social cognitive career theory has focused on the importance of self-efficacy, outcome expectations, and goals as variables in academic and career choices. Learning experiences have been shown to affect individuals' sense of self-efficacy and their views of what will occur in future events (outcome expectations). These factors do not exist in isolation; they are affected by external barriers, such as limited financial resources and lack of occupational information. Supports such as parental and teacher encouragement can help individuals to overcome barriers. These supports and barriers have an influence, together with self-efficacy and outcome expectations, on the development of interests, choice goals, actions taken to realize goals, and actual career attainment and successes. As a result of a significant body of research, social cognitive career theorists have been able to describe a detailed process of career development. Much of this research has studied social cognitive career theory in the context of gender and culturally diverse populations. Familiarity with this model can be useful for counselors in attending to and supporting the self-efficacy beliefs of their clients and helping them deal with barriers to career goals.

References

Adachi, T. (2001). Career development by university students: Social cognitive career theory. *Japanese Journal of Educational Psychology, 49,* 326–336.

Ali, S. R., & Saunders, J. L. (2006). College expectations of rural Appalachian youth: An exploration of social cognitive career theory factors. *The Career Development Quarterly, 55*(1), 38–51.

Bandura, A. (1986). *Social foundations of thought and action: A social cognitive theory.* Englewood Cliffs, NJ: Prentice Hall.

Bandura, A. (1997). *Self-efficacy: The exercise of control.* San Francisco: W. H. Freeman.

Bandura, A. (2000). Social cognitive theory: An agentic perspective. *Annual Review of Psychology, 52,* 1–26.

Bandura, A. (2002). Social cognitive theory in cultural context. *Applied Psychology: An International Review, 51,* 269–290.

Bandura, A. (2006). Toward a psychology of human agency. *Perspectives on Psychological Science, 1*(2), 164–180.

Bandura, A. (2007). Much ado over a faulty conception of perceived self-efficacy grounded in faulty experimentation. *Journal of Social & Clinical Psychology, 26*(6), 641–658.

Betz, N. (1992). Counseling uses of career self-efficacy theory. *The Career Development Quarterly, 41,* 22–26.

Betz, N. (2006). Basic issues and concepts in the career development and counseling of women. In W. B. Walsh & M. J. Heppner (Eds.), *Handbook of career counseling for women* (2nd ed., pp. 45–74). Mahwah, NJ: Erlbaum Associates.

Betz, N. E. (2007). Career self-efficacy: Exemplary recent research and emerging directions. *Journal of Career Assessment, 15*(4), 403–422.

Betz, N., Borgen, F. H., Kaplan, A., & Harmon, L. W. (1998). Gender and Holland type as moderators of the validity and interpretive utility of the Skills Confidence Inventory. *Journal of Vocational Behavior, 53,* 334–352.

Betz, N. E., & Hackett, G. (1981). The relationship of career-related self-efficacy expectations to perceived career options in college women and men. *Journal of Counseling, 28,* 399–410.

Betz, N. E., & Hackett, G. (1997). Applications of self-efficacy theory to the career assessment of women. *Journal of Career Assessment, 5,* 383–402.

Betz, N. E., & Hackett, G. (2006). Career self-efficacy theory: Back to the future. *Journal of Career Assessment, 14*(1), 3–11.

Betz, N. E., Hammond, M. S., & Multon, K. D. (2005). Reliability and validity of five-level response continua for the Career Decision Self-Efficacy Scale. *Journal of Career Assessment, 13*(2), 131–149.

Betz, N. E., & Luzzo, D. A. (1996). Career assessment and the Career Decision-Making Self-Efficacy Scale. *Journal of Career Assessment, 4,* 413–428.

Betz, N. E., & Taylor, K. M. (2000). *Manual for the Career Decision Self-Efficacy Scale and CDMSE-Short Form.* Unpublished instrument. Columbus, OH: Ohio State University.

Brown, S. D., & Lent, R. W. (1996). A social cognitive framework for career choice counseling. *The Career Development Quarterly, 44,* 354–366.

Brown, S. D., Lent, R. W., & Gore, P. A. (2000). Self-rated abilities and self-efficacy beliefs: Are they empirically distinct? *Journal of Career Assessment, 8,* 223–235.

Chaney, D., Hammond, M. S., Betz, N. E., & Multon, K. D. (2007). The reliability and factor structure of the Career Decision Self-Efficacy Scale-SF with African Americans. *Journal of Career Assessment, 15*(2), 194–205.

Chang, A. (2006). Ethnic identity and social cognitive determinants of Korean American career choices in the science and non-science domains. *Dissertation Abstracts International Section A: Humanities and Social Sciences, 67/3-A,* 835.

Chronister, K. M., & McWhirter, E. H. (2003). Applying social cognitive career theory to the empowerment of battered women. *Journal of Counseling & Development, 81,* 418–425.

Cinamon, R. G. (2006). Preparing minority adolescents to blend work and family roles: Increasing work-family conflict management self efficacy. *International Journal for the Advancement of Counselling, 28*(1), 79–94.

Constantine, M. G., Wallace, B. C., & Kindaichi, M. M. (2005). Examining contextual factors in the career decision status of African American adolescents. *Journal of Career Assessment, 13*(3), 307–319.

Coogan, P. A., & Chen, C. P. (2007). Career development and counselling for women: Connecting theories to practice. *Counselling Psychology Quarterly, 20*(2), 191–204.

Cunningham, G. B., Bruening, J., Sartore, M. L., Sagas, M., & Fink, J. S. (2005). The application of social cognitive career theory to sport and leisure career choices. *Journal of Career Development, 32*(2), 122–138.

Flores, L. Y., Navarro, R. L., Smith, J. L., & Ploszaj, A. M. (2006). Testing a model of nontraditional career choice goals with Mexican American adolescent men. *Journal of Career Assessment, 14*(2), 214–234.

Flores, L. Y., & O'Brien, K. M. (2002). The career development of Mexican American adolescent women: A test of social cognitive career theory. *Journal of Counseling Psychology, 49*, 14–27.

Fouad, N. A., Smith, P. L., & Zao, K. E. (2002). Across academic domains: Extension of the social-cognitive career model. *Journal of Counseling Psychology, 49*, 164–171.

Gushue, G. V. (2006). The relationship of ethnic identity, career decision-making self-efficacy and outcome expectations among Latino/a high school students. *Journal of Vocational Behavior, 68*(1), 85–95.

Gushue, G. V., & Whitson, M. L. (2006a). The relationship among support, ethnic identity, career decision self-efficacy, and outcome expectations in African American high school students: Applying social cognitive career theory. *Journal of Career Development, 33*(2), 112–124.

Gushue, G. V., & Whitson, M. L. (2006b). The relationship of ethnic identity and gender role attitudes to the development of career choice goals among Black and Latina girls. *Journal of Counseling Psychology, 53*(3), 379–385.

Hackett, G. (1995). Self-efficacy in career choice and development. In A. Bandura (Ed.), *Self-efficacy in changing societies* (pp. 232–258). Cambridge, UK: Cambridge University Press.

Hackett, G., & Betz, N. (1981). A self-efficacy approach to the career development of women. *Journal of Vocational Behavior, 18*, 326–339.

Lent, R. W. (2001). Vocational psychology and career counseling: Inventing the future. *Journal of Vocational Behavior, 59*, 213–225.

Lent, R. W. (2005). A social cognitive view of career development and counseling. In S. D. Brown & R. W. Lent (Eds.), *Career development and counseling: Putting theory and research to work* (pp.101–127). Hoboken, NJ,: John Wiley.

Lent, R. W., & Brown, S. D. (1996). Social cognitive approach to career development. An overview. *The Career Development Quarterly, 44*, 311–321.

Lent, R. W., & Brown, S. D. (2002). Social cognitive career theory and adult career development. In S. G. Niles (Ed.), *Adult career development concepts, issues, and practices* (3rd ed., pp. 78–97). Columbus, OH: National Career Development Association.

Lent, R. W., & Brown, S. D. (2008). Social cognitive career theory and subjective well-being. *Journal of Career Assessment, 16*(1), 6–21.

Lent, R. W., Brown, S. D., Brenner, B., Chopra, S. B., Davis, T., Talleyrand, R., & Suthakaran, V. (2001). The role of contextual supports and barriers in the choice of math/science educational options: A test of social cognitive hypotheses. *Journal of Counseling Psychology, 48*, 474–483.

Lent, R. W., Brown, S. D., & Hackett, G. (1994). Toward a unified social cognitive theory of career and academic interest, choice, and performance. *Journal of Vocational Behavior, 45*, 79–122.

Lent, R. W., Brown, S. D., & Hackett, G. (2000). Contextual supports and barriers to career choice: A social cognitive analysis. *Journal of Counseling Psychology, 47*, 36–49.

Lent, R. W., Brown, S. D., & Hackett, G. (2002). Social cognitive career theory. In D. Brown & Associates (Eds.), *Career choice and development* (4th ed., pp. 255–312). San Francisco: Jossey-Bass.

Lent, R. W., Brown, S. D., & Larkin, K. C. (1986). Self-efficacy in the prediction of academic performance and perceived career options. *Journal of Counseling Psychology, 33,* 165–169.

Lent, R. W., Brown, S. D., Nota, L., & Soresi, S. (2003). Testing social cognitive interest and choice hypotheses across Holland types in Italian high school students. *Journal of Vocational Behavior, 62,* 101–118.

Lent, R. W., Brown, S. D., Schmidt, J., Brenner, B., Lyons, H., & Treistman, D. (2003). Relation of contextual supports and barriers to choice behavior in engineering majors: Test of alternative social cognitive models. *Journal of Counseling Psychology, 50,* 458–465.

Lent, R. W., Brown, S. D., Sheu, H., Schmidt, J., Brenner, B. R., Gloster, C. S., et al. (2005). Social cognitive predictors of academic interests and goals in engineering: Utility for women and students at historically black universities. *Journal of Counseling Psychology, 52*(1), 84–92.

Lent, R. W., Brown, S. D., Talleyrand, R., McPartland, E. B., Davis, T., Chopra, S. B., Alexander, M. S. Suthakaran, V., & Chai, C. (2002). Career choice barriers, supports, and coping strategies: College students' experiences. *Journal of Vocational Behavior, 60,* 61–72.

Lent, R. W., & Hackett, G. (1987). Career self-efficacy: Empirical status and future directions. *Journal of Vocational Behavior, 30,* 347–382.

Lent, R. W., & Hackett, G. (1994). Sociocognitive mechanisms of personal agency in career development: Pantheoretical prospects. In M. L. Savickas & R. W. Lent (Eds.), *Convergence in career development theories: Implications for science and practice* (pp. 77–101). Palo Alto, CA: Consulting Psychologists Press.

Lindley, L. D. (2005). Perceived barriers to career development in the context of social cognitive career theory. *Journal of Career Assessment, 13*(3), 271–287.

Luzzo, D. A., & McWhirter, E. H. (2001). Sex and ethnic differences in the perception of educational and career-related barriers and levels of coping efficacy. *Journal of Counseling & Development, 79,* 61–67.

Navarro, R. L., Flores, L. Y., & Worthington, R. L. (2007). Mexican American middle school students' goal intentions in mathematics and science: A test of social cognitive career theory. *Journal of Counseling Psychology, 54*(3), 320–335.

O'Brien, K. M. (2003). Measuring career self-efficacy: Promoting confidence and happiness at work. In S. J. Lopez & C. R. Snyder (Eds.), *Positive psychological assessment: A handbook of models and measures* (pp. 109–126). Washington, DC: American Psychological Association.

Özyürek, R. (2005). Informative sources of math-related self-efficacy expectations and their relationship with math-related self-efficacy, interest, and preference. *International Journal of Psychology, 40*(3), 145–156.

Perrone, K. M., Sedlacek, W. E., & Alexander, C. M. (2001). Gender and ethnic differences in career goal attainment. *Career Development Quarterly, 50,* 168–178.

Schaefers, K. G., Epperson, D. L., & Nauta, M. M. (1997). Women's career development: Can theoretically derived variables predict persistence in engineering majors? *Journal of Counseling Psychology, 44,* 173–183.

Solberg, V. S. (1998). Assessing career search self-efficacy: Construct evidence and developmental antecedents. *Journal of Career Assessment, 6,* 181–193.

Springer, S. H., Larson, L. M., Tilley, B. P., Gasser, C. E., & Quinn, A. C. (2001). The development of an educational and career outcome expectancy scale. ERIC Report ED 462657, 24pp.

Taylor, K. M., & Popma, J. (1990). An examination of the relationships among career decision-making self-efficacy, career salience, locus of control, and vocational indecision. *Journal of Vocational Behavior, 22*, 63–81.

Tilley, B. P. (2006). The development of the revised version of the Educational Outcome Expectancy Scale. *Dissertation Abstracts International: Section B: The Sciences and Engineering, 66/8-B*, 4503.

Waller, B. (2006). Math interest and choice intentions of non-traditional African American college students. *Journal of Vocational Behavior, 68*(3), 538–547.

Weiss, K. I. (2001). The social cognitive model of career choice: A cross-cultural analysis (Doctoral dissertation, State University of New York at Buffalo, 2001). *Dissertation Abstracts International: Section B, 61/9-B*, 6502.

CHAPTER 15 | CAREER DECISION-MAKING APPROACHES

CHAPTER HIGHLIGHTS

A Spiritual Perspective on Decision Making

A Cognitive Information–Processing Approach

The Role of Occupational Information

The Role of Assessment Instruments

Applying the Theories to Women and Culturally Diverse Populations

Counselor Issues

There have been many different approaches to the study of career decision making. Some early models followed a business decision-making approach. This approach suggested that there is a right way of making decisions in organizations, and if individuals would apply it to their own career decisions, they would be able to make good choices. Other early approaches did not rely on an organizational model; rather, they tried to model an effective way to make career decisions. These models have had relatively little impact. Of more recent interest has been a focus on understanding the process of career decision making and understanding the role of thought processes and decision making.

This chapter explains two categories of decision-making models: descriptive and prescriptive. Descriptive theories describe or explain the choices that an individual makes when deciding on career choices. In contrast, prescriptive decision-making theories focus on an ideal approach to decision making. Descriptive theories tend to be based on studies of adolescent or adult decision making, whereas prescriptive theories originate with psychological decision-making theory or observations of cognitive decision-making processes. These two categories lead to two different ways of viewing career decision making.

This chapter presents one descriptive approach, followed by a prescriptive approach. One descriptive approach is that of spirituality in career development. In presenting this approach, I include the work of Anna Miller-Tiedeman, Bloch and Richmond, and Sunny Hansen. Miller-Tiedeman explains that life and career are totally related and proposes the Lifecareer Process Theory. To further explain a spiritual approach to career counseling, I have integrated seven spiritual concepts that Bloch and Richmond describe that relate to career choice and work adjustment: change, balance, energy, community, calling, harmony, and unity. The spiritual approach to counseling shows how individuals can transcend their ordinary lives and connect with inner meanings found deep within themselves. Hansen has a holistic approach to life planning that she calls Integrative Life Planning, which is based on six broad life tasks.

In contrast to the spiritual approaches of Miller-Tiedeman, Bloch and Richmond, and Hansen, Gary Peterson and colleagues developed the cognitive information–processing approach, which is prescriptive. In their model, which is based on cognitive science, Peterson and colleagues examine how decision-making skills can be used to help clients integrate information about self and occupations and make good career choices. A central aspect of their model is a career decision-making approach that starts with communicating the problem, analyzing information, synthesizing alternatives, evaluating or valuing alternatives, and executing action plans.

Spiritual approaches to career decision making have become more popular in recent years, but little research related to their concepts has been found. The cognitive information–processing approach of Peterson and colleagues also is relatively new, being initiated in the early 1980s, and little research has been applied to this model. These approaches provide two very different views of career decision making. In a sense, they are opposite from each other. The spiritual view is philosophical, affective, and broad; the cognitive information–processing view is specific and detailed and is based on psychological research.

A SPIRITUAL PERSPECTIVE ON DECISION MAKING

A number of counselors and authors have taken a spiritual approach to work and decision making about work (Duffy, 2006). These writers see work not as a mundane task or as a job that one has to do, but rather as a place in which one's spirit can be nourished and one can develop oneself. From this perspective, individuals' spirits can greatly affect their lives, their choices, and the type of individuals they will become. *Spirit* can be seen as an essential principle that gives life to physical being (Savickas, 1997). Individuals can be seen as trying to become more complete and more whole as they develop their spiritual selves. Individuals' motivations provide a direction for them in their lives and making their decisions. Spiritual energy and motivation often is expressed in work through needs, values, and interests. Counselors and writers using a spiritual perspective often are implicit rather than explicit in their discussion of needs, values, and interests. Limited research shows a positive relationship between spiritual and religious well-being and job satisfaction (Robert, Young, & Kelly,

2006). Another study demonstrates that individuals who have a strong spiritual relationship with a higher power tend to be more confident in making career choices and more open to exploring occupational possibilities (Duffy & Blustein, 2005).

A spiritual approach to career decision making may or may not include a religious point of view. Many writers take a broad, nonreligious view of spirituality. However, other writers integrate their theological beliefs with their views of career decision making. For example, Huntley (1997) and Rayburn (1997) illustrate how Christianity provides a framework for helping some clients understand their careers and career decision-making processes. Fox (2003) describes the involvement of the Protestant Church in career guidance from 1960 to 2000. Stoltz-Loike (1997) uses Judaism as a perspective to understand careers and career decision making. This section presents a broad spiritual perspective rather than one using a specific theological view. Unlike most career development theories, a spiritual perspective has not been developed using objective criteria. In this chapter, I combine the general spiritual overview of Miller-Tiedeman (1997, 1999; Duffy, 2006) with seven spiritual concepts, as explained by Bloch and Richmond (1998; Duffy, 2006). Then, I describe the broader holistic worldview of Hansen (2001, 2002; Skovholt, Hage, Kachgal, & Gama, 2007) that shows how spirituality and awareness of social values intersect with each other to provide a model of career decision making that combines self-awareness with awareness of others.

Perhaps the best-known author writing about spirituality is Miller-Tiedeman (1988, 1989, 1992, 1997, 1999). As the founder of the Lifecareer Foundation, Miller-Tiedeman focuses on the importance of viewing life-as-career. From her perspective, life is one's career; that is, a career is not a job. Her view can be characterized as valuing the intelligence and experience of individuals.

Miller-Tiedeman's point of view is referred to as Lifecareer Theory. In this theory, she shows how individuals should accept themselves, their feelings, and beliefs and approach decision making in a way that reduces stress and increases motivation. Rather than being afraid of change, they should appreciate the surprise and newness that comes with change. Rather than focusing on right and wrong answers, they should appreciate information that comes from different aspects of choosing. The counselor's role is not to advise or direct, but rather to help individuals listen to themselves and appreciate their intelligence and experience by using their intuition. This focus is present oriented; that is, it encourages individuals not to dwell in the past or speculate on the future.

LIFECAREER THEORY (MILLER-TIEDEMAN)

Lifecareer Theory states that individuals are able to process information and make decisions in a process that flows. Using a perspective similar to that of constructivist theorists (Chapter 11), Miller-Tiedeman sees each individual as his or her own theory maker. Implicit in this view is deep respect for the individual and the individual's life process. From this point of view, you are not looking for a career, you have one. Life is your career. By trusting inner wisdom that comes from your intellectual ability, previous experiences, and intuition into past experiences, you can experience your career. Because your life is your career, you can flow with it, not fight it or work against it. In essence, you are doing what you want to do, not what others think is best for you. In emphasizing the importance of listening to one's self, Miller-Tiedeman distinguishes between personal and common realities.

PERSONAL AND COMMON REALITIES

Reality concerns the awareness of one's career decision making (Miller-Tiedeman & Tiedeman, 1990). The question of whether a decision or act is realistic is a matter of opinion. The question is: Realistic to whom? Tiedeman and Miller-Tiedeman (1979) specify two types of reality: personal and common. *Personal reality* refers to an individual's sense of what is right. It is a feeling that the decision or direction to be taken is correct and appropriate to the decision maker. In contrast, *common reality* is what others say the individual should do; for example, "You would be a good teacher," "You can get a better job than that," and "You can't get anywhere without a college degree." Common reality also includes the opinions of experts.

SPIRITUALITY (BLOCH AND RICHMOND)

When individuals experience the wholeness of living, they experience spirituality. Thus, spirituality is not brought into one's life; rather, it develops. Understanding yourself and your whole being can also help you to relate to others in a nonviolent and effective way. In doing so, individuals reduce stress in their lives and become more relaxed.

Lifecareer is *the dynamic, lived-in-the-moment process defined by each person in individual moments* (Miller-Tiedeman, 1997). In Lifecareer Theory, the client, not the counselor, determines what does and does not work. Individuals experience their feelings, thoughts, physical self, and spiritual self in a harmonious way. Clients are helped to reflect on their lives in a serious and deep way. They are shown how trusting in one's life helps in the development of a career in a natural and relaxed manner. In doing this, counselors can listen for themes or issues that are important in clients' lives.

In their book, *Soul Work*, Bloch and Richmond (1998) describe seven themes that individuals can use to better understand their lives and the career decisions that are a part of their lives. These seven themes reflect a spiritual approach to career decision making. They include change, balance, energy, community, calling, harmony, and unity.

CHANGE   Change is inevitable, occurring at many times throughout one's life career. When change occurs by chance or through seemingly unconnected events, it can be called *synchronicity* (Guindon & Hanna, 2002). Being open to changes that occur in work can give individuals opportunities that they previously had not considered.

Change can be internal or external. Internal changes may occur through anxiety or dissatisfaction with aspects of a job. On the other hand, when one feels excited by aspects of one's work and seeks new challenges, then that is a positive internal change. In contrast, external events may force change on people, regardless of whether they desire it. The classic example is being fired or losing a job because a company is going out of business. Change may come about through the experience of losing a loved one or a valued coworker.

Regardless of whether change is internal or external, there are likely to be many feelings and emotions. Being able to identify and be aware of feelings is important for individuals coping with change. Sometimes change brings about disruptions in physical being. Working the night shift can clearly bring about changes in sleeping and other physical functions.

Individuals often cope with change by keeping current in their field or by attending workshops. From a spiritual point of view, another way of coping with change is through identifying strengths and acting on them. Strengths may be physical, interpersonal, emotional, verbal, analytical, or moral. All of these strengths provide ways of coping with distress or the surprise of change.

BALANCE   Sometimes, individuals seek a balance in their lives; other times, it is a natural inclination to maintain a balance among work, play, and other activities. Individuals often seek out a balance in relationships with others. An excellent example of this is the dual-career family, in which individuals seek achievement at work while maintaining a good relationship with their partner. Circumstances in our lives cause us to seek a balance among the many roles that we may play, such as that of child, spouse, homemaker, parent, citizen, and worker. Super's roles (Chapter 9) describe more aspects of balancing circumstances in our lives. Another area of balance is the relationship with one's self. Are interests and values being met? Are only a few of them being met and the others ignored? Individuals often ask themselves these questions to develop balance in their lives.

Bloch and Richmond (1998) suggest some ways to bring about more balance in life. They state that by changing one's view of time, one may be able to stop procrastinating and experience the moment. Weighing the importance of the different tasks that we work on may help in doing this. Sometimes, changing views of authority, parents, supervisors, and teachers may help to balance the demands that are placed on us. By changing the way we talk and the messages we give ourselves, we may be able to change our views of authority and our views of how we will spend our time. Changing from I can't do that to I can do that can alter the balance in life. Likewise, changing the way we behave, whether it is in our relationship with others or in doing tasks at work, can also alter the balance in life, bringing about a greater feeling of equanimity.

ENERGY   To bring about change and balance in one's life, there must be energy. Energy exists throughout the universe. Physics and biology observe energy in different ways. The way individuals approach their careers can be measured or viewed by the amount of energy that they generate in their work.

There are many different sources of energy. Some individuals are energized by being with others, whereas others are energized by being alone. For some, music, painting, theater, film, and books generate energy. Sports and physical activity can be yet another source of energy. When individuals love their work, the work generates energy. Individuals who approach work in such a way that they are totally involved are often said to be in the flow. When they are in the flow, they are doing what they can to the best of their ability, fully enjoying it and fully immersed in their work. In this way, energy often brings about more energy rather than tiredness.

COMMUNITY   Bloch and Richmond (1998) identify three types of communities in which individuals are likely to participate: communities of companionship, communities of culture, and the cosmic community. The community of companionship includes immediate and extended family, as well as close friends. The community of culture may include neighbors, classmates, coworkers, and individuals with whom one shares leisure or professional interests. Cosmic communities are those that concern large ideas such as the environment, the dying poor, the homeless, taxation, and many others. Not only are there many different types of communities, but there are many different ways in which individuals connect with them.

Individuals have many different styles of relating with each other. For example, Chapter 6 contrasts the way extraverts and introverts deal with the external and internal world. Individuals vary in their need to be included or recognized by others. Some have strong needs for belonging and contact, whereas others do not. For some, being in control of others and influencing others is important, whereas other individuals are content to listen and follow the suggestions of authorities. Individuals also differ in their need for support, warmth, and love. Work is a means of interacting with one's community. Certainly, work provides the opportunity to feel included, to be in control, and to feel needed and cared for.

CALLING   Calling is about hearing your own song and singing it out loud and clear (Bloch & Richmond, 1998, p. 128). Although traditionally calling used to mean to be called by God to a religious occupation, calling can refer to finding one's ideal work (Fox, 2003). A similar definition is that a calling carries with it a sense of purpose, in that it is the work that one was meant to do (Hall & Chandler, 2005, p. 155). Dreher, Holloway, and Schoenfelder (2007) designed an inventory, The Vocation Identity Questionnaire, to measure an individual's sense of calling. Finding one's calling is to recognize one's interests, skills, values, and abilities and apply them to productive work. When individuals find their calling, they find much joy in their work. However, some individuals are not aware of how much joy they find in their work until they stop doing it, for example, for a vacation or because of a transfer to a new occupation. When people have found their calling, they are truly absorbed by their work and are in the flow. Trait and factor theorists refer to matching interests, abilities, and values with an occupation; career counselors who take a spiritual point of view may help individuals find their calling.

Recently, research on the concept of calling has focused on the relationship of calling to career choice issues as well as examining individuals' calling to different types of professions. For college freshmen, having a calling was shown to be related to being decided, being comfortable about career choice, and being clear about choice-related issues (Duffy & Sedlacek, 2007). The call to teach has been described as having a strong feeling towards students and about an area of knowledge (Buskist, Benson, & Sikorski, 2005). There is a desire to positively influence students. A study of adult educators who worked in steel mill learning centers found that they did not intend to become adult educators but felt a strong, even passionate, appreciation of and commitment to their students (Rose, Jeris, & Smith, 2005). According to Rose et al. (2005), the steel mill educators' view of their career was explained better by Miller-Tiedeman's Lifecareer Theory than by other career development theories. For young musicians who saw music as their calling, two important factors in feeling called to music as a profession were being very involved in music and receiving encouragement from others (Dobrow, 2006). Research on calling provides an insight into spiritual or emotional aspects of career choice that other theories do not.

HARMONY   Whereas calling refers to knowing your ideal work through knowing yourself, harmony refers to finding the work that will bring about a true sense of appreciation and understanding. Searching for information about education and occupations helps individuals to find harmony. But this is not enough; individuals must know that their work and their current career is producing harmony by meeting their interests, values, and abilities.

Harmony not only comes from work but from meditation or stillness. Individuals find harmony when they have a sense of meaningfulness in their life and a way of knowing that comes from quiet self-examination. Bloch and Richmond believe that through meditation individuals will find harmony between their internal search for their interests, values, and abilities and their external search for information about occupations.

UNITY   To believe in unity is to trust the universe. To trust the universe is to be prepared to deal with changes that occur and to believe that the universe is one whole entity. For most religions, a goal is unity, that is, a sense of union with a higher power. Bloch and Richmond refer to ways that individuals can achieve unity of career, of spirit, of energy, and with others. Unity of career refers to feeling a sense of flow or being totally involved in one's work; that is, to be a part of, not apart from, the work. Unity of energy can be seen by the feeling of being connected to one's work and one's world and to intentionally bring about changes in one's career to increase harmoniousness. Unity of spirit refers to feeling connected with one's self (being fully aware), being connected with one's partner and friends, feeling a sense of belonging with one's community, having a sense of connection with one's culture, and having a sense of being connected to the universe. Interpersonal unity comes from involvement with others.

These seven concepts provide a spiritual way of viewing how individuals can achieve job satisfaction and satisfaction in their lives. The concepts of change, balance, energy, community, calling, harmony, and unity are ways that counselors can view their clients' struggles with their lives and careers—Lifecareer. How counselors can help clients by using a spiritual point of view is the subject of the following section.

A SPIRITUAL APPROACH TO CAREER COUNSELING

A spiritual approach to career counseling may seem vague and unclear. However, Miller-Tiedeman (1997) makes several suggestions that can be helpful to counselors in using the Lifecareer Theory when working with clients. These suggestions reflect her profound respect for the client and the client's role in decision making that affects his or her life career.

- Let clients know that they have a career, and that it is their life. Listen to their narration of their life career and provide information where helpful.

- Help clients respect their lives and process their decisions. Decreasing their anxiety through relaxation techniques or meditation may be helpful.
- Let clients know that they, not the counselor, are the best judge of whether something is working. That is, emphasize the importance of personal rather than common reality. Not only does the counselor not judge the client's reality, the counselor encourages clients not to pass judgment on their own reality. Rather, they should accept what they have done so they can discover their potential to do more.
- Encourage students to learn through their experience and to assess this experience. This assessment may lead to developing three or four plans that can be modified each semester so that individuals can apply their decision making to important events.
- When using assessment instruments, be careful that tests and inventories (common reality) do not interfere with students' exploration of educational or occupational opportunities.
- Help clients set intentions without placing time restrictions on them. Intentions or desires may change from time to time. Some may be stable, whereas others may disappear. If clients want to track their intentions, they can write "intention" on one side of the paper and "date completed" on the other side. This way they can follow what their intentions are and keep track of their decision making. Or, they may wish to just jot down ideas and look at them from time to time to see if they merge into a direction to follow.
- If you are enthusiastic about change, your clients are less likely to feel afraid to change and more likely to feel excitement in making career decisions. This focus on change will help students take action and worry less about the outcome of their decisions. Thus, the focus should be on taking action now, rather than worrying about the outcome. In this way, the counselor concentrates on the present, not the future or the past.

These suggestions value the client and the client's Lifecareer. The counselor assists clients with the flow of their careers and does not interpret or judge. The counseling approach is to help clients be less judgmental and more self-aware. As they become more self-aware, they can focus on understanding changes in their lives, creating balance, being aware of their energy, understanding their relationship with their communities, developing a calling, and being at harmony with this calling. In following this spiritual approach, they can strive to achieve unity in their lives. The following case example serves to show how a counselor might apply a spiritual approach to career counseling.

A CASE EXAMPLE OF SPIRITUAL COUNSELING

Bonnie is an 18-year-old high school senior whose father is Caucasian and mother is Japanese. At the suggestion of her parents, Bonnie has come to talk to her high school guidance counselor about her future plans. An excellent student with A grades in most courses, Bonnie had originally planned to stay at her home in Madison, Wisconsin, and attend the University of Wisconsin at Madison. Her excellent grades in science and math suggested to her parents that a career in engineering or medicine might be appropriate for her. However, Bonnie disagrees. She has been active in student government and the honor society. But her first love is acting. She has had major roles in high school productions over the last three years. Furthermore, she has appeared in the chorus and in minor roles in community productions in Madison.

Conflict has developed between Bonnie and her parents about her future plans. Bonnie would like to go to Hollywood to try to get a job in acting or modeling. Her parents are frightened that Bonnie will be taken advantage of, or that harm will come to her when she leaves home. They much prefer to see her stay at home and enter the University of Wisconsin. Bonnie's counselor has decided to use a model that is consistent with Lifecareer Theory. The following dialogue is an excerpt from a counseling session between Bonnie and her counselor:

CL: My parents are really bugging me at home. I can't stand it. They drive me crazy. They're always telling me what will happen to me next year if I leave home.

CO: Tell me more. [The counselor wants to learn more about how Bonnie perceives the current situation.]

CL: I love acting. I know that this is what is going to be my future. I've been acting for the last five years. I just get this wonderful feeling when I am out there in front of an audience. Even when I am auditioning and rehearsing it's great. It's like this is me. This is what I am going to be and what I am now.

CO: You feel so energized by acting; it's such a fulfilling experience. [The counselor is struck by Bonnie's energy and reflects this back to her.]

CL: Yeah, we did *Guys and Dolls*, and I played the role of the Salvation Army woman. It was great. I got to sing, dance, act, and work with a demanding director. That's what I look forward to. I sure don't look forward to math class.

CO: Right now acting is just what you want to do. It's for you. [At this moment, now, Bonnie sees her calling. It is clear that it is acting. Whether this will be her calling in the future is unclear. But now the counselor honors her decision about acting.]

CL: Yeah, it seems great to me, but not to my parents. My mother is always saying to me, You should be a doctor.

CO: How does that fit for you? [The counselor wonders whether that is an occupation that would create harmony for Bonnie. Right now, she wants to focus on Bonnie's views, not her mother's.]

CL: I don't know. How can I tell? My mother keeps bugging me.

CO: Well, let's take a look and examine this. [The counselor is trying to help Bonnie achieve harmony, to be open to change, and to examine her interests, values, and abilities.]

CL: I really don't like biology, and I don't like being with sick people. Of all the courses that I have, I probably like biology the least. I mean, I like figuring out problems. Don't get me wrong, that's fun. But trying to deal with sick people and all their ailments is not something that I want to do.

CO: It's really clear that medicine does not interest you now. It seems like this is also creating problems between you and your mother. [The counselor observes the disharmony between medicine and Bonnie and between Bonnie and her mother.]

CL: This is really difficult. My mom and I used to get along real well. Now there is tension. I don't like being home the way I use to like it. When I am at school in the evening working on plays, it is a relief for me.

CO: It's so hard for you to be at odds with your mother now.

CL: It really is. *(Crying)* I miss her. I miss my mother. I miss the closeness that we had. I don't know what to do. This is really tearing me apart that we can't talk the way we use to.

CO: This dilemma is eating at you. You want so much to be with your mother, and at the same time have her agree with your choice. [The counselor frames the problem for Bonnie and is aware of the lack of balance that this is creating in her life.]

CL: It's so hard to do what I want, to try out acting the way I want to.

CO: The way you want to?

CL: Yes, I really don't want to go to college next year. I want to try acting and see what I can do; maybe later I will go to college, but I don't want to now.

CO: Trying acting would give you the feeling that you were doing what is best for you. [The counselor is encouraging Bonnie to try something out and is not making a judgment about her success or potential.]

CL: Yes, I know it is difficult to get an acting job. I really want to try. I know I might fail. But, that's possible, people may not hire me. I may not get an agent.

CO: You're willing to try. You know that your choice may work or may not work. [The client is encouraged to continue, and her plan, her life career, is supported. The counselor does not take sides or interfere with Bonnie's perception of her internal reality.]

CL: But then there is my mother. I keep worrying about her. She means so much to me. She worries about me so.

CO: I know you're worrying. I wonder if you have impressed your mother with the strength of your passion for acting and your willingness to consider something else only if it doesn't work out.

This example may cause some discomfort to parents and counselors. It illustrates the emphasis that counselors, using a spiritual model, particularly that of Miller-Tiedeman, put on the client in making decisions for his or her life. The counselor is patient and continues to discuss with Bonnie the dilemma between doing what she wants to do with her career now and the potential of hurting her mother. When the counselor sees Bonnie again, Bonnie's perception of her personal reality may have changed. The counselor does not pass judgment; rather, the counselor encourages Bonnie to look at her inner self and to make decisions that she is comfortable with.

A Holistic Approach to Life Planning (Hansen)

Sunny Hansen (1997, 2001, 2002; Goodman & Hansen, 2005) has developed a model that focuses on ways to make society a better place while helping individuals with their career concerns. Hansen has traveled widely to countries such as Australia and Japan, showing how the Integrative Life Planning approach represents a worldview of career development. Reflecting her interests in gender and multicultural issues, Hansen looks at changes in the workplace, families, and society as they affect each other. In her approach, she views work similarly to Bloch and Richmond and Miller-Tiedeman but focuses on the societal context for change in life roles. In her approach, she identifies six critical life tasks.

Task 1: Finding Work That Needs Doing in Changing Global Contexts

Increasingly, clients and counselors will find it helpful to have a worldview that goes beyond looking at just the local job market or even that of their country and includes an awareness of changes in societal and economic conditions in the world (Amundson, 2005). There is a need for individuals to understand technology and the use of computers and information processing. Together with this emphasis on technology, Hansen stresses a value system that emphasizes the need to understand cultural and gender diversity, to reduce violence, to reduce poverty, and to advocate human rights. Related to this idea is that of striving for global responsibility (Nakamura & Watanabe-Muraoka, 2006).

TASK 2: WEAVING OUR LIVES INTO A MEANINGFUL WHOLE   Hansen emphasizes the roles of men and women that go beyond their working life. She believes that counselors working with career concerns need to help their clients integrate work and their personal lives. This reflects her emphasis on values such as treating others with respect, being flexible in relationships, and considering social, intellectual, physical, spiritual, and emotional roles of clients. Like Super, Hansen sees work as one of several important roles, believing that all roles should be woven together and considered as interrelated. Similar to Super (Chapters 7–9), Hansen's approach is integrative of life roles. Like Miller-Tiedeman and Bloch and Richmond, Hansen emphasizes the spiritual aspect of career development.

TASK 3: CONNECTING FAMILY AND WORK   Hansen believes that an important integrative life-planning task is to help clients understand how family relationships impact work. In career counseling, counselors may attend to a number of family issues and concerns such as attitudes toward child care, importance of work and family to both partners, sharing tasks at home, marital satisfaction, stress, and power in the marital relationship. In the 1970s, Hansen developed BORN FREE to study and to address gender-role issues across cultures. An important aspect of BORN FREE studies the effect of gender-role stereotypes on individuals and on work. Suggestions to employers as to how they can assist in helping individuals connect family and work include creating more flexible work arrangements, varying scheduling and time away from a career, developing more home-based work, and viewing a person's work–family choice as flexible, rather than as a one-time decision. Hansen stresses that the family must not always fit around work; that is, work can also fit around the family.

TASK 4: VALUING PLURALISM AND INCLUSIVITY   Hansen believes that an important aspect of career development to which both counselors and clients should attend is the valuing of cultural diversity. She believes that counseling professionals need to truly understand the importance of valuing diversity and at the same time understand their own biases and attitudes. As they expand their worldview, clients are likely to develop one that will allow them to function in a multicultural environment. Hansen challenges traditional assumptions about career development. Recognizing that not all individuals have many choices in their lives because of racism or sexism can help clients and counselors work with both individual and societal limitations. A population that Hansen believes is often neglected is that of immigrants and refugees. With such individuals, it is particularly important to attend to cultural diversity.

TASK 5: MANAGING PERSONAL TRANSITIONS AND ORGANIZATIONAL CHANGE   Individuals need to be aware that there are many transitions that take place in life—graduation, marriage, layoffs, new jobs, and so forth. For example, Hansen sees the growth of outplacement counseling as an indication of the abundance of transitions that are currently occurring in the workplace. Individuals must deal not only with details of transitions, but the stress and effects that these transitions have on families. Counselors can assist clients in managing the many wanted and unwanted transitions in their lives. Both clients and counselors can be aware that even when decisions are made purposefully by clients about transitions, these decisions may be rational, intuitive, or a combination. Clients in a rapidly changing world often are dealing with uncertainty in their decisions. Thus, societal changes can influence the degree to which a career decision is emotionally and rationally based.

TASK 6: EXPLORING SPIRITUALITY, PURPOSE, AND MEANING For Hansen, exploring spirituality is an important and critical task that is central to the lives of many individuals. Often, it can mean a yearning for a higher power, something larger than one's self, or it can mean an acknowledgment of others and their importance. For example, individuals who explore their spirituality and value it highly may be involved in doing volunteer work with the homeless, with children, or with older individuals. This can provide a sense of connectedness with others and an internal sense of the value of life. In discussing this task, Hansen emphasizes Asian values such as Zen meditation, which provides an opportunity to reach higher levels of consciousness, as well as other methods for doing so. By exploring one's life purpose, work can become more meaningful.

In her Integrative Life Planning approach, Hansen shows how many important life concepts are tied together. She sees individuals as exploring their identity, which is affected by their ethnicity, gender, social class, disabilities, and so forth. This exploration is related to social, intellectual, physical, spiritual, and career development concerns that are related to each other. These factors impact life roles such as romantic and family relationships, work, learning, and leisure, which all affect clients' career decision making.

Hansen emphasizes the importance of considering gender and cultural diversity issues when dealing with clients' decision-making process. Returning to the example of Bonnie from earlier in this chapter, Hansen, as does the counselor in the example, would attend to family concerns and issues. Hansen might also discuss gender issues that affect Bonnie (because she is female) and how her Japanese and Caucasian cultural heritage impacts her career decision making. Helping Bonnie achieve harmony in her life, balancing Bonnie's concerns with those of her mother, and dealing with Bonnie's energy are consistent with Hansen's attention to spiritual issues in career counseling. From a social context point of view, Hansen believes that counselors can help influence organizations to develop flexibility in the workplace and to develop flexible and humane leadership models. Thus, Hansen encourages counselors to take a holistic and humanistic approach to career counseling and also to make an impact on the world of work.

The essence of spiritual approaches to career development is seen through the work of Miller-Tiedeman, Bloch and Richmond, and Hansen. In Miller-Tiedeman's view of career development, life is career. Her work strongly emphasizes the value of the human being in making decisions and in appreciating a person's ability to decide for himself or herself. Many of Miller-Tiedeman's strategies for helping students in career decision making are to support and encourage them to take action and to listen to their inner selves. Bloch and Richmond provide another dimension to a spiritual approach by describing themes of change, balance, energy, community, calling, harmony, and unity. These themes can provide useful ways of mapping the direction of the decision making. These themes emphasize the importance of the human spirit in career development. Hansen also emphasizes spirituality but places it in the context of the family, gender equality, multiculturalism, and the world of work.

A COGNITIVE INFORMATION–PROCESSING APPROACH

Whereas Miller-Tiedeman and colleagues emphasize the importance of the human spirit in career decision making, other theorists focus on a cognitive approach to choosing careers and making career decisions. Starting in the early 1980s, Gary Peterson, James Sampson, Jr., Robert Reardon, and Janet Lenz, who are all professors and practitioners at Florida State University, turned their attention to how individuals think about careers and how their thought processes affect their career decision making. They were concerned not only about helping individuals to learn about their interests, abilities, values, employment preferences, and the world of work, but also about helping individuals understand the way that they think and how that influences their career decision making. They believe that individuals can profit from questioning their belief systems about themselves and occupations and from learning effective strategies for making career decisions. In addition, they show how their theory can be applied to employment decision making that is, choosing from one or more job offers. In their work, Peterson and his colleagues (Peterson, Sampson, Lenz, & Reardon, 2002; Peterson, Sampson, Reardon, & Lenz, 2006; Sampson, Reardon, Peterson, & Lenz, 2004) have been influenced by research in cognitive science, the study of human thinking processes.

The early work on cognitive information processing (how people think) was done in the 1970s. Peterson and his colleagues were particularly influenced by the work of Hunt (1971), Newell and Simon (1972), and Lackman, Lackman, and Butterfield (1979). In their study of how individuals learn and process information, Peterson and his colleagues observed the learning involved in mathematics, physics, verbal analogies, and approaches used in taking intelligence tests. All of these subjects have in common the study of the learning process when there is a specific correct answer. In career development, the client and counselor must work out an appropriate strategy when often a correct answer is unclear. In *Career Development and Services: A Cognitive Approach* (Peterson, Sampson, & Reardon, 1991), research from cognitive information processing is applied to a theory of career development. This approach can best be summarized by the following question: What can we do as career counselors to enable individuals to acquire self-knowledge, occupational knowledge, career decision skills, and metacognitions to become effective and informed career problem solvers and decision makers?

Assumptions of a Cognitive Information–Processing Approach

Unlike theorists who take a spiritual approach that describes the client's way of decision making, Peterson and his colleagues take a prescriptive point of view. That is, they prescribe or suggest ways that individuals can think about career decision making that will improve their ability to make good career decisions. From Miller-Tiedeman's perspective, they are helping individuals incorporate common reality information into personal career decision-making concerns. The four assumptions that Peterson and colleagues make about applying career information processing theory to career concerns reflect this prescriptive approach. These assumptions are as follows:

1. Both affect and cognitive processing are important components of career decision making. Anxiety, confusion, depression, and other emotions may be part of the decision-making process for many individuals. Peterson and colleagues do not deny the importance of emotions in career decision making, rather they examine how human emotions interact with information processing. Some critics have mistakenly labeled this approach as one that deals only with reasoning, not emotions (Sampson, et al., 2004).

2. To make adequate career decisions, individuals must not only know themselves and the world of work, but they should also have information about thinking and how it affects decision making. Knowledge of career decision making helps individuals to recognize, to find, and to analyze occupational information, as well as information about themselves. This then allows them to formulate and evaluate career choice possibilities (Peterson et al., 2002).

3. Information about self and the world of work is continually changing. There are cognitive structures such as schemas (ways of grouping and networking learned information) that develop and grow throughout the life span.

4. By improving their information–processing capabilities, clients can improve their career problem-solving abilities. Individuals' career decision-making abilities will improve if they can develop specific decision-making skills, as well as higher level executive control processes, which deal with acquiring, storing, and retrieving information about self, occupations, and other areas.

These four assumptions can help in understanding the pyramid of information processing that is the core of the cognitive information-processing approach. This pyramid describes the important relationship between knowledge about self and occupations and decision-making skills.

The Pyramid of Information Processing

The approach to career development of cognitive information processing theory is best illustrated through the pyramid of information processing. This pyramid is based on Robert Sternberg's (1980, 1985) approach to understanding human intelligence. Figures 15.1 and 15.2 illustrate this pyramid. Figure 15.1 shows the theoretical components of cognitive information–processing theory. Figure 15.2 shows how these components translate into a client's thinking.

The three basic components of cognitive information processing are knowledge domains, the decision-making skills domain, and the executive processing domain. The knowledge domain consists of knowing one's self and knowing about occupations and world of work options. In the decision-making skills domain, individuals learn about how to make decisions. In the executive processing domain, clients become aware of how their thoughts influence their decisions. In describing the

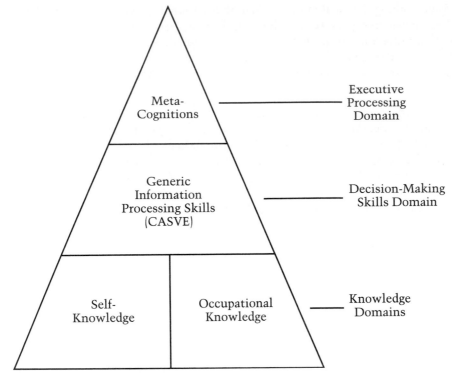

FIGURE 15.1 | PYRAMID OF INFORMATION-PROCESSING DOMAINS IN CAREER
DECISION MAKING.

Source: From "A cognitive approach to career services: Translating concepts into practice" by
J. P. Sampson, Jr., G. W. Peterson, J. Lenz, and R. C. Reardon in *Career Development
Quarterly*, pp. 67–74. Copyright © 1992. Reprinted by permission of The National Career
Development Association.

pyramid of information-processing domains, I first focus on the base of the pyramid, the knowledge domain, and next go to the decision-making domain, and,
finally, to the executive processing domain. To illustrate the cognitive information–
processing approach to career development, I use a case example.

Parnell is an African American college freshman from Cincinnati, Ohio. He is
attending a small, predominantly African American, religiously affiliated college near
Nashville, Tennessee. Parnell is the son of middle-class, college-educated parents.
Both parents are accountants and work together in their own accounting firm.
They are active in Parnell's church and have supported the church through financial
gifts and service in various capacities. Parnell has a musically talented younger sister
who is completing eighth grade. When at church functions, Parnell often has heard
about how his parents are upstanding citizens and do so much for their community.
Parnell has felt the pressure to be a model citizen and to follow in his parents foot-
steps in the church. Although his parents have not pushed Parnell to go into
accounting, they have shown him how well the profession has improved their own
lives and how it has provided a good home for their family.

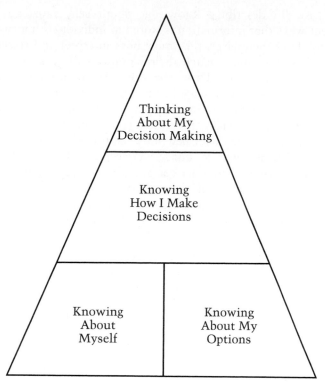

FIGURE 15.2 | THE FACTORS INVOLVED IN CAREER CHOICE.

Source: From "A cognitive approach to career services: Translating concepts into practice" by J. P. Sampson, Jr., G. W. Peterson, J. Lenz, and R. C. Reardon in *Career Development Quarterly*, pp. 67–74. Copyright © 1992. Reprinted by permission of The National Career Development Association.

When Parnell started college, he thought that he might go into accounting like his parents. He started off with economics and accounting courses in his freshman year. Because he had done well in all of his subjects in high school, he thought that this would be a practical career. Living on the college campus and taking the courses, boring though they seemed to him, was going along relatively smoothly for Parnell. However, the weekend before he was to go home for Thanksgiving vacation, he went off campus to meet some of his friends. His friends were at a party, where they had been drinking, when Parnell joined them. Previously, Parnell had only had a drink or two, but this time was an exception. When he got back to college and went into the student lounge, he was inebriated and in good humor. As friends would walk into the lounge, he would greet them by heaving a chair in their direction and purposely missing them. Although he did not do any damage to individuals, he damaged the walls of the lounge. His parents were furious when they found out. This was the first time that he had truly provoked their anger. He was to meet with a counselor to discuss both his career direction and his inappropriate behavior when he returned from Thanksgiving break.

SELF-KNOWLEDGE   In describing knowledge about self, Sampson et al. (2004) present different ways that information is stored in individuals' memories. For individuals to learn about themselves, they must both interpret and reconstruct events. To interpret events, they must match their sensations of present events with episodes stored in their memories. These episodes contain subjects, actions, feelings, objects, and outcomes. Episodes related to present events are linked across time to help us have a view of ourselves. Reconstruction involves interpreting past events to put them into a current social context. Sometimes, individuals may look at past events to compare these events with new information. This provides a new look at ourselves or an embellishment to our self-concept. Self-knowledge comes from information about previous school performance, previous work performance, interactions with other individuals, and observations about past events. From a career development perspective, the self-knowledge domain may include scores on interest inventories, ability tests, grades, as well as reactions to school, work, and leisure.

For Parnell, the pertinent information in the self-knowledge domain is dislike of economics and accounting. From a more positive perspective, it included his enjoyment as a day camp counselor in working with young children and playing tennis and soccer. Good grades in school and strong religious beliefs also are part of this domain.

OCCUPATIONAL KNOWLEDGE   Throughout their lives individuals acquire information about the educational system and occupations. They structure and organize this information into related concepts. Schemas are ways of organizing information that is relevant to education and occupations so that meaningful connections can be made. When individuals learn new information about occupations, they are continually combining new information with older information. They may acquire new information that more specifically describes an occupation, such as accounting, or they may learn information that ties occupations together, such as economist and accountant. These two processes are important in acquiring occupational knowledge.

For Parnell, occupational knowledge was somewhat limited. He heard much about his parents work, because they would sometimes describe it at dinner. He learned that accounting was not just numbers, and that it also entailed consulting with others and helping them in difficult situations. He also seemed to have a clear idea about roles of ministers and teachers through his exposure to them at school and at church. However, his knowledge of science, health, the trades, and other areas of the world of work was quite limited.

The two knowledge domains that have been discussed (self and occupational) correspond directly to trait and factor theory. Self-knowledge corresponds directly to Step 1 in trait and factor theory (Chapter 2): gaining self-understanding. The occupational knowledge domain corresponds to Step 2 of trait and factor theory: obtaining knowledge about the world of work. It is the decision-making skills domain and the executive processing domain of cognitive information–processing theory that set it apart from trait and factor theory, as well as other theories.

DECISION-MAKING SKILLS   The capabilities that enable individuals to process information about themselves and occupations are referred to as generic information–processing skills (Sampson et al., 2004). These skills are known by the acronym CASVE (*c*ommunication, *a*nalysis, *s*ynthesis, *v*aluing, and *e*xecution).

These skills are outlined in a cycle and represent the skills that Peterson and colleagues believe characterize good decision making. Figure 15.3 shows the five skills in relationship to each other. Figure 15.4 shows how each of these skills is represented in the way clients think about themselves and occupations when making good decisions. These five skills are described in some detail below, and instances of how they may occur in counseling sessions with Parnell are given.

1. **Communication** When individuals get input from within themselves or from the environment, the communication process starts. Individuals become in touch with internal or external information signals. This is when they become aware of

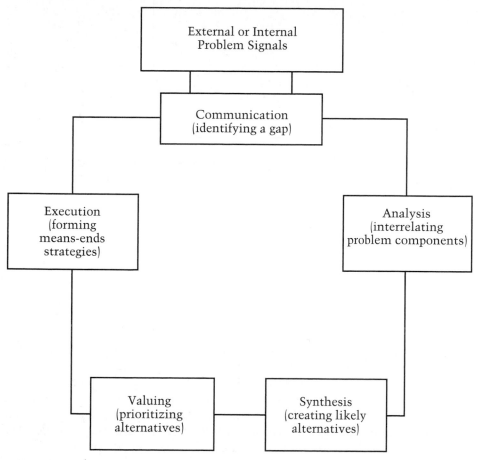

FIGURE 15.3 │ THE FIVE STAGES OF THE CASVE (COMMUNICATION, ANALYSIS, SYNTHESIS, VALUING, EXECUTION) CYCLE OF INFORMATION-PROCESSING SKILLS USED IN CAREER DECISION MAKING.

Source: From "A cognitive approach to career services: Translating concepts into practice" by J. P. Sampson, Jr., G. W. Peterson, J. Lenz, and R. C. Reardon, in *Career Development Quarterly*, pp. 67–74. Copyright © 1992. Reprinted by permission of The National Career Development Association.

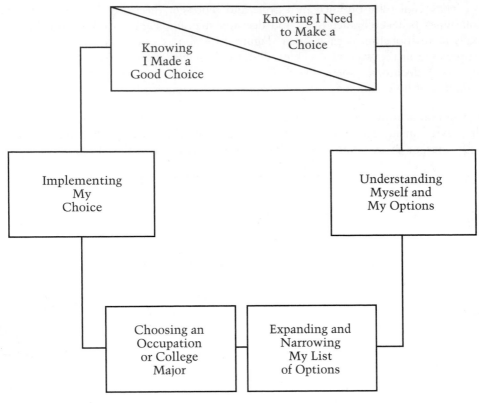

FIGURE 15.4 | A GUIDE TO GOOD DECISION MAKING.

Source: From "A cognitive approach to career services: Translating concepts into practice" by
J. P. Sampson, Jr., G. W. Peterson, J. Lenz, and R. C. Reardon, in *Career Development
Quarterly*, pp. 67–74. Copyright © 1992. Reprinted by permission of The National Career
Development Association.

a problem, such as one they may have previously denied the existence of. Individuals
start to examine themselves, their environment, and the problems that exist. They
become aware that they need to act on information or to make a choice.

In Parnell's case, the signals were rather clear. One blatant external signal to
Parnell was the letter from the Dean of Students placing him on probation for damaging the dormitory lounge. If that signal were not enough, his mother's angry
phone call was another. Regarding his career development, the internal signal of
his dissatisfaction and boredom with accounting and economics was yet another
indication. These signals communicated to Parnell that he needed to make the
choice to do some things differently. In talking to his counselor, the communication
phase emerged in the following way:

CL: When I first came to college, I thought, no problem, I'll just go into accounting like
my parents. That's easy. They have a great business, and I can work with them.

CO: But then some things happened. [The counselor gets a hint of some strong internal
communication messages.]

CL: I was just aware that things weren't working out.

CO: Can you tell me more about that, Parnell? [The counselor wants to learn more about problems emerging in the communications stage.]

CL: I admitted to myself that accounting was really boring. The exercises that we had to do, the class assignments, the classes themselves, everything. At first this scared me. I didn't like it. I mean, I wanted to like accounting. I didn't like the fact that I didn't like accounting.

CO: It sounds like somewhere you said to yourself that you needed to rethink your career choice.

CL: Yes, I need to figure out something else. What else can I do? I need to know that.

CO: We can work together to help you figure out alternative career choices. [The communication stage focuses on becoming fully aware of the problem and starting to do something about it.]

This short dialogue is consistent with the major goal of the communication stage. Peterson et al. (2002) suggest that there are two particularly important questions for clients at this stage: What am I thinking and feeling about my career choice at this moment? and What do I hope to attain as a result of career counseling? (p. 436).

2. **Analysis** Examining the self-knowledge and occupational knowledge domain is a part of the analysis phase. Individuals attend to causes of the problem and reflect on the problem. Reexamining values, interests, skills, employment preferences, and family situations is a recommended part of the phase. Learning new occupational information and reexamining old information also is suggested. In addition, clients are encouraged to consider their approach to making decisions and to understand how positive and negative thoughts might influence their decision making (Sampson et al., 2004).

In Parnell's case, the analysis phase included examining his interests and skills. Parnell was eager to take the Strong Interest Inventory. As he examined the results that indicated interests in social service and teaching occupations, he could understand why his interests would match those of teachers and social workers. However, the low score on accounting surprised him at first, because he was so familiar with the occupation. When the counselor pointed out that the low score represented lack of interest in doing the types of activities that accountants do, he understood the score had to do with likes and dislikes, not familiarity. The scores helped him understand why he was currently undecided. He had to look at different aspects of himself and consider different occupational information than he had before. In the following dialogue, Parnell and his counselor are discussing Parnell's inventory results:

CL: I thought it was interesting that I scored so high on teaching.

CO: What was interesting about that? [The counselor is interested in how Parnell analyzes information in the self-knowledge domain.]

CL: Well, it got me thinking about teaching I had done. I guess I haven't done formal teaching, but I really like teaching the kids at the day camp how to swim and how to play sports.

CO: You seem excited when you talk about teaching the children. [The counselor is aware that emotional excitement can be a part of the analysis phase; it may not be purely an intellectual process.]

CL: Yes, it was lots of fun because I felt a sense of reward in helping children learn things that they felt good about, like how to play baseball.

CO: Sounds like as we talk about this you're learning more about yourself. [In more technical terms, the counselor is referring to Parnell's analyzing his self-knowledge domain.]

Counseling with Parnell may include many discussions of various aspects of his interests, abilities, values, and employment preferences. By examining these areas, Parnell is analyzing his self-knowledge and occupational knowledge domains and how they relate to each other.

3. Synthesis   When information is analyzed, then individuals can pursue courses of action. Thus, they are taking information and synthesizing it through elaborating or crystallizing what they have analyzed. Elaboration (or expanding) refers to creating many possible solutions, even unlikely ones. Individuals may brainstorm or create metaphors so that they can generate many possible actions without having reality considerations limit the possibility of interactions. There is time for reality constraints later. Crystallization (or narrowing) is the opposite of elaboration in that it refers to limiting potential options through the application of reality constraints such as finances and ability (Sampson et al., 2004). Occupations that do not fit a person's interests, abilities, values, or employment preferences may be eliminated. Further use of occupational and educational information can help the client in the crystallization process.

Parnell's synthesis occurred after considerable analysis. At first he was somewhat reluctant to explore options other than accounting and credit managing. Parnell explored options such as social work, psychology, occupational therapy, high school social studies teacher, and others. By elaborating on the information that he had analyzed, Parnell was able to examine occupations he had not previously considered. The counselor reassured Parnell that whether he could actually enter the occupation or get good enough grades to go to graduate school was to be considered later, not now. After generating so many opportunities, the counselor and Parnell could crystallize or narrow options. Parnell felt that as a freshman he did not want to limit his options too much. He thought that he could do well enough to go to graduate school in education or social work, but he was not sure. In this way, Parnell was limiting possible courses of action, and thus being consistent with the synthesis stage.

4. Valuing   As potential options are crystallized or narrowed, the client can evaluate or value possible actions or career directions. The client then can evaluate occupational or other choices in terms of a tentative first choice, second choice, and so on. In essence, the client is asking: What is the best choice for me now? How will it affect my future life and the people who I care about? How will it affect my community? In some cultures, the relationship between a career option and spiritual and cultural values also is important. This may refer to specific educational or occupational possibilities, job areas, or even specific positions, depending on the nature of the question the client seeks to answer (Sampson et al., 2004). In valuing, clients consider both the self-knowledge and the occupational knowledge domains. This phase may include considering job opportunities, qualifications, job duties, costs of education or training, and so forth.

For Parnell, the valuing stage gave him an opportunity to consider many of his actions. He evaluated not only his career concerns, but also previous actions, as shown in the following dialogue:

CL: I don't know if I'm ever going to live down that chair flinging thing.

CO: It really has had a big impact on you. You've done a lot of thinking about yourself since that happened. [The counselor is aware of the evaluation process that Parnell is going through.]

CL: Yes, it's not just that my mother has brought it up each time I talk to her—really embarrassing—it's also that I know that if I do something like that again, I may never be able to go to graduate school, and that's something that I really want to do.

CO: It's good to hear how you're thinking about that incident. [The counselor comments on the valuing that Parnell is doing.]

CL: I have to be careful, at least somewhat, so I can do those things that are important to me.

Parnell also examined his values as they related to his career choice. At this point, he considered advantages and disadvantages of several occupations: high school social studies teacher, elementary school teacher, and social worker. As he considered these, he further explored the field of social work and considered being a social worker in the school system and a related career—probation or parole officer working with adolescents. He chose probation and parole work as it fit with his view of himself and how it would affect his family and community. If he found that he did not like social work courses, as was the case with accounting, he would consider taking courses in education.

5. Execution   Once choices have been evaluated or have undergone the valuing process, then a plan or strategy can be formulated to implement the choice. This is done by taking small and intermediate steps. Individuals examine how they can try out a choice and see if it fits them. Sometimes, executing refers to finding volunteer work or part-time work, or taking specific courses or training. At other times, deciding where to send résumés or spending time with someone doing a specific job may be appropriate (Sampson et al., 2004). Depending on an individual's career concern, different types of actions may be appropriate. For individuals who are upset about the way they are being treated in their current job, possible actions might include strategies for talking to coworkers or supervisors, or possibly hiring a lawyer.

Parnell, near the end of counseling, had decided that he was interested in doing parole or probation work. The counselor helped Parnell find out more about probation work in the local community. After doing that, Parnell was able to talk to a probation counselor about his work and to arrange a volunteer experience while he completed his initial courses in social work.

The CASVE process does not end here. Individuals may then act on or execute a particular choice, with actions resulting from this choice. They may have problems with following through on their plan, or unanticipated results may follow. They then recycle through the CASVE cycle, beginning with the communication phase and examining their exploration experiences. In addition, unanticipated events, which Sampson et al. (2004) call serendipity, may cause individuals to recycle through the CASVE cycle. Obtaining occupational information may occur in an interview (analysis or synthesis) with a probation officer. This would be an example of partially recycling through the CASVE cycle.

Parnell performed well in his courses and enjoyed his volunteer work. He completed his degree and obtained an entry-level position as a probation officer. His personal experience with drinking and with being disciplined for his disorderly behavior helped him to relate to his clients who were arrested as a result of a first offense. Although his parents had initial misgivings about his occupational choice, they became increasingly pleased by his decisions as he experienced success and enjoyment in his work.

The Executive Processing Domain

The top section of the pyramid of information-processing domains (see Figures 15.1 and 15.2) refers to higher order functions. This is called executive processing because individuals examine how they think, feel, and act. Peterson et al. (2002) and Sampson et al. (2004) describe three major ways of thinking about decision making. These include self-talk, self-awareness, and monitoring and control.

1. Self-Talk   Similar to expectations that we have of ourselves, self-talk refers to the internal messages that we give ourselves about career choice and other issues. Self-talk can be positive or negative. Positive self-talk includes thoughts such as I can make good career decisions, or I can find the information that I need about an occupation. Similarly, positive self-talk can refer to academic performance such as "Although I did poorly on the last exam, I can study more effectively this time and do better." Negative self-talk is associated with difficulties in making decisions. It can include comments such as "I never do anything well," "I won't be able to get a job as a teacher," and "No one will want to hire me." If individuals use positive self-talk in their decision making (communication, analysis, synthesis, valuing, and execution), they are able to make better and more appropriate career decisions than if they use negative self-talk.

When Parnell thinks about his career decision making, he uses both positive and negative self-talk. The first two comments below reflect positive self-talk; the last two reflect negative self-talk.

> I can explore many alternatives to accounting as a possible occupation for me to choose. I can control my drinking in a party situation and avoid having problems. I will never be able to be a successful social worker. I have been in trouble once, and I will probably be in trouble again.

2. Self-Awareness   Individuals can be more effective problem solvers when they are aware of what they are doing and why they are doing it. Being aware of one's career decision-making strategy and process is much more helpful than not being aware of it. When one is aware of one's decision making, negative self-talk can be labeled, and then changed. Also, when self-aware, individuals can more easily follow the CASVE process by being aware of what they think and how they feel about their current situation, how they analyze information about their choices, how they synthesize alternatives, how they prioritize and value alternatives, and how they execute their plan by taking action.

The following brief dialogue indicates that Parnell is self-aware:

CL: I wouldn't have thought it, but since I got put on probation for the study lounge incident, it's changed my outlook on how I choose careers.

CO: That's interesting. Tell me more about how that incident has changed your career decision-making thoughts. [The counselor picks up that this is an indication of Parnell being self-aware and wants to reinforce and follow up on his self-awareness.]

CL: I guess it made me more aware that I could have control of myself. I could choose when to drink and when not to drink, or how much to drink. I could choose which occupations to explore and which occupations not to explore. I could also choose to be scared of what my mother might think if I am not an accountant, or I could choose not to be scared.

CO: That's a great way that you put it. You are aware of the choices that you make and the types of choices that you could make in the future.

3. Monitoring and Control Individuals are able to monitor the way in which they go through the CASVE process and are able to control how much time they give to each of these phases. When clients can monitor and control accurately, then they know how much information they need to analyze a career choice before moving to the synthesis stage. They then will know how much time is needed to synthesize information to create alternatives, and then how much effort and time is needed to evaluate (valuing alternatives). They then can move to an action plan and execute the decisions that they have made. Clients who are not able to monitor and control their decision-making skills may spend too much or too little time in any one of the five stages. For example, individuals who are anxious or indecisive may spend much time gathering data (analysis) but feel unsure in synthesizing this information and are reluctant to move toward making a career choice. Counselors can help clients by providing encouragement and support in their monitoring and controlling of how they go through the CASVE process.

Focusing particularly on Parnell's career decision-making skills, his counselor was able to help him move from one phase to another. Parnell was anxious about not having enough information to make a list of alternatives (analysis). His counselor was able to help him decrease his anxiety by pointing out the positive decisions that he had made in the past. As Parnell proceeded in the career decision-making process, he developed more and more confidence in his ability to monitor his own decision making and to execute his career plans by talking to teachers and counselors.

To review the pyramid of information-processing domains in career decision making, you may find it helpful to start at the top—the executive processing domain. Individuals can control the way they make decisions through the way they talk to themselves, through self-awareness, and through monitoring and controlling their career decision-making process. This career decision-making process includes communicating the problem, analyzing information or data, synthesizing by expanding and narrowing alternatives, valuing advantages and disadvantages of options, and then prioritizing them, and executing a plan by taking a variety of actions. The information that is used in the decision-making skills domain is that of self-knowledge and occupational knowledge. This entire process provides a view of career decision making.

MATERIALS FOR COUNSELORS AND STUDENTS

For better use of the cognitive information–processing theory with clients and students, Reardon and colleagues have developed four methods. They have provided a wide variety of materials, including a workbook for college students in an undergraduate career development course and Web-based materials. To help counselors better understand their clients, they have classified individuals into three major categories with regard to decision making: decided, undecided, and indecisive. To help in understanding clients' negative decision-making approaches, the researchers have designed three scales that make up the Career Thoughts Inventory: Decision-Making Confusion, External Conflict, and Commitment Anxiety. They also suggest a structured seven-step approach to service delivery using the cognitive information–processing approach. These four methods are described next.

MATERIALS FOR STUDENTS   Not only has the cognitive information–processing approach been developed for career counselors but it has also been applied to the design of workbooks and online materials for clients. Reardon, Lenz, Sampson, and Peterson (2005) have developed *Career Development and Planning: A Comprehensive Approach* to be used by students in career-planning classes or workshops for college students. This book includes chapters on assessing values, interests, and abilities that cover the knowledge domain illustrated in Figure 15.1 on page 430. Also, there are two chapters on career decision making that follow the CASVE model described in Figure 15.4 on page 434. A Web-based approach called *Career Decision-Making Tool* (O'Connor, Peterson, Sampson, Reardon, Lenz, & Darabi, 2005) has been developed for the America's Career Development Resource Network sponsored by the United States Office of Education. This program, designed for high school students, follows the general method of the CASVE model and is meant to be used with other materials in the classroom or in workshops. It covers career decision making and assessment of abilities, values, and interests.

CLASSIFICATION OF CAREER DECISION-MAKING STYLES   Consistent with their approach to career decision making, Peterson and his colleagues have developed a system of classifying individuals into three major categories with regard to decision making: decided, undecided, and indecisive. Some individuals are decided and need to get information to confirm their decision, others need help to implement it through action, and yet others have made a decision to hide the fact that they are undecided, being reluctant to acknowledge this fact. Some undecided individuals may need more information to make a choice, others are lacking self or occupational information to make a decision, and yet others have many talents and interests that make choosing difficult. In contrast, the indecisive individual is one who has a maladaptive approach to career decision making, in general, and usually has considerable anxiety (Sampson et al., 2004). Such individuals may need more counseling sessions to discover their abilities and interests than those who are undecided.

Parnell's career decision making could best be categorized as undecided–developmental. That is, he needed more information about himself and occupations to make a career decision. As he gathered this information through the counseling process, he moved to decided—implementation, meaning that he still needed some help in implementing his career decision making.

CAREER THOUGHTS INVENTORY   To help clients in dealing with negative thoughts about career decision making, Sampson, Peterson, Lenz, Reardon, and Saunders (1996a) have developed three scales that make up the Career Thoughts Inventory: Decision-Making Confusion, External Conflict, and Commitment Anxiety. They also have developed a workbook that can be used with the Career Thoughts Inventory (Sampson, Peterson, Lenz, Reardon, & Saunders, 1996b) to help clients identify, challenge, and alter negative career thoughts. Clients can act by exploring career options. This can lead to changing negative career thoughts to positive ones.

Decision-Making Confusion indicates the difficulty that individuals have in initiating or sustaining career decision making. This may be because of anxiety or other emotions related to career decision making, or it may be because of a lack of understanding about how career decisions are made. The Decision-Making Confusion Scale relates to difficulties involved in the CAS phases of the CASVE cycle.

Commitment Anxiety refers to the fear or anxiety that comes with the difficulty in implementing a career choice. This scale is associated with the valuing phase of the CASVE cycle.

External Conflict refers to the difficulty in balancing one's own views of information about one's self and occupations with the views of others. When individuals have difficulty in balancing the input of themselves with that of others, they may be reluctant to be responsible for their career decision making. The External Conflict Scale also relates to difficulty in the valuing phase of the CASVE cycle.

The Career Thoughts Inventory workbook uses the scores from each of these scales and helps individuals deal with negative career thoughts that might interfere with the career decision-making process. The five sections of the workbook show one way in which cognitive information–processing theory can be implemented in career choice issues. The sections are as follows:

Section 1: Identifying the extent of negative career thoughts

Section 2: Identifying the nature of negative career thoughts

Section 3: Challenging and altering negative career thoughts and taking action

Section 4: Improving one's ability to make good decisions

Section 5: Making good use of support from other people

Counselors who use the Career Thoughts Inventory may find the workbook to be helpful in dealing with clients who have negative career thoughts that impede the decision-making process (Sampson, Peterson, Lenz, Reardon, & Saunders, 1998). The Career Thoughts Inventory and the workbook can be used within a seven-step service delivery sequence.

SEVEN-STEP SERVICE DELIVERY SEQUENCE   Sampson et al. (2004) recommend a seven-step approach to service delivery using the cognitive information–processing approach. The seven steps represent a structured model for career counseling that is more organized than most of the other approaches described in this text. The steps are as follows:

Step 1: Initial interview. Information is gathered about the context of the client's career problem. Rapport is established with the client, and the pyramid of information-processing domains and the CASVE cycle are explained.

Step 2: Preliminary assessment. A screening instrument such as the Career Thoughts Inventory is given to a client, and readiness for counseling is assessed.

Step 3: Define problem and analyze causes. The problem is clarified and defined so that client goals can be developed.

Step 4: Formulate goals. Together, the counselor and the client establish client goals based on the career problem examined in Step 3. Goals become the basis for an individual learning plan described in Step 5.

Step 5: Develop individual learning plan (ILP). Together, the counselor and the client develop an ILP that lists the activities that are to be completed by the client to achieve his or her goals.

Step 6: Execute individual learning plan. With the help of a counselor, clients follow through on the individual learning plan that is integrated with the CASVE cycle.

Step 7: Summative review and generalization. After the client has completed the ILP, client and counselor discuss progress toward solving the problem identified in Step 3.

In following this seven-step model, counselors may use a variety of counseling techniques. Many of these may be cognitive in nature. Questions that challenge and support clients may be used. When individuals are anxious, relaxation or guided imagery may be used. Not all counselors who use the cognitive information–processing model will choose to use this seven-step process.

THE ROLE OF OCCUPATIONAL INFORMATION

For each of the two decision-making theories that have been discussed, occupational information is used in different ways. When a spiritual approach is applied to career choice, occupational information is an important aspect of it. However, the occupational information may be obtained through a variety of sources. Individuals not only use occupational libraries, but also their own job experience, discussions with other people, and job interviews. Career theorists taking the spiritual point of view emphasize the role of the client in evaluating the opinions of others.

In cognitive information–processing theory, occupational information plays a significant role; it is covered in the occupational knowledge domain at the base of the pyramid of information processing. When individuals analyze and synthesize information that is related to career decision making, they are weighing information related to occupations, as well as information related to self. Classification systems, such as those described in Chapter 2, may help individuals organize occupational information so they can synthesize and evaluate it.

THE ROLE OF ASSESSMENT INSTRUMENTS

As with occupational information, the two different decision-making approaches take two different views of assessment. Career counselors who use a spiritual approach to helping individuals with career choice and work adjustment problems may find tests and inventories to be helpful. However, they are careful to help their clients rely on their own views of assessment results and not be overwhelmed by what appears to be expert advice. Counselors using this approach may use nontechnical terms to explain the limitations of tests and inventories (reliability and validity). For such counselors, assessment is likely to play a relatively minor role.

Career counselors who use cognitive information–processing theory are likely to find that tests and inventories are helpful in this process. The Career Thoughts Inventory may be used as a measure of readiness for career decision making. A case study illustrates how it can be used to assess readiness with a veteran of the United States Army who wishes to enter the civilian work force (Clemens & Milsom, 2008). Assessing confusion about decision making, anxiety about committing to a choice, and reluctance to assume responsibility for decision making can help counselors decide how to work with clients as they progress through the CASVE cycle. Tests and inventories are likely to be widely used in helping clients learn about themselves (the self-knowledge domain).

APPLYING THE THEORIES TO WOMEN AND CULTURALLY DIVERSE POPULATIONS

In general, career decision-making theories do not offer different recommendations for women or people from culturally diverse populations. Counselors using a spiritual approach to career counseling are aware of wide differences in spiritual values of clients. Religious values and theological considerations may influence the way that clients respond to comments by the counselor. Although counselors who use a spiritual approach are aware that concepts such as change, balance, energy, community, calling, harmony, and unity are useful constructs to apply in counseling of many clients, they are likely to be flexible and be aware of great differences in spirituality among women and culturally diverse individuals. For example, some clients may feel a calling, whereas others do not. A study of 11 Christian women describes the meaning of being called both to motherhood and career for women in the sample (Sellers, Thomas, Batts, & Ostman, 2005). Another study of 12 African American college students describes the close interaction between their spirituality and their career development (Constantine, Miville, Warren, Gainor, & Lewis-Coles, 2006). Miller-Tiedeman, in particular, emphasizes the importance of considering the individual and not having societal norms unduly pressure clients. Understanding and responding to relevant issues related to gender and culture are likely to be an important part of Hansen's approach to career counseling. She also is concerned about access that women and cultural minorities have to occupational information.

Counselors who use cognitive information–processing theory may apply it to all clients. For example, using a racially diverse sample of college freshmen, Osborn, Howard, and Leierer (2007) found that a six-week career-development course significantly reduced dysfunctional career thoughts irrespective of gender and ethnicity. However, counselors should be aware that the CASVE model represents a Western scientific point of view. In the CASVE cycle of knowing, there is a need to make a choice through understanding self and occupations; expanding and narrowing a list of occupations; choosing an occupation, program of study, or job; and implementing that choice. Peterson and his colleagues (Sampson et al., 2004) understand that clients often are constrained in their career choice by prejudice and stereotyping as a result of group membership. However, they also point out that group membership (religious, social, or cultural) may provide opportunities for networking and mentoring. As clients discuss information about self and occupations (the knowledge domain), counselors are able to respond to clients' concerns, about discrimination.

Because relatively little research has been done on any of these theories with regard to gender or cultural diversity, it is difficult to provide more information about gender and diversity issues. Research on a spiritual approach to career development is sparse and difficult to do because of the complexity of concepts and the difficulty in defining them. Because the cognitive information–processing approach to career development is relatively new, little information exists with regard to gender and diversity. However, there is potential for research in this area.

COUNSELOR ISSUES

When using the spiritual approach to career counseling, counselors focus on the client's internal decision-making process. Often, counselors will be aware of how different their own decision-making process is from that of their clients. The counselor does not want to encumber the client with "shoulds" that will interfere with the client being able to make decisions that are best for him or her. Furthermore, if the counselor's own personal decision-making reality is so strong that it interferes with the client's decision making, the counselor's effectiveness will be limited. Miller-Tiedeman (1997) cautions counselors not to impose their own view of common reality onto clients, but rather to attend to the client's personal reality. Hansen's (2002) emphasis on culture, gender, and family is a reminder to counselors to attend to how these variables are different for themselves and for their clients.

In cognitive information–processing theory, counselors may wish to avoid imposing too much structure on clients. Some counselors might find the seven-step service delivery sequence (Sampson et al., 2004) to be useful for some clients, but modify it for others. Deciding which inventories to use to assess client readiness, or whether to assess it at all, are issues that counselors may need to consider. In a cognitive information–processing approach, there is an emphasis on helping clients make career choices, as well as improve their career decision-making skills for use with future career concerns.

SUMMARY

This chapter has compared two types of career decision-making approaches: spiritual and cognitive information processing. In presenting a spiritual approach to career choice and work adjustment, I have focused on Miller-Tiedeman's Lifecareer Theory. To further illustrate a spiritual approach to career counseling, I have explained Bloch and Richmond's seven spiritual concepts: change, balance, energy, community, calling, harmony, and unity. Hansen's holistic approach to life planning goes beyond their views by presenting a world view of career development that emphasizes culture, gender, and family, as well as spirituality. All of these approaches focus on the client's view of decision making and personal reality that describes his or her decision-making process.

In contrast, the cognitive information–processing approach to career development takes a prescriptive approach to career decision making by describing a method of choosing careers that will improve the client's decision-making ability. The cognitive information-processing approach describes five sequential decision-making skills: communication, analysis, synthesis, valuing, and execution. The cognitive information–processing approach emphasizes understanding decision making and developing decision-making skills to process self-knowledge and occupational knowledge. Materials that have been developed for this theory are also explained. This chapter presents an emphasis on career decision making that is different from other approaches because other chapters do not focus as much on the decision-making process.

REFERENCES

Amundson, N. (2005). The potential impact of global changes in work for career theory and practice. *International Journal for Educational and Vocational Guidance, 5*(2), 91–99.

Bloch, D. P., & Richmond, L. J. (1998). *Soul work: Finding the work you love, loving the work you have.* Palo Alto, CA: Davies-Black.

Buskist, W., Benson, T., & Sikorski, J. F. (2005). The call to teach. *Journal of Social & Clinical Psychology, 24*(1), 111–122.

Clemens, E. V., & Milsom, A. C. (2008). Enlisted service members' transition into the civilian world of work: A cognitive information processing approach. *The Career Development Quarterly, 56*(3), 246–256.

Constantine, M. G., Miville, M. L., Warren, A. K., Gainor, K. A., & Lewis-Coles, M. E. L. (2006). Religion, spirituality, and career development in African American college students: A qualitative inquiry. *The Career Development Quarterly, 54*(3), 227–241.

Dobrow, S. R. (2006). Having a calling: A longitudinal study of young musicians. *Dissertation Abstracts International Section A: Humanities and Social Sciences, 67/5*-A, 1808.

Dreher, D. E., Holloway, K. A., & Schoenfelder, E. (2007). The Vocation Identity Questionnaire: Measuring the sense of calling. *Research in the Social Scientific Study of Religion, 18*, 99–120.

Duffy, R. D. (2006). Spirituality, religion, and career development: Current status and future directions. *Career Development Quarterly, 55*(1), 52–63.

Duffy, R. D., & Blustein, D. L. (2005). The relationship between spirituality, religiousness, and career adaptability. *Journal of Vocational Behavior, 67*(3), 429–440.

Duffy, R. D., & Sedlacek, W. E. (2007). The presence of and search for a calling: Connections to career development. *Journal of Vocational Behavior, 70*(3), 590–601.

Fox, L. A. (2003). The role of the church in career guidance and development: A review of the literature 1960-early 2003. *Journal of Career Development, 29*, 167–182.

Goodman, J., & Hansen, S. (2005). Career development and guidance programs across cultures: The gap between policies and practices. *The Career Development Quarterly, 54*(1), 57–65.

Guindon, M. H., & Hanna, F. J. (2002). Coincidence, happenstance, serendipity, fate, or the hand of God: Case studies in synchronicity. *Career Development Quarterly, 50*, 195–208.

Hall, D. T., & Chandler, D. E. (2005). Psychological success: When the career is a calling. *Journal of Organizational Behavior, 26*(2), 155–176.

Hansen, L. S. (1997). *Integrative life planning: Critical tasks for career development and changing life patterns.* San Francisco: Jossey-Bass.

Hansen, L. S. (2001). Integrating work, family, and community through holistic life planning. *Career Development Quarterly, 49,* 261–274.

Hansen, L. S. (2002). Integrative Life Planning (ILP): A holistic theory for career counseling with adults. In S. Niles (Ed.), *Adult career development: Concepts, issues and practices* (3rd ed., pp. 57–75). Columbus, OH: National Career Development Association.

Hunt, E. B. (1971). What kind of computer is man? *Cognitive Psychology, 2,* 57–98.

Huntley, H. L. (1997). How does "God-Talk" speak to the workplace: An essay on the theology of work. In D. P. Bloch & L. J. Richmond (Eds.), *Connections between spirit and work in career development* (pp. 115–136). Palo Alto: CA: Davies-Black.

Lackman, R., Lackman, J. L., & Butterfield, E. C. (1979). *Cognitive psychology and information processing.* Hillsdale, NJ: Erlbaum.

Miller-Tiedeman, A. L. (1988). *LIFECAREER: The quantum leap into a process theory of career.* Vista, CA: Lifecareer Foundation.

Miller-Tiedeman, A. L. (1989). *How NOT to make it and succeed: Life on your own terms.* Vista, CA: Lifecareer Foundation.

Miller-Tiedeman, A. L. (1992). *LIFECAREER: How it can benefit you.* Vista, CA: Lifecareer Foundation.

Miller-Tiedeman, A. L. (1997). The Lifecareer process theory: A healthier choice. In D. P. Bloch & L. J. Richmond (Eds.), *Connection between spirit and work in career development* (pp. 87–114). Palo Alto, CA: Davies-Black.

Miller-Tiedeman, A. L. (1999). *Learning, practicing, and living the new careering.* Philadelphia: Accelerated Development.

Miller-Tiedeman, A. L., & Tiedeman, D. V. (1990). Career decision making: An individualistic perspective. In D. Brown, L. Brooks, & Associates (Eds.), *Career choice and development: Applying contemporary theories to practice* (2nd ed., pp. 308–337). San Francisco: Jossey-Bass.

Nakamura, M., & Watanabe-Muraoka, A. M. (2006). Global social responsibility: Developing a scale for senior high school students in Japan. *International Journal for the Advancement of Counselling, 28*(3), 213–226.

Newell, A., & Simon, H. (1972). *Human problem solving.* Englewood Cliffs, NJ: Prentice Hall.

O'Connor, D. L., Peterson, G. W., Sampson, J. P., Jr., Reardon, R. C., Lenz, J. G., & Darabi, A. (2005). *Career decision-making tool: A Web-based tool for learning the career decision-making process - student guide, instructor guide, and train-the-trainer guide.* Tallahassee, FL: The Florida State University Center for the Study of Technology in Counseling and Career Development, the Florida State University Learning Systems Institute, and the America's Career Development Resource Network sponsored by the United States Office of Education. [see also http://www.acrnetwork.org/decision.htm.]

Osborn, D. S., Howard, D. K., & Leierer, S. J. (2007). The effect of a career development course on the dysfunctional career thoughts of racially and ethnically diverse college freshmen. *Career Development Quarterly, 55,* 365–377.

Peterson, G. W., Sampson, J. P., Jr., Lenz, J. G., & Reardon, R. C. (2002). Becoming career problem solvers and decision makers: A cognitive information processing approach. In D. Brown & Associates (Eds.), *Career choice and development* (4th ed., pp. 312–369). San Francisco: Jossey-Bass.

Peterson, G. W., Sampson, J. P., Jr., & Reardon, R. C. (1991). *Career development and services: A cognitive approach.* Pacific Grove, CA: Brooks/Cole.

Peterson, G. W., Sampson, J. P., Jr., Reardon, R. C., & Lenz, J. G. (2006). Cognitive information processing in career development and counseling. In J. Greenhaus & G. Callanan (Eds.), *Encyclopedia of career development*. Thousand Oaks, CA: SAGE.

Rayburn, C. A. (1997). Vocation as calling: Affirmative response or "wrong number." In D. P. Bloch & L. J. Richmond (Eds.), *Connections between spirit and work in career development* (pp. 163–184). Palo Alto, CA: Davies-Black.

Reardon, R., Lenz, J., Sampson, J., & Peterson, G. (2005). *Career development and planning: A comprehensive approach* (2nd ed.). Mason, OH: Thomson Custom Solutions.

Robert, T. E., Young, J. S., & Kelly, V. A. (2006). Relationships between adult workers' spiritual well-being and job satisfaction: A preliminary study. *Counseling and Values*, 50(3), 165–175.

Rose, A. D., Jeris, L., & Smith, R. (2005). Is adult education a calling? Shaping identity and practice in steel mill learning centers. *Teachers College Record*, 107(6), 1305–1334.

Sampson, J. P., Jr., Peterson, G. W., Lenz, J. G., Reardon, R. C., & Saunders, D. E. (1996a). *Career Thoughts Inventory manual*. Odessa, FL: Psychological Assessment Resources.

Sampson, J. P., Jr., Peterson, G. W., Lenz, J. G., Reardon, R. C., & Saunders, D. E. (1996b). *Career Thoughts Inventory workbook*. Odessa, FL: Psychological Assessment Resources.

Sampson, J. P., Jr., Peterson, G. W., Lenz, J. G., Reardon, R. C., & Saunders, D. E. (1998). The design and use of a measure of dysfunctional career thoughts among adults, college students, and high school students: The Career Thoughts Inventory. *Journal of Career Assessment*, 6, 115–134.

Sampson, J. P., Jr., Reardon, R. C., Peterson, G. W., & Lenz, J. G. (2004). *Career counseling & service: A cognitive information processing approach*. Belmont, CA: Brooks/Cole.

Savickas, M. L. (1997). The spirit in career counseling: Fostering self completion through work. In D. P. Bloch & L. J. Richmond (Eds.), *Connections between spirit and work in career development* (pp. 3–26). Palo Alto, CA: Davies-Black.

Sellers, T. S., Thomas, K., Batts, J., & Ostman, C. (2005). Women called: A qualitative study of Christian women dually called to motherhood and career. *Journal of Psychology & Theology*, 33(3), 198–209.

Skovholt, T. S., Hage, S. M., Kachgal, M. M., & Gama, E. P. (2007). An interview with Sunny Hansen: Pioneer and innovator in counseling and career development. *Journal of Counseling & Development*, 85(2), 216–226.

Sternberg, R. J. (1980). Sketch of a componential subtheory of human intelligence. *Behavioral and Brain Science*, 3, 573–584.

Sternberg, R. J. (1985). Instrumental and componential approaches to the nature of training on intelligence. In S. Chapman, J. Segal, & R. Glaser (Eds.), *Thinking and learning skills: Research and open questions*. Hillsdale, NJ: Erlbaum.

Stoltz-Loike, M. (1997). Creating personal and spiritual balance: Another dimension in career development. In D. P. Bloch & L. J. Richmond (Eds.), *Connections between spirit and work in career development* (pp. 139–162). Palo Alto, CA: Davies-Black.

Tiedeman D. V., & Miller-Tiedeman, A. L. (1979). Choice and decision processes and career revisited. In A. M. Mitchell, G. B. Jones, & J. D. Krumboltz (Eds.), *Social learning and career decision making* (pp. 160–179). Cranston, RI: Carroll Press.

THEORETICAL
INTEGRATION

PART | IV

Counselors rarely use one theoretical orientation to career development without at least making some use of other theories. The ability to combine theories when working with a client may make a counselor more flexible in meeting a wide range of client needs. Lapan and Turner's approach to career counseling with children and adolescents illustrates a method of integrating several theories covered in this text. Some career development theories meet the needs of certain types of clients more than do others; for example, some are better than others for adolescent clients. The purpose of Chapter 16 is to describe the many ways that theories can be used in combination. Other issues such as group career counseling, using the Internet, and job search strategies also are addressed.

THEORIES IN
COMBINATION

CHAPTER HIGHLIGHTS

Combining Theories

Noncounseling Applications of Theories

Special Counseling Issues

Use of Assessment Instruments in Theories

Occupational Classification Systems and Career Development Theories

How Theories Apply to Career Development Issues of Women

How Theories Apply to Cultural Diversity Issues in Career Development

Counselor Issues

The previous chapters have explained how a particular theory or theories can be used in counseling. These chapters have looked at theories in isolation. However, it is possible to combine theories to fit both one's theoretical counseling orientation and the work setting. Although some counselors rely on one theory for their career counseling, others use two or more. Either approach can be very helpful; it is not necessary to integrate theories. Much of this chapter concerns the appropriateness of different combinations of career development theories for individuals in specific age ranges.

Throughout this book, the emphasis has been on using career development theory in individual counseling. This focus has been used to illustrate the application of theory. However, counselors often are in situations where there is not sufficient time for individual counseling, or other methods may seem more appropriate. This chapter addresses those situations. Noncounseling uses of career development theory, such as in administering self-help and computer materials, are described in this chapter. Some counselors work with career groups, either by choice or because career groups are an efficient way of providing career services to large numbers of clients. Different approaches to career group counseling are explained.

Two special applications of theory have not yet been addressed. The first is using career development theory when career counseling issues are not the presenting problem. The second concerns the implication of career development theory for job search or placement strategies. Because most of this book focuses on career choice and work adjustment, it is fitting to also include information about implications for job search strategies. Although most career development theories have not addressed this issue directly, giving job search assistance is an important role for many counselors.

Topics that have been covered throughout this book include the roles of assessment and occupational information, the career development of women and culturally diverse populations, and the counselor issues raised by specific theories. For each of these topics, comparisons are made among theories.

Before discussing ways to combine theories, it will be helpful to review the theories discussed in this book. To do so, I have developed Table 16.1 to summarize the major concepts covered in each theory. I have separated the concepts by theory and by chapter. This table has several purposes. It can be used for studying the materials in this book. Also, you may use it to refresh your memory of the theories when you are reading about ways to combine theories. When doing career counseling, this table can be useful in reminding you of the various theories and their approach to career development. Using Table 16.1 can serve as a reference; you can then find more detail about the theory in the text.

COMBINING THEORIES

To discuss how theories can be used with each other in counseling, I have categorized them into three groups: trait and factor theory, life-span theory, and career decision-making theories. The trait and factor theories include general trait and factor theory (Chapter 2), Stage 2 of trait and factor theory—occupational information (Chapter 3), Lofquist and Dawis's work adjustment theory (Chapter 4), Holland's typology (Chapter 5), and Myers–Briggs type theory (Chapter 6). With regard to lifespan theory, the focus here is mainly on the work of Super (Chapters 7–9), but also includes that of Gottfredson (Chapter 7), Erikson and Vondracek (Chapter 8), Atkinson, Morten, and Sue (Chapter 9), and Hopson and Adams's theory of transitions (Chapter 10). For purposes of comparison, I will include among career decision-making theories Krumboltz's social learning theory (Chapter 13) and social cognitive career theory (Chapter 14), as well as the spiritual approach to career decision making and the cognitive information–processing perspective from Chapter 15.

Two theories that do not fit neatly into any of these categories are those of constructivist approaches (Chapter 11) and relational approaches (Chapter 12). There are different reasons for not including these theories in this section on combining theories. The constructivist theories focus on the subjective perceptions of the client. Constructivist and narrative counseling attend to the clients' stories of their lives.

TABLE 16.1	AN OUTLINE OF THEORIES, THEIR CONCEPTS, AND OTHER IMPORTANT TOPICS FROM CHAPTERS 2–15

CHAPTER 2

TRAIT AND FACTOR THEORY

Step 1: Gaining self-understanding
    Aptitudes
    Ability
    Achievement
    Interests
    Values
    Personality

Step 2: Obtaining knowledge about the world of work
    Types of occupational information
    Classification systems
        Holland's classification system
        Dictionary of Occupational Titles system
        Occupational Information Network (O*NET)
        Enhanced Guide for Occupational Exploration (GOE)
        Standard Occupational Classification Manual

Step 3: Integrating information about one's self and the world of work
    Test and inventory manuals
    Matching patterns of scores
    Computer guidance systems

CHAPTER 3

OCCUPATIONS: INFORMATION AND THEORY

The United States labor market
Social and economic approaches
Youth employment
The effect of the work on the individual
Status attainment theory
Human capital theory
The structure of the labor market
Women and discrimination in the workplace
    Gender segregation
Culturally diverse individuals
    Discrimination in the workplace

CHAPTER 4

WORK ADJUSTMENT THEORY

Step 1: Assessing abilities, values, personality, and interests
Abilities: General Aptitude Test Battery (GATB)
    General learning ability
    Verbal ability
    Numerical ability
    Spatial ability
    Form perception

(Continued)

TABLE 16.1 | CONTINUED

Clerical ability
Eye/hand coordination
Finger dexterity
Manual dexterity
Values: 20 needs are grouped within 6 values in the Minnesota Importance
   Questionnaire (MIQ)
     Achievement
        Ability utilization
        Achievement
     Comfort
        Activity
        Independence
        Variety
        Compensation
        Security
        Working Conditions
     Status
        Advancement
        Recognition
        Authority
        Social status
     Altruism
        Moral values
        Social service
        Coworkers
     Safety
        Company policies and practices
        Supervision—Human relations
        Supervision—Technical
     Autonomy
        Creativity
        Responsibility
Personality styles
   Celerity
   Pace
   Rhythm
   Endurance
Interests develop from values and abilities

Step 2: Measuring the requirements and conditions of occupations
Ability Patterns (GATB)
Value patterns (Minnesota Job Description Questionnaire)
Combining ability and value patterns (Minnesota Occupational Classification System, MOCS)

Step 3: Matching abilities, values and reinforcers
  Use MIQ, GATB, MOCS
Adjustment style
   Flexibility
   Activeness

(Continued)

TABLE 16.1 | CONTINUED

Reactiveness
Perseverance

CHAPTER 5

HOLLAND'S THEORY OF TYPES

Holland assigns people and work environments to specific categories
Realistic
Investigative
Artistic
Social
Enterprising
Conventional
Combination of types
Explanatory constructs
Congruence
Differentiation
Consistency
Identity

CHAPTER 6

MYERS-BRIGGS TYPE THEORY

A theory of personality rather than a theory of career development
Focuses on styles of decision-making
Perceiving and judging
Perceiving
Sensing
Intuiting
Judging
Thinking
Feeling
Combinations of perceiving and judging
Sensing and thinking
Sensing and feeling
Intuition and feeling
Intuition and thinking
Extraversion and introversion
Extraversion
Introversion
The 16 type combinations
Dominant and auxiliary processes

CHAPTER 7

CAREER DEVELOPMENT IN CHILDHOOD

Super's model of the career development of children
Curiosity
Exploration
Information

(Continued)

TABLE 16.1 | CONTINUED

(Continued)

TABLE 16.1 | CONTINUED

The role of occupational information
  Psychtalk
  Occtalk

CHAPTER 9
LATE ADOLESCENT AND ADULT CAREER DEVELOPMENT
Role salience
  Differences in the importance of work to different people
  Importance of work depends on life stage
Life roles (Salience Inventory)
  Studying
  Working
  Community service
  Home and family
  Leisure activities
Indicators of the salience of life roles (Salience Inventory)
  Participation
  Commitment
  Knowledge
  Values expectations (Values Scale)
    Ability utilization
    Achievement
    Aesthetics
    Altruism
    Autonomy
    Creativity
    Economic rewards
    Lifestyle
    Physical activity
    Prestige
    Risk
    Social interaction
    Variety
    Working conditions
Adult life stages
  Exploration
    Crystallizing
    Specifying
    Implementing
  Establishment
    Stabilizing
    Consolidating
    Advancing
  Maintenance
    Holding
    Updating
    Innovating
  Disengagement
    Decelerating
    Retirement planning
    Retirement living
  [Recycling (returning to a previous stage)]

(Continued)

TABLE 16.1 | CONTINUED

Super's life stages for women
    Stable homemaking career pattern
    Conventional career pattern
    Stable working career pattern
    Double-track career pattern
    Interrupted career pattern
    Unstable career pattern
    Multiple-trial career pattern
Bardwick's stages
    Ages 30 to 40—women with children not wanting to delay career, trying to balance
      professional role with childrearing
    Ages 40 to 50—more autonomy more, independence
    Ages Over 50—career accomplishments
Stages of minority identity development
    Conformity
    Dissonance
    Resistance and immersion
    Introspection
    Synergetic articulation and awareness

CHAPTER 10

ADULT CAREER CRISES AND TRANSITIONS

Definition of transition
Definition of crisis
Schlossberg's four types of transitions
    Anticipated
    Unanticipated
    Chronic hassles
    Nonevents
Hopson and Adams's classification of transitions
    Voluntary
    Involuntary
Categories of career transitions
    Normative role transitions
    Anticipated and voluntary
Louis's five categories of normative transitions
    Entering or reentering the labor pool
    Taking on a different role in an organization
    Moving from one organization to another
    Changing professions
    Leaving the labor pool
Boundaryless and protean careers
Career Transitions Inventory
    Readiness
    Confidence
    Control
    Perceived support
    Decision independence

(Continued)

TABLE 16.1 | CONTINUED

Nonnormative career events
Persistent occupational problems
Hopson and Adams's model of adult transitions
    Immobilization
    Minimization
    Self-doubt
    Letting go
    Testing out
    Search for meaning
    Internalization
Career crises affecting women
    Temporary reentry into and leave-taking from the labor force
    Sexual harassment
    Tills's five levels of sexual harassment

      1. Gender harassment
      2. Seductive behavior
      3. Sexual bribery
      4. Sexual coercion
      5. Sexual assault

    Victim's response to sexual harassment
      Internally focused strategies
      Externally focused strategies
    Gutek and Koss's four stages of reacting to sexual harassment
      Confusion and self-blame
      Fear and anxiety
      Depression and anger
      Disillusionment
Career crises affecting culturally diverse populations
    Discrimination
    Atkinson, Morten, and Sue's model

CHAPTER 11

CONSTRUCTIVIST AND NARRATIVE APPROACHES TO
CAREER DEVELOPMENT

Constructivism
Postmodernism
Narrative career counseling
    Agent
    Setting
    Action
    Instrument
    Storytelling
    Goals of assessment in narrative career counseling

    Narrative career counseling
    Cochran's narrative career counseling
      1. Elaborating a career problem
      2. Composing a life history
      3. Eliciting a future narrative

(Continued)

TABLE 16.1 | CONTINUED

4. Reality construction
5. Changing a life structure
6. Enacting a role
7. Crystallizing a career decision
Savickas's career construction theory
  Vocational personality—Holland's theory
  Developmental tasks of career adaptability—Super's theory
  Dimensions of career adaptability
      Concern
      Control
      Curiosity
      Confidence
Life themes
  Lifestyle
  Early recollections
  Five major life tasks
Reviewing counseling goals
The life portrait

CHAPTER 12

RELATIONAL APPROACHES TO CAREER DEVELOPMENT

Roe's theory
Attachment theory
  Three types of responding
      Secure pattern
      Anxious–ambivalent pattern
      Avoidant pattern
Parent–child career interactions
  Joint action
  Parent Involved Career Exploration (PICE)

    1. Introduction
    2. Pattern identification exercise (PIE)
    3. Discussion of school preferences and performance
    4. A perspective on education and labor market possibilities
    5. Planning the next step

Family systems therapy
  Enmeshed family
  Disengaged family
  Genograms
Phillips's developmental–relationship model
  Actions of others
      Nonactive support
      Unconditional support
      Information provided
      Alternatives provided
      Push/nudge
      Forced guidance
      Criticism

(Continued)

Table 16.1 | Continued

Self-directedness
Confident independence (false confidence)
Unsuccessful recruitment
Insecure use of others
Cautious
Seeking information about self
Weighing options
Sounding board
Systematic

CHAPTER 13

KRUMBOLTZ'S SOCIAL LEARNING THEORY

Bandura's reinforcement theory
Triadic reciprocal interaction system
Genetic endowment
Environmental conditions and events
    Social factors
    Educational conditions
    Occupational conditions
Learning experiences
    Instrumental
    Observational
Task approach skills
Client cognitive and behavioral skills
    Self-observation generalizations about abilities
    Self-observation generalizations about interests
    Self-observation generalizations about values
    Generalizations about the world
    Task-approach skills used in career decision-making
Counselor behavioral strategies
    Reinforcement
    Role models
    Role-playing
    Simulation
Cognitive strategies for counseling
    Goal clarification
    Counter a troublesome belief
    Look for inconsistencies between words and actions
    Cognitive rehearsal
Social learning theory goals for career counseling
Three criteria that influence goals of career counseling
    Need to expand capabilities and interests
    Need to prepare for changing work tasks
    Need to be empowered to take action
Planned happenstance theory
    Skills helpful in dealing with chance career opportunities
        Curiosity
        Persistence

(Continued)

TABLE 16.1 | CONTINUED

      Flexibility
      Optimism
      Risk taking
Four steps in planned happenstance theory
    1. Normalize planned happenstance in the client's history
    2. Assist clients to transform curiosity into opportunities for learning and exploration
    3. Teach clients to produce desirable chance events
    4. Teach clients to overcome blocks to action
The role of occupational information
      Job experience kits
      Computer simulation of occupations
The role of assessment instruments
      Values and interest inventories and ability tests
      Career Beliefs Inventory has 25 scales

CHAPTER 14

SOCIAL COGNITIVE CAREER THEORY

Based on Bandura's social learning theory
Uses triadic reciprocal interaction system
Self-efficacy
Outcome expectations
Goals
Contextual factors
      Barriers
      Supports
The social cognitive career model of career choice
      Self-efficacy → Interest
      Outcome expectations → Interest
      Interest → Choice goals
      Goals → Choice actions
      Choice actions → Performance outcomes
      Performance outcomes → Learning experiences → Self-efficacy/Outcome expectations
      Outcome expectations → Choice goals → Choice Actions
      Self-efficacy → Interest → Choice Actions → Performance Outcomes
      Contextual influences
Social cognitive model of the development of interests
Social cognitive model of performance
Social cognitive model of work and life satisfaction

CHAPTER 15

CAREER DECISION-MAKING APPROACHES

Descriptive theories
Prescriptive theories
A spiritual perspective on career decision making
Lifecareer theory (Miller-Tiedeman)

(Continued)

TABLE 16.1 | CONTINUED

Personal and common realities
    Personal reality
    Common reality
Spirituality themes (Bloch and Richmond)
    Change
    Balance
    Energy
    Community
    Calling
    Harmony
    Unity
A spiritual approach to career counseling
    Let clients know their career is their life
    Client knows what works and what doesn't
    Clients learn to assess experience
    Clients set intentions without placing restrictions
    Counselors are enthusiastic
A holistic approach to life planning—Hansen

    1. Finding work that needs doing in a global context
    2. Weaving our lives into a meaningful whole
    3. Connecting families and work
    4. Valuing pluralism and inclusivity
    5. Managing personal transitions and organizational change
    6. Exploring spirituality and life purpose
A cognitive information–processing approach
Assumptions of the cognitive information–processing approach
Self-knowledge
Occupational knowledge
Decision-making skills
    Communication
    Analysis
    Synthesis
    Valuing
    Execution
The executive processing domain
    Self-talk
    Self-awareness
    Monitoring and control
    Career decision-making types
Seven-step service delivery system
The role of occupational information
    Spirituality
    Cognitive information–processing approach

These approaches are more subjective than trait and factor theory, decision-making theories, or developmental theories, and are therefore hard to compare. Relational approaches may be used with other theories to examine how others influence clients' career choice. However, they tend to play a secondary rather than a primary role in helping clients make career decisions. For purposes of comparison, Chapter 3 will be treated as a continuation of Chapter 2, as it provides more detail about the second stage of trait and factor theory (occupational information). Because these theories do have much to offer, they are alluded to in later sections of this chapter. Before discussing ways to combine theories, it will be helpful to examine how Lapan (2004) and Turner and Lapan (2005) have combined theories into a practical method for helping children and adolescents with their career development.

Lapan (2004) and Turner and Lapan (2005) have made use of many of these theories in developing a contextually responsive career-counseling system for young people from kindergarten through high school. In this approach, Lapan (2004) and Turner and Lapan (2005) describe six interrelated tasks that are based on several theories covered in previous chapters. They have developed a practical approach that shows how to use these methods in individual and group career counseling, classroom-based education, computer guidance programs, and community programs. This contextually responsive career counseling system is described briefly below as it relates to theories covered in this text.

1. Lapan and Turner suggest that helping clients develop self-efficacy beliefs (social cognitive career theory, chapter 14) can be helpful to children and adolescents in their attitudes toward school subjects and occupational choices. Furthermore, attending to these self-efficacy beliefs can help students deal with barriers that affect outcome expectations and career goals.
2. Developing vocational identity (concepts explained by Vondracek and his colleagues in Chapter 8) can help children and adolescents develop a sense of their own uniqueness regarding their interests, abilities, and values.
3. Lapan (2004) explains how it is important for children and adolescents to develop work-readiness skills. These skills include the ability to build effective interpersonal relationships; interact well with people from diverse cultures; develop positive working habits; develop basic skills for interacting with employers; and become creative, motivated, and open to opportunity.
4. Lapan (2004) and Turner and Lapan (2005) show how Gottfredson's theory of circumscription and compromise (Chapter 7) and trait and factor theory (Chapter 2) help students develop a better understanding of themselves and the world of work. These theories can be helpful in examining ways to prepare students for the transition from school to work.
5. Helping students crystallize valued vocational interests is seen as an important dimension of assisting students in career decision making. Super (Chapters 7 and 8) addresses this issue from a developmental point of view, whereas Holland addresses this from a trait and factor perspective.
6. Another aspect of the contextually responsive career counseling system is to help students to achieve academically and to value lifelong learning. This emphasis on continual learning and being motivated to improve one's work performance reflects Super's emphasis on growth in the establishment and maintenance stages of adult career development (Chapter 9).

In their writings, Lapan (2004) and Turner and Lapan (2005) provide various activities and exercises to help children and adolescents develop a foundation for career development that can be used throughout their lifetime. The methods that they suggest for helping students consider both the student's needs and the counselor's expertise. They also show research support for the methods that are used in their contextually responsive career counseling system. In the next sections, I will show how specific theories can be integrated with each other, although the description is not as systematic as Lapan (2004) and Turner and Lapan's (2005) approach.

COMBINING LIFE-SPAN THEORY WITH TRAIT AND FACTOR AND CAREER DECISION-MAKING THEORIES

Because it encompasses the entire life span, Super's life-span theory has received considerable attention. Super's theory is compatible with trait and factor and career decision-making theories. Such theories focus on career choice or work adjustment at a particular point in time. Therefore, it is helpful to examine which trait and factor theories and career decision-making theories are most useful at which stage in the life span. Such an approach is compatible with Super's (1990) suggestions for counseling, which incorporate Holland's model, as well as trait and factor approaches. Figure 16.1 examines seven theories in terms of their appropriateness for different age groups according to Super's life stages. The solid line shows when, in an individual's lifetime, the theory is likely to be most useful. The dotted line shows when it is likely to be helpful, but not as pertinent. The following sections discuss the applicability of non–life-span theories to life-span theories in relation to childhood, early adolescence, late adolescence and adulthood, and adult career transitions.

CHILDHOOD   The developmental models of Super (1990), and Gottfredson (2005) provide information about the career development of children. Trait and factor and career decision-making theorists have little to say about this period. Super's (1990) emphasis on the development of curiosity, exploration, and information leading to the development of interests, an accurate time perspective, and a self-concept is a helpful view of the career development process of children. Gottfredson's (2005) focus on orientation to size and power, gender roles, social-class variables, and self-awareness provides an interesting insight into the development of career choice. Because career selection and work adjustment are inappropriate at this age, developmental life-span theories provide useful information for the counselor that is not provided by trait and factor and career decision-making theories.

EARLY ADOLESCENCE   During early adolescence, the convergence of life-span theory and other theories becomes murky. Super's (1990) work emphasizes the importance of career maturity, which is desirable before career selection takes place. Super's concepts of career planning, which include career exploration, decision making, world-of-work information, and knowledge of preferred occupation, focus on the readiness of the individual. Erikson's theory of identity also has been applied to vocational identity by Vondracek and colleagues and provides concepts that describe vocational readiness. According to developmental theorists such as Super, it is at the point of vocational readiness that trait and factor and career decision-making theories are useful. For trait and factor theorists, with the possible exception of Holland, readiness for self-assessment is not a focus. The age group that is the focus of concern for the concept of readiness for career selection is adolescence from the 8th grade through the 12th grade. The Career Development Inventory (Super, Bohn, Forrest, Jordaan, Lindeman, & Thompson, 1971;

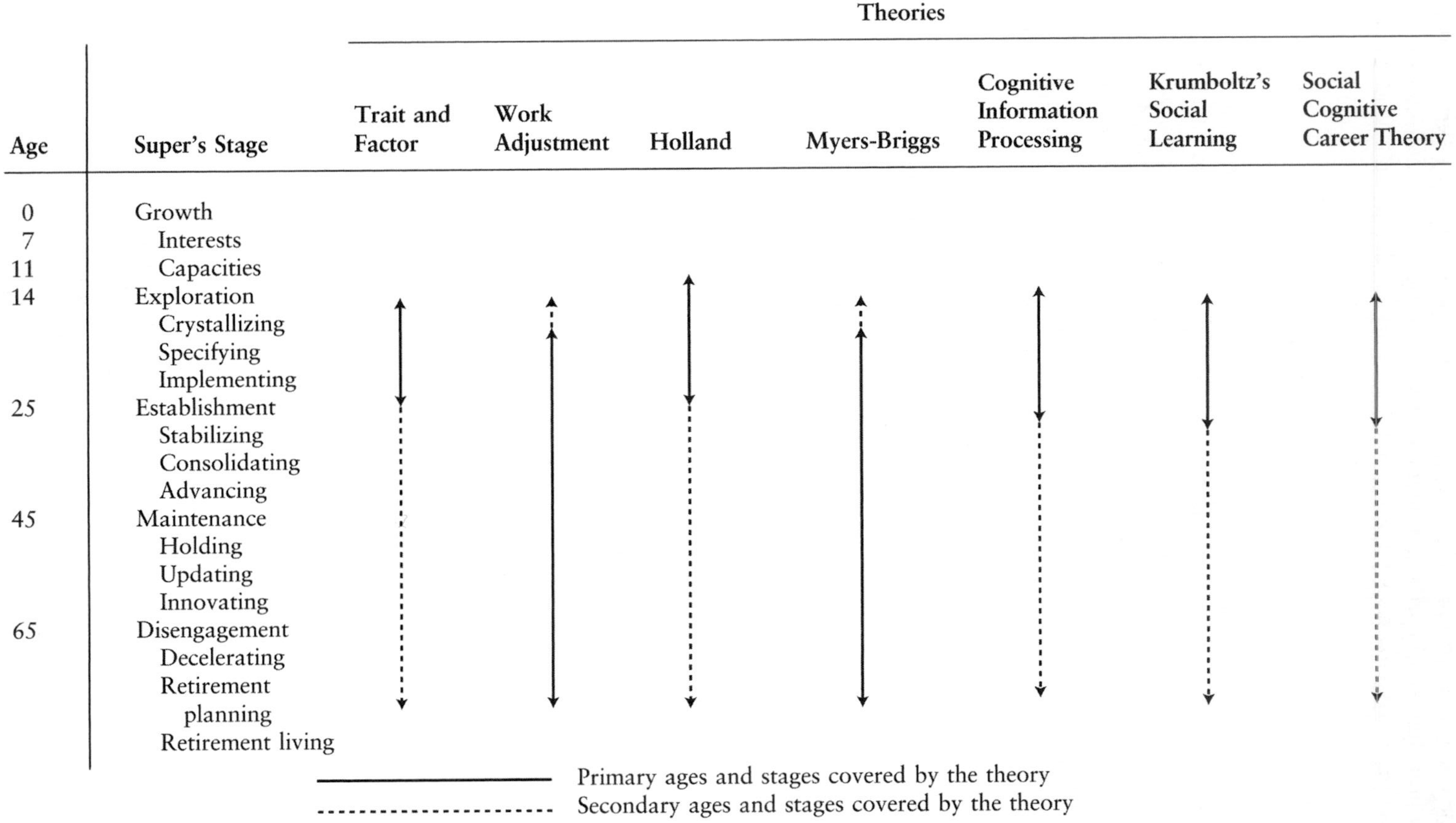

FIGURE 16.1 | How Various Career Development Theories Relate to Super's Life-Span Stages.

Thompson & Lindeman, 1981) was developed to determine maturity and readiness to explore careers. Vondracek's (2007) concept of vocational identity is another way of examining how ready clients are to make career choices. Often, trait and factor and career decision-making theories are used with this age group without measures of readiness. Whether students who may be only partially ready to explore career alternatives can benefit from trait and factor theory or career decision-making approaches is unknown.

LATE ADOLESCENCE AND ADULTHOOD   In high school and college, counseling for career choice is common. With regard to trait and factor theories, some counselors use a variety of tests and inventories measuring interests, abilities, personality, and/ or values that follow the general trait and factor model. Others find Holland's six personalities and environments to be quite useful. Because the concepts of the Myers–Briggs theory are rather complex, that theory rarely is used with high school students. The work adjustment theory of Lofquist and Dawis can be used with high school students but rarely is. To benefit from the use of work adjustment theory, the client should have experience and knowledge of work-related values and needs. Most high school students have had limited work experience. In terms of decision-making theories, most are applicable to high school students, as well as college students. Cognitive information processing and Krumboltz's social learning theory, which emphasize faulty beliefs, may be appropriate for high school students, who may have many misconceptions about career selection. These views about correcting inaccurate information to make career decisions are somewhat similar to Super's notion of having accurate occupational knowledge and information about career decision making. Also, social cognitive career theory emphasizes the importance of self-efficacy in the career choice process, an issue important to high school students.

ADULT CAREER DEVELOPMENT   Super's stages of adult career development as described in Figure 16.1 provide a way to view trait and factor and decision-making theories. The stage of exploration, which includes the substages of crystallizing, specifying, and implementing, is the stage in which trait and factor and decision-making theories are most likely to be used. However, Super's concept of recycling would suggest that exploring one's career can occur at almost any age for adults. Certainly, general trait and factor theory, as well as the theories of Holland and Myers–Briggs, can be useful in career selection, as work adjustment theory can be. The decision-making theories of spiritual and cognitive information–processing approaches fit Super's exploration phase. In social learning theory, task-approach skills are likely to be used in Super's crystallizing and specifying substages of exploration. In spiritual approaches to career decision making, many of the processes described by Miller-Tiedeman (1999) concern understanding one's self and committing to this understanding, which is consistent with Super's crystallizing and specifying substages of exploration. In cognitive information–processing theory, the communication and analysis phases of the CASVE cycle (Communication, Analysis, Synthesis, Valuing, Execution) would correspond with the crystallizing subphase. Synthesis and valuing might most resemble the specifying substage, and execution is comparable with the focus of the implementing substage. All of these theories, including Super's theory, provide a means to understand adult career decision-making processes.

In the establishment, maintenance, and disengagement stages, work adjustment is an important issue. Although Holland's theory and general trait and factor theory may address this issue, the work adjustment theory of Lofquist and Dawis and the Myers–Briggs typology are specifically concerned with ways of helping individuals adjust to work concerns. Work adjustment theory does this by attending to the congruence between the needs, values, and abilities of the client and the reinforcers offered by the job. Myers–Briggs type theory examines work adjustment by attending to the judging and perceiving patterns of the client in comparison with those of his or her colleagues and other aspects of the work environment. These approaches are appropriate to retirement issues, as well as problems that arise at work. The decision-making theorists provide a model that is helpful not only in career choice, but in decision making in general as well. Therefore, the approaches of Krumboltz, social cognitive career theory, Miller-Tiedeman (spiritual approaches), and cognitive information processing contain elements that can be used at any phase of the career adjustment process, such as when a worker experiences conflicts with his or her superior and must decide how to resolve them.

Also related to the establishment, maintenance, and disengagement stages is the approach to crises and transitions proposed by Hopson and Adams (1977). They recognize that problems arising from being fired or laid off, sexual harassment and other crises can be serious for an individual. This appears to be particularly true for those individuals who see their role as worker as being important, and who are in the establishment or maintenance stages as described by Super. Hopson and Adams suggest that individuals react to crises in this sequence: shock and immobilization, minimization and denial, self-doubt, letting go, testing options, searching for meaning, and integration. For some counselors, it may be helpful to look at issues such as job loss from the point of view of Hopson and Adams's transition theory, work adjustment theory, and the perceiving and judging focus of the Myers–Briggs typology. For example, whether an individual deals more in the inner world or the outer world (introversion/extraversion) and senses or intuits may be related to how he or she deals with the initial shock of job termination and the minimization phase. Often, several different theoretical points of view will add to the counselor's understanding of a career crisis.

COMBINING TRAIT AND FACTOR THEORIES

Can a counselor use more than one trait and factor theory without being confused or possibly confusing the client? Briefly, the answer is yes. A lengthier answer can be arrived at by examining Table 16.2. Each trait and factor theory emphasizes certain traits and factors more than others. For example, general trait and factor theory allows the counselor to emphasize aptitude, interests, values, and personality in any way that he or she wishes to do so. Many tests and inventories are available in each of these categories (Table 16.2 provides a sample of some of these). It is up to the counselor to emphasize those tests and inventories that seem most appropriate. Holland's system suggests use of either the Self-Directed Search or the Vocational Preference Inventory, which are measures of interests and/or self-estimates of competencies. Work adjustment theory stresses measurement of aptitudes and values with the General Aptitude Test Battery and the Minnesota Importance Questionnaire. For career selection purposes, the Myers–Briggs typology is an incomplete trait and factor theory, focusing on personality measurement. Because these theories emphasize different traits, it is quite possible to use them in combination.

For example, using Holland's Self-Directed Search with the Myers–Briggs Type Indicator provides information about work personality as measured by interests and self-estimated competencies (Self-Directed Search) and perceiving and judging style (the Myers–Briggs Type Indicator). Similarly, either or both of these theories could be used with work adjustment theory. As more theories are used, the addition of more concepts might create confusion for both the client and the counselor. In general, however, there seems to be little overlap in the approaches of general trait and factor theory, Holland's theory, work adjustment theory, and the Myers–Briggs typology.

Combining Career Decision-Making Theories

Unlike trait and factor theories, which tend to differ from each other because they measure different characteristics of individuals, career decision-making theories tend to describe the same process. Therefore, it is unlikely that a counselor would wish to use more than one career decision-making theory in counseling. Krumboltz's social learning theory uses behavioral and cognitive interventions, as does cognitive information processing theory. Social cognitive career theory has as its emphasis self-efficacy, outcome expectations and goals as well as supports and barriers. In contrast, the spiritual approach of Miller-Tiedeman and others emphasizes the subjective experience of the client. Furthermore, the Myers–Briggs typology can be seen as a theory of career decision making because it focuses on making perceptions about events, and then judging or deciding about those events. If a counselor does decide to use a career decision-making theory in counseling, it is important that the theory fit the counselor's orientation, as well as the client population.

The Counselor's Choice

Each of the theories described in the preceding pages has been supported by varying amounts of research. In general, these theories are clear and concise. For the counselor, they offer a tested approach to understanding and helping clients with career problems. Whether a counselor uses one theory or several in the conceptualization of client issues is a personal decision. There is no information to suggest the most appropriate number of theories to use.

NONCOUNSELING APPLICATIONS OF THEORIES

Practical considerations, such as a large caseload and little time available for career counseling, often require counselors to look for methods other than individual counseling to help their clientele with issues of career selection. Some noncounseling interventions can serve as a way of identifying those individuals who might profit from further counseling. In some cases, noncounseling materials are offered as the only career selection aid. Four noncounseling applications of theories are described

TABLE 16.2 | TESTS AND INVENTORIES ASSOCIATED WITH SPECIFIC CAREER DEVELOPMENT THEORIES

Theory	Test Type					
	Aptitude	Interests	Values	Personality	Decision Making	Maturity and Development
Trait and factor theory*	Scholastic Assessment Test	Kuder Career Search	Study of Values	California Psychological Inventory		
	Differential Aptitude Tests	Strong Interest Inventory	Values Scale	Sixteen Personality Factor Questionnaire		
	General Aptitude Test Battery	California Occupational Preference Survey				
	Armed Services Vocational Aptitude Battery					
Holland's typology		Self-Directed Search				
		Vocational Preference Inventory				

Theory			
Myers–Briggs typology	Myers–Briggs Type Indicator		
Work adjustment	General Aptitude Test Battery	Minnesota Importance Questionnaire	
Super's life-span theory		Values Scale Salience Inventory	Career Development Inventory
Cognitive information–processing theory			Carrer Thoughts Inventory
Krumboltz's social learning theory			Carrer Beliefs Inventory

*Trait and factor theory can make use of many tests and inventories. Examples are presented here.

here: screening methods, paper-and-pencil materials, computerized guidance systems, and the Internet.

SCREENING METHODS

Some theorists have developed tests or inventories that screen for the clients who will benefit most from counseling. Another use of screening is to separate clients into groups by test and inventory scores so that appropriate counseling interventions can be offered. One example of a screening instrument is Super's Career Development Inventory (Super et al., 1971). Depending on how a student scores on this instrument, he or she can be referred either to counseling for career choice or to information that will increase the level of his or her vocational maturity, so that he or she can then be assigned to a career-selection intervention. Holland's Self-Directed Search can be used in a similar manner. Those students who are not able to arrive at a series of acceptable career alternatives through the Self-Directed Search can be scheduled for individual or group career counseling. Although many other inventories and tests are not normally used in this manner, it might be possible to do so.

PAPER-AND-PENCIL MATERIALS

Most theories do not offer materials designed to be used in place of counseling. Holland's Self-Directed Search is a notable exception. Holland (1997) believes that help in selecting an occupation can be provided through easy-to-use inventories and supplemental materials, so that, in many cases, counseling will be unnecessary. The Self-Directed Search is designed so that individuals can score, as well as interpret, the inventory themselves. Professionals should not be necessary, except in situations where the results of the Self-Directed Search are confusing or incomplete. In addition, Holland developed *The Occupations Finder*, which lists hundreds of careers sorted by Holland's three-letter codes. Thus, a student can look up in *The Occupations Finder* the three-letter code that he or she received on the Self-Directed Search and locate careers that exactly, or nearly, match that code. Also, Holland (1985) has written an easy-to-read, eight-page booklet called *You and Your Career* that advises students on how to understand the Holland six-type system and how to make career decisions. Many educational systems have used these instruments to provide career assistance to their students. Counselors wishing to use these materials need to consider the cost effectiveness of these relatively inexpensive materials and the merits of a system that does not stress a counseling approach to career selection.

COMPUTERIZED GUIDANCE SYSTEMS

Since the early 1970s, computer-assisted guidance systems have become an integral part of career counseling (Harris-Bowlsbey & Sampson, 2001). Although these systems are designed to be used as an adjunct to counseling, they are occasionally used similarly to Holland's Self-Directed Search. For example, a computerized guidance system can be assigned to individuals so that they may select appropriate careers. If this method is not sufficient for an individual, then counseling may be offered. Two systems are particularly well-known and have been highly developed: DISCOVER (ACT, Inc., 2007) and SIGI[3] (VALPAR, 2007). Both systems follow the trait and factor method in that they help individuals assess their abilities, interests, and values. Then, the systems provide occupational and educational information for the people using the system. A match is made between the self-assessment of the individual and occupational information. Clients then go on to select the occupations that would fit them best. SIGI[3] emphasizes the values aspect of self-assessment, whereas DISCOVER uses some portions of Super's developmental life-span theory in its approach.

These descriptions do not do justice to the sophisticated interactive nature of these programs. Both have large databases of occupational information. Their self-assessment sections are, in many ways, similar to paper-and-pencil assessments of interests, self-estimated competencies, and values. Evaluating SIGI and SIGI PLUS (earlier forms of SIGI[3]) and DISCOVER, Peterson, Ryan-Jones, Sampson, and Reardon (1994) reported no practical differences in effectiveness between the systems. Brake (2001) used DISCOVER with 54 adolescents in foster care. He reported that students who used the full DISCOVER system listed more jobs after completing DISCOVER than those who just completed inventories as a part of DISCOVER. Studying 33 at-risk high school students, Bleier (2007) found that DISCOVER and career counseling helped students improve their overall grade point average. Kratz (1998) studied the use of SIGI PLUS and found that SIGI PLUS was assigned after an interview with a client, but often there was no counseling provided after the client had completed SIGI PLUS. Kratz questions the appropriateness of using SIGI PLUS in this manner. SIGI PLUS and DISCOVER are systems that take several hours to complete. Evaluation of these instruments is limited and presents unique questions for researchers due to the interactive nature of these instruments (Fowkes & McWhirter, 2007). Other systems are available on the Internet.

INTERNET

Many types of career assistance are likely to be found on the Internet (Boer, 2001; Harris-Bowlsbey & Sampson, 2005). Assessment inventories (Appendix B), career information (Appendix C), and career counseling or coaching are available over the Internet (Harris-Bowlsbey, 2002). Many of the tests and inventories described in this text can be taken over the Internet (Appendix B). Costs for these vary from publisher to publisher. Studying the Self-Directed Search (SDS), Barak and Cohen (2002) reported that high school students preferred taking the SDS over the Internet rather than scoring it themselves. Taking tests and inventories over the Internet is likely to increase in popularity.

Keeping up with the many career information Web sites can be a difficult task (McCarthy, Moller, & Beard, 2003). For example, some of the Web sites in Appendices B and C may have changed addresses or may no longer be available. To provide an overview of Web sites, I have selected some of the more common ones and divided them into the following categories in Appendix C: career counseling organizations, education and internships, job postings, and occupations. The most important career counseling organization, the National Career Development Association, is listed together with information for counselor certification. Most colleges, universities, and other training institutions have their own Web sites. I list directories of institutions, as well as lists of internships for students. Job postings have been popular for job seekers. America's Job Bank and Monster.com are two of the more well-known job listing services. The *Occupational Outlook Handbook*, which frequently is mentioned in this text, is listed together with job definitions to be found in the O*NET (*Occupational Information Network* online).

Providing career counseling over the Internet raises several ethical issues (Mallen, Vogel, & Rochlen, 2005; McCarthy, Moller, & Beard, 2003). Questions about confidentiality arise, as do questions about the accuracy of information and following professional counseling standards. These issues require research and study. An evaluation of an Internet-based career planning system was done in Croatia (Sverko, Akik, Babarovic, Brcina, & Sverko, 2002). In this study, career management advice was given to several thousand individuals. A sample of 2,064 individuals found the advice to be helpful. Harris-Bowlsbey (2002) believes that the ethical issues involved in career counseling over the Internet will receive much attention in the next few years.

SPECIAL COUNSELING ISSUES

A number of counseling issues have implications for career development theories. One important concern is group counseling. Sometimes, because of preference, and often because of limited time, counselors choose to use career group counseling rather than individual counseling. Most of the theories that have been discussed in this book lend themselves to the group approach. Another issue that arises is career counseling as a related concern. Some counselors work in a setting where they deal with personal or family problems to which career issues are related. For example, they may rarely do counseling for career choice and more often do work adjustment counseling as a part of other issues. Selecting a career development theory to use in that case may be different than if one's major responsibility is career counseling. Another issue that occasionally faces counselors is changing the career development theories that one uses when one changes work settings. For example, if a counselor changes from a job in which he or she has worked with children to one in which he or she is working with adults, the career development theory that the counselor uses may be different in the two settings. Another duty of counselors is placement and job search counseling. The theories that have been discussed in this book have implications for helping people locate a job once they have decided about the career that they wish to pursue. Although these issues do not apply to all counselors, they do arise for many.

GROUP CAREER COUNSELING

The concepts and materials that career development theorists provide for counselors can be applied in most group settings. In a meta-analysis of a variety of career interventions, methods that used a counselor were more effective than those that used noncounselor interventions, such as computer guidance systems without counseling (Whiston, Brecheisen, & Stephens, 2003). This study also shows that structured career workshops and groups were more effective than nonstructured workshops and groups. In his review of career group counseling, Kivlighan (1990) reports that most studies of career groups demonstrated that a primary purpose was imparting information to clients. Other purposes included helping clients in vocational exploration and in developing career decision-making skills (Herr, Cramer, & Niles, 2004). Some features of group counseling that are not available in individual counseling are motivation from peers, an opportunity to learn from the experience of peers, and the opportunity to help and be helped by people who are in a similar situation. Also, groups can be designed for specific populations, such as those with disabilities (Zunker, 2006), adults transitioning from welfare to work (Clow, 2005), and displaced homemakers (McAllister & Ponterotto, 1992). Career groups have been used internationally; for example, career groups have been used in China with college students (Wang, Li, & Wang, 2006) and with Chinese youth immigrating to urban areas in the United States (Shea, Ma, & Yeh, 2007). Herr, Cramer, and Niles (2004) find that role-playing certain situations and using a board game such as the Life Career Game, in which people can play different roles, are excellent group career counseling techniques. Whether the goal of group career counseling is career selection or work adjustment, career groups can fulfill many of the functions of individual career counseling.

Trait and factor theory can be adapted rather easily to a group counseling format. If using general trait and factor theory, the counselor must select the tests and inventories that will be used for the group. Interpretation of tests and inventories can be done in a group, with the counselor suggesting meanings of the results and other group members adding input. Similarly, the materials developed by Holland can be used in a group setting. Because they are particularly easy to understand, they can be used with clients with a wide range of ages and abilities. The Myers–Briggs Type Indicator is used widely in group settings, with both career and other issues or in structured exercises (Tieger & Barron-Tieger, 1992). In discussion, group members can give feedback to each other about their views of the person's type. Discussion of the kind of work setting that would fit a particular individual's type can be instructive. Although Lofquist and Dawis's work adjustment theory often is thought of in terms of individual vocational rehabilitation counseling, it, too, can be used in career groups. Administering the General Aptitude Test Battery and the Minnesota Importance Questionnaire for discussion and interpretation in a group may be quite conducive to exploration. However, the counselor needs to be prepared to make suggestions to the group as to which occupations would match their individual abilities and values.

Developmental theory can be used in several different ways in group counseling. With adolescents, career maturity issues, which include career planning, career exploration, and finding out about the world of work, can be a focus. Furthermore, Super's (1990) rainbow enables adolescents to examine where they have been and what they might expect in the future. Looking behind and looking ahead also can apply to adults. Adults who are contemplating making career changes or are experiencing work adjustment problems may find it helpful to examine the importance of various roles in their life, such as worker, leisurite, citizen, and student. Looking at life roles in the context of the stages of exploration, establishment, maintenance, and disengagement can help clients see how they compare with other members of the group in terms of the similarity and dissimilarity of their life situations, a process that will give them a sense of understanding about their own life situation. Super's theory also supplies a context for understanding career crises such as firings and layoffs.

Career decision making often is used in a group format. Krumboltz's social learning theory has been used in a group format called DECIDES (Krumboltz & Hamel, 1977). In a spiritual approach to group career counseling, group members can discuss their feelings about career choice and encourage each other to freely explore career options. Cognitive information–processing theory has been used at Florida State University as a structure for a course that uses group procedures that are oriented toward student career development (Reardon, Lenz, Sampson, & Peterson, 2006). Krumboltz's social learning theory and the cognitive information–processing theory have manuals that group leaders can use that follow a structured format.

Career Counseling as a Related Issue

For counselors who do career counseling infrequently or have clients who present work adjustment problems, certain theories may be particularly appropriate. In terms of trait and factor theories, the Myers–Briggs typology and Lofquist and Dawis's work adjustment theory may be particularly helpful. The former emphasizes perceiving and judging styles, whereas the latter emphasizes abilities and work-related values that directly correspond to job issues. These theories may provide useful insights into work adjustment difficulties, such as problems with colleagues or superiors and difficulties with job requirements. Another theory that is particularly helpful for working with career issues when they are a related concern is that of Super. By assessing how important the work role is in comparison with that of student, citizen, leisurite, and family member, the counselor can put career issues into a useful perspective. The career stages of Super also provide a way of understanding the kinds of work-related problems that adults experience. For adults in a career crisis, Hopson and Adams's theory provides guidelines in understanding the career process. For children, Super's and Gottfredson's developmental theories can be particularly valuable, because they can be used to examine exploratory gender-role behavior that other theories do not address (see Figure 16.1 for a comparison).

Changing Work Settings

The ages and ability levels of the clients may determine the type of theory that the counselor chooses. For example, if a high school guidance counselor who has used Super's concepts of vocational maturity together with Holland's typology moves to a community college setting in which he or she is dealing with returning adult students, his or her choice of theory might change. The counselor might wish to use Myers–Briggs typological theory in addition to Holland's theory, or might wish to replace Holland's theory with the work adjustment theory of Lofquist and Dawis. In general, counselors might be less likely to change their theory of counseling or psychotherapy when they move from one work setting to another than to modify the career development theory that they use.

Placement Counseling

Most career development theorists have been more concerned with career selection and career adjustment than they have been with issues of finding a job. However, many authors have written job search books to help individuals find employment. Most notable of these books is *What Color Is Your Parachute?* (Bolles, 2008). This book, which is updated each year, is designed for adult job hunters and career changers. It deals with issues such as finding out about the labor market, where jobs are, how to get leads, how to write résumés, and how to conduct one's self during job interviews. Many writers, such as Bolles, emphasize the importance of developing a network of people who can help in the job search. Most of the advice is practical and not related to theory.

However, one method of helping unemployed adults find work is quite practical but also based on theory. Azrin and Besalel (1980) have developed the concept of the "job club," based on the behavioral principle of positive reinforcement. Focusing on professionals who had lost jobs, Azrin developed a structured approach so that members of the job club could reinforce each other's progress in job seeking. The effectiveness of this approach has been shown with young adults with modest cognitive impairments (Black, Tsuhako, & McDougall, 1998), with welfare recipients (Brooks, Nackerud, & Risler, 2001), executive job seekers (Kondo, 2005), and with counselor education students (Rutter & Jones, 2007). The action-oriented approach of Azrin to getting a job once one has lost a job contrasts with the approach of Hopson and Adams (1977), which emphasizes understanding the stages of a crisis. Although these approaches are different, they are not incompatible. Hopson and Adams provide a way of understanding a crisis that may help in knowing when is the best time to implement an action-oriented program such as that of Azrin. Azrin's focus is on looking for work when one has experienced a job crisis. The career development theories discussed in this book offer a way of viewing both crises and more normal transitions that occur when individuals graduate from high school or college, and then look for work.

One approach to finding a job can be extrapolated from Holland's theory. Often, people who are looking for work are encouraged to sell themselves to employers, to develop a network of contacts that can help them find a job, and to be assertive in their job search. This type of behavior is most similar to that of the Enterprising individual, who often enjoys persuading others and selling. The assertive approach recommended by many job search strategists may be more difficult for Realistic, Conventional, and Investigative types to use. A counselor, when assisting a client in the job search process, may wish to consider his or her client's Holland type and how that person can develop an appropriate job search strategy.

Using the Myers–Briggs typology, individuals who deal with the outer world (extraversion) may be more comfortable in using assertive job search strategies than those who deal with the inner world (introversion). Similarly, those individuals who take a sensing approach to finding information about job openings may have a different style from those who take an intuiting approach. For example, those who acquire information about the job market based on intuition or introversion may be depressed by the difficulties that they are facing, because they may not focus on the job market itself but rather on their own reactions.

Super's concept of role salience can be helpful in career placement counseling. Clients vary as to how much they value the worker role in contrast to that of student, leisurite, citizen, or homemaker. This notion of role provides an opportunity to put the entire context of the job search into perspective. The stage theory of Super also provides a broader context within which to view job search strategies. The job search process itself fits within the specifying and implementing substages of the exploration stage.

Because the job-hunting process often is seen by an individual as a process of many rejections, social learning and cognitive information–processing approaches can be useful. Reinforcing the job search process itself, rather than its outcome, is an important part of a behavioral approach. Because individuals might be discouraged as they start to look for work, attending to inaccurate beliefs and correcting them is part of the role of the counselor using social learning theory or cognitive information processing. These perspectives and those of other career development theorists offer an interesting approach to the job search process that is different from the pragmatic approach of most job search books.

USE OF ASSESSMENT INSTRUMENTS IN THEORIES

Career development theories vary as to the importance of tests and inventories in the conceptualization of client career problems. In general, trait and factor theories rely more heavily on assessment use than does life-span theory, which, in turn, uses assessment instruments more than career decision-making theories. A comparison of test and inventory use is provided in Table 16.2 (p. 470), listing the trait, factor, or characteristic measured for theories described in this book. Part of the success of trait and factor theory relies on the ability of test and inventory developers to accurately measure traits such as aptitudes, interests, values, and personality. General trait and factor theory requires that career counselors select assessment instruments that are reliable and valid. Matching the measured traits and factors of a client with characteristics of a job is the essence of applying trait and factor theory. Holland's typological theory also measures traits and factors, but it categorizes them into six types that then are matched with environmental types. There are several inventories, such as the Strong Interest Inventory, that provide scores for the six types. In addition, Holland's Vocational Preference Inventory and Self-Directed Search are designed to provide scores for the six types so that matching can occur with occupational environments. The Myers–Briggs Type Indicator gives information to the counselor about the personality type of the client. Those counselors who use the Myers–Briggs type theory in their work rely heavily on the Myers–Briggs Type Indicator to assess personality style. Perhaps the most precise use of assessment occurs in work adjustment theory. Client scores on the General Aptitude Test Battery and the Minnesota Importance Questionnaire are matched with the ability patterns and needs and values reinforcer patterns of more than 1,700 occupations. It is fair to conclude that, without accurate measurement of traits and factors, there would be no trait and factor theory.

For life-span theory, assessment serves the purpose of identifying important developmental issues that individuals must face. Super's Career Development Inventory assesses the developmental phase of career maturity. Super's Adult Career Concerns Inventory assesses the extent to which adults are concerned about issues relating to the exploration, establishment, maintenance, or disengagement stage, or to any of the substages. In general, inventories that measure developmental tasks or stages are less precise than those that measure traits and factors. The reason is that life-span issues are broader and less predictable than measurements of aptitudes or interests. However, such instruments can still be useful in conceptualizing career concerns.

Career decision-making theory focuses on the process of selecting occupations. Although tests and inventories can be used by counselors using a spiritual approach, they are used cautiously so as not to detract from the individuals' self-assessment and career development. Cognitive information–processing theory uses the Career Thoughts Inventory to assess client confusion and anxiety about making career decisions, as well as to assess how individuals balance their own views with outside information. Krumboltz believes that values inventories can help individuals in the process of clarifying values. Aptitude tests and interest inventories can help in identifying alternatives and in discovering probable outcomes of these alternatives. In addition, the Career Beliefs Inventory provides assistance in assessing inaccurate beliefs that clients may have that interfere with the career decision-making process. Thus, for career decision-making theories, as well as for other theories of career development, the purpose of the theory and the role of assessment are highly related.

OCCUPATIONAL CLASSIFICATION SYSTEMS AND CAREER DEVELOPMENT THEORIES

The development of classification systems for occupations has been associated with trait and factor theory because occupations must be classified so that they can be matched with measured traits and factors of individuals. The focus of various classification systems differs widely. For comparison, Table 16.3 lists the groupings used in three classification systems (*O**NET Occupations, the *Dictionary of Occupational Titles*, and the *Guide for Occupational Exploration*) and cross-classifies them by Holland's system. This provides an opportunity to see how the four systems relate to each other. The 12 categories of the *Guide for Occupational Exploration* represent a more detailed categorization system than Holland's system. The 17,000 occupations listed in the *Dictionary of Occupational Titles* have as their primary classification the 8 categories listed in Table 16.3. The predominance of Realistic occupations in this first level of the *Dictionary of Occupational Titles* categorization is indicative of the large number of Realistic occupations in the definitions. The nine categories of O*NET (*Occupational Information Network* online) are similar to those of the *Dictionary of Occupational Titles* (DOT); they are listed in Table 16.3 to provide comparison with those in the DOT. The *Dictionary of Holland Occupational Codes* provides a Holland code identification for each of the occupations listed in the *Dictionary of Occupational Titles*. How career development theories make use of classification systems is the subject of this section.

As previously stated, classification systems are essential for use in trait and factor theory. Those counselors who use a general trait and factor theory can choose from classification systems that fit the tests and inventories they wish to use in counseling. For Holland's theory, it is essential to use his classification system. In contrast, work adjustment theory categorizes occupations according to the system of the *Dictionary of Occupational Titles*. However, because this system is no longer being updated, counselors increasingly make use of the O*NET (*Occupational Information Network* online) that is available on the Internet. In general, the theories or tests that counselors select are likely to dictate the classification system that the counselor will use.

For life-span theory, classification systems become important when career selections are to be made. When that occurs, life-span theorists incorporate developmental

TABLE 16.3 | COMPARISON OF HOLLAND'S CLASSIFICATION SYSTEM TO THREE OTHER SYSTEMS

	O*NET Occupations	Dictionary of Occupational Titles	Guide for Occupational Exploration
Section 1	Executives, managers, and administrators (E)	Professional, technical, and managerial occupations (A, E, I, S)	Artistic (A).
Section 2	Professional and support specialists, financial specialists, engineers, scientists, mathematicians, social scientists, social services workers, religious workers, and legal workers (I, E, S, A, C)	Clerical and sales occupations (C, E)	Scientific (I, R) Plants and animals (I, R) Protective (S, R)
Section 3	Professional and support specialists, educators, librarians, counselors, health care workers, artists, writers, performers, and other professional workers (S, A, I)	Service occupations (S, R) Agricultural, fishery, forestry, and related occupations (R)	Mechanical (I, R) Industrial (R) Business detail (E, C)
Section 4	Sales workers (E)	Processing occupations (R)	Selling (E)
Section 5	Administrative support workers (C)	Machine trades occupations (R)	Accommodating (S, E, R)
Section 6	Service workers (R, E, S)	Structural work occupations (R)	Humanitarian (S)
Section 7	Agricultural, forestry, and fishing workers (R)	Miscellaneous occupationsBenchwork occupations (R)	Leading-influencing (E)
Section 8	Mechanics, installers, repairers, construction trades, extractive trades, metal and plastic working, woodworking, apparel, precision printing, and food-processing workers (R)		Physical-performance (A)
Section 9	Machine setters, operations, and tenders; production workers; hand workers; plant and systems workers; transportation workers; and helpers (R)		

*Letters in parentheses represent the Holland code that roughly corresponds to the occupational grouping: (R) Realistic, (I) Investigative, (A) Artistic, (S) Social, (E) Enterprising, and (C) Conventional.

concepts, as well as trait and factor theory. Therefore, life-span theorists are likely to make use of classification systems in the same way as trait and factor theorists.

For career decision-making theorists, the selection of tests and inventories, which may be a secondary part of counseling, will determine the occupational classification system to be used. The classification of occupations is not a major emphasis of career decision-making theorists.

HOW THEORIES APPLY TO CAREER DEVELOPMENT ISSUES OF WOMEN

Much of the information about the career development of women has come from lifespan theory rather than from trait and factor or career decision-making theory. It is life-span theory that draws attention to gender-role issues that affect career development in childhood, adolescence, and adulthood. Knowledge of gender-role stereotyping and gender-role issues of women in various stages of their lives can help in work adjustment and career selection. In contrast, the information available from trait and factor and career decision-making theories about gender differences is minimal. However, recent research on social cognitive career theory as it affects women is a notable exception.

With regard to trait and factor theory, some research shows differences in the interests and abilities of men and women. It is often difficult to separate learned from genetic characteristics. For example, if women do more poorly in math than men, is that poor performance because of a lack of innate ability or because of socialization that women are not as good in math as men? Research reviewed in Part Two of this textbook suggests that the latter is true. Similarly, in Holland's typology, women predominate in the Social and Artistic areas. This is a reflection of socialization rather than misclassification in using Holland's system. This information should not be used to suggest that women whose personalities are Realistic or Investigative are in some way aberrant and should be considering other occupations. There are some differences between the scores of men and women on the Minnesota Importance Questionnaire, which is an important component of work adjustment theory. Lofquist and Dawis (1984) suggest that it is the individual's needs that are important, not those of women or men in general. A similar conclusion can be reached about the Myers–Briggs typology. Although women tend to predominate in the feeling category and men in the thinking category (Myers, McCaulley, Quenk, & Hammer, 1998), this fact may have few implications for individual counseling. That men and women, in general, may differ on various traits cannot be generalized to the individual client, who may have interests, aptitudes, and personality patterns that are atypical of those of other women.

With regard to career decision-making theories, there are some findings that can be useful in counseling women. In his social learning theory, Krumboltz emphasizes the importance of role models for women. He points out that, although groups, such as women, may have limited control over environmental conditions, there are ways through collective action that cultural biases such as gender discrimination can be changed. Social cognitive career theory investigates how environmental factors affect the way women learn about their academic and career competencies in the process of making career choices. The spiritual career decision-making perspective focuses on the individual's own developmental process or subjective experiencing rather than emphasizing issues of gender role. That is not to say that these theorists consider gender-role stereotyping unimportant.

A major focus of the chapters in Part Two of this textbook is examining the life-span development of women. Gottfredson's attention to the impact of gender role on career choice at ages 6 to 8 years has been instrumental in emphasizing that the career choices that men and women make in their adolescence and adulthood are different. Gottfredson's concepts of circumscription and compromise are useful in highlighting these differences. Chapter 8 explains the impact of the educational system on gender-role stereotyping of adolescent women. In adulthood, the career development of women often is more varied than that of men, with family and child care considerations leading to varied patterns of leaving and reentering the labor force. In addition to these concerns, women are far more likely than men to face sexual harassment issues in the workplace. Knowledge of these issues can help counselors provide an enlightened approach to working with women who have career choice or work adjustment problems.

HOW THEORIES APPLY TO CULTURAL DIVERSITY ISSUES IN CAREER DEVELOPMENT

In general, there has been less research on the career development of nonwhite people than on women. Trait and factor theory, as well as career decision-making theory, has provided relatively little information about varying characteristics of nonwhite populations. One difficulty in interpreting the research in trait and factor theory is that it is important not to apply generalizations about the interests, aptitudes, and personalities of a group to an individual client. Social learning theory emphasizes environmental influences on the importance of role models who have the same cultural background as the client. Social cognitive career theory focuses on concerns about self-efficacy that can affect the career development of people from diverse cultural backgrounds, as well as women. Other career decision-making theories do not focus on cultural background.

Perhaps the life-span perspective has the most to say about issues affecting culturally diverse populations. In general, minority children may be prevented from, or may have limited access to, exploratory activities that help them acquire information that leads to career maturity. In the United States, nonwhite adolescents with high aspirations may be thwarted from achieving them because of limited access to educational and occupational opportunities. Research discussed in Chapter 3 suggests that nonwhite adolescents in the United States are more likely to find jobs with limited potential for advancement and to encounter job discrimination. Negative attitudes toward work can be the result of a historical pattern of experiencing discrimination from one generation to another. The work of Vondracek and his colleagues emphasizes the importance for counselors to be aware not only of the individual's vocational identity but also of the context of the individual's historical and social situation. The minority identity development model of Atkinson, Morten, and Sue (1998) can be helpful to counselors in understanding how people from culturally diverse populations may react to a variety of work situations. The Atkinson, Morten, and Sue model suggests that minority group members may start in a stage of conformity and move through dissonance, resistance, emergence, and introspection to a stage of synergetic articulation and awareness. This theory is useful in understanding how minorities relate to their own group, as well as to the majority group. Although not a model of career development, it has direct applicability to issues of job selection and work adjustment.

The need for counselors to attend to issues of women and culturally diverse populations in career development is highlighted by the research of sociologists and economists (discussed in Chapter 3). They document, over and over again, that women and nonwhite employees in the United States receive less pay than white men for equal work and may be denied access to jobs that are likely to lead to advancement and higher pay. The sociological and economic theories of career development draw conclusions about broad groups from their studies of large numbers of people. However, for the individual counselor, the research is a reminder to look for attitudes within one's self that may hinder the career development of a female client or a client of another ethnic group.

COUNSELOR ISSUES

Career development theories not only provide a means of conceptualizing the client's concerns but also suggest a perspective on client–counselor issues. From a trait and factor point of view, it is often helpful to look at the traits and factors of the client and compare them with those of the counselor. In a life-span perspective, a contrast between the counselor's life stage and that of the client can be helpful in counseling situations. With regard to decision-making theories, being aware of the contrast between the decision-making style and progress of the client and that of the counselor can be instructive.

Trait and Factor Theories

In general, when using trait and factor theory, it is helpful for the counselor to be aware that the abilities, aptitudes, personality, values, and interests of the client are likely to be different from those of the counselor. Appreciating a wide range of interests, abilities, and values can be helpful to the counselor in working with many problems.

From the point of view of Holland's typology, the less congruent the counselor's type is with the client's type, the more likely it is that the counselor will have to deal with a value conflict. For example, a counselor who is primarily Social in orientation may not enjoy organizing and working with numbers as does a person who is Conventional.

With regard to the Myers–Briggs typological theory, researchers (Yeakley, 1983) point out the importance of using a communication style that is similar to that of the client. For example, if the counselor's primary way of perceiving is through sensing and the client's way of perceiving is through intuiting, each will be looking at events from a different point of view. It is important for the counselor to adapt to or understand the client's communication style.

Lofquist and Dawis, in their theory of work adjustment, view the client and the counselor as serving as environments for each other. As environments, they reinforce each other and meet each other's needs in different ways. An awareness of both his or her own needs and those of the client can help the counselor in offering appropriate reinforcers for the client. For example, if the client has a need for responsibility, it may be helpful for the counselor to let the client act independently and make little acknowledgment of the counseling process to achieve a satisfactory result. This might mean sacrificing the counselor's own altruistic needs. Although trait and factor theory generally is not thought of as encompassing approaches that have an impact on the client–counselor relationship, it is clear that all of these theories can be viewed in this manner.

LIFE-SPAN THEORIES

Life-span theory draws attention to the different roles and stages of the client and the counselor. For example, a 65-year-old person who is counseling a 15-year-old is working with someone whose interests, exploratory behavior, and self-concept are at relatively early stages. For the counselor, focusing on the client's issues and not on his or her own will cross the large generational gap. Similarly, counselors often work with clients in crises. Knowing that each individual in each crisis is different will help the counselor to refrain from applying his or her own experience with a crisis to that of the client. Also, being aware of gender-role issues when the client is of the other gender can help the counselor focus on the needs and issues of the client. For example, being aware of a client's early experiences with gender bias in school may affect how the counselor assists the client with career selection issues.

CAREER DECISION-MAKING THEORIES

Implications of career decision-making theories for counselors vary. Krumboltz and Baker (1973) pointed out that counselors who use social learning theory should be careful that their counseling skills match the needs of the client. Furthermore, they believed it is important for the client and the counselor to have mutually agreeable goals. If a counselor is expert in working with a specific type of client but chooses to work with a very different type of client, that behavior may be unethical. For social cognitive career counselors, being sensitive to the barriers that affect client's self-efficacy, outcome expectations, and career goals requires awareness of stereotypes about women and culturally diverse populations. A counselor who uses a spiritual approach to career development should be clear about the subjective experience of the client's career decision making, which might be vastly different from that of the counselor. Appreciating the client's unique individuality is one of the main goals of the spiritual perspective on career decision making. In contrast, the cognitive information–processing approach can be quite structured; therefore, the counselor should be certain that the structure does not preclude discussion of atypical matters affecting career choice.

SOCIOLOGICAL AND ECONOMIC APPROACHES

The implications of sociological and economic perspectives on career choice (Chapter 3) are quite different from those of the psychological approaches. Sociological and economic research on career development factors points out the inequalities that exist for culturally diverse populations and women as they deal with the labor market. Rather than assume that these apply to each client, the counselor can use this information as background from which to evaluate the client's individual issues. Furthermore, the research of sociologists and economists into cultural and gender issues can serve as a guide to evaluating one's own values and prejudices.

CONCLUSION

The theories that have been discussed in this book provide useful approaches to problems of career choice and work adjustment. In many cases, the theorists and many of their colleagues have spent 20, 30, or more years developing, evaluating, and refining their theories. Through research and evaluation, they have modified and strengthened their work, at the same time providing tests and inventories for counselors to use. In addition, recent theorists have developed perspectives and insights into the career-development-choice process that provide new ways for counselors to view their clients. The continuing research into, and the development of, revised and new theories is evidence that career development theory will continue to offer new and better tools and ideas for counselors to use. Implicit in the work of these theorists and researchers is the importance that they attribute to careers and career problems. They have great respect for the role of the counselor, whose work can significantly improve the client's satisfaction with his or her life.

REFERENCES

ACT, Inc. (2007) DISCOVER (Windows). Iowa City, IA: Author.

Atkinson, D. R., Morten, G., & Sue, D. W. (1998). *Counseling American minorities: A cross-cultural perspective* (5th ed.). Boston: McGraw-Hill.

Azrin, N. H., & Besalel, V. A. (1980). *Job club counselor's manual: A behavioral approach to vocational counseling.* Baltimore: University Park Press.

Barak, A., & Cohen, L. (2002). Empirical examination of an online version of the Self-Directed Search. *Journal of Career Assessment, 10,* 387–400.

Black, R. S., Tsuhako, K., & McDougall, D. (1998). Job club intervention to improve interviewing skills of young adults with cognitive disabilities. *Journal for Special Needs Education, 20,* 33–38.

Bleier, J. K. (2007). The impact of career counseling plus DISCOVER (internet version) on the academic achievement of high school sophomores at risk for dropping out of school. *Dissertation Abstracts International: Section B: The Sciences and Engineering, 68/2-B,* 1294.

Boer, D. M. (2001). *Career counseling over the Internet.* Mahwah, NJ: Lawrence Erlbaum Associates.

Bolles, R. N. (2008). *What color is your parachute?* (38th ed.). San Francisco: Ten Speed Press.

Brake, R. G. (2001). The effects of DISCOVER career guidance software on career decision-making self-efficacy of adolescents in foster care. *Dissertation Abstracts International: Section B, 62/5-B,* 2477.

Brooks, F., Nackerud, L., & Risler, E. (2001). Evaluation of a job-finding club for TANF recipients: Psychosocial impacts. *Research on Social Work Practice, 11,* 79–92.

Clow, R. B. (2005). Experiential career exploration: Qualitative examination of a group-based intervention. *Dissertation Abstracts International: Section B: The Sciences and Engineering, 65/11-B,* 6040.

Fowkes, K. M., & McWhirter, E. H. (2007). Evaluation of computer-assisted career guidance in middle and secondary education settings: Status, obstacles, and suggestions. *Journal of Career Assessment, 15*(3), 388–400.

Gottfredson, L. S. (2005). Applying Gottfredson's theory of circumscription and compromise in career guidance and counseling. In S. D. Brown & R. W. Lent (Eds.), *Career development and counseling: Putting theory and research to work.* (pp.71–100). Hoboken, NJ: Wiley.

Harris-Bowlsbey, J. (2002). Career planning and technology in the 21st century. In S. G. Niles (Ed.), *Adult career development: Concepts, issues, and practices* (3rd ed., pp. 157–165). Columbus, OH: National Career Development Association.

Harris-Bowlsbey, J., & Sampson, J. P., Jr. (2001). Computer-based career planning systems: Dreams and realities. *Career Development Quarterly, 49,* 250–260.

Harris-Bowlsbey, J., & Sampson, J. P., Jr. (2005). Use of technology in delivering career services worldwide. *The Career Development Quarterly, 54*(1), 48–56.

Herr, E. L., Cramer, S. H., & Niles, S. G. (2004). *Career guidance and counseling through the life span* (6th ed.). Boston: Allyn & Bacon.

Holland, J. L. (1985). *You and your career.* Odessa, FL: Psychological Assessment Resources.

Holland, J. L. (1997). *Making vocational choices: A theory of vocational personalities and work environments* (3rd ed.). Odessa, FL: Psychological Assessment Resources.

Hopson, B., & Adams, J. D. (1977). Towards an understanding of transitions: Defining some boundaries of transition. In J. Adams, J. Hayes, & B. Hopson (Eds.), *Transition: Understanding and managing personal change.* Montclair, NJ: Allenheld & Osmun.

Kivlighan, D. M. (1990). Career group therapy. *The Counseling Psychologist, 18,* 64–79.

Kondo, C. T. (2005). How a job club benefits executive job seekers: A tale of hares and tortoises. *Dissertation Abstracts International Section A: Humanities and Social Sciences, 66/5-A,* 1594.

Kratz, L. E. (1998). The use of the SIGI PLUS computer-assisted career guidance system as a career counseling intervention. *Dissertation Abstracts International, 59/3-A,* 0737.

Krumboltz, J. D., & Baker, R. D. (1973). Behavioral counseling for vocational decision. In H. Borow (Ed.), *Career guidance for a new age* (pp. 235–284). Boston: Houghton Mifflin.

Krumboltz, J. D., & Hamel, D. A. (1977). *Guide to career decision-making skills.* New York: Educational Testing Service.

Lapan, R. T. (2004). *Career development across the K-16 years: Bridging the present to satisfying and successful futures.* Alexandria, VA: American Counseling Association.

Lofquist, L. H., & Dawis, R. V. (1984). Research on work adjustment and satisfaction: Implications for career counseling. In S. Brown & R. Lent (Eds.), *Handbook of counseling psychology* (pp. 216–237). New York.

Mallen, M. J., Vogel, D. L., & Rochlen, A. B. (2005). The practical aspects of online counseling: Ethics, training, technology, and competency. *Counseling Psychologist, 33*(6), 776–818.

McAllister, S., & Ponterotto, J. G. (1992). A career group program for displaced homemakers. *Journal for Specialists in Group Work, 17,* 29–36.

McCarthy, C. J., Moller, N., & Beard, L. M. (2003). Suggestions for training students in using the Internet for career counseling. *Career Development Quarterly, 51,* 368–381.

Miller-Tiedeman, A. (1999). *Learning, practicing, and living the new careering.* Philadelphia: Accelerated Development.

Myers, I. B., McCaulley, M. H., Quenk, N. L., & Hammer, A. L. (1998). *MBTI Manual: A guide to the development and use of the Myers-Briggs Type Indicator* (3rd ed.). Palo Alto, CA: Consulting Psychologists Press.

Peterson, G. W., Ryan-Jones, R. E., Sampson, J. P., Jr., & Reardon, R. C. (1994). A comparison of the effectiveness of three computer-assisted career guidance systems: DISCOVER, SIGI, and SIGI PLUS. *Computers in Human Behavior, 1,* 189–198.

Reardon, R. C., Lenz, J. G., Sampson, J. P. Jr., Peterson, G. W. (2006). *Career counseling and planning: A comprehensive approach.* (2nd ed.). Mason, OH: Thomson.

Rutter, M. E., & Jones, J. V. (2007). The job club redux: A step forward in addressing the career development needs of counselor education students. *The Career Development Quarterly, 55*(3), 280–288.

Shea, M., Ma, P. W., & Yeh, C. J. (2007). Development of a culturally specific career exploration group for urban Chinese immigrant youth. *The Career Development Quarterly, 56*(1), 62–73.

Super, D. E. (1990). A life-span, life-space approach to career development. In D. Brown, L. Brooks & Associates (Eds.), *Career choice and development* (2nd ed., pp. 197–261). San Francisco: Jossey-Bass.

Super, D. E., Bohn, M. J., Forrest, D. J., Jordaan, J. P., Lindeman, R. H., & Thompson, A. S. (1971). *Career Development Inventory.* New York: Teachers College: Columbia University.

Šverko, B., Akik, N., Babarovic, T., Brcina, A., & Sverko, I. (2002). Validity of e-advice: The evaluation of an Internet-based system for career planning. *International Journal for Educational & Vocational Guidance, 2,* 193–215.

Thompson, A. S., & Lindeman, R. H. (1981). *Career Development Inventory: User's manual* (Vol. 1). Palo Alto, CA: Consulting Psychologists Press.

Tieger, P. D., & Barron-Tieger, B. (1992). *Do what you are: Discover the perfect career for you through the secrets of personality type.* Boston: Little, Brown.

Turner, S. L., & Lapan, R. T. (2005). Promoting career development and aspirations in school-age youths. In S. D. Brown & R. W. Lent (Eds.), *Career development and counseling: Putting theory and research to work.* (pp. 417–440). Hoboken, NJ: John Wiley.

VALPAR, International. (2007). SIGI^3. [Computer Program]. Tuscon, AZ: Author.

Vondracek, F. W., & Skorikov, V. R. (2007). Vocational identity. In V. B. Skorikov & W. Patton (Eds.), *Career development in childhood and adolescence* (pp. 143–168). Sense Publishers.

Wang, W., Li, C., & Wang, X. (2006). Effect of group psychological guidance on university junior class students' career decision-making. *Chinese Journal of Clinical Psychology, 14*(6), 649–651.

Whiston, S. C., Brecheisen, B. R., & Stephens, J. (2003). Does treatment modality affect career counseling effectiveness? *Journal of Vocational Behavior, 62,* 390–410.

Yeakley, F. R. (1983). Implications of communication style research for psychological type theory. *Research in Psychological Type, 6,* 5–23.

Zunker, V. G. (2006). *Career counseling: A holistic approach* (7th ed.). Belmont, CA: Brooks/Cole.

Appendix A

CACREP STANDARDS

This Appendix lists the 2001 Council for Accreditation of Counseling and Related Educational Programs (CACREP) standards for career development. Also listed is the third draft of the proposed standards for 2009. More information about these standards can be found at the CACREP Web site http://www.cacrep.org/.

For each of the standards I have indicated the chapter, and where appropriate, page numbers in the Fifth Edition of *Applying Career Development Theory to Counseling* that have information related to each standard.

2001 CACREP STANDARDS FOR CAREER DEVELOPMENT

4. CAREER DEVELOPMENT—studies that provide an understanding of career development and related life factors, including all of the following:

a. career development theories and decision-making models:

Every section of each chapter is related to this standard.

b. career, avocational, educational, occupational and labor market information resources, visual and print media, computer-based career information systems, and other electronic career information systems:

There is a section in most chapters, titled "Occupational Information," that describes how each career development theory makes use of occupational information of a variety of types. Furthermore, Chapter 2 describes different types of occupational information (pp. 40–41) and several occupational classification systems (pp. 41–52). Chapter 3 provides a summary of the United States labor market and information about sociological and economic theories as they pertain to occupations and the labor market. Information about computer guidance systems can be found on page 15 of Chapter 1, page 54–55 of Chapter 2, and pages 472–473 of Chapter 16. Information about use of the Internet will be found on pages 473–474 of Chapter 16 and in Appendix C.

c. career development program planning, organization, implementation, administration, and evaluation:

Career programs for children are described in Chapter 7 (pp. 212–213), along with information about school-to-work programs. Information about placement programs is in Chapter 16 (pp. 476–478); information about out-placement programs can be found in Chapter 10 (pp. 291–292). Information about program and evaluation can be found in Research and Evaluation courses.

d. interrelationships among and between work, family, and other life roles and factors including the role of diversity and gender in career development:

Part Two, Chapters 7–10, discusses the relationship between work, family, and other life roles. The role of relationships in career development is the subject of Chapter 12. All chapters have sections on the role of diversity and gender in career development.

e. career and educational planning, placement, follow-up, and evaluation:

Information about placement programs is in Chapter 16 (pp. 476–478); information about outplacement programs can be found in Chapter 10 (pp. 291–292). Information about program and evaluation can be found in Research and Evaluation courses. Information about school-to-work programs is described in Chapter 7 (pp. 213–215).

f. assessment instruments and techniques that are relevant to career planning and decision making:

A brief introduction to basic assessment concepts such as norms, reliability, and validity is included in Chapter 1 (pp. 13–14). Although all chapters (except Chapter 3) discuss assessment instruments related to a specific theory, Chapter 2 provides information about the most commonly used assessment instruments.

g. technology-based career development applications and strategies, including computer-assisted career guidance and information systems and appropriate Web sites:

Information about computer guidance systems can be found on page 15 of Chapter 1, page 54 of Chapter 2, and pages 472–473 of Chapter 16. Information about use of the Internet will be found on pages 473–474 of Chapter 16 and in Appendix C, which lists Internet Web sites.

h. career counseling processes, techniques, and resources, including those applicable to specific populations; and

Chapter 1 (pp. 8–16) describes general counseling skills needed for career counseling. Examples of career counseling are described in most chapters to show how counseling skills are used with a specific theory. Counseling skills specific to a theory are described in Chapter 11, "Constructivist and Narrative Approaches to Career Development" and in Chapter 13, Krumboltz's Social Learning Theory." Some counseling processes and resources are described in chapter sections on culturally diverse populations and women.

i.   ethical and legal considerations.

Chapter 1 (pp. 17–18) gives a brief overview of ethics as they relate to career development and career counseling. Ethics courses provide much more thorough coverage.

CACREP STANDARDS 2009 3RD DRAFT FOR CAREER DEVELOPMENT

4. CAREER DEVELOPMENT—studies that provide an understanding of career development and related life factors, including all of the following:

a.   career development theories and decision-making models:

Every section of each chapter is related to this standard.

b.   career, avocational, educational, occupational and labor market information resources, visual and print media, and career information systems:

There is a section in most chapters, titled "Occupational Information," that describes how each career development theory makes use of occupational information of a variety of types. Furthermore, Chapter 2 describes different types of occupational information (pp. 40–41) and several occupational classification systems (pp. 41–52). Chapter 3 provides a summary of the United States labor market and information about sociological and economic theories as they pertain to occupations and the labor market. Information about computer guidance systems can be found on page 15 of Chapter 1, page 54–55 of Chapter 2, and pages 472–473 of Chapter 16. Information about use of the Internet will be found on pages 473–474 of Chapter 16 and in Appendix C.

c.   career development program planning, organization, implementation, administration, and evaluation:

Career programs for children are described in Chapter 7 (pp. 212–213) along with information about school-to-work programs. Information about placement programs is in Chapter 16 (pp. 476–478); information about outplacement programs can be found in Chapter 10 (pp. 291–292). Information about program and evaluation can be found in Research and Evaluation courses.

d.   interrelationships among and between work, family, and other life roles and factors including the role of multicultural issues in career development:

Part Two, Chapters 7–10, discusses the relationship between work, family, and other life roles. The role of relationships in career development is the subject of Chapter 12. All chapters have sections on the role of diversity and gender in career development.

e.   career and educational planning, placement, follow-up, and evaluation:

Information about placement programs is in Chapter 16 (pp. 476–478); information about outplacement programs can be found in Chapter 10 (pp. 291–292). Information about program and evaluation can be found in Research and Evaluation courses. Information about school-to-work programs is described in Chapter 7 (pp. 213–215).

f.   assessment instruments and techniques that are relevant to career planning and decision making, and

A brief introduction to basic assessment concepts such as norms, reliability, and validity is described in Chapter 1 (pp. 13–14). Although all chapters (except Chapter 3) discuss assessment instruments related to a specific theory, Chapter 2 provides information about the most commonly used assessment instruments.

g.   career counseling processes, techniques, and resources, including those applicable to specific populations:

Chapter 1 (pp. 8–16) describes general counseling skills needed for career counseling. Examples of career counseling are described in most chapters to show how counseling skills are used with a specific theory. Counseling skills specific to a theory are described in Chapter 11, "Constructivist and Narrative Approaches to Career Development" and Chapter 13, "Krumboltz's Social Learning Theory. Some counseling processes and resources are described in chapter sections on culturally diverse populations and women.

Appendix B

TESTS AND THEIR PUBLISHERS

Test or Inventory	*Publisher or Distributor*
ACT Assessment Program: Academic Tests	American College Testing Program
Adult Career Concerns Inventory	CPP (Consulting Psychologists Press)
Armed Services Vocational Aptitude Battery	Department of Defense
Assessment of Career Decision Making	Western Psychological Services
California Occupational Preference Survey	Educational and Industrial Testing Service
California Psychological Inventory	CPP (Consulting Psychologists Press)
Career Beliefs Inventory	CPP (Consulting Psychologists Press)
Career Decision Scale	Psychological Assessment Resources
Career Development Inventory	CPP (Consulting Psychologists Press)
Career Thoughts Inventory	Psychological Assessment Resources
Differential Aptitude Tests	Psychological Corporation
General Aptitude Test Battery	Nelson Assessment and Guidance Group
Kuder Career Search	National Career Assessment Services, Inc.
Minnesota Importance Questionnaire	Vocational Psychology Research
Minnesota Job Description Questionnaire	Vocational Psychology Research
Minnesota Multiphasic Personality Inventory	Pearson Assessments
Minnesota Satisfaction Questionnaire	Vocational Psychology Research
Minnesota Satisfactoriness Scales	Vocational Psychology Research
Myers–Briggs Type Indicator	CPP (Consulting Psychologists Press)
Rorschach	Psychological Assessment Resources
Salience Inventory	CPP (Consulting Psychologists Press)
Scholastic Assessment Test	Educational Testing Service
Self-Directed Search	Psychological Assessment Resources
Sixteen Personality Factor Questionnaire	Wonderlic, Inc.
Strong Interest Inventory	CPP (Consulting Psychologists Press)
Study of Values	Houghton Mifflin–Riverside Publishing

Test or Inventory	Publisher or Distributor
Thematic Apperception Test	Pearson Assessments
Values Scale	CPP (Consulting Psychologists Press)
Vocational Interest Inventory	Western Psychological Services
Vocational Preference Inventory	Psychological Assessment Resources

Publishers' Addresses

American College Testing Program, P.O. Box 168, Iowa City, IA 52243–0168, www.act.org

CPP (Consulting Psychologists Press), 1055 Joaquin Road, 2nd Floor, Mountain View, CA 94043, www.cpp.com

Department of Defense, 2834 Green Bay Road, North Chicago, IL 60064, www.asvabprogram.com

Educational and Industrial Testing Service, P.O. Box 7234, San Diego, CA 92167, www.edits.net

Educational Testing Service, Rosedale Rd., Princeton, NJ 08541–6736, www.ets.org

Houghton Mifflin Company, One Beacon Street, Boston, MA 02108, www.hmco.com

National Career Assessment Services, Inc., 302 Visions Pkwy, Adel, IA 50003, www.kuder.com

Nelson Assessment and Guidance Group, 1120 Birchmount Rd., Toronto, Ontario, M1K5G4, www.assess.nelson.com

Pearson Assessments, P.O. Box 1416, Minneapolis, MN 55440, www.pearsonassessments.com

Psychological Assessment Resources, 16204 N. Florida Ave., Lutz, FL 33549, www.parinc.com

Psychological Corporation, Society for Human Resource Management 1800 Duke St., Alexandria, VA, www.shrm.org

Vocational Psychology Research, Department of Psychology, University of Minnesota, 75 East River Road, Minneapolis, MN 55455, www.psych.umn.edu

Western Psychological Services, 12031 Wilshire Boulevard, Los Angeles, CA 90025–1251, www.portal.wpspublish.com

Wonderlic, Inc., 1795 N. Butterfield Road, Libertyville, IL 60048, www.wonderlic.com

Appendix C

WEB SITES

Career Counseling Organizations

National Career Development Association	www.ncda.org
National Board for Certified Counselors	www.nbcc.org
The Association of Computer-based Systems for Career Information	www.acsci.org

Education and Internships

College Net	www.collegenet.com
College and Universities	www.collegesource.org
Peterson's Education Center	www.petersons.com
College and University Career Centers	www.jobweb.com
Corporation for National Service	www.nationalservice.org
Internship Programs	http://internshipprograms.com

Job Postings

America's Job Bank	www.ajb.dni.us
CareerBuilder.com	www.careerbuilder.com
Hotjobs (Yahoo)	http://hotjobs.yahoo.com/careertools
Monster.com	www.monster.com
Nation Jobs Online Job Databases	http://nationjob.com
Spherion	www.spherion.com/corporate/careercenter/home.jsp

Occupations

America Career Info Net	www.acinet.org
CareerJournal.com	www.careerpath.org
(The Wall Street Journal)	
Careers: US News	www.usnews.com/sectons/business/careers/
Occupational Outlook Handbook	www.bls.gov/home.htm
O*Net (Dictionary of Occupational	www.doleta.gov/programs/onet/
Titles [DOT])	
Princeton Review	www.princetonreview.com

Author Index

Subject Index